Women on Waves

WOMEN ON
WAVES

A CULTURAL HISTORY OF SURFING:

FROM ANCIENT GODDESSES AND HAWAIIAN QUEENS

TO MALIBU MOVIE STARS AND MILLENNIAL CHAMPIONS

JIM KEMPTON

PEGASUS BOOKS
NEW YORK LONDON

WOMEN ON WAVES

Pegasus Books, Ltd.
148 West 37th Street, 13th Floor
New York, NY 10018

First Pegasus Books cloth edition July 2021

Interior design by Maria Fernandez

ISBN: 978-1-64313-724-7

10 9 8 7 6 5 4 3 2 1

Printed in the United States of America
Distributed by Simon & Schuster
www.pegasusbooks.com

To the women on waves everywhere:

Goddesses, queens, world changers, trailblazers, visionaries,

record breakers, stylists and joyous enthusiasts—Long may you ride.

Preface

Run the World, Girls

If ever there has been a subject so ripe for exploration, or so appropriate for recounting, the history of women's surfing is it. Bold, beautiful and breathtaking, the adventures and achievements of women waveriders is an epic that has gone unsung too long.

Any history is a serious undertaking. But women's surfing was made more difficult by the dearth of original sources that were readily accessible. Digging deep and assembling disparate pieces of this collective saga was painstaking but rewarding. It quickly became clear that much that has been written about women surfers is inaccurate, and most has been written by men—and from a male point of view. Recent material often tended to be superficial and peripheral.

A decade ago, when I embarked on a women's exhibit at the California Surf Museum, it was an eye-opening experience. Jane Schmass, our historian and Julie Cox, our museum manager at the time, were major contributors to the exhibit. For nearly two years we read, researched, and compiled content about the women's achievements in surfing. Had the framework we assembled back then not been accessible, this book would have taken far longer.

While we chronicled the foremost figures of surf culture, the struggles and barriers that faced women in the modern era (1900 to today) were never really addressed. Nor were the vast number of women who contributed to this progress; we only presented surfing's key moments and major stars.

Once neck-deep in writing this book, it became obvious that women's surf history is a history of surfing itself. Women have been embedded in the heart of wave-riding from its ancient origins.

Over my decades in the surf culture—at *Surfer* magazine, TransWorld and the major women's brands I worked for—I met and became friends with many of the most remarkable women who surf. I had championed them over the years and was inspired to tell their stories in one volume. What surprised me was the ocean of new discoveries and little-known achievements that unfolded. Wave after wave of captivating stories began to take form. Like the template of a surfboard blank being sculpted, each layer revealed a more beautiful and significant shape. In the decade since my first research, women's surfing has swept forward like a rising swell, gaining height and strength each year.

This book is meant to be a definitive history of surfing—and intended to be seen from the women's perspective, though of course I acknowledge my own male gender as the author. Rarely has a sporting activity carried so much athletic prowess, mental preparation, danger and sheer beauty as the act of surfing.

As a microcosm of the world at large, women waveriders have experienced similar struggles other females have faced—across many social domains. Surfing, however, presents distinctive aspects.

Unlike "Run the World (Girls)," Beyoncé's girl power anthem that played on every platform and in stadiums worldwide, the act of riding a wave is frequently done without an audience and outside of the competitive arena. Most sports are performed in a contest format. The extremely subjective nature of surfing is often more effectively experienced without the constrictions of rigid formal rules. In surfing, judgment should recognize the ballet-like "attitude dancing" that women *in particular* excel at creating. Wave-riding is essentially a free-form activity whose acceptance did not become widespread until the mid-20th Century. Unlike child-rearing, warfare or marriage, where social norms have been established for millenniums, surfing's gender roles and expectations are neither clear nor constant. Traditions are still in an evolutionary stage.

The origins of surf culture are from a distant world, distinctly dissimilar from the technology-driven, specialized functions of our current social structure. To understand the true relationship of women on waves—and its future potential—a look at surfing's ancient past is necessary. And *that* requires a return to the beginning.

The Sport of Queens, the Realm of Goddesses

1099–1899

"Surfing is not just an activity. It is a part of the Hawaiian way of life."
—Princess Victoria Ka'iulani

It's Good to Be Queen

In 1905 the world's oldest known surfboard was discovered in Hawaii. It dated back to the early 1600s. And it belonged to a woman.

Pristinely preserved in a cool dry burial cave on the Big Island's Kona coast, this *papa he'e nalu* (Koa wood surfboard) is believed to have been the prize possession of Princess Kaneamuna, a 17th Century Polynesian royal. It had been carefully placed next to her tomb along with a land toboggan (or *papa holua*) which appears to have been her version of "sidewalk surfin'."

Like Egyptian Pharaohs, Hawaiian royalty were often buried with their beloved possessions, and these were Princess Kaneamuna's favorites—one for *he'e nalu* (surfing), and one for *he'e holua* (coasting on a sled.) On the steep hill just behind the royal village of Ho'okena, her subjects matted the long native Pili grass to make a smooth, high-speed course for sled sliding. This was no substitute for wave-riding, though. Princess Kaneamuna had surfboards custom-made for her amusement—and rode them well.

Hawaiian queens and princesses often had their own private surf spots and were among the best waveriders in their realm.

One particularly fine surfing location was reserved for a single *ali'i* woman: "a special surf at Waikiki that was taboo to everyone but the Queen." Daring to ride on the royal lady's waves, one young man was "severely beaten and nearly put to death."

Women were equal to the men both in status and respect when out in the waves. Most of the early images from Europeans initial voyages show women frolicking with minimal garments in the surf, while their counterparts in England and Spain wore six layers of clothing and shunned exposing even a sleeve to the shoreline sun.

From a historical vantage point today it conjures an almost comical juxtaposition: about the time Queen Anne Boleyn's head was rolling into the executioner's basket, Kaneamuna was rolling across the pristine surf off the Kona coast, while her entire kingdom watched and cheered. It was good to be queen. At least in Hawaii.

Women, Bloodlines and Surfing

Historical references to surfing and women are as old as the Polynesian culture itself. Like the culture of ancient Greece, the legends go back before any actual living figures. One of Hawaii's greatest deities—Pele, the volcano goddess—was celebrated in Polynesian mythology as a surfer of big waves. But more recent inquiries have found something unique in royal lineage.

Studies of Polynesia's historical mythology disclose a fascinating revelation: both women and surfing are central to the ranking of hereditary descendants. When ancient deities and heroic mortals met to compete and procreate, the genealogy of the royalty was determined by the goddesses and queens who represented *wave-riding*. Polynesian bloodlines split as various groups migrated to different regions and islands. But much of the spoken history remained intact. In each linage the highest bloodline was determined by the *female* descendants. And the dynamics of chiefly relationships were revealed through their connection to *surfing*.

In the Tahitian legend of royal descent Huauri, the goddess of the waves, holds the supreme regal bloodline. In the Hawaiian version the royal lineage is traced from the surfing deity Hinahanaiakamālama. They are "the ones who ride atop the highest crest of her parents line." Consider the poetic theme of lovemaking that surfing implies: Hina is the female in Hawaii with which to ride this wave of high bloodline, just as Huauri is the one to surf with upon reaching Tahiti.

And just as significantly, the position of surfing deity is held, not by a god, but by a goddess.

Hawaiian female surfers were not just goddesses—though their history has a murky entanglement with mythology. The earliest known record of a female surfer describes a prominent Oahu chieftess named Mamala. As a *kupua*—a demigod or heroine with supernatural powers—she could take the form of a beautiful woman, a gigantic lizard, or a great shark.

Ke-kai-o-Mamala, the ocean west of Waikiki off the coast of Honolulu, broke "straight out from a beautiful coconut grove . . . [at] Honoka'upu," wrote Finney and Houston, in their 1966 surf history *Surfing: The Sport of Hawaiian Kings,* "and provided some of the finest waves in Kou"—in what is now the port area of Honolulu.

Mamala, by all accounts, was a wonderful waverider. She could surf the roughest waves with skill and daring and apparently liked to paddle out to the outside breaks when the Kona winds blew into the bay of Kou. Crowds would gather on the shoreline to cheer and applaud her for her extraordinary skill.

Watching her surf, they would clap and shout in recognition to her extraordinary riding. The Mamala break was named after her and even today maps show this name on the outer reaches of Honolulu harbor.

A legend explaining the name of Sunset Beach on Oahu's North Shore tells the story of a woman who was known for her ability to catch octopus. Asked by a chief to go to a particular reef in Paumalu, she was met on the beach by an old man. He told her that there was a catch limit at this reef, and that she must not exceed it. The woman agreed, but once in the water she disregarded the warning. Suddenly, a large shark appeared and attacked her, taking off both her legs. Later, when her body was examined, the people saw the marks left by the shark's teeth. They knew that she had been punished by the guardian of the reef. After the incident, the area was named Paumalu, "taken by surprise."

One surfing love story involved a supernatural woman who lived in a cave overlooking the North Shore. A prince of Kauai' came to surf in the breakers at Paumalu Sunset Beach. A Bird Maiden who lived in a cave above watched him surf, then sent her bird messengers to bring a *lehua* lei to him and bring him to her. After months together as lovers, the surfing season came around again. He promised to never kiss another woman but broke this vow when a lovely female came up after his surfing and put an *ilima* lei around his neck. The birds brought word back to their mistress. She ran to the beach, tore off the *ilima* lei and reclaimed him with her *lehua* lei. The Bird Woman ran back to her cave, with him in hot pursuit. He never caught her but turned to stone halfway up the mountainside.

Liberty, Equality, Sorority

If the women's struggle for liberation and equality casts a long, dark shadow over western societies, there was nothing but sunlight for the first female surfers in Hawaii. The oral histories and ancient myths were filled with tales of women riding their long Koa olos across the surf.

English writer Isabella Bird was the first European woman to describe surfing after visiting Hawaii in 1876: "It really is a most exciting pastime, and in a rough sea requires immense nerve. The surfboard is a rough plank shaped like a coffin lid, about two feet broad, and from six to nine feet long, well-oiled and cared for."

Females of all ages, abilities and classes rode waves in traditional Hawaiian culture. These surfing women were seen as spiritually and physically powerful and commanded great respect in society. As historians Finney and Houston noted in *Surfing: the Spirit of Hawaiian Kings*, "a large percentage of *wahines* of early Hawaii were skillful surfers, and sometimes champions. Early engravings of the sport are full of half-dressed females perched on surfboards at the top of a curling wave."

Modern surfing's portrayal of women as bathing beauties sitting on the beach faithfully watching their masculine mates ride the wild surf could not be more opposite from the origins of surf culture. In every ancient depiction women appear in prominent—often even primary—roles. Thomas Thrum published an article in 1896 entitled "Hawaiian Surf Riding." A well-known journalist of the time, he wrote, "Native legends abound with the exploits of those who attained distinction among their fellows by their skill and daring in this sport, indulged in alike by both sexes; and frequently too—as in these days of intellectual development—the gentler sex carried off the highest honors."

His observation is supported from the first European account of Hawaii, by Captain Cook. Cook described how a "princess" (meaning a woman of the *ali'i*—other accounts call such women "chieftess") "paddled her board through heavy surf to catch a ride in the rolling waves," and observed that women were equally ready "to place themselves on the summit of the largest surge."

In the beginning there was Sex, Surf, and Spirituality All in One

As Brigham Young University–Hawaii Assistant Professor Isaiah Walker has observed, "Although these particular historical figures were beautiful women who surfed with little to no clothing, these stories do not simply convey them as objects of male sexual desire.

"Female surfers are celebrated as empowered people in the waves," Walker notes. "While some are remembered for their grace, style, and dominance in competitive surfing, others were known as bold and powerful surfers—even regulating men in lineups."

Sex, power, pleasure and courtship were intricately intertwined with the act of surfing. And women claimed an equal if not the lion's share of mother ocean's sensual, sacred experience.

When a man and woman rode in on the same wave sexual indulgence often followed.

In one of Honolulu's first Hawaiian language newspapers, the *Nupepa Kuokoa*, an article appeared 1865 describing *Ka Holomana Kahiko* (Ancient Sports of Hawaii). In that December 23rd issue the journalist J. Waimau wrote that at surfing contests held in older times, the men, looking like "a company of soldiers of that day," would wear red-dyed *malo* (loincloths) and assemble on the beach. Women would make their way to the beach in matching red-dyed *kapa* skirts. Then, "they go and join together with the men in surfriding."

Those who spoke of surfing with their intimate partners include Palani and 'Iewale of Kahana, Pili A'ama and Kapū'ewai of Waimea, Oahu. Even the youngest of the goddess Pele's clan, Hi'iaka, surfed on Kauai, with the high chief Lohi'au, after (as the story is told) she helped revive him from near death.

More formal courtship was also carried out in the surf, when a man or woman tried to woo and win a mate by performing on the waves. "Hawaiian legends abound in tales of thwarted and successful love affairs," wrote Ben Finney, "and surfing played a part in many of them." Passionate adventures of champion surfers and famous courtships that began on the edge of the ocean were recorded in Hawaii's abundant oral history. They indicate women's significance in the unwritten but extensive surfing literature of the Polynesian people.

Many women surfers who displayed skills in the surf, attracted the highest ranks of kapu chiefs with their beauty and mana. Kinahanaiakamālama, wife of King Aikanaka, who rules in Rarotonga and the Tuamotuan Islands, was known as an excellent surfer.

Chiefesses like Kamelamela of Kealohilani, Keleanuinohoana'api'api of Maui, Hinahanaiakamālama of Hilo, and Māmala of Kou Harbor in Honolulu all surfed with their suitors at some point in their stories. This correlation hints at the literary evidence presented about surfing women within Polynesian oral traditions. One obvious observation: surfing has always exuded a strong sensuality and part of surfing's allure to *both* sexes is its inherent erotic context.

Royal Courts and Supreme Courting

King David Kalakaua, the Hawaiian Kingdom's last male sovereign, ruled the nation from 1874 to 1891, championing a sport which had almost been extinguished by Western influence. Known as the "Merry Monarch," Kalakaua is credited with helping revive the ancient traditions of both hula, and surfing. He also set down a number of Hawaiian stories, many of them relating to women surfing.

One of the most intriguing is the story of Princess Kelea, the beautiful sister of Maui, the ruler of that island territory. As Kalakaua told it, Kelea, "the surf-rider of Maui," while surfing Lahaina was abducted by a chief named Kalamakua and taken to be married to Lo-lale, the King of Oahu. On the way Kalamakua stopped at his own fiefdom on the West side of Oahu and took Kelea surfing—more than likely at the great break of Makaha. Kelea and Kalamakua both shared a love of surfing and in the time they spent getting over to the Honolulu side where Kelea was to be married to his King, a secret romance began. Marriage to Lo-lale, the high chief of Oahu proved problematic. Lo-lale didn't surf, and worse yet didn't even like the ocean. Living inland at Lihue, Kelea was miserable, only finding happiness on the rare trips to the coast. Soon she was planning her getaway. Stealthily commandeering a sailing vessel Kelea slipped through the reef pass, escaped from the King's clutches and headed back to her native Maui. She made one stop though—on the West side. She paid a visit to her abductor Kalamakua and instead of punishing him, Kelea rekindled their romance and swept him away to surf with her back on Maui.

Queens of the Stone Age

As the Sport of Kings, surfing has always retained a regal status. But in reading the original texts of these histories, queens appear to be better known for their surfing prowess than kings.

During the time of the Hawaiian Monarchy, the entire royal family—chieftesses, princesses and queens—were all recognized as formidable surfers.

The most famous surfer of this period was Kaahumanu, a wife of King Kamehameha the Great who ruled from 1782 to his death in 1819. Ka'ahumanu was known as an expert surfer and an influential woman in the culture. An 1822 engraving shows the image of a tall, voluptuous woman.

Both Ka'ahumanu and her husband Kamehameha were dedicated surfing enthusiasts. According to Hawaiian historian John Papa II, they liked to surf Kooka, a break located at Pua'a, in north Kona, "where a coral head stands just outside a point of lava rocks." Clearly the regal women who surfed these reefs or (like Kelea) escaped marriage to surf were no timid wallflowers.

And although these particular historical figures were beautiful women surfing with little to no clothing, these stories do not convey them as objects of male sexual desire. Instead, the stories portray them as agents in history, women remembered for their surfing abilities, prowess, mana and character. Female surfers like Kelea, Ka'ahumanu, Mamala, and many others are central characters in epic legends from centuries ago.

Beyond Hawaii, women surfing in the waters of Tahiti, Aotearoa (New Zealand) and Rapa Nui (Easter Island) are also mention in native surf lore. Teuira Henry (1847–1915) was an early female ethnographer who published her grandfather John M. Orsman's manuscripts of recorded Tahitian legends. In Tahiti, Henry observed, "Fa'a he'e, (surf-riding) was highly popular with young men and women," and that "surfriding is still practiced to some extent." Even the

Boatswain's mate on the 'Bounty,' James Morrison, wrote in the first description of Tahitian surfing that "all sexes are excellent" and that "the children also take their sport in the smaller surfs."

Polynesian ethnographer William Ellis noted there is even mention of a patron deity that presides over surfing in Tahiti prior to Western contact. Ellis tells us about "horue or faahee" (surfing) of which "Huaouri was the presiding god."

Moses Manu's translation of Keaomelemele, the grandchild of Mo'oinanea, abounds with surfers like Punahoa, 'Ōhele, and Keaomelemele herself, who surfs famous breaks and then bathes in the famous fresh water pools of the islands. Keaomelemele enjoyed surfing nightly after completing intensive days of training in chant and hula at Waolani on Konahuanui (Oahu). It appears that Keaomelemele's surf sessions followed by the bathing in these fresh water pools restored her energy. Manu describes the time spent as rests between hula sessions, but it is almost like surfing is meant as a form of cross training.

Ranging from just a few pages to epic oral poems, stories of such women made a prominent mark on Hawaiian society for generations.

Over the centuries, as Hawaii's economy became increasingly driven by tourism, marketing entities faced the challenge of assuring visitors that Hawaii's natives were safe and accommodating hosts, deftly marketing the islands with images of passive, lifeless, scantily-clad native hula girls. Next to such imagery, the historical reality of empowered female surfers became nearly invisible.

Thanks to contemporary female surfers (including modern pioneers like Rell Sunn and others), by the 70s Hawaii began to see a restoration of surfing's true roots.

Japan's Senoshi Surfing Girls

While the act of standing upright on a surfboard appears to be first performed by the Polynesians, only recently has it been verified that Japan had a two hundred year tradition of body boarding. And this wave-riding included females.

From the mid-Edo Period (1603–1867) Japanese style wooden boats developed a then-new technology of timber processing that used removable floor boards called *Itago*. Fishermen's children took these *Itago* out of the boats and used them as boards and bodyboards. The practice was commonly known as *Itago-nori*, meaning "floor board riding."

Dokurakuan Kanri, a *haiku* poet from Sakata, in Northeastern Japan, provided the oldest written documentation of Itago-nori in his diary after visiting Yuno-hama Beach in 1821 and seeing children playing "senoshi," a local word meaning wave-riding.

By the 1880s, beaches became popular venues for healthy exercise and leisure activities. From then until the onset of World War II, Itago boards became more of a wave-riding tool than a boat floorboard and were widely produced and commonly ridden along the coastlines of Japan. Surprisingly, there are unmistakable images of young women using these wooden crafts with waves breaking in the background.

Princess Victoria Ka'iulani

Defying a ban on surfing to keep Hawaiian heritage alive, the courageous 'Island Rose' fought for her beloved kingdom like a wave-riding warrior

With the destiny of a kingdom on the line, Princess Victoria Ka'iulani, heir to the Hawaiian Crown, entered the American White House in Washington, D.C. She had just sailed from the British Iles where she had been riding her surfboard in the waves at Brighton Beach, on England's southern coast. It was 1893, a momentous year for Hawaiians.

Face-to-face with the 24th President of the United States, the Princess rose up with all her regal grace and presented an eloquent and emotional plea: "Four years ago, at the request of Mr. Thurston, then the Hawaiian Cabinet Minister, I was sent away to England to be educated privately and fitted to the position which by the constitution of Hawaii I was to inherit. For all these years, I have patiently and in exile striven to fit myself for my return this year to my native country. I am now told that Mr. Thurston will be in Washington asking you to take away my flag and my throne. No one tells me even this officially. Have I done anything wrong that this wrong should be done to me and my people? I am coming to Washington to plead for my throne, my nation and my flag. Will not the great American people hear me?"

Grover Cleveland, the American President, was moved. He would, he promised, take her case to the Congress and demand that they honor the legitimate Hawaiian Monarchy and refuse to recognize the January 17, 1883 coup led by a contingent of powerful American businessmen attempting to annex the Hawaiian Islands. Congress's decision would determine her fate and Hawaii's future.

Brilliant, beautiful and betrayed by American financiers, Ka'iulani was no pedantic princess. Classically educated at Great Harrowden Hall, in Northamptonshire, England, she spoke several languages, wrote poetry in English, Latin and Polynesian and was a child prodigy in art and music composition.

But first and foremost, the princess was a surfer. Known to ride a long wooden board, (a particularly heavy and demanding one at that), she had a reputation for outstanding performance in big surf. Women, particularly those of Royal blood, were noted for their prowess and power on the waves. The Hawaiian Monarchy had surfed with passion until the late 1800s when wave-riding became almost extinct as a sport.

The evangelical missionary's religious dogma had become the preeminent cultural power in the land—and for the most part they had succeeded in removing surfing from the everyday lives of the Hawaiian people. But Princess Ka'iulani—the second in line for the succession of the Hawaiian Crown—was a notable exception. Disregarding the missionary's efforts to eradicate all wave-riding activities, she continued to surf daily in full defiance of the western restrictions imposed on the Hawaiian culture.

"She was an expert surfrider around 1895 to 1900," recalled early 20th Century surfrider Knute Cottrell, one of the founders of the Hui Nalu surf club at Waikiki in 1908. Riding a "long olo board made of 'wili wili' hardwood Ka'iulani was the last of the traditional native surfers at Waikiki."

There is a strong case to be made that surfing was saved from extinction by this brave, bold woman—a royal princess no less. If Duke Kahanamoku is rightfully the man who introduced surfing to the world, then Princess Ka'iulani might be the savior who made that possible.

Born Princess Victoria Ka'iulani Kawekio I Lunalilo Kalaninuiahilapalapa Cleghorn on October 16, 1875, the Crown Princess was named after Queen Victoria and her maternal aunt Anna Ka'iulani, who died young. Princess Ka'iulani's life and legacy are a testament to her love of the Hawaiian people in their hour of need. Ka 'iu lani means "the highest point of heaven" or "the royal sacred one" in the Hawaiian language.

Descended from her first Cousin Kamehameha the Great, the founder and first ruler of the Kingdom of Hawaii, Ka'iulani's mother was known as Likelike, the sister of the last two ruling monarchs. Her father was the prominent Scottish businessman Archibald Scott Cleghorn. Because Princess Ka'iulani was second in line to the throne after her elderly and childless aunt, the young girl was expected to eventually become queen.

Being the first 'hapa haole' (half western) successor to the monarchy was not easy. A mixed marriage does not always run smoothly, and Princess Ka'iulani's parents struggled with the clash of their respective social traditions.

Expecting to be the master of the household, Cleghorn's staunch Victorian male chauvinism clashed with the Hawaiian nobility's belief that regardless of gender, royalty's decisions should rule supreme.

Her Mother's Deathbed Prophecy

When Ka'iulani was just eleven years old, Likelike fell ill and never recovered. Legend has it that a large school of bright red fish—an omen of death in her family—massed close to shore and that Likelike predicted her daughter would never marry and never become queen.

The reigning monarchs, King Kalākaua and Queen Kapi'olani, talked with Cleghorn and the Princess about preparing her for her royal role with a British education.

Sent to Northamptonshire, England in 1889 at the age of thirteen, Ka'iulani was given a private education, excelling in her studies of Latin, Literature, Mathematics and History. She studied French and German and took lessons in tennis and cricket. Growing up knowing the landscape painter Joseph Dwight Strong from her uncle's court, and Isobel Strong, a lady in waiting under her mother, she showed an early talent for art and took several trips to Scotland and France to study.

Isobel was the stepdaughter of Scottish novelist Robert Louis Stevenson, of "Treasure Island" fame. Ka'iulani and Stevenson became good friends and he called her "the island rose" in a poem he wrote in her autograph book.

Moving to Brighton in 1892 felt like a fresh start for Princess Ka'iulani who continued to study in England for the next four years. Surfing was her great joy, and there is explicit evidence that she surfed the beaches of Brighton on England's southern coast quite frequently. Chaperoned and tutored by a Mrs. Rooke who set up a rigorous curriculum, the resort by the sea pleased the princess with its consistent surf. As Mrs. Rooke, reported, the Princess "loved being on the water again, the bracing sea air giving her renewed energy."

Arranging for her to have an audience with Queen Victoria as part of a trip around Europe, her Hawaiian overseers had to suddenly cancel all plans in late January of 1893. It was the news of that moment which had brought her to the White House to plead with President Cleveland. A short telegram announced the shocking message: 'Queen Deposed,' 'Monarchy Abrogated,' 'Break News to Princess.'

Refusing to remain idle while the nation she loved was illegally stolen from her people, she gave a fiery impassioned statement to the English press and headed for the American capitol.

It was to be a bitter experience. Treating Ka'iulani with contempt, the pro-annexation press referred to her in print as a half-breed, calling her "dusky," although she was saved from the blatantly racist treatment repeatedly given to her Aunt, the Queen of Hawaii.

Typical of the time, "positive" accounts of the Princess' appearance often tried to emphasize what was thought to be "white" about her.

Occasionally, even her British father, Archibald Cleghorn, was disparaged by American writers fearing Great Britain as a rival for possession of the Islands.

A Queen without a Country

Returning to Europe to finish her education, her world further imploded when her cherished childhood friend, Robert Louis Stevenson died. And then came the news that a new Republic of Hawaii had been established—in her absence and against her will. Despite her exhortations to U.S. President Grover Cleveland, who brought her plight before Congress, her efforts could not prevent the annexation of her homeland.

Arriving back in Hawaii, she now found herself an heir without a throne. The day Hawaii was annexed as a territory of the United States—August 12, 1898—citizen Ka'iulani and her aunt, the Hawaiian Kingdom's last monarch, wore funeral attire to protest what they considered a criminal coup d'état. "It was bad enough to lose the throne," Ka'iulani wept, "but infinitely worse to have the flag go down."

Shortly thereafter her half-sister, Annie Cleghorn, and her English guardian, Theophilus Harris Davies, both died, leaving the princess without close friends or family; a stranger in a strange land, adrift and abandoned. A great sadness overwhelmed her. In heartbreak, her health started to decline.

She thought the warm familiar waves of Hawaii would help her recover. But her condition continued to deteriorate. Even the new house her father had built for her couldn't lift her spirits as she struggled to readjust to the loss of her future kingdom, vanished like a windswell.

Urged by her father to continue making public appearances, the futility of her efforts instead caused her to become more withdrawn and emotionally exhausted.

In a stalwart effort to find a path forward a glimmer of future contentment shone: she found a fond companion—and announced her engagement to Hawaii Prince David Kawānanakoa. But even that was not to be. Riding in the mountains of Hawaii in late 1898, Ka'iulani was caught in a storm and came down with a fever leading to a fatal case of pneumonia. Princess Victoria Ka'iulani Kawekio I Lunalilo Kalaninuiahilapalapa Cleghorn would die soon thereafter of inflammatory rheumatism on March 6, 1899, at the age of twenty-three.

Her mother Likeliki's ominous prediction had finally come true: Ka'iulani was never able to marry and would never become queen. She was the last in a line of tragic Hawaiian royals whose sovereign nation was usurped by would-be colonials. It was an irony compounded by the fact that America had only a century before thrown off the bonds of a foreign power and demanded self-rule themselves.

One silver lining in her legacy remains: fighting valiantly but vainly to save her country, Princess Ka'iulani preserved a precious piece of Hawaii that every waverider so cherishes: she kept on riding waves—and in so doing saved surfing for all generations to come.

2

Death, Resurrection, and the Road to Emancipation

1900–1925

"Women, like men, should try to do the impossible, and when they fail, their failure should be a challenge to others."

—Amelia Earhart

Suffragette City

In the eight years following Princess Ka'iulani's death her efforts to keep surfing alive were rewarded. Duke Kahanamoku and his five brothers, the Kaupikos, Keaweamahis families and others, revitalized the sport by continuing to introduce visitors to the art of wave-riding.

The year 1907 was an auspicious one for surfing: Alexander Hume Ford, a journalist from Chicago moved into the grass shack adjacent to the Old Seaside Hotel on the beach in Waikiki, soon founding the Outrigger Canoe Club. After experiencing a wave-riding session with Ford, Jack London wrote *Riding the South Sea Surf,* on a visit to Hawaii. Surf pioneer George Freeth gave the first California surfing exhibition in Redondo Beach. Legendary Edison Electric company cameraman Robert Bonnie showed his then sensational film footage of surfing to mainland audiences as far away as New Jersey. *Surfing had been discovered.*

But a little-known story of an Australian water-woman who visited the East Coast of America made headlines around the world for challenging the laws for women's swim wear. Her "trial of the century," as it was called then, had a profound influence on women's sports performance that broke a major barrier.

And as the tightly-bound taboos of the Victorian age began to loosen, surfing spelled emancipation for the bold—and sinfulness to the pious. The beach was society's frontier and wave-riding the definition of freedom itself.

Annette Kellerman
The First Million Dollar Mermaid Risked Jail to
Win Women's Opportunities and Stand for Athlete's Rights

On an October afternoon in the autumn of 1907 water-woman Annette Kell-erman stepped onto the stretch of cool gray sand at Revere Beach that looked across the shoreline of Boston's teeming metropolis. Along its strand thousands of onlookers watched as this athletic, intrepid "Australian Mermaid" stood defiantly as uniformed city police surrounded her to serve an arrest warrant for indecent exposure.

Kellerman, a professional swimming performer was soon to become the most famous water-woman of her age for wearing a black wool swim outfit which—although covering more flesh than a neoprene spring suit of today—was considered so scandalously skimpy it was deemed a criminal offense by the tradi-tional upper-class Brahmins of Boston.

She had brought her splashy act to America that year, traveling as an "under-water ballerina"—an ancestor of synchronized swimming. Billed as "The Diving Venus" at New York City's heralded Hippodrome, she wore her skintight suit customized to accentuate her body and improve her performance. Her swimming costume in the Big Apple didn't, however, pass the straitlaced Boston muster. The slightly shortened sleeves and legs of her form-fitting design were so shocking she might as well have appeared nude. "Banned in Boston" did not become a glib axiom without good reason.

It should be noted that Boston was hardly the only beachfront where restric-tions were in place: in her home country women were forbidden to swim during daylight hours, a ban that had only begun to be listed in 1902. Swimming zones were still segregated for men and women and suits had been until just a few years before essentially similar to the requirements in Boston—long, wool and cumber-some. Victoria's rules were even more restrictive and for the most part France did not have an extensive beach culture this early.

All of that was a moot point once Kellerman defied the social norms there at Revere Beach. Within minutes of making her emergence onto Boston's most conservative stretch of shoreline, Kellerman was arrested. Thrown into the Boston jail, the incident became front page headlines and set up a challenge of precedent-setting proportions. The trail was followed by millions around the globe. The outcome would ignite a firestorm setting women's water sports ablaze.

But Kellerman was stubborn, flamboyant and fearless, and took her indecency case to court. Her argument to the judge was both legitimate and reasonable: "A competitive athlete needed to have the most efficient swimsuit design in order to achieve peak performance," she contended. It didn't hurt that the 1900 Summer

Olympics in Paris had introduced women's events—even if it was only golf, tennis and croquet.

Kellerman posited that practical long-distance open-ocean swimming garb was essential to attain top results. In Chicago, she "created a new record swimming from the government pier in Lake Michigan to Hyde Park crib, a distance of six miles," as well as doing a 72-foot dive from the topmast of a steamship. In Boston harbor she swam twelve miles "from Charlestown bridge to Boston light," breaking "all records for this course by a good half hour."

Salacious and sensible in equal measure, Kellerman demanded a legitimate legal opinion about the very nature of women's competitive performance. It attracted both scorn and support.

The trial became a cause célèbre, with newspapers around the world covering the story. Which was more important—performance or propriety? It was a powerful legal argument, an audacious challenge by one of the most colorful women of the age.

In the end the judge agreed with Kellerman, marking a milestone in the legal fight for women's sports. Across the globe every woman who went near the shoreline suddenly found a heroine both socially and sexually, vaulting her into international celebrity. In a single controversial incident Kellerman landed in jail, on the front-page and into the history books. With talent, tenacity and public relations genius, Annette Kellerman made herself a global mega-star, daringly undoing the oppressive girdle of 19th Century society.

Challenging Race, Roles and Gender

Women surfers in the early decades of the 20th Century all knew Duke Kahanamoku. As Hawaii's aloha ambassador, the five-time Olympic medalist was one of modern surfing's earliest first-person observers of women's surfing. Since many of the early lifestyle adopters surfed alongside him in Hawaii, he knew these intrepid women as well as anyone. This vanguard of the re-emerging surf culture was the new century's image of travel adventure in a rapidly shrinking world.

Duke and Tom Blake (another giant in early surfing) were among the few surfers who documented women in the early years of the sports revival. In *Hawaiian Surfboard*, Tom Blake noted that Duke Kahanamoku was the first 20th Century surfer to tandem ride a surfboard.

"Leslie Lemon was the first to stand on Duke's shoulders," Blake noted. "Miss Marion 'Baby' Dowsett and Beatrice Dowsett were the two girls who first rode with Duke, three on the same board, the full length of Canoe surf."

Kahanamoku founded the Hui Nalu in 1911 as the first surf club for local Hawaiians as well as men and women of European decent. It included two outstanding women surfers, Mildred 'Ladybird' Turner, and Josephine 'Jo' Pratt. It is arguable that these women—joining an all-inclusive, mixed-ethnic surfing club—were among the first groups to challenge the racial codes of the world's white ruling class.

"Josephine Pratt was the best woman surfboard rider in the Islands during 1909–10 and 1911," wrote Tom Blake, who arrived in the Islands afterward, but had gotten the word from others. "She surfed Canoe, Queens and small first break."

It is arguable that these women—joining an all-inclusive, mixed-ethnic surfing club—were among the first groups to challenge the racial codes of the world's white ruling class.

In early 1910, Alexander Hume Ford (a Scottish-Hawaiian surf enthusiast) arranged a surfboard contest and canoe races at the other surf club in Hawaii—the venerable but all-white Outrigger Canoe Club—for a cruise line whose ships would be making two stops in Hawaii. Four silver cups were made for the race and were known as the Frank Clark Cups. Only one cup was actually awarded—and it was for the Best Woman Surfer at the Outrigger Canoe Club. The winner was Josephine C. Pratt. It was the first trophy bestowed by the Club and is believed to be the first surfing trophy ever awarded. And it appears to be the first modern surf contest won by a woman.

And as Duke Kahanamoku spread the sport of surfing around the world, another woman a continent away would answer a call to become part of its colorful history.

Australia's Inspiration

Standing in the crowd that Saturday morning in 1914, fifteen-year-old Isabel Letham heard the request she couldn't resist. Duke Kahanamoku, the greatest Olympic swimming star of the era stood before a crowd of thousands gathered at Sydney's Freshwater Beach. He called out to the waiting audience with a simple offer: Would any of the young ladies in the audience like to come out and ride with him?

Sparked by the excitement, she stepped forward and raised her hand. It was a decision that would alter the course of her life—and Australian watersports as well.

Following a record-smashing Gold Medal performance at the 1912 Stockholm Olympics, Duke Kahanamoku set out on a worldwide tour giving swimming and surfing demonstrations in California and New Jersey. Now he had traveled by ship to Australia to do the same for the mass of enthusiasts in this water-crazed nation.

Isabel Letham was an accomplished bodysurfer and competitive rough water swimmer herself. The *Hawaiian Star Bulletin* claimed that "As far as features go,

Miss Lethem is the prettiest swimmer to come out of Australia. As for diving, she is another Annette Kellerman." When the statuesque Hawaiian chose Isabel to do a tandem demonstration with him, she caught a wave that would be remembered as one of the great moments in Australian beach history.

"He paddled on to this green wave and, when I looked down it, I was scared out of my wits. It was like looking over a cliff. After I'd screamed 'oh no, no!' a couple of times, he replied: 'Oh, Yes, yes!' He took me by the scruff of the neck and yanked me on to my feet. Off we went, down the wave."

That performance—or performances, since there are more than one version regarding location, number of waves ridden, size of crowd and exact date—has become a romanticized piece of Australian folklore. For more than a century that moment introduced surfing to the nation—and Isabel Letham became its legend.

But in 2014 surf historians discovered a reality that has given the achievement a different unexpected twist. Combing through old newspapers they identified Tommy Walker as the real first surfer in Australia, riding a board he bought for $2 in Waikiki during a trans-Pacific crossing.

The *Telegraph*, Australia's newspaper of record in that era, describes surfing at Manly beach in Sydney on January 1912, three years before Letham's historic day at Freshwater: "A clever exhibition of surfboard shooting was given by Mr. Walker, of the Manly Seagulls Surf Club. With his Hawaiian surfboard he drew much applause for his clever feats, coming in on the breakers standing balanced on his feet or his head."

But even more dramatic was the discovery of another *female*—Isma Amor—who was also considered an outstanding waverider three years before Isabel Letham rode with the Duke into Australian history.

In 1959 Manly Life Saving Club biographer Reg Harris wrote: "in the 1912–13 season a number of . . . members decided to persevere and master the art [of surfboard riding]. They included . . . an outstanding woman surfer, Miss Isma Amor."

A photograph published in the *Sunday Times* in Sydney on March 1st, 1914 pictures a woman standing upright on a surfboard cutting through a broken wave. The caption reads: "Sydney can boast of possessing several young ladies (notably Miss Amor, of Manly) who can 'shoot' the breakers in the method in vogue here almost as expertly as the best men exponents."

This uncovering of Amor via close reading of archival sources disrupts the linearity of the Kahanamoku/Letham surfing story. Yet it enriches the history of Australian surfing, opening another chapter not only for women's surfing history but also for the development of Australian beach culture more broadly.

Why did Amor disappear and Letham sustain? Researchers surmise that Amor was forgotten mainly due to her marriage in 1920 which uprooted her to an inland locale disconnecting her public association with surfing from that time onward.

Isabel Letham, by contrast, not only continued her aquatic career, but managed to flourish. In 1918, Letham sailed to America and was able to make a living teaching swimming, diving and water fitness. She initiated San Francisco's first ever swimming competitions and coached at the University of California, establishing a women's competitive swimming program that is still in place today.

Working in the San Francisco Bay Area in the mid-20s, Letham attempted to introduce the highly successful Australian lifeguarding techniques in her community. As many times as she tried, her efforts were repeatedly dismissed. Local politicians simply would not accept the viewpoints of a female, no matter how expert.

Whether Letham was the first surfer or even the first woman surfer in Australia is to miss the point. She was to Australian surfing what *Gidget* was to American surfing: the catalyst that caused wave-riding to catch fire both on the beaches and in the imagination of the world. Letham was not the first Australian surfer but she was the central figure in popularizing the sport of surfing down under. Letham herself never claimed to be the first nor did she aggrandize her lifelong surfing passion as the media did.

Returning to Australia in 1929 Letham was still surfing at age sixty-two. In her late 70s, she helped organize the Australian Women's Surfriders Association and served as its patron. "There's no reason why girls should not be as good on surfboards as the boys. I'm all for them," she proclaimed.

Her energy and enthusiasm helped inspire a shy 12-year-old newcomer, Pam Burridge, who later went on to win a World Title. Burridge adored Letham, and Letham admired her young protégée as if she were her own.

When Burridge won the inaugural women's championship in May of 1990, Isabel was there. "I know I should be home with my knitting, but I've waited sixty-five years for this," she proudly exclaimed.

In 1993, this first lady of Australian surfing who had carved her own lifestyle, and revolutionized swimming techniques, was inducted into the Australian Surfing Hall of Fame. When she passed away just two years later, beach lovers from around the world scattered her ashes outside the surfline at Freshwater Bay where she first rode with the great Duke. Something even more moving about this unique woman links Australia's surfing lineage: the connective tissue of womanhood. Shortly after Letham died, her protégé World Champion Pam Burridge gave birth to her first child, a daughter. Her name, naturally, was *Isabel*.

Girls On Film

As interest grew, film, music and magazines began to present a view of the idyllic island life. "Auntie" Alice Nāmakelua, a renowned expert in "slack key" guitar played and recorded songs in front of the breaking waves at Waikiki. "On the Beach in Waikiki" topped the radio play lists in 1917. But they frequently missed their mark eschewing authenticity for glamour, veering toward exaggeration and sometimes outright distortion.

The silver screen was equally as influential—and inaccurate. Although surfing had only been introduced to Southern California by George Freeth in 1907, less than a decade later Hollywood was churning out a plethora of films set in Hawaii, many of them Annette Kellerman productions. Commercially focused as these movies were, they shaped the public's perception of surf and beach lifestyle as much as the surf films of the 60s did for the 'Baby Boom' generation. Betty Compson, one of Hollywood's leading movie stars, went on location in Hawaii to film *The White Flower* in 1922. She played a hapa-haole (half-white) woman who fell in love with a pineapple company executive, and the plot thickened from there.

Popular publications like *Sunset* magazine quickly took advantage of the American public's fascination with all things surfing, especially in Hawaii. While magazines, films and music spread the romantic image, athletes like Hawaiian Josephine 'Phena' Hopkins Garner rose to the top level of actual sport performance. "I used to spend all my days out there in the surf from eight o'clock to until lunchtime," Garner recalled. "Change the bathing suit. Rest for an hour. Back out on the board again till five o'clock—every day." It was not surprising when she entered the women's 1917 Surfboard Championship at Queens surf that she took home the title. Garner and her colleagues Ruth Scudder Gilmore and Gerd Hjorth set swimming records while spending their leisure time riding waves. Garner was prophetically connected to her idol, Annette Kellerman for swimming a breaststroke in Kellerman's style—and the judges eliminated her for it. Along with Lillie Bowmer Mackenzie these women successfully entered the Hawaiian surf community from the teens into the early 20s.

Hawaii was not the only place women entered the formative surfing scene. Ever since 1915, when teenager Dorothy Becker stunned locals by becoming the first woman to perform a headstand on a board, Santa Cruz has been home to an ever-growing, tight-knit network of surfer girls. Soon, more women joined Becker, including Mabel Hathaway-Jeffreys, who, in 1922, rode a redwood board made by Duke Kahanamoku himself.

Heather Price, South Africa's first surfer, took her place in history (albeit unknowingly) as the first ever person recorded to stand-up surf with a photo appearing in a local newspaper in 1919.

While on a holiday in Cape Town, she reportedly borrowed a board from two American Marines. The two men had solid-wood, Hawaiian style surfboards and were kind enough to introduce Heather to stand-up wave-riding. Once again an entire continent had been introduced to surfing by a woman. Photographs of her surfing can still be found on collectable postcards from the era.

Hawaii was now successfully exporting surfing's allure. England, South Africa and Australia, as well as America had been introduce to wave-riding. Film and literature and popular music had integrated surfing into their storylines. "The ultimate pleasure" as Captain Cook's 1778 ship's log described it, was now being rediscovered by the western world. It would not be long before surfing would turn that world upside down.

Surfing's Great Mystery Queen
Agatha Christie—the World's Best Selling Author—was a zealous Surfer

Agatha Christie was struggling up the beach at Waikiki, exhausted, board-less and nearly naked. The most successful mystery writer of all time was having a wardrobe malfunction that would have sent most of her novel's fictional characters to a watery grave. It wasn't *Murder on the Orient Express*, but Christie felt like she was getting killed by the surf at Queens.

In this, her second session of surf in Hawaii her silk bathing suit—which covered her from shoulder to ankle—had been ripped from her body by a thumping outside set.

"It was a catastrophe," she wrote in her diaries. "My silk bathing dress was more or less torn from me by the force of the waves. Almost nude, I made for my beach wrap."

Undeterred by an experience that had left her stripped of her suit *and* dignity, she did the only thing any good fashionable women would: she went *shopping*.

"I had immediately to visit the hotel shop and provide myself with a wonderful, skimpy, emerald green wool bathing dress, which was the joy of my life, and in which I thought I looked remarkably well. Archie thought I did too."

Christie and her husband Archie had sailed into Honolulu harbor just two days earlier, August 6th, 1922. They had checked into the stately Moana Hotel and gone to their room to settle in. As they gazed out onto the beach below they saw surfriders catching waves directly out front. They jumped into their beach attire, rushed out to the sand, rented boards and paddled out. It was to be a serious learning experience.

And Then There Was Surf

Agatha Christie had an astonishing talent for writing detective novels. Her short story *And Then There Were None* is the world's best-selling mystery. With over

100 million copies sold, Publications International lists the novel as the world's sixth best-selling title of all time. But writing aside she was also one of the most adventurous women of her age—and she found her passion for surfing every bit as fervent as her enthusiasm for entrancing murder plots.

In the summer of 1924, she and her husband Archie had taken a side trip from their planned round-the-world sailing route specifically to try the surf in Hawaii. This was the leg of their voyage they had been most excited about when they had set sail on an eight-month global sojourn that had taken them to South Africa, Australia and New Zealand. They had been introduced to surfing in Cape Town, and as Agatha wrote about her experience in a novel, published two years later, *The Man in the Brown Suit*: "Surfing looks perfectly easy. It isn't. I say no more."

"The surf boards in South Africa were made of light, thin wood, easy to carry, and one soon got the knack of coming in on the waves. It was occasionally painful as you took a nosedive down into the sand, but on the whole it was great fun."

But they had really only tried prone surfing in Cape Town. In Hawaii they would learn the fine art of standing upright on a board—and learn the power of Hawaiian waves even on the gentler South Shore of Oahu. It would be a memory that set her on a course for life.

"It was a bad day for surfing—one of the days when only the experts go in—but we, who had surfed in South Africa, thought we knew all about it. It is very different in Honolulu." She would recall.

"I was not as powerful a swimmer as Archie, so it took me longer to get out to the reef. I had lost sight of him by that time, but I presumed he was shooting into shore in a negligent manner as others were doing. So, I arranged myself on my board and waited for a wave."

"The wave came. It was the wrong wave. In next to no time I and my board were flung asunder.

"When I arrived on the surface of the water again, gasping for breath, having swallowed quarts of saltwater, I saw a tiny board floating about half a mile away from me, going into shore."

She assumed she was in for a long swim—but her luck held, just as it did in her books.

A young American surfer retrieved her board for her with some advice as well: "Say, sister, if I were you I wouldn't come out surfing today. You take a nasty chance if you do. You take this board and get right into shore now." It was no put down, just good council from an experienced surfer to a novice.

As Christie noted, "I followed his advice."

Yet she came back the next day. And the day after that. She continued to surf every day getting better and better as she put the requisite time in.

"After starting my run, I would hoist myself carefully to my knees on the board, and then endeavor to stand up. The first six times, I came to grief. . . . [but] Oh, the moment of complete triumph on the day that I kept my balance and came right into shore standing upright on my board!"

"Agatha Christie is probably one of the first British 'stand-up surfers,' along with Edward, the Prince of Wales, who also surfed in Waikiki in 1920 and held a short reign as King Edward VIII of England before abdicating the throne to marry the love of his life American beauty Wallis Simpson," noted researcher Peter Robinson from the Museum of British Surfing.

"In the early 20s very few British people were surfing and the only one we know about earlier than her, standing up, was Prince Edward," Robinson said.

"It certainly shows a new aspect to her life, she clearly had a passion for the sea and was one of the first wave of new surfers," he continued. "She was such a prolific writer that people tend to associate the image of an older lady writing books. But when she was younger she was actually a very accomplished surfer, and one of the first I know of from the UK."

Agatha never gave up her love for surfing. There was, she wrote, "Nothing like it. Nothing like that rushing through the water at what seems to you a speed of about two hundred miles an hour . . . until you arrived, gently slowing down, on the beach, and foundered among the soft, flowing waves."

There may be no more famous woman whose pursuit of adventure resulted in her becoming one of the earliest surfers of her age. But there was no mystery about what drove this astonishing woman to ride the waves. "It was," she wrote in later years, "one of the most perfect physical pleasures that I have ever known."

3

Rediscovering the Supreme Pleasure

1926–1941

"So that the monotonous fall of the waves on the beach, which for the most part beat a measured and soothing tattoo to her thoughts seemed consolingly to repeat over and over again."

—Virginia Woolf, *To the Lighthouse*, 1927

Waves of Glamour
Hawaii Sells Surfing To Promote Tourism

At the turn of the 20th Century, Hawaii was a distant fantasy to most anyone but sailors and ship captains. Yet the allure for experiencing the romantic dream of South Sea Island adventure was irresistible. Seeing a profitable opportunity, Walter Chamberlain Peacock opened the Moana Hotel in 1901, nurturing a trickle of tourists making passage on three-masted schooners—an often uncomfortable and sometimes hazardous passage. Travelers to Hawaii who wanted to learn the secrets of the sea were taken surfing and canoeing by the Beach Boys—skilled Hawaiian water-men trained to take the inexperienced "haole" guests into the waters of Waikiki.

That trickle became a stream when the 51-passenger steamship *Lurline* was replaced by the 146-passenger S.S. *Wilhelmina*. Matson Lines opened the Royal Hawaiian Hotel in 1927 and added increasingly larger, faster liners to their Hawaiian and Pacific service.

Sensing an untapped demand, American tourism brokers promoted Hawaiian visits using exotic images of women riding waves in Hawaii. Hotel brochures, Chamber of Commerce ads, steamship line menus, and vinyl record sleeves displayed women on surfboards wearing less than conservative swimsuits. Beckoning both sexes alike, these surfing images became icons of the Hawaiian lifestyle.

The lure proved irresistible to a small but growing number of adventurous women. Most often they were affluent, but some enlisted as stewardesses on passenger ships or served as nurses, secretaries (or almost any available job) to chance a glimpse of Diamond Head, smell the plumeria-tinted air and maybe catch a wave—or at least "sunbathe" in the latest swim fashions.

Lighting the Torches of the Roaring 20s

Wading into the Pacific Ocean on a clear cold New Year's Eve in 1926, Faye Baird was more than a little nervous. For starters she was carrying a ten foot, 110 pound redwood surfboard on her back as she entered the shoreline. There was no wetsuit to seal out the 55 degree temperature on both land and sea—only a scratchy wool bathing suit. The winter sky had darkened early and was now turning a shade of blue black.

Joining her—and already neck deep in the surf—was her partner Charlie Wright, a lifeguard from Ocean Beach just a few miles south. He was carrying two lit waterproof flares above his head trying to get as far past the shorebreak as possible to prevent the torches from getting soaked before they reached the outside lineup. In the moonlight Faye could see head-high waves rolling through on her right. But what gave her the most pause were the hundreds of people packing the Promenade, crowding the dunes. Hundreds more were following her to the water's edge. The magisterial Mission Beach Ballroom had just been completed. For their grand opening Faye and Charlie had been hired by the owners to give a New Year's Eve surfing demonstration for their patrons. That audience had now swelled to over a thousand people. *That*, she thought, *is what makes me nervous.*

Faye closed her eyes for a moment remembering the wave she had caught a few years before at north Pacific Beach—one that she rode all the way to shore, right through Crystal Pier. All she would think about at the time was dodging the barnacled pilings. It had thrilled her to death.

Tonight, with 1927 just a few hours away, she and Charlie Wright would attempt to paddle into one of the outside waves; she would leap onto his shoulders and raise the flares to light their dance on this aquatic stage. It was a starring role for a plucky, precocious fifteen-year-old. And she was ready for her star-turning debut.

A native San Diegan, Faye Baird learned to swim at Creelman's Bathhouse on Fifth Avenue near the San Diego bay before she was five. She loved the water and had trained to be a distance swimmer ever since. In those days swimming was one of the sports that girls *could* do. As a young teenager she found she preferred the buoyancy of saltwater and soon became an accomplished competitor, a regular in the annual Silvergate Swim Classic. But then surfing got in the way. Her family moved into a cottage in Ocean Beach, and there Faye met Charlie Wright—a husky, handsome city lifeguard.

He owned a heavy redwood surfboard, and without much effort he talked her into going out on it. It was love at first ride. At least for her and the solid, ten-foot plank. Within the season she was riding waves in any conditions with ease.

She was a natural in the surf—a great swimmer, at home in the ocean, completely hooked. The bigger challenge, she found, was getting the board to and from the water. Charlie's board was a three-inch-thick redwood. Faye learned to position it upright, lean it against her back, carry it on her shoulder blades to the water and drop it in. She most often rode solo—but she especially enjoyed tandem sessions with Charlie.

Faye Baird was more than likely the first female San Diegan to surf—and possibly one of the first in all of California. Looking back a century later, it was a remarkable achievement.

But for a girl in the Jazz Age, being a *surfer* hardly seemed groundbreaking—women in 1927 were wearing short skirts, bobbed hair and heavy makeup, pushing the envelope of the era's social acceptability. Black jazz music was the rage, and the sexually implicit Charleston was the dance craze. Young "flappers" flaunted their newfound freedom in an economic boom that was louder than the Tommy-guns of the Prohibition rum runners along the nation's beaches. Baird took little notice; surfing was simply something she loved.

Hollywood noticed, though. Young, athletic and seemingly fearless she had already received offers from the studio moguls to come under contract as a stunt-woman. Once again she was thrilled to death. Hollywood was on the horizon.

Her mother, however, was having none of it. She was not about to allow the naïve fifteen-year-old to take off for the footlights. Faye chafed, but her mother was resolute. And in the light of the "Me Too" movement of 2018, Faye's mom may have been a lot smarter than she seemed to her daughter. Predators prey in every era.

Back on the Promenade, the Mission Beach Ballroom crowd was growing restless. They wanted to see this new-fangled surfing thing before the evening got too cold. The Ballroom's owners were hosting a huge party, and after this publicity stunt was over, the festivities would move inside. The flappers and their consorts on the Promenade were getting chilled—and all were ready to dance.

Outside in the lineup Faye was losing body heat. "Maybe we should go in," Charlie offered. Faye Baird brushed the idea away. She'd not spent her entire childhood swimming and two whole summers surfing to disappoint this gathering.

The crowd began to make noise. A set had appeared—a fairly big one. Not knowing how wave-riding worked they cheered for the first wave in sight. Charlie scanned the set then paddled them into the down-the-line position, nodding to indicate this was the one they would take.

Charlie paddled; Faye kept the flares from touching the water. Almost immediately the tandem team began to glide diagonally with the wave. Seconds later
Faye and Charlie were standing; both hands extended upwards with the glaring
red flares sparkling and smoking as they lit the riders for the crowd. Flashbulbs
popped, lighting the shore like strobe lights. As they shot across the breaking wave
heading straight for the pier a thousand onlookers roared their approval. Even out
in the water the applause sounded loud, Faye would remember later, talking to the
newspaper journalists. They rode three waves in all. The audience was ecstatic.

When they finally stepped back onto the sand Faye was shivering uncontrollably.

As the throng headed for the Ballroom, Charlie gave Faye a coat. "Maybe we
should get you home," he offered.

"Home!" That was not the plan Faye had in mind.

She knew this was a moment in Southern California history; she wanted to
savor it. What she could not know was the other events this New Year 1927 would
usher in: Amelia Earhart flying an airplane across the Atlantic, Virginia Wolfe
writing her masterpiece *To the Lighthouse*, Coco Chanel reinventing global fashion
and Zelda Fitzgerald embodying *The Great Gatsby's* Jazz Age madness.

But Faye Baird *did* know one thing—she knew what she wanted to do: "I
brought a change of clothes, she told Charlie. Let's go to the party. I plan to
dance the New Year in."

Spoken like a true surfer. In *any* age.

Breaking the Taboos

Faye Baird, Isabel Latham and Agatha Christie were not the only change agents
of their era. By the 30s American women had begun to push different limits.
Hastened by the 19th Amendment to the U.S. Constitution, women won more
than just the right to vote. Social norms like traveling abroad alone, wearing
revealing beach attire, exhibiting overtly athletic activity and interracial marriage
were still verboten on the mainland. But in Hawaii women found these activities
far more acceptable. Surfing introduced scores of young men and women to the
Polynesian culture. Women in the 30s became enchanted by the open, tolerant
freedom Hawaiian society permitted.

While alluring, the idea of pulling up stakes to experience a culture still foreign
in society's eyes was an audacious move—and it could still risk scandal back home.
None-the-less, those who did make the journey were noted, if for nothing more
than their appearance in such an exotic locale.

Tom Blake, who has been credited with the invention of both the surfboard
fin and surf leash, was also author of *Hawaiian Surfriders, 1935,* the first book

strictly dedicated to surfing. His comments on the women are the most definitive observations of the era: "Among the best known at surfboard paddle racing since 1915 are Beatrice Newport, Dot Hammond, Mildred Slaight, Babe Gillespie, Olga Clark and Marchien Wehselau." An early Outrigger Canoe Club member Wehselau—an Olympic swimmer and expert surfer—was documented riding her solid wood board in big surf at Waikiki in the early 20s.

By the early 30s, Beatrice Newport had risen to top slot among the females surfing Waikiki. "Miss Beatrice Newport was the best woman surfrider along about 1930," wrote Blake. "Since her time no girl has come near to the mastering of surf-riding as she did except perhaps Cecily Cunha."

Newport was appreciative of Blake's praise, but even more enthusiastic about his newly developed hollow board, a breakthrough design that reduced surfboard weight by more than half.

"The Hollow Board," she was quoted as saying "is delightful, fast, light and sporty to ride."

As for Cecily Cunha, the woman mentioned as Newport's equal, her prowess in the waves was not surprising although her story is. Her father Emanuael Cahuna arrived from the Azores on a whaling vessel in the late 1800s. He built a two-story beachfront home at the intersection of Kapahula and Kalakawa Avenues, in what is now downtown Waikiki. His daughter Cecily "was a great swimmer and surfer," wrote her neice May Kunha Ross in 1996. "She rode old wooden boards and surfed right in front of the house." It was hardly surprising given her own private beach with some of the best waves in the Honolulu area, that she would not rise to the top of the ranks of Hawaiian water-women.

By the mid-30s surfing had been fully revived in Hawaii. But back on the west coast, it was new and largely the province of a select few men and a handful of women. In California Mary Kerwin surfed the Hermosa Beach pier. Martha Chapin, the sister of pioneer surfer Gard Chapin—and step-aunt to the notorious 60s surf icon Miki Dora—rode the Palos Verdes Peninsula breaks with the men who founded California's oldest surf club. Doc Ball, a pioneering photographer who documented much of the intial California surf scene, took images and notes about the women surfers of his time. Patty Godsave was a standout who, Doc Ball wrote, "used to ride tandem with one of the guys, either Pete Peterson or E.J. Oshier."

Tandem was a popular activity for women of the 30s both in Hawaii and California. Doc Ball photographed Marion "Cookie" Cook and Ann Kresge riding tandem with male partners as well as surfing solo at San Onofre.

Californians Ethel Harrison and her brother Lorrin "Whitey" Harrison— who had discovered new surfing Meccas at Dana Point and San Onofre in 1933—succumbed to the allure of Hawaiian surf life as well.

Growing up in Corona del Mar, Ethel and Whitey started surfing in 1925. Managing to stow away to Honolulu on more than one occasion, he and Ethel eventually travelled as stylish passengers on a trans-Pacific Ocean liner in 1935. The two surfed, made friendships with the local Hawaiian surfers and saturated themselves with island beach culture. Lorrin eventually returned to California, bringing with him tikis, palm frond beach shacks, and ukulele music of Hawaii. He promptly implanted these cultural icons into the nascent surfing culture of San Onofre. Ethel, meanwhile, had fallen in love, marrying full-blooded Polynesian Joe Kukea, a descendant of Hawaiian royalty. She remained to raise a family in the 40s and become one of the finest women surfers on Oahu.

San Onofre Surfing Wahines
The First Women's Surf Club

Back in California an attractive group of fun-loving females formed the San Onofre Surfing Wahines in 1938. As the first exclusive club of women surfers they broke some taboos themselves. A scrapbook of the Wahines club—uncovered in 2020—shed new light on the previously unknown activities of women surfers in the pre-WWII era of California. The 75-page scrapbook—filled with newspaper clippings and dated journal entries—described the women's dance parties and wild escapes at the secluded beach.

It also included photographs. A group photo by Harvey Walters identifying club members Mary Jo Best, Eleanor Roach, Jean Olsen, Irene Chovan, Helen Hughes, Marion Chovan, Dorothy Hackett, and Ruth Sizemore was dated May 15, 1938. Another image shows part of the group in an old topless Model T Ford, proudly displaying a T-shirt with their club's name.

David F. Matuszak, author of "San Onofre: Memories of a Legendary Surfing Beach," released a second edition, adding 50 new pages to the now 1,550-page history book about the iconic surfing beach after learning about the San Onofre Surfing Wahines. Notes in the scrapbook also describe building the first beach hut down on the sand. Matuszak confirmed the evidence: "There are pictures of these women up in the rafters, hammering away and building the first shack."

Many of the photographs are believed to be taken by iconic surf photographer LeRoy Grannis. Although not confirmed, the scrapbook makes references to "Granny" the nickname Grannis was commonly known by. Ruth (Grannis) Sizemour was a sister of Leroy Grannis, adding probability to the supposition that he was the photographer. The San Onofre Wahines discovery was considered a major addition in documenting West Coast women's surfing in the 30s.

Dueling Dukes
Hero Duke Kahanamoku Taught Heiress Doris Duke
How to Surf—and a Lot More

In the late 30s billionaire heiress Doris Duke was the world's richest woman. Olympian Duke Kahanamoku was its most famous Hawaiian. The torrid, tragic story of these two mavericks would have made a Paramount Studios screenplay. He taught her how to surf and she taught him that being crazy wealthy could sometimes lead to becoming—well, just crazy. They were a match made in paradise—or purgatory depending on the viewpoint. Their matching height (both 6'1") matching names, and matching fame made them natural bedfellows—in more ways than one. Passionate, athletic and charismatic, both the Duke and Ms. Duke were reluctant celebrities, generous givers—and both experienced bittersweet lives.

Ardent, unrepentant surf lovers, they were romantically involved in a time when Hawaiian men did not mix with rich white society ladies—at least not in the public eye. A jazz pianist, who served a brief stint as a war correspondent, Doris was an unbridled bohemian who flaunted society's restraints. She left the world a philanthropic legacy of 1.3 billion dollars—and a string of lovers from Rio to Washington, from Hollywood to Santo Domingo.

He left the world the gift of surfing—and a string of competitive records that held for half a century.

They were celebrated by friends: Iconic surfboard designer Dale Velzy made Doris a yellow-tinted Pig model surfboard; fashion designer Claire McCadell made her a striking two-piece striped swimsuit. John Wayne gave Duke parts in his films.

The couple surfed in front of *Shangri-la* her opulent mansion in Honolulu, and she threw parties inviting Duke's brothers and friends. But the two Dukes' relationship was far more troubled than their public personas would indicate, and their romance—as with so many beachboy-celebrity trysts—ended in misfortune.

"In July 1940, Doris gave birth to a daughter named Arden, who died one day later," wrote eminent historian Michael Beschloss in a 2014 *New York Times* article. "Biographers have argued that the baby was almost certainly Kahanamoku's."

Three weeks after the birth—his timing perhaps provoked by dread of a public scandal—Kahanamoku married Nadine Alexander, a Cleveland-born dance teacher at the Royal Hawaiian Hotel. Doris Duke reportedly gave the newlyweds about $12,000 (now over $200,000), which they used to purchase a house not far from her own.

Like Duke himself, Doris would suffer because of who she was—scandals, rumors, more attention than she wanted. But as her biographer Sallie Bingham wrote "nothing could prevent her from seizing that moment in the Hawaiian surf—exulting in doing what she wanted, claiming her place in the world—as a figurehead, a beacon, a woman with 'too much money, too much power and too much imagination.'"

Yet as liberating and idyllic as Hawaii was for many women, storm clouds were forming over Europe and Japan. These same women who had broken new ground on the beach would find even more change in the impending global conflict that shook civilization and changed women's roles forever.

On December 7th, 1941 just minutes from Waikiki, the balmy waters of Pearl Harbor would experience the start of a cataclysm from which there was no escape. The gates of an old world order would be blown off their hinges. For women drawn to surfing, the coming World War would end up leaving the entrance to equality open wider than ever before.

4

A New Rising Swell
1941–1950

"We cannot direct the wind, but we can adjust the sails."
—Dolly Parton, country music icon and activist

Testing the Waters in a New Era

The cataclysm of World War II brought unprecedented upheaval to American society. Millions of women who joined the workforce for the first time discovered talents and confidence they had never known. Born from a resolute determination forged in the armament factories of the American war machine, women for the first time became full-time skilled laborers—at jobs which could not be spared for men needed in combat.

Like their male counterparts, women serving in the military passed through the California shores and on to Hawaii on their way to and from the Pacific Theater of war. They saw the beach, touched the surf and felt the magic.

Returning from service, a wind of aspiration emboldened self-confident women as they explored the changing moral codes and pushed the envelope of acceptable behavior. In the August 1950 issue of *Life* magazine, a large photo essay captured the nascent yet already robust surfing lifestyle at San Onofre featuring many of the women who surfed there year-round, raising their children right on the beach.

"It was a new, fabulous opportunity for women to experience a freer, more independent life," said Stephanie Becket, whose mother was one of those San Onofre women.

Equal opportunity was still not on the radar, but smart, self-assured women seized prospects where they could. Whether in film roles, signature swimsuit lines, stunt work, tandem competition or sheer power surfing, the plucky 40s and 50s women took full advantage of the chance to experience their emerging newfound freedom.

A new rising swell was sweeping into the country's landscape. In the coming decade it would transform the culture of surfing—and of America itself. And trailblazing women waveriders would help pave the way.

Mary Ann Hawkins
The 20th Century's First Female Superstar
Her Last Ride

On a beautiful April morning in 1983 Mary Ann Hawkins paddled out to surf for her last time. Alone. She was not ending her storied career or commemorating one of her competitive triumphs. Surfing's first superstar was not performing as a stunt-double for megastars like Elizabeth Taylor in *Giant* or Shirley Jones in *Oklahoma* as she had in many films of the past. She was not celebrating the anniversary of her 1938 feature in *Life* magazine, or her record-breaking 880 meter race in the 1933 Swimming and Diving Championships.

Entering the water from in front of her beachfront Mokuleia home on the far western corner of Oahu's North Shore, sixty-three-year-old Mary Ann Hawkins was beginning her final surf session to memorialize one of her greatest losses—one which all her triumphs could not salve.

Hawkins had certainly garnered enough achievements in her lifetime. Regarded as the undisputed standout woman surfer of her era, between 1935 and 1941 Mary Ann won every surfing and paddling event she entered. In 1936 at the first-ever all-female paddleboard race Hawkins finished first. On the same day she won the half-mile swim. Those impressive victories were simply sequels to her honors for all around swimming and diving: 37 first-place ribbons were draped on her parent's mantel piece. Personable, talented and tough, she was also gifted with possessing "the figure and looks of a movie star" with "grace personified in the water." Nonetheless she was no child prodigy; Hawkins had been a sickly youngster and had spent decades in the water fighting for every hard-earned success.

On that last day as she paddled out for the last time Hawkins' grief did not come from a disappointing competitive result. Despite "breaking records for breaking records," not all her challenges could be overcome with talent, courage and determination. Some were tragedies beyond individual control. While Mary Ann Hawkins may have been the supreme surfing female of her generation her life would suffer the greatest heartbreak a woman can endure—twice.

A Pre-ordained Destiny
Meets an Irresistible Force

Her childhood was idyllic enough: born in Pasadena in 1919, Mary Ann was winning trophies for swimming and diving with the Pasadena Swimming Club by the age of ten. At fifteen, she set a new record for the AAU 880-yard freestyle and became the Junior National Half-Mile Open Champion. A gifted swimmer with Olympic-level skills, Hawkins' road to a successful swimming career seemed almost pre-ordained.

But a glimpse of Duke Kahanamoku was all it took to detour Mary Ann onto the wave-riding path whose ultimate destination would make her the first great 20th Century water-woman: "I was about 10 when I saw Duke in the pool in Pasadena," Hawkins remembered. "He was this big, beautiful Hawaiian man, making bubbling noises with his mouth and making everyone laugh. Duke would have been around thirty-three. He fascinated me and I'll never forget the first time I saw him."

In 1934 Mary Ann competed with the Ambassador Hotel Swim Team in an 880-yard paddleboard race and won—*against men*. That same year, her family bought a home in Costa Mesa, near Newport Beach—a gathering spot for early California boardriders.

"The first surfers I saw at the Corona del Mar jetty were Gene 'Tarzan' Smith, Lorrin 'Whitey' Harrison and Preston 'Pete' Peterson—all great surfers. I fell so in love with surfing and bodysurfing, I never really swam my best from that time on."

One of Mary's contemporaries—and an excellent surfer herself—was Pete Peterson's wife Alice Peterson. Her daughter Lisa Peterson is the second in a three generation lineage of exemplary surfing women along with her daughter Elsie. Lisa's father Pete Peterson was the male equivalent of Mary Ann Hawkins: the most dominate surfing figure of his era. Lisa—who visited San Onofre faithfully every summer and surfed every rideable day—remembered a story her mother Alice told her when she was a small child. "There was a contest with only men that Mary Ann decided to enter. When Mary Ann was told women couldn't compete with the men she responded: 'Yes we can!'"

Mary entered the competition and—like many subsequent events—beat the men handily. "This was a woman with plenty of grace," Peterson remarked, "but she was not to be daunted by fools—of any gender."

Hawkins' stay at Costa Mesa and as a regular at Corona del Mar was brief; she and her mother moved to Santa Monica in 1935. Now—immersed in the world of wave-riding—she got her own board—almost unheard of for a woman in the mid-30s. Although part of the beach scene, few took to riding other than tandem. The weight of surfboards was considerable; they had to be literally dragged up and down the trail at places like Palos Verdes Cove. At the time, Hawkins probably weighed less than her surfboard. Surfing in Santa Monica, she fell in with a group that included Bud Morrissey, Hoppy Swarts, Leroy Grannis, Barney Wilkes, Tulie Clark and E.J. Oshier—all future surf legends—and her surfing improved.

Her first marriage was to one of those legends, surfer/shaper Bud Morrissey. They had a daughter, Kathy, but family life did not deter her drive to be the ultimate water-woman.

In 1939, Hawkins "was invited to compete in the 1939 Duke Kahanamoku Swim Meet in Honolulu." It was a big jump at eighteen, but she took the steamship ride to the Hawaiian Islands and competed in the Pacific Aquatic Festival. She won the women's half-mile and the 880-yard and broke a record in the 220-yard. More importantly for her, however, was the chance to surf Queens and meet Duke Kahanamoku, who had inspired her as a young girl. "My very favorite surf spot in all this world is Canoe Surf in Waikiki," Mary Ann declared many years later. "In 1939, when I was over there, Duke helped me in every way. He'd always have me get to his right, he'd coach me. . . . Duke and his brother and I were a team together. He picked me to team with him, to surf against the Australians." That surfing competition was cancelled, but Hawkins came home with her most cherished memento: a photo of her shaking hands with Duke.

Fame and Fate

She won the Pacific Coast Women's Surfboard Championships in 1938, 1939 and 1940, dominating the competition. *Life* and *Argosy* magazines featured her girl-next-door good looks in articles, which in turn opened doors in Hollywood. She stunt-doubled for Esther Williams in *Million Dollar Mermaid* and Dorothy Lamour in *Beyond the Blue Horizon*. She even broke her ankle jumping from a burning haystack for Shirley Jones in *Oklahoma*.

After World War II, Hawkins became a regular at Malibu, riding a custom board made by the area's preeminent shaper, Joe Quigg. "I absolutely loved it," she recalled, "and that board seemed to pick up waves all on its own. Unfortunately that board was stolen. . . . Then I had Velzy make me a board."

Her surfing life continued to succeed unabated; her married life less so. By the late 40s her first marriage to Bud Morrissey had ended.

Like Elizabeth Taylor the movie star she doubled for in films, Hawkins married a number of times. And like Taylor, the one she seemed most fond of would come to a sudden, tragic end.

In 1950 she married a water-man named Don McGuire. That marriage produced a son, Rusty, and appeared to be as perfect a match as her friends had seen.

But all too shortly her world came crashing down when McGuire—while boating to Catalina Island with a Hollywood stuntman named Paul Stader—drowned. The boat foundered about 10 miles off Catalina. Stader made it to safety, but McGuire did not, leaving Hawkins with two children, one an infant.

A Hopeful New Start in Hawaii

In 1955 Hawkins married Fred Sears, a movie director with a long, respectable string of credits including the first rock and roll picture *Rock Around the Clock*. Her marriage with Fred Sears was short. A year after the marriage ceremony, they split. Hawkins was once again a single mother of two: Rusty McGuire and Kathy Morrissey. She moved the family to Hawaii in 1956 to work on another movie.

"She befriended Henry Kaiser who owned what would become the Hilton Hawaiian Village," recalled Robin Grigg, one of the most accomplished water-women of the 50s, and one of many surfers influenced heavily by Hawkins' earlier breakthrough success and style.

"Mary Ann surfed Canoes as much as possible," Grigg continued, "and was hired to do a water show at the Hilton Hawaiian Village during a time when air travel was opening the Hawaiian Islands up as a world-renowned vacation spot."

Hawkins also performed water ballet in an underwater swimming show at the Reef Hotel in 1960. The performances often featured special appearances by her friend Esther Williams, beachboy Sam Kahanamoku and the legendary father of surfing, Duke Kahanamoku.

"Kaiser built her a special pool that was only two or three feet deep and was heated to 90 degrees," explained Robin Grigg, who moved to Hawaii with Hawkins that same year. "Mary Ann began teaching swim classes at Kaiser's hotel and she specialized in teaching very young babies to swim."

A Lasting Legacy

For thirty years, from 1956 to 1986, the Mary Ann Sears Swim School in Waikiki instructed thousands of babies to hold their breath while swimming under water and breathe on the surface. Comfort in the water came naturally to Hawkins but she believed this affinity was natural to all humans, and she proved it by taking children as young as six weeks old from the bottom of the pool to the top and teaching them what she believed they already instinctively knew how to do.

Hawkins's baby swimming technique was (in its early stages) quite controversial. The National YWCA, the American Medical Association and the American Academy of Pediatrics all thought her practices with babies less than three years old would lead to ear infections, water intoxication and other viral infections. Their fears were never borne out by the reality and Hawkins perseverance prevailed.

Slowly, over the years, her work with children drew the attention of writers both in Hawaii and nationally. She was credited with developing a whole new advance in swimming development. An entire generation of swimmers had been taught her techniques right there in Waikiki.

"Who knows how many lives Mary Ann saved," pondered surf writer Ben Marcus, "and who knows how many future surfers—known and unknown—she introduced to the ways of the water?" More than a few it appears.

"I took a class as a child," recalled Dale Hope, a Hawaiian legend who as a toddler learned to swim at Hawkins' side. "She changed the way people related to the water."

"She was our neighbor back when I was a child," remembered Patti Paniccia, another surfer who grew up to compete professionally as an adult. "Everyone knew she was a magical swim teacher."

Hawkins' personal life was going well too. Her son Rusty and daughter Kathy had grown into successful adults. Rusty, like his father, was a waterman working on boats. Hawkins remarried, this time to Jack Midkiff. They moved to a beach house on the northern part of Oahu at Mokule'ia, living happily for seven years.

Then tragedy struck again—and in almost exactly the same way it had the first time. Her son Rusty McGuire who—like his father before him—died in the water, drowning in a tugboat accident in Alaska.

Bereft, Hawkins decided the best way to help heal the pain was to do what she loved the most—and what they loved doing together. When she began that final paddled out from the beach house at Mokule'ia she was saying goodbye—a surfer's fond farewell.

"The last time I surfed was to remember Rusty," Hawkins' confided. "I just felt that if I got out in the water again maybe I'd be closer to him, closer to God, because Rusty hadn't yet been found. . . . It was so lonely, because quite often Rusty and I had boogie boarded out there. So that was actually the last [time]. . . . I was ever on a board, and when I caught a wave, I didn't stand up because I wasn't in condition anymore to do that."

Mary Ann Hawkins lived another ten years. Despite tragedy and tumult, she earned the legacy of surfing's first female superstar and led a paradigm leap in water safety.

Her memorial, held at the ultra-respected Outrigger Canoe Club, was attended by hundreds and eulogized by every newspaper columnist in the Islands.

Unquestionably the greatest female surfer in the first half of the 20th Century, Hawkins's achievements and influence were cherished by a generation of women who followed her. But her most important statement—the image of that last ride to shore—may be her most memorable.

A Calm Between Two Storms
After the Bang; Before the Boom

In the 40s Hawaii saw a new set of women surfers, many introduced at the vener-ated *Outrigger Canoe Club*. After four years of world war, the nation was aching for fun and relaxation. Surfing was an elixir. Waikiki was a welcome, familiar venue. Nearly forty years after its founding, the *Outrigger* would again be a center for women's surfing.

Pat Honl, Anita and Doris Berg, Helen Haxton, and Pat Barker were con-sidered the best young waveriders caught in the spell of Hawaii and surfing. In a 1998 Outrigger Canoe Club oral history session Pat Barker talked about teaching Humphrey Bogart to catch swells in front of the Royal Hawaiian hotel where she worked. "Not much of a surfer but he was the nicest man!"

Working was just a means to an end, though. Evidently, even back in the 40s the "surf virus" was a common excuse for ditching your job to ride waves: "Every time the surf was up "all of us knew what was going to happen: 'Sorry, I'm sick today!'" Pat Barker laughed "When the surfs up, forget going to work. Lord, that was fun."

There were many others: Eva Hunter, Gwen Davis and Yvonne "Blondie" Boyd could be found sampling the breaks from Queens to Populars, but their appearance was not an everyday commitment. Keanuinui Kekai's *was*. Unquestionably one of the most outstanding Hawaiian woman surfers of the era, she married Rabbit Kekai, one of the greatest beachboy surfers of Waikiki. Rising to prominence in the post-World War II period, Keanuinui remained a top talent well after she remarried to another noted surfer of the time, Dave Rochlen, an early giant in the surf clothing industry.

"Keanuinui Rochlen was one of surfing's little-known treasures," wrote Sam George for *Surfer* magazine in 1999, "emerging as one of the hottest female surfers and all-around water-persons in Waikiki. Keanuinui excelled in all the traditional beachboy arts. She became one of the top steersmen competing in Hawaiian long-distance outrigger races." Other regulars included Ivanelle Mountcastle, Pam Anderson, and Jane Wiley, all outstanding riders.

The post WWII era also saw big changes in surfboard design—and the women of Waikiki were among the first adaptors. In 1948 Anita Berg received a "surfboard of my own for my sixteenth birthday . . . it looked like a big wooden spoon in shape. I think it was Richard Willett of Waikiki Surf Club that shaped it down and made it a really fast board. It was 11'6"."

Joe Quigg, one of California's preeminent shapers of the 40s, brought the first fiberglass-sealed balsa surfboards on a 1947 trip to Hawaii. It was state-of-the-art equipment at the time, half the weight of other boards. The first Hawaiian to own one was Pat Honl, whose Outrigger Canoe Club nickname was "surfer girl."

Helen Haxton went from a very heavy redwood plank in 1945, to a big hollow board about twelve feet long in 1948. Her later board would be a balsa-fiberglass, nine-foot board that "came into style from the *Tarzan* film, starring Johnny Sheffield ('Boy'). He brought the spoon-shaped balsa board from California and ours were patterned after it but shaped in a modern sleek way." Returning to the beach with these huge 80-pound hollow boards, they would undo the metal plug to drain the water as they carried them the 50 yards to the locker.

"If a woman wanted to be treated with respect and surf where the waves were larger, invading the space where the guys surfed, they had to know how to surf, follow the rules and be able to carry their own boards down to the ocean. Doris Berg explained. "We refused to be considered a bunch of wimps, so we always carried our own boards."

Pam Anderson was apparently no wimp—she told the Outrigger Canoe Club that only a handful of the girls surfed really big waves, which included her surf pals Pat Honl and Pam Barker. But the girls who rode the really big stuff were Ethel Kukea and Vi Makua. *Their* time for glory would be coming.

Nearly everyone who surfed the beaches of Hawaii remembered this as a special time—after the world war ended, before the deluge of tourism truly began.

"I went to work for United Airlines in San Francisco and they eventually transferred me back, so I worked in the United office right outside the Outrigger Canoe Club," Pam Barker laughed. "I was able to spend my lunch hour surfing. It was *just great*. I was very fortunate."

Years after her surfing adventures Helen Haxton often found herself yearning for the "good old days" at the 'old' Outrigger site.

"The surf was right there in front of you (Canoes and Queens) and one could spend the whole day out there having the time of one's life. Surf in the morning . . . come in for lunch . . . and surf again until dark."

Wahine Wanderlust
Adventurers of the 50s
1949–1959

Just Add Water

The 50s proved an inescapable fact: the nectar of surfing was irresistible. The seed that spread from Hawaii germinated wherever passionate waveriders carried it. Surf enthusiasts grew like spring wildflowers and traveled like dried food—the common requirement was "just add water."

Wave-riding blossomed in the most unlikely places: Near the mouth of the Necanicum River in Oregon circa 1940, there are authenticated photographs of a woman identified as Geraldine Mathis being pulled along on her *surfboard* by a car driven along the smooth hard sand.

In Cornwall, on England's west coast Betty Hunt led the British beach lovers to try wave-riding very early on with enthusiasts Marylyn Ridge, Lyn Connelly and Dee Delaney following suit. In Peru, the sport took root within the robust beach culture of the upper class. Despite shark danger South Africans flocked to the surf along its coast. And in Australia's predominately coastal population, an entire beach lifestyle bloomed—from Sydney north to the Gold Coast and south to Victoria.

But nowhere was the attraction stronger than in the birthplace itself: Hawaii, and then California by proxy. Locals, transplants and visitors alike were caught up in surfing's sheer delight—what the first observers described as "the ultimate pleasure."

Freed from the provincial constraints of previous generations, women caught the new rising swell and were carried across the globe.

Climbing Kilimanjaro and Surfing Jeffreys Bay

Examples were everywhere: Native Californian Donna Matson was the first woman to climb Kilimanjaro and surf Jeffreys Bay, South Africa's premier point wave. She didn't consider herself to be a good surfer, she "just liked it" well enough to end up surfing all over the world—including Hawaii before it became a state. While on South African assignment in the mid-50s, she saw the waves at Jeffrey's Bay and inquired if she could rent a board. The locals pointed to the nets out in the ocean, told her there were sharks out there. While declining to rent her a board, the local surfers *did* take her out to surf tandem—encouraging her to surf, refusing to permit her to go out alone.

Matson traveled extensively in Africa, South America, Asia, the Middle East, and Europe. As the first American woman to climb Mt. Kilimanjaro, she hiked and snow-skied on five continents, working as an elementary school teacher, a global oceanic research diver and as an adventure cinematographer—at one point spending eight months lugging heavy camera gear around to do a story on Machu Picchu in Peru.

Peru: A Hawaiian Safari to South America

Even in Peru women had a hand in introducing surfing. The first foam board reached Peru in March of 1957. Betty Heldreich, Ethel Kukea and Ann Lamont brought it as a gift for Carlos Reyy Lama who was hosting his Hawaiian friends.

Betty Heldreich, who had been surfing for years at Makaha, first met Peruvian surfer and renown playboy Carlos Dogny when he had judged the Makaha International in 1956, the third year of the event and first year women had been welcomed to compete. "Incredibly 110 contestants signed up," Heldreich's daughter Vicky wrote in *Wave Woman*, her beautiful memoir of her mother Betty.

"Between eight and ten thousand spectators flocked to Makaha on January 15 and 22, 1956. There were no hotels of any sort on the West Side, but people camped on the beach. Her mother Betty entered the contest along with friend Ethel Kukea who had come over years earlier with her brother Lorin 'Whitey' Harrison. Whitey (a name given to him by his Hawaiian friends) had returned to share the gift of aloha culture with the Southern California surf world, Ethel had married and made a life in Hawaii.

Betty Heldreich and Ethel Kukea were two of the best waveriders in the early 50s Hawaii scene. They entered the Makaha International contest "Women's Surfboard Riding" division—along with several dozen other competitors—including Violet Makua, Joan Kalahiki, Esther Kalama and Christy Donaldson. Even legendary icon Mary Ann Hawkins, and Cynthia Hemmings (the sister of future world champ Fred Hemmings) registered to compete. Few in number, these women were nonetheless all outstanding athletes.

But with their competitive spirit in high gear Ethel and Betty took first and second in the event.

Carlos Dogny, who was there to judge the Makaha International, took notice. Vicky Heldreich wrote "He was impressed with the women he saw surfing in the big powerful waves in Makaha. Back in Peru he convinced his fellow Club Waikiki members that they should bring surfing women to Miraflores to stir interest among the women of Peru."

Dogny was, for 50s Hawaii, quite a swashbuckling character. Vicky Heldreich described Dogny in her memoir as "The son of a French army colonel and a Peruvian sugarcane heiress, who had learned to surf under the tutelage of Duke Kahanamoku during a 1938 visit to Waikiki."

Dogny invited Heldreich and Kukea along with the other winners of the Makaha event to form a team and surf in the 1957 World Contest in Lima. The team would spend a month in Peru; Betty had to promise her daughter Vicky that she would bring her on the next visit to South America—with the condition that Vicky would win the Makaha Championship the following year. She was not the only one who would feel the pressure to perform. The entire Hawaiian team was nervous about an international event in a distant spot they had never surfed. They were front page Island news; expectations were high.

The Hawaiians boarded a Pan American Airways flight, arrived amid national fanfare in Peru and were wined and dined by Lima' elite social class.

The reigning Peruvian surf princess of that era was Sonia Barreda, a statuesque surfer of power and grace. Considered the first great female surfer in Peru, she did most of her surfing in the 50s. In later years her two children Gordo and Flaco would become among Peru's most notable surfers.

As with the visiting surfers in years to come the connection was immediate and enduring.

"In Peru we were treated like royalty—lots of wonderful, lavish parties," Heldreich remembered. "But the surfing conditions were very challenging: Ethel, Rabbit and I were out at least a half-mile from shore, and the wind was behind the waves. There was no sand on the beach, only these big rocks, so they placed spotters on the shore to catch the boards and protect them from being dashed to pieces."

The event was an international sensation carried on news broadcasts as far away as Australia and Europe. When the contest was over it was Heldreich who took home the three-foot silver trophy and had vivid recollections of the trip: "Ethel was actually the better surfer," she told California Surf Museum historian Jane Schmauss. "I was just lucky, I got the best waves when we were out there"

Makaha Matriarchs

Returning to Oahu, Heldreich and her daughters Vicky and Gloria lived on the beach while they built their pre-fab home on the Makaha beachfront lot she had purchased the year before. It was at Makaha that she met a young Rell Sunn.

"After I would wipe out, my board would go all the way in," recalled Heldreich, "and by the time I swam to shore, Sunn often had my board and was playing around in the shorebreak. She was a beautiful little girl, and I knew she'd be a good surfer."

Ethel Kukea and Betty Heldreich were surrounded with a group of early women who loved surfing. They included Keala Stubbard. Del Wong, Jane Kaopuiki, Marge Phillips, Joan Kalahiki, Christie Danials and Mozelle Angel. Mozelle was married to legendary surfer, diver and fisherman Jose Angel, and she was no slouch in the water herself. The stretch of breaks west of Sunset Point were cheaper than housing in Haleiwa and they had a house right on Pipeline. They surfed all along the breaks from Rocky Point to Rockpile in the late 50s, on a largely empty beach.

Mozelle Angel's good friend Anona Naone Napoleon was another of the early pioneers of North Shore surfing in Hawaii, By the time she was 18 she was trying to qualify for the 1960 Rome Olympics in the two person kayak event. Married to the legendary Nappy Napoleon, one of the original beachboys, she was an expert in surfing, paddling and—obviously—two man kayak. Along with two other women in 1954 she gained respect for being the first women to paddle the Kaiwi Channel—a grueling 41-mile stretch of open ocean separating the Hawaiian Islands of Molokai and Oahu—considered the pinnacle of long-distance Hawaiian outrigger canoe racing. A noted educator and committed historian, she developed teaching methods specific to Hawaiian students.

Napoleon remembered surfing breaks the length of the North Shore in the late 50s, including Waimea.

But it was Ethel Harrison Kukea who would end up the most influential of the early women surf pioneers, coming from one of the most prominent early California families and marrying into one of the most prominent Hawaiian surf families.

Her brother Lorrin "Whitey" Harrison had met Hawaiian Joe Kukea during Whitey's first trip to the Islands. A full-blooded Polynesian and direct descendant from Hawaiian royalty, Joe Kukea had the good looks and regal bearing of a chieftain. Ethel, also tall, regal and athletically gifted, fell for Joe soon after she arrived in the Islands.

"Joe and Ethel were pen pals in the 30s. It was popular to have a pen pal those years," Whitey's daughter Rosie Harrison wrote in *Let's Go, Let's Go*, a biography of her father. "After he and Ethel had corresponded so many years it was as though they were in love almost before they actually met." Ethel's parents were apparently not supportive.

"I'm not sure that her mother ever forgave her for running away to marry Joe," daughter Rosie wrote. "But, I can't imagine two people more beautifully suited to each other."

"Having already learned to surf in California," wrote surf historian and former *Surfer* magazine editor Sam George, "Ethel Harrison married into Oahu's surf-centric Kukea family and became the dominant figure in Hawaiian women's surfing during the late 50s. Ethel is perhaps competitive surfing's earliest female role model, winning back-to-back Makaha International contests, considered then to be the sport's world championship."

It was Ethel's innate charm and natural leadership that got women into the event to begin with. The Makaha International Surfing Championship was the largest contest in the 50s, but there was no women's division. Ethel gathered six enthusiastic contestants then approached the officials pleading for a chance to compete in the 1955 event. The judges acquiesced to her quiet strength and irresistible smile. Ethel made the finals and went on to be a three-time champion.

Strength was a trademark characteristic in these pioneering surfers. Physical strength to compete against men, emotional strength to deal with the many challenges and mental strength to out-think their male counterparts. And there was no stronger woman in the rising swell of the late 50s than Marge Calhoun.

Santa Cruz Matriarchs

While Marge Calhoun wore the crown of the surf kingdom, surfing capitals sprung up in each region where aficionados gathered to enjoy the burgeoning sport. La Jolla, San Onofre, Malibu, Santa Barbara and Santa Cruz all established their own close-knit enclaves. Women were part of each community.

Shirley Templeman and Pat Fassio were two of the earliest to surf Santa Cruz. Fassio (whose maiden name was Collins) was born in Santa Cruz in 1925—just five years after women gained the right to vote and nearly half a century before the Title IX act revolutionized women's sports. One of only two women surfing with Santa Cruz club members in 1941, Fassio would borrow their boards to ride at Cowell Beach.

A decade later Rosemari Rice and Earlyne Colfer were surfing Cowell's and Steamer Lane—popular Santa Cruz surf spots—before crowds, before wetsuits and leashes, when boards were hard and heavy.

As a teenager in the late 50s, Colfer remembered swimming hundreds of yards in the chilled water for a lost board.

"I would get out of the water so cold I'd go into my Volkswagen and turn on the heater full-blast, and then go home and take a warm shower until the hot water ran out," Colfer said.

Rice remembered having to fight for respect in a male-dominated sport. Out-of-towners gave her the stink eye when they saw a female surfing their local break. But Rice wouldn't stand for any nonsense. She played as hard as the boys.

She recalled one run-in at the Hook—near 41st Avenue in Capitola: "I had these young kids who just kept dropping in front of me. 'These kids just keep burning me,'" she told her husband and board shaper Johnny Rice. "He looked at me and said, 'Well, run them over, then,' and that's what I did. And I've got the skid marks to prove it."

Malibu Matriarchs

Of all the women who surfed around Malibu during the 50s, one of the best was Shelley Merrick. Nicknamed the 'Latigo Girl' her family moved to Malibu from Texas in 1946, where she grew up in front of a mostly-private right point at Latigo Shores, taking her first ride on a big redwood board when she was only ten years old. She never stopped for the next sixty years.

Access to those uncrowded waves in the late 50s, coupled with ongoing surfboard innovations propelled Merrick into the 60s contest circuit where she became the second woman on the Dewey Weber Surf Team, competing in the West Coast and United States Championships at Huntington Beach.

Moving to Savannah in 2002 she worked as the Coordinator of Special Events at Armstrong State University. Still surfing until her passing in January of 2015, she was a longtime Surfrider Foundation activist and educator, dedicated to teaching young students about the ocean and its importance to the planet.

Another early standout who moved away was Margo Scotton—but not before she met a movie star. Born in Long Beach, California in 1948, she started surfing at age eight in the South Bay of Los Angles riding waves in Redondo, Hermosa and Manhattan Beach.

Scotton's fondest memory was of beloved 40s character actor Andy Divine (best remembered for playing cowboy Roy Rogers' sidekick) presenting her trophy for second place in a 1959 event in San Clemente when she was just eleven.

Her description of the beloved film star was "that very large man, Jingles, on the western TV show." Scotton recalled that Joyce Hoffman won the contest—as usual. "Whenever she was in Southern California I always got second—she was so fast at getting to the next wave." Scotton moved to Santa Fe, New Mexico in the mid-80s.

San Onofre Matriarchs

When using the tin outhouses and cooking on open beach fires were considered luxuries by women at San Onofre, Gwen "Honey Babe" Waters was riding waves there. Demure in appearance, Waters' vivaciousness was on full display in the early 50s—hunched on her kneeboard, a tightly-reserved feminine coil that sprang free upon contact with swells.

Another accomplished surfer who could be found performing the hula for every special occasion and teaching Sunday School on the bluff above the break at Old Man's, Liz Irwin was an icon at San Onofre for more than six decades. She and her husband Jim were a cornerstone of the San Onofre Surf Club, spending countless hours on the beach in the early days of the Club. In the 50s. "She was the Duchess of San Onofre," said Stephanie Becket, who was in her Sunday School classes as a child. "An eternal icon."

These women were the embodiment of Hawaii's care-free surf culture. They were an elixir to western women yearning to break free from the constricting corsets of 50s status quo. It offered a powerful opportunity to expand athleticism, adventure and attitude in an exciting new way. If a women's place was in the *home*, these audacious women found themselves most at home in the inviting waves of San Onofre, Sydney, Santa Monica and Waikiki.

6

Hollywood Malibu Magic

Marilyn Monroe Rides the Wild Surf, a Pack of Feisty Females Claim Malibu, and a Surfboard Made for a Film Starlet Starts a Design Revolution

1945–1958

"I have learned over the years that when one's mind is made up, this dimin-ishes fear; knowing what must be done does away with fear."
—Rosa Parks

Cashing in the Malibu Chip

Les Williams was in a hurry. Rushing to catch some late afternoon waves at Malibu, he had skipped the last hour of work to add time to his surf session. Arriving in the parking lot, he could see the swell running across the cobbled beach and the light wind catching the face. As he leapt out of his car, he suddenly realized he had forgotten the one thing he needed most—*his surfboard.* He knew most of the surfers would already be out in the water, but as he hustled onto the sand his eye caught Darrylin Zanuck sitting at first point with her board in tow.

Williams knew her surfboard was a smaller balsa board built for a girl.

But he was desperate. Cajoling Darrylin into letting him borrow it, he paddled out into the line-up. The very first ride was a revelation.

"I'd never experienced anything like the sensation it produced," Williams told me in an interview in 2004. "It was so light, so responsive; it was like riding a magic carpet. Before the session was over, I was running circles around the rest of the crew!"

His first reaction was to stride onto the beach and demand why Darrylin had never let him ride this miracle before?"

"It's a girl's board," she replied. "You never asked." Williams went straight to shaper Joe Quigg and asked to try one. Quigg had just finished a board for his girlfriend and soon to be wife Agnes. Both he and Matt Kivlin (the two pre-eminent Malibu shapers of the era) had been shaping lighter, shorter boards for their girlfriends for some time.

Darrylin Zanuck, who had stolen actor and surfer Tommy Zahn away from Marilyn Monroe, surfed regularly at Malibu. At Zahn's request Joe Quigg created a surfboard for her. Traditional design called for a redwood-balsa plank—heavy and un-maneuverable. Quigg fashioned a *balsa* board covered in fiberglass and resin. Shorter, lighter, and—equally important—it fit in the back of Ms. Zanuck's chic Chrysler convertible.

"She was really the first girl to buy a surfboard and buy a convertible and stick the surfboard in the back and drive up to Malibu and drive up and down the coast and learn to surf," Quigg recalled. He dubbed the board the "Easy Rider," but it has gone down in history as the "Darrylin."

Williams claimed to be the first to discover the inherent properties that made these boards perform, but it didn't take long for the secret to be uncovered. Suddenly, the boards that were being built for the female surfers were being "borrowed," and the girls found it tougher and tougher to get their own boards back. The "Malibu Chip," a board that revolutionized surfing, had been launched.

"That board," commented master board builder Joe Quigg, "busted the whole surfing thing wide open. That unique shape allowed for bottom- and top-turns that held closer to the curl. The surfer was where he or she needed to be in the wave."

The performance properties of shortboards that transformed the sport were discovered when men tried riding boards *shaped for women*.

Inadvertently, women had requested an innovation that became one of the most important design developments in the history of wave-riding equipment.

The Actors Studio

As an early epicenter of surfing, Malibu—with its perfect, gentle peeling waves and beautiful shoreline—was a magnet for surfers, actors, dreamers and occasionally, desperados. Proximity to an urban metropolis and Hollywood's film-making industry, Malibu's secluded location quickly became a haven for the surfing set and the movie crowd. The heady mix of bohemian freedom and media-soaked fantasy provided a gathering spot close enough to Hollywood for actors to drive to work. For those who wanted to surf it was the perfect actors studio. Television actor James Arness of *Gunsmoke* fame, Hemmingway's screenwriter Peter Viertel, and even Marilyn Monroe—when she was still Norma Jean Baker—were regulars in the surf. Mary Ann Hawkins, 40s surfing superstar, now earning frequent roles as a stunt woman, moved to Malibu to be near her work.

"I used to surf with Peter Lawford, Debbie Reynolds and Robin Grigg," Hawkins, daughter Kathy remembered. "They were my babysitters on the beach while my mom was working in Hollywood."

The rest of the nation was not as idyllic as Malibu. In Montgomery, Alabama, Rosa Parks refused to give up her seat on the bus to a white man. Interracial couple Richard and Mildred Loving had to marry secretly, breaking Virginia's racial laws.

Racism and misogyny were only marginally better in California. Los Angeles had an after dark curfew for Black people in white neighborhoods. Hollywood film and recording studios employed the "casting couch" a blatant form of male power abuse, the cover charge for entrance into the entertainment business.

Nonetheless, actresses and vocalists offered hope by portraying strong roles—or singing about them. Hard experience only encouraged more determined efforts to attain dreams that were now substantially more visible.

Actress Lucille Ball created and starred in *I Love Lucy*—a revolutionary television comedy that was the number one series from 1951 to 1957. The first woman entertainer to co-own her own show's production company with her husband, she created the template that all sitcoms continued to follow.

In films like *The African Queen* Kate Hepburn depicted a strong unshakable woman whose strength and dignity powered the most popular movie of the era. And in music a sultry, self-confident Peggy Lee—the most independent woman in the music business—sang her most famous tune "Fever." For the daring few women discovering wave-riding it would soon correlate to "*surf* fever."

In a society still stilted with an almost complete male dominance, the surfing culture afforded females more options than most. Women surfers from Maui to Malibu showed their athletic prowess and remarkable free spirit while demanding surfboards whose design—when discovered by men—ended up revolutionizing the surfing world.

The Women of Malibu
In the ferment of Mid-century America,
Surfer Girls Lead the Charge

Kathy "Gidget" Kohner is the most famous of the women of Malibu, but she was not the most experienced surfer, nor the first. Darrylin Zanuck—the daughter of Hollywood film mogul Darryl F. Zanuck—was one. Her boyfriend at the time Tommy Zahn, an actor, well known surfer, and all round water-man had asked Malibu shaper Joe Quigg to build a board for her. This shorter, lighter balsa board was adopted by a squadron of women to progress rapidly, driving performance at an unexpected pace. In the late 40s, this crew included Robin Grigg, her best friend

Aggie Bane, Vicki Flaxman, and Claire Cassidy. Robin Grigg remembered her first trip to Malibu in the late 40s, "a little gremmie sneaking through a hole in the fence at the Rindge Estate." She often received rides to the beach from young struggling actor Peter Lawford who was part of the small crew at Malibu. Tommy Zahn took her under his wing and introduced her to Joe Quigg who built her a board, a 60 pound 10' square tail, that she and Aggie Bane both rode.

Grigg and Aggie Bane had been friends since sixth grade in Sunday School. They had both spent their summers at the beach, swimming, prone paddling and surfing. During the winter of 1950, Aggie met Joe Quigg, fell in love, and married soon after. Joe and Aggie enjoyed taking road trips together, selling the newly-made "girl" boards up and down the coast. Shortly thereafter Quigg also fashioned a similar board for Vicki Flaxman, perhaps the most talented "Malibu Surf Girls" of the 50s. This 9'6" board was so light and responsive that by the end of the summer, "Vicki was surfing," Quigg acknowledged, "better than most of the men."

Flaxman, perhaps the most competitive of the crew, started surfing in earnest during the summer of 1950. Tall and muscular, with an athlete's poise, she hoisted her board and carved turns in the water with equal grace.

Wanting to prove their skill in the water, she coaxed her friend, Aggie Bane, into racing the lifeguards' paddleboards for such a distance that the girls returned to the beach with the inside of their upper arms scratched and bleeding from the workout.

Claire Cassidy, described by the others as the sweetest of the bunch, played ukulele and organized a women's surf club, Hele Nalu ("going surfing" in Hawaiian). Gregarious yet nonchalant, she apparently was wholly unfazed by the male surfers and their advances.

"She was," Joe Quigg observed, "the original independent woman surfer." Although a small group, these women had an effect on the progression of women's surfing far greater than first realized.

As a result of having these new-type Malibu Boards, explained Jeff Duclos in his definitive article on Malibu women surfers of the time, "Vicky Flaxman and Aggie Bane represented the counter-counterculture at Malibu, riding alongside he-men on custom, trimmed-down balsa boards designed by Aggie's boyfriend (and future husband) Joe Quigg.

Historian and *Surfer* editor Sam George contended that "it was the use of these ladies' lightweight boards by Quigg and Les Williams that is credited with sparking the entire movement toward shorter, lighter surfboards."

Joe Quigg agreed: "That's what helped Vicki look better than most men out there, because they (the girls) got those boards first. And, oh, they (the men) were jealous. A lot of people don't want to admit that, but a lot of big name Malibu guys did not like women out there looking that good."

"The guys at Malibu were really nice to us, with the exception of Simmons, of course, and Buzzy Trent," Vicki Flaxman attested. "When we first learned, there were only two breaks at Malibu: There was a mid-break and there was the point. We learned at mid-break and the guys would let us in the waves—except for Simmons who would never let any girl in a wave and Buzzy Trent, who wasn't very nice about it either."

The lighter, shorter boards the girls rode met with skepticism from other areas of California, and in some cases produced outright derision. The Malibu crew was intent on proving the validity of the design—and of their female contingent as well. On a trip to Baja they stopped in the upscale San Diego suburb of La Jolla to attend the Windansea Surf Club's annual luau celebration. As surfing's elite from all over California gathered for the festivities, the Malibu crew saw their chance. Surf historian and Los Angeles culture doyen–Craig Stecyk account in the *Surfer's Journal*: "The Malibu elders sense vindication is at hand. Vicky Flaxman is taken aside and told that she will become the first [mainland] female to surf outside Windansea."

"Everybody was dazzled because we had these balsa boards," Vicki Flaxman remembered. "It was nearly 10 feet. The biggest waves I'd seen at Malibu were maybe six-to-eight feet. It was breaking way outside and I wasn't anxious to go out there. But the guys talked me into it. They kept telling me I had to go out there and take off from the point. 'No girl's ever done it,' they said. "So I said 'O.K., if you guys don't take off and don't leave me out there by myself.'"

But once out in the lineup, her compatriots vanished. Flaxman found herself out in the ten foot faces on her own. "Her first wave results in a hideous wipeout and a long swim," Stecyk wrote.

Pummeled and tired, Flaxman was ready to quit. "I said: 'That's it. I'm done,' she acknowledged. "But they *insisted* I go back out."

"On her next wave Flaxman takes off far outside and adroitly maneuvers all the way to the beach, where she gingerly steps off onto the sand," Stecyk recounted in the *Surfer's Journal*.

"The entire beach crowd breaks into applause upon Vicky's dismount," Stecyk concluded. "History had been made, and a point had been proven." Personifying the strong, independent women of the 50s these surfers lived the life that would soon be exposed to the world.

As important as it was, the era was short lived. "We all had other things going on in our lives besides surfing. Surfing was something we did that pulled us together and set us apart," Robin said.

Robin's brother surf legend Ricky Grigg summed up their significance: "When the idea of 'Gidget' came along," Grigg observed, "the writer, of course, picked his daughter. You can't blame him for that. But the idea of it was: *the young girl at Malibu*. That could have been Robin, or Vicki or Aggie. In fact, it was all three of them."

Les Williams would go on to become a founder of the San Onofre Surf Club, compete in countless contests and even grace the cover of the Beach Boys first album, *Surfin USA*. Joe Quigg and Matt Kivlin would become historic Malibu shaping icons. Darrylin, Aggie, Claire, Robin and Vickie would be nearly lost in the mists of time. Like many 50s surfers they were overshadowed as the Gidget boom produced a whole new cast of modern surfers.

In the faded photographs of surf lore, it would be easy to overlook one thing: *women* had been the catalyst for the shortboard revolution. As Jeff Duclos who wrote the definitive story *Women of Malibu*, for *Longboard* magazine told me, "These women, on surfboards designed by Joe Quigg and Matt Kivlin, started the evolution of high performance surfing."

But it was not just about design innovation. This was a whole new set of options for lifestyle independence.

"They may not be recognized as pioneers today," Ricky Grigg concluded, "because . . . all the attention is on what's going on at the moment. But, when you think back, *they were the ones*."

Good Ride, Norma Jean
Marilyn Monroe as Part of the 40s Surf Scene

A local Los Angeles girl in the post-WW II years, Norma Jean Baker loved the beach—particularly Malibu. She dated Tom Zahn (an aspiring actor and top surfer of the 40s) and although she rode waves with him and enjoyed the surfing lifestyle, she was primarily focused on modeling and acting. In 1947, some show-business friends who lived in the Malibu beach colony gave the young model her stage name: Marilyn Monroe. Images from some of her first modeling shoots show her posing on the cliffs above Malibu point.

Beach parties at Malibu included film stars Gary Cooper, Peter Lawford and starlet Darrylin Zanuck, along with the era's surfing superstars Pete Peterson, Whitey Harrison, Dave Rochlin and Tommy Zahn. Along with Monroe, Zahn was also dating Darrylin Zanuck, the daughter of 20th Century Fox movie mogul Darryl Zanuck.

For career advancement Zahn knew Zanuck was a better bet than Monroe and the relationship with Marilyn slipped away. But he remembered Monroe from her days surfing with him at Malibu.

"She was in prime condition. Tremendously fit. I used to take her surfing up at Malibu, tandem surfing, you know, two riders on the same surfboard," recalled

Zahn. "I'd take her later, in the dead of winter when it was cold, and it didn't faze her in the least; she'd lay in the cold water, waiting for the waves. Marilyn was very good in the water, very robust, so healthy, a really fine attitude toward life. I was twenty-two when I met her, and I guess she was twenty. Gosh, I really liked her."

When Zahn asked Joe Quigg to make a "novice girls' board" for Darrylin Zanuck his new surfing girlfriend, Quigg produced a board now known as "The Darrylin Board." The design is now seen as the transitional concept that bridged "big and heavy" to "light and fast."

Had a romantic tussle gone slightly differently, that board might have been "The Marilyn Board"—and Marilyn Monroe would have been a goddess of surf as well as film.

The Calhoun Dynasty
Marge, Robin and Candy Were the Icons of the 50s/60s

Marge Calhoun took up the mantle of the Malibu women like a fire takes up the oxygen in a room. It is hard to overestimate the impact Calhoun had on women surfers. A towering figure of independence, strength and talent, "Marge was the first woman in the surf culture who could do it all," Rell Sunn told me in 1985. "She could be married but have her own career, raise fabulous daughters but remain athletically competitive; she could socialize with men from all walks of life and still be respected and adored."

"Marge showed women how many things they could be by *being so many things*," explains Terry Eselun, who knew Calhoun and was a good friend for many years. "Marge worked as a stunt double for Ether Williams, worked with Roy Rogers on TV, she cofounded the first surfing association, became a contest judge" Eselun continued. "She rode huge waves and won the Makaha International which was then considered the World Championships. She was the first lady of surfing in the 50s."

Born in Hollywood in 1926, Marge Booth learned to swim at the Deauville Beach club next to the Santa Monica Pier. She took to the ocean almost immediately, but surfing was a long way off.

In 1942 Marge married Tom Calhoun. Returning to post-war Los Angeles, Calhoun's water skills found a place in Hollywood. Her charisma became apparent almost immediately. "Frank Capra came to my house in Santa Monica Canyon, looking for me," Calhoun said, of the revered film director producer and writer who became the creative force behind some of the major award-winning films of the 30s and 40s. "He wanted me for a Frank Sinatra movie called *Hole in the Head*."

Calhoun began surfing at the late age of thirty-one, when her husband Tom had legendary Malibu shaper Joe Quigg make Calhoun a 10-foot, 27 pound custom balsa board in 1955. When she caught her first wave at Malibu she realized her destiny. "Surfing is an exciting, challenging sport, with a minimum amount of equipment required—you only need a board, a bathing suit, and a piece of wax. Nature provides everything else."

Learning to ride that board at the Malibu Colony she became friends with Darrylin Zanuck. Calhoun was tutored by Darrylin along with some of Santa Monica's greatest water-men, including Peter Cole, Ricky Grigg and Buzzy Trent.

In Hawaii, she toured around with friend Eve Fletcher and—on a lark—entered the women's division of the 1958 Makaha International Surfing Championships. She won.

Marge Calhoun's two daughters, Robin and Candy were the media darlings of the newly-emerging surf magazine industry. Photos of the tall, beautiful, athletic women with sun-streaked hair graced every publication for years. They shared waves with the best riders of the day and left an indelible impression.

"They were America's surfing sweethearts," noted *Surfing Illustrated* publisher and Hang Ten originator Duke Boyd in his 2012 book *Legends of Surfing*. "They epitomized the spirit of surfing and brought a sense of legitimacy to a sport that was suffering from a mischievous beach-bum reputation." Candy was also a top bodysurfer, the first woman to be pictured *bodysurfing* both the Newport Wedge and Hawaii's Banzai Pipeline.

Through the 50s and into the 60s, the Calhoun's were the mother/daughter model of good surfing, good health and good fun. When the girls were grown, Calhoun continued to surf and promote the sport she loved. She became an active contest judge, and a cofounder of the U.S. Surfing Association. Calhoun retired from surfing and moved to the Central Coast in the 80s. In 2003 she was inducted into the Huntington Beach Surfing Walk of Fame, as the "Woman of the Year."

She passed away in 2017 at the age of ninety-three. Her influence was immeasurable to the generation of waveriders who came after her.

The Disappearing Act

On a hot summer day in the late 50s a young Eve Fletcher drove her British Racing Green Austin Healy to legendary surfer Marge Calhoun's house in Santa Monica. Loading their boards into Calhoun's van they took off for the beach, leaving Calhoun's husband Tom and a group of surfing's merriest pranksters to commit mischief. In an era when practical jokes were a deep part of the surfing culture, the caper this group played on the unsuspecting women was elaborate even for their talents: Removing the molding and then the large picture glass front window of the Calhoun's house, they propped 2" x 8" timber into the opening and slowly drove Eve's sports car onto the boards up into the gaping hole and carefully into the home's living room. Replacing the window and molding, the crew cleaned up and waited for the girls' return.

Arriving at the driveway, seeing her car was missing, Fletcher panicked.

"It's gone!" She sobbed. "It's been stolen!" Racing to the kitchen phone to report a car theft, a distraught Fletcher and Marge were met by the jokers who quickly ushered them into the living room. "There's my car!" Fletcher yelled in relief. Then realizing the prank was on her, Fletcher paused. Calmly turning to Marge Calhoun—with no hint of irony—she remarked, "*It looks really good next to your red leather chair.*"

One of the first women to come to Hawaii in the 50s, one of the first to join the storied San Onofre Surfing Club, Eve Fletcher saw the modern era of surfing from wooden boards to jet skis. Radiant and unflappable, she had the looks of movie star Grace Kelly and the insouciance of feminist Gloria Steinem.

Born on the East Coast, Fletcher moved with her family to the San Fernando Valley at age ten, becoming an avid swimmer when her parents joined the local country club. After college Disney's Imagineering department hired her as an animation supervisor where she contributed to *Cinderella, Alice in Wonderland,* and other Disney films.

Fletcher met actor Johnny Sheffield (who played Boy in several Tarzan films) who introduced her to surfing at San Onofre. Lured by surfing's thrill, she became a San Onofre Surfing Club member back when the membership was as exclusive as a back entrance key to Disneyland.

Notorious for wearing a knitted white wool cardigan in the dead of winter (in lieu of a wetsuit) Fletcher's grace on the beach and enthusiasm in the water made her a fond fixture for more than one generation of waveriders.

Fletcher continued at Disney through 1989 working on *The Little Mermaid* before receiving the Animation Guild's Golden Award in 2005.

Featured in the documentary, *Surfing For Life*, Fletcher was seventy-five and still surfing almost daily.

"I want to keep surfing as long as I can," Fletcher told me at a California Surf Museum exhibit opening in 2014. "You're never too old to be stoked!"

Eve Fletcher's memorial was held November 12, 2020 on her ninety-third birthday.

"No one had more enthusiasm than Eve," recalled Don Craig, a former President of the San Onofre Surf Club at her memorial where her ashes were scattered at sea off Dana Point. "She lived the surfing life."

Groundswells and Undercurrents

The expansion of America's post-WW II prosperity launched surfing's modern age. As adventurous Americans explored the new "leisure" society, the beach became a focal point. Surfing's small coastal enclaves in California and Hawaii were seen as youthful pockets of exotic activity, but too offbeat for acceptance in the mainstream's social conformity.

Fed by the newly burgeoning media of television and the proliferation of women's magazines, the 50s more often than not rewarded the embrace of traditional gender roles, where women's identities as wives and mothers were still expected to give the appearance of acquiescence.

But beneath the platitudes of television shows like *Father Knows Best* and *Leave it to Beaver*, the decade saw a smoldering discontent with the status quo—particularly among young people. Below the surface was a powerful groundswell—not just a wave but a set of waves—rock & roll radio waves, a tide of new technology, undercurrents of the sexual revolution and the long-simmering surge of the civil rights movement.

The biggest wave would be the Baby Boomers themselves—the largest generation of Americans ever. It would soon roll onto the continental shelf of American society like a tsunami—crashing headlong into the shallow reefs of hypocrisy and walls of bigotry. Marge Calhoun, Vicki Flaxman, Robin Grigg and the other surfers of their day were creating a lifestyle based on non-conventional roles and a disregard for restrictive traditions. Asked how she got the courage to seize that independence Calhoun responded, "If you look out there and think, 'Gee, I wish I could go out there'—just do it!" "If you have the desire for anything, do it!"

The women of Malibu were an early signal that Marge Calhoun was the future—and she lived by this credo. Calhoun was an inspiration to women surfers—but the desire for increased independence bubbled everywhere. As the incomparable R&B singer Etta James' 1959 signature song would say: *"At Last!"*

As the coastlines became beachheads, surfing symbolized free expression; women would join the ranks of the freedom riders—on real waves of change.

Gidget Goes Global

A Movie Introduces Surfing to the World But Real-life Women's Roles Remained Stereotypical

1959–1969

"A good woman is one who loves passionately, has guts, seriousness and passionate convictions, takes responsibility, and shapes society."
—Betty Friedan, iconic American activist
and author of *The Feminine Mystique*

The Original Gidget
Kathy Kohner's Malibu Summer Sparks a Wildfire

Making her way onto the beach and into the Malibu surf domain was a young teenager, so obviously unfamiliar with the scene she was immediately noticed. It was June 27, 1956, a day destined to change Malibu history forever.

"I remember the first time Gidget came down the stairs at Malibu," wrote Mike Doyle in his autobiography *Morning Glass*, "She was only about five feet tall, weighed less than a hundred pounds, and was carrying a borrowed surfboard that was so big, one end of it was dragging in the sand.

"She really caught our eye because there weren't a lot of girl surfers then. Tubesteak said, 'Gee, here comes a girl.'"

"Tubesteak" was Terry Tracy, Malibu's reigning regent, the character on which the future movie's Big Kahuna would be based.

"Somebody else started giving her a hard time, saying 'Whatta ya think you're doing? Don't you know girls can't surf?'

"Gidget (whose real name was Kathy Kohner) stopped halfway down the stairs, practically in tears. Tubesteak, who had a soft heart and needed a girlfriend, went over and said, 'Hey, it's okay if you surf. Come on down.'"

"According to Tubesteak himself," wrote 1966 World Champion Nat Young in his 1983 *History of Surfing*, "about the last week in June 1956 he, Mickey Munoz and Micky Dora were standing on the incline above Malibu, checking out the waves, when a young surfer in a baby-blue ski parka pulled a new Velzy/Jacobs board from the rear of a Buick convertible and headed off down the path. "'Hey,' shouted Dora, hassling the new arrival. 'Go back to the valley, you kook!' shouted Munoz. Tubesteak told the others to shut up and went to help and discovered the new arrival was a girl! A very short girl!

"'For Chrissake,' mumbled Tubesteak, 'it's a midget, a girl midget, a goddamn gidget!'

The girl was not amused. 'I'm not a gidget,' she yelled. 'My name is Kathryn—and you can keep your filthy hands off me, you creep.'

"Tubesteak laughed. 'Hey Gidget, see you around.'

"That," wrote Nat Young of Tubesteak's acceptance of Gidget into the Malibu fold, "was a statement which was to mean more than Tubesteak thought."

Kathy Kohner was one of the few young women of the late 50s who had been entranced by the waves and those who rode them. Begging her parents for rides, she frequented nearby Malibu for the next two summers. Kohner met the surfing elite of the era—who had already set the surfing tradition of adopting nicknames as a badge of induction: Moondoggie, The Kahuna, Tubesteak, the Masochist and Da Cat.

Tracy's palm frond shack on the beach at Malibu was a royal residence perfectly fit for the lost boys of Los Angeles, an actual Neverland for a motley clan of wayward waveriders. Like the Big Kahuna character in the movie, which was largely based on Tracy, Tubesteak was both a mentor and a nemesis to the petite tomboy he had christened the Gidget.

Unintimidated by the surfers or the ocean, the 5-foot, 95-pound tenth grader surfed with passion. Determined to be accepted into the surfing crowd at Malibu, she repeatedly raided her family's refrigerator to share groceries with the regulars.

When Kohner showed the talent and tenacity to become a surfer, she was admitted to the nascent confederation of coastal bohemians creating their own new world.

For two summers she hung out at the beach, surfed, made friends and kept a meticulous diary of her adventures. Kohner dreamed about turning her diary entries into a "real" book, and she sought advice from her father, Frederick, a Jewish immigrant from Czechoslovakia, nominated for a 1938 Oscar in the Original Story category. Taking note of Kathy's stories and even listening in on her phone conversations (with her permission, she maintained) he turned his daughter's stories into an original coming-of-age novella that shed first light on the surfing phenomenon along the beaches of Los Angeles.

Although English was his second language, he was able to capture his daughter's lively, natural teen slang, adding to the book's timeless authenticity. The result was a best-selling 1957 novel, *Gidget—the Little Girl with Big Ideas*, which quickly sold half a million copies.

Like the movies own characters, Kathy Kohner's active surf life only lasted a few summers. Enrolling at Oregon State College she drifted from her beach friends and after graduation, gave up surfing altogether. But she continued to be part of the larger culture of surf and beach lifestyle, engaging in speaking tours and a film about her life. Duke's ocean view restaurant in Malibu bestowed an honorary title Ambassador of Aloha. *Surfer* magazine ranked her No. 7 on its list of the 25 most influential people in surfing. "Once a surfer, always a surfer," she laughed. "I'm still here, and I am Gidget." In 2011, she was inducted into the Huntington Beach Surfing Walk of Fame continuing to maintain an iconic perch in the list of surfing greats. "It was the time of my life" she later conceded when I interviewed her in 2011. "If that changed the world, it is good enough for me."

Hollywood Introduces Surfing to the World

Gidget the movie immortalized the golden years of the 50s, but also ended them. The movie version of the 1957 coming-of-age novella had a star-studded cast and was a hit movie at the turn of the decade—the same year Dick Dale and the Del Tones began playing "Surfer Stomp" dances at the Rendezvous Ballroom in Newport Beach, Brian Wilson got a C grade for a high school musical composition called *Surfin'* and Jack O'Neill moved his surf shop from San Francisco to Santa Cruz to make the first commercially-made wetsuits.

Gidget the movie ignited the fuse that would detonate the 60s. The nascent lifestyle enjoyed by a small tribe on the continent's edge would become the passion of every beach-loving teenager from Malibu to Miami.

The film was a serious effort by Columbia Pictures to turn the popular novel into a box-office hit. Sandra Dee starred as Gidget the zany, loveable ingenue making her an overnight sensation. Future Oscar-winner Cliff Robertson starred as the Big Kahuna and while the producers originally wanted Elvis Presley to play Moondoggie, they chose James Darren, a teen heartthrob of the era. Those three characters formed the screenplay's love triangle: "troublesome teen" Francie "Gidget" Lawrence, smitten by Moondoggie, college-kid in-limbo Jeffrey "Moondoggie" Matthews seduced by the free and easy existence of a surf bum, as defined by Robertson's Big Kahuna.

Shot on location at Leo Carrillo State Beach (substituting for Malibu) *Gidget* gave the world a Technicolor view of all the thrills and spills of the surfing lifestyle; with top surfers of their day Miki Dora and Mickey Muñoz doubling the surfing for the stars. The film portrayed surfing—as Gidget blurts out to her parents—as "the absolute ultimate!"

A promotional poster from the original *Gidget* movie showed a scene where actress Sandra Dee is practicing her balance on her bed. Perhaps typical of that time period in American culture, the sampler on the wall reads: "To be a REAL woman is to bring out the BEST in a man." Early 60s Hollywood *and* surfing both lagged behind more progressive sectors of society regarding women.

Gidget—Hollywood's first attempt at a surf film—was a nationwide hit. It would produce five sequels, a television series and spawn a host of surf exploitation movies aimed at the vast new youth audience who instantly adopted at least the *trappings* of the beach lifestyle.

Although Hollywood's subsequent efforts were laughable; the generation they aimed at already had their own take on surfing—and it didn't include beach blankets, the effect Gidget had on the youth movement across the globe is hard to overstate. Seemingly overnight surfing went from the obscure pastime of a happy few, to a worldwide sensation. Malibu would never be the same. And neither would surfing.

What was the Feminine Mystique's Main Message?
You Don't Own Me

From 1959 to 1963 surfing's popularity exploded. In the four years between Hawaii Statehood and the assassination of JFK, surfing vaulted from obscure underground pursuit to a worldwide sporting craze.

As the 50s closed, an unexpected film set the youth market ablaze, sweeping this new audience like a firestorm. The catalyst was a petite Southern California teen nicknamed Gidget.

Based on the summer surf escapades Kathy Kohner shared with her father—a Hollywood screenwriter—her stories became the framework for a best-selling novel and then a film recounting her surfing experience at Malibu. The reverberations would echo across the entire Boomer generation. Exposing the irresistible thrill of riding waves to a global audience, it changed the perception of sport forever.

Gidget was released in late 1959 in the midst of a commercial and social shift brought on by the youth market. Chart-topping songs departed from "Where the Boys Are," a smarmy, yearning ballad by Connie Francis and just three years later caught the "Heat Wave," a feisty 1963 power-rocker by Martha and the

Vandellas. When Betty Friedan's groundbreaking feminist text, *The Feminine Mystique*, came out in 1963, it was widely credited with sparking the second-wave feminist movement.

Women began entering new roles, making statements challenging the status quo. In *The Days of Wine and Roses*, 1962's most acclaimed film, actress Lee Remick won one of the film's five Academy Awards tackling the previously taboo subject of alcohol addiction. Audiences flocked to see the film; critics rewarded her with a Best Actress nomination.

Aussie hip hop artist Grace and rapper G-Easy had a 2015 hit with "You Don't Own Me." But Lesley Gore's original version was 1963's most personally courageous statement on pop radio—by a seventeen-year-old sensation collaborating with her black producer/mentor Quincy Jones who himself would go on to become a giant in the recording industry. Women singers, writers, and actors came into their own.

But surfing's early 60s image lagged behind, continuing to portray a sport dominated almost exclusively by young men. Females, especially younger ones, were seen as spectators not participants. In *Surfer Girl*, the Beach Boys sang "I have watched you on the shore" making it clear that females were *not* companions on the water. A small number of women had always been a part of the wave-riding cadre, but as the legions of teenagers took to the beaches the vast majority remained for the most part shore-bound.

Among the thorns some roses bloomed nonetheless: Judy Dibble, from Ocean Beach, California, would follow Marge Calhoun's giant footsteps and win the Makaha International Championships in 1960 and 1961. Pamela Maloche would start the first female-exclusive surf club in the South Bay. And fifteen-year-old Linda Benson—the first great 60s superstar—was filmed riding Waimea Bay.

Surfing Waimea at 15 on a Borrowed Board
Linda Benson Was First Great Surf Star of the 60s

For a moment Linda Benson hesitated. She was paddling out at Waimea Bay. Though it broke only a handful of days a year it was now definitely showing in the 15 to 20 foot range. This was her first trip to Hawaii. Waimea was then the biggest known wave in the world. Unlike the men out in the lineup—who had studied it for a decade before challenging it, the break was completely unfamiliar to her. She was only fifteen years old. And she had gone out *on a borrowed board*.

A set came. Fred Van Dyke—already a legend at Waimea—took off.

"He made it to the bottom, got hit by the exploding whitewater and wiped out," Benson remembered. Moments later the two pieces of his snapped board popped up. Fifteen long seconds later Fred burst through the white foam gasping. A second wave feathered, and John Severson—the soon-to-be founder of *Surfer* magazine—dropped in. Halfway down the face he hit a four-foot piece of chop and was chucked off. Luckily his board was still intact but had washed in. As Benson stroked toward the outside lineup, Severson swam past her heading in. Linda saw him look over, shake his head at her and shout. "You're crazy!" It made her pause, watching the last two waves of the set go unridden.

Just two winters before, a group of intrepid wild men had ventured out to catch waves there for the first time since 1943 when a huge swell had caught surfers Dickie Cross and Woody Brown in a monstrous 35-foot set. Cross and Brown paddled all the way from Sunset Point looking for a safe spot to reach land. As they attempted to ride a wave in, Waimea Bay closed out. Woodie managed to make it to shore that evening. Dickie Cross's body was never found.

Spooked by old Hawaiian legends and this recent tragedy, it took the next challengers a decade and a half to try again.

But on this day in 1959 John Severson made it back to the beach easily and went about setting up his movie camera next to another storied film maker of the era, Bud Browne. Both of them planned to film her for their next surf movie. A year later Severson would publish the first issue of Surfer magazine and become a titan in the surfing pantheon. But for the moment he just wanted to document this diminutive towheaded teen doing something very, very extraordinary.

Benson had nothing to prove but nothing to lose either—except possibly her life. She took a deep breath. "I figured, I'd just give it a try," she laughed.

Then she continued to paddle to the outside.

Born in 1944, Benson grew up at Moonlight Beach, in Encinitas California when it was a tiny beach town of warm sand, gentle surf and uncrowded waves: "When I was eleven I used to stand on the cliffs above the beach and watch my older brother Charlie surf with his friends," Benson said. "I thought it was the neatest thing I'd ever seen."

At twelve, Benson's father bought her a waterlogged 8'6" balsawood board for twenty dollars. She took to it fast and in three years Benson won the first U.S. Championships held at Huntington Beach. Dale Velzy, one of surfing's seminal characters and prominent board makers, sponsored her one-way to Hawaii. Once there she had taken to the Hawaiian waves and Island lifestyle immediately. Entering the Makaha International Championships—then considered the World Title of surfing—she followed in the footsteps of her heroine Marge Calhoun and won the event on her first try. Three days later she found herself at Waimea.

Now, sitting in the unpredictable line up, Benson was looking to go after just about anything—as long as it avoided getting caught inside.

Another set came. She angled her board toward the shoulder and stroked hard. "It wasn't a huge day by Waimea standards," she said. Some of the waves were breaking around 18 feet. "I can remember the steepness, the speed of the wave, and the spray of water on my face from the wind. It nearly blinds you. I felt the drop and hoped I could stay on. The wave was maybe 15 feet." She stayed on and rode it all the way to the channel. Then she caught a few more just to make sure nobody took her for a big-wave one-hit wonder.

That is perhaps not remarkable in today's 70-foot benchmarks. But this was 1959. This was the outer realm of challenge. This was a fifteen-year-old girl on a first trip to Hawaii, using a borrowed board.

It was a sensation.

She would go on to be the first big female star of the 60s—a tiny surfing pixie from Encinitas, California, whose visible joy of performing set the early 60s standard.

No one title could be bestowed on Linda Benson. She was the queen of the small wave performance, a brilliant competitor, a big wave pioneer and a free-surfing free spirit. Benson was the first female to break the gender barrier when she appeared on the 1963 cover of *Surf Guide* magazine. The first woman surfing stunt double, she was an equal with the men but always keep her innocence and her friendships with other women. Petite, adorable, and superbly talented, she was the whole package—wrapped with a humble presence.

During the ten years following her win at Makaha, Linda went on to win four additional U.S. Championships, in 1960, 61, 64 and 68. Corky Carroll, who won the men's side in many of her title years, christened her the Godmother of Surfing.

In 1965, Benson took a job as a flight attendant with United Airlines—a nearly perfect choice for her. After thirty-eight years with United Airlines, in a career that afforded her the opportunity to surf all over the globe, surfing remained her favorite pastime. And talking about that 1959 day at Waimea still brought a smile to her face.

8

The Surfing Life

1959–1969

"Kaptain" of Industry
Nancy Katin Launches the Surf Trunk Business

Corky Carroll knew exactly what he wanted. "Mrs. Katin, I need a pair of surf trunks that can *last*. Will you make me a pair?" It was 1959, Carroll was an energetic neighbor kid asking Nancy and Walter Katin for a specially made pair of trunks for surfing. Surfers like Corky put serious stress on regular swim trunks, and they rarely held up.

"Come on in," Nancy Katin said. "We'll see what we can do."

As Mike Doyle told the story in his autobiography *Morning Glass*, "Nancy sewed Corky a pair of red trunks out of 16-ounce drill canvas. She sewed them the same way she sewed her boat covers—zigzag stitching, double and even triple seams. Corky loved them, but they were so stiff that he wore them for two years before they broke in enough that they wouldn't stand up by themselves. And after three years, he was still wearing them."

Custom surfwear required resourcefulness from surfers during the 50s. Some went to the Salvation Army and bought cheap sailor pants and cut the legs off to fit. The lucky few who went to Hawaii would come back with custom trunks from the Japanese-Hawaiian tailors turned surf-trunk makers: M Nii in Makaha on Oahu's westside or the Outrigger Canoe Club in Waikiki or Take's in Honolulu. On the North Shore the H. Mura store in Haleiwa even allowed surfers to pick out their personal fabric and patterns. The owners would sew up trunks and shirts in the back room. In California there were "beach moms"—up and down the coast—who used their seamstress skills to make surf trunks for neighbor kids.

One of those women, Nancy Katin—a tiny, chain-smoking entrepreneur—had a business in Sunset Beach, California, making canvas boat covers with her husband, Walter. The Katins had no children of their own but they loved kids and welcomed them anytime they came by. The 1959 visit by Corky Carroll was the first.

By the early 60s, Corky Carroll had become an international surf star, winning multiple National Championships and setting a high profile. He had traded his stiff canvas for a pair soft red cotton trunks—still triple-stitched by Katin. Hundreds of local surfers were coming to Katin's little shop asking for a pair of surf trunks just like Corky's. "It was a spontaneous walk in business," explained Jericho Poppler, who lived close by in Seal Beach, and knew the Katins well. "They didn't have to advertise; it was all word of mouth."

As demand for surf trunks outstripped boat covers, Walter and Nancy opened a retail outlet in Surfside, California. During the first half of the 60s, Nancy Katin and two Japanese seamstress' turned out thousands of pairs of custom surf trunks, quickly moving into cotton and nylon and other materials more pliable than canvas.

Catalina Sportswear bought Kanvas by Katin in the later 60s, but Nancy, dissatisfied with the quality of product they produced, bought it back from Catalina. When husband Walter Katin died in 1967 Nancy continued on, making trunks for the next two decades that were, as Jericho Poppler claimed, "bullet-proof." Katin sponsored a surf team contest in Huntington Beach, "back when they were about the only prize money competitions in the USA," Poppler remembered.

In 1978 the Katin Team Challenge became the spark that set the fiery return of competition surfing when international surf stars from Australia, South Africa and Hawaii showed up to surf for their brand's team in the contest.

"I used to wear white clam diggers that I cut off above the knees," Carroll remembered. "I had a pair of customs from the Cotton Shop in Seal Beach. When I went to Hawaii I had both M Nii's and Take's over there. But to my knowledge Katin was the first real solid custom boardshort company in California. Nancy made me that original great pair and the demand just took off." Corky looked pensive. "Man, I wish I would have gotten a percentage for that!"

Nancy died in 1986 and left the business to one of her loyal employees, Sato Hughes, who for twenty-five years, had faithfully built product for her.

Out of her back cutting room on the beach in Huntington Katin created a multi-million dollar brand based on the authentic understanding of the customer.

It was another first for women in surfing: The surfing craze had been started by a diminutive teenage girl. The shortboard innovation had been a woman's request. The surfwear industry had now been launched by a tiny entrepreneur. In surfing it appeared, small was beautiful.

Surfing was growing like kelp beds in California's Channel Islands. Between 1959 and 1962 the surfing population went from under 5,000 to nearly half a million. The sales of surfboards multiplied ten-fold. In little over three years more than fifty surfboard brands opened retail outlets in California, Australia, Hawaii, and the eastern seaboard of the USA and surf clubs, for boys and girls, continued to spring up in California Florida, and Hawaii.

Join the Club
To get into the club, women decided they needed
to start their own

As surfing gathered momentum surf clubs began to spring up in beach towns up and down California's coast. While long a staple of Australia's beach-centered society, surf clubs in California had been limited to lifestyle enthusiasts. (Palos Verdes and Santa Cruz surf clubs date back to the 30s, La Jolla Windansea from the late 40s and San Onofre from the 50s.) But the 60s brought a burst of new surf clubs—most of which were predominately male. Feeling shut out of the action, at least two groups of women formed female-exclusive surf clubs of their own.

Although the Vahine Kai woman's surf club had been formed in the early 50s, the California Coast Girls Surf Club was formed in the fall of 1961 by Pamela Maloche, then a student in the South Bay of Los Angeles County. Its members were teenage girls drawn from area high schools, including Bishop Montgomery, the Torrance public high schools and Hermosa and Manhattan Beach.

Another woman's surf club, the Piling Peekers, was started in late 1962 by Jan Johnson, a sixteen-year-old sophomore at South High, also in Torrance.

Open to girls between thirteen and nineteen who were devoted to surfing and had good academic records, the Peekers drew their membership from a similar pool of coastal South Bay high schools as Meloche's group.

Johnson was not so much intent on proving that female surfers were the equal of males (club members were quick to acknowledge the advanced skills of many male surfers) but simply to show that women deserved a shot at the waves too.

Club member Rosemari Reimers-Rice became the first female to earn a spot on the prestigious Dewey Weber Surf team. Several others won trophies in various competitions.

This was an era when the South Bay was headquarters for board manufacturing. The beaches of Hermosa, Redondo, Manhattan and the Palos Verdes peninsula were surf epicenters for the surfboard industry, organizations and clubs. Two of the best women surfers from the area were Margo Scotton, a finalist in the First Annual United States Invitational Surfing Championships in 1964 and Josette Lagardere who would avenge a painful loss against Australia. Both belonged to the female exclusive Peekers Club.

A similar environment sprang up on the East Coast, where clubs were more informal, but the members made lifetime friendships and created a culture that would continue for decades. In Melbourne Beach Florida where beach girls of the early 60s were called Bettys, the traditional role was for females to sit demurely in the sand.

But there were those like Kathy Anderson who refused that sedentary role. She had caught the surfing fever and when she met surfers Mimi Munro and Linda Grover in 1963 at a Daytona Beach competition they became Bettys of a very different sort. Joining the boys and competing in hundreds of contests the trio was among the first female surfers on the East Coast. Competing against each other never tested their friendship. They squabbled over boyfriends, but never over surfing. Lisa Muir-Wakley joined them, forming a loose club of surf sisters. Muir-Wakley, a standout from the Gulf coast region of Pensacola, would compete for the next three decades traveling to Puerto Rico, Hatteras and Corpus Christi, before embarking on a ten year stint in Hawaii starting in the mid-70s.

The "Bettys" all continued to surf as frequently as possible while passionately maintaining their lifelong friendship that began as young teens in 1962.

In the summer of 2001 Anderson opened her Melbourne Beach surf school with contests to make surfing more accessible to women. They christened them the "Betty Series," to poke fun at society's expectations of women. That same year Lisa Muir-Wakley was inducted into the East Coast Surf Hall of Fame. Mimi Munro was the Surfing Hall of Fame 2007 Woman of the Year.

Another Daytona Shores local Renee Eisler started her career when she was recruited by Dick Catri for his prestigious Hobie surfboards team, traveling the East Coast and appearing in *Sports Illustrated* and *Life* magazines. Invited to the World Contest in California—an experience that fueled her travel passion—she enrolled in the Scholastic Seas voyage, a campus afloat cruise ship where she was able to surf Africa, Portugal and the Caribbean. Upon her return she moved to Hawaii and finished college at UH with a degree in art with a minor in Hawaiian surfing, and then a stint with the Peace Corps where she had a chance to surf in Brazil and the Virgin Islands.

But perhaps Linda Grover has the best story: in 2003 her daughter April—a professional surfer herself—made her debut on the MTV series *Surfer Girls*. The Club had carried on into the second generation.

"It's all about girl power," her friend Anderson said.

In Australia, where clubs were a way of life, that power did not win inclusion—or their own clubs either. Historian Leonie Huntsman describes the formation of—and resistance to—women's lifesaving clubs from as early as 1908; Australian historian Ed Jaggard contends that women competed nationally in surf lifesaving from the 20s onward. Yet academic writing on surfboard riding has focused on male participation, and no documentation of women-exclusive surf clubs seems to appear until the formation of the Australian Women's Surfing Association in 1980.

Although surfing grew exponentially in the 60s, it remained a primarily male domain. While surfing had reached the shores of five continents, outside of France, Peru, Australia and the USA women were not participating on any significant level. Gidget had gone global but Madison Avenue advertising exalted Sandra Dee's beach outfits over serious surfing. The 1960 Jantzen Swimwear advertising campaign titled "Just Wear a Smile and a Jantzen" took the country by storm. Sponsors like Kodak, Ford Motor and United Airlines invited "Smile Contest" winners from each state to an annual contest in the Hawaiian Islands. Top contestants were featured in advertising campaigns.

Innovation in design and styling was a hallmark of the decade. Fabrics included knits and wovens in quick-drying synthetics. Natural fibers were often blended with man-made yarns. The conversion to foam and fiberglass accelerated mass production of surfboards; these new product developments were now able to fill the rapid rise in demand. The Baby Boom generation, now in its teens, saw surfing (like rock & roll) as exclusively their own. Surfing's popularity saw a rapid growth spike.

Regrettably, few female surfing athletes were part of this dramatic expansion. A number of regions that would provide outstanding women surfers in later years had not yet begun to involve women on waves just yet. Asia, Africa and most of Europe and South America have scant records of female surfers throughout the period from 1950 to 1980. The prevailing attitudes toward female athletes did not expedite the flowering of women on waves. Surf travelers to Mexico and Central America would not see native female surfers until the 90s.

France and Peru were the two bright spots, and once again a surf club would be part of the success: the exclusive Club Waikiki in Miraflores—the beachfront suburb of Lima Peru—was world famous in its early years, proudly holding the first-ever international surf events in the late 50s, including women in every category. The Lacanau Surf Club in coastal Aquitaine and the Cotes de Basques surf club in Biarritz, France, both founded in 1968 and 69 were elite surfing clubs. Among the first members in Lacanau were Gisèle Bidon and Nadège Guillet, both respected boardriders of their era.

France's premiere female surfer of the 60s, Marie-Christine Delanne, remembers surfing with screenwriter Peter Viertel and his Hollywood film star wife Deborah Kerr in 1959, just after Viertel had discovered the waves of the Basque coast during the filming of Hemmingway's novel *The Sun Also Rises*, in Pamplona Spain. Delanne gave lessons to Lucia Bosè, another film star, while they were on their adventures to Pamplona for the famous running of the bulls. Famous bullfighter Luis Miguel Dominguin had left superstar Ava Gardner to marry Bosè amid tabloid headlines. A heady, romantic era, party life in the 60s was legendary.

"We used to go out at night, dance like mad and drink till dawn," Delanne said. One time she remembers going surfing after partying all night, as the sun was just rising. "I paddled out and before I could catch a wave I vomited on my board. Around me, the boys were dead laughing. Not very proper, but funny memories!"

Brilliant and whimsical, Delanne needn't have been concerned with propriety. She not only set a record of six French National Championships but became a highly respected environmental scientist in later life. She used her big wave courage for other purposes too: As a journalist she wrote a highly influential book *Guerre du Golf, la sale guerre propre*, an investigation into "the dirty truth" of the Gulf War, which had significant impact on French politics in 2000.

She starred in 1967's *Au Sommet de la Vague* (At the Crest of the Wave) one of the rare French surf films during the Avant-guard era of French cinema. Her younger sister Marie-Paule won a French National title and her youngest sister, Marie-Pascal, married Tom Curren and raised a daughter who also became a National Champion. But the exhilaration of the 60s surf boom remained a highlight. Her six titles remained a record for decades, and her European contemporaries considered her the Joyce Hoffman of French surf history.

"There were no more than 20 or 25 surfers in those earliest times," recalled Delanne. But the number grew exponentially by the mid-60s. Other pioneering surfers who started with Delanne included Françoise Cazayous, Florence de la Clergerie, Kati Tardrew and Sylvie Campagne.

Delanne moved to a picturesque French Village in the Pyrenees foothills in 2012. In what she considered her last big achievement, she raised a young African refugee.

"My life has been very happy," Delanne reminisced. "But I think those early surfing days in France have been mostly forgotten."

A Forgotten Early Competitive Master

While Joyce Hoffman became one of the best known and celebrated surfers of the 60s, regional stars in California were sometimes forgotten. In the blur of rapid changes and newsworthy incidents during the early 60s, perhaps no one has been more overlooked in historical annals than Nancy Nelson. Born in 1947 in San Clemente, California, Nelson got her first surfboard at age twelve. A phenomenal competitor, Nancy placed third in the Makaha International Surfing Championships contest while living with her family in Honolulu for eight months in 1961. Nelson subsequently won the Makaha International Surfing Championships in 1962, 1963 and 1965, placed second in the 1962 West Coast Championships, finished third in the 1963 West Coast Championships, and was a runner-up in both the World Surfing Championships and the United States Surfing Championships in 1965. Moreover, Nancy placed third in both the 1964 and 1965 Surfer

Poll Awards as well as placed third in the 1966 International Surfing Hall of Fame Awards right behind fellow champion female surfers Joyce Hoffman and Joey Hamasaki.

Asked about competing in such a male dominated sport Nelson responded "If girls like athletics like I do, I see no reason why they should just have to sit on the beach and look pretty. Besides, who said it was just a man's sport? I don't like all the restrictions that men seem to think are necessary for women."

Her competitive record certainly legitimized her point.

Leaving the competition scene in the late 60s, Nelson soon after moved to Hawaii and ran a photography business in Honolulu. But she made long-term stays in Montana, Ireland and California—all distant from surf—perhaps due to her lack of recognition as a champion surf personality. She died of breast cancer in 2013.

Peru's Surfing Women

With Peru hosting international surf festivals as early as 1957, when Peru again invited surfers from around the world in 1962, excitement took the nation by storm. "Surf fever was running rampant among the Peruvians men and women alike." In February of 1962 the Peruvian press published articles alleging that Gladys Zender, the 1957 Peruvian Miss Universe was considering participating on the national women's team. Thousands of people took to the beaches in hopes of catching a glimpse of her in her bathing suit.

She certainly wasn't the only beauty on the beach—or the only athlete. "Mainie Rey, Eva Eyzaguirre and Pilar Merino all enjoyed waves together," noted Peruvian surf pioneer Carlos Dogny. "Along with Sonia Barreda, Ice Kessel, Olga Pardo, Carmen Velarde Pastorelli and Lucha Velarde, the Peruvian women's surf movement was a force to be reckoned with."

There was also a small group of girls from Lima in the early 60s who were enamored with the surf culture from the North American perspective. They didn't care about competition at first, enjoying the sense of freedom the new sport afforded them—and the connection to the ocean in summer and winter alike.

Jonchi Pinzas described the experiences of early surfing in Peru: "We surfed without wetsuits in wintertime and without leashes." Walking downtown toward the Makah and Waikiki clubs in the mornings, friends would often lend them club members' boards. Then they would walk with the boards past the small waterfalls along the steep cliffs and surf a spot called Breakline at the Barranquito beach. The posse included Peruvian surf matriarch Sonia Barreda, her daughter Liliana, Ana Maria del Carpio, Marjory Cannock and Eve Terry.

Not content to surf the Lima, they began exploring the coastline: "We were the first girls to surf in Chicama," Pinzas remembered. "And on an exploratory trip I stayed at the Cabo Blanco Fishing Club and we were the first to surf what is now known as the Cabo Blanquillo." Not only was the Casa Blanco Fishing Club a legendary resort where everyone from Ernest Hemmingway to Paul Newman went to find big game fish, but the wave at Casa Blanquillo was considered one of the best in the world.

"What was really cool was to go down south of Lima to El Silencio and Cerro Azul," Jonchi Pinzas continued, recalling some of the early adventures.

"I remember those days at Cerro Azul beach," recalled Liliana Barreda, "when one was happy to hear the engine of another car from afar and you'd say to yourself 'Jonchi is here, cool!'

"We were all free without any leashes, nor wetsuits no sunscreen, no people," she continued. "Oh and by the way," she added emphatically, "the few girls who surfed back then *had first priority to catch a wave!*"

Jonchi Pinzas and Marjory Cannock remembered traveling down to Pasamayo to the international invitational event the Peruvians were hosting.

"Before the opening of the World Championships we met Jimmy Blears and Corky Carroll, and they lent us their boards. We surfed really good waves!"

Almost exactly four decades after the 1965 World Contest in Peru, Sofia Mulanovich would become the most prominent female surfer in Latin American.

It would be a long road for female surfers. But along the way their achievements became part of surfing's unsung legacy. And in the 60s the *real* women's surf story was just beginning.

First Editions
The 60s

"Why is it that surfers are some of the strongest advocates of ocean conservation? Because they've spent time in and around the ocean, and they've personally seen the beauty, the fragility, and even the degradation of our planet's blue heart."
— Sylvia Earle chief scientist of the National Oceanic and Atmospheric Administration (NOAA)

No decade in the 20th Century experienced more change than the 60s. Opening with Sandra Dee's "Gidget," an innocent teen, it exited with Jane Fonda's "Barbarella" a bizarre space traveler from the 41st Century. Annette and Frankie were replaced by Sonny and Cher. True Romance became Free Love. Acceptance of new social behavior itself was changing at an accelerating pace.

Eighteen-year-old songwriter Carol King penned "Will You Love Me Tomorrow?," the number one hit for the Shirelles in late 1960—a paeon to the perils of pre-marital sex—making them the first all-female group to summit the top of the music charts.

And in surfing there were notable achievements even if they were simply women exceling in spite of their restraints.

To count the number of women's firsts that happened in the 60s would strain the most jaded of surf historians. But there were many memorable moments, some triumphant, some forgotten and some virtually unknown.

Three Fistfuls of Firsts
1. Queen of Clubs: the First Surf Club Just for Women

In the fall of 1961 the California Coast Girls Surf Club was formed by Pamela Maloche, then a sophomore at Narbonne High in Harbor City. She also became the club's first president. Maloche founded the club shortly after moving with her parents to Balboa Peninsula in Newport Beach from the Inland Empire.

Her early years were spent living on the beach in Balboa, where her parents ran vacation cottages. Maloche spent almost every day in the Newport Beach shorebreak, completely hooked on the emerging beach lifestyle.

After forming the surf club, she continued to surf throughout the next three decades, becoming a thoughtful and active personality in the surf culture.

2. Surfing's First Woman Stunt Double

The first woman stunt double in surfing, Linda Benson had seen family fame as a child. Her father had been a drummer for the Tommy Dorsey Orchestra, the biggest band of the 30s. Even before her string of contest victories she rode waves disguised as Sally Fields during Sally's reign in the early 60s. She served as a stunt double for Deborah Walley in *Gidget Goes Hawaiian* (1961), and for Funicello in *Muscle Beach Party* (1963) and *Beach Blanket Bingo* (1965), substituting for the movies' stars in big surf and small. *Surf Guide* magazine published a 1963 cover shot with a coverline reading "World's Greatest!" Although it was not *Surfer*, Benson's photo was the first women to appear on a surf magazine cover.

3. The Cover of *Surfer* Magazine
Linda Merrill Makes it First

In 1964, *Surfer* magazine took a leap and published this stunning watershot of stylish goofy-foot Linda Merrill, the very first woman to appear on the cover of surfing's premier magazine. Daughter of San Onofre surf pioneer Benny Merrill, Merrill was a natural, learning to swim at four from the great water-woman Mary Ann Hawkins. By the time she was a teenager Merrill had teamed with all-around water-man Mike Doyle and won the tandem divisions of the West Coast Championships at Huntington Beach, and the Makaha Invitational in 1963.

At 5'2" with an hourglass figure, Merrill was the classic stylist, displaying ballet-like artistry as she danced from the tail to the nose on playful waves in the early 60s.

4. The First World Champ

The seeds planted by Duke Kahanamoku and Isabel Letham in 1914 blossomed fifty years later in the form of Phyllis O'Donnell. Born in Sydney in 1937, O'Donnell didn't start surfing until 1960, at the advanced age of twenty-three, learning on the Sydney beaches, mentored by Australian surfing great Snowy McAllister.

Most Australian surfers lived in Sydney at the time, but O'Donnell moved to the Gold Coast of Queensland, where she rode waves in isolation at Snapper Rocks. In 1964 O'Donnell was a surprise winner of the Australian National Titles, and that qualified her to surf in the first World Amateur Surfing Championships at Manly, one of her native breaks. For a ten-year period from the early 60s Phyllis was a dominant force in women's surfing. A World Champion, eight-times Queensland Champion, and three-time Australian Title winner (1963–65) talent and dedication took her to the top.

O'Donnell was twenty-seven when she won the first World Title in 1964 and was still a strong a competitive presence into the 70s, remaining a revered icon.

The All Girls Surfriders Club of Lennox Head continued to run an annual Ma Bendall Memorial Interclub Contest with other Australian women's clubs, to honor surfing's first women's world champion.

5. Fender Bender
First Mainstream Sponsorship

Californian Elizabeth "Banzai Betty" Carhart was a Laguna Beach surfer considered one of the best of the early 60s. A friend and one-time paramour of multi-time National Champion Corky Carroll, Betty could hang with the best of the boys. She has been credited as the first female surfer to garner a mainstream professional sponsorship by appearing in the ads for Fender Guitar, promoting their new Jaguar model which achieved its most noticeable popularity in the surf music scene. Nineteen-sixties advertising for the Jaguar often had beach themes, underscoring the brand's effort to appeal to surf musicians. Photographs for the campaign, done by icon Bob Perine, included bikini-clad girls on sandy beaches holding Jaguars. The Beach Boys' Carl Wilson is featured in one early publicity photo.

6. The First Star Rises in the East

The East Coast Surfing Hall of Fame described Mimi Munro as "Joyce Hoffman of the East Coast and the female version of Gary Propper," and by that they mean she was the first female dominant surf star to come from the Eastern Seaboard.

Decades before fellow Floridian surf stars Lisa Andersen and Frieda Zamba made their mark, Mimi Munro was paving the way for women from the east coast of the USA. Born in 1952 in Ormond Beach, Florida, Munro was Florida State Champion at twelve and then won the East Coast Surfing Championships in 1965 and 1966. She traveled to California to compete in the 1966 World Contest (placing third), then took a trip to Hawaii with her hero, Joyce Hoffman. Mimi Munroe came onto the scene like a hurricane and left just as suddenly. She won three East Coast Championships by the time she was fourteen.

The diminutive goofy-foot didn't like the big surf of Hawaii, and back in Florida, she was teased and bullied for being a 'Tomboy' causing problems with school and her grades. By sixteen she became disillusioned and went off to finish school. She married in her twenties and had four children.

Decades later, when one of her daughters began dating a surfer, Mimi tried surfing again at thirty-eight and was immediately reinvigorated. Entering the 33rd Annual Easter Surfing Fest in 1997, Mimi won the longboard division. In 2007, Munro was recognized for her 60s performances when she was awarded the 2007 Woman of the Year award by the Huntington Beach Surf Walk of Fame.

7. South Africa's First Star

Although she was by no means the first woman to stand on a board in South Africa—Christine "Bippo" Muller—is considered to be the first South Africa woman surfer in the modern era. Using Jeffreys Bay as a home base, Muller travelled to California and Hawaii in 1966 and became quite well known as a big-wave rider surfing sizable waves with famous male friends in the Islands. Big wave legend Greg Noll made her a semi-gun for Sunset, which she rode for months when the North Shore was comparatively uncrowded. "That was a beautiful board. She told Jeffreys local journalist Bruce Gold in 2016. "I could ride in three foot waves or ten foot waves." Part of the very early group at Jeffreys Bay, she was introduced to the *Endless Summer* crew and spent time with Miki Dora—the black knight of the 60s surf culture—during his five year encampment at the fabled right point.

8. America's First Surf Organizer
Brought a World Contest to the USA

In 1966, "Miss" Billy Riley—a petite blond with an Oklahoma accent—persuaded San Diego's city council to host a World Surfing Contest. The manager of the Half Moon Bay Hotel on Shelter Island and a respected civic activist, Riley convinced

City officials that a world surfing championship was just the thing to help put San Diego on the global tourist map. It would be no easy mission. San Diego had barely recovered from a wild ruckus in the fall of 1961, when thousands of raucous surfers descended on the area around Windansea Beach in La Jolla, trampling private property and creating public nuisance scenarios (read: consuming alcohol and changing clothes in public). But with Riley's relentless cajoling the City eventually approved the contest. Now considered one of the seminal events in surf history (ushering in the short board era with Australian Nat Young's vertical-performance victory) it was a model success.

Irresistible and tireless, Riley secured free hotel rooms and arrangements to feed two hundred surfers from eleven countries, for several days. Local Chevrolet dealers loaned cars for transportation around town, and the first-place finisher was awarded a sporty Camaro.

The first female president of the San Diego Hotel-Motel Association and first woman director of the San Diego Chamber of Commerce, Riley took no chances with a repeat of 1961: "I gathered a whole bunch of surfers together in the parking lot at the Bali Hai," Riley said, "and told them that we expected them to represent the surfing industry and establish themselves as an honorable group of people."

Bringing Duke Kahanamoku as the event's host and guest of honor insured her request was honored: participants respected the father of modern-day surfing and rewarded Riley with picture-perfect behavior.

"This whole thing was wonderful," Riley recalled. "Everyone was at their best, and the contest went off beautifully."

Mostly forgotten in the sweep of history, an entire epoch might have played out differently without her vision and persistence.

9. The First Woman's Signature Model

Remembered for her graceful, flowing style, Joey Hamasaki was born and raised in Honolulu, taking up surfing at the age of ten. Her considerable skills vaulted her onto the world stage as one of the dominant performers of the early to mid-60s, where she stood out among her Nordic rivals.

"Joey was a lone Japanese-American role model," Sam George wrote in *Surfer* magazine in 1999. "Her technique was artful and her personality reticent, but her wave-riding was sensational."

Wardy Surfboards introduced the Joey Hamasaki signature model in 1966, one of the earliest boards endorsed by a woman.

Hamasaki petitioned to be able to surf in the men's division in the 1966 Malibu Invitational, but she was denied. She easily took the women's division. Still steamed at not being able to compete against the men, Joey, shortly after the men's final, rode a wave all the way through to the pier that was so elegant, and showed so much command, that it stopped the awards ceremony until she kicked out.

A career highlight for Joey came in 1967, when she beat both rising talent Margo Godfrey and master Joyce Hoffman to win the East Coast Surfing Championship at Virginia Beach. "Joey was unbelievable," Hoffman claimed. "She had moves and style *nobody* else had at the time." Hoffman herself was among the first women to have her own "model" surfboard as well.

In an age when gentlemen still preferred blondes, Joyce Hoffman was the poster girl from central casting. But had it not been for Hoffman's talent, this small, shy whisper-voiced Hawaiian powerhouse might have been the best female of her era.

From Cover Girl to Surf Culture Maven

In 1966, The *Los Angeles Times West* magazine featured a svelte blond on the cover and proudly announced the article "The New Wave of Surfing Girls" inside. The California women who had turned to the ocean to help stay in athletic shape thought Mary Lou McGinnis exemplified a new breed: competitive surfer and film star.

Historians have noted that throughout the 60s, it was not uncommon for Drummy to pop up in various Hollywood films, including beach movies with Frankie Avalon and Annette Funicello. She stunt-doubled for Sharon Tate in the 1967 *Don't Make Waves* with Tony Curtis and became the first women to star in her own feature surf film *Follow Me*, which put her on a Bruce Brown-style journey through Japan, Morocco, Spain and India.

In 1970 Mary Lou married Steve Drummy and brought up a family of notable surf riders. Beginning to surf competitively in 1959, she continued her competitive career all through her child-raising days.

Once her career performing in front of surf judges and movie critics wound down, Drummy turned to the other side of the clipboard and began running surf events full time, organizing countless events and serving as a frequent judge.

Drummy was a founding member of the Malibu Surfing Association and in 1965 won the Santa Monica Mid-Winter Surfing Championships, defeating up-and-coming star Margo Oberg.

In 1975, Drummy helped found the Women's International Surfing Association (WISA), which ran the first all-women pro contest at Malibu. She worked alongside Jericho Poppler, Mary Setterholm and Shannon Aikman to pick up industry vanguard Hang Ten Sportswear as a sponsor. She was W.I.S.A.'s first president and ran the organization until it merged with the Western Surfing Association (W.S.A.) in 1994. With Midget Smith, her long-time partner of 20 years, she continued to organize WSA competitions and, to this day, remains at the helm of the longest-standing amateur surfing organization in America. She was awarded the 2015 Surfing America Midget Smith Judging Award for her longstanding commitment to competitive surfing. Honored with a Lifetime Achievement Award at 2003's Action Sports Retailers Trade Show, it's a safe bet that American competitive surfing might not be where it is today without the devotion of this California original. Her commitment to the sport and her contribution to competitive surfing landed her a coveted spot on 2016's Surfing Walk of Fame.

11. Ringing Ten Bells

From the mid-60s to the mid-70s Gail Couper became an almost unbeatable force on the Australian surfing circuit. Born in Melbourne in 1947, Gail, the daughter of surf contest administration pioneer Stan Couper, started surfing when she was fourteen, after moving to Lorne in Victoria.

Inspired by the surfing of fellow Victorian Wayne Lynch, Couper won her first State Title just three years after taking up surfing. It marked the start of an unprecedented dominance of surfing events. Couper won fourteen Victorian State Titles and won ten Bells events every year from 1966 onward, missing just once in 1969.

On the world stage, Couper also made a mark reaching the semi-finals of the World Championships in 1964, fourth two years later and the semi-finals again in 1968.

"Bells is the most iconic spot on Tour when it comes to women's surfing history," said World Surfing League Deputy Commissioner Jessi Miley-Dyer.

"Gail Couper has won the event ten times, but not all of them were within the professional era. She's one of those women within the sport that didn't get all the recognition that they deserve—for being a mold-breaker and someone that really paved the way."

12. As Easy as ABC—or ESA

Janice Domorski was crowned the 1968 Women's Champion of the ESA's first full competitive season. It was there that the East Coast built the foundation for a huge and colorful part of the surfing culture. Attending the 1968 World

Contest in Puerto Rico she was described as "The only competitor riding a wide-tailed v-bottom board (with a blue nose patch), seen in the ABC Television coverage, is Janice Domorski from Virginia Beach, representing East Coast of the USA." She was inducted into the East Coast Surfing Hall of Fame in 2000.

13. We're Tops Down Under

The fierce but respectful rivalry between the two great surfing nations of Australia and the United States was already in full swing when Josette Lagardere turned the tables on the brash, brilliant Aussies by winning the 1969 Australian National Championships as an American expatriate. It was an ironic twist to the famous headline Tracks magazine founder John Witzig had crowed (We're Tops Now!) when Nat Young had stolen the show from the Californians at the 1966 World Contest in Ocean Beach San Diego.

A nimble, blond regular-foot originally from Redondo Beach, California Lagardere had already earned a distinguished reputation winning the 1966 Laguna Swimwear Masters contest and a finalist berth in the '66 World Contest as well. Along with 1964 World Champ Australian Phyllis O'Donnell, she had worked at the Dewey Weber shop in the Los Angeles South Bay learning the trade and honing her skills . When Josette relocated to Australia and won the 1969 Women's Australian National Title at Margret River, Western Australia, she could claim that upset avenged the 66 contest where fellow Dewey Weber sponsored Aussie Nat Young had dominated the competition in America.

14. The First California Female Surf Shop Owner

Barbie Baron opened Offshore Surf Shop in late 1969 and both she *and* the shop became beloved fixtures in the North County surf community.

Growing up on The Strand in Oceanside Baron started surfing in junior high. Turning pro at age eighteen Baron made it to the top 10 in the U.S. ratings and "that's when I realized there was no real money to be made in surfing for women at that time, and I decided to open the shop," she said.

"I borrowed fifteen hundred dollars from a bank and opened my doors," Barbie said.

The Offshore shop originally opened off Cleveland Street in Oceanside, and after moving the shop several times Barbie partnered with Scot Tammen and in 1978 they moved the shop to its beachfront location on Pacific Coast Highway.

"The shop was like me, small but mighty," says Barbie. "It was 800 square feet, attached to Harbor Fish south, and has the best view possible." Baron retired in 2015 after forty-five years in the business.

15. The First Emmy-winning Surfer

Linda Spheeris was a surfer of the 60s who competed on the West Coast circuit. She was a regular at Doheny surfing with legends Joey Hamasaki and Dee Dee Aravelos.

In 1993, Linda received the Heroic Act Award, given to non-lifeguard persons by the United States Lifesaving Association (USLA) who risked their lives in an extraordinary degree in a rescue of another person.

Linda worked in film and television as an Art Director and Production Designer for many years. Her credits include *Falcon Crest*, *Point Break* and *Planes, Trains & Automobiles*.

Honorable Mention
First Female State Lifeguard

With Joyce Hoffman there are many firsts. And technically this effort was achieved in 1972. There were, of course, prior women lifeguards—in pools and waterparks both private and municipal. But her success as the first surfer lifeguard is unusually significant in that it was awarded by the State of California and that she was required to make the team competing—exclusively—with *the men* for the job. This was man on man, head to head trials, and only the fittest survived.

"She was in unbelievable shape, Del Mar lifeguard teammate Tom Cousins told me in 1973. "She was as good as *any* of the guys."

In film, sports and music women could claim "first's" in many areas. But those often simply highlighted the dearth of opportunities in the past. In 1967 Aretha Franklin turned Otis Redding's R&B masterpiece "Respect" on its head—and into one of the most powerful female anthems of all time. It was a mandate for change, defining the missing ingredient women sought. That demand would not be met for some time.

Big Girls Don't Cry

1962–1967

"Surfing is such an amazing concept. You're taking on Nature with a little stick and saying, 'I'm gonna ride you!' And a lot of times Nature says, 'No you're not!' and crashes you to the bottom."
—Jolene Blalock, Actress *Star Trek: Enterprise*

"Big Girls Don't Cry" by the pop group the Four Seasons spent five weeks at number one on the 1964 Top 40 radio charts. Inspired by a line in the film noir *Slightly Scarlet*, starring John Payne and Rhonda Fleming, it became a statement of women's mental and physical toughness for the younger generation. When Payne's character slapped the woman played by Fleming, he asks her what she thinks about being slapped. She got up, composed herself, and defiantly replied, "Big girls don't cry." Younger women knew exactly what the maxim meant: they weren't hitting back, but they were no longer taking it lying down either.

It was a milestone—and the 60s would provide many more, especially in surfing: Ten-foot, fifty-pound balsa logs evolved into five-foot slivers of fiberglass. Phyllis O'Donnell won the first World Contest in Australia, and a tiny teenage Margo Oberg took on big Sunset.

As the world turned upside down in the tumultuous upheaval of the late 60s, surfing rode the cutting edge wave of a cultural sea change. Women, for the first time, were beginning to see themselves as a driving force: Joyce Hoffman became the first multiple World-Title holder, first female state lifeguard, first cross-trainer. And then there was the decision to ride Pipeline.

Personal Best

Joyce Hoffman knew she was in trouble. She had just successfully ridden three waves at Pipeline and then took a drop too steep and wiped out hard. Now, still dazed from the punch of Pipeline's explosive lip, she was caught in an intense riptide. Disoriented, in an unfamiliar place, she was not sure which way to swim. The current made getting to shore hard but letting the rip carry her made getting caught by a larger set an unattractive alternative. "Nobody feels very safe on their first go out at Pipeline," attested Butch Van Artsdalen, known as one of the best Pipe surfers ever. *This was Hoffman's first session.*

It was a good size day, she remembered—with serious conditions. Legendary photographer LeRoy Grannis was shooting, and Bud Browne was filming with his movie camera. John Pike, an early Pipeline pioneer had just got smashed on the reef, nearly ripping his ear off and tearing open his shoulder. Joyce's mother, watching from the beach saw Pike, stumbling into the shore, blood pouring out of his mutilated ear.

In later decades there would always be a couple of dozen other surfers—and a trained lifeguard—all watching out for one another. Medical aid would be just a few minutes away. Except this was *not* the 2000s—*it was 1962.* Medical help was in Honolulu. Only two other surfers were in the lineup—and they had Pipeline worries of their own. This was no ordinary situation.

The good news was that this was no ordinary woman either. She would win an unprecedented three National Surfing Championships in a row. And then two back-to-back World Titles. She would ride Hobie's first and only woman's signature model—her own. Her paddling prowess was unmatched. And in a macho era that had never even heard of "Women's Lib," she would become the first female beach lifeguard in San Diego's history. Before Gloria Steinem had graduated from college Joyce Patricia Hoffman had ridden 15 foot Makaha, met the President of Peru, and been featured in full-page ads for Triumph sports cars.

A natural athlete, Joyce knew from early childhood she would pursue some sport professionally—she just wasn't sure which one it would be. Track and field, tennis and skiing were serious considerations, but when her mom married waterman Walter Hoffman and he took Joyce surfing, the catalyst jelled.

Walter and his brother Phillip "Flippy" Hoffman were regulars at Malibu and frequent flyers to Hawaii, and what had started out as a pleasant pastime became a passion for the gifted, driven young woman. Giving up all other sports, Hoffman trained like the athlete she was—running, weight training and paddling—techniques that were ahead of the time but true to her competitive nature. The preparation served her well as she took contest after contest.

All of a sudden Joyce's image seemed to be everywhere. In a two year period during the mid-60s she would grace the cover of *Life, Look, Vogue, Seventeen* and *Sports Illustrated.* The *Los Angeles Times* would name her 1965's "Woman of the Year" for outstanding achievement in sports, the only surfer to ever receive that honor. The two-time World Champ was the alpha female during the longboard era of the early to mid-60s, arguably the world's best-known and most successful surfer of her time. The success led to global exposure, giving women's surfing a much-needed shot in the arm and opened doors for the next generation of competitors.

Now she had just experienced the thrill of Pipeline—and the price that is often extracted like a pound of flesh.

"The only reason I went out there was because Bud Browne was filming, and I wanted to be recognized as the first woman documented surfing Pipeline," Joyce admitted. "Thank God Bud got it on film. I lost my board, got caught in a monstrous rip, and my mom had to send my all-time hero, Phil Edwards, out to help me in." That was the last time Hoffman had to be rescued. At least from the surf.

"We all knew her because she was under the tutelage of Phil Edwards," said Herbie Fletcher, soon to be brother in law, and surf legend himself.

Phil Edwards was the reigning surf deity. Joyce slid effortlessly under his spell.

"There was nothing like watching Phil," she contended. "He was so classic, a true one-of-a kind guy. He was—next to my dad—the biggest influence on my surfing."

"I'm sure she learned from watching me." Edwards, always understated, doesn't add he was considered the greatest surfer of his era. But he does realize Joyce benefitted from his being there.

"She was a power surfer. I guess all great surfers are power surfers," he offered. "I was just there to witness her extraordinary talent."

The beachbreak in front of her house was a great training ground for her career.

The first contest she entered was the 1962 San Clemente Surf Capades. She won the women's event and won the tandem event with her father. She was thirteen. From then on losing was a rarity. From 1964 to 1967 she dominated women's surfing like no other. "She would leave every morning at 6 A.M. to practice," recalled legendary surf photographer Leroy Grannis. "It was eight hours a day, every day." Her obsessive dedication paid off. In 1965 she won 10 of 12 contests in the major competition circuit, a record unequaled in all of surfing by a woman *or* a man. Jericho Poppler saw it like the Beatles placing five hits in the top music slots. "She was at the apex." Leroy Grannis agreed. "She was the one."

"She brought surfing up to the level of skiing or golf," Jericho Poppler declared emphatically. "Just a total ambassador. Of course her family was key to her, a big help."

All in the Family

"There's no doubt my family, particularly my dad has been my greatest asset in success," Hoffman conceded. "My folks took me to Hawaii, to the contests; it was always the whole family." The family, in this case, also happens to be one of the most celebrated surfing clans in the world. There is her late uncle Flippy, big-wave rider and water-man extraordinaire, and his son Marty a "former WSL World Tour competitor." There are her nephews Christian Fletcher (who—depending on what historian is speaking—either invented, innovated, or popularized the aerial maneuver); and Nathan, one of the sport's most respected and debonair big wave hell-men. Their father Herbie Fletcher (Joyce's brother in law) is one of the most prominent and colorful characters in the sport, an artist as well as long-standing surf businessmen. Fletcher's wife (Joyce's sister Dibi) is renowned for her art, most of it depicting surf culture in mediums ranging from colored resin paintings to impressionist island scenes. Joyce's brother Tony surfs well. Even youngest sister Robin surfs, even though she focused on riding horses. And her nephew Grayson joined the ranks as a top rated performer as well. Which brings us to her father, big Walter, the sultan of surfwear, pioneer of Makaha, Waimea and world exploration. "All the girls in the family can surf," Hoffman Patriarch Walter has explained when asked about his family. "Joyce just went beyond. She was a natural. In her character is the ability to really get into something full on. She's just so competitive by nature."

Joyce Hoffman's reputation for competitiveness was legendary. "She was my role model for competition," Jericho Poppler has attested. "I wasn't savvy. I tagged onto Joyce and from her I learned how to compete. How to understand competition."

Mary Lou McGinnis, a top surf star and contestant in Joyce's era, agreed: "She was the most competitive woman *ever*," McGuiness stated. "She set the example for all the girls to come."

"Joyce was a lot of fun, but I never saw her *surf* for fun," Jericho Poppler has observed. "She knew how to handle herself as a champion," Poppler explained. "It was her style." Her style, by most observers, was raw aggression coupled with exacting wave knowledge and natural physical prowess. "My hero was Phil Edwards; I tended to emulate him," she said in an interview in 1990. "The women before me—Linda Merrill, Candy Calhoun, Linda Benson—tended to not pattern themselves after the men. It was precedent setting in more ways than one: I came from the hard-core athletic, not the grace that perhaps they had." Her brother-in-law Herbie Fletcher was more blunt. "She was the best because she hung with all the best surfers. She changed the way girls surfed."

Perhaps Leroy Grannis summed it up best: "In those days nobody had women's contests at Sunset Beach. Joyce could ride it with the best of them. She surfed contests like a guy. But she's a lady."

Her mom always maintained it was all hard work, confidence and determination. "It runs in the family," she claimed.

Family has obviously played a major role in her life. Joyce's dedication to her own daughter is a reflection of the support she received herself. "Samantha is the best thing that ever happened to me," she has attested numerous times in interviews. 'Nothing in all the sports compares to her. Even back in the day."

What *was* it like back then, particularly for women? After all, it was a different time, one that has almost disappeared. Just knowing people didn't always bring you acceptance; it took all of Joyce's iron will to pry her way into the top of a male-dominated sport.

"When I first started surfing, women were not always appreciated in the water. There were many occasions where I was physically challenged, yelled at, chased out of the water," she remembered. "Guys cutting me off, shooting their boards at me, just letting me know I wasn't welcome out there." She has admitted it was a hard time for women—and it shaped her attitude toward the sport early on.

"I learned really quick the only way to overcome that was to gain their respect. You had to get good enough so that whether you were a woman or not they would respect your abilities and share the water with you."

Once a woman demonstrated true grit, things changed. "As soon as they saw you could keep up, that you had talent, then it turned completely around. When they saw you were competent, you were serious, they wanted nothing more than to help you."

A Golden Age?

Was it more difficult back then? More macho, less equal? "Probably," was Joyce's answer. "There are a lot more good women now. Guys are used to seeing them."

Leroy Grannis, who had shot surfers since the 40s, saw machismo as a consistent attitude. "Men have always looked down their noses at women surfers," he commented.

What other people thought was not a concern for Joyce Hoffman. She had a plan and she stuck to it. At an early age she had decided she wanted to do something serious. "I was going to be the best at something . . . for as long as I can remember," she told me back in 1998. Hoffman was a "straight A" student, a model citizen, a world champ. And suddenly she had become a national celebrity.

Karen MacKay remembers Hoffman's effect in those days. For her sixteenth birthday in 1966 Karen's mom purchased a new surfboard at Montgomery Ward's department store in Houston Texas. The store hosted an appearance with Joyce Hoffman, current World Champion, in the sporting goods department, promoting surfboards in the Gulf. "After meeting her, my passion for riding waves was lit, MacKay said. She made me feel confident to compete and meet other women surfers—I saw it as my life." Apparently the inspiration was effective; MacKay went on to become a two-time Gulf Coast champion and win the 1977 U.S. National title at Huntington Beach. MacKay would go on to serve on the Board of The Gulf Surfing Association, U.S. Surfing Federation, organize the WISA Texas Chapter and become the 1993 Board of Director President for The Surfrider Foundation. She credits Hoffman for hers and others' motivation.

"Joyce was a role model for women athletes," MacKay claimed.

The compulsive drive to achieve took Hoffman to the very top of the surf world, but not without a price. Being a blond surf goddess was never a role with which she felt comfortable, though she played the part superbly.

Hoffman was philosophical about it: "That was what they expected of you, and so I just did it. The sport needed it and I was willing." But the pressure of being a perfect role model was taking its toll. In 1971 she won the U.S. Championships in Huntington Beach for the fifth time, and after years of dominating women's surfing, walked off the scene and disappeared.

"There was nothing left to prove," she thought. And nothing left to gain. "Nobody was giving out any money. You could win a television set, and I got to drive a great car because my sponsor was Triumph. But there was nothing you could sink a professional career into." Contest surfing would not see her again for more than a decade. There would be more expectations and more roles to play. Marrying her longtime boyfriend who had just finished architecture school, she shunned the limelight that had almost scorched her. She had a daughter and tried to settle into the suburban good life.

But there was a restlessness that she could not subdue. Old desires to compete and new ones to experience a different life came powering back in. As if one life was not enough, Hoffman sought another challenge. She would find part of her fulfillment in the *other* great 60s sub-culture in California—*motor sports*—but it was short lived after a near-fatal accident.

But her redemption after the accident and her search for a renewed sense of purpose outside of competition came in part by coming back to the place she started—surfing.

Her brother-in-law Herbie Fletcher invited her to a contest, shaped her a surfboard and gave her a week to prepare. For seven days in a row she "practiced like mad, so I could win the thing." She remembered. "And luckily, I *did*." She won nearly every contest she entered in fact but ran into the same old roadblocks: "no money, still no place to go."

She found she needed to give it up in order to not be obsessive about winning. From that point on she surfed mostly for fun.

In the early 2000s Hoffman moved to San Juan Capistrano, just minutes from her beach road childhood home. She took on managing a horse farm and continued to surf, living a quiet life of tranquility. Finding the balance between sport, family, fame and career, she made a lasting peace.

"Everyone has so much respect for her," family friend and surf legend Mickey Munoz said. "The thing I respect about Joyce the most is that she has continued to be her own person. She doesn't flaunt anything. She doesn't hide anything. She just lives an honest life."

The Golden Age

Sex, Lies and Videotape

The 60s

As Hoffman's career attested, surfing received an astounding amount of mainstream coverage during the mid-60s in both international and domestic media. Hollywood's depiction of the surfing life was met by surfers with titters. The much maligned "Beach Party" movies including *Beach Blanket Bingo* and *Muscle Beach Party* made clear the film industry's embarrassing lack of understanding about surfing. As bad as they were, their depictions were harmless save for the subservient stereotypes and poses of the scantily-clad starlets. In 1965's horror film *The Beach Girls and the Monsters*, surfers were brutally murdered—the mystery being whether the culprit was a sea monster or one of the teens jealous parents. Along with *The Horror of Party Beach*, and *How to Stuff a Wild Bikini*, this was a mercifully short-lived exploitation genre hoping to cash in on the surf craze crossbred with titillating sex and terror. Caught between the collapse of the helpless damsel of the 50s and the women's movement yet to come, these typified the era's oblivious misogyny. Even big budget epics like *Ride the Wild Surf* using real surfers as stunt doubles and real footage of big Waimea Bay never quite captured the accurate essence of surfing.

But as general audience films faded from the scene, surf filmmakers capitalized on their authentic knowledge of the niche market of real surfers.

Bruce Brown's seminal surf documentary, *The Endless Summer*, was the first large-screen 35 millimeter film about surfing, and was a sensation at the box office, introducing two women to the world: Hawaiian Bernie Ross and Australian Pearl Turton. "Bernie Ross," *Surfer* editor Sam George wrote, "showed an aplomb in North Shore power that few Mainlanders—male or female—could match."

Ross was the only woman to be featured actually surfing in the film, and—although her performance was strong (Haleiwa in solid size)—the segment had been shot years before the film debuted.

Pearle Turton was another story. Surf champion and cultural critic Cori Schumacher has rightly pointed out that while Turton—the first nationally recognized champion in Australia—was *featured* in the *Endless Summer*, the way they presented her "was absolutely ridiculous and embarrassed the heck out of her," she admonished. "Just after showing the heroics of men surfing Waimea, the boys decide to surf a Sydney break when Pearl walks by in a bikini bottom that shows the top of her crack," declared Schumacher. "The entire section is a ridiculous portrayal of 'boys will be boys' and 'girls are there to ogle' goofiness that diminishes and trivializes Pearl."

Its doubtful Brown was an intentional misogynist; he and his wife surfed, rode motorbikes and raced in Baja shoulder-to-shoulder for nearly fifty years together, one of the great love stories of surfdom. And to be fair, Turton had appeared on the cover of *Australian Women's Weekly* and done live broadcasts in a national television studio wearing only her bikini. But she was also an established surf star having won the Australian National Titles a year earlier. The salient point that Schumacher drives home so convincingly is that Turton was not treated like a professional athlete, but a cheesecake—a product of the times perhaps, but women were simply not given equal respect then that they demanded in the 21st Century.

Rancho Humboldt
The Woman who Introduced Surfing to Ecuador

On a warm windless day in 1962, Dorothy Jurado stood at her bedroom window that looked across the beach and the small fishing village to the first of five long pointbreaks. The sand was gray and speckled white, and the water was clear in the shallows and deep blue in the Humboldt Current that ran parallel to the coastline of her family's property. The waves broke along the shoreline and the sunlight danced on the foiled ridge of swell. But what Jurado saw was a lone surfer riding a fiberglass surfboard rising and dropping with the wave pocket, gliding along the crisp clean swell line. She had never seen a surfer before, never seen a foam and fiberglass surfboard, had only ridden scraps of balsa that washed down the rivers from the sawmills. The 1960 Ecuadorian backstroke champion with a long lean six-foot frame, Dorothy Jurado had spent much of her life in the water. That day she swiftly swam out to the lineup, curious to meet the rider and inspect the equipment.

She encountered Piti Block, one of Peru's first modern surfers. He had been exploring the coast in search of the perfect wave and thought he had found it here in Ecuador where the summer is already endless. In short shrift she convinced Piti to let her try his shiny new 9' Hobie. Her first ride was as addicting as the ocean itself.

Soon Piti was dating Jurado's cousin and leaving his board at her family's home as an excuse for return visits. The second of five children, Jurado was born into a well-to-do family in 1940 and had spent her weekends bodysurfing and bellyboarding as well as competitive swimming in the waves in front of her home; when her father died just months before her chance meeting with Piti, she dropped swim competition and took her passion to surfing exclusively. Athletic and statuesque, Jurado quickly became Ecuador's top surfer—man or woman. The grand-daughter of Emilio Estrada, who had been Ecuador's president, her family's two miles of beachfront property housed one of the largest and most luxurious hotels in South America. A fervent waverider and surf culture maven, Jurado immediately began to spread the surfing lifestyle to other locals. She was also vivacious and athletic—a shoo in for an invitation to Peru's Championship in 1964. There she met many of the early surf stars from Hawaii and California as well as Peru. The future World Champion, Hawaii's Fred Hemmings recalled her as "Ecuador's premiere and pioneer surfer from the 60s."

Surfing's top stars began to pay visit's to her mother's home as much to experience the gracious hospitality as to surf the first-rate point waves which broke in front of her welcoming beachside residence. Among her star-studded visitors was a seventeen-year-old Joyce Hoffman. "*The Endless Summer* had just come out," remembered Hoffman. "We loved traveling for new surf and the South American hospitality was hard to match anywhere."

The surfers found the area pristine, almost from another time. "Deer would walk into the house like pet dogs," Greg Huglin wrote in 2014. "The swimming pool was full of a million lobsters." There were virtually no local surfers and miles of unexplored surf spots.

Not long after her father died, Dorothy's mother decided to build a weekend-only restaurant on the beach in front of her house to feed friends and visiting surfers.

The entire family (including her younger sister Silvia, a 1974 Miss Ecuador) worked the enterprise. Christened Chabela's it had a worldwide reputation for good food, holding surfing contests and hosting surf guests from around the globe.

After years of surfing in the intense equatorial sun, Jurado contracted sun blindness causing serious retina damage to her eyes. She eventually had to quit surfing but appears to have lost none of her appetite for the waves.

For more than seven decades Dorothy Jurado continued to promote surfing in her native country and welcoming all those who love the surfing lifestyle—enhanced by the Ecuadorian hospitality. In her stretch of beach the innocence and exhuberence of the 60s still continued to prevail.

All through the eras Dorothy remained the center of the action, all smiles and aloha spirit, still the young Olympic hopeful who swam out to meet Piti Block in 1962. "You can see the happiness on her face and the love she bestowed on her countless friends," Greg Huglin wrote summing up the person and her place in surf lore. "She is the glue that holds the whole tribe together and the matriarch who brought the surfing lifestyle to her country."

The Twain *Shall* Meet

While contests had been a part of surfing since the days when Hawaiian Queens would wager their lovers life on a single ride, modern surfing competition became widespread for the first time during the mid-60s. By 1967 Joyce Hoffman had already won a World Championship at the 1966 World Contest in San Diego. As the current queen of the waves—along with Linda Benson, and young teen Margo Oberg, Hoffman created the public perception of California as the dominion of surfing's female royalty.

But one contest turned the conventional wisdom on its head: the 1966 East Coast Surfing Championships. A year earlier Florida surf impresario Dick Catri had formed a team of East Coast surfers sponsored by Surfboards Hawaii, one of the several big board manufacturers looking to fill the new regions' surfing demand. His team included three teenage women: Cocoa Beach prodigy Mimi Munro, Kathy LaCroix of Jacksonville and Renee Eisler of Daytona Beach, Florida, all top competitors of their time.

Poet Rudyard Kipling famous verse read "the east is east, and the west is west and never the twain shall meet." But in this case they *did*—with surprising results. Held in Virginia Beach, the event was billed as a West Coast/East Coast showdown. Covered by both leading magazines, *Surfer* and *Surfing*, nearly 10,000 spectators jammed the beach to witness the intercoastal duel. It was the largest crowd ever for an east coast event—and the oddsmakers had Californians as the heavy favorites.

But Catri's team was one of the most talented rosters to ever fill a lineup, and when the smoke cleared the East Coasters had swept the titles in nearly every category. Mimi Munroe won the women's division, and the three girls took home five of the many trophies the easterners had claimed.

Surfer magazine declared "for the first time—East Beats West!" It was a triumph for the East Coast—and the Floridian women had been the *dark horse* performers in the runoff.

Surfing's Golden Age of Innocence

Was there ever a Golden Age of Innocence? As with most history it depends on who and where you were at the time. And often who and where you were when the history is written. Looking back decades later, women spoke about their experience with a very different perspective.

International competitions continued to build and starting with the 1964 World Contest in Australia the tournaments almost always included a women's division. In this age of relative innocence, events were not so much cutthroat competitions as they were gatherings of the tribe. Contests often resembled tailgate parties at the beach, an excuse for the younger competitors to get out of town and the families to enjoy a destination experience mom, dad and the kids all loved.

"Results were immaterial," Rell Sunn told me at her home Thanksgiving Day in 1981. "There was no money to win and no career to develop. So pride was the only value to wager."

Pride could be a strong motivator though: Although she never received the media attention World Champ Phyllis O'Donnell did, Dorothy Vidgen (formerly De Rooy) a modest, easy-going surfer from northern Sydney captured *five* NSW surfing titles—1960, 62, 64, 65 and 66 and in 1964 just missed out on a podium finish at the World Surfing Championships at Manly, finishing fourth. Vidgen and surfing compatriot Marilyn Bennett were both totally involved in the mid-60s surf world. While they were lucky enough to ride their home breaks of Long Reef and Collaroy with a tight group of accepting and respectful surfers, they also recalled a broader disrespect toward women board riders and regarded themselves as pioneers. At the contests, Vidgen remembered "cringing at the way photographers would shoot wet bikini shots" of her on the beach rather than her prodigious skill in the water. "The media and the contest promotors wanted 'the look'—*put the board as close to your bosom as you can* scenarios," she told the Pittwater News in an interview in 2019. "It didn't matter if you could surf well, they wanted cheesecake images. They wanted you to look good and focused a little too much on those who did—it didn't matter about skill, we were just being exploited. I didn't like any of those photos," she continued. "I always felt the girls were tacked on as an extra and not taken seriously—they were there because of the way they looked, wearing bikinis—that sort of thing. Its unlike today where the girls are just doing amazing surfing and given credit for it."

But it did not deter either of the women from their passionate dedication: "I just loved surfing so much . . ." Vidgen confessed. She married shortly after winning her third NSW Title. Vidgen and her husband built a yacht and departed for a ten-year adventure sailing for waves.

Surfers like Margaret Smith from then remote South Africa were completely unknown outside their native country. Smith, a long-time resident on the False Bay coast, was an early pioneer of women's surfing. A Springbok (South African National sports team athlete), she earned her colors after winning the South African Surf Championships in 1966. Smith along with Sally Sturrock and Christine Muller, laid the foundation for a new era for South African women surfers. "I remember the Beach Boys and rock n' roll," National Surf Champ Sally Sturrock told the Cape Argus newspaper in 2010. "*We* wore baggies to keep our bikini bottoms from falling off. These days it's the *fashion*."

And luckily, each time a Springbok team was chosen to surf in international competitions, at least two women were included. Pippa Sales, a plucky Springbok from Muizenberg Beach (where Agatha Christie had first tried surfing 50 years before) was selected to represent South Africa at the World Surfing Championships in Ocean Beach California. Sales and Sally Sturrock, who also hailed from the Cape Town area, were the girls on the South African team of eight. "It was the time of our lives!" Sales told the media back home.

And although their level of surfing prowess was often less than that of their overseas counterparts, the spirited waveriders that *did* travel abroad—Philippa Hulett, Marlene Webb, Christine Muller and Pippa Sales, to name a few—were positive representatives for an isolated nation in a distant and troubled global sphere. And while the obvious ugliness of apartheid and restrictive gender roles cast a dark shadow, these groundbreaking females did much to open South African eyes and added some appreciated sunlight for the women surfers in their home country.

"The 60s was a special time, even with all that was going on in our country," said Christine Muller. "We were free to travel the world, surf, live the life we wanted. It was *new*."

Even Dorothy Vidgen admitted that these early years of modern surfing were in some respects golden.

"I was lucky in that way—to have a decent go in the beginning." And despite the Chauvinism from promoters and media, the surfers themselves "were really just all friends at the beginning—we were just a group of people who all loved to surf. At a reunion I went to just a few years ago, with so many of us catching up, that's what stood out—we weren't male or female or surfing stars—we were surfing for the passion of it—for the waves, for the sense of freedom that gave. And in that we were all just mates."

Shop Around

Fellow females were far fewer in the early 60s. That was true particularly on the North East Coast of the USA. With its short season and frigid winters there was no mystery why Maine's surfing population remained small. The rugged conditions did *not*, however, stop entrepreneurs like Linda Peters from opening surf shops. Peters began surfing in 1962, opening the Bikini Surf Shop in Maine's York Beach the following year in the basement of her parent's house. She was a sixteen-year-old high school student. Her sister Susie ran the beach rentals while mom Ellen Peters did the books. Her dad John—a wealth of weather knowledge and local lore—sold boards and fixed dings. John's homespun style and proclivity for gaffs earned him a loveable rapscallion's reputation as the 'Archie Bunker' of the Southern Maine surfing community, adding to the shop's draw. Linda opened her second shop in Old Orchard circa 1966–67. It was a family affair that flourished with the times.

Both sisters married icons of surf culture: Linda to Floyd Smith, the "Smith" in the original Gordon and Smith Surfboard brand and creator of Surfboards Australia. Susie, the older daughter, married Warren Bolster, one of the most prominent surf photographers to ever come out of the East. "It was an early enough period, with such a small cadre of committed characters that unions like these felt like noble dynasties," noted Sandy Ordille, later considered part of the patrician-class of Eastern surf culture herself. "In those days accomplished surfers were heroes and heroines of a magic kingdom."

Linda Peters was certainly not the only woman surf shop owner on the East Coast with a reputation for welcoming wayward surfers. In Indialantic, Florida, Shagg Catri along with her legendary ex-husband Dick, brought a warmth and comfort to patrons of Shagg's Surf Shop, one of the oldest and most influential on the entire East Coast. Gathering a fabled team of the very best Eastern surfers of the 60s and early 70s, they beat the top California surfers in a head to head match-up that elevated the East's reputation worldwide. Shagg's became a central hub for surfers, shapers and visiting surf royalty; a magnetic zone for finding new innovations and the latest local surf news. It expanded to manufacturing, retail and wholesale sales, a veritable empire in Indialantic.

But the shop and its ever-present owner was more than that. Shagg was "the glue that held things together, at the shop, the factory, the foam warehouse and her own home with three lovely, young daughters," Greg Loehr attested at her induction into the East Coast Surfing Hall of Fame in 2012. "Her easy manner always gave the feeling that being at Shagg's was like being home with mom."

Some women simply made their own opportunities. Gerry Stewart, a young surfer from Long Island New York, joined the Bunger Surfboards team and became one of the East Coast's first 'sponsored' performers, and "an outright pioneer in the East," wrote Sam George in 1999. Traveling on Bunger Surfboards promotional tours—as well as competing in the early East Coast Championships and earning modeling jobs—Stewart was a prototypical pro long before the term was ever applied to any surfer, let alone female.

Shop ownership was no requirement for legend status. Renee Whitman, the first East Coast women's surfing champion ever—and daughter of Daytona Beach Florida surfing pioneer Dudley Whitman—has frequently reminisced about her days living in Hawaii. Whitman remembered surfing alongside Duke Kahanamoku, his brothers, and other legends that she met while traveling with her father, who was among the very first surfers in Florida back in the late 30s.

But for the longest time the women's club was a gang of no more than three. "You just didn't see women in the lineup in those days," Whitman recalled. "There weren't career opportunities." Contests offered winners a television set; second place might be a steak dinner.

"When I see what girls have going on now," she told *Surfer* magazine in 2004, "I'm amazed."

Whether it was the age of innocence or the age of obliviousness, the eight years 1962–69—was likely the zenith of amateur surf competitions. And in those years a cast of truly great competitors came on the scene: In 1968 a sixteen-year-old prodigy named Margo Godfrey took the women's top prize at the still-heralded Makaha International surf contest in Hawaii and then topped it off by winning the 1968 World Contest in Puerto Rico, establishing her as surfing's new wunderkind. Linda Benson claim her fourth USSA title and a plucky but tragic Judy Trim won the Australian National Titles.

In 1969 the newly formed Eastern Surfing Association's 6-event contest season crowned Ocean City's first world-class surfer, Barbara Bellyea. The United States Surfing Championships were won by East Coast starlet Sharron Weber, and Rell Sunn's sister Martha Sunn took home her second top trophy at the Makaha International. While Australia's National Titles were being secured by Californian Josette Lagardere, another Californian—once again the phenomenon Margo Godfrey—showed her big wave skills to clinch the Smirnoff World Cup Championship at Sunset Beach, Hawaii.

The coming decade of the 70s would see vast changes in design, technology, style and attitude—a *revolution* it would be called. For the women it would culminate in something closer to a *revolt*.

12

Surrealistic Pillow

1967–1972

The Next Level

Margo Godfrey Oberg had fallen on a wave and lost her board in a critical heat in her battle for another contest win in Australia. Until that slip-up she had been leading on the scoreboard. With only fifteen minutes left to compete against five other women the long swim into the shorebreak could mean elimination for Oberg. The board was floating halfway between the takeoff spot and the rocks. The next set would wash it in. Margo was stroking furiously but it was almost impossible for her to reach her board before the next set of waves did. Margo Oberg remembered that her "board was washing toward the rocks, and I was screaming at my husband Steve to grab it."

But suddenly the crowd began to cheer, with the enthusiasm of a drunken bar crowd watching a stripper. Steve Oberg, Margo's coach, critic and husband had stripped down to his underwear, and was racing into the shorebreak to retrieve her lost board. Splashing out into the waves he dove repeatedly to get to her board before it washed in another 60 yards to shore. Racing against time Margo was plowing toward him herself, now sensing that all was not lost. Using both hands Steve Oberg launch the board from the tail shooting across the 15 yards between them. Margo grabbed the rails and made a frantic return to the lineup. "They just went wild," remembered Margo Oberg. "The 5000 spectators on the beach couldn't believe it!"

As he exited up the beach from the water the crowd gave Steve Oberg a standing ovation. As might be expected in any history worth re-telling, Margo Oberg went on to win the heat. And the contest.

I'll Take You There

Calling Margo Oberg a competitor is akin to calling Wolfgang Mozart a musician. For skeptics of the claim that in her era there was no equal, consider this: Margo Godfrey Oberg retired in 1970 having taken the surf world by storm, winning every major amateur championship, securing a World Title, placing number one in the Surfer Poll, pioneering women's big-wave riding and completely dominating four years of global competition. *Before* finishing high school.

Athleticism was just the start of her wave-riding gifts; during her twenty-year reign at the top of the surf world she was dominant in every category of women's surfing. Perhaps her greatest contribution was proving performance parity in an unmistakable fashion. For the first time in modern surf history a women succeeded in a number of men's divisions and in areas of the sport others had not mastered. Yet for many observers she would remain the waif-like wunderkind—the same slight, agile, endearing girl with a mouthful of braces that caught the eye of iconic water-man Mike Doyle.

Observing her remarkable talents for the first time in 1964, Doyle proclaimed "There's the future world champion." Margo's ability to execute carving turns and link them together was a landmark of the time. "She had a stand-up-straight style and dropped low in her stance when she was about to cut back," Doyle asserted. "She was the first in my mind to *be better* than most of the guys."

Doyle's instincts turned out to be remarkably accurate about the young prodigy, who was born in Pennsylvania in 1953, and moved with her family to La Jolla, a southern California coastal village. She took up surfing at La Jolla Shores in 1963 and in her first contest—as a ten year old—she won the twelve-year-old Boys Division. Her extraordinary competitive spirit had been awakened; by age thirteen Margo Godfrey was ranked fourth in the world, qualifying as a finalist in the 1966 World Contest in San Diego.

In 1968, the wispy-thin ninth-grader scored title victories in the California, Makaha, and East Coast Surfing Championships, then topped off the year by winning the World Contest held in Puerto Rico.

The next year she swept all four AAAA-rated events and became the first woman to earn a cash prize—three hundred and fifty dollars—in the 1969 Santa Cruz Pro-Am. She had, at that point, won every event on the map.

But in 1970, at the World Contest in Australia, Margo came in a close *second* to Sharron Weber. It was a devastating blow to a naïve high school junior who had been touted as the new heir apparent to reigning queen of surf Joyce Hoffman.

"I didn't know how to handle the loss," she admitted to me in an interview at the *Surfer* magazine offices in 1981. "I was crushed and embarrassed and just suddenly wanted to hide away."

Experiencing the anguish of defeat for the first time, Margo stepped back from the competitive circuit, re-evaluating the bewildering consequences of international fame and fortune before her first prom.

In 1972, after a whirlwind courtship, Margo Godfrey married Steve Oberg and they moved to Kauai, where she enjoyed the seclusion of an outer island, which suited the shy, introverted side of her personality. But immersed in the power of Hawaiian swells she discovered a penchant for riding bigger waves, and husband Steve nurtured her self-confidence, focus, and competitive strategies much like Mike Doyle and her friend U.S. Champion Corky Carroll had previously. Soon she was a regular fixture at Sunset Beach on the North Shore of Oahu.

For women's surfing Margo Oberg singlehandedly fulfilled the promise of the Staple Singers, 1972 gospel-powered anthem: "I'll take you there!" She also joined the Pentecostal church—part of the early 70s movement that swept the nation. She struggled with the faith as with other things in her life: "My wild side wanted to party, the other side wants to go to church." She did a bit of both.

Baby Come Back

Beginning in 1975, after a five-year hiatus, Lightning Bolt, the leading brand of the era, enticed Oberg back full-time into the competition arena with a substantial contract. That same year she and six other women competed in the men's Smirnoff contest. Oberg placed first among the women and third overall, against the best male professionals in the world. Oberg's competitive record boosted women's surfing to a level of respectability it has yet to exceed.

When the #1 hit single "Baby Come Back" came out in 1977 it played like Margo Oberg's theme song. That same year the IPS added a women's crown to the year-old tour. It would be the first Professional World Surfing Title and there was little doubt that it would be Oberg's.

In 1978, she won the Stubbies and the Bells contest, and came in first in the *Surfer* magazine poll (which she'd won in 1968, a decade before.)

Astonishing her competition from the late 60s to the early 80s, winning the World Championships in 1968, 1977, 1980, and 1981, Margo's four undisputed World Titles set a record that would not be surpassed for nearly a quarter century.

The only woman included in the 1985 *Surfer* magazine feature titled "25 Surfers Whose Surfing Changed the Sport," she retired from full-time competition at age twenty-nine, but continued to compete professionally until 1991, when she finished fourth in the world championships.

Throughout all of this she simultaneously owned and operated the Margo Oberg Surfing School on Kauai, wrote a book on contest strategy, had two children and became a Pentecostal Christian.

Instinctively good-natured but psychologically frail, born with a dichotomy of shyness and intense competitiveness, she struggled with numerous issues throughout her life. But her proclivity toward private demons does not diminish the achievements nor change the fundamental strength of her successes—including the almost singular accomplishment—her exceptional ability to perform on the top level with *any* competitor, male *or* female.

As surfing author Jason Borte pointed out in his 2000 Surfline biography of Oberg, she "not only dominated women's surfing over three decades, she was considered worth watching by even the most hardened sexists."

She was inducted into the International Surfing Hall of Fame in 1991, and the Surfing Walk of Fame as that year's Woman of the Year. In 2000, Oberg was ranked 99th on the *Sports Illustrated* list of the Top 100 Women Athletes of the 20th Century. In 2001, she was inducted into the Hawaii Sports Hall of Fame.

In 2018, she received the "Silver Surfer Award," a lifetime achievement award from the California Surf Museum.

Still revered by her contemporaries, she remains in many critics' eyes, the most influential woman in surfing history.

Missing in Action

The troubled iconicity of Margo Oberg often overshadowed just how much other women achieved both after and even during her emergence. Gail Couper took the 1971 and 72 Australian National Titles back-to-back and won an astonishing *ten* Bells Beach events during Margo's reign. But outside of Australia Cooper barely received a mention. Sharon Weber, unquestionably one of the era's most overlooked masters, earned six Hawaii state titles during the late 60s, finished runner-up to Margo Godfrey in the 1968 World Surfing Championships and won the U.S. titles in 1969 before taking two World Championships in 1970 and 72. Her first came in Victoria, Australia and her second in San Diego. Despite all her accolades, Weber was never once profiled in any of the surf magazines of that time.

In 1973, Weber cancelled a trip to South Africa protesting the country's apartheid policy and the government's opposition to her "dark-skinned" Hawaiian teammates. Less than a year later, after a somewhat abbreviated competitive career, Weber retired from professional surfing and opened a tire business on Kauai. A 2001 interview quoted her saying, "I only know three things—how to surf, how to change a tire and how to golf."

In the same period Nancy Emerson came on the scene, moving from California to Hawaii and quickly making a strong impression in the women's ranks.

Frustrated with the politics of competition she retired from contest surfing after the 1969 Makaha Championships, moving to Maui and opening her first surf school a few years after. But her retirement would be short, and her contest record would lengthen.

Returning from a surf adventure in the remote Marshall Islands she was invited to the 1976 Pro Class Trials, promptly winning the event and qualifying for the World Cup title. "I was one of only two girls totally sponsored to go on tour in 77, 78, and 79, when I reached number six in the World Tour ratings," Emerson told me in a 2020 interview. "Jack Shipley at Lightning Bolt supported me with equipment too." Back on the Pro Tour in 83, Emerson was in the finals regularly again. By 85 she had started the Longboard tour in California and Hawaii while still continuing to open surf camps. Over the decade Emerson built a veritable surf school empire with six locations scattered from Maui and Malibu to Japan and San Clemente.

Emerson went on to open surf schools and clinics in Chiba, Japan, Honolulu, Fiji, and Australia. Sampling the lifestyle in Malibu Maui and Palm Beach Australia, she eventually settled on the Gold Coast with a successful surf camp chain. Featured in the *New York Times, Outside* magazine and the *L.A. Times*, she founded Island Vision, a film production company that did work for Honda Motors, Coke, and Sony. Later she would do work on the *China Beach* TV series and Hollywood blockbusters *Eye of the Tiger, North Shore* (1887) and *Waterworld* (1995). "Nancy has lived about three lifetimes more than the average person," noted Jeannette Prince. "What a life."

But in her prime competitive seasons Emerson's performance beacon never had the chance to shine free of Oberg's glaring spotlight. During Margo's streak from 1966–1969 Nancy Emerson either won or took the top three positions in over forty contests as an amateur. In any other circumstance she would have been given far more accolades from the surf culture. For women like Emerson it must have seemed as if the media thought no one else but Oberg existed.

Linda Davoli was another high-achiever whose myriad successes were shrouded in the shadow of Margo's spectacular ascent. Described in *Surfer* magazine as "very possibly the finest woman surfer in the world," Davoli was the first woman to win the East Coast Championships at Cape Hatteras North Carolina, in 1971. Two years later she would take the title at the United States Surfing Championships—the first East Coast surfer of either gender to do so.

"We thought of her as the ultra-uber competitor," said Shannon Aikman, "smooth, fast and stylish."

She entered the pro ranks in the late 70s spending three years in the top-five of the ratings before dropping off the World Tour while still in the lead.

At one point this talented, attractive, Brigantine, New Jersey native was ranked third in the world, and won the 2001 ESA Senior Women's ESA Championship—thirty years after winning her first Eastern's title.

Davoli starred in Hal Jepsen's 1975 surf film *Super Session* and while filming an episode of the acclaimed television series *American Sportsman* in 1980, she became the first woman to ride the fabled "G-Land," Indonesia's perfect point break, Garjagan. Davoli's big wave performances matched her reputation for proficiency in large swell conditions. "We surfed 12 to 15 foot Himalayas one year when Sunset was closed out," marveled fellow East Coast legend Greg Loehr. "She had all the skills."

Considered by most critics to be East Coast surfing's greatest women of her era, she was inducted into the East Coast Surf Legends Hall of Fame in 2002. Yet for all her achievements she was rarely given the coverage one would have expected, and little was done to correct her lack of recognition.

Some women were left out of the spotlight altogether. Elaine Davis, originally a Florida native, came to Hawaii, starting in the forgiving waves of Oahu's South Shore, and worked her way from the smaller Hawaiian breaks of Rocky Point and Velzyland to eventually ride Pipeline and Sunset. Her big wave bravado was as impressive as any women in the early 70s, particularly at Pipeline. Even though she was a goofy-foot, she limited her appearances to the relatively uncrowded days. "So many people get hurt there," she said. "You've really got to be confident about taking off." That confidence got her respect from the top pros but no recognition from the world at large. She deserved far more.

Another unheralded Hawaiian in that era was Dale Kimura Dahlin, an early big-wave rider. Living just across the street from the Haleiwa Surf Center, her classic power was the female counterpoint to Barry Kanaiaupuni's "make the radical look easy" approach. Dahlin's lack of recognition most likely came from the fact she was raising two children and rarely surfed beyond Haleiwa, a spot distant from shore and rarely frequented by surf photographers.

Oberg's dominance may have stifled her peers, but the younger generation saw her as the pinnacle to reach for. Koral and Melanie McCarty, two of Kuai's top longboarders, remembered studying Oberg's performances at Hanalei Bay near where they all lived. Inspired by her surfing, the sisters received personal encouragement from Oberg as well.

"If anyone had an influence on my early career choices it was Margo," said Rochelle Ballard. "She taught me how to improve my surfing, but she also gave me advice that helped ultimately set my direction." Considered a protégé who took the baton of big-wave riding from Oberg, Ballard said, "At the end of high school she took me under her wing and prepared me for the next step in my career—big waves and barrels."

Distance did not diminish Oberg's impact on her generation. Across the globe surfers of both sexes marveled at Oberg's ability.

Roger Mansfield, a British surf champion and leading authority on British women's surfing, recalled an incident while surfing on the British team at the 1970 World Championships in Australia: "We arrived at Bells Beach after a straight drive from Sydney. There weren't many other surfers out, just a handful further up the point. One was really good, reed-thin and swooping into waves with a beautiful, graceful style. I wondered who it could be, as I knew I was about to meet many of the international surf heroes I idolized. With fading light the mystery surfer raced past, turning with speed and poise. It was Margo Godfrey (later Oberg) from the USA, destined to become four times Women's World Champion. I never treated women in the waves with any double-standard from that day on."

Women of the Surfing Tribe:
English Surfers in the Late 60s

Mansfield did not discriminate after seeing Margo, but he *did* go on to co-author *The Surfing Tribe*, an impressive history of surfing in Britain.

"By the mid-60s in Cornwall, England, Jill Costa, Maureen Burnett, Janice Pearce and Annette Hughes were keen surfers," Mansfield wrote in 2011. "Annette was petite and agile and caught the attention of Rod Sumpter, who was looking for a tandem surfing partner." Sumpter, the United Kingdom's multi-title international surf star entered them in the tandem event at the 1968 World Championships in Puerto Rico. Representing Ireland (a somewhat controversial move in itself) the couple made the final and finished fourth, a triumph for the United Kingdom.

Rod Sumpter was a major figure in British surfing, winning titles, shaping surfboards, and later producing seven surf films. His relationship with another Cornwall resident, Simone Renvoize would play a crucial role in the growth of British surf culture, notably surf films and magazines.

Although Simone Renvoize did not surf, she had a long love affair with surfing (her mother managed the largest surf shop in England), and her networking talents brought together the most unlikely combinations. Following her breakup with Rod Sumpter, she married Paul Holmes, who later became the editor of *Surfer* magazine. Together with surfer Fuz Bleakley, they published *Surf Insight* magazine and ran Aqua Gem Surf Flicks, a company showing surf films. The driving force of the company, Renvoize's greatest coup was to persuade legend George Greenough to let Aqua Gem show his films *Crystal Voyager* and *The Innermost Limits of Pure Fun* at the London Electric Cinema in Britain's capital.

Britannia Rules the Waves

Margo's era also introduced Cornish surfer Gwynedd Haslock, the first truly dominant British female. The solid, supple regular-footer's impressive string of performances among the men culminated in the British Surfing Association adding a women's division to the British Championships in 1969. Six girls competed, including outstanding surfer Beth Mottart, but were no match for Haslock. "Surfing and competition didn't really feel like a comfortable mix," Mottart observed about herself. "I was too nervous."

Haslock's nerves, meanwhile, were steely, collecting five British titles from 1969 to 1976 sticking consistently to her trusty 9-foot *Bilbo* brand shape from Newquay. She reigned supreme as national champion into the 70s with graceful, consistent surfing, competing with standouts Jill Jennings from Somerset, Lynn Daniel from Devon and Judy Heyworth from St. Agnes.

Women's increased acceptance attracted new participants and the pioneer group soon faced a generation of shortboarders. Stylish goofy-footer Sarah Newling was the youngest member of that core competitive cadre. Influenced by her elder brother, Tigger, who by the late 60s was one of Britain's most high profile surfers, the family home at Rosmerrin was frequently in the press or on TV, as the media had latched onto them as Britain's archetypal surfing family. Sarah became the British Women's Champion in 1971, having just married Australian surfboard-builder Mickey Mac. Shortly thereafter the couple departed to live in Australia. But both Newling and Haslock paid homage to Oberg's textbook style and contest savvy. "I idolized Margo," Hadlock attested.

Back on the East Coast of the USA other women were trying to make their mark in a time when Margo Oberg seemed to suck the oxygen out of the room. Barbie Belyea was a late 60s, early 70s standout gaining a title in the legendary ESA East Coast Tour Championship Series of 1969. Always a top performer she represented the ESA at the 1970 ISA World Championships. Held at Johanna, near Bell's Beach Australia, Belyea notched an impressive third place finish. For perspective, this equaled the 1966 feat of Mimi Munroe as the highest placing World Championship position by an east coast surfer up to that time. Belyea's nickname, "Bubbles," was penned by prolific writer and East Coast surf star Bruce Valluzzi who traveled with Barbie Belyea and Mike Tabeling to the World Contest in 1970.

Like so many others, Barbie Belyea's outstanding performance (at a World Contest Margo didn't even attend) was overlooked partly because of media laziness, partly because of the interest in men covering the men's events, and partly because of the blinding spotlight Oberg seemed to possess effortlessly.

"There was really only one woman who could match Margo, and that was Lynne Boyer," said Jodi Young Wilmott, who surfed against them both for a decade. "Lynne took two World Titles during Margo's long reign. Nobody else was even close." (Note: Boyer, who came to stardom in the late 70s is covered in Chapter 16, A Trio of Heartbreaks.)

After many years of surfing the New Jersey's harsh winter waves Belyea moved to Kona, Hawaii.

So it would be inaccurate to say that Margo overtook *everyone*—in fact besides Boyer there were many standout successes. And, in deference to their overlooked record, it is notable that although Martha Sunn, Becky Benson, and Joyce Hoffman are considered an era ahead of Oberg, they won the 1970 and 71 Makaha, and 1971 U.S. Championships, respectively—long after they were supposed to have seen their peak period of achievement. But from 1968 onward the attention was overwhelmingly Oberg's.

13

Short-boards, Short-sighted, and Short-changed

1969–1975

"Let us begin the revolution and let us begin it with love: All of us, male and female, black, white, and gold, have it within our power to create a world we could bear out of the desert we inhabit—for we hold our very fate in our hands."

—Kate Millet, *Sexual Politics* (1969)

The Circle Game

The twelve months of 1969 saw a man land on the moon, *Easy Rider* land on theater screens and half a million youths land at Yasgur's farm in Woodstock. Science, film and music underwent a transfiguration. Experiencing this cataclysmic year in real time, everyone under the age of thirty knew the world had permanently changed in fundamental ways. Surfboards had gone short, hair had gone long and society had momentarily leapt dizzyingly beyond its boundaries. In surfing, a fifteen-year-old female prodigy would win a World Contest amidst a design upheaval that mirrored the myriad changes throughout the social structure.

From 1969 to 1975 a banner era opened for women in the arts: Joni Mitchell's *Circle Game*—a poetic ode to life's phases—was a landmark artistic album. Ellen Burstyn's Oscar-winning voyage of self-discovery as a widow and mother starting a new life in *Alice Doesn't Live Here Anymore* gave a true-life look at the struggles of women in a post-modern world. And Judy Blume wrote the groundbreaking, taboo-trampling young adult novel, *Are You There God? It's Me, Margaret* in 1970. Generation after generation has read and loved and taken solace in these works of music, film and literature.

Unfortunately, those years would be not be nearly so progressive or creative for women's surfing. The journey of self-discovery would be strewn with sharp coral heads of frustration and disappointment

The early 70s marked a period that future leaders in the women's surfing community consider the "Dark Ages"—years in which optimism regressed and sexism ran rampant. "Take Another Little Piece of My Heart," Janis Joplin's anguished rasp and yowl was the era's musical lament for women's surfing.

"Why is surfing considered a man's sport, and why are women the minority in surfing?" asked surf visionary Mary Setterholm in a 1974 *Surfer* magazine article. "Surfing, which started out to be a cultural gathering of artists, has evolved into a state which reflects the paranoia, the prejudices and the hostilities of society as a whole." Male resentment toward female surfers echoed a larger societal push-back against demands of feminists and minorities.

"A lot of girls come up to me and say 'Gee, I wish I could surf,'" 1977 Australian Women's Champ Jill Sanotti told *Tracks* magazine. "When I ask them why they don't, they say they're scared the guys will laugh at them."

Australia seemed to be particularly strong in exuding male dominance.

Hawaiian locals may have exuded hostility toward visiting surfers in general but the centuries-old cultural deference toward women surfers was still mainly intact.

"The guys in Hawaii take us surfing with them," Hawaiian transplant Elaine Davis told *Tracks* magazine on a trip to Australia's Gold Coast. "Here they stare at us like we're freaks."

"Women here are intimidated," said Nancy Emerson, who had been a Maui resident since 1961. Emerson *did* nonetheless move to Australia where she built a thriving surf school. But Emerson is the kind of women who is rarely intimidated—and she surfed better than most the men even back in that day. But the coasts of the U.S. had their own method of marginalization: while Australians may have laughed the girls out of the water, California employed the freezeout approach.

"I had so many friends around the world it was never a problem," 60s surf star Mary Lou Drummy told me, remembering the early contest days. "But I was witness to the ugliness that could happen back then. It was definitely *there*."

Linda Davoli, the era's premiere East Coast female had perhaps the most succinct assessment about the male surfers of the day: "Less beer and more manners is what they need."

Economic marginalization persisted as well. Purse winnings for female surf competitions were a fraction of those won by their male peers, while bikini contests generally drew far more attention than women's surf battles.

All-male judging panels scored their performances. All-male magazine staffs wrote their profiles. And with little coverage in the surf publications, sponsorship was harder to come by.

"Women's competitive surfing," Jericho Poppler had famously declared, "would be a lot better *if women were running it*." But they were *not* running it. They were running in circles. And the louder the talk, the less action they got.

While the outspokenness of Setterholm, Poppler and Drummy might have chaffed male counterparts, it led to the creation of the women's surf organizations in California, Hawaii and Australia—established as a bulwark against hostility and indifference toward female surfers. But that was still in the future. For the half-decade between Woodstock and the end of the Vietnam War, women's surfing seemed to go round and round in the circle game.

Killing Me Softly

The reality was this: despite the unequal treatment, despite the dissatisfaction from so many of the competitors, the long-established events were still the only viable venues and they were—at least for the amateur side of things—well run and well organized.

In 1970 Martha Sunn won the Makaha International, Judy Trim took the Australian National Titles and Laura Powers was victorious at the United States Surfing Federation in California. And although the 1970 World Surfing Championships in Victoria, Australia, was plagued by poor surf and turbulent skies, American Sharon Weber took home the titles sending Margo Oberg into a self-imposed retirement. At the first East Coast Championships to be held in Cape Hatteras NC, 1971 Linda Davoli was the winner. For the next thirty years these championships were held at the Cape. The 1972 Australian National Titles saw Gail Couper victorious while returning 71 ESA champ Linda Davoli took the ESA East Coast season titles once again.

The farewell nail in the coffin of international surf contests however was the 1972 World Surfing Championships in San Diego, California. Poor surf, inadequate funding, unruly participants and controversial judging calls marred an altruistic effort by the organizers and helped cement a resistance to competitive surfing for half a decade—at least in California.

Competition was *not* the only benchmark for a growing global involvement among women on waves. In 1972 one of the first television commercials featuring a female surfer was filmed at La Pampilla beach, Peru. It showcased Jonchi Pinzas—who starred with her brother—surfing in an ad for Audaces (meaning bold) cigarettes. The tag line under the two Peruvians was titled "They are bold!"

Women surfers were emerging from a number of nations—England, South Africa, and notably, in *France.*

Perhaps surfing's most influential French female of the 70s and 80s was Maritxu Darrigrand, whose coastal roots were in Bayonne, France.

The daughter of a Superior Court Judge, she was raised in Cameroon and the Ivory Coast, two African nations closely allied to France. An inveterate traveler, she visited surf and snow resorts in the USA and traveled to Tahiti, Hawaii and Mauritius, where legendary surfer and Chart House restaurant founder Joey Cabell pushed her to take up surfing. Through Cabell, Darrigrand met Ironman champion Mike Doyle in Snowbird, Utah, where he was popularizing the mono-ski (the forerunner of the snowboard) and fell in love with it. She brought mono-ski back to Chamonix—France's skiing epicenter—and introduced the concept to Europe.

Intrepid and blasé, Darrigrand employed her natural talent to become a top athlete in skiing and surfing—and the business that followed. Bitten by the boardsport's thrill, Darrigrand became partners in an enterprise showing surf films in Biarritz, ground zero for surfing in France. "It was always packed," remembered Oscar-winning filmmaker Greg McGillivray, whose surf films were shown there frequently. "When they connected surf films, ski films and skateboard films they had a serious business." The events helped create a French surf culture in the process.

Darrigrand's athleticism won her the 1979 French National Surf Championships with a nonchalant self-confidence. Then, in 1982—on a surf trip to Australia—she met the owners of the still-developing Quiksilver sister-brand Roxy. That same year she opened the company's French branch, beginning a career that would have influence throughout Europe and beyond. By 1999 she was virtually running the brand's French division. The business rapidly grew into a major beachwear label in Europe, and Darrigrand was the strategic catalyst.

Roxy's founder and President Randy Hild attested to Darrigrand's impact: "The biggest thing she did was to start the Roxy Jam. It was more than a contest, it was a women's beach festival that included art, music and other board sports where everyone got together and celebrated the lifestyle." The annual events were significant for Roxy's worldwide image, but their popularity reflected something far deeper: a worldwide hunger among women for not just fashion but a social ethos that was all their own.

"Maritxu was one of the people that made the women's surf boom happen globally," said four-time World Champion Lisa Andersen, who was just starting out when they met. "She had a huge impact on me."

Darrigrand continued as a major branding influence in France throughout the first two decades of the 2000s. Retiring in 2016, she became the president of Keep A Breast, a woman's breast cancer foundation closely aligned with the surf culture.

Industrial Strength Britain

In the United Kingdom surf culture was flourishing as well. The coast had historically been used for commercial ventures—seaports, shipbuilding yards, tin mines and trading centers. But as coastal living became more fashionable around the world, watersports bloomed. UK shorelines became centers for a new lifestyle, with surfing creating the same allure it held in Hawaii.

As a child, nineteen-time Welsh Champion Linda Sharp grew up in the shadow of the Port Talbot industrial complex on the south coast of Wales, between the British Steel Works—a Petro-chemical refinery—and the motorway. Although industrialization often polluted the local water, she learned to surf at thirteen, in a competitive, masculine environment. Sharp quickly developed into such a top performer at the local break at "Avon," many began referring to it as "Linda's Left."

In 1971 Sharp and two other women persuaded the Welsh Surfing Federation to include a Women's Division. When the season finished Sharp had won. "I was always very competitive by nature," she asserted, "and embraced the challenge." She won multiple titles but then chose to take a three-year break in her competitive career to study Physical Education in Kent.

Returning to the surf full time in 1975, Sharp won both the Welsh title and British Championships, defeating long-time champ Gwynedd Haslock. That same year Sharp travelled to Biarritz, France, winning the European Women's title and becoming the first woman's triple champion in European surfing.

Inspired by Hawaiian winner Lynn Boyer, she entered the 1980 World Championships in Biarritz, advanced all the way to the finals, finishing fifth. Not since Rod Sumpter's fifth place in 1966 in California had a British team member reached a World Championships final. Solidified as Britain's new star, Sharp nonetheless spurned turning professional, continuing to focus on a teaching career.

Through the 80s and much of the 90s, Sharp worked as Secretary of the Welsh Surfing Federation as well as the Executive Committee of the BSA and European Surfing Federation Secretary. Her twenty-year career dominated British competitive surfing. Retiring in the late 90s she remained in her beloved Porthcawl with her husband and daughter—enjoying life as a surfing family. British historian Roger Mansfield called her the most successful and influential British women's surfer of all time. "Her pure determination to win was amazing," declared top Welsh shortboarder Mark Vaughan. "She's been an inspiration to us all."

Ain't No Mountain High Enough

Inspiration was emerging in the U.S. as well. Certainly there was the story one woman had to tell, full of heartbreak, despair and then remarkable transformation. Her name was Mary Setterholm.

If ever there was a tail of tragedy and redemption, Setterholm would qualify for the role. Born in Los Angeles, Mary's dad left home when she was a baby—and ended up in jail. Her mom, working while earning a law degree, would leave Setterholm and her five brothers and sisters with a babysitter.

"This woman would put us in a backyard dog pen area and just leave us there," Mary said in an October 29, 2009 National Public Radio interview.

Enduring constant beatings, the darkness was complete when the babysitter's son and his friends gang-raped Setterholm several times.

"I would really, really, really fight back sometimes, and I never won, not once, Setterholm recounted years later. "But I fought. I fought. I never let them just have me."

Rebellious and emotionally frail from the trauma, she was a serious discipline problem at the Catholic school she attended. Her teacher, a nun, beat her numerous times; once when she was twelve she was beaten so badly she fainted, seeing the cross of Jesus on the wall, and finding solace in the message of forgiveness. Then a priest who she had trust in sexually abused her. Setterholm—emotionally devastated—said she feared she would lose faith in humanity.

Surfing was her escape. When her family moved to the toney Orange County beach town of Corona Del Mar, she thought she could break free of the psychological damage. When she discovered the waves of Newport and Huntington Beach, her natural affinity for surfing was obvious almost immediately. Only fifteen, the victim of years of abuse, the ocean became her sanctuary—as it had been ever since she was six years old. But for a bewildered and ravaged teenager, it was not enough.

The connection between childhood sex abuse and teenage prostitution is well-known in medical research. Setterholm succumbed to the delusion tens of thousands of abused girls believe: that taking money for sex provided a sense of control in a world where she had so little. Setterholm started hitchhiking to the beach, and "that's when I turned my first trick." After an enraged "john" nearly killed her, she retreated from the abuse, focusing intently on surfing.

Competing in the Western Surfing Association in the 3A and 4A divisions in the early 70s, she rose through the rankings and began to excel. During high school, she met Shannon Aikman, a fellow surfer and kindred spirit. They became good friends, and Aikman—from a solid, well-to-do Newport Beach family—set a positive example for Setterholm.

In high school Setterholm made sporty bathing suits for women and, along with Aikman, rode their bikes nine miles with board under arm "every day from Corona Del Mar to Huntington Beach to train at the pier." Their dedication vaulted both into a higher level of performance. Then at only seventeen, Mary Setterholm won the 1972 United States Championships. Her confidence soared.

In 1974 Mary graduated from Corona del Mar High, ready to find her path. Aikman helped Setterholm schedule a trip to Hawaii to surf and talk about a professional women's circuit with the pro surfing directors. When she returned to California she presented her peers with the idea of creating a woman's organization of their own.

Along with Jericho Poppler, she "was the key protagonist in the founding of WISA."

Setterholm married and had five children, worked as a designer for Body Glove, and eventually landed back in Manhattan Beach.

"Mary is one of the most intelligent people I've ever met," declared Shannon Aikman, who, after spending many years in high school—and beyond—maintained a strong friendship with Setterholm. "If her circumstances had been different she might well have been a Harvard Law graduate or a Surgeon General—anything she wanted," said Aikman. "She's that smart."

Setterholm continued to be close to her children, even attending Loyola Marymount University earning a bachelor's degree in theology. In 2004, she and her daughter Marion Clark founded the Surf Academy surf school for women and her daughter continued the Academy's work. She founded Serenity Sisters in 2009 to help homeless and abused women and get them to shelters.

In the decades to come Setterholm would come to be seen as an early example of breaking away from the path of addiction and despair. Surfing was her roadmap.

The eastern seaboard had inspirational stories too. Riding her grandmother's wooden ironing board was the first surfing experience for Nanci Polk. It convinced her of two important things: She loved surfing and she needed a *real* surfboard. Growing up in Charleston, South Carolina she went straight to 12th street in Folly Beach entering competition as a thirteen-year-old in 1964. Polk flew up the ratings ladder, winning or placing in most nearly every event from New York to Florida. When the ESA centralized their championships at Cape Hatteras, Polk won the title in 1972. A cross-country trip to the U.S. Championships in Huntington Beach later that year with fellow surfer Jerre Weckhorst garnered a semi-final placing and sparked a lifelong partnership.

Graduating from the College of Charleston with a Marine Biology degree in 1974 she began teaching at U.S.C. in Beaufort, and with Jean-Michael Cousteau teaching marine ecology in Hilton Head for six years. She founded the first Sea Turtle Nesting and Stranding study on Hilton Head which continued for twenty years in a career that included starting the marine mammal stranding network through the South Carolina Department of Natural Resources.

But her unrequited passion for surfing inspired Polk and Weckhorst to open the first authentic surf shop on Hilton Head Island. Coaching and mentoring for twenty-five years, their shop introduced hundreds of kids to surfing while developing a great local surf team. Returning to competition in 1985 Polk won most of the E.S.A. district and regional contests for the next seven years.

A year after Polk rode her ironing board, Pam Hill caught her first wave 330 miles down the coast in Ormand Beach, Florida. Not long after, in 1967, she picked up her first trophy—at the Daytona Beach Junior Championships, just one beach down from her hometown. Although she remained a regular competitor until 1997, Pam began contest directing in the 80s, and became the ESA's Southeast Regional Director, a job which appeared ideally suited to her vision. "She never missed an Eastern's Championship," clamed regional surf director Lisa Rosselli. "And she has competed in it over forty times." Though her commitment has been to ensuring contests are run smoothly and fairly, her passion has always been fostering the careers of young female surfers. "The Girls Division is way bigger than the Boys Division now," she noted.

"I never had children," Hill explained. "The kids in the ESA were my family." Greg Loehr agreed. "Pam's busy role hasn't stopped her from helping out," he said in April 2020, "or from being sought out by other events around Florida, like the National Kidney Foundation's surf festival. She's as stoked as when she won that first trophy."

The fun was there even when the technology was still primitive. Contest admin team members remembered Pam Hill and her friend Ormand Beach surfer Marilyn Austin making pitchers of blended drinks while they all hand-copied the heat sheets late into the evening.

"Surfing has been my life." Hill concluded. To prove the authenticity of her statement she added, "I *still have* that first trophy I won in 1967."

Technology was changing every aspect of life at an accelerating pace from 1969 to 1974. The "transition" era saw boards and bathing suits go from small to tiny. Music went from radio to 4-track, 8-track and cassette player in a few short years. Studio production was revolutionized. If the internet had been invented in 1971 *Tapestry* by Carole King would have gone globally viral on the day of its release. A monumental collection of songs from a great artist who had finally fought her way from backstage songwriter to the very top of the rock star world, it was music filled with women's power and vulnerability.

But surfing was not riding that wavelength. A backlash in response to the disastrous 1972 Amateur World Contest had set contest surfing—and women's participation in the sport—back on its heels. Short boards made entry-level learning more difficult. Localism's virulent strain had grown so ugly, venturing outside of hometown breaks had become a risky undertaking. It would be a future era before women surfers would feel the ocean move under their feet.

So Far Away

Thousands of miles across the Northern Pacific, Guam—home of America's formidable B52 nuclear bomber base—also held a number of explosive reef breaks. As surfing's popularity grew, so did the surf population of the Marianas Islands. While Lynn Vignetti and Elaine Davis—already well-known surfers of their era—spent time exploring the reefs of the tiny atoll, there were few who started surfing at Talafofo Bay, the only mellow Waikiki/San Onofre spot on the island. Nella "Twinks" Allen (now Webster) rode some hollow waves at the Boat Basin (an Ala Moana-style wave). A sunken Japanese submarine provided an infrequent excellent but mellower spot called Umatac for Maggie Pier, Kathy Bogen and Sharon Sawyer. But only one standout surfer called Guam home. Considered the Queen of Rick's Reef, the premiere break on the island, Tanya Jump had a solid stance from the top of the point that earned her deserved respect at the close of the longboard era. As shortboards transitioned her reputation only grew.

Carla Rowland, who later became the head instructor at the Surf Institute, gave an impassioned address recalling her early days, particularly during this period: "For a couple years, I was one of the few women seen in the lineup in the water on a regular basis, not to mention the youngest, and this definitely had an impact on the person I was to become. This clan of nomadic surfers, I discovered, was a culture in and of itself with rules, rewards, and punishments. No matter how beaten up I would feel, no matter how low they would bring me—I would have to remind myself that I could never give up, I would never let them push me off my beach, they could never take away surfing from me. Time and time again, I felt defeated or alone, but through the struggle I discovered the importance of perseverance and holding true to one's core values, morals, and dreams. Those times where I stood my ground may have imposed moments of alienation; however, in the long run, I have discovered those moments have garnered me more respect than anything else. I have not only managed to hold my own in this male-dominated sport but have also found many creative outlets and varying means of success, as well as developed much of who I am through surfing. Perhaps you can say this experience has made me calloused. I think it has made me stronger, wiser, and more enlightened to the world around me."

"Tough and talented with a hard shell and a soft heart" Rowland often remained in the shadows of the 90s "missing the spotlight" she deserved.

The Big Short

Although things would get better in the future, the first half of the 70s had been a disappointment in many ways. Shortboards had taken away women's advantage of grace and elegance and sidelined the entire division of tandem surf. Surf industry power brokers had been short-sighted, failing to cater to an unserved market. And after a period of being virtually shut out of competitive opportunities the female professionals were feeling *short-changed*, unable to make progress. Barbara Streisand had a #1 hit on Billboard's Hot 100, the theme song to the film *"The Way We Were."* Women in the coming era were more intent on the way they *would be*—in the future.

There was one woman though, who *no* one could keep out of the spotlight. She took United States Surfing Championships by storm, and after going on a winning streak mid-decade, drove straight into the big Hawaiian surf, winning the 1976/77 Smirnoff World Pro-Am Surfing Championships back-to-back in sizable surf at Sunset Beach and Haleiwa. In the coming era a feisty Jericho Poppler would lead a glorious, sometimes chaotic crusade bent on attaining opportunity, legendary fame, and controversial celebrity, like an approaching Category 5 hurricane.

Visionaries Breach
the Barricades
1975–1982

"I have met brave women who are exploring the outer edge of possibility, with no history to guide them and a courage to make themselves vulnerable that I find moving beyond the words to express it."
—Gloria Steinem, American social political journalist, and cofounder of *Ms.* magazine

Without Victory There Is No Survival

Jericho Poppler was for once, speechless. She had just been made an offer she couldn't refuse. And maybe couldn't take either.

As the 1979 World Cup of Surfing's ceremonies opened, a huge swell hit Oahu's North Shore. Giant breakers poured over the outside reef, sending plumes of spray swirling two stories into the air as whitewater smashed through the lineup. When big, stormy swells come from both the north and west the sound is like artillery fire erupting on the coral reef.

Jericho Poppler—a veteran of the first world tour in 1976—had won two Smirnoff World Pro-Am contests in a row in 1976 and 77. Full of finesse in the water and flamboyant on land, she was no demure damsel. Standing next to Poppler was Hawaii's own surf royalty—Rell Sunn, a native Hawaiian and leader in the women's surfing movement.

An ABC Wide World of Sports television crew sat anxiously, waiting to film an event they had invested a significant amount of studio time and money to capture. Fred Hemmings, the thick trunked, square-jawed contest producer, had just made Poppler and Sunn a proposition. For the last hour Hemmings had stood staring into the lineup, studying the conditions of the pounding swell. His competition director Randy Rarick had crouched beside him, timing the intervals between sets, watching the rip currents in the wide, foam-speckled channel that swept back out in the Northern Pacific.

Clustered on the beach a score of male competitors also watched, many muttering under their breath that these were not conditions for a surf contest. And behind them a handful of women huddled among themselves, wondering if they would have a chance to join the competition. Some of the women were apprehensive. No contest site is more intimidating than big stormy Sunset with both west and north peaks generating powerful one-two punches.

Margo Oberg, Lynne Boyer, Becky Benson, Linda Davoli were less concerned. Bad conditions for the women's division of a contest was nothing new. This handful of women had surfed here many times. They had also experienced the beatings this wave could dispense for even the slightest miscalculation. But the question now was whether they would even have a chance to compete at all.

Taking the initiative, Jericho Poppler and Rell Sunn approached Fred Hemmings and Randy Rarick. The women's question was careful, but the challenge was in the tone: "Will the girls get to compete?"

Hemmings shrugged. They all knew if the men's heats were delayed until the surf calmed down there might not be time for the women's heats to run.

Hemmings looked at the women. "Okay," he said, accommodatingly. "You want to compete? Here's your chance. Let's go. Right now."

Now?

"Yeah. *Now.* The swell is supposed to clean up and get good, but only for a couple of days. Just enough time to complete the men's competition. This is your chance."

Hemmings' victory at the 1968 World Championship a decade earlier in Puerto Rico had solidified a long career—one that stretched from playing football for Punahou (Hawaii's most prestigious college prep high school) to serving as a Hawaii State Senator. As a young surf star, he had been chosen for the Duke Kahanamoku Surf Team, an honor afforded only three other legendary surfers of that era. Born and raised in Hawaii, of Portuguese Irish decent, Hemmings could paddle an outrigger canoe as well as he could ride big waves at Makaha. He was by his own words "a businessman." Two years earlier he and Rarick had cobbled together a fledgling professional surf tour for the first time in the sport's history. He was not—as his friends would attest—"prone to frivolity."

"But Fred, these are the worst conditions you could have for a heat!" Sunn was taking the reasoned approach, aloha style. "For some of these girls its dangerous," she protested.

"Hell," interjected Jericho, "it's dangerous for most of the guys! I mean look at them—most of them just want to walk away right now."

"Exactly," Hemmings retorted. "So, here's your chance. If you don't go now, you're not getting another one. Take it or leave it."

From Hemmings' perspective the offer seemed generous.

To the women it felt like a direct dare: *can you handle this stuff like the big boys?* "Do we get thirty minute heats like the guys?" Jericho knew they needed it. In many events the women's heats were shortened. Shorter heats expedited the competition but increased the difficulty of determining a clear winner.

From behind Hemmings, Randy Rarick caught their eye and nodded slightly—a gesture that silently said, *yes, longer heats like the men. And the lifeguards will be watching as well.*

Poppler and Sunn went back to the women's huddle to strategize. A line had been drawn in the sand and they either stepped over it and committed completely—or they walked away. Decision time was immediate; the conditions for the next several hours would not improve, only become worse and more problematic. The minutes ticked by, the television crew growing visibly more restless.

The vote came. Almost wordlessly the first heat of women picked up their boards and began paddling into the sloppy, storm-addled surf. Not one of them walked away.

The brinksmanship had provided everyone what they needed. The camera crew was elated. The male competitors were relieved. Hemmings and Rarick were pleased, having solved TV network's demands and the women's entreatment all in a single swoop.

The only anxiety was for the intrepid surfers paddling out. They would surf in the worst conditions. They would forgo their forebodings for a chance to prove their mettle in a battlefield loaded with incoming ordinance of big treacherous waves. But they too would be vindicated: the ABC television footage would be shown nationwide. The prize money, meager as it was, would be awarded. And taking on one of the region's most formidable waves satisfied some deserved personal pride.

The characters in this tense 'world summit' were seminal players in the future of surfing. Rell Sunn would become the spear point in a revival of Hawaiian female surfing. It would earn her the title "Queen of Makaha," as in the ancient days of Polynesia—and inspire a generation of girls. Randy Rarick would go on to direct pro surfing's most prestigious Hawaiian competitions for the next four decades. He and Hemmings would set the cornerstones to take their fledgling professional surfing organization to the level they had dreamed of for both men and women. And Jericho Poppler and Rell Sunn would go on to cofound Women's Pro Surfing, inspiring respect, credibility and pride to female surfers across the globe.

On that day one more barrier had been breached. And although it would be a long time before women's contest conditions would see real change, the moment was a small, clean victory in a generation of stormy struggle.

The Birth of Women's Professional Surfing

The feminist revolution that swept America in the 70s had surfing's women at its forefront. Not that the male surfers were paying much attention. Winston Churchill's epic statement, "without victory there is no survival," when it came to surfing, came with the realization that women were losing battles.

A woman had not been on the cover of a surf magazine since 1964, and there was virtually no coverage of women outside the shot of a cute bikini or a girlfriend saving her boyfriend's board from the rocks. A retrograde narrowing of the surf culture in the early 70s—dominated by aggressive territorialism and an anticontest mind-set—dampened the competitive contest scene and discouraged many women's participation for several years. Beyond the established stars—or women who already knew how to surf well—the intimidation factor pushed females to the sidelines.

That all changed dramatically in 1975. Dead center in the middle of the decade women stormed surfing's gates like beautiful barbarians. For the first time they began to seriously organize to benefit women—demanding their own voice, own place and equal opportunity.

Television's sitcom sensation of the 70s—*The Mary Tyler Moore Show*—presented the first independent career woman on television. Absurd as it sounds in retrospect, meek Mary Richards was then a radical character: unabashedly single, and more interested in pursuing her profession than nailing down a fiancé.

Pop star Gladys Knight had a top hit in 1975 titled "I've Got to Use My Imagination." Professional women needed exactly that to enter the power realm and get their piece of the action. That same year Junko Tabei of Japan became the first woman to reach the peak of Mount Everest. "For surfers, there were many more mountains that needed to be scaled," said early professional Shannon Aikman, laughing as she made the point. "For us it was just the beginning of the climb."

It would be no easy ascent to the summit. While many men welcomed the women and supported their goals, there was a substantial regiment of resistors, many of whom zealously guarded the gates of masculine control. As women entered the water looking to be treated as equals, men often felt threatened in this changing social milieu. Even more frequently some saw themselves as protectors of their turf—*or surf* as this watery realm was defined.

Attempting professional careers was a lesson in both the joy and frustration of making money from a previous labor of love. It was lonely too—in the beginning it was a small, visionary cadre—initially consisting of little more than two dozen revolutionary trailblazers in total.

"You're on the road constantly, like a performer," Jericho Poppler admitted. "There's no prize money, no sponsorship, no support. It's tough." Steely resolve, executive leadership and masterly negotiating skills were required to pick the entry locks of the good-old-boys castle. "Pro surfing," Poppler stated pointedly, "would be a lot better if women were running the show." Drama ensued, the result of a rapidly changing culture encountering radical redefinition. Dull it was *not*.

Surfing's feminine mystique had been unveiled and the genie was not going back in the bottle. For some men it was future shock. For women, it was a brave new world.

Jericho Poppler
A Woman Over the Influence

Perhaps no other women of her generation drove the women's surfing movement with the incorrigible audaciousness of Jericho Poppler. Although she entered the line-up in an era when the presence of women wasn't always appreciated, Poppler managed to hold her own in any boy's sand box. "She wasn't afraid to challenge the masculine line-ups with a bit of attitude but still keep her style quite feminine and fluid," 7-time World Champ Stephanie Gilmore observed in 2012, "and that's something I really admire about her surfing."

Savvy and sassy, Poppler looked the part of a confident, attractive, well-toned athlete. Perhaps more importantly she knew how to favorably present herself and other women surfers to the media. Born in Long Beach on December 13, 1951, Jericho Poppler took up surfing at age nine when she caught her first wave at Doheny; soon her extroverted exuberance and athletic talent found her the spotlight. Choosing University of California Irvine so she could surf nearby Newport Beach, her graceful style succored by years of ballet training earned her the sobriquet "Wave Dancer." Light and lyrical, Poppler's dance style was smooth but potent—like the taste of a dry Martini.

One of the first full-time pros, Poppler was at the vanguard of many of surfing's biggest issues for women. As the seeds of professional surfing germinated, women were often left in the weeds, almost entirely neglected. Women's events were few and far between and lacked any real influence. "It was a constant struggle to find sponsors and get media attention," said 1982 World Champ Debbie Beacham. "Jericho was the one who pushed and shoved to correct these inequities. She busted down the door. The word 'no' was not an option."

In an effort to enable women's empowerment, Poppler helped create the Women's International Surfing Association (WISA, 1975), which was the first all-women's competitive organization. The "Golden Girls," a promotional group she helped found, sought to put women's surfing issues in the spotlight.

"She's done a lot," said Shannon Aikman, who was there in almost every pivotal moment in the California women's movement. "She was founding member of the Surfrider Foundation and an ardent environmentalist." Poppler also started "Kids for Clean Waves," an annual contest that includes educational outreach programs, complete with beach clean-ups.

"She found time to work with the Surfers Environmental Alliance and the Algalita Marine Research Foundation," Aikman added. "Jericho was the spearhead."

Throughout her long and varied career, Poppler has remained "eternally youthful, outspoken and passionate." Her patrician sensibility and flamboyant style are singularly her own. A young Kim McKenzie remembered while competing for the first time at the 1972 World Championships in Ocean Beach: "Jericho stayed in the same room as Gail Cooper and me. She was so popular that the phone never stopped ringing. Jericho has been a legend since the moment she arrived on this planet."

Yet first and foremost Poppler shines as a strong skillful surfer. Rated #2 in the Professional Tour in 1979, her competitive record stands as one of the best in history, spanning the length of the modern era. She was the U.S. National Champion in 1970 and twenty-two years later won the Women Women's Pro Longboarding title in 1992.

Inducted into the Huntington Beach 1999 Surfing Walk of Fame, Poppler's legacy is beyond debate. "Jericho is like a Duchess from the 17th Century," her friend Rell Sunn told me in a 1987 interview. "She was empowered, entitled, impossible and incredible. There is only one Jericho."

But like all heroines there is an Achilles heel which carries the sad fortunes as well as the grand triumphs. Her daughter Sophie, a world champion paddler, short boarder, longboarder and stand up paddleboard surfer was the one of her six offspring who followed Poppler's extroverted lead. In a tragic twist of fate while traveling in Hawaii the young prodigy died in an auto accident. Gorgeous and vivacious, Sophie's motto "Be a local wherever you go" was a positive calling cry for her generation of young confident, spirited surfers.

Break It Up

In 1975 punk poet Patti Smith debuted *Horses*, a rock album so startling in concept and so empowering in execution it was an instant sensation on rock radio. With fiercely literate lyrics and simple, mesmeric music, her defiant declamation made clear that a new brand of female was crashing the party.

Inspired by the chutzpah and charisma of artists like Smith, women competitors—who felt stifled, even sidelined—decided to establish a league of their own. They named it WISA—the Women's International Surfing Association.

"Break it up," Patti Smith wailed on *Horses*, and that is exactly what these revolutionaries did.

"WISA was born because every alternative had been shuttered," said Poppler. After holding numerous conversations with other aspiring competitors, California proactivist Mary Setterholm scraped up the funds for a ticket to Hawaii. Her mission was to meet with Fred Hemmings hoping for an invitation to enter the rapidly developing pro surfing boom. Setterholm, a more than capable leader, felt she could convince Hemmings to fashion a contest circuit with a fair opportunity for women.

It was not to be. Setterholm felt she got nowhere with Hemmings and returned home believing the only option for the women was to go it alone. On a cloudy Saturday afternoon a determined group from all over California decided to take the future in their own hands and make it work for women properly. It was not a secession since there wasn't much to succeed from. But it was a statement; a commitment to the cause.

Formed on International Woman's Day, March 8, 1975, in the back sewing room of Nancy Katin's Seal Beach surf shop, Californians Jericho Poppler, Mary Setterholm and forty other surf culture mavens conceived a visionary ideal: to raise the level of women's surfing in all areas—performance, sponsorship, media attention. The original WISA Board of Directors included Terry Eselun, Shannon Aikman, Duline McGough, Karen Mackay, Mary Lou Drummy, Pam Maher, Jan Gaffney, Linda Westfall, Catherine Rosset and Liz Irwin.

Mary Lou Drummy was elected as the first president. She would prove to be ideal for the job. "Reflecting back, it was a strong choice," said Setterholm. "I was pulling up stakes for the East Coast. Jericho was about to head out on the coming World Tour. Mary Lou kept us on track."

Drummy, along with her competition director Linda Westfall, had the operations skills and political diplomacy to harness the maverick nature of surfers into a coherent professional contest structure. The first year produced amateur events at San Onofre, Huntington, Newport Beach, Salt Creek, and an impressive professional contest at Malibu. WISA's first year was a success both for the statement they made and the media coverage it garnered. When the International Pro Surfers world tour added a women's division in 1977, WISA's international stature became more of a strong regional organization who—like all aspects of surfing—was just becoming savvy to the commercial opportunities afforded by sponsors and brand supporters. Despite continuing to run excellent events through the 80s, WISA struggled to attract adequate sponsor funding.

Building the Foundations of Surfing's World Tour

The Hawaiian Women's Surfing Hui was a parallel organization founded in the very same time period as the movement in California. Headed by Hawaiian surfers Linda McCrerey, Sally Prange, Patti Paniccia, Jeannie Chesser, Lynne Boyer, Laola Lake, Claudia Nuuhiwa, Becky Benson, Debbie Montgomery and Rell Sunn, it may have even precluded WISA as a professional women's surf organization.

They met in Linda McCreary's beach house near Backyards, and the early meetings were part surf organization, part charitable planning and part excuse to party.

"We had so much fun back then," recalled McCrerey. "Guy surfers would show up with food, music,and surf films. We called them 'Friends of the Hui.' We had lots of laughs."

It was not all parties. Plenty of work got done.

"We wanted to do good things for the community," Jeanie Chesser told me. "We set up amateur contests for the kids at Chun's Reef and Waikiki."

"We started the Haleiwa Menehune Surf Contest (just for kids)," remembered Claudia Kravitz. It was still going strong forty-five years later.

But there was another reason the activities centered around McCrerey's beach bungalow: a reliance on McCrerey's useful talents. Already a college graduate, McCrerey had a few years of professional, office experience as a newspaper reporter and University of Hawaii marine advisory specialist; she possessed organizational skills and real world experience most of the younger surf women in the group were lacking.

"Linda drew up our incorporation papers to file for non-profit status," Laola Lake, a cofounder and surf pioneer, explained. "She was the adult we needed."

Sharp, assertive and fervent, Linda McCrerey took care of business.

Patti Paniccia saw the value: "She knew how to submit grants, contact supporters, how to run meetings." McCrerey agreed to serve as the Hui's first President and using her skills, the organization took off. "She was indispensable," added Becky Benson who surfed on the very first World Pro Tour. "I really don't think we could have done it without her." The organization turned out to be indispensable too. "If it hadn't have been for Paniccia and her crew," remarked Randy Rarick, the man behind professional surfing's birthing, "the Women's Pro circuit could have been delayed by a decade."

I Want Candy

The first Hawaiian Women's Surfing Hui surf event was an Expression Session in March 1975, and it started with an immediate problem—if an amusing one in the end. Unlike regular contests, Expression Sessions precluded winners or losers. The women assumed this freestyle performance format would help them garner the attention of the surf magazines and attract sponsors. They chose Rocky Point on Oahu's North Shore as their venue. Rocky Point had always been a favorite of locale lensmen. Almost an outdoor studio, the wave is photogenic, the lighting nearly always good and the reef breaks close to shore, making it easy to shoot. The girls wanted to make it simple and attractive: Images for photographers, exposure for competitors.

But as the event opened, few photographers arrived. And certainly none of the A-listers. "The magazines won't buy photos of women," the photographers explained somewhat sheepishly. "So, we can't afford to spend time and film money shooting you."

The only sponsor that reached out was a company called CandyPants. They made edible underwear. CandyPants wanted the women pros to show up wearing CandyPants as part of a Waikiki sidewalk display. "I think they were cinnamon-flavored," remembered Patti Paniccia. "And I kept wondering what they expected us to tell people on that sidewalk! We joked among ourselves: 'Excuse me, Mr. and Mrs. Waikiki Visitor, hungry?'"

Sponsorship, prize money and media coverage were hardly the only challenge women surfers faced as they began to assert their new-found possibilities. Disgruntled male waveriders, broken contracts, a derisive media and even physical hostility met them from the start.

The First Women's Pro

The $8,000 Hang Ten Women's International Professional Surfing Championships held at California's famed Malibu point, was the first internationally recognized women's professional surfing event. It was a significant achievement to get a major non-public event at one of the most popular State beaches, let alone one solely for women. While the *non-public event* part "went really well, the *solely for women* part did not," remembered Shannon Aikman, who made it through the quarterfinals of the competition.

As the finals began in outstanding surf conditions, male surfers—who had paddled out in the lineup during the break following the semifinal event—refused to exit the water. In the *finals* of the *very first* official professional women's surf event the organizers were confronted with open defiance. Bullhorns, State permits and judges pleading did not deter the men from attempting to take the best waves and give the women no quarter. Finalists Margo Oberg and Linda Wolfe were forced to carve around the crowd to compete for the $1,500 first place purse.

"They weren't *that* intrusive," Margo Oberg told me with a laugh. "We just surfed around them." Her tolerance was admirable—although it probably helped that Oberg won the event.

"I remember that first WISA contest, the Malibu Pro in 1975," recalled Terry Eselun, who was a top competitor at the time as well as a major figure in running contests. "The guys wouldn't get out of the water." That, however, was not the only time: "At Salt Creek it happened again, and my ex-husband got unto a full on altercation with a guy just trying to clear the lineup. It was tense, to say the least." Although the contests were a big hit with the competitors, the media largely ignored them. Likewise, the men's organizations provided little support.

To the women organizers the snub was a disappointment—they felt a legitimate achievement was being unreasonably disregarded. The Women's International Surfing Association had done a great job finding contest sponsors. California-based, the WISA leaders had held successful contests, the first pro events solely comprised of women. They awarded real money, hired excellent judges and showed the surfing world what women could do. Those, they soon discovered, were just the beginning of their challenges. That same year, Rarick, Paniccia and Hemmings would construct the first professional world tour. Six women would make the journey. But whatever positive advancement was happening in the USA, the rigid attitudes at some of the foreign tour destinations were barely short of dismissive. Despite the best efforts of the organizers who partnered with the IPS, that first year contest circuit—particularly for the women—was understandably chaotic. The WISA Pro Circuit in California or the Hui in Hawaii could never have prepared the female surf competitors for the chaotic—and sometimes comical—reality they would meet on tour.

15

The First World Surfing Tour
Around the World
in 80 Dismays

As the women's pro surfing's initial tour debuted in 1976, aspiring women pros saw this moment as their *time*. Popular culture had begun to acknowledge issues of gender inequality, showcasing strong, independent women seeking parity in the workplace. Wouldn't surfing, a vanguard of the new social order, be a natural beneficiary? *That* apparently, depended on gender. Only six women made it halfway around the world to Africa on that first world tour: Becky Benson, Jericho Poppler, Patti Paniccia, Sally Prange, Rell Sunn and Claudia Kravitz. Surprises were abundant.

The Women's Chapstick Pro—held in conjunction with the Men's Gunston 500 in Durban South Africa—was the first stop. Durban's coastline provided plenty of waves and the women had been promised prize money—albeit far less than the men. But two days before the event, the Chapstick sponsors asked to meet with the female competitors. "Look," they said, "we don't have prize money," remembered Becky Benson, whose family was a pillar of the Hawaiian surfing community where five of the women were from. "We didn't think you would really show up . . . come all the way to South Africa." She laughed remembering the sponsors next sentence: "So we want to propose that we hold a nationwide raffle that will provide prize money. And the winner will get his choice of having a *personal date* with whichever one of you *he* desires."

The women (as was often the case) were at first at a loss for words. A *personal date?* They were *athletes*, not *escorts*. After discussing it the women refused. Sally Prange, a civic-minded, effervescent personality who had been teaching classes in snorkeling and surfing at the Haleiwa Surf Center, was baffled. "We said 'no,'" Sally Prange remembered. "And they came up with a mere pittance in total prize money—about $1,000, which was only half of the minimum required for a women's event to be sanctioned by IPS."

Like many events in the early years, prize money didn't cover their hotel rooms, let alone their flights. And because the men had brought their wives (which meant they each got a room to themselves instead of bunking up with another guy) there was a shortage of hotel rooms for the women. Jericho Poppler spent the night in a space under the stairs, hoping the bedbugs were the worst thing that could happen in a nation already seething from apartheid and reeling from international sanctions. It was bad enough they didn't have rooms. But then there were no rental cars either. Rell Sunn and Jericho Poppler were not having it. They marched down to the local Avis headquarters and—between their chutzpah, charm and cheek—convinced the rental car company to comp them one of the nicest models on the lot. So did Patti Paniccia and the other girls in the band of sisters.

"You should have seen the look on the boys faces!" remembered Jericho Poppler still smirking fifty years later. The tough conditions and the women's bold response must have been a stimulant: the next day Poppler won the contest.

At least the South African contest sponsors did their best. The media on the other hand was not nearly so sympathetic—in some cases coverage seemed almost worse than being ignored. As the women competitors put on surfing performances the likes of which some host countries had never seen, they became a force to be reckoned with.

The Media Circus

As tales of the women's exploits preceded them, the media began clamoring to do interviews. It seemed exciting—a big step forward. The pros figured if nothing else the coverage would be positive and might bring them some sponsorships. They overestimated.

The first journalist to interview them was from a mainstream magazine—a good sign they thought. The first question out of the interviewers mouth was, "Have you ever surfed naked?"

"Rell Sunn jumped in with that answer," recalled Patti Paniccia, "and God bless her for it because I was so stunned, I really didn't know what to say. Sunn said 'NO. THAT'S STUPID. It would be too scratchy. It would just chafe you and it would hurt.'" The journalist used her quote but omitted the part about his question being stupid.

At the next contest a newspaper article actually managed to cover the women's results as well as the men's. The reporter noted that the women surfers had caused "a wave of excitement" on tour . . . "but women are still traditionally tied to hearth and home. And the women surfers must go back to their husbands again, to the lonely hot stove and the children." For young, ambitious female athletes who were traveling the world—surfing big waves and earning a living in a career they loved—the sentiment seemed out of another age.

"It was prehistoric!" Becky Benson laughed, remembering the incident. What really flabbergasted the troupe, though, was this: *a woman wrote that article.* It evidenced a presumption held by many people at the time as to where women belonged. And it certainly was not in the ocean.

The Girls in Ipanema

The thousands of spectators that thronged Arpoador on Brazil's famous Ipanema beach on opening day was beyond anyone's imaginings. Rio de Janeiro, the next stop on the circuit, was short on prize money but long on interest—and like South Africa, the girls were the main attraction. The women's prize money was again far short of plan, but at least they were sure to get what had been promised. And fairly enough, they had been forewarned. Rico de Souza, a top Brazilian surfer and owner of a surf shop in town, had done the best he could with the prize money and at least he had been up front that he couldn't meet the IPS purse requirements. He made up for it with Brazilian hospitality.

"He literally put up his own money to cover our prize purse," said Jericho. "He was a knight in shining armor, and we were the Snow Whites the promoter had hoped for. He was a truly good man. And we didn't forget it."

Jericho took a third place in Rio. She had won the second event in South Africa as well as the first, and now had two firsts and a third under her belt. She, like the rest of the girls, was broke and bedraggled—but not beaten.

The best part was, said Jericho, the girls in Brazil "got introduced to a bunch of strong, fun-loving women, we got to compete, and everyone saw the possibilities they never dreamed of before."

Becky Benson won the Rico Women's Pro with more than twenty thousand enthusiastic Brazilian fans crowding the waterfront cheering the tall and tan and young and lovely girls surfing Ipanema. With an entire nation's eyes on the event, it was a portent of the potential this new world tour concept might offer.

But Becky Benson's win on the world's most famous beach brought little fanfare back home. Benson, a three-time Hawaii State Champion had been raised to surf big wave without self-promotion. When her family moved to Hawaii in 1967, her father "Colonel" Benson, had bought surfboards for the kids and a camera for himself. His footage would soon show up in over a dozen surf films. Every weekend and many afternoons, her Dad took her, along with her sister Blanche, to the beach, taking photos and eventually becoming their "coach."

(Blanche, it should be noted, was an outstanding surfer herself, who consistently surfed big Sunset with the coaching of legendary Hawaiian big wave brothers Eddie & Clyde Aikau. Blanche won the 1969 World Tandem title with Bob

Moore and then thirty-eight years later, at the age of fifty-four, won the World Tandem title again with Kalani Vierra.)

While at home in big waves Benson was feeling her way when it came to a career. In 1976, Benson entered her first professional contest, the Lancers World Cup, and placed second to Margo Oberg. "I missed first by a half point," she said. "Performing so well in my first pro event gave me a lot of confidence." By the end of the first season the diminutive, dedicated blonde was ranked number three on the World Tour and had claimed a string of victories.

But she had joined the world tour immediately after high school graduation, having also just enrolled in college. Trying to balance the two became a struggle and after traveling on the circuit for three years, she decided to return to college full time.

"The decision really upset my Dad," she remembered. "Since he had always been so supportive, I felt bad disappointing him," Benson said. "According to my Dad, I could go to college *anytime*, but I could only be number one in the world at *that* time. He didn't want me to give up the opportunity to win the World Title."

Like many of the still-teenage pros, Benson enjoyed traveling but deeply missed family and friends. And looking toward the future at the time, there was no realistic path to make a living from surfing. "Prize money was next to nothing," she laughed. "We surfed because we loved it, not for the money." Of course not many gifted surfers retire completely. Six years after that first world tour she won the 1982 U.S. Championships at the OP Pro in Huntington.

A throng of contestants showed up from both California and Hawaii for the WISA Hang Ten at Malibu, the next stop for the women on this first circuit of international competitions. Two relative newcomers placed well: San Diego rising star Debbie Beacham took third and Hawaii's hot challenger Lynne Boyer won the event. Jericho Poppler took second, reaching the top three slots of every event. Unfortunately WISA did not apply for IPS sanctioning.

The return to Hawaii for the final leg of the tour proved anti-climactic. Poppler won the Smirnoff for the second straight year, Godfrey won the Offshore Masters and Boyer won the Lancer's World Cup. The trio were the indisputably hottest competitors of 1976, with each of them rating in the top three positions for all but one event. The final results turned out to be far more complicated—and eventually far more controversial. Due to the lack of minimum required prize money only the Hawaiian leg of the tour was sanctioned, thereby eliminating the four international events where Jericho Poppler had won two and placed second and third in the others. It seemed unfair to award a World Title for unsanctioned events that many of the top women had not even entered. Yet it also seemed unfair to award the title from ratings based on points at only three contests—all held in Hawaii. The resultant decision left the woman's title unnamed for the first year's Pro Tour.

The frantic race "around the world in 80 dismays" as Poppler would describe it, turned out to be a "wild-goose chase." For the ensuing half century claims have been made and arguments debated. Who *would* have had the most points? Why was a male champion picked but not a female? The various disputes remained unresolved, but one uncontestable fact remains—no title was awarded in 1976.

The whirlwind journey around the globe had nevertheless proven two things: international interest in women's surfing was massive—but in the U.S. it garnered little more than a footnote. American media—both mainstream and surf—had barely noticed. In other nations the women had met with front page headlines and tens of thousands of spectators. There was a *market* it would seem—but there was no *marketing*. Yet.

The Golden Girls
Marketing and Media Mavens Reach the Airwaves

Passion was an unquestionable characteristic of the early pros. But determination to make it pay was equally important. The origins of Women's Pro Surfing started with a few visionaries and the realization they needed to market themselves to generate commercial value. The Golden Girls was the brainchild of 70s surf stars Shannon Aikman, Debbie Beacham, Brenda Scott, Lisa Tomb, Candy Woodward, Betty Depolito and the irrepressible Jericho Poppler. An ingenious marketing concept, it combined the firepower of an entire group of high-profile female surfers to promote themselves "collectively and individually as pro women athletes."

Their first volley—in 1977—hit the bulls-eye. They surfed well, looked good and caught the attention of ABC's Eyewitness News. Other networks followed. The surf media couldn't ignore the rockets' red glare either. The Golden Girls helped to raise the profile of women's surfing out of the 70s and into the 80s, an achievement as seminal as any in surf history. It was, as Shannon Aikman would later contend, "the defining moment when the profile of women surfers came into focus."

Hawaii Calls

Although WISA made headlines and the Golden Girls made great TV, in that same period Hawaiian surfers founded their own organization: the Hawaii Women's Surfing Hui. It would soon play a big role in women's surfing. Patti Paniccia took the role of Pro Competition Director, and rather than hold their own contests, the Hui opted to work directly with Fred Hemmings. "He was the one major surf contest organizer at the time, running more events than anyone," explained Paniccia.

For the Men's Smirnoff Pro in the early 70s, held in big waves on Oahu's North Shore, Hemmings had invited one woman and one woman only to compete against the men—Laura Blears.

Already a popular celebrity, Blears had won the 1972 Makaha Invitational and claimed the title of Hawaii's number one female surfer that same year.

The darling of the Waikiki Beachboys in her childhood, she'd surfed alongside her father, a British professional wrestling champion, world-class surfer in his own right and survivor of a World War II merchant ship sinking at sea.

In the era prior to the Pro Tour, Laura Blears was perhaps the most successful female to parlay her surfing performances into commercial prominence and profitability. Her victory at the 1973 World Pro Am netted her a stint as a Smirnoff vodka girl, posing in a white swimsuit on a surfboard for a promotional poster that was sent to every drinking establishment in the Hawaiian islands. She appeared on a national television program *What's My Line*, a popular network show whose panel members attempted to identify the profession of guests. Her acting ability proved strong—none of the experts recognized Laura as a world-class surfer.

For three straight years she was a star competitor on ABC's Wide World of Sports' *Challenge of the Sexes* as well as *Superstars*. Competing with the likes of NFL football star Dick Butkus, NBA legend Kareem Abdul Jabbar, and record-holding baseball icon Hank Aaron, she was winning thousands in prize earnings. Described as "blonde, attractive, with a great figure," by surf historian Jane Schmauss, her most sensational achievement was when she posed surfing "in the buff for *Playboy* magazine in a three-page feature." Her illustrious father Lord James Blears was in complete support, advising her to "go for it." At every opportunity Laura Blears did just that. The first woman to compete in the Smirnoff World Pro-Am Surfing Championships in 1973, a TV star, a Hawaiian hero who would go on to management in the Duke's restaurant group, Blears loved it all. She was Hawaii's surf diva, and this was her allegro in the spotlight.

The Points of it All

As deserving as Laura Blears was, the stark reality was obvious: the invitation to the Smirnoff contest was the event producer's singularly personal choice; there were no points forming a criteria to determine a female's qualification to compete.

At a Hui meeting, the women suggested *Maybe one of us could open a dialogue with Fred Hemmings*. Patti Paniccia was voted the women's envoy. Over the next several years, Paniccia worked with Hemmings to create a rating method defining who would receive invitations to his contests. The ranking structure aimed at distributing invites in a fair and consistent manner. It included invitations for WISA. The Hui began to run open qualifying contests whose top placers could receive invitations as well.

In 1976, Fred Hemmings formed International Professional Surfers (IPS), the first professional governing body of the sport, setting the stage for the initial World Pro Tour and laying the foundation for today's World Surf League (WSL). He summoned Paniccia.

"I'm going to ask Randy Rarick to head up a men's division," Hemmings told her. "Why don't you join with us and run a woman's division?"

Paniccia saw it as an opportunity for the women—and for her own career as well: "We'd already been working together on the contest criteria and invitations," remembered Paniccia. "It was really just a matter of formalizing my work under this newly created entity—the IPS." Patti said yes, and dove in. "I made $100 a month," she told me chuckling. "Neither Fred, Randy nor I made much money. Fred was paying both of us out of his own pocket. For all three of us, it was a labor of love."

In 1978 Patti Paniccia left her Hawaiian childhood home to begin Law School at Pepperdine University just up the road from Malibu. She had worked for nearly a dozen years as the Hawaiian faction's leader of women's pro surfing. Her consistent effort had formalized the ratings process, entrenched the women in the International Professional Surfers world tour and helped establish sponsorship requirements for the women's events. Her presence and persistence was missed.

But as rock diva Debra Harry reminded everyone "I'm not the kind of girl who gives up just like that. *Oh, no.*" Less than a year later Rell Sunn and Jericho Poppler formed the WPS—Women's Professional Surfing. Unlike the Pro Tour organization, it functioned more like a union to represent the women in the triangle of interests between sponsor, contest operators and competitors.

"It was small but potent," said two-time World Champ Lynn Boyer, another of the founding members of the alliance. "At that point we were just trying to find a path."

But to the struggling women surfers, that initial path meant everything. "It was something the women had to do and Rell and Jericho really fought for us," Australian hopeful Pam McKenzie recalled. "The men were out there to make a living, but we were pushing the envelope and doing whatever we could to be included. For us it was so much bigger."

Go Your Own Way

The women visionaries of the 70s breached the barricades that had restrained their participation since the beginning of modern surfing. It was a sign of the times: In other areas women made significant leaps in achievement too: Millions more women entered the workforce. At the 1976 Summer Olympics in Montreal, Canada, Nadia Comăneci, a fifteen-year-old Romanian gymnast, won three gold medals and was the first gymnast to be awarded a perfect score of 10 for gymnastics. In the state of Indiana, American Janet Guthrie was the first woman to compete in the 1977 Indianapolis 500 automobile race. Throughout the decade advances in civil rights and increased emphasis on women's issues continued to push change.

In the next five years women would grace *Surfer* magazine's cover three times and have more coverage than in the entire period before and after that era, even if it would be a momentary high point. Competition improved as well. Not long after women in California and Hawaii formed organizations, Australia followed suit: In 1978 a group of women broke away from the Australian Surfrider's Association, and—headed by Queensland surf shop owner Gail Austin—founded the Australian Women Surfriders Association.

"We were tired of being given the runoff surf when the conditions were poor," admitted AWSA organizer Robyn Burgess. Isabel Latham, the Australian surf icon who had ridden with Duke Kahanamoku on his first trip to the country, and Phyllis O'Donnell the first Women's World Champ, were both founding members. Future World Champion Pam Burridge was the federation's first national champion. The AWSA set up branches in each state of the nation and in 1982 the 300 member organization merged with the Australian Surfriders Association again and received full and equal voting power.

But for women's professional surfing overall, success would take longer than any of the visionaries anticipated. Million-dollar contracts and Olympic medals would be a half-century away. For all the revolutionary fireworks and creative talent, the surfers had expended, two events starkly contrasted the overall women's athletic movement to that of surfing in the 70s: On September 20, 1973 at the Houston Astrodome, tennis legend Billie Jean King won the infamous "Battle of the Sexes" match against tennis gadfly Bobby Riggs, with 30,000 people in attendance and millions watching around the globe. As King dismantled both Riggs and male assumptions on LIVE television, the ambitious women surfers watched what they hoped was their own future to come.

Yet seven years later, in June of 1980 at the Men's World Contest Tour stop at the Bali Pro in Indonesia, New Jersey's pro phenom Linda Davoli became the first woman to surf one-on-one against a man in a major professional surf event. There were 300 people on the beach. She lost by a score of 74.0 to 60.6—just one good wave from victory. But there was no television.

16

Heart Full of Soul

A Trio of Heartbreaks

1982

"Strong women aren't simply born. We are forged through the challenges of life. With each challenge we grow mentally and emotionally. We move forward with our head held high and a strength that cannot be denied."

—Alysia Helming, novelist

A fierce feminine power permeates surfing, an emotional magnetism as strong as Odysseus' sirens, as dramatic as Venus' birth from the sea. Every woman who has ridden waves has experienced heartbreaks and triumphs related to the ocean's energy—the sea itself is considered feminine in language. The three women in this chapter were friends, rivals, competitors. Each confronted heartbreak and triumph in different ways. But their stories cross age and time with a universal experience that the surfing life can bring.

Rell Sunn
Hawaii's Beloved Heart of the Sea

As the caravan of autos turned onto the highway toward Makaha the radio stations dedicated the day to surfing's queen, playing pure Hawaiian music in weeping mist, Hawaiian heavens crying in the somber overcast of a February day on the Ewa side of Oahu.

When the growing motorcade that wove its way west finally reached the beach at Makaha, the sky opened up in brilliant sunlight as if ancient gods were paying tribute to the woman many of us considered the female equivalent of Duke Kahanamoku himself. Many hundreds had already gathered, but the long string of cars continued, arriving at a scene fit for any monarch: on the beach a large pavilion tent housed hundreds of photographs, mementos and awards chronicling the remarkable life of the joyous water-women we affectionately remember as both Auntie Rell and the Queen of Makaha. The haunting slack key music of Brother Noland filled the air. Out in the channel the E'ala (a replica of the giant canoes used by Polynesia royalty) rocked gently in the deep water. Head-high waves poured through the lineup, seemingly without a lull, as if to match the unending line of mourners meeting them at the shoreline. Even the sky of Waianae respectfully reserved its outpouring of sorrow until the service was over. It let the nearly 2,000 members of her tribe shed their own tears.

One of a Kind

There has never been a woman in the history of surfing like Rella Kapolio-ka'ehukai Sunn.

While the surfing Hawaiian queens are buried in time and myth, riding waves alongside Rell Sunn reminded a viewer of how ancient Polynesian royalty might have presented itself.

Born in Makaha, on Oahu's west side in 1950, she learned to surf from the time she could walk. It was Rell's prescient grandmother who christened her with the middle name Kapolioka'ehukai, which means "Heart of the Sea." Her bloodline came from three cultures: Asia from her father; Europe and Polynesia from her mother. It gave her the unique blend of character traits that embody Hawaii itself: zen-like Chinese love of beauty, fiery Irish passion, regal Hawaiian grace.

When she was a little girl growing up on the shore of Makaha, she found a glass ball washed up on the beach. She asked her father what it was. He told her that most glass balls were tied together by big nets that worked to catch fish. But sometimes one of these balls would break free and float all over the oceans traveling on the waves to many shores. Sunn told me it seemed that her father was somehow telling her what her life would be like. And whether he knew it or not, *he was*. Sunn would break free of all the conventional constraints of modern life, becoming a thoroughly progressive woman, an iconic surf star and an archetypical earth mother.

Surrounded by water-men famous and anonymous, Sunn took to the sea, following a path blazed by her older sister Martha, a Makaha International contest winner herself. As a teenager Sunn rode big waves before women were supposed to do such things.

She knew the father of surfing—the late great Duke Kahanamoku, and was mentored by all the giants of Hawaiian surfing. Studying the ancient customs of old Polynesia, she became a cultural historian, well-respected hula dancer and a keeper of the Hawaiian surfing traditions.

Her athletic feats were legendary: she was a black belt martial artist, but devotion to joy and harmony cloaked that talent.

"Rell was capable of decking the most sniveling perpetrators of violence," said Jeff Divine, a paramour of Rell's in the 80s. "Her skills were debilitating."

A diver who learned her tricks from consummate water-man Buffalo Keaulana and Buzzy Trent, she could free-dive 80 feet and bring home dinner for the neighborhood. She earned a degree in Cultural Anthropology from the University of Hawaii, authored books, worked as a computer operator and physical therapist, hosted a radio program, taught hula and paddled with championship teams as a member of the Hawaiian Canoe Club.

Auntie Rell

Sunn raised her daughter Jan on her own as a single parent, never missing a chance to take her on a trip to Tahiti or teach her the ways of the sea.

Perhaps she will be best remembered for walking in the footsteps of the strongest of her mentors, the legendary Duke Kahanamoku, acting as Hawaii's surfing ambassador to the world for nearly thirty years.

Her home was the embodiment of the little grass shack—a south seas beach cottage filled with classic surfboards, glass balls, tapa-cloth, sea shells, grass mats, Koa wood carvings and Hawaiiana bric-a-brac. Rattan furniture with tropical prints, treasures from around the world, Champs Elysees French designers to Hotel Street thrift stores. Her home was always an open door.

"I stayed with Rell at Makaha and it was the time of my life," said World Champion Lynne Boyer. "That's where I really learned to surf. She taught me so much about the ocean."

On Thanksgiving a Kalua Turkey was always cooking and visitors arrived from far and wide. On Easter she would paint eggs and then hide them in the tide pools making the older kids dive to the bottom crevasses while the younger ones scrambled in the shallows.

No one built more foundations for the surf world or gave back more to it than Rell Sunn. For twenty years the Rell Sunn Menehune contest for kids nurtured every youngster who set foot on a surfboard on Oahu. As the first female lifeguard in Hawaii, she was a woman of such strength and ability that no one even kept count of the many lives she saved. A champion who never touted her wins, Sunn was the very essence of feminine grace coupled with fearless performance.

Queen of Makaha

It was Margo Oberg who first christened Sunn the Queen of Makaha.

"She was just so *regal*," observed Oberg, the most dominant competitor of her era. It seemed so *appropriate*. But also, *no one* would beat her at Makaha. We were all in awe of Rell."

"Women owe Rell a debt of gratitude," declared Jericho Poppler, a long-time friend and fellow surf pioneer. "Rell was a leader in the environmental movement serving as the voice for Hawaii's Surfrider chapter, and a pioneer of women's professional surfing."

Together, Sunn and Poppler turned heads.

"Aside from their great ability, Rell and Jericho were the most glamorous girls who have ever done the tour by far," *Surfer* editor Sam George wrote. "They were a talented dynamite combination."

George remembers first meeting Sunn in Australia during the 1977 at Bells Beach contest just after she had done a radio interview to stir up some interest for the event. "Rell told the radio announcer, 'We want all of you Aussie surfers to come down and watch the contest. We'll be rootin' for all the locals!' Rell had no idea what rootin' meant in Australian slang, but it was a four letter sex word. The whole population just went crazy!" Sam George recounted. "They packed the beaches the next day. Two beautiful girls rooting for Aussie surfers? That was something to see!"

"She had beauty, elegance, extreme coordination and a very sophisticated surfing style," observed Keoni Watson, one of the youngster she mentored into a successful career as a big-wave rider and surf brand sales rep. "I was always in awe that she never seemed to do things for her own benefit. She just loved to be involved with people—and loved helping them have fun."

Native Hawaiian Rell Sunn changed the visibility of women in surfing during the early 70s, deeply connecting to her culture's values of spirituality in surfing, caring for the ocean and engagement with the community, noted Nancy Naples, Distinguished Professor of Women's Gender, and Sexuality Studies at the University of Connecticut. "She was a powerful influence on other Native Hawaiian women who subsequently followed her lead, reclaiming knowledge that surfing was traditionally an equal opportunity sport where women and men both surfed difficult waves."

No Surrender

Cancer claimed an equal opportunity randomness as well. When Sunn first saw the symptoms of sarcoma she denied its danger and waited far too long to get treatment. The cancer eventually ravaged her over fifteen years, but she never complained, never withdrew, never surrendered. Instead she focused on other people's problems and made her own life an exemplary statement of grace, a tribute to her indomitable will.

She had spent a lifetime helping others—saving lives, mentoring kids, offering a spare room for the night, giving gifts for no particular reason. Now that spirit came back from all who loved her. The community raised funds, threw benefits, found specialists that might help.

As repeated sessions of chemotherapy devastated her body causing her hair to fall out, Sunn's sensitivity to her appearance caused personal anguish. She wore a skull cap for protection but also to cover the hair loss she was embarrassed about. When she didn't want to come out one day the entire top crew at Makaha—Brian Keaulana, Mel Pu'u, Brian Keaulana, Lance Ho'okano, Dennis Gouveia—all of the respected water-men, came to get her, all wearing skull caps to make her feel better.

"That was so sweet," Sunn recalled, adding the inevitable touch of humor: "Buffalo (Keaulana, the surfing patriarch of Oahu's Westside) tried to do it, but he couldn't get it over his hair. He looked like a clown!"

For fifteen years Sunn tried every therapy, every treatment every regimen to beat the insidious disease. At every turn there was hope. And accolades: Sunn was inducted into the International Surfing Hall of Fame in 1991. In 1996 she earned a place in the Huntington Beach Surfing Walk of Fame and was presented with the Surf Industry Manufacturers Association's prestigious Water-man Achievement Award. In 1997 she was inducted into the Hawaii Sports Hall of Fame.

In 1998 Hawaii lost a treasure and surfing lost a queen when Sunn died at age forty-seven after a long, brave battle with breast cancer. But she had been serene to the last, cheerful, generous and upbeat. She had even planned her memorial, exactly as she wanted.

The Sea Takes Back its Heart

Standing on the beach back at Makaha, Sunn's memorial was a reminder of all that seemed noble and joyous and eternal about the Hawaiian way of life. As Conch shells signaled the beginning of the service, the Cazimero Brothers sang, accolades were spoken, and a hula all about Sunn followed. By the finish the dancers were in tears. The crowd wept with them; big 200 pound Hawaiian men with tears streaming down their faces. As Rell's daughter Jan thanked the crowd—grief-stricken but composed with grace—she transformed from the little girl mourners had watched grow up, into a woman with the stately strength and character of her mother.

The final ritual—scattering of ashes—was pure royal Hawaiiana. Like official palace guards, the Keaulana family and their clan gently loaded the family into the big wooden canoe and delicately paddled them through the shorebreak, around the regal E'ala and into the lineup. As they scattered Rell's ashes conch shells trumpeted and a throng of 2,000 on the beach cast flowers and leis into the water; a carpet of plumeria bobbing on the shoreline, sweet perfume and echoing conch shells filling the salt air.

Turning back toward the beach, the canoe caught the first wave of a big set, shooting precariously through the whitewater like an apparition. A massive cry went up from the crowd, a combined shout of triumph, a joyous rhapsody and a final wail of pain. Simultaneously, more than 500 surfers hit the water, a tribe of admirers honoring Sunn by riding a wave for the Queen at her beloved beach, each one sharing the heart of the sea. Nothing could have pleased Rell Kapolio-ka'ehukai Sunn more.

Jeannie Chesser
Tragic Kingdom

Jeannie Chesser's grin has been compared to a certain cat. But, as her good friend Rell Sunn once told me, "much warmer, kinder, more beautiful. And much more loyal."

Chesser's path intertwined joy and sorrow, more sorrow than her sunny public persona would ever show. There was great pleasure too, and Chesser's son Todd was her greatest joy.

Chesser began surfing in South Beach Miami in 1964. Within a year she had won her first contest—in a 1965 hurricane swell at South Beach. She was fourth in the World Amateur Surfing Championships in France in 1980 and in California again in 1986. By 1992 she had earned the title of U.S. National Surfing Champion. Cheshire was Hawaii State Amateur short board women's champion several times, her last title was in 2001. Contest surfing was a joy and bore the fruit of her talent.

But sorrow came to her door with no warning. In 1970, when son Todd was only two years old, her husband died in a fatal car crash. From then on surfing wasn't always just about having fun; for Chesser it became part of what kept the horizon bright and depression at bay.

"Surfing helped me get up in the morning," she said. It enabled her to "manage each little sadness that came along." A year after losing her husband, Chesser and Todd moved to Hawaii in search of the life she dreamed of living. Once there, both built their world around wave-riding.

Surfing on a nearly daily schedule at Ala Moana Bowls, the Chesser's lived on a boat in the harbor in 1973, in the urban center of Hawaiian surf culture.

"Jeannie was the queen of Ala Moana in those days," stated Jericho Poppler. "No one ruled that place like her—all the local guys adored her."

To maintain her livelihood Cheshire worked multiple jobs—lifeguarding and judging surf contests both amateur and professional events. She started airbrushing that same year, eventually working full time for a multitude of the best Hawaiian surf brands.

While Todd's surfing prowess expanded, Chesser began to earn income from her other passion: art. From a young age, Chesser was always drawing and painting. Her mom got her into making jewelry as a teenager and she started airbrushing in her early twenties.

Chesser grew into a skilled artist, creating ocean themed jewelry and paintings of ocean scenes. But surfing had always been her focus. And her son had always been her closest companion.

Her son Todd had been a prominent member of the Momentum Generation which included World Champ Kelly Slater, style icon Rob Machado, director Benji Weatherly, Jaws expert Shane Dorian, wild man Kalani Robb, XXL winner Taylor Knox, the world traveling Malloy Brothers, and Pat O'Connell, star of *Endless Summer II*. Initially setting up camp at the Hill house near Laniakea, the camaraderie (and craziness) among the crew began to grow. But when they moved their quarters to the Weatherly's Pipeline beach house each winter, their surfing and teenage antics were documented by a then unknown film director, Taylor Steele. The Momentum generation eventually spawned a feature length film by the same name. That once-in-a-generation collective of talent was anchored by Chesser's son, the legendary Todd Chesser. Like Jason's mom Barbara Weatherly Lancaster, Jeannie Chesser opened her heart and hospitality to the entire Momentum gang, doting on them all, a pack of feral cats bent on being their era's changing of the guard.

Total Eclipse of the Heart

The Chessers' world seemed good, almost magical. Surrounded with close friends, by 1997 Todd was one of the big wave category's brightest stars; on a trajectory toward a long, exciting career. Engaged to his sweetheart, Janet Rollins, Todd was planning to marry in the late summer of that year. He was writing stories for *Surfer* magazine. The most recent one had been titled "Tragic Kingdom."

Like a mother lion, Chesser had brought her son to a place in the world where both felt confident at last. The future lit a bright fuse. No one could have predicted that flame would be suddenly extinguished.

But on an inauspicious February 13, 1997, with a huge winter swell pounding the North Shore's Alligator Rock, Todd Chesser got hit by a wave and disappeared.

After a frantic search, his friends found him, tried to keep him breathing but a second outside set tore him loose from them. By the time his friends found him washed up onshore he had drowned. Although heroic rescue efforts were made by the North Shore lifeguards, he died in the hospital. He was just twenty-eight.

It was a Tsunami of grief for the Hawaiian surf community and the reverberations were felt around the globe. Like the Bonnie Tyler song, for Chesser it was a total eclipse of the heart.

Not long after his death, Todd's best friend Benji Weatherly brought the grieving mother on a trip to Tavarua, Fiji's luxury island surf resort.

"It really helped me to renew my spirits," she confessed "It was a blessing."

But Chesser's trials were not over. Ten years after Todd's death, Chesser was diagnosed with Merkel cell carcinoma, a rare form of skin cancer, and underwent surgery, radiation and chemotherapy. At the peak of her cancer battle, she was still trying to surf while undergoing chemo and radiation. "Even if I couldn't stand up after a treatment, I would lay on my board and turn in the whitewash. I never stopped."

Retiring from commentating and judging, she continued airbrushing and designing jewelry. Her work has been displayed in the Hawaii State Art Museum gift shop.

Art also became a therapy, helping to mend some of the heartbreak life dealt her.

"Creating art takes you to a meditative space," Chesser confided in 2020. "Surfing does the same thing."

"When I surf or make art it helps tune out everything and just focus on the moment." And it would appear, it helps the healing too.

Lynne Boyer
Artists Proof: The Lady Vanishes

At the peak of her career, with two World Titles and a decisive string of other victories, Lynne Boyer—the most photographed surfer of her era—executed a vanishing act that perplexed the surfing world for more than a decade. Like the remake of Alfred Hitchcock's *The Lady Vanishes* in the 1979 thriller—released the same year she claimed her second World Title—her disappearance from the competitive arena in 1985 was so mystifying—and so complete—it was as if, as journalist Greg Ambrose wrote "she had pulled into a wave's deep, dark tube and never emerged."

The cause was a cautionary tale of struggle and secrets; a portent to the following decades, just as her influential style would be for future female competitors.

"Lynne was radical," her rival Margo Oberg observed. "She was pretty, and new and really good. Yeah."

With a fiery red mane of hair, brightly airbrushed ribbon-patterned boards and an electrifying style both in big waves and small, Boyer had burst upon the competitive scene in 1975, winning the Hawaii State Championships at eighteen. Just three years later she won her first World Title.

"Her entrance into the ranks of pro surfing was considered a sensation," Shannon Aikman said, remembering Boyers' very first professional contest at the Hang Ten Pro Championships at Malibu in 1976, which she won. "She had flown out to California, won the event and then went straight back Hawaii to sign onto the women's tour."

Boyer immediately impressed judges, spectators and competitors alike with her performances in the big powerful North Shore waves.

She was equally noticed for her aggressive approach, executing multiple maneuvers rather than the more conventional big sweeping turns.

Reticent in conversation, Boyer found fluency in her descriptive statements on the wave face. Her style was almost instantly compared to that of Larry Bertlemann—who had redefined 'radical' surfing by incorporating low-stance, rail-to-rail skateboard-like influences.

The daughter of a military family, she was born in Allentown, Pennsylvania, unconnected to surfing until her family moved to Hawaii in 1968.

"My dad was an oncologist in the Army," Boyer related, "so we lived on military bases and eventually wound up here in Hawaii when I was about eleven."

"I used to stay with Rell Sunn at Makaha and it was the time of my life," Boyer remembered. "That's where I really learned to surf. My whole thing was catching the biggest wave and I had one of my worst experiences there on a 15-foot day.

"I got caught inside, saw stars, and just barely made it. That kind of humbled me about big waves. But when it came time to prove myself at Sunset, that experience *really helped*."

Like most of the top women before her, Boyers rise in the pro ranks was meteoric. Icons like Benson, Hoffman, Oberg and Poppler vaulted into the arena and usually were required to knock off the reigning champ in the process.

Ebullient yet intensely competitive, Boyer immediately found herself in a fierce rivalry with the most dominant surfer of her era, the formidable Margo Oberg.

"The moment Lynne came on the scene there were just these titanic duels, one after another, usually in the finals of every contest," declared Debbie Beacham who would win a title herself soon after. "Lynne and Margo were like two giants of their time with everyone else just watching their combat."

Kim Mearing—another future world champion—would recall Boyer's influence: "I had an art class in junior high, and I had pictures of Lynne Boyer. When we had to do an art project, I would draw pictures of her—a collage type of thing. She was one of my idols."

Boyer and Oberg engaged in epic duels pushing the level of excitement in woman's competitive surfing to new heights. The rivals contrasted in style, but both found their performances rewarded—Oberg taking the World Title in 1977 and 80, while in between, Boyer won two back-to-back in 1978 and 79.

"Lynne turned pro just after the first full year of the World Surfing Tour," said Sandy Ordille, who was on the tour through the years of Boyer's ascendency. "Those first few years were wild, it was literally *anything goes*. At the same time there was a lot of pressure on Lynne—both professionally and personally."

"Lynne was very shy, but I think she was the best in her time," Ordille contended. "I think it made her conflicted."

Boyer's inner conflicts were certainly not noticeable at the time. With her perpetually crinkled smile and upbeat modesty, she appeared to possess what some described as the charm of an Irish leprechaun.

Boyer could be as mischievous as she could be competitive. "She beat me at the Bells contest in Australia one afternoon," Ordille recalled. "And that night she was making out with Mark Richards, the best surfer and cutest Aussie who I adored," Ordille remembered. "I was crushed on both counts."

I'm Coming Out

But Lynne Boyer held a secret. In the 80s while many freedoms had been hard won, there remained a prejudice against gays—repressive and often cruel.

"I never felt like I fit in," she admitted in 2020. "It was so hard, and it made me feel—well, depressed I guess."

For all their excesses, the 80s were still resistant to the concept of different sexual orientations. "I had a lot of secrets and I couldn't really share them—not to competitors and not to the media."

Diana Ross sang "I'm Coming Out" as a diva coming out from under her record producer's thumb, announcing her new artistic freedom. For Boyer that song's title had a whole different meaning.

"I was afraid that no one would like me," she confessed. "So I just hid it—and it was a hard way to have to live."

In light of the celebratory statement of self-disclosure the term *coming out* came to symbolize, it seems heartbreaking that a vivacious and gifted young twenty-something would bear the agony of a struggle that framed her era in a clandestine darkness.

"Lynne was fabulous," marveled Jericho Poppler, "This light on her feet, strawberry blond with an aggressive style and a blinding smile. But she had a deep relationship that didn't work out. When they broke up I think it was a huge heartbreak."

The frenetic pace of the new international surf circuit, the closeted secret of numerous competitors, and the casual acceptance of excess found almost any tour—music, politics or surf—filled with the decadence of *Miami Vice*, television's most sensational show of the era.

"The combination of endless travel, bursts of easy money, partying and ego-stroking adulation could drive even the most talented individuals into murky territory," wrote Robin Hill in 2019. "Turns out Lynne fell into the trap."

The end result was a disappearing act that was one of the most surprising and disheartening in women's surfing.

"I just sort of felt heartbroken," Boyer recalled. For over a decade Boyer worked in small surf shops, grocery stores, remaining incognito. In the ensuing years, Boyer began painting—partly as passion and partly to salve the pain. She had always enjoyed sketching and drawing, but now she began to turn her attention to art as her primary focus. Her thick but delicate oils of Hawaiian landscapes began to attract attention. And her joy for riding waves returned.

"I began surfing again," she told me. "But it took me thirteen years to beat the demons and really be able to enjoy it." Her painting improved and she began to sell her work in galleries. By the mid-2000s she was making a living from her work. There is a frailty to her emotions that has imbued her paintings with a slightly wistful realism that reflected her struggle and triumph even if unconsciously.

Time did wonders for Boyer. Restructuring a confidence in her inner core and maturing into middle adulthood, she spent her time painting in her studio below the two-story home near Honolulu. It was her artist's proof.

"Life is good," she concluded in 2020. "I live in a great place. I'm in a strong, loving relationship. I love to paint, I love to surf. It's the perfect proof that there is life after surf stardom."

17

Some Girls

The Women of the 70s Shattered the Fiber Glass Ceiling

The 70s

"Surfing frees everything up, it's just the best soul fix. Whatever it takes, you're gonna do it, because nothing else in the world can give you that kind of self-esteem."

—Rell Sunn

The *Some Girl's* album by the Rolling Stones was the soundtrack to the scorching summer of 1978. It ruled the airwaves and played in every surf house till the record grooves wore out. Among many breakout female athletes of the period, Pro tennis great Billie Jean King was cited most frequently as the biggest inspiration to the women on waves. "We all saw her as the model for success," said Candy Woodward. "She was who everyone looked to," added Terry Eselun. "Billie Jean showed everyone what could be done," Jericho Poppler concluded. "She was the kind of breakout in sports we *all* wanted." In the memorable year of 1975, tired of the roles as beasts of burden, as the Rolling Stones would put into song, the whip came down. Even though it did not turn the surf world *completely* upside down, the 70s revolutionaries inspired an army of younger girls in years to come. But there were *some girls*—the girls in this chapter—who were there when this glass ceiling shattered.

Respectable

While the male surf stars of the 60s and 70s often developed reputations as mavericks, wild men and even outlaws, the women tended to be far more responsible, a generality to be sure, but certainly not an anomaly in the larger spectrum of male/female analysis. The number of women who transitioned into accomplished professions in the non-surfing world seemed far higher than the men who more often sought to continue within the surf industry in pursuing their careers.

Patti Paniccia, an early competitor in the fledgling Hawaiian pro scene, built careers as a professional surfer, then an attorney, broadcast journalist, law professor and finally a mother of two.

A less spotlighted personality of the era, Paniccia was nonetheless a highly-ranked surfer during the 70s and early 80s, one of six women who competed on the first women's World Pro Tour in 1976.

Focused and ambitious, she cofounded the Hawaii Women's Surfing Hui in the early 70s, and as competition director, established a qualifying contest system for invitations to Hawaii's pro contests. Working with Fred Hemmings, alongside Randy Rarick, she launch the Women's Pro Tour for International Professional Surfing (IPS), the initial pro surfing association and precursor to the ASP and today's World Surf League (WSL).

Leaving Hawaii to obtain a law degree, Paniccia then started her career as a professional TV news reporter for more than a decade, most recently at CNN's Los Angeles Bureau. In the 20-teens she began lecturing as an adjunct professor at Pepperdine Law School in Malibu, California, specializing in Gender and the Law. As board member to the Surfing Heritage Cultural Center, she gave talks on surf history. "Her contribution to the women's pro development only became fully recognized in the 20-teens," Fred Hemmings contended.

In 2018, she was awarded a David McKibbin Excellence in Teaching Award.

Emotional Rescue

The women of the 70s often wore multiple hats and were central in the forefront of action by virtue of their sheer presence. Energetic and effervescent Shannon Aikman was a "major figure in the women's surfing movement from its inception through many of its most important moments," observed her esteemed contemporary Mary Lou Drummy. As one of the first professional women surfer's, Aikman competed for nearly a decade on the International Professional Surfers World Tour (now the WSL) where she was rated in the top three California contestants for five years.

A founding board member of the Women's International Surfing Association she was one of the earliest women to travel internationally in the mid-70s establishing a reputation in Biarritz France.

In 1977 Aikman cofounded the seminal women's organization, the California Golden Girls, with Jericho Poppler, building a team of surf stars dedicated to creating awareness for women in professional surfing. "Shannon deserves a lot of kudos for her work with the Golden Girls," said Jericho Poppler. "And it was actually her dad who coined the name."

Aikman was also the recipient of the prestigious County of Los Angeles Commendation for "creating a platform for women to excel in the sport, pioneering modern day women's professional surfing."

Introduced to surfing in 1969, in front of her family's Hermosa Beach house, she was a mere 80 pounds when she got her first board. The Aikman family moved to Balboa Island where Shannon rode her bike daily up to local breaks Blackies and 36th Street in Newport Beach. Attending Corona del Mar High School, she met Mary Setterholm, becoming adolescent surf buddies, surfing and training together. It was Setterholm who encouraged Aikman to surf her first contest at age fifteen. In 1974, age sixteen, Aikman started the Corona del Mar High School surfing team where "seventy-five guys showed up for qualifying." Her high school was among the first to establish surf teams. Aikman drafted members from the school's other sports. The football coach, she remembered, "grumbled that I was taking his team away." She was inducted into the Surfing Walk of Fame in Huntington Beach in 2016 along with her other founding members of the Women's International Surf Association.

Like the Founding Fathers of the American Revolution, most of the women who achieved a lasting legacy were in some way involved with the seminal organizations and manifestos in the surfing revolution of 1975, which helped advance women's issues forward significantly. Additionally, they tended to be women of character, whether Karen Mackay from Texas, Hawaiian Rell Sunn or Linda Davoli from New Jersey.

Terry Eselun, a behind-the-scenes figure who set the stage for many of the competitive and social advancements of the 70s, also held that reputation. The youngest finalist to compete in the 1965 U.S. Championships in Huntington Beach, the intrepid sixteen-year-old placed fourth in some of the largest waves in the contest's history.

That natural self-confidence prepared her for what was unpredictably coming next. The second wave of feminism was sweeping the nation from sports to politics: tired of being treated as second-class citizens of the sea, surfers formed their own organization: the Women's International Surfing Association.

"In 1975, Jericho Poppler and I co-directed, along with WISA, the First Hang Ten Women's Championship in Malibu, California," Eselun remembered. "Without any experience, but excited and groping in the dark, we created a budget, found sponsors, secured radio time; I even managed a 'live' gig on Regis Philbin's television show to talk about women's surfing."

For the first time, women had their own professional event with prize money. "I don't think we realized then how amazing it was," Eselun remarked, "but that first pro event proved to be the stepping stone for contests to come."

Charming and self-reliant, Eselun honed her writing skills, taking a role as a chronicler of the surf culture doing interviews and recording stories of historical note.

In later years Eselun expanded her interests abroad, earning respect as a world traveler too. "I've traversed the Virunga Mountains to see the gorillas of Rwanda, journeyed to Mt. Everest Base Camp, hiked the Inca Trail, and climbed to the top of the Great Pyramid to see the sunrise," Eselun said, "but I've always considered Huntington Beach to be home." "Her contributions have never been fully acknowledged," noted Shannon Aikman.

"Terry earned respect from her peers," attested Jericho Poppler. "Respect she *deserved*."

Respect was also something earned—particularly in Australia—by hard work winning the regard of male counterparts. As former *Surfing* magazine editor Nick Carroll would observe from his early years back in his native country: "There were two local girls surfing at Newport" (one of Sydney's premiere wavefields) "and they totally won us over. They were part of our tribe, they actually became human to us boys because they decided to surf. Anyone who'd tried to mess with them we'd have kicked the person's teeth in, like, literally. One of them has sadly died (Kay Jarman), the other is still a great surfer and board/SUP racer (Julia Farmer, now Magliano). Other women in the water, Jenny Steen at Avalon, later Pam Burridge of course, and then Toni Sawyer."

In Hawaii the same could be said—respect was what everyone had for highly-regarded surfers Toni Stickler and Suzanne Walker; Lani Gay and Big Island's Sherri Carney.

Stephany Sofos who—like many of these women—had started in the 60s or early 70s. She remembered the South Shore crew: "We all surfed together in those days—Heidi Hemmings, Sharon Bintliff, Kaiulu Downing, Kisi Haine, Evie Black and Tracy Phillips," recalled Sofos, "but my two heroes were Tracy Phillips and Evie Black." Described by Jericho Poppler as "pretty, blond and a great athlete," Evie Black was one of Hawaii's greatest hopes, winning the 1974 Hawaii State Championships. With tutelage from the legendary Rabbit Kekai she was from Poppler's perspective, "slated to be the next world champion."

What happened? "I was going to turn pro but my grandfather who was a very wise old man, was a very strong believer in going to college." In 1973 she had graduated from Punahou Prep School. Her grandfather said: "Well, you can be a beach bum, or you can go to college and I'll pay for it," she laughed. "I gave up the possibility of turning professional and by the time I'd gone through four years at USC and University of Hawaii I had lost my interest in competition."

Respect was also due to Hawaii's longtime supporters and promoters of women's surfing: Linda Sugihara of Town & Country Surfboards and Aunty Moku and

Luana Froiseth. These women watched the evolution of the modern surf culture—the powerful melding of the California spark and the Polynesian bloodlines.

Another Way

Juxtaposing the desire to continue surfing while finding a successful career was a major effort for the women of the 70s. As the surf culture expanded, women discovered that winning contests was not the only avenue available.

"Worked the bars and sideshows along the twilight zone," the Rolling Stones sang on *Some Girls*, and that is exactly what these young women did—worked as waitresses, scientists, coaches and stuntwomen. Some like Barbie Baron, opened surf shops. Others were able to find jobs that fit their lifestyle: dedicated Huntington Pier local Dulane "Twinkle Toes" McGaugh worked as a steward instructor for United Airlines, frequently hopping quick flights to Hawaii on good swells.

Business talent like Nancy Emerson started surf camps. Others managed high school surf teams, established a surf organization, or like Sandi Undraitis (of Summer Girl fame) became surf clothing designers.

Perhaps the earliest of these West Coast surf entrepreneurs was Catherine Marie Rossett. Born in 1922, Rossett was in her 40s when she taught herself to surf. Soon she began shaping and glassing her own surfboards out of her single car garage in Carson, under the trade name "El Bandito."

Rossett moved to Seal Beach in 1971, quickly becoming a fixture at Bolsa Chica in Huntington Beach and a founding board member of WISA. No longer building boards she started "Bag Lady" surfboard bags and "Yankzee" surfboard leashes, she continued to surf, searching (like so many women of the time) for the balance between making her means to her surfing end and making ends meet.

A good number of the surfers in the era became artists or teachers, giving them flex time to still chase waves. And more often than not they fused one or more of these occupations to create their own custom lifestyle path.

Some lucky few even became professional surfers.

Before they Make Me Run *Road Gypsies*

California's surf mecca was a lure that sent generation after generation of Easterners to make a run for the Hollywood hills and on to Hawaiian footlights—even if their paths took a circuitous route.

For Sandy Ordille the initial run was from Ocean City, New Jersey to Satellite Beach, Florida, a desperately needed break from parental chaos and icy winters. Her good friend Mary Anne Hayes had found an abandoned beach cottage in a relatively empty coastal stretch with a surf spot right out front. She found the owner and negotiated a forty dollars a month rent.

Industrious and entrepreneurial, Hayes had once used curtain cords to fashion a surf leash. She was adept at shaping surfboards, ding repair, and sewing up shirts for Oceanside Surf Shop in Cocoa Beach. She even took a job with a drive-away car company to supplement her travel expenses.

Hayes had competitive skills—she would later win the Eastern Surf Championships back to back in 76 and 77—and a worldly view beyond her years. Ordille—eyes fixed on a competitive surf career—had met her mentor.

Gregarious and intrepid, Ordille had something to prove. In a beach town where iconic film goddess Grace Kelly had used her brother John's hollow-wood kook box to "surf as well as the boys," Ordille had huge pride in her hometown. She had gotten the City Council in Ocean City to approve an ordinance "so members of her surfing community could ride waves all year round." It had been the biggest accomplishment of her life. Now she had set another goal: to prove "you didn't have to be wealthy or famous to become a professional surfer—that you could conquer California reefs and ride big waves in Hawaii." But those dreams would require a complex strategy.

When Hayes (who was half a dozen years older) agreed to become Ordille's legal guardian in 1972, it provided the first step—a beach house environs with a wave any teen surfer would covet. And just as importantly it gave Ordille step number two: a way to finish high school without missing a single good swell.

Competing in ESA events up and down the Eastern Seaboard, 'Snidely'— Ordille's childhood nickname—honed her skills at every opportunity, using the break out front of Hayes's beach house as a private training grounds. Working weekends at a local restaurant, Ordille saved her earnings for step number three—the cross country trek East Coast hopefuls knew was a prerequisite to making their mark in California and beyond.

But it was Hayes who devised the opportunity to make that trip. Discovering an auto delivery service that paid the way for driving cars to the west coast, Hayes found one headed for Southern California.

"We took off for the West Coast in a big blue Cadillac loaded with boards, made the cross country run and delivered it to San Diego," recounted Ordille. "Little did we know, the guy who owned the Caddie also owned the San Diego Chargers! We got a good tip when we dropped *that one* off."

In the youth explosion of the 70s, Beat author Jack Kerouac's manic highway odyssey *On the Road* captured an entire generation of East Coast surfer girls who were born to run while Bruce Springsteen was still living in the back of Tinker West's Jersey surf shop.

"Everyone had to do that coast-to-coast drive at least once," recalled Ordille. "It was a rite of passage."

Contemporaries of South Jersey greats Linda Davoli and Barbie Belyea, Ordille and Hayes formed a loose-knit but tightly connected Eastern expat community, adopting the gypsy lifestyle in California's hotbed surf community of San Diego county. They included Kirstin Wilkinson, Diane Rynasko and Barbie Belyea.

This cadre of interesting ragtag roustabouts made their defining west coast debut in 1972 as singing sensation Roberta Flack released "The First Time Ever I Saw Your Face." For surfing newcomers on the world stage the song fit.

For one, it would be the last time—at least at the beach. Although Wilkinson was an outstanding surfer she chose a musician's role in Nashville rather than pursue the surf life. Wilkinson's own life might have made a screenplay itself: On one of the many road trips out west "Kirsten got out of the car in Nashville, walked into town, and never left," recalled Ordille, marveling at her boldness. Thirty years later she could be seen playing violin and leading the string section on the Country Music Awards. *All the Pretty Horses*, the acclaimed film starring Matt Damon, won her a Grammy for writing and performing the music.

Diane Rynasko, who later settled in Malibu to make her mark, eventually became the president of the Malibu Surf Club under her married name Dianne Sanders.

Hayes, who loved the wild drives more than anyone, could always see the opportunity too. As Ordille recounted, "Mary Anne would buy cars in Wyoming on our way out, drive them to California, fix them up and sell them for good profit!"

"Barbie had come out to college at UCSD, so she had a dorm room," Hayes explained. "The rest of us piled into an apartment, riding waves every day, working in restaurants and surf shops at night."

Hayes had taught Ordille about board building and ding repair back in Florida; together they worked out of the shed on the side of the Pacific Beach surf shop just behind the alleyway of their apartment. Ordille trained for Hawaii on the La Jolla reefs while Hayes sewed up board shorts under the label of Blue Dolphin, even opening a shop.

Nicknamed "M80" like the firecracker, Hayes's energy propelled her entrepreneurship but drove her restless spirit too.

"She was a road trip person, couldn't sit still, always on the road," Ordille attested. "Florida, San Diego, Hatteras, Hawaii, Mexico—and then back to Jersey to win two East Coast Championships."

Following Hayes departure, Ordille found a beach house for rent in La Jolla just steps from Windansea, the city's most coveted reef break. Her mother (now reconciled with the idea of a pro surfing daughter) moved out to live with her and Ordille immersed herself into the local surf community, becoming a charter member of California's storied Windansea Surf Club.

But Ordille remained focused on a pro surf career and shortly thereafter qualified for the 1977 Women's World Tour. For a half dozen years she traveled the world maintaining a top ten position in the pro rankings and in 1978 became the first woman to surf man-on-man heats against the men, in the Stubbies Pro contest in La Jolla, reaching the quarterfinals. Moving to Hawaii she was mentored by shaper Bill Barnfield, got a degree from the University of Hawaii and surfed big Sunset Beach. Continuing to compete through the next dozen years, Ordille placed a strong second in the Marui Pro as late as 1989.

Returning from the Islands to California in 2012, Ordille was inducted into the East Coast Surfing Hall of Fame in 2016.

"My father disowned me because I made the decision to go on the IPS rated Women's Pro Surf Tour," Ordille confided. "The Hall of Fame award was *redemption*."

But there was something more. In 2020 the Ocean City, NJ Town Council "awarded me a founding member honor" for the 7th Street Surfing Beach approval in 1970. "*That* award," said Ordille, "was *legacy*."

Linda Westfall didn't run away from home, but she did run away from school a few times, hitching a ride with a friend to paddle out at Huntington Pier. Plucky and petite, she grew up in Granada Hills and began *surfing* in Malibu in 1965. Westfall graduated from California State University Long Beach in 1974 with a degree in Physical Education and Social Science and went on to teach for twenty-seven years as an activities director in Lake Elsinore. But she never stopped surfing, successfully competing in the WSA events until WISA formed in 1975, eventually providing her strong organizational skills as Competition Director. When husband Dirk died suddenly from a heart attack in 2009, Westfall continued to run "The Mill," the family pizza and pasta restaurant with her daughter in Murrieta where they had lived for twenty years. She was inducted into the Surfing Hall of Fame in 2016.

When the Whip Comes Down *Competitors*

There were many ways to get to California, but everyone knew that cross-country shuttle was a ticket to ride. Lynn Vignetti Thomas—a respected Hobie Team rider and the 1969 East Coast Women's Champion, married into the industry. Soon after meeting top surfer/shaper Joey Thomas, the couple wed and Vignetti set off on a successful west coast career in both surfing competition and as President of her husband's Thomas Surfboards in Santa Cruz. In 1975 the Women's International Surfing Association (WISA) was formed running pro and amateur events. Agile and strategic, Vignetti-Thomas quickly became a tour fixture; for the next decade (1975–1984) she claimed numerous titles along with number one rankings in 1978 and 1981. Through that decade Thomas showed a competitive toughness, landing top ten placings every year of her prolific career.

Competitive toughness, however, was not a required trait to be in the thick of the competition. For many women contests were simply the organized excuse for a gathering of the tribes, collectively enjoying the festivities. For Jeannette Prince, incentives for competing in local California events included the camaraderie that emanated through the other families like spareribs smoking on makeshift beach BBQs. Her own family was seen as the model of surf lifestyle.

Iconic longboard champion Joel Tudor's clan were close friends, and the kids of these families were immersed in an almost fantasy-like atmosphere. Deeply committed to their church, school and Cardiff Reef, the Prince family enjoyed the surfing life. For a moment it all seemed perfect.

Prince's Garden Grove childhood had been a traditional Orange County upbringing: bedrock conservative. Her Pacifica High School surf crowd was far less so, an eclectic, surf-crazed crew who funneled straight down Superior Avenue to Coast Highway, a four minute drive ending at the River Jetties between Newport and Huntington where Prince cut her teeth on the estuary's sandspit barrels. She spent the 80s decade exploring the San Diego reefs at Sunset Cliffs and began competing in the WISA events, then in the 90s with other dedicated women constructing their own events for fun, friendship and self-esteem.

"We were road pavers," Prince said. "We were the women who built a foundation for the next generation."

The "next generation" was lucky enough to catch the explosion of brands willing to sponsor riders, underwrite contests and support the women's side of the business. Prince was the first to admit, "When the boom time came, I just kept surfing because I didn't want to miss all the fun!"

It was, at that point, all in the family. At the 1998 French Surf Festival—that first that included women—she and her daughter Cori made it to the finals. No one had known they were mother and daughter but as word traveled through the audience crowds began to cheer for Mommy or Cori. "We ended up taking first and second in the event and the media went crazy," Prince remembered. To the delight of their compatriots it continued to happen frequently "to the point that in California we had a reputation," Prince laughed. "We were a dangerous duo!"

Prince represents an entire category of women competitors who enter contests as much for the social camaraderie and family friendships as for any sense of ranking that might be bestowed. Among her peers, her popularity was unmistakable; Prince remained one of the most admired and well-liked women of her generation. And always a champion of her children, Prince remembered all her descendants—her daughter Cori included. "Everything Cori has ever done, she set her mind to being the best," Prince said. "She was never selfish. Cori spoke up for issues before *anyone*."

Just My Imagination
Artists

As women moved into the mainstream of the surfing industry, artists started to explore their imaginative talents, applying them to an expanding variety of surfboard artistry. Jeanie Chesser and Lynne Boyer are two who have painted their way to an artistic living.

Laura Powers found a successful business applying her art directly to surfboards.

When Powers won the 1973 USSF (United States Surfing Federation) National Championships at Malibu, California she was already a veteran in the surfboard manufacturing industry. Starting right out of high school in 1966, Powers was glossing boards for a shaper in Southern California. As she gained experience, she found opportunities to explore her talents using pigmented resins to create unique surfboard art. From the beginning her work was adopted predominately by female surfers.

Powers married and moved to Santa Cruz, where she began to dabble in the emerging art of air-brushing. To make ends meet, she worked in as many as five surf shops at one time, honing her skills, and becoming fluent in many styles of artwork. By the time she moved to Hawaii in 1987, she had enough experience to land a job with renowned shaper Glen Minami. As the 20th Century closed Powers had become a full-fledged independent artist creating artwork predominately displayed on surfboards. "Girls are really making it a boom for business," Powers noted to the Honolulu Advertiser in 2004. "They like the flowery designs and the feminine colors. They're different than guys."

Understanding being "different than guys" was a prerequisite for many women of the 70s, or at least *artistically* different. Born in the West Indies island of Curacao, Simone Riddingius lived in Holland for three years and started her deep relationship with wave-riding in 1964 when her family moved from the Netherlands to California. She met surfer Denny Auberg, a lifeguard at Malibu during her teen years camping with her family. Auberg would later write the screenplay to *Big Wednesday*, the major Hollywood film depiction of his brother Kemp, Lance Carson and other Malibu greats in the early 60s.

While Auberg gave her tips in the lineup and taught her guitar, Riddingius soaked in the entire cultural milieu emanating from the beach life, incorporating it into her own creative personality.

"I was always mesmerized by the breaking waves," Reddingius remembered. "I'd watch the surfers carrying their boards, waxing them up, and then dancing on the waves. I wanted that lifestyle." After learning on a decrepit one-dollar longboard, she bought a shorter board and, "before you knew it, my girlfriend and I were ditching school to go to the beach."

Shock-white blond and effortlessly engaging, Reddingius turned out to be an archetype of 70s surf style: after high school she moved to Santa Barbara trading Malibu for Rincon, exploring music, shooting budding future surf stars Kim Mearig and Tommy Curren; then vagabonding to Maui through the 90s making jewelry, shooting Jaws and sampling the counter-culture.

In 2000 she won the Masters' Division of the Margaritaville Malibu Women's Longboard Open. A surfing photo of her from the event published in Wahine Magazine, "was the highlight of my contest career," she laughed. Twenty-two years after moving to Maui she returned to Santa Barbara, freelancing as an engineer, opening a photo gallery and playing music once again with Denny Auberg and the Wrinkled Teenagers.

Miss You
Memorials

Like many of her generation Judy Trim was born too early to prevent the heartache of gender-based intolerance. A much-loved surfing individual, Trim burst on the surf scene at fifteen, an impressive teenager at Sydney's Dee Why Point at a time when few women were out there.

Trim's joyfulness was infectious and her old 1938 Buick was the subject of one of John Witzig's most iconic surf photos of the era. Her white swimsuits and later her white boardshorts were part of her confident persona. A standout Australian female surfer when social codes were far more severe, she won the Australian National Titles in 1970. When she came out as gay at eighteen, Judy was stunned by the negative response. The "darker flip side to surf culture" was still in ascendance in the 70s and "the backlash crushed her naïve optimism." Even with the empathy of friends who knew her public life was difficult, she often turned to substance abuse to quell the emotional pain. Yet she spoke up for gay rights when hostility was still widespread.

But in the face of all that Trim's vitality, humor and love of life came through. Still beloved by the many surf friends, she passed away in 2014 at age sixty-four, after tragically breaking her neck in an accident four weeks earlier. Sadly Trim's trials came too early in history to overcome the despair of prejudice she endured.

For those whose luck fit the societal expectations, a life well-lived received more positive rewards. Founding member and the first treasurer of W.I.S.A, Pam Maher grew up in Long Beach, the daughter of a military family. Graduating from Pasadena High School, she returned to the beach in the later 60s, falling in love with the surf lifestyle. Maher earned a nursing degree and worked at Hoag Hospital in Newport Beach. Her family eventually set down roots in Belmont Shore, developing a close friendship with the Poppler's, a distinguished surfing family who lived on the Peninsula.

In 1975 Jericho Poppler asked Maher to become the first treasurer of the newly forming W.I.S.A board "and Pam happily accepted."

Warm and dedicated, Maher served the surf organization for years. She died unexpectedly from a heart attack in 2004. "Pam was a tremendous asset to the Board, in addition to helping behind the scenes running the contests," Terry Eselun wrote in her affectionate memorial of Maher. "Pam was also a fantastic cook and often brought food to those often long WISA meetings," said Eselun. "But mostly she was just a loving heart."

Described as a surfer's surfer from Cocoa Beach, Diane Sanders Rynesko moved out to California in the 70s with the surf crew of eastern road gypsies, eventually settling in the Los Angeles area where she became a fixture at Malibu. At her paddleout those from her home town remembered her proud family of surf sisters. Her sister Lorraine Guthrie (Mama G, as she was known) was a well-known local photographer in central Florida. Those who knew her from Malibu remembered a trophy winning club president who was a mentor to dozens of young devotees. "Diane had a way of making you feel important, a part of a larger dynamic and that you had a job to do just by being yourself and being present," wrote Cori Schumacher, who grew up under her wing. "She always had her eye out for female longboarders, especially those of us who grew up competing in the coalition contests in the early 90s. She rallied behind women's longboarding at every opportunity and was an integral part of where we are today." Sanders-Rynasko had ceremonies on both coasts, a tribute to a long life well-lived.

If some girls lived long full lives others were a bursting nova that left the starlight dimmer with their passing. Lori Faggothy surfed in the first WISA Pro in Malibu in 1975, a sixteen-year-old representing Hawaii. A troubled soul, Faggothy died by her own hand in 2011. "She was a beautiful, vibrant, talented surfer," said Shannon Aikman, a friend who surfed against her in the Malibu event. "We remember her still."

Though some memories are half a century past, some girls fire was burning brightly much more recently. Hailed by the French Surfing Federation as an "outstanding educator" who "transmitted her passion for surfing and the ocean," rising star Poeti Norac had moved from the Vendée region in France, to Queensland's Sunshine Coast to continue her lifelong passion of chasing waves. Norac learned surf with her father Bruno at age six in the seaside town Les Sables d'Olonne, specializing in longboard surfing after switching from shortboard, and had competed for ten years. A finalist four times in France's national championships, she came second in 2018 and third in 2016. She also won ten victories in the Coupe du France. She died in an accident on February 2020.

Far Away Eyes
Travelers

Women traveling globally to surf was a relatively rare occurrence previous to the mid-70s. But the World Contest Circuit was an open invitation for women to experience international travel unchaperoned but with a protective buffer provided by the proximity of other competitors and event itinerary.

The Golden Girl's arrival at the Australian leg of the WTC Tour was—by all accounts—something approaching a Rolling Stones concert on the beach. The *Miami Vice* decadence of the late 70s had been fully embraced by the surfing population in general. But there had been nothing like this before on the women's side when it came to ground-breaking performances, high visibility and untrammeled hedonism. Apparently the Bells Beach contest in 1978 was a combination of *The Bachelorette* and *Sex in the City*. For many of the "girls with faraway eyes" it was their first trip away from home and they experienced the thrill of no parental supervision and the *anything goes* attitude of the late 70s.

"It was crazy but so fun," Aikman recollected fondly.

"I stole Brenda Scott's boyfriend while Lisa Tomb stole my boyfriend!"

"Lynne was very shy, but I think she was the best in her time," declared fellow competitor Sandy Ordille. "She beat me at the Bells contest in Australia. And at the same time she was making out with Mark Richards, the best surfer and cutest Aussie who I adored," Ordille remembered. "I was crushed on both counts."

The craziest of stories remain untold. As Jericho Poppler insisted, "What happened in OZ stayed in OZ."

A traveler to Costa Rica, Nicaragua, Puerto Rica and El Salvador, Jo Pickett may have given up travel and competitive surfing decades ago, but her competitive drive never slowed.

Pickett, a former U.S. national shortboard, U.S. senior women's, Eastern Surfing Association champion, became a popular surfing coach in Wilmington, North Carolina.

"Jo was a legend in these waters," Lisa Rosselli once declared. "And she's a lovely person, fun to be with and hot in the water." For decades she continued to shares waves with the very surfers she had mentored over her years in the surf at her Crystal South surf camp in Wrightsville beach.

Her three children—Leilani, Airlie and Doug—became surfers and camp coaches themselves. Pickett could not have been happier.

"The combination of the human spirit with the ocean energy . . ." she remarked in 2018, her voice trailing off in wonder. "There's not a more beautiful thing in the world to watch."

At the 2017 Wahine Classic, that beauty proved too much for Jo to bear from the shoreline. Spur of the moment, she jumped on her board and paddled out to surf in a heat against Leilani. The beach crowd cheered as mother and daughter split waves. "We're competing," Leilani says, "but, at the same time, there's an *understanding*. She's not going to cut me off." Neither Pickett won. But neither cared. The moment was victory enough.

Adventure Girl

Respectability—and the impact successful women surfers had on the world at large—was still being explored by the 70s innovators. While competitive surfing offered women a shot at stardom it also forced the competitors to acquiesce to the demands of an event system dominated by the males. Candy Woodward took a different route. "I wasn't interested that much in competition," explained Woodward. "All I really wanted was to get uncrowded waves and travel the world." That approach took her to New Zealand, Tahiti's outer islands, Hawaii, Mexico and Australia. Halfway around the world at Fiji's Cloud Break off Tavarua Island, she volunteered with Dr. Mark Renneker and the Surfers Medical Association to provide care for the local villagers.

"She was the 'Adventure Girl,'" her friend Shannon Aikman explained. "A good competitor but always on her own quest—independent, private, a little mysterious—and very stylish."

Candice "Candy" Woodward first learned to surf at Torrance Beach on a 10' longboard when she was eleven. Given the moniker "Soul Surfer" by *Surfer* Magazine she was one of a handful of accomplished California female surfers during the 70s and 80s. Steve Sakamoto, a surf photographer who was one of *Surfer* magazine's top shooters told me Woodward was "the easiest subject to shoot, because her ability was so exceptional."

Margo Oberg, who watched Woodward for years, agreed: "She was the best goofy-foot in California."

Known for her prominent cheekbones and piecing green eyes, Oberg's smooth, high-performance style soon became part of a new element in the growing surf culture: women who could "keep up with, and even out-surf the guys in the line-up."

Did that present challenges? "Sure," Woodward conceded. "But I don't want to dwell on that side of things," she replied, pausing. "I can tell you though, there were times when the local boys at Point Dume met us with sticks and rocks and told us to go back up the trail.

"The thing about being a female is you have to prove yourself," She mused. "And the problem compounds when you travel because you have to prove yourself *everywhere you go*. And each time you travel to a different spot you have to prove yourself again. And again. *Over and over.*"

But the adventurer wanted it all and saw no reason to trade one goal for another.

"I gambled," she admitted, laughing, "that I could figure out how to build visibility for the women surfers, travel around the world, earn a reputation, compete in contests, get a college education and be a success."

It was a good bet. In the 80s, Woodward helped introduce women's surfing to the mainstream media, surfing in national and international television commercials for RCA Television, filmed in Hawaii by the legendary George Greenough. Her surfing images were also part of RCA's marketing campaign appearing in *People*, *Life*, *Reader's Digest*, *Time*, *Newsweek* and *Vogue*. From there Woodward began working with a prominent British fashion and sports photographer Tony Duffy, who submitted her surfing and modeling photos to international magazines that highlighted lifestyle trends, beauty, fitness, photography and sports. It didn't hurt of course to have movie star looks and a model's body.

An original member of "The California Golden Girls," Woodward was also a skillful competitor, winning the 1979 San Diego WISA Championships, and the 1980 WISA Pro Division State Championship. Woodward made numerous appearances in *Surfer* magazine, the *Los Angeles Times* and other periodicals.

Graduating from Cal State University Long Beach's Physical Therapy Program, Woodward would later became a Board Certified Professional Ergonomist.

"I kept surfing through all my studies. There was a time," she chuckled, "when I was so stretched between studies and surfing, I was stashing my surfboard in the medical departments cadaver room."

Starting an ergonomics consulting firm, she also built a business designing and fabricating specialized ergonomic products for laboratories and Biotech companies. In 2018 she was inducted—as the Female Legend—into the Hermosa Beach Surfers Walk of Fame.

"Candy was the inspiration for the Roxy events I produced," Allan Seymour confided. It was poise, athleticism, grace, beauty. I didn't care about the winning and losing. "I wanted to showcase what Candy had."

What Woodward "had" observers agreed was "one unmistakable ability," whether in a physicians' office, a remote island chain, an international contest, or just surfing with the regulars at her home break: Woodward was "fondly respected by both the men and the women on waves."

Proof? She was the first and only female pro surfer to be inducted into the prestigious Haggerty's Surfing Club. And for those who understood the protectively fierce character of that insular club, it was no frivolous induction—and might have been the most telling accomplishment of all.

Professionalism
Goes Feminine
1982–1993

"The cure for anything is saltwater: sweat, tears or the sea."
—Isak Dinesen, author of *Out of Africa*

Saltwater, Sweat and Tears

The women who envisioned professional surfing in the 80s had the same dream of professional surfing as those who came before them: a way to travel the world, surf great waves, and win enough money to finance the next competition in Australia, Japan, South America, Hawaii or South Africa.

All around them they could see women claiming their future. The Go-Go's rose to the top the Billboard album charts—the first all-female arena-level band to write their own songs and play their own instruments. "Walk Like an Egyptian" by the all-girl Bangles became the biggest selling single of 1987. In film, *Aliens*, James Cameron's seven-Oscar nominated blockbuster, showcased Sigourney Weaver's role as a strong resourceful woman persevering in the face of insurmountable odds. The 80s saw women make huge strides in politics as well. Sandra Day O'Connor became the first woman appointed to the Supreme Court in 1981. Geraldine Ferraro was the first female vice presidential candidate for a major party in 1984.

No doubt these achievements were further inspiration to the Women's Professional Surfers (WPS) formed in 1981 by founders Debbie Beacham and Jericho Poppler, Rell Sunn, Lynne Boyer, Margo Oberg, Cherie Gross, Linda Davoli, Patti Paniccia, Becky Benson and Brenda Scott. *That*, many observers would say, was a pretty impressive group themselves. It must be added that Cheri's mother Gwen Gross received near unanimous praise for her administrative role in the organization's fledgling first years. Efficient, detailed and diligent, she was as Debbie Beacham would say, "the real adult in the room." The pro surf posse had built a foundation on saltwater, sweat and tears. But now the possibility of a sustainable women's pro circuit had finally begun to feel cautiously real.

Over the course of history, women's world champions have tended to dominate for multi-year periods. Joyce Hoffman, Sharon Webber and Lynne Boyer each won a pair of World Titles. Margo Oberg, Frieda Zamba, Wendy Botha, Lisa Andersen and Carissa Moore all won four. Steph Gilmore and Layne Beachley took seven World Titles apiece.

Since the initial Word Surfing Champions were first crowned in 1964 there have been 17 women champions. But in the brief era between 1982 and 1993—the period between Margo Oberg and Lisa Andersen's reigns—six different women claimed the throne. Their stories—and this era—are among the most intriguing.

Managing to win a World Title while managing the Women's Pro Surfing organization

In 1980 during a warm-up session at Haleiwa, Debbie Beacham dropped into a 12-foot wave-face, and took a hard wipeout, cracking one of her ribs. Determined not to be sidelined by something as frivolous as broken bones, she had surf-guru sports physician Dr. Greg Mattson tape her up, and three hours later, paddled out into 15-foot Sunset for the Offshore Masters surf event. On her third wave her board snapped in two. She swam the 100 yards to the beach to retrieve another board and continue, but (mercifully) the heat clock ran out.

If that gives the impression that Debbie Melville Beacham is a character of quality and unwavering determination, it would be dead-on accurate. But Beacham had something else: the ability to make apple cobbler without overturning the apple cart.

The white-hot fire lit by women determined to redefine pro surfing in the mid-70s had subsided somewhat—some thought that the spirit of "girl power" movements like WISA and the Hawaiian Women's Hui had been co-opted by a strain of less confrontational coalition-builders that would douse the fiery potential of the earlier radical leaders.

Debbie Beacham was in no disagreement with these skeptics. She knew full-well that surfing was, in her own words, "the most ego-driven, male-dominated sport on the planet." But when Beacham took over the Women's Professional Surfers organization her soft-spoken restraint and non-adversarial style got the members more money, more coverage, and more control—without bludgeoning those she negotiated with. In retrospect Beacham and the second wave of pros who shepherded women's pro surfing in the mid-to-late 80s, not only kept the fragile structure from unraveling, but did so while continuing to address central concerns of inclusion and self-determination, resetting the parameters for women as agents of their own expressiveness in ways that are still being played out in wide-ranging endeavors including marketing, film and non-profit efforts.

Managing to win the 1982 World Title while managing the Women's Pro Surfing organization was no easy feat; tactful diplomacy coupled with hard-as-nails smarts were all required. If rock star Pat Benatar's "Hit Me With Your Best Shot" defined the necessary sacrifice of the era, it was Beacham who took the blows—but pulled no punches herself.

In 1985 Debbie took a position at *Surfer* magazine where I had been publisher a few years earlier. She took on the sales and marketing of the magazine the same way she took on the fight for women's values—with a poet's heart and a warrior's armor.

Not that she was immune to the emotional price. In the face of endemic surf-world sexism—which may have peaked when the surf media began to run *Sports Illustrated* style swimsuit issues—the powerlessness she felt could bring her to tears. As hard as she had worked for women's surfing, the demeaning stereotypes seemed ascendant at every level of surf media.

But she persevered: with indie film director Donna Olsen, Beacham co-produced the first all-women surf documentary *Surfer Girl*. Filmed in Tavarua Fiji, it depicted the passion and problems of women surfers against a backdrop of perfect South Pacific swells. Awarded the Silver Plaque Award for Cinematography at the Chicago International Film Festival, it appeared on numerous television channels over the years.

Her efforts were often altruistic: helping to organize the Legend's Luau in San Diego, which has raised ten million dollars for cancer research, Beacham continued to contribute to the surf culture as an inspiration, still remaining an active participant.

But Beacham's tenure at the head of the Women's Pro movement will likely be her most lasting legacy, picking up where the revolutionaries left off. The bold pioneering women of the 70s had pierced the power structure previously organized and run by men. But it would take the resolute and tenacious effort that Beacham brought to the table to sustain the hard-earned progress those visionaries had made. For nearly a decade Debbie Beacham was both a top competitor *and* the president of the Women's Professional Surfing association (WPS). That she did so while navigating a marriage and raising two children who have traveled the world with her, illuminates the increased workload required from women of substance in western culture. To be effective *and* respected *and* feminine—she had to be, as Sade sang, a *smooth operator*—just what was needed for the turbulent decade she piloted.

First of the New School Champs
A True California Girl

The next world champ could not have been a greater contrast. The 80s began with Margo Oberg winning the title for two years in a row at the ages of twenty-seven and twenty-eight, and then twenty-nine-year-old Debbie Beacham finally breaking Oberg's stranglehold in 1982. But beginning in 1983, a New School of women surfers entered the competitive arena producing a cadre of young world champions through the rest of the 80s. Kim Mearig, still a teenager in her title year run, would set the standard of both performance and good manners.

Affable and demure with her close friends, Kim Mearig's fierceness in competition and quiet grace in victory was a laudable trademark. The very embodiment of a California surfer—blond, fit, tan—the Santa Barbara native was quickly noticed.

Surfing since age twelve, she was riding shapes by alpha shaper Al Merrick and competing at the amateur level by fourteen, often sharing the limelight with schoolmate Tom Curren. "We went down to Huntington for the NSSA Nationals when we were sixteen," Mearig recalled. "We both won and got picked for the National Team, but at the time, we didn't even know what it was." Mearig also claimed victory in the 1981 West Coast and United States Championships, as well as defeating California's top women in pro/am events up and down the coast.

Propelled by the new tri-fin Thruster surfboards and inspired by the rise of her hometown friend and hero Tom Curren, Mearig was twenty years old when she won the 1983 World Title and took home a "whopping" $5,800 in prize money. But she signed a lucrative deal with Ocean Pacific that made her the highest-paid female professional surfer on record. She maintained a position in the Top 8 and narrowly missed a second crown in 1985 to Frieda Zamba and in 1988 to Wendy Botha. As writer Jason Borte observed, "While her peak came well before the 90s boom in women's surfing, she was one of the first professional women surfers to earn a good living. Her popularity garnered a *Surfer* Poll victory and inspired a generation of girls who would break down the barriers."

"Kim was someone I looked up to," declared future world champ Lisa Andersen. "She had a really smooth style and I even copied her pink and yellow Victory wetsuits." Mearig married and had a child the year after her title run and within a few years gave up the tour.

Three years into retirement, Mearig returned to Huntington in 1993 to reclaim the Ocean Pacific World Cup title before permanently abandoning competition in favor of motherhood.

East Coast's Greatest Maverick

When a young, virtual unknown from Flagler Beach Florida arrived in Solana Beach, California for the 1983 Mazda Pro, her eye-opening performance became the shock of the new. Taunt and explosive, rookie Frieda Zamba stunned the crowd with powerful 360 degree maneuvers in the final—and won the event so effortlessly the women's ranks were barely able to comprehend the performance. It was just a prelude, as it turned out, to a much larger symphonic assault. Within a year of her professional debut, Zamba had become the youngest woman to win a professional World Tour event and then at nineteen, the youngest world champion surfer in history.

Most surf careers follow an arithmetic curve. Frieda Zamba's was exponential: Small, light—and very fast—Zamba won five of ten events en route to her first World Title in 1984, and then repeated in 1985 and 1986 and again in 1988. Her husband Flea Shaw, a mentor and coach, shaped her boards and helped shield her from the attention even as her star shined.

Chalking up five straight *Surfer* Poll wins Zamba remained an understated maverick, shunning the limelight. As Matt Warshaw wrote in 2003, "Zamba presented something new in the sport: an aggressive female who knew where to find the speed and power." She set the stage for the string of strong, confident women in her decade and was a key link in the chain that connected the East Coast passion to its emerging competitive power. In 1998 she was chosen Woman of the Year at the Surfing Walk of Fame. After her professional career she and her husband built a successful surf school business in Costa Rica. Considered the East Coast's greatest maverick, Frieda Zamba won four World Titles—quietly—and, in the consensus of her peers, with modest simplicity.

Courageous Cover Girl Wins Four World Titles

Posing for *Playboy* and winning four World Titles may seem incongruous, but South African Wendy Botha was the rare combo of tough competitor and controversial sweetheart. Petite and supple at 5'4" and 115 pounds, Botha won the women's world surfing title in 1987 and 1989 when she became Australia's first female professional champion and set a competitive record (seven) for most victories in a single season for a man or woman. Winning the title again in 1991 and 1992, she matched the historic string of four titles set by her forerunner Frieda Zamba. After her first world championship, she changed her citizenship to Australian to avoid international apartheid sanctions and set off on her four title quest.

"Wendy could have been any kind of athlete she wanted," observed Layne Beachley. "She chose surfing. Her surfing is a reflection of her era."

Raised in the distant state of then apartheid South Africa, she initially struggled with the contest circuit's relentless travel schedule.

But her aggressive, radical performances immediately garnered notice from the judges—and the rest of the surfing world—at every stop.

Outspoken and brash at times, Botha created controversy in 1992 when she posed nude in *Playboy* magazine, claiming to show the world what surfing does for the female body. The response was contentious, but it was, nonetheless, the first issue of *Playboy* ever to sell out in Australia.

"It might be an indictment of surfing," wrote journalist Tim MacDonald, "but Wendy Botha is better known for her spread in *Playboy* than for her incredible sporting achievements. That fact says a lot about the pro surfing reportage. . . . that due to a male-dominated and generally uninterested surf media, some of surfing's greatest champions have been ignored. In such a way, the world of Wendy Botha, one of surfing's most-dominant competitive forces in the late 80s, remained off the map. And as a result, a great story of competitive tragedies, fierce rivalries and immense achievement has largely been undocumented."

Botha retired from the Pro Tour in 1993, moving to New Zealand where she married national football star Brent Todd. There she had two children, and co-hosted a sports TV show for several years, but eventually moved back to Australia. Botha even competed again, mainly for fun, in a few WQS events. The controversy about *Playboy* became a minor blip on the radar screen of a stellar career. Recognized in later years as an undeniable athletic talent, she was inducted into the Surfing Walk of Fame in 2017.

A Queen Too Soon
the First Great Australian Pro

A decade of rapid progression in women's surfing was capped off as Isabel Letham protégé Pam Burridge won the Women's World Title in 1990. Hailed in her homeland as the Queen of Australian surfing, Burridge burst onto the scene as an enfant terrible—crushing her Australian competition—but spent much of the decade battling a variety of personal crises. Problems not-withstanding, Burridge maintained an overall ranking through the 80s that was only bettered by the extraordinary four-time world champion Frieda Zamba. The year she won her World Title, Burridge earned a total of $36,395 in prize money—$20,000 more than the entire tour offered at the start of the decade.

Although her smooth, almost laconic style appeared to look too easy, Burridge surfed hard and finished strong. But the Australian press created immense pressure for her to win the Women's World Title which had never been won by an Australian since the start of the World Tour in 1976. When she fell just one or two spots below the top spot for five years in a row an unforgiving national media spewed a torrent of critical coverage. As Burridge struggled with a goal unattained, falling short of expectations from an unrelenting media, she drank hard, played hard and partied hard—going through more wardrobe changes than David Bowie. Enamored with music, Burridge released a single, "Summer Time All 'Round the World" in collaboration with Australian hard-rocker Damien Lovelock, under the name Pam and the Pashions. But by 1989 her indulgences had spiraled into a destructive and debilitating low point for a warm, articulate girl who had dropped out of high school at fifteen to pursue her dream of pro surfing. In the ensuing year she met Mark Rabbidge, her future husband—a mature, respected shaper and surf coach—who, working together on equipment, training and strategy helped her get clean, strong and focused. This concentrated effort was the positive catalyst for a year of self-confident performance on the competitive circuit. In a startling and well-received comeback she won the 1990 World Title and dispelled the personal demons that had tried to crown her a queen too soon. She continued to compete through 1998 and retired after remaining in the top eight rankings for fifteen years—a record that still stands. Inducted into the Australian Surfing Hall of fame in 1997, she and her husband started Feisty Girl Surfboards. She had two children, naming her firstborn Isabel in honor of her childhood surfing idol Isabel Latham, the first lady of Australian surfing.

"Pam was always in search of something she couldn't quite find," observed Australia's premier surf chronicler, Nick Carroll. "She won a World Title and it freed her up to begin to become her true self. There's something special about Pam that places her in a very rarefied space in surf culture, she is a true keeper of the flame."

The Triumphant Underdog

Going into the final contest of 1993, Pauline Menczer thought she had the World Title locked up. She had won three of the first eleven events and was holding a slim lead with the last contest just weeks away. A fiery five-year tour veteran, Menczer had come close to winning her first world crown in 1991 and 1992, but was edged by wonder-woman Wendy Botha, a recent immigrant from South Africa. This season, she thought, she *had* to prevail, even if the odds were stacked against her. And stacked they were.

Menczer's challenges were multiple—not only was she broke and sponsorless, she was also facing some of history's best competitors (three of them would hold World Titles of their own.) But it was not just foes and finances she was battling.

Her biggest adversary was physiological rather than fiscal: She suffered from crippling arthritis, so intense that friends would often push her around in a shopping cart to save her the anguish of trying to walk.

Menczer had already spent $25,000 of the $30,000 winnings she'd accumulated just getting around the world to the events. He performances had given her the lead. And then suddenly two weeks before the final contest of the year she was struck with an arthritic attack so debilitating she was confined to a wheelchair. "I couldn't even brush my own hair," she recalled of her pre-finals attack. "My body just shut down."

Menczer was no stranger to poverty or pain. Her father and grandfather were both killed in separate car accidents when she was only five, leaving Menczer's mother to take care of four children and a grandmother on a monthly welfare check. Raised by a single parent in the Sydney suburb of Bronte, she learned to surf at thirteen on one half of her brother's broken board. Instantly obsessed with riding waves, she began to enter competitions, raising money to pay for travel and entry fees by collecting aluminum cans, baking cakes and selling toffees through her hometown high school.

But at fourteen the arthritic condition erupted.

"At first I didn't know what was going on. I'd wake up and my knees were all swollen, and that rheumatoid arthritis has now turned into osteoarthritis," she recalled, grimacing. "Even the year I went for the World Title I could barely walk."

Menczer was not daunted: "As talented as she was," stressed the next World Champion Lisa Andersen, "to appreciate Pauline's achievements, you have to recognize that her career was built as much on *perseverance,* as it was talent."

Possessed of a powerful, athletic style and no shortage of courage, she won her way to a berth in the world amateur championships in Puerto Rico in 1988 and, at just eighteen, came home amateur champion.

"I thought 'this is great, this is what I want to do for a living,'" she said. "And not long after that I turned professional."

She quickly joined the professional ranks that same year and finished fifth in her first season on the tour. She immediately became a title contender almost winning in 1991 and 92, pushing through the pain of serious joint inflammation.

Now in the final event of her best shot for a title, ranked number one by a thread, she was nearly completely immobile. Relying on sheer willpower, Menczer began paddling in a pool a week before the contest, to keep her strength before competing. On the day of the competition the surf was big, stormy, windblown Sunset, a challenge for any surfer let alone one in her condition. Summoning pure grit Menczer squeezed past her rivals heat after heat, and in the finals narrowly scraped by to gain her World Title.

"Menczer's 1993 championship win remains one of the sport's great underdog stories," former *Surfer* editor Matt Warshaw told me in 2020. "To this day." Yet despite her world crown Menczer never received the attention or sponsorship dollars her peers did before and after. She felt she knew the reason but remained philosophical.

"I'm not sure why I didn't, maybe because I was never a groupie," she told ABC news. "A lot of people thought it was because I didn't have the look that the surfing community wanted—the big boobs, blonde hair, blue eyes, whereas I was this dark-haired, freckle-faced kid."

It is hard not to imagine that if Pauline Menczer had the coveted looks of Lisa Andersen she would have garnered far more sponsorship and media attention from an industry run almost entirely by men. But her courage and talent stand.

In 2017 she was inducted into the Australian Surfing Hall of Fame, an honor both fitting and long overdue. And despite the obvious inequities between men and women's looks—still inherent in society—her triumph in the face of adversity made her a legend among her legion of peers and friends worldwide.

Smooth Operators

Heading up the women's tour in the period from the early 80s to the early 90s was something like an on-the-job apprenticeship, with no training manual and no coach. Debbie Melville Beacham had taken on the position with much appreciated sensitivity, and the bravery to adjust in the heat of battle. But along with her a whole cadre of women organizers began to fill in the ranks, inventing the professional structure and style like a recipe from scratch. As the depth of talent expanded so did the solidity of the professional programs.

Alisa Schwarzstein Cairns worked alongside Beacham helping to enhance professional competition in the embryonic decade of the 80s. Serving on the board of directors for ten years, Cairns and many other strong surfers built solid foundations which are still cornerstones in the pro contest structure.

After her first glimpse of surfing at the age of nine, Alisa Schwarzstein-Cairns leapt into local NSSA events, then going on to a world amateur championship by the age of fifteen. From there, it was a seamless transition into the pro ranks and in 1984, Cairns was named ASP Rookie of the Year. Her best result was a fourth in the world in 1986 but she held a solid position in the top eight for four years. As the coach of the Laguna Beach High School surf team Alicia mentored then up-and-coming future greats Taylor Pitz and Leah Pakpour, along with other aspiring competitors. She eventually married her legendary N.S.S.A. coach, the controversial Ian Cairns in 1996 and the couple raised twin boys just blocks from her parents' house in Laguna Beach.

A member of the Surfing America ISA Masters Team that won the team gold medal in 2011, and the team silver medal in July 2012, her career spanned thirty years of dedication to the sport, as a competitor and then behind the scenes. In recognition of her lifetime commitment to pro surfing, Schwarzstein-Cairns received the "Woman of the Year" award from the Surfing Walk of Fame in 2012.

Like Schwarzstein-Cairns, Betty Depolito had a successful career both as a competitor and event organizer but focused her career in Hawaii, producing and directing the first ever Women's Surf competition at Pipeline in 2010. The California West Coast Champion and California Golden Girl traveled the world as a top ten–rated international surfer. "Banzai Betty" (so named for her early Pipeline performances and willingness to charge) pioneered women's surfing videos and produced the first ever DVD in the 80s. Depolito began in the television field as an ESPN reporter. She went on to work as a technician and media & marketing professional, producing and directing many surf competitions including the Eddie Aikau, the North Shore Tow-In and the Pipeline Women's Pro. For several years in the 20-teens she produced Women's Sports TV and an online show for women called FlHi Girls Sports TV and continues to organize women's surfing competitions. A member of the California Golden Girls she became an event marketing and organizing expert, remembered for her tenacious efforts to bring back the women's events to Hawaii's North Shore. As Keala Kennelly observed, "Betty loves wave-riding and she has fought so hard for women's opportunities in surfing."

Depolito was certainly not the only woman of the era to evolve from passionate participant to powerful administrative role—sometimes unexpectedly. Meg Bernardo could almost qualify as surfing's accidental operations director. When Bernardo enrolled in the Newport Surf School in 1980—which was owned and operated by Australian expatriates Peter Townend and Ian Cairns—her casual introduction to the Aussie surf stars would prove to be a fateful occurrence.

Less than eighteen months after her surf school lessons, she was hired by the Bronzed Aussie's in 1982 to handle administrative duties for the NSSA. It would be the beginning of a lifelong career. Four years later and now a seasoned veteran of competition management, the burgeoning professional surfing tour (then called the Associated Professional Surfers) offered Bernardo the job of Operations Director for the ASP in 1986, operating the Pro Tour from a small headquarters in Huntington Beach. By 1995 she had shifted her role to Special Events Manager for the ASP Tour and when in 1999, the ASP moved its international headquarters to Coolangatta, Australia, World Champ Peter Townend would enter her life again, this time in 2000, hiring her as the Administrative Director of the newly-created, SIMA-backed Surfing America, the North American amateur surfing organization. But she would go on to become the General Manager at World Surf League, capping a storied career in competitive surf organizations. "Meg was like all of us—she dove in and learned on the job," Debbie Beacham said of Bernardo. "But she became one of the most well-loved and valuable administrators in pro surfing."

By 1989, the ASP World Tour (led by Beacham and her colleagues) had expanded to fourteen events with sponsors ranging from Italian fashion brand Forenza and Pert Shampoo to Diet Coke and Pepsi. The women's total prize money amounted to $272,000, more than the 1980 Men's *and* Women's divisions *combined*. This significant leap in the number of events and the amount of prize money pushed the performance level of women's surfing during the 90s as a younger, more international crew of women surfers stood on the shoulders of the women who had worked hard (and surfed hard) to build women's pro surfing in the previous two decades. In her cry for a chance at freedom 1988's unforgettable "Fast Car" songwriter Tracy Chapman sang what all women were hoping:

> *"I had a feeling that I belonged.*
> *I had a feeling I could be someone. Be someone. Be someone.*

Love is a Battlefield
The 80s

Jodie Cooper felt the crack of the fist as it hit her head. It was a hard punch and it nearly knocked her off her board.

For Keiki Beach Park, the sideline sandbar sitting just to the right of the lifeguard tower at Pipeline, it was an otherwise typical day. With a fading north swell running, many of the world's best surfers were concentrated in a confined area—on Oahu's North Shore—battling for a scarcity of hollow barrels pouring through the lineup, and Jodie was caught in the middle.

California's Bud Llamas caught a good wave. Another rider blatantly took off in front of him. With the typical aplomb of a Huntington Beach local used to dealing with drop-in artists, Bud—an affable, popular U.S. National Champ—carved around the intruding surfer and continued riding in front of him. It was a common circumstance and ordinarily nothing to worry about. Only this was not Huntington Beach. And this was no ordinary surfer. It was Johnny Boy Gomes—one of Hawaii's best surfers—and one who commanded the most intimidating presence on the North Shore.

With menace that had become a trademark, Gomes shot his board at Bud's head, just missing a potentially severe contact. They both came up in the soup right next to Jodie Cooper, boards and cords tangled together. Immediately Johnny started punching. Everyone nearby scattered, knowing what was coming next. It was not something they wanted to witness. Experienced waveriders just put their head down and paddled away, avoiding the situation—and its consequences.

Jodi Cooper knew Johnny Boy—knew his positives and knew the dark side as well. But she knew his attack on Llamas was wrong, knew he should stop. "Oi, Johnny Boy, leave him alone!" She heard herself shouting. "Stop it, leave him alone; chill out." "He let go of Bud's hair, swung his board around, paddled over and whacked me in the head," she remembered. "Everyone just took off, no one stood up for me—every big surf star was out there—everyone saw it, but they didn't want to get smacked in the head themselves. He hit me and tried to humiliate me and said get out of the water."

Defiant in the face of physical assault, Jodie stayed out another half-hour catching several more waves just to salve her own pride.

For two years after that Gomes harassed her—on the beach, in the water, even in public spaces.

"If you act like a man, I'm gonna treat you like a man," Gomes told her. Once at the 7-Eleven in Haleiwa, he came up and threatened to kill her. Finally she'd had enough.

"The next time he confronted me was at Sunset car park and I lost it. I was yelling 'Are you going to stab me or are we going to deal with this?' I just let it rip," she confessed. "He didn't say or do anything and from that day on he left me alone. But it was a heavy two years."

Although this became a less frequent occurrence in the future, any female who confronts a dominating male in the lineup still takes a potentially dangerous chance—even when totally in the right.

Remembered as the best big-wave rider of her generation, Jodie Cooper had a late start to surfing, first learning on the solid beachbreaks around Albany, a small town on the remote southern tip of Western Australia when she was sixteen. "Three years later Jodie earned Rookie of the Year status and finished at number six in the world," wrote Reggie Elliss in *Surfing World Australia*. Cooper stayed on tour for eleven years, winning seven events, never finishing below fourth on the ratings. But the World Title always evaded her. Number two in 1985 ended up being her best result.

One of the first high profile surfers to come out as gay, Cooper fought her fair share of battles over the years. And that's on top of having to deal with a shark attack, a punch in the head from Johnny Boy Gomes and some pretty horrendous online bullying during her time as an event commentator. But she also had plenty of classic highlights like stunt surfing for Lori Petty in the Hollywood surf blockbuster *Point Break*.

"Jodie's energy and stoke made her very popular among both tour surfers and the public," wrote Nick Carroll for *Surfline*. "Sharp, intelligent and not afraid of a party, she was the first to cheer on a disheartened competitor—and there were a few of those in the 80s, when women pro surfers were held in high contempt by their male counterparts."

Cooper quit the world tour in 1994, having appeared in the Top 8 eleven times and, at twenty-nine, was the oldest woman to win an event.

After injuring her back, she retired in 2002 and moved to Bondi Beach in Sydney.

The *Jodie Cooper Award* (first awarded in 1999) is presented to the Western Australian Female Surfer of the Year. She was made a Life Member of the Association of Surfing Professionals in 1994 and in 2001 was inducted into the Western Australian Hall of Champions.

Jodie Cooper's run-in with Johnny Boy was not her last encounter with surf rage from a male. In 2019 a Sydney surfer was convicted of assaulting her in the water after cutting her off on a surf mat. The trial was divisive, but the overwhelming sentiment supported Cooper who had continued to be a beloved figure in Australian surfing culture. Her popularity comes from her courage and kindness—her candidness about her sexuality, and her willingness to stand up to the bullying that she finds untenable in today's world. Jodie Cooper has loved surfing. And like it or not, her rock music contemporary Pat Benatar reminded us all: "love is a battlefield."

Sharon Wolfe-Cranston certainly looked at the surf zone as a battlefield—and with good reason. One of the first damages she suffered was from a shark attack while surfing Patrick Air Force Base, near her hometown in Florida. "It tore off a good chunk of big toe," she attested. "I was on crutches for four weeks."

But that was just first blood. Johnny Boy Gomes gave Wolfe-Cranston a taste of male chauvinism just as he had Jodi Cooper. "He would take off on me, paddle in front of me, just hassle me in every way possible," she recalled. "And the surf was total junk—not even worth fighting about."

Wolfe-Cranston didn't run easily though. Most of her surf companions were male, friends from Florida she grew up with.

"I remember a guy paddling up to me and commenting 'You surf pretty well for a girl!'" she recalled. "I beat him in the next event."

She won the Girl's division in 79; that same year she took the U.S. Championships, and the World Amateur title in France the following year. Her streak continued, winning Junior's division in 81, the women's title in 82. Surf pundits were touting her as the next international star to emerge from the East Coast.

But in 1982 her mother was diagnosed with cancer.

"She had always been there for me," Wolfe said. "I felt I had to take care of her when she needed *me*." Unable to balance the responsibilities of parental care with the intensity of international competition, Wolfe dropped off the contest circuit for nearly six years. "I didn't party, I hardly surfed, I just had to do my duty," she explained. Her mother passed away when she was just twenty-four. Still fueled with the same passion she'd channeled as a teen, in 1988 she committed to a comeback. Supported by a crew of friends at Florida's renown surfboard brand Quiet Flight (who she felt listened to and respected her) Wolfe-Cranston worked together to craft winning board shapes. In 1991—more than a decade after winning national five titles—she won her sixth, in the women's senior championship event.

"Sarcastic and hilarious" by her friends consensus, she nonetheless could not have been "a nicer or more humble champion."

Purple Hearts, Friendly Fire

Competitive surfing can leave casualties on the battlefield. Tricia Gill's amateur career culminated in her selection as one of two women representatives of the United States at the 1984 amateur World Championships, where she placed second. But turning pro that same year, she received a hard wound. At the 1986 O.P. Pro Gill was eliminated by her coach and manager, former World Champion Debbie Beacham. It was her worst experience.

Gill hadn't caught her quota of four good waves and when Beacham saw a good one coming, she yelled for Gill to take it. Gill's performance would have clinched the victory. But the judges, unable to hear what had gone on between mentor and protege, ruled that Beacham had priority on the wave and Gill had committed interference in taking it.

"I thought, 'There goes my whole life,'" Gill said. "I just couldn't comprehend that I'd lost my biggest event—against Debbie—on an interference call."

On top of it all it had been her birthday. "I cried so long I couldn't believe it," Gill recalled. "I was devastated."

"It was such an unfortunate ruling," said Beacham, who was as disheartened as Gill.

At 5'1", Gill was one of the most diminutive women on the Pro Tour, but using her combined power and control, she cracked the World Tour Top 20 in 1990,

"She had a wonderful, unique style," observed Beacham. "She could put every part of her body into every move she made."

"I don't know if you could say I have a beautiful style," Gill reflected later, "but I like it and you can tell it's a girl's style. I like to look smooth but also real aggressive."

The Margo Slayers

Another battle brewed in the winter of 1981. Margo Oberg had been the most dominant force in women's pro surfing for more than a decade, winning an unprecedented number of events and three of the first five titles from the outset of the WPS rating system. But giants begat giant killers, and in the culminating events of the 1981/82 season, a number of young upcomers attempted to overthrow the queen. Rell Sunn dubbed them the "Margo Slayers."

They were an impressive assemblage:

The first challenger was Sharon Holland—the "Ozzette Machete"—a moniker given to for her aggressive competitive attitude in general and her big wave acumen in particular. Holland—no stranger to big Sunset Beach—made an immediate impact and continued to impress through four consecutive winters of North Shore big wave performances. A native of Australia's steel town Wollongong, home to many top surfers, she had no shortage of talent to study. Friendly on land, feisty in competition, Holland was just seventeen on her first visit to Hawaii. Her sheer determination lent an edge in larger waves—but not enough to take out Oberg.

Debbie Bowers, a striking 6' blonde from Eva Beach on Oahu's Westside, was Rell Sun's vote for Rookie of the Year among the young candidates for "Margo Slayer" status in the winter of 1981. In the Women's Masters, her very first contest—she took third place, appearing to be a serious threat. But working shifts as a cashier at the grocery store, and as a model for one of her sponsors, decelerated the momentum of her attack. A member of the Makaha Surf Club, Bowers was well-respected by the local community, always ready to help fundraise for a good cause. Riding mainly larger boards for bigger surf where she felt particularly at ease, she brought high hopes but was eventually unable to bring the aggression and acumen required to get herself beyond a top ten rating.

Winning both the Pro Trials and the Women's World Cup that winter, Cherie Gross established herself as a capable contender against Oberg. Her amateur career culminated with a 1978 U.S. Championship title before she turned pro. By the end of 1980 she was rated seventh in the world and looked like a legitimate opponent. But Gross opted not to travel the circuit in 1980 and 81. Her broad range of interests may have slackened her focus on the obsessive goal required to be a slayer in the pro ranks, and Gross explored a career in design and drama.

Although she was only sixteen years old in 1981 Pam Burridge was already being touted as a giant killer even then. She had been on a terror in Australia for eighteen months as the highest rated pro in the country. Pundits gave her solid odds to bring home the gold. But it was not her time yet either. Although destined for a World Title, she would have to wait until Margo retired from the scene before taking her rightful place on the throne. As Debbie Beacham asserted, "There was really only one woman who challenged Margo during her reign—Lynn Boyer." And despite Rell Sunn's fervent hopes, for the next two years no pretenders to the throne could snatch the crown from Margo Oberg's supremacy. Lynne Boyer had done it in 1978 and 79. It was one of surfing's greatest rivalries. But Boyer was the only one to best Oberg in her prime. Retiring after back-to back wins in 80 and 81 Oberg left the field of battle to a determined Debbie Beacham.

The Queen of Pleasure Point

Robin "Zuef" Hesson encountered another kind of fight—at a moment when she had the surrealistic experience of *being present at her own memorial service*. In

May 2013, her many supporters staged a paddle-out (a surfing tradition to honor the passing of a beloved surfer). As she stroked her way through the shorebreak, hundreds of friends expected it would be the last time they would see her. After two long and painful bouts with breast cancer, Hesson's friends and doctors saw the end of her twenty year battle as eminent. Hesson did not. "All of us are here to celebrate my life," she joked. "It's a reverse birthday."

"We called it Love Fest 2013," her friend Alayna Nathe said. "We thought she would just crash. But for four of five days after, she was wide awake and high off the experience. She called it *the best day of her life.*"

The woman everyone knew a 'Zuef' lived another two months—with the same strength and joyfulness she was renowned for.

Robin Janiszeufski Hesson was married to iconic big-wave rider Frosty Hesson, who had already lost his second wife Brenda. In his book *Making Mavericks* (later made into the iconic film *Chasing Mavericks*) he dedicated an entire chapter of his memories to Zuef. It was a true friendship that evolved into love.

"She was incredibly intelligent, and our exchanges became a little more interesting every time we had a conversation," her husband remembered.

With her distinctive mass of sun-bleached hair identifiable from the cliffs of Santa Cruz, Hasson became an icon of the 90s surf scene there. But it was her solid surfing style and wholehearted generosity that helped inspire a generation of younger women into the lineup.

Radio listeners knew her as the drive-time voice of the surfing reports on KPIG (107.5 FM). But her friends and neighbors in Pleasure Point knew her as an ever-present source of strength and comfort. Compassionate and kind, Hesson seldom addressed her cancer, preferring to focus on others instead.

"She rarely spoke about her *own* issues," said longtime friend Nell Newman, the president of Newman's Own Organic, and daughter of actor Paul Newman. "She always wanted to know how *you* were."

Working her entire career as a critical care hospital nurse in Oakland and Berkeley, she also volunteered for charitable programs like Ride-a-Wave. She loved playing music and singing, often with her good friend and neighbor Ashley Lloyd.

Amy Mihal, the co-owner of Village Yoga downtown, said Zeuf"s physical strength was an indication of a deeper reserve: "Yes, she was strong, but that physical strength had to come from somewhere. And with her, it was from a spirit that remained strong and pure, despite the pain that most of us would not be able to endure."

"She was a huge influence on my life," said Sally Smith-Weymouth, the owner/operator of the famed Paradise Surf Shop in the Pleasure Point area. "She was always there to help me focus on what was positive and what was good."

80s Ladies

Meanwhile up and down the coast of California new faces emerged—often as siblings. Liz Benavidez may be the only surfer inducted into the Redondo Beach Walk of fame whose first surfboard was shaped by her fellow inductee Pat Ryan. She might also be the first sister and brother duo who both competed in the professional surfing ranks; her sibling Mike Benavidez had a successful career in pro surfing as well. But Liz stood out so well because she fit in so well. Gregarious and determined, from the day she first surfed she ran with a pack of slightly older males who both nurtured and challenged her.

"Liz is the sweetest person in the world," said Jericho Poppler. "Unless you were in a heat against her!"

Concise and compact, with a radiant smile, Benavidez developed a powerful style, winning the prestigious Stubbies Surf Classic in her rookie year. She continued to rank in the top five on the professional tour through 1988. Benavidez's favorite contest wave was Sunset Beach, where she and her friend and former World Champ Kim Mearig frequently free surfed—with and against one another.

The only identical twins to surf professionally, Jorja and Jolene Smith were an effervescent duo who dominated the National Scholastic Surfing Association during the 1983 and 1984 seasons. Some referred to their two year reign as "Twins Peak." Raised in the burgeoning beach town of San Clemente, California, their mother was a fixture at Surfing magazine during their heyday. Jolene was a goofy-foot and Jorja a regular; their front-side stance when riding a wave was the easiest (and sometimes *only*) means of distinguishing one from the other. Ubiquitous and welcomed figures on the booming amateur surf contest circuit of California's go-go 80s, the twins brought a sunny, hometown disposition to the rapidly evolving surf culture when surf brands, flush with profits, saw sponsorships and support as worthwhile investments. Graduating to the pro ranks, they had solid performances in their years on the World Tour. With Jorja holding a top four position in the rankings and winning the circuit's opening two events in 1988, they were an inspiration for women looking to combine fun and career options.

Lynn Smith, another San Clementean with the same name but no relation—combined inspiration and innovation in a similar manner but focused it on art and business. The daughter of legendary water-polo coach Jimmy Smith she was in her own words, "raised in the water."

"My dad was inducted into the swimming Hall of Fame the same year as surf pioneer Tome Blake," she remembered. "The only vacation we ever took was to the beach."

In high school she became friends with Tom Morey and his wife-to-be Marcha, learning to body surf while her father took Stanford to a National Championship in water polo. Many women of the period were introduced to wave-riding through vacations to the beach. Families like Rosalie Burris's would rent a beach house in seaside towns like Encinitas for extended summer stays.

Moving to southern Orange County in 1971, Smith became friends with Shirlene Diamond (a future 1978 surf champion and colorful character in the West Coast surf scene) and through her soon met many of the era's surf stars—Darlene's husband Daryl Diamond, *Endless Summer* star Robert August and BC Surfboards owner Brian Clark. She was also friends with Tom and Pat Longo who were making Raisins swimwear.

"I designed some hats with an embroidered heart on it—and they were a hit," she remembered. "Then the owner of the Hobie stores Dick Metz started ordering from me and shortly after I started getting orders for 10,000 pieces."

Smith started Have-a-Heart, one of the first women's lines in 1978 and built a rep force and a thriving local business. But surfing with Tom Morey, Corky Carroll and surfboard factory owner Jeff Basham proved far more interesting. Smith became an art teacher in 2002, and married Basham in 2012. Her students included a dozen future surf champions, and her company inspired many to connect with the surf business. "It was fun while it lasted," she said of her own company, in 2020. "And *surfing* is *still* fun."

Other women leading the Orange County California attack were Missy Prior, Susan Davidson, Cathy Hawkins and Susan Mills.

But one woman surfer combined an impressive combination of progressive medicine, surfing and other watersports as well. Originally from Ohio, Lori Malkoff was accepted to the Pre-Med program at UC Irvine at sixteen years old. Introduced to surfing while earning a B.S. degree in Biological Sciences with cum laude and Phi Beta Kappa honors, she quickly fell in love with watersports, becoming a nationally-ranked athlete in swimming, water polo and surfing. Completing a Medical Degree at UC Irvine in 1985, Malkoff took post-doctoral training in Family Medicine. A sponsored surfing professional since 1989, she practiced Family Medicine for well over three decades, Certified by the American College of Sports Medicine as a Health and Fitness Instructor, Malkoff was one of very few Medical Doctors in the U.S. to be trained as a Feldenkrais Teacher and Practitioner but continued to compete occasionally in selective surf events.

Bright Northern Lights

"In the colder extremes around Santa Cruz, a group of women gained notoriety for their big waves and competition skills," wrote Kate McKnight in *Surfer* magazine in 1981. "Brenda Scott-Rodgers, Lynn Thomas and Laura Powers Noe are pushing their abilities on the most knarly of waves." Noe was described as a "classic throwback to her Malibu days," applying her surfing heritage to the set waves of Santa Cruz. Thomas was a threat to "win any contest she surfed in."

Brenda Scott-Rodgers was a particularly major figure in the Santa Cruz surfing community, a status she maintained for more than four decades. The daughter of "Doc" Scott, a legendary surfer and physician who was a pioneer in ear damage from surfing cold waters, her father designed Doc's Pro Plugs to protect the inner ear from the boney growths that result. Scott-Rodgers overcame Northern California's frigid water, powerful waves and macho atmosphere to become one of the city's most outstanding surfers in a town that produced an abundance of them. Although her two sisters and two brothers surfed, it was Brenda whose talent was immediately visible.

The Scotts' home on Lighthouse Avenue—just two blocks from top surf spot Steamer Lane—was a beacon for topflight international surf professionals throughout her early years. Dinners and happy hours were gatherings often referred to as "a surfer United Nations taking place in their front room."

"Brenda was like a big sister fellow Santa Cruz," remembered friend and local Karen Gallagher, who first left home by traveling with Scott-Rodgers.

Scott-Rodgers seemed to be drawn to all her father's aptitudes.

"Brenda was a powerhouse in big waves," observed two-time World Champ Lynne Boyer. At just twenty-one Scott-Rodgers won the 1978 World Cup in big surf at Sunset Beach, Hawaii and gained notoriety as International Surfing Professionals' prestigious Rookie of the Year.

"She was one of the early members of the women's professional ranks," noted Shannon Aikman who was a colleague in those years. "And she is one of the nicest, kindest, sweetest women in the world."

From the Scott's family compound she built a solid and respectable reputation. By 1981 she reached number three on the professional standings and excellence in big waves. But as early as 1979 Scott had recognized the need to create a means to support herself on tour and have something to fall back on once she had retired from professional surfing. Cofounding Hotline Wetsuits, she achieved not only an athletic legacy but an entrepreneurial one as well.

"This was at a time when, according to Brenda, the idea of women's wetsuits styles and models barely existed and women simply wore men's suits to surf," wrote Sally McGee in *Liquid Salt* magazine. "Brenda introduced Hotline to the U.S. market and for many years she was the surf industry's only female CEO."

Farther down south, San Diego's small-town surf culture found an epicenter in Ocean Beach where Paula Reynolds followed her surf pioneer father as a top competitor in WSA and WISA events from the late 70s–80s. "Paula was a strong, enthusiastic surfer," remembered her friend Cher Pendarvis, who spoke with Reynolds and other women athletes on a panel at Palomar College in 2019.

In San Diego's North County, other lesser-known talents like Swami's Surfing Club members Joyce Sisson and Diane Brummett-Hansen continued the tradition of the glory years in North County. Debbie Dicapua, a strong competitor from Oceanside placed third at the 1980 World Amateur Contest in France.

Yvonne Willette, Shelly Darrow and Sandy Hood stood out. Cynthia Foos, Patty Willis and Susie Stevenson drew "clean lines, co-existing with males in a harmonious atmosphere."

Body English

At the dawn of the 80s the British Isles came into their own. Like American blues music, Great Britain embraced surfing's boom almost immediately. But it was not until the Reagan years that "surfing went ballistic. In the UK, glossy full-color magazines like *Wavelength*, *Surf Scene* and *Carve* were launched, reflecting the growing popularity of surfing," the British Surfing Museum declared in 2015.

Like American Margo Oberg, British superstar Linda Sharp had a profound effect on the generation of young women coming into surfing in the late 70s and early 80s. "If she can do that, then so can I," thought upcoming talent like Eden Burberry, Shelly Matthews, Jill Moss and Arlene Maltman. And so they did. Moss became British Champion in 78 and 80, and Maltman in 84.

But Newquay star Eden Burberry was the outstanding example. So totally excited by the first WSLP event at Fistral Beach in Cornwall she later received some coaching from Sharp herself. Heavily influenced by Sharp's confident stance as an internationally recognized surfer, Burberry surfed with the top Newquay male surfers, always pushing her surfing to their level. She went on to claim five British titles and the European Championships in Portugal. It made her a superstar in Newquay, and a well-known name throughout Europe. Eventually drawn to the more powerful, warmer waves in the Canary Islands, she moved to Lanzarote where she continued to surf recreationally for many years. But Burberry will always be best remembered for her fluid and aggressive 80s style that set the standard for a new guard of European professionals.

Gallic Glory

Just across the channel surfing was experiencing an explosion of popularity in France brought on by the country's passion for individual sports and spurred by the invasion of Australian and American surfers drawn to the Basque coast for its plethora of waves and quality of life. An immediate attraction between the Anglo men and French women resulted in numerous marriages. It also helped stimulate the increased interest in surfing for women. Marie-Pascale Delanne married Tom Curren and in 1986 was runner up in the European Championships. Christine Sanford was a strong performance surfer as was Emmanuelle Joly who later won an ISA World Amateur Championship.

But it was Cathy Monge who went to the 1982 World Amateur event in Australia and placed ninth, remaining a force in French surfing matched only by the extraordinary streak of Anne-Gaëlle Hoarau, a French surfer from Réunion Island who dominated the French surf scene from the mid-80s to the mid-90s winning three ISA World Championships in 1986, 90, and 92.

Desperately Seeking Surfing

Madonna's 1985 film *Desperately Seeking Susan* was a trendy comedic thriller about mistaken identity and women's vulnerability. But it struck a chord for many independent women who identified as much with the stars of the movie as the roles being portrayed. The credibility and confidence of the early surf professionals was as important to the success of the fledgling pro organization as the experience or the positions these women held. Across the surfing world from California and Hawaii to France and Spain, there was a unified sense of opportunity.

"Women wanted pro surfing to work," Sandy Ordille declared. "There was a trust, a solidarity we all could feel." The early years of professional surfing were memorable, if for nothing else, the open camaraderie that bound the motley yet still intimate collection of competitors, judges, coaches and organizers together in the common goal of increased opportunity. Hope and promise filled the vocabulary among women's conversations at event after event, time after time. The material girls were stepping out over the borderline. They were coming out and willing to work hard for the money.

Somebody Bring Me
Some Water
1981–1992

*"Surely woman rose from the frothy sea, as resplendent as
Aphrodite on her scalloped chariot."*
— Margot Datz, *A Survival Guide for Landlocked Mermaids*

Shove Me In The Shallow Water
Before I Get Too Deep

Standing on the broad lawn of celebrated photographer Peter Beard's Montauk
Long Island simple shingled home, Rell Sunn and Jericho Poppler surveyed
the panorama—the sweeping ocean view; the sandy cliff at the lawn's end that
dropped fifty feet into the sea, avant-gard jazz floating in a cloudless summer
haze. Entering through the front gate (the words "Land's End" carved into its
wood) the crowd of Hampton millionaires, artists and surfers mixed like those
in a Pointillist painting or one of Beard's own works.

The scene seemed surreal for two women who had scraped together enough
savings to buy plane fare and were fighting it out for the $1000 prize purse which
would get them back home without over-drafting their bank accounts.

Perhaps the world's most celebrated photographer at the time, Beard was
married to Cheryl Tiegs who Sunn and Poppler had met that afternoon at the
Hampton Bay Classic surf contest; the first WSL event on the East Coast. She
had invited them back to a party at her home with Beard. Described as America's
first supermodel, Tiegs had already made multiple appearances on the covers of
the *Sports Illustrated Swimsuit Issue* and *TIME*; her 1978 "Pink Bikini" poster,
was even then an iconic image in pop culture.

On the first day of the 1981 Hamptons Bay Classic the number of New York
celebrities had the surfers star struck: Ralph Lauren strolled the beach with
a bevy of models. Iconic artist Julian Schnabel and proto-punk band Velvet

Underground's Nico cured their curiosity mingling with the surfers along with socialites and luminaries from the New York hipster scene.

With all the local Long Island star power on hand the sensation women surfers caused upon arrival surprised even the most jaded of paparazzi.

As had been the case almost everywhere they went, the women pros were huge attractions. Jericho Poppler and Rell Sunn were the most dazzling, the Irish Countess and Island Queen emitting their own mega-wattage. Feted by the local elites it was a week of champagne and lobster, esoteric jazz music and private art collections to rival the Louvre. "That trip was so wild!" Poppler recalled.

"For two surfer girls on a shoestring," Sunn conceded, "it was putting on the Ritz."

I Want What She's Having

The 80s was a heady decade. When the Go Go's released 1981's "Our Lips Are Sealed" (a straight-up story of lead guitarist Jane Wiedlin's affair with the lead singer of the Special's) the song climbed to number 20. Their album "Beauty and the Beat" was the first album by an all-girl band to hit number one in America where it stayed for six weeks. The 80s expanded brand-new roles on the silver screen—Meg Ryan's faux orgasm scene in *When Harry Met Sally* created one of filmdom's most memorable lines. "I want what *she's* having!" It was 1989—the first time that subject had ever been broached in mainstream film—and it became a touchstone statement about women's freedom for decades after.

Molly Ringwald became a star in the 1986 box office smash *Pretty in Pink*, and 1987's *Dirty Dancing* did the same for Jennifer Grey, portraying regular girls doing something extraordinary.

Television broke new ground too. Two of the most influential women-led sitcoms of the 80s—*Murphy Brown* and *The Cosby Show*, with Claire Huxtable—were dramatically modern characters. Their divergent dialogues about politics and social mores were eerily similar to the 80s culture wars. Huxtable's role centered on a working mother in an upscale black family; Murphy Brown—liberated, WASP and single—was a news anchor at a fictional CBS network TV news station. Despite their differences, they both significantly contributed to furthering women-led sitcoms as a genre—and the larger conversation about women, gender and ethnicity.

Surfing had its contribution to breaking stereotypes, even if in a small way. Sharon Schaffer may have done some extraordinary work as an actress and stunt double in *Star Trek: The Next Generation* and *Star Trek IV: The Voyage Home*. But where this vivacious goofy-foot Californian from Marina Del Rey truly broke new ground was as the first African-American female professional surfer in the United States. Astute and multi-talented, Schaffer was a role model for aspiring surfers of color everywhere.

The Kiwi Queen of Surf

It was not until the 80s that the wave-rich island nation of New Zealand produced a world class surf star—and it was as might be expected—a woman. Pauline Pullman dominated New Zealand surfing as perhaps no other Kiwi until the turn of the millennium—taking the first of six New Zealand Women's Surfing Championships and represented her home country at Four World Championships, placing fifth in the World at the 1982 event in Australia. Continuing to contribute to the Kiwi surf culture, she served as New Zealand's head judge, contest director, and was President of the prestigious North Coast Boardriders. With a Diploma in Architectural Technology, she helped build boats with Sir Peter Blake, and captained a 48' offshore sailing catamaran, exploring surf spots throughout the SW Pacific. In 2002, twenty-five years after her first championships, she won the ISA World Masters event.

Four on the Flor-ida

The "Reagan Years" saw the U.S. Eastern Seaboard once again in the forefront of the surfing world. Four Florida standouts from that decade were inducted into the East Coast Surfing Hall of Fame. Each of them had an exceptional story to tell, and unique achievements far beyond their surfing skill: overcoming crippling disease, earning a Master's degree in Mathematics, becoming the first National Champ from East Coast and founding a beloved women's organization.

Adele Fabe, two-time ESA East Coast Women's Champion (80 and 81) was a profile in courage. Competing in the Men's Division, Fabe pushed the limits of women's surfing in the process. While her dogged determination appeared to be her greatest strength, her cutting-edge surfing and dedication to training proved to be her not-so-secret weapon. An unfortunate injury in 1982 cut short a promising pro career. The next decade saw her battling CRPS, a disabling, painful disease. These challenges led to teaching disabled and military members to surf and later to founding CRPS/PAIN, the Adele Faba Foundation to help others with the crippling affliction. The subject of numerous films and museum exhibits for her contributions to surfing and charity, Fabe started the Women's Surfing Initiative, the largest archive on women surfers. She was featured in *Surfing Florida: A*

Photographic History published in 2014 and in 2015 WISA Women's International Surfing Association recognized Fabe—including her as a member working on future fundraising projects to further women's surfing. In 2020 she was inducted into the East Coast Surfing Hall of Fame.

Not many surfers become college professors, professional sand sculptors or Gold Medal winners in the World Surfing Games. Tall, talented and tack sharp, Christel Roever became all three. Beginning in 1982, Roever won the National Scholastic Surfing Association National title, and then the Women's ESA championships three years in a row in 83, 84, and 85 while leading the ESA All-Star team. In 1986 she added the U.S. Championships to her resume and later that year helped the U.S. win gold at the world games in England. "Christel had the discipline *and* the desire," observed Lisa Rosselli, a fellow competitor who went on the be a regional director. "When she really wanted it she got it." After earning a BS in Math Education from Florida Institute of Technology in 1986 she worked as a professional sand sculptor and competed in the World Championships in British Columbia three times.

"Christel was really smart," noted Lisa Rosselli, a college alumni herself. Roever returned for a master's degree in Mathematics at the University of Central Florida in 1995 and was then granted a professorship at Daytona State College. She still continued to surf however, founding the "Women of the Waves" event and winning the Divas division (35+) at the 2008 Sisters of the Sea Contest in Jacksonville. And in 2014 she was inducted into the East Coast Surfing Hall of Fame.

Isabel McLaughlin had one of the most passionate surf families of her era. Growing up in the Shortboard Revolution she and her three sisters lived in the water, fishing, water skiing, swimming and diving. Her sisters Cathy and Margaret competed at the local club pool where their oldest sister, Louise, lifeguarded. Their mom would take them to surf every day of the summer—along with girlfriends Joan Bailey and Lisa Scarborough—dropping them off in the morning and picking them up late in the afternoon. Starting at 10th Street, they then moved up to Crawford Avenue, and when good enough, honed their talents at Sebastian Inlet, amidst a tough pack of males.

Her first big win came at the Women's Division of the 1974 Florida State Championship in Daytona Beach. What was more remarkable was her win in the contest's Super Heat, which included the winners of all the other divisions, both women *and* men.

Qualifying for the East Coast Championships in Cape Hatteras along with younger sister Cathy, Isabel won the event with her sister finishing third. Both then qualified to surf in the 1974 U.S. Championship held in Cape Hatteras that year.

Isabel's historic win there made her the first East Coast women to ever win a U.S. title. Sister Cathy Baldwin finished sixth.

Meanwhile unbeknownst to Isabel, her sponsor Charley Baldwin entered her against the men in the inaugural 1988 ASP East Pro Tour. Baldwin nicknamed her "secret weapon." Under Baldwin's coaching ("yelling" she laughed) Isabel beat team riders at the National Kidney Foundation event and then went on to an equal ninth at the next ASP East event. She ended that year placing *an equal 17th on the ASP East Men's Tour.*

"The guys didn't like it, but I just did what I always did, surfed against the guys, like I did every day at The Inlet," she chuckled. "It's competitive, and I was used to proving myself."

Buoyed by competitive success, Baldwin encouraged McLaughlin to join the women's professional tour. Isabel decided to finish her education at the University of Central Florida instead, earning a degree in Biology. "I needed something more stable than surfing.

Baldwin went on the teach at her high school alma mater, New Smyrna Beach High School—and was nominated Teacher of the Year in 2004. Involved with charitable Women of the Waves events, Isabel remained an inspirational figure to young up and coming girl competitors, most notably World Champs Frieda Zamba and Lisa Andersen.

Debra Swaney was yet another of the great Jacksonville Beach surf community and memorable East Coast women. As a two-time U.S. Champion (1986–1988) and four time East Coast Champion (1985–1988) she competed in the 1988 World Contest and placed thirteenth.

Active in the surfing community leading the EPIC surf clinics for women, Swaney continued to surf after her competitive career finished, traveling frequently to her family surf house in Costa Rica. A founding member of Sisters of the Sea, she was inducted into the East Coast Surf Hall of Fame in 2018.

Sweet Dreams Are Made of These

Not everything in the 80s was about the contest circuit. Many enterprising women set off to surf destinations with no more than the packs on their backs. They established businesses, supported projects and invented careers.

Karen Gallagher got her first job at the fabled Santa Cruz surf maker NHS and learned how to patch dings on the side. But at seventeen, she took off with local Santa Cruz colleague Brenda Scott, following the pro circuit in Australia, then on to Hawaii. She was going to visit for a week. She stayed forty years.

A girl alone on the North Shore was not common in 1979. But Gallagher knew retail, could work with resin and surfed better than a lot of guys.

"After working at NHS the bad boys on the North Shore weren't that intimidating!" laughed Karen.

Being Waimea surf legend Fred Van Dyke's niece couldn't have hurt her odds either. Using her chutzpah and her uncle's reputation she wrangled a job in retail at the Sunset Surfboards shop in the Kammies complex right across the Kamehameha Highway from Sunset Beach.

Soon she was working at the Country Surfboards in Haleiwa too, both owned by surf entrepreneur Ed Searfoss. She bought the store from Ed in 1981, renamed it Sunset Beach Surf Shop and became a fixture on the north shore for the next fourteen years. Then, in 1995 her shop was unexpectedly robbed, the interior set fire and irreparably burned. Shocked, stunned and strapped for income Gallagher returned to Santa Cruz for a year to regroup with her daughter. But the siren call of the Islands brought her back the following season. Ed Searfoss once again gave her a job—this time in the Country Surfboards in Laie.

She also worked as a judge for the NSSA, Xcel wetsuits and Pipe bodyboard events too. A colleague pointed out that she was making "half what the guys doing the same work were making," she remembers. "So I asked the organizers why I wasn't getting the same pay as the guys," Gallagher told me. "And the next day they told me I was fired."

"That was not just the north shore, not just the surf industry, it was pretty much the whole world at that time," says Nancy Emerson who was hustling up work to surf in those days too. "You could take it or leave it, but you didn't buck it—if you wanted to stay employed."

Gallagher decided the most steady work was teaching surf lessons—which she continued to do until 2020. "Karen is one of the true independents," says Bernie Baker, a lifelong resident and legendary media maestro on the North Shore. "She has made a surfing life here—without fuss or fanfare—but she's really one of the mainstays in this area's surf history."

Wild Things Run Fast

California was hardly the only departure point for wave searchers. Two-time New York State shortboard champ Indy Callaway moved out from Long Island to San Diego and made a name for herself in the reefs and coves of La Jolla. She forsook her architectural degree to build the surf industry instead, managing the Pacific Sunwear surf shop in Orange County and top surf lensman Aaron Chang's photography business in the 90s.

"I learned to surf in beachbreak," Indy laughed. "I knew how to drop in and pull into a close out tube long before I had ever learned to surf a long point wave!"

New Jersey surfer Lisa Rosselli came out to California when, as the publisher of *Surfer* magazine, I drafted her as the East Coast editor.

"My parents were reluctant to buy a surfboard," Roselli told the audience at her induction into the New Jersey Surfing Hall of Fame. "They had been told by a respected family friend that surfers were a 'bad influence.'" "Looking at all my closest friends, and myself in the mirror," she told me later, "I realized they were—well, *mostly right*."

Attending college as a Marsh Scholarship recipient, Rosselli earned a reputation for her caustic but irresistible sense of humor.

Codirector of the Eastern Surfing Association's South Jersey District, and a lion of the venerable organization for four decades, Roselli started surfing in the sixth grade shortly after her parents bought a house at the beach in Wildwood Crest, the next beach down from Cape May, New Jersey. She met Joe Grottola and got her first surfboard when she was eleven. They married in 1988, and for the next thirty-five years never stopped surfing.

"We were so free in those days," Roselli said reflecting back. "We lived by a different set of rules and values."

Frank and feisty, Rosselli's commitment to good work matched her intelligence. In response to a 2002 article in *Blue Crush* by Sam George, Rosselli wrote a retort saying most men love to surf with women. It was published in *Time* magazine, then the most important publication in the world. "Sam made it sound like men don't really like to surf with women," Rosselli said. "I wanted to set the record straight."

An art teacher for twenty-five years in the New Jersey School System, Rosselli became an icon for her service to the ESA as well. "When I was a little girl I chose surfing as my life, and surfers as my family," she remarked at her induction into the New Jersey Surfing Hall of Fame in 2018. "And I can't thank you enough for choosing me back."

Floridian Melody DeCarlo was older when she started surfing, but it didn't keep her from winning a "Betty's Series" contest started by East Coast pioneer and surf organizer Kathy Anderson, a hero of DeCarlo's.

"When I first started competing I had younger women say, 'I can't believe you're still surfing at thirty!' joked DeCarlo. "Now, half the surfers in the water are over that age."

In 2016, Melody DeCarlo (who served for a decade as President of the Florida Surf Museum and produced dozens of local charity events like Surfing Santa) received the Surfer of the Year award given to the "one lady who has continuously gone above and beyond with her community both in and out of the water." In 2019, DeCarlo—proving it is never too late to start surfing—placed first at the regional Water-man's Challenge in the Women's Longboard Over-Fifty division.

"Once surfing gets hold of you, it becomes your life," Melody declared.

That sensibility—of surfing for the pure joy of it—has been a stronger pull on the women's side than the men's.

If lifestyle is truly a key component of surfing's appeal it started very early in the modern era. Dreama Carroll was a cliff diver at the Falls at the top of Waimea Valley when she started surfing in Hawaii. "A lot of the media never saw how good she was," Karen Gallagher told me in 2020. "She was a regular fixture in the Sunset Beach lineup for decades." The wife of shaper Tim Carroll and mother of former pro Nathan (whose Sunset performances were considered exceptional) Dreama personifies the intricate involvement in a total life based around surfing. She even took up foiling—the controversial and exhilarating hybrid of surfing and hydrofoil technology, foil surfing replaces the traditional fin at the bottom of a surfboard with a much longer, hydrodynamically designed fin called a blade. "Dreama is so immersed in wave-riding she even mastered a new development like foiling," Gallagher marveled, "in her *fourth decade* of wave-riding!"

Returning from a decade in Hawaii, Hawaiian Women's Bodybuilding Champ Allison Brundage caught the attention of Sunset riders when she appeared seemingly out of nowhere to ride what in the 80s was considered impressively sizable waves. Using her own diet and workout regimen designed for peak competitive performance in sports, she made rapid progress in an era when cross-training was not yet widely understood.

On Maui, Melissa Proud won the 1887 U.S. Championships and made the American World Amateur team and the following year she was chosen along with one other woman to represent the USA on the World Amateur Surf Team, an honor that "was one of the highlights of my life."

"Melissa was another one of the Takayama team members, mentored by Donald, who were so dominant for so long," said her contemporary Jeannette Prince. "She was an L.A. champion and Maui and Oahu too."

In 2008 Proud had been crowned by her Maui Surfer Girl peers as the "Queen of Honolulu," riding 12 foot waves and long hollow tubes. Her performances earned her a wild card spot at the Billabong Pro Maui, competing on the Pro Tour with the world's best professionals.

In Australia Carley Smith took enough late drops and deep barrels to earn a reputation as a star along the cobbled points of the East Coast. Renee Hyman, whose famous shaper father Nev helped guide her though the winding points of Queensland, was equally distinguished. Leann Gervais from Canada made a name for herself in the Vancouver Island region.

On the Eastern seaboard a similar scenario was unfolding: Floridian Kira Shepparo ranked number one three years in a row in the Eastern Surfing

Association's Central Florida division. Florida transplant Nicole Grodesky who had moved to California, proved the adage that Eastern surfers needed to cross coasts to build a career where the media would take notice.

Florence and the Machines

Fathers are universally mentioned when surfers credit their mentors. But are mothers as important a component to success? Alex Florence—a longboarder, skater, model and dirtbiker, who would become a world traveler, single mom, college graduate—would test the question.

Growing up on America's East Coast, watching movies like *Beyond Blazing Boards* (about surfing's evolution during the mid-80s) and surfing with her brothers and sisters in oversized wetsuits, Alexandra Helen Florence decided she was "going to be one of *those* girls."

Maverick by nature and surfer at heart, Florence took a daring (her parents would call it *dangerous*) journey attempting to find success using the rare combination of passion, luck, and chutzpah.

At sixteen, the starry-eyed New Jersey surfer girl loaded a backpack, skateboard and a few hundred dollars and flew to Hawaii. Hitch-hiking from Honolulu to Haleiwa, she was picked up by a nineteen-year-old girl, and—on the drive across the island—offered a job as an extra on *North Shore*, a Hollywood production which would eventually become a cult film among the surfing population worldwide. It would be the beginning of a series of lucky breaks which created a family dynasty.

Arriving as a young, attractive, free-spirit, Florence and was quickly swooped up into the lifestyle she had always dreamed of. Taken in by the locals as one of their own, she moved to Kauai for a year, then decided to explore Indonesia, hopping a ferry from Bali to Lombok, ending up in Garjagan where she contracted such a severe case of malaria, she was forced to return home.

Her wanderlust would not be stilted. Shortly after recovery, she took a job on a cruise ship. After cruising the Caribbean for six months she traveled on to Europe with the man in the triad. After months of traveling with a friend they became lovers—and John-John was born in 1990. They remained a couple and Florence bore two more children. When the relationship eventually ended she move back to Oahu.

Uncertain and struggling financially, a sense of exhilarating freedom and future opportunity nevertheless motivated her life path. Florence remembered—as journalist Derek Rielly wrote—"driving her Valiant, the ex-husband gone, John, five, Nathan, three, Ivan, a baby at one-and-a-half, looking over at her little boys and saying: 'What do you guys want to do? We don't have to do anything or be anywhere? We can stay out till 10:30! We can go to thrift stores!'"

Within the next two years Herbie Fletcher, a pioneer of Jet skis in the surf, began towing a young John-John into Pipeline waves—at the age of seven. Over the next decade a bevy of Pipeline legends would help the Florence boys enter the Pipeline lineup.

But Alex Florence had more than surf on her mind. Exploring her dreams once again, she acquired student loans and "in the late aughts," went to night school for a degree in English Literature. "As time went by" middle son Nathan devoured her class reading lists as she brought books home. From their rented house at Rocky Point near Sunset Beach, Florence took in boarders, frequently as many as ten at a time, squeezed into their three bedrooms—anything required to remain in their home and keep the family fed.

Mom Becomes Mom-John

As John-John's reputation grew, Florence acquired the moniker Mom-john, initially used by water photographers Darren Crawford and Todd Messick. Others started referring to the quiet mother as Mom-john because although Florence was always surfing and on the beach with the boys, no one actually knew her name.

Even though Florence has always disliked the alias, after ten years she opted to simply embrace it. "Kind of how you would deal with a bully at school," Florence explained.

Modest and soft-spoken, Florence succeeded as a working and surfing mom, keeping her family close and instability at a minimum. But in 2000, when her landlord returned to inhabit her home himself, she suddenly found herself vulnerable and without a secure abode for her family.

Once again luck and chutzpah seemed to enter the picture. While out on a stroll with John-John (now a precocious ten-year-old) contemplating their potentially dire circumstance, she saw her *real* dream house right at Pipeline. Believing fortune favors the bold, Florence stopped to ask the owner about the home's availability and found herself serendipitously ensconced at the most coveted location in the surfing world—directly in front of Pipeline.

Over the next two decades her sons would go on to become top Pipeline riders, John-John winning two back-to-back WSL World Championships in 2016 and 17 and the consensus choice as successor to Kelly Slater. By any measure Florence was a successful mother raising a family. In the surfing world she was successful at raising a dynasty.

What I Am

The 80s were characterized by both advancement and backlash for women. Social issues like reproductive rights and affirmative action were in retreat. But by 1984, half of undergraduate college degrees were being awarded to women, and women were earning 49 percent of all master's degrees and about 33 percent of all doctoral degrees.

By decade's end women were filling even more roles that had previously been men's domains. Melissa Ethridge's 1988 chart-topping "Somebody Bring Me Some Water" was a passion-powered torch-torrent, proof that the new female cadre of hard-rocking singer-songwriters could match any man in the genre.

"What I Am," Eddie Brickell's 1988 breakout hit was the lyric of the era—existential, self-effacing and casually decadent. The band's folky jazz sound was a breath of fresh air for those recovering from a decade of big-hair bands. It fit the times and the general mood of the women's surfing movement.

As east coast surf legend Ella Chalfant reminded everyone in her famous soliloquy: "When you paddle out, everything is both forgotten and remembered. I will never forget all the memories and lessons I have had and learned," Chalfant noted. She started surfing in 1967 and "never stopped since," she said, ending with her most memorable line: "You can't buy happiness, but you can buy a surfboard."

"Which," as Lisa Rosselli adamantly added, "is *almost as good*."

Just A Girl

Feminine Mystique Reaches Its First Destination

1993–1999

"The most courageous act is still to think for yourself. Aloud."
—Coco Chanel

Nothing Compares to You

The 20th Century's last decade was a powerful testimony to how far women's surfing has come. In the cusp of the new millennium, new benchmarks were set. Women paddled into huge waves and were towed into even bigger ones. One courageous star even learned to excel using just a single arm.

Sometimes, the most powerful path forward in an unjust world is letting it all out.

California beach girl Gwen Stefani decked herself out in clothes as sports-functional as they were sexy and sang about the very limits placed upon her as a woman fronting an all-male band in No Doubt's "Just a Girl."

Fortunately some doors *unlocked* in the surf world: *Wahine*, the first all-women's surf magazine, was launched by Elizabeth Glazner and Marilyn Edwards. The first all-woman's surf shop, Ilona Wood's Water Girl, opened in Encinitas, California in 1995. That same year And Isabelle "Izzy" Tihanyi opened Surf Diva, the first all-women's surf school in La Jolla, California.

In 1997 the East Coast Wahine Championships debuted in Wrightsville Beach, North Carolina; Las Olas surf camp for women was founded near Puerto Vallarta by Bev Sanders.

Doors in more mainstream areas started to find keys as well. Before Ellen DeGeneres was the host of a popular talk show, she was the goofy, slacks-wearing heroine at the center of her own television series *Ellen,* a beloved sitcom—but it became a legendary one when, on April 30, 1997, DeGeneres's character came out as a lesbian, to an audience of forty-two million. Two weeks before, DeGeneres herself had come out with a *Time* magazine cover and the headline, "Yep, I'm Gay," and then spoke about her sexuality on Oprah.

The O.J. Simpson trial was a reminder that rich, powerful men—with good lawyers—still wielded the dominating force in society. And while women made progress, the specter of ice skater Tanya Harding's brutal, envy-fueled attack on Olympic hopeful Nancy Kerrigan was a tragic reminder that women could be bad too. Surfing set a much higher standard. "Don't Think With Your Dick" was the title of Jodi Cooper's first and only surf magazine article in 1994—and (to use an appropriate phrase) it pulled no punches.

In the mid-90s a charismatic young surfer rose to the top of the competitive field. She would set a new paradigm for performance, style and feminine mystique. In her era nothing compared.

Runaway Champion
Lisa Andersen Dominates the 90s

When Lisa Andersen ran away from home at sixteen years old, she left a note to her mother saying she was going to become the women's world surfing champion. Unsure if such a title even existed, her overriding desire to break free from her restraints drove Andersen's determination to aim for dreams still unclear but all-consuming. Fueled by her passion for wave-riding she went west hoping to find the answers that had eluded her in her Florida hometown.

Born March 13, 1969 in New York, Andersen learned to surf at Ormond Beach at age thirteen. Her parents thought surfing was to blame for her school truancies, bad grades and other teenage troubles; her father going so far as to break one of her surfboards. It was the culminating act that drove Andersen to cross the country to Huntington Beach. She worked part-time as a waitress and slept wherever she could—sometimes in less-than-ideal situations.

"When Lisa first came on the scene she had to be 'groomed' for a while," noted an earlier top pro Nancy Emerson. "She was untamed—but committed in the deepest way."

"Of course I was a little wild," admitted Andersen. "*I was sixteen.*" As she crashed onto the scene rising like a tsunami, Andersen allowed herself to be *groomed*. But not *tamed*.

Her raw talent was noticed by people along the way—people who took her surfing, mentored her, and entered her into contests.

"My big break came with Quiksilver," she remembered. "I begged Bruce Raymond (the International President of the brand) for just a plane ticket." Raymond bought her a flight and put her up at his family's house.

"While I was there, with all the Quik bigwigs watching I won the contest. That was my real start."

After one successful year as an amateur, she turned pro at age seventeen and won the World Pro Tour's 1988 Rookie of the Year award. Once on the Pro Tour, she remained in the top ten of the rankings for several years but was unable to reach the ultimate title.

Then came her first child—daughter Erica in 1994—an experience so empowering for Andersen it seemed to catapult her into a league of her own. Nothing seemed to stand in her way competitively after that. From 1994 through 1997 she won four consecutive world crowns. In 1996, she was the first female in fifteen years to be featured on the cover of *Surfer* magazine. She won the *Surfer Poll* award six times and was named one of the "25 Most Influential Surfers of all Time." *Sports Illustrated* also named her one of the "Top Female Athletes of the 20th Century."

"Women's surfing *IS* Lisa Andersen," stated former world champion Pauline Menczer in 1997 after Andersen's fourth title. "The rest of us might as well not even be here."

As if to prove Menczer's accuracy, Andersen was featured on the cover of *Outside* magazine, the world's largest sports publication, with a full profile inside.

"Pauline was one of my favorite competitors," Lisa said in an interview for this book. "We would actually cheer each other on in heats we had," she laughed. "She was fierce but so fun."

In the period Andersen began her assault on the World Title, she began dating (and would end up marrying) Brazilian Renato Hickel, the WSL senior judge. While no one doubted her superior talent, it ostensibly held the appearance of conflict of interest—especially if you were competing against her. Hickel recused himself from judging her heats and ultimately withdrew from the women's events completely, becoming Andersen's coach and manager.

For four years Andersen's ascent seemed unsurmountable. But in July of 1998 Andersen herniated a disc in her back, which plagued her all year and continued to be a problem for the rest of her career.

Andersen's influence in women's surfing history extends far beyond contest results. Her powerful, stylish surfing, natural look and innate charisma were irresistible to the surf world—and to Quiksilver who sponsored her in the early 90s. Needing suits that were functional and fashionable, Lisa helped design a women's style of boardshort, which launched the Roxy brand.

"In the four decades of professional surfing not one other woman has had the impact Lisa did," said Jodi Wilmott, a former pro and longtime World Tour executive. "She didn't just change people's perspective, she *stylized* the image of women surfers." But her success was not always matched by monetary reward. "I never made that much money," Andersen said. "People think I was making huge salaries, but the reality was I lived paycheck to paycheck."

In 2001 Andersen had another child, Mason, and in 2005 she became the global brand ambassador for Roxy, which allowed her to become a coach, businesswoman, enforcer of contest guidelines and still be a mentor to the women on the Pro Tour and aspiring girl surfers all around the world.

"The generation she influenced weren't looking for a leader, they were looking for a dream," Wilmott explained. "Lisa had so much mystery, just by being reserved. That allowed her followers to envision surf life for themselves, any way they wanted it."

Her second marriage—to former professional baseball player Tim Shannon in 2008—was covered by *People* magazine. Her visibility rose, her privacy was bruised.

In 2019 she was given the Silver Surfer award at the California Surf Museum's Annual Gala alongside her good friend and mentor three-time World Champ Tom Curren.

Andersen shared similarities with her friend and colleague Curren, who, like Lisa, dominated the top levels of both competition and free surfing. Both were lone Americans holding the pinnacle positions—surrounded by Australians who ran like a leap of leopards pinning all of the next five rankings.

"In 1995 and 1996, the USA's Lisa Andersen was the peerless world champ, wrote Nick Carroll, a peerless surf journalist himself. "But second, third, fourth and fifth—were Australians." They were an impressive septet: Layne Beachley, Pauline Menczer, Neridah Falconer, Lynette Mackenzie, Kylie Webb, along with Michele Donoghue in 95 and Trudy Todd in 96.

In this period a group of the young hot male surfers, most-notably eleven-time World Champ Kelly Slater, became known as the Momentum Generation and were made immortal on the silver screen by a 2018 film of the same name. Andersen and this crew who competed against her in the 90s, were their counterparts.

Kylie Webb, touted in her early years as the next Australian sensation, and considered a potential threat to Andersen's dominance, surfed brilliantly in small and medium surf yet was never able to excel in bigger waves and eventually quit the tour at the height of Lisa's reign.

Neridah Falconer—who came from Macksville, a small village of eight hundred in northern New South Wales—was a fighter when it came to jockeying for waves with the boys. "I've never kissed anyone's arse to get what I have," she told Alison Smith, in *Surfing Girl* magazine. "There are battlers out there and I'm one of them."

There was no denying the fierceness of Falconer's determination. In 1996 she took first place in the amateur World Surfing Games. She won the prestigious

Triple Crown title in 2002 against Hawaiians in sizable surf. But she got into a post-heat shoving match at a contest in South Africa in 2001 with fellow Australian Lynette Mackenzie. No stranger to physical confrontations, Mackenzie had engaged in other altercations and was known for her explosive temper. She'd been ranked number three on the Pro Tour in 1994—the same year Lisa Andersen won the first of her four consecutive titles. A competitor with a string of titles, she was nipping at Lisa's heels. But in 1999 just two years before her incident with Falconer, Mackenzie had been involved in another highly public fight, becoming the first surfer in the women's division to ever be fined and sanctioned for violence at a WSL event. "What sets you off?" an interviewer asked her. "Just about everything," she retorted.

Trudy Todd prowled between third and fifth place during Andersen's entire winning streak, capturing the Triple Crown in 1999 and nearly toppling Lisa's last title run.

Other women made waves: Alessandra Vieira won the World Amateur Title at the International *Surfing* Association (ISA) games in 1994 and 1998 respectively, as did Kathy Newman in 1990. Belinda Hardwick (nee Godfrey) from Australia's Mid-Coast region scratched into the top sixteen ratings after winning numerous events as an amateur and then taking the 2000 Rookie of the Year award. Chris Zeitler, a UCSD University graduate from San Diego was a top California competitor.

Perhaps the most dramatic entry in this era was Brazilian Maria "Tita" Tavares, who began surfing at five on a board carved out of a discarded wooden door and was still riding it when she entered her first contest three years later. A prodigy in small surf, Tavares was raised in Titanzinho, a small fishing village on the eastern horn of Brazil; at nineteen she captured the Pan American amateur championship. By 1999—her first year on the world tour—she would finish the season at number six and be named Rookie of the Year. Slender and flashy, she was one of the first females to regularly complete aerial maneuvers successfully. Christened the "Brazilian bombshell" by journalist Carol Hogan, the diminutive Latinx would peak in 2000 at number four on the world ratings.

Hawaii fielded exceptional talent as well. In 1997 surfer model Malia Jones graced the cover of *Shape* magazine and followed up with a two-page spread in *People* magazine's "50 Most Beautiful People" issue. The mainstream attention and acknowledgment served notice that a genuine movement was in process: the rise of the *new surfer girl*.

But like other mega-stars before her, "Lisa Andersen blocked out the sun for other women of her era," contended Jodi Wilmott. "She was like a total eclipse, inadvertently taking the whole spotlight. All eyes focused on her."

Good looks, natural talent and strong will are not faults, but they could be troubling, nonetheless. "I used to wonder 'Why do I feel so guilty' for my accomplishments," Andersen recalled thinking. "Other people have demons. *I am my own private demon.*"

The attention may have been excessive, but her opponents were equally intense. Layne Beachley and Pauline Menczer were testimony to the competition Andersen faced—both became World Champs soon after her retirement.

And Andersen was an exception, not only in talent but in level of support. Discounting Andersen's ground-breaking lucrative contract with Roxy, these other women, all Australian, were still struggling in the mid-90s to earn an adequate living from their professional career path. Layne Beachley became her most consistent adversary—a fearsome competitor, equally driven. Coming in twice as runner up, Beachley and Andersen's rivalry was one of the fiercest in competition history.

As much as any athlete of her generation, Andersen's performances and career have remained essential maps, blueprints and touchstones, setting standards by which we measure how deep a woman's emotional barriers can pushed, or how much invention her career can contain.

Her back injuries, the intense level of competition and her sometimes personal uncertainty kept her humble nature intact. In 2019 Andersen had another back surgery and went back to her home town in Florida contemplating a permanent move back to Ormond Beach. "As they say," Lisa laughed, 'You can take the girl out of Florida, but you can't. . . .'"

Throughout the late twentieth and second decade of the 21st Century she was one of the most powerfully charismatic surf stars of record, the indelible voice of a female juggernaut, whose longevity prevailed past every major difficulty celebrity can create. Andersen's shadow flickers across each new advance, seemingly at every turn.

The entirety of surfdom seems to have acknowledged her influence. As her successor, Layne Beachley knew her intense competitiveness. But with respectful generosity, arch-rival Beachley defined Andersen's largest contribution: "Lisa Andersen made it OK to be a strong, beautiful woman in a man's world."

From 1994 to 1997 and Andersen surfed hard and fast, and ushered in another change to her sport—the move away from bikinis to board shorts. "Bikinis have a tendency to fall off," Andersen said. "I've lost many a suit and still do, which is no good when you're free-surfing and no good at all in a heat. Technical problems are the last thing you want in a competition."

As Lisa was ascending the contest ranks, she used whatever men's boardshorts she felt were lucky or functional. Quiksilver sponsored Andersen in 1992 and that allowed Lisa to cherry-pick boys shorts from the warehouse. But she needed something better: "I think how Roxy came about is I noticed other girls wearing boy's long 'boardies' in Hawaii—I knew what I needed and saw that other girls might need them too. It all grew from there."

Lisa was "a human pincushion" at first, working with Roxy president Randy Hild to adjust scalloped-leg Quiksilver boardshorts to find the right length to ward against wax rash, but also be comfortable, functional, and suited for a woman's body.

"In 1995 I was the Roxy poster child as the World Champion and it just exploded from there," Andersen said.

"I guess we were right, there was a need out there for trunks for women that were functional and feminine. They say that Roxy saved the surf industry, or at least launched the whole women's era. It's a multi-million dollar business which was shocking to me and still is, but I am proud of how Quiksilver and Roxy and Randy Hild and I collaborated to develop something we thought was needed."

"The lifestyle, fashion, and healthful attractiveness of women's surfing has come of age because of women like Lisa simply being herself and doing what comes naturally. Roxy grew to a 750 million dollar brand—bigger than all the men's brands," said Randy Hild, who was Roxy's first President. "But," he adds, "just like the women themselves, the achievements often went unnoticed."

Writer and champion surfer Cori Schumacher credits Andersen with popularizing the "board short," which boosted the industry and led to more attention for female surfers and athletes: "This shift ignited a wildfire of all-girl surf schools, girl surf movies, and female surf lifestyle clothing lines across surf brands."

Roxy was certainly not the only surf company to sponsor women, but it was the most coveted. Quiksilver had started the brand in 1990—the first extensive, fashion line of surfwear made specifically for women—and established an official Roxy team a few years later. The first member was four-time world champ Lisa Andersen.

Before Roxy, wetsuits custom tailored to women were practically nonexistent. Andersen, who'd worn men's board shorts and wetsuits early in her career, had demanded better gear, designed for the female form. Roxy obliged with what were essentially smaller versions of men's wetsuits, cut to similar tailoring.

The year 1992—also known as "The Year of the Woman"—made great strides in politics. It saw the election of four women to the U.S. Senate—Barbara Boxer, Dianne Feinstein, Carol Moseley Braun (the first black woman elected to the Senate) and Patty Murray. A year later, Janet Reno became the first woman to serve as United States attorney general.

Alanis Morissette's 1995 album *Jagged Little Pill* exploded the myth that women couldn't be rich, wild and wondrous all at the same time. Her collection of songs released on Maverick Records showed women as strong street-smart survivalists. That same year Sarah Gerhardt charged thirty-foot Mavericks, verifying that surfing women were of that same gritty grace.

Women's surf opportunities flourished across the board in this new decade. Although the International Surfing Association was re-organized in this period, there were still some outstanding women who were lesser known than their contemporaries who became huge stars.

As the 1990 Amateur World Champion, Kathy Newman surfed some of the best swells in the world—and against some of the finest surfers. But there is one wave she couldn't wait to ride: Australia's first gay and lesbian surf contest. Newman had gone on from her World Amateur title to a respectable pro career. But the Coastout Festival at Coffs Harbor was one of personal pride.

"It is acknowledging that gay men and women not only surf, but that they can be very competitive in the water," Kathy said.

Alessandra Vieira considered Brazil's first great modern pro, won the 1994 ISA World Amateur Champion at fourteen.

Brazilian Alcione Silva, the 1998 ISA World Amateur champ became a surf coach in her native country. She had trained with some of Brazil's top male competitors and when she left the circuit she joined them in the elite school to help the next generation advance.

"There was the whole 90s boom in the surf world," explained Serena Brooke, whose career paralleled the peaking economic expansion. "There was the Hollywood aspect with *Blue Crush*. There was the women's boardshort revolution with Roxy. We started getting stand-alone events on the World Championship Tour. The world was thriving economically at that point, there were a lot of girls-only surfing magazines as well."

The 90s was the first decade where women could not only grow but prosper as well. It would set the stage for the new millennium and unprecedented changes to come.

A League of Their Own

Contests, Camps, Shops, and Factories

The 90s

"The most alluring thing a woman can have is confidence."
—Beyonce

Boomtown

Mary Hartman was hardly the starstruck type. But when *Mick Jagger* walked into her store, she admitted, "you tend to notice."

Hartman, who had just opened her landmark women's surf shop Girl In The Curl, had plenty of reservations when she entered the retail business in 1997. But any misgivings Hartman had about establishing one of the first girls-only "core" surf shops were laid to rest after receiving a call from the concierge of a nearby resort hotel, warning that a VIP was on the way to her Dana Point, California, store. "Don't tell your staff or call your friends," the concierge admonished.

"Of course the minute we hung up I started screaming to my staff and calling every friend I knew!" Hartman laughed.

"Jagger was in my store for forty-five minutes with his daughter, her nanny, and a bodyguard standing outside the door," recalled Hartman about the encounter. "It was all about his daughter. He spent 500 dollars on her. And he bought a sarong for himself. I asked him if he would wear it onstage. He said it would fall off." Surf chic had arrived center-stage.

The boom that hit the surfing world in the 90s was not like upticks in prior periods—where women were allowed to compete, or organizations were formed—but where women were still an adjunct afterthought added to placate those who were willing to speak out.

The surge of the 90s spread across every facet of surf culture from women's exclusive surf shops like Hartman's to women only surf camps, clothing brands

(beyond bikinis) and even surfboard manufacturing. Competitive events accelerated as well.

Often some of these were interwoven, moving several facets forward simultaneously. In February 1990 an historic event occurred at Pipeline: for the first time
ever, a group of women got to ride waves there all by themselves. The performances
were eye opening to many who had never seen women ride the place. Billed as
the first annual World Championship of Women's Bodyboarding the event was
organized by Hawaiian big wave bodyboarder Carol Phillips.

No newcomer, Phillips had been the first woman to compete against the men
at the Banzai Pipeline, the founder of the North Shore Surf Girls Surf School was
appointed in 2005 to a four-year term on the Hawaii State Commission on the
Status of Women by the Governor of the State of Hawaii. "My mother raised six
kids and was a really wonderful influence," she said. "I grew up believing I could
do what I wanted, that there were no limitations to being a woman."

In that same year, WISA president Mary Lou Drummy put together an
eight-contest circuit for 100 active members, but over the next few years lack of
sponsorship continued to be a challenge.

This issue—of professional athletics and lack of sponsorship in women's
sports—became the storyline of a popular film. Bolstered by an impressive cast,
including Tom Hanks, Madonna, Rosie O'Donnell and Geena Davis, *A League of
Their Own* became a phenomenon of its own, grossing over $107 million. The 1992
box office smash succeeded in educating a global audience about an unprecedented
gender experiment in the male-dominated history of baseball.

Meanwhile, amateur competition was flourishing, particularly on the East Coast.
Establishing a contest structure driven by amateurs who operated like professionals,
the Eastern Surfing Association was gaining the reputation as the most efficient
surfing federation in the world, running hundreds of events and adding thousands
of members. Although founders Doc Couture and Cecil Lear were the tireless and
talented leaders of the multi-state coalition of local districts, the organizing aptitude
was more often found in women like Lisa Rosselli, Pam Hill, Laura Bren, Kathy
Phillips, and in particular, the late great Betty Marsh. Neither Couture nor Lear
ever shirked from offering praise for their directors. "The women directors are the
heart of the organization," Lear assured any journalist who would ask. "You can't
give them enough credit. No women, no ESA. Simple as that."

Of the 25 districts comprising the ESA, nearly three quarters are directed or
co-directed by women. Michelle Sommers, ESA's 2020 executive director or Amy
Rose (whose uniquely named district is *Southern North* Carolina) coordinated with
Virginia's Jeanine Montgomery to put on events rivaling rock concerts or car races
for the complexity of logistics. In the 90s girls flocked to the contests creating an
atmosphere resembling tailgate parties at national sports arenas.

Surfing magazine editor Nick Carroll traveled east to provide the most extensive championship coverage of the decade as Jennifer Pulaski took the ESA Women's crown in 1996.

The "good-natured but intense rivalry" between ESA districts "created epic competitive clashes" barely known outside the byzantine district clans that operated more like the Iroquois Confederacy than the National Football League: When I-5 Hurricane Floyd postponed The Easterns for the first time in thirty-two years, North Carolina's Sarah Willis upset Jamie Dewitt in the Girls Division; Florida answered back via Junior Women's champ Kelly Hutchinson, giving the crowd entertainment worthy of a Wimbledon tennis match.

But the dedication to the organization, the zealous, selfless work done by the women of the Eastern Surfing Association was always in a class by itself—and the contests, camps, shops and factories that evolved during the 90s became a league of its own.

But the third-wave feminism that this decade has come to be remembered for was a contradictory experience at the time. It was, on one hand, all about girl power and sex positivity. The 90s were full of shows about superhuman women—*Buffy the Vampire Slayer, Charmed* and *Sabrina the Teenage Witch.* Women could offer reason as well as magic. The portrayal of *X-Files* lead character Dana Scully—an upwardly mobile, physically strong, skeptical scientist with a brilliant mind—was, for many women, a defining TV experience of the decade. Decades later, educators recruiting women into STEM programs would talk about the "Scully effect." On the other, it was the ultimate pornification of the female body. Sex trafficking skyrocketed, the press demeaned women who sought influence and in Victoria's Secret stores and on the pages of Cosmo, consumerism masqueraded as female empowerment.

Beachwear for women finally took on a more functional design while creating a fashion-forward look that is all its own. This ethic spawned an explosion in active young female participants who suddenly saw the chance to enter a cool beach environment. At the same time, as the new leaders of the Associated Surfing Professionals became seasoned veterans, and recreational aficionados moved into full adulthood, they built a foundation for the next generation—becoming role models as well as icons.

Happy Campers

When Bev Sanders met her husband Chris in a Lake Tahoe bar he was doodling drawings of snowboards on a cocktail napkin. Fascinated, she joined him and began making snowboards in their garage in 1985, marrying, and ultimately founding Avalanche Snowboards. Snowboarding's popularity exploded in the late 80s and as their brand rode the surge, Sanders took to championing the women snowboard performers.

On a trip to Hawaii she took a lesson from Nancy Emerson and became immediately enamored with wave-riding. Emerson, who had one of the earliest surf schools in Hawaii, encouraged Sanders to try the idea herself. Going back to the cocktail napkin concept, Sanders eventually interested her husband in coming with her to Costa Rica. There she created Las Olas Surf Safaris in 1997, the first all-inclusive surf vacation for women.

"Bev built it the same way she did for the snowboards," said Nancy Emerson, remembering the passion Sanders had. "She put together some hot friends, hired a photographer, and marketed the idea to her huge rolodex of friends." It was an idea whose time had come.

That same year "Sunset" Suzy Stewart opened her surf school on Oahu's North Shore when there were few choices on that side of the island. Renowned as Oahu North Shore's only female city and county lifeguard, her business took off almost immediately.

Surf Diva, which had opened just a year earlier in 1996, provided surf lessons, gear, and even a foundational text for 21st Century female surfers. Employing a how-to narrative in the vein of authors like Generation X's Douglass Copeland and with graphic novel stylings, *Surf Diva: A Girl's Guide to Getting Good Waves* (2005) might be the "closest thing to a 'feminist manifesto' that a trade press book might offer," argued Comer. In every region others followed. Surf Sister Surf School was founded in 1999 in Tofino British Columbia, by Canadian Jenny Stewart and run by Krissy "Surf Momma" Montgomery. Mary Setter-holm founded her Surf Academy in 2000, growing it to over eighty full-time instructors. In 2003, Lulu Agan came up with the idea of creating experiential vacations that combined her passions: surfing, yoga, cooking & wellness. After spending more than a decade as a full-time private chef she decided to blend top-quality, healthy food with her dedication to leading a healthy lifestyle, eventually expanding to Hawaii, Nicaragua, El Salvador, Anguilla, Sri Lanka and Thailand.

Bev Sanders, meanwhile, continued to innovate—in other areas as well as surfing. A proponent of sustainable transportation, Sanders purchased a General Motors EV-1 in 1992, and wrote an article entitled "Don't unplug the electric car" for the *San Francisco Chronicle* in 2003.

In 2005 she started Artista Creative Safaris, an encaustic and acrylic painting vacation for women. Sanders launched Jennifer's Journey, a women's travel website, in honor of her sister, Jennifer Maher, who died from cancer in 2007.

As demand leapt, the "women's exclusive" movement spawned a whole new business model, which began evolving like a Harvard Business case study. It would not be long before the retail store concept would follow the same path.

Attention Shoppers

The girls-only surf shop trend began on April 6, 1996, when Ilona Wood-Anderle opened WaterGirl in Encinitas, California. WaterGirl was a result of Wood-Anderle's desire to own her own business while keeping an eye on her young daughter. But she was the first to capitalize on surfing's burgeoning popularity with women.

"I saw the surfing business as a whole on the rise," recalled Wood-Anderle.

"People thought I was crazy. One guy told me not to bother with a cash register because it would be so slow. I didn't even tell my family about it at first. But I realized that the real market was not the hardcore male surfer, because they don't buy clothes and usually order boards from a shaper. The real customer was one who loves the ocean and identifies with the culture." Wood-Anderle's perception was accurate. WaterGirl was an instant success.

Others recognized the opportunity. Isabelle "Izzy" Tihanyi and her sister Coco opened the influential Surf Diva shop in La Jolla in 2004, at once symbolizing the sport's growth among women and a new sensibility. "We grew up with punk, not boomers burning bras," noted Tihanyi in 2002. "With Madonna, the Queen of Capitalism, she had a *huge* effect when we first saw her! And Latifah and other rappers, and Gwen Stefani—all of them with confident empowerment, and all of them with their own lines of products."

Tihanyi even named their shop Surf Diva "because those women who had influenced us—gave inspiration—that's what they were—divas."

"Title IX (the 1972 amendment to the federal Civil Rights Act barring sexual discrimination in education, including sports) gave girls the freedom to participate in traditional male-dominated sports—including surfing," noted Marie Case, Board-Trac partner and managing director. "Women have the confidence today to do things that were less acceptable or unheard of in the past, like surfing and opening surf shops."

Benefiting from institutional changes like Title IX, and a new positive image of capitalism, both the Tihanyi sisters had competed on UCSD's women's surfing team and had an ambitious vision.

Their parents were immigrants—father from Hungary, mother from France—and that helped drive their dream of making it big in the U.S. They expanded into their own clothing line, with sister Coco handling the retail. Their business represented an updated version of earlier waves of feminism.

Indefatigably enthusiastic and unpretentiously erudite, the Tihanyi sisters owed some of their success to simply working hard and doing a good job. The other was being ahead of the curve and flexible. The result was not only growth in their own business but a domino effect on others.

"It was exciting to realize that over 100 surf camps have started up from instructors that trained with us," Tihanyi said. "We felt like a tree with all these beautiful branches."

Two years later, Sally Smith opened Santa Cruz's Paradise Surf Shop, with surf partners Kristina Marquez, a legal assistant by training, and Alayna Schiebel who had run a surf shop on the North Shore for twelve years. Schiebel had a pedigree of surf royalty: her mother was San Onofre surf queen Gretchen Van Dyke and uncle Fred Van Dyke a legendary Waimea big wave pioneer who had founded the Duke Kahanamoku surf contest.

Though Smith related to an earlier form of feminism that aligned with counterculture boomers more than Tahanyi's pro-capitalist Generation X, together the two businesses helped to create what surf culture scholar Krista Comer described as "new politicized constituencies of both girls and midlife women surfers" linked locally, regionally and globally through their respective outreach programs, particularly those dedicated to coastal stewardship, environmentalism, anti-racism and women's rights."

The timing for women retailers was ripe: of the 2.26-million surfers in 2002, a solid 25 percent of those were female, compared with sixteen percent just two years prior. The action-sports research firm Board-Trac found that from 1999 to 2002 the number of females surfing regularly rose 220 percent, while the total number of surfers globally actually declined. Based on the numbers, the emergence of core surf shops owned by women for women was a simple lesson in supply and demand.

"The surf industry acknowledged that women exist and have an impact," Marie Case explained. "Roxy was able to secure more retail real estate and became one of the triggers that opened up the gates for girls in this industry."

With or without Roxy, women's emerging role in surf-retail ownership was inevitable. Wood-Anderle utilized an aggressive publicity campaign, published a WaterGirl newsletter, became an advocate on controversial issues (including a well-publicized battle with a clothing company that used anti-girl slogans.) She also started a surf team of local schoolgirls and operated a modest surf school to nurture present and future clients: "When you get involved in the community, they feel an attachment to you, and they'll patronize your store."

Interest from other surf entrepreneurs was instantaneous. A surf school operator since 1985, Mary Hartman immediately paid a call to the WaterGirl shop. Hartman had entrepreneurship in her bones. Before starting her surf school she had started a successful boat repair business in the Dana Point Harbor—not exactly a dainty occupation.

"My mother owned a retail shop in this area my whole life," she noted. "I grew up in a store."

Like others who visited WaterGirl, Hartman immediately saw the template had been drawn. The dimensions of the template, however could be modified to fit a personal vision.

"I was so excited I decided to open my own shop in Orange County and call it Girl in the Curl," Hartman remembered.

Like the majority of the shops, Hartman's surf school was an integral facet of her operation—and a significant volume of her income. "They go hand in hand," she stressed. "They complement each other."

The response to the expanding new "women's surf" category was a slow build. But it served an underappreciated but intensely loyal clientele. Catering to an ever-increasing demographic, women's surf shops provided moral support and a welcome sanctuary for those who have felt intimidated by the confines of the traditional male-run surf shop. Trying on a wetsuit or asking a guy questions about surfboards was often an uncomfortable—even humiliating—experience.

"A lot of women still don't feel comfortable going into a surf shop where there's a guy behind the counter and the woman wants to try on a wetsuit," explained "Saltwater" Sally Smith of Paradise Surf Shop in Santa Cruz in 2003. "Our women clientele are stoked to come in and get input from women surfers."

Sunshine Makarow, publisher of *Surf Life For Women* agreed: "Women's shops tend to be more helpful and welcoming, especially to surfers just starting out."

"They are more friendly and more willing to explain the basics."

Although girls-only surf shops are a relatively new phenomena, their business models complement the overall trend in surf retail to diversify. In the process they take full advantage of the difference in buying habits between men and their female counterparts, the dominant shopper of the species.

"When women shop they like to experience the whole process, and they like to shop in groups," observed Caroline "Coco" Tihanyi, co-owner of Surf Diva in La Jolla, California. "Guys like to be on a mission and buy what they need—they put blinders on. Girls, on the other hand, are much more spontaneous."

Tory Strange of Girl Next Door in St. Augustine, Florida considers his store a "pro shop for girls who surf," rather than a boutique with some surfboards thrown in. "The girls behind the counter love surfing and like to talk surf," said Strange.

As expected, girls' surf shops generally have the upper hand in women's soft-goods selection compared to guy shops, with more space devoted to the full range of women's sizes. "We look at women of all ages and try not to pigeonhole them into junior sizes," emphasized Robin Holton of Aloha Paradise in Jacksonville, Florida.

The result was not only growth in their own business but a domino effect on others. From a corporate standpoint, women's surf shops provided a captive audience for women's brands.

Larger labels—with their own chain of retail outlets—did not miss the opportunity either. Candy Harris, who was Billabong Girls's brand manager noted "Any retailer who makes a point to hire a well-informed, style-conscious sales staff and creates a comfortable environment has a better chance at attracting female consumers."

Roxy's VP of Sales then was Deanna Jackson. She concurred: "Women's-only stores can be a more girl-friendly, inviting place to shop."

The industry eventually backed the women's movement by offering more junior lines. But initially it was difficult for women's surf shops to secure the most coveted product. Several store owners experienced what they termed "corporate discrimination." Paradise's Sally Smith said getting product in the store is one of the biggest challenges facing women retailers. "We had a lot of vendors who didn't think we'd make it, and also the neighboring shops would block us from getting the top brands," said Smith.

Hartman remarked that it was only after she sent a personal "love letter" to Quiksilver CEO Bob McKnight along with a petition signed by four thousand girls that Girl In The Curl was able to get Roxy's attention. "My surf team was in the finals of Roxy-sponsored contests and they still weren't selling to me," Hartman recalled. "When they finally opened up, I got this huge credit application in the mail, nine pages or something. It was like, do you want a blood sample, too? But when it finally happened, the business took off."

While WaterGirl prompted a run of girls' core surf shops, some were short-lived. Like retailers in general, mismanagement rather than market saturation was the cause. Often it was misunderstanding the appeal they offered. "The shops that are still open are core women-owned businesses, with women surfers running the show who can sell a board as easily as sunscreen with a tint in it to even out your skin tone," Hartman said.

Terry Kraszewski of Ocean Girl in La Jolla argued that the era's sagging economy and competition from department stores were additional obstacles. "A lot of the department stores have recognized the surf trend as fashion and now stock most major surf brands. It's hard to compete with that buying power."

Women's stores that catered to the female appeal persevered—and continued to thrive. Empathy, support and feminine deference became an attractive aspect of customer service. "It's like a sisterhood here," contended Hartman in 2020. "We had a couch and pillow that girls would grab and cry on when they broke up with their boyfriends or had fights with their husbands. It built a safe haven."

No Business

"I tried to keep up with the supply and demand," Bonnie Raitt lamented on "No Business" from her exquisite 1991 album *Luck of the Draw*.

The demand in the decade heading into the millennium seemed to grow by the day. As shops thrived more product was needed; creativity flourished, opportunities expanded—along with risk.

Seeking a simpler life—and more honest way to make a living—sometimes requires risk-taking—and the sacrifices to achieve the goals. Marine Mausse and her young family left France for a more idyllic existence in Bali. "We sold our furniture, our boards and our cars," she once told *Herewith Media*. "We closed our bank accounts and phones, we booked one-way plane tickets and left," Mausse remembered. "We needed to feel every second intensely and see the real side of things."

While in Bali, Mausse created Dolphin Love, a brand whose pieces are only available in small batches of thirty pieces maximum, and the vintage cuts are hand-sewn by two seamstresses in Bali. Made from Italian fabric, the designs were inspired by bright retro florals, sometimes mixed with gold velour and animal prints—risky but rewarding.

Risk-taking would have been Kassia Meador's middle name. From flash-dancing on the nose of her longboard to break-dancing in Hainan, Meador was always ready to gamble on her personal strength to build an independence in her lifestyle. A professional surfer since age seventeen, Kassia Meador sacrificed her sponsorships in 2013, forsaking a safe corporate environment to build her own brand, one aimed at generating "the highest vibe [in the] lowest impact way."

Bold and buoyantly fervent, Meador risked financial security to serve her higher purposes. Her brand—Kassia Surf—touted sustainability practices like a wetsuit recycling program inviting wearers to "empower yourself and your community to expand your mind, body and soul through healthy active lifestyle choices and experiences."

The 90s boom created an environment that institutionalized an entire new category—beach lifestyle fashion. It would continue far into the following decades.

Another surfer/artist Amanda Chinchelli collaborated with fashion brands like Moschino Jeans, Quiksilver and Seea while she remained in Italy using her native coastline of waves as inspiration. Resmini's work has appeared in *Elle* Italy, *Glamour* Italy, *Foam* and *Desillusion*.

Leaving her home in Italy to join her boyfriend (now husband) in San Francisco, Chinchelli didn't plan to pioneer an entire new genre of women's surf apparel. But creating Seea in 2011, she did just that. Chinchelli told Lauren Hill author of the book *She Surf,* "I was offended by the sexualized images of women in the surfing world. It felt necessary to create a product designed for women, by women."

Seea produced a full range of surfwear options, from bikinis to rashguards to spring suits, and "almost any woman could find a fit and pattern to complement her taste." All pieces are made within seventy miles of their San Clemente head-quarters, and most of the line is made from recycled, upcycled or natural materials.

A former designer for Patagonia, J. Crew and Deus Ex Machina, Erika Seiko Togashi was no novice when she established September The Line. In fact, you can see influences of all those brands in her own label. Founded in Tokyo, Japan at the turn of the century, the line was an outcome of her dissatisfaction with surfwear options. Moving from New York to Bali, Togashi spent more hours surfing than ever, and realized at the same time that she wanted international distribution and sourcing.

Sturdy, stylish and sensible, Togashi's suits were built to withstand duck dives and wipeouts without any wardrobe malfunctions.

Searching for an appealing, American-made board bag, professional free surfer Anna Ehrgott decided to create her own—from material she sourced at a thrift shop. As word spread, custom orders for homemade creations swelled the surf shop where she worked.

Ehrgott named the brand Sagebrush, sourced unused fabrics from other busi-nesses, and expanded the line to include scrunchies, snowboard bags and adjustable masks—allowing her to achieve parallel dreams of owning her own business and traveling the world to surf.

There would be bumps in the road and ups and downs of economic cycles. But the pavement laid down in the 90s provided a foundation for what was possible as these women explored the next era in surf business.

The Resurgence of Glide

A Longboard Revival Offered Attractive Alternatives of Artistry and Grace

1982–1999

"I am constantly amazed at how courageous and radical speaking the truth is."

—Melissa Etheridge, singer/songwriter, activist

Women's Elegant Style and Infectious Camaraderie Elevated a 80s Longboard Renaissance

The late 60s shortboard development was a genuine revolution. The adaption was swift and universal. Across the globe shapers and surfboard manufacturers responded to the overwhelming new demand, dropping virtually all production of longer equipment. The consequences were numerous: boards over 7'10" became obsolete. The old longboard culture with its emphasis on footwork, glide and elegant poses was replaced by the quest for maneuverability, tight pocket positioning and vertical rather than horizontal trajectories on the waveface. Riding inside the tube replaced riding the nose as the most radical performance maneuver.

A new culture sprang up, in sync with—and sometimes at the forefront of—the global youth movement of music, dress and worldview—more idealistic but simultaneously often more dogmatic. Many older surfers dropped out. Many Vietnam veterans returning from the war found the extreme drop in size—and attitude as well—too difficult an adjustment. For beginners, learning was much more difficult on tiny equipment. But the rise of the baby boomers and the subsequent surge in wave-riding's popularity easily replaced the attrition rate of surfing's first modern generation. These factors—coupled with the development of the leash and improved wetsuits—made surfing far more crowded and considerably less friendly.

Nowhere was the effect more pronounced than for the women. Hostility in a more crowded lineup, aggressive competition for waves and the physical power requirements of shortboard surfing shifted the atmosphere toward a masculine environment neither best-suited nor welcoming to women. Within the few short years from 1967 to 1969 the nearly total disappearance of longboards resulted in a visible reduction to an already scarce female minority in the water. The shortboard's absolute supremacy in equipment choice predominated for more than a decade from the late 60s to the end of the 70s.

Walking on Sunshine

The renaissance began as a whisper in the early 80s. By mid-decade modest numbers of iconoclasts in Hawaii and the U.S. Mainland chose a return to longboards. A marked alternative to the status quo, this small band of revivalists ferreted out single-fin, nine-foot wave-riding relics—at garage sales or in dusty rafters. It was the only means of acquiring these longer models that had been unfashionable for over a decade. Clark Foam, still the dominating blank manufacturer of the day, was producing no blanks big enough for shapers to even *make* a longboard.

Like "Walking on Sunshine," the euphoric, upbeat 1985 hit by Katrina and the Waves, longboarding's attraction for women was immediate and irresistible.

"I hadn't ridden anything but shortboards for fifteen years," recalls Sheri Crummer, a veteran competitor and photographic chronicler since the early 60s. "The moment I entered a longboard competition I remembered what I was missing for so long in surfing."

Trendiness was superfluous—the elegance of glide, the nuances of trim positioning and the smooth transitions (synonymous with longboarding in the 60s "Golden Era") enticed surfers to enthusiastically adopt neoclassical equipment. Most regions that embraced the new longboard pulse had sustained a deep and lasting traditional surf culture established long before the onset of its dark ages (1969 to 1985).

Foremost was the South Shore of Oahu, which had maintained an almost religious longboard artform since the time of 100-pound koawood planks. And the generally softer, rolling waves of the South Shore were far more conducive to longer board lengths. In the previous decade young talent like Rell and Martha Sunn from the west side of Oahu began to remind Hawaiians of their deep roots in the lengthier genre. Nancy Emerson considered by many to be one of the preeminent talents of her time returned to longboarding. Already a seasoned shortboard pro and established surf school developer, Emerson decided to start the Hawaiian longboard series. Met with immediate support, it gave disparate enthusiasts a gathering place to celebrate tradition. Anna

Moody, a Kihei, Maui local, was a perfect example of the talent that "surfed with Lopez-style grace."

San Onofre, the southernmost tip of Orange County California, had also maintained a Hawaiianesque surf culture since the 30s. Like Waikiki the long, slow-rolling waves at "San'O'" were usually the prescribed preference for classic longboards. Access to San Onofre was for many years limited to members of the elite San Onofre Surf Club where a very colorful but relaxed lifestyle had evolved. Little changed as the beach became public in the 70s, and surfers were already well-versed in the benefits of traditional longboards. But by the 80s surfers like Nancy Duesler and Pauline Lutton—women from the first families of San Onofre, where much of the early California surf culture had emanated—were nearing the end of their active surf careers. It was a moment when a second generation of classicists emerged, setting off a significant revitalization.

Karen Williams, whose father was a legendary board rider and San Onofre fixture, was one of the first women to reintroduce longboards. Laurie Craig, Jean Vetter and Diane Jappe were notable standouts from prominent families as well. Wendy Irwin, another daughter of first generation California surfers, was becoming an outstanding competitor and beach advocate. Her mother Liz Irwin was one of the "matriarchs" from the classic founders period of the San Onofre Surf Club. Liz had been an elegant longboarder—and like many others Wendy had returned from shortboarding. Nearly all of the women who reverted to the longer lengths were in fact surfers whose parents (and even grandparents) had ridden classic nine-foot plus shapes themselves. Lisa Peterson, Lori Roth, Jamie Gee and the Becket sisters were all part of long-time San Onofre families from the 50s whose parents were iconic figures in the Southern California surf culture.

Malibu, too, was again home to a crew of girls styling on traditional "logs" as the shortboard generation dismissively called them. Brittany Leonard and Carla Rowland were among those leading the resurgence, choosing heavily glassed, leashless single fin equipment.

Shy and sometimes quirky, Leonard was an "independent thinking blonde" known for her elegant footwork. Her sister Courtney by contrast was dark haired and talkative.

Rowland, who would later go on to become the head instructor at the Surf Institute, remembered enduring "years of battling to hold my ground and earn my right in the testosterone-filled lineup."

"Being a woman, I was not just discriminated against, but also required to prove myself on a regular basis." As Rowland described it, "There were rock wars, wrestling matches, I was 'pantsed' in front of crowds, called names, lied about, 'snaked' on waves, I was even told that my place in the hierarchy that possessed the point was on the same level as the 'groms' the kids."

It was never easy for women in the water, but the reintroduction of long boards intensified the conflict. Deep-seated resentment festered within a 70s generation struggling with increasingly crowded lineups.

Despite the resistance, increasing board length was out of the bag and nothing could stuff it back in. "It was too late to reverse course," switch artist Sherry Crummer declared. "Even Baja regulars could be seen riding the tip" at the peninsula's classic point breaks "on small days between swells."

Hordes of SoCal and East Coast surfers began surfacing at Saturday garage sales in search of pristine fifty-dollar treasures. The infectious enthusiasm even spawned a short resurrection of surf music and classic surf movies.

As interest grew, dedicated aficionados began to penetrate the conformity entrenched by a decade of shortboard domination—and women were a major faction of the vanguard.

San Onofre, by now in full-length bloom, saw women like Julie Whitegon and Sheri Crummer—who had previously been shortboard competitors—move to the longer lengths with even more contest success.

Together Again

By the early 90s there was a bona fide, well-entrenched scene, exuding camaraderie like Janet Jackson's ode to sisterhood "Together Again." It was reflected in surfers like Diane Sanders who had broken into the crowded third point at Malibu, eventually becoming the L.A. Women's Champ. Her life was cut short in 2009 by a rare form of breast cancer—but not before inspiring a generation of upcoming women.

"She always had her eye out for female longboarders, especially those of us who grew up competing at the coalition contests in the early 90s," proclaimed Cori Schumacher, one of longboarding's most articulate representatives. "Diane rallied behind women's longboarding at every opportunity and was an integral part of where we are today."

On smaller days, the frequently uncrowded inside cove sections at Cardiff and Swami's to the south, Rincon, and Steamer's Lane to the north would see women like Jane "The Lane" McKenzie from Santa Cruz, Santa Barbara's Simone Reddingius and Jeannette Prince in Encinitas, displaying the kind of feminine grace that was immediately attractive to other women in the lineup. Nearby in San Diego's North County, Prince's daughter Cory Schumacher—who had been surfing all of her life on longboards and shortboards alike—was the stand-out young girl at Cardiff Reef. Gifted with both natural athleticism and an exceptional intellect she was soon to become a much more prominent figure in the surfing culture.

These enthusiastic members of the longboard reawakening often enjoyed the shunned sections of reefs and points by themselves—contemporary shortboards of the time being unsuited to small point wave conditions.

In Australia Sandy Carlson won ten longboard titles along the cobbled points of the Sunshine Coast. Colleen Dean and Julie Moxy were among those redis-covering Broken Heads, Noosa and Crescent Heads, revered for their longboard qualities that were now returning to vogue. Jeannie Shanks from New Zealand connected with the women from California and Hawaii, a bond that continued for decades.

On America's eastern seaboard a similar scenario was unfolding: Floridian Lisa Muir-Wakley returning from a decade in Hawaii, was once again a Pensacola standout. Mimi Munro, a child prodigy in the 60s returned to the scene as well. "It was like they saved a spot in the lineup for me all those years," she said.

In New Jersey, Mary Anne Hayes and surfer musician Sandy Smedley re-examined their earlier roots.

In Hawaii, the scene was customarily low-key, but the performances could often be impressive. Kristin Cole dazzled the North Shore. Waikiki beach girls Pinoi Makalena and Lori Saxman were standouts in Honolulu while Desiree Desoto and Martha Sunn continued to perform exceptionally at Makaha. Sunn, Desoto and Makalena, all from storied Hawaiian surf families, would go on to become mentors to young surfers for years to come.

In every region good surfers had their favorite surf spot. In California Jen Smith, a very young Windansea Club member, took to the La Jolla reefs, while Mary Bagalso preferred Oceanside's peaks. Jill Nakano (who later became a successful surf instructor) started at Tourmaline Surf Park but became a regular at Bolsa Chica and the Cliffs after transplanting to Huntington. Kelly Sloan, a member of the U.S. Surf Team in the 90s, drove out from inland Vista to excel at the Oceanside jetties, a consistent semi-finals performer. Top trim expert Debi Trautvien loved the lines at Rincon while Melvis Morris (who had mentored many of the younger upcomers) adopted Seaside Reef as her own.

For this burgeoning breed of new longboarders, acceptance in the lineup would be a few years off. Disdain for riding equipment considered archaic often triggered ridicule and in some cases outright contempt. But the capacity for longboarders to pick off every good set wave from the outside was really the unstated but more worrisome threat.

For women, one positive outcome became apparent: as surfing's populace reaffiliated with the lost artform, a large cadre found it an attractive alternative, incorporating a return to style and grace that many had been longing for.

Longboards expanded competition opportunities for women too: the United States Surfing Federation included a women's longboard division. The Coalition of Surfing Clubs (a revival in itself) hosted contests up and down the coast of California. Mary Schwinn was the Malibu Club kingpin while Maka Pua'a proudly represented the Maui contingency. Schwinn became the vice president of the Malibu Boardriders Association. "Mary dominated first and second point Malibu in the late 90s and early 2000s," remembered Jeannette Prince.

The Roxy brand—enjoying a reign in women's beachwear—held just-for-fun events at San Onofre, directed by surf culture impresario Allan Seymour. Together Roxy and Seymour lit a flame for young women. Quickly labeled as "Roxy girls" young beach lovers were suddenly allowed to simply experience the joy of the waves; high-performance was not required to gain acceptance in the culture. In fact the movement created its own cultural rituals; the most important was exhibiting a carefree attitude with playful intensity. From both a social and commercial standpoint offering *inclusiveness* as an essential component of surf lifestyle was pure genius.

Have I been blind? Have I been hypnotized, mesmerized by what my eyes have found? Natalie Merchant asked, as she stalked the streets of New York, shooting photographs with a Leica M3, writing the song lyrics to "Carnival," her top ten Billboard hit in the summer of 1995.

The world may not have been looking but they could no longer be blind. By the mid-90s the increased presence of women in the line-up was finally undeniable: In Southern California alone, the number of longboards fast approached a 50/50 ratio to shortboards, and the increasing number of women in the lineup helped tip the scale. Female-exclusive surf camps like Surf Diva in La Jolla and Las Olas in Mainland Mexico flourished. Hot young boardriders like Tanya Booth, a San Onofre State Park Lifeguard's daughter, became the poster girl. (Literally, the San Onofre Classic used her image for the event poster in 1996 and 2000.)

By the summer of 1995—spurred by a deluge of marketing dollars from an influx of new women's surfwear companies who followed Roxy into the marketplace—thousands of females boldly ignored the entrenched stigma that surfing was "only for the guys," and entered the lineup. Retail demand had grown strong enough for the world's first all girl surf shop to open—Watergirl in Encinitas—and the trend would continue across the spectrum.

As World Champion shortboarder Lisa Andersen became the first woman on the cover of *Surfer* Magazine in over fifteen years, and Madeleine Albright made history as America's first female Secretary of State, the longboard groundswell was as historic as anything else that was happening in women's surfing—or perhaps in national politics.

Up and down the West Coast the trend was expanding. Younger girls living inland of Malibu, including Kassia Meador and Ashley Lloyd, noticed the trend and followed suit. These two women would become major figures in the longboard and general surfing culture in decades to come. But in the late 90s they were eager teenagers getting their first taste of surfing's unmitigated joy.

No Cruel Summer

For Kassia Meador that taste came in summer of 1997, when she was fifteen and her parents started dropping her off at First Point Malibu. While the shortboard revolution of the 70s and the Pro Tour of the 80s had continued to grow, the world-famous, right-peeling break had returned to its classic roots; as those who were longtime students knew, First Point was practically *engineered* for longboarding. Meador immediately became captivated, quickly mastering the fundamentals and developing her own style.

"She was *so* distinctive," contended Joel Tudor, a two-time world longboard champion. "No one could miss her performances."

Joining the Malibu Surf Club, she traveled to competitions up and down the coast. The Ace of Base trio may have had a huge 1998 radio hit singing about summer's oppressive heat and the misery of romance, but Meador and her companions had no "Cruel Summer." For them it was more like "All I Wanna Do Is Have Some Fun" by Sheryl Crow. Over the next few years, Meador surfed nearly every day, from dawn till dusk. Wave-riding became no ordinary love.

Her first invitation to an international surf competition came from the Rabbit Kekai 1999 Longboard Classic in Costa Rica. Her parents didn't have the money to send her. So Meador bought candy at Smart & Final discount grocers and sold it to her classmates at a markup. She made $1,500—enough for the ticket to Costa Rica.

Using the same tactic, she covered her own travel expenses to a competition in Noosa, Australia, where she caught the eye of renowned longboard shaper Donald Takayama. Takayama was in the water with Jeff Hakman, cofounder of Quiksilver. Takayama offered to shape boards for Meador. Hakman helped secure her a sponsorship from Roxy.

Within a few short months, Meador was on a surf-adventure vessel in the Indian Ocean, exploring the Maldives island chain. She was skipping her senior prom but turning heads with her frenetic footwork.

Implementing a wildly free-spirited and original style, Meador would grip the nose with her toes and suspend herself in full trim, spin around and cross-step backward to reposition the board for additional feats of gravity. These elegant performances earned her media attention and bolstered the appeal of longboards for women. "Kassie was like a magnet," fellow Malibu girl's crew member Julie Cox remembered. "She had so much style, she could make you laugh and at the same time be very entrepreneurial."

Her timing seemed ideal: supported by the vibrant *Longboard* magazine, heightened general media coverage and a boom in women's surf-specific fashions, longboarding's rekindled popularity accelerated the acceptance of women's surfing as a whole.

To the mass of women competing on longboards across the globe all that was missing now was an event worthy of being called a world contest.

Hank Raymond, organizer of the Costa Rica Longboard Classic, stepped in to fill that longstanding void. His self-proclaimed World Title event—the Toes on the Nose Women's World Longboard Championship—was the first women's longboard world championship since the short board revolution of the late 60s. Held annually in Costa Rica from 1999–2003—in conjunction with the Rabbit Kekai Classic—the Women's World Longboard Championships (WWLC) became the world's longest-running women's-only surf competition to date.

Acceptance and opportunity encouraged a new wave of women into the professional career path. But for many it would come with a price.

Beauty Is A Beast

As market demand created a commercial boom, opportunities expanded—for women with the right "characteristics." But the results of this new stardom had its dark side. Unlike the men, females were not judged strictly on their athletics—they were required to have other qualities as well. It was a confusing and sometimes debilitating juxtaposition. A few years before Meador's rise, Veronica Kay also joined the Roxy team as both a competitor and model. Bright and effervescent, she was fourteen at the time. "My weight went up and down, between focusing on surfing and modeling," Kay remembered. "I would have a model body and be really skinny, then I'd try to paddle out and be like, 'Oh, my God, I'm not strong enough.' Then you focus on being an athlete, but you're like, 'I don't look as good in a bathing suit.' It messes with your head."

That a graceful, talented, compellingly candid woman, who became the 1997 National Scholastic Surfing Association Champion at seventeen, should have insecurities about her appearance strong enough to "mess with her head" illustrates the added struggles women face compared to their male counterparts.

No matter that Kay had traveled the world as professional athlete and brand ambassador for the largest company in surfing and became a fashion editor for a Newport Beach magazine—the apprehension about looks was endemic among women in surfing. The worry was pervasive regardless of sexuality. Keala Kennelly, then a top-ten ranked shortboarder with a record-breaking resume in big-waves, still felt compelled to conceal her sexuality during her brand-sponsored years on the Billabong team. "I was definitely trying to femme it up," Kennelly divulged.

"For most brands you need to be feminine and straight and pretty if you want to be sponsored."

Tanya Booth, a beautiful stylist from a long-time San Onofre surfing family, was crushed when her sponsorship was not renewed. Allen Seymour, who had created the Roxy longboard events and had helped her obtain her patronage, saw the emotional damage: "No matter how gorgeous you are or how well you surf, no matter how many other reasons the brand might have for cutting back on budget," he lamented, "when a young impressionable girl gets cut, she can take it to mean she isn't pretty enough."

Another Roxy team member from the tweens decade, Julie Cox, remembered the pressure. "I'm 5'10" and skinny, so I was the accepted stereotype, but I saw much more talented people *not* getting sponsorships," Cox recollected. "There weren't that many brands supporting women. If you fit the Roxy mold and rode for their team, you were stoked. But if you didn't, you were out of luck."

Cox, whose elegant style in and out of the water brought her many admirers, balanced the competing demands better than most.

Conventional beauty was not the *only* thing—but it was often a big part of a long-term career with many of the surf labels. What was remarkable was how each of these women found a path to success by not giving up.

Veronica Kay would move to New York, train with Dani Crooker (one of the most avant-garde yoga instructors in the tri-state area) and eventually became the only other instructor of her method—DCM, a fusion of hot yoga boot camp, cross fit and total body fitness.

Kassia Meador would start her own brand—targeting a distinct set of consumers for women's surfwear—drafting a fresh blueprint for female pros struggling to earn a living. Julie Cox would create her own surfboard line and innovative hybrid surf shop—part women's social club, part surf school and part travel destination—serving a myriad of female needs.

From Ocean Beach, California to Ocean City, New Jersey, pods of women surfers now filled the line ups.

Young daughters of surf families entrenched in the lifestyle slipped into the mix. Jennifer Tracy, Kirstin Moore and Molly and Amanda Hulsizer, all found their way around the breaks of San Onofre.

The renewed enthusiasm for longboards in the first half of the 90s felt like a paradigm shift, but it was really a blast pattern: a series of eruptions; real progress, yet only partially representing the female side where the Roxy brand exploded. As surfing's cultural foundation itself splintered into divisions—longboard, big-wave, professional competition, amateur rankings and even stand-up paddling—the options expanded.

Into this fractured landscape came a diverse array of events and new names who took on the challenge of expressing self-aware womanhood in very different ways.

As the Millennium clock crossed midnight a new dawning began.

Turbulent Indigo
The 90s

As wave-riding's popularity grew in the 90s the larger issue of women's roles and rights began to become a more controversial issue in the waves. Why were the women not being represented in the surf? Certainly one barrier was the antagonistic environment in the lineup. For beginners, whether men or women, there had never been much mercy given. Learning to surf in crowded, intimidating arenas always required perseverance. And the pressure intensified when it came to competition.

Statistics show that since the very beginning fewer women than men compete in contests. Virginia Beach and parts of Florida were an exception, and 90s surfers like Amy Smith and Robin Forti competed successfully in local and state contests.

"Historically, there never have been too many girls," stated Kathy Phillips, administrative director of the Eastern Surfing Association. The question was—what created the significant barrier to entry? Jeff Phillips, director of the Maryland District of the ESA, had an explanation: the sport "takes a lot of time, money and effort all year long."

Kelly List, Holly Hopkins and other women disputed that contention. Among the small corps who rode the waves along Ocean City, Maryland's beaches, they experienced the issue first hand.

Conceding that the sport is physically demanding and requires significant time and contest fees, they saw more provocative reasons for women's reticence.

"I know it's hard to believe, but that [sexism] does exist," asserted Hopkins, a junior government major at the University of Maryland, College Park.

"Guys don't look at you as surfers," List argued in 1992. "They don't look at what you can do on a surfboard. They look at you as someone to be picked up. It's disgusting and it's demoralizing." Hopkins said: "I think a lot of girls still see it as a 'guy' sport. They feel intimidated and don't feel like they can fit in," Hopkins added. "There's no place in the lineup for girls."

That may have been the prevailing sentiment, but determined females found their way into the surf despite the resistance. Bianca Valenti, whose audacity was legendary, put it concisely: "As a woman, you have to constantly prove yourself, whereas a guy—even of lesser experience—will paddle out and no one will say anything. Now I get cheered on [by the guys], but it took me a while. Psychologically, it was the hardest thing to deal with that hungry pack of wolves while I earned my place."

The 90s was the first generation of established professionals on the women's side. The previous decade had built a foundation and in the exploding surf market of the go-go 90s "lots of possibilities seemed to be on the table—if you were willing to fight for them," said Layne Beachley. But for women it was often paid for with far more sacrifice: the accepted response when it came to determining the competition schedule was the refrain, as Beachley famously declared, "the waves are shit, so send the girls out."

"My generation challenged the status quo," Beachley said about the circumstances she and her colleagues endured. "We'd sell candy for plane fares, we'd hitch-hike to the next event."

Like Joni Mitchell's exquisite album *Turbulent Indigo* about the trials of being an artist, the women of the 90s navigated society and the ocean's deep blue turbulence with grit and ingenuity.

"We would sleep in our board bags at contest sites because we couldn't afford proper accommodation."

"But we were resourceful!" Beachley continued. "I mean sometimes we'd buy a dozen pair of Levi's or Hawaiian shirts and sell them in France to cover the train ride down from Paris," Beachley recalled. "We put up with intolerable situations that no current professional ever had to experience."

One of the first women to prove women's potential to a wider audience, Keala Kennelly was once asked why more women didn't do the same. "They've been discouraged all their lives," she answered. "They were told they couldn't. I was told my whole life that women can't ride big waves; women can't get barreled; women can't surf Chopes or Pipe. I got told that I *can't* so often. And if I had listened to people's opinions, I wouldn't have accomplished even *half* of what I've in my career."

Shape Shifting

If any area of the surfing culture would be described as male-dominated, surfboard-building would seem most likely. Female stars, photographers, contest organizers, retailers, journalists and beachwear makers existed (no matter how small in numbers) from the start. But the factory was a place *exclusively* reserved for men. Turbulence erupted with any attempt to enter the sanctity of the shaper's temple. The shortboard revolution and the subsequent backyard garage builders opened the first chance to crack the code.

Cher Pendarvis may have been the first woman documented as a board-builder from start to finish. Her boards were usually original twin-fin shapes appropriately named for their fish shaped tails and ability to move with superior speed through the water. Fish shapes, first imagined by kneeboard maestro Steve Lis in the late 60s, were confined to the local Sunset Cliffs aficionados until the 1972 World Contest in nearby Ocean Beach, California. The design's validity was proven when Jimmy Blears won the World Championship on a Fish he borrowed from the underground crew at Sunset Cliffs. "We made Blears's Fish here," Pendarvis recalled in 2020. "I helped glass it and make the fins. David Nuuhiwa placed second on a fish of his own design."

The world outside surfing took notice, even if belatedly: The Autry Museum in Los Angeles held a California Designing Women Show from August 2012 through January of 2013. It showcased female designers from 1896 to 1986. Cher Pendarvis was one of the recipients of the prestigious Henry Award, which recognizes excellence in design and was awarded by the design community. She won for a 1976 surfboard she designed—the only surfboard featured in the exhibit. Pendarvis felt honored by the award, but added, "it meant a lot to have surfing represented in the show with all the other wonderful awards." Pendarvis constantly deferred to the importance of surfing rather than ruminating on her own contributions. But her place in surf history was set as hard as a double coat of resin.

There was, however, a women in the surfboard manufacturing sector even earlier, although not engaged in the traditional process. In the late 60s the British surfboard industry in Cornwall employed the first woman at the *Bilbo* surfboard factory, founded by Bill Bailey and Bob Head (hence Bilbo.) Rose Holmes, Bill Bailey's sister-in-law, became responsible for the company's revolutionary molded board production. Aimed at the general public, this was a cheaper starter surfboard for the novice. It was rapidly nicknamed "the pop-out" by the surfing establishment and considered too crude and un-personalized for advanced surfers. In Southwest England, Rose became known as "the Popout Queen."

Carving a Path for Today's Female Shapers

Only since the mid-90s had women chosen sanding blocks and planers as tools of their trade, and exchanged long hours spent covered in foam dust for their daily bread. Most remember Shannon McIntyre—who trained with now-established master of the craft and former college classmate, Chris Christensen—as the first woman to make a career from shaping surfboards beginning in 1995.

From a historical view, Pendarvis and McIntyre carved the path for today's female shapers. After McIntyre, a handful of women emerged to take their places in the craft and culture of surfboard building: Ashley Lloyd (Santa Cruz), Molly Logan (Huntington Beach) and Dessa Kirk (San Diego) trained independently under shaping legends like Bing Copeland and Skip Frye: they all were inspired by their mentors to earn their laurels as accomplished board-builders. In a largely male-dominated space, a growing number of female voices have risen in the surfboard shaping world.

A Melody Shaping Mama

Female shaper Ashley Lloyd was the forefront of the small but growing number of women earning a living making boards. A graceful longboarder, she established herself as both a surfboard shaper and singer/songwriter musician. Living in Santa Cruz, California, Lloyd first made a name for herself gracefully riding traditional "single fins" across Malibu's beloved First Point. In the early 2000s, fellow Malibu surfer Danny Tarampi asked Lloyd if she'd be interested in learning the art of shaping. She said yes, becoming one of the most significant and popular women shapers; one of the select few females who shaped boards for a living. Featured in the movies *Girls Rip* (2005), *Dear and Yonder* (2009) and *Women and the Waves* (2009) Lloyd then teamed up with Bing surfboards and shaped the original "Ashley Lloyd" and "Dear and Yonder" models. She also shaped under her own Ashley Lloyd Surfboards label in Santa Cruz. A seasoned water-woman and former professional surfer, Lloyd became an environmental activist who committed to making boards using less volatile chemicals. Lloyd's creations are Ecoboards, meaning they're "all green certified" by the Sustainable Surf Organization for using bio-based epoxy resins and less toxic materials.

She married Alex Thompson, a fellow surfer and musician, and in 2014 her first child, Odin, was born, and she began sharing waves with him by age four. An accomplished musician, she played in a band called the Shapes with her husband and partner Alex, who also glasses and finishes her shapes. In her era, she became perhaps the best-known woman shaper in the business.

Artist, Sculptress, Surfer, Skateboarder

Mentored by legendary San Diego surfer and surfboard shaper Skip Frye, Dessa Kirk became known for her tall, graceful metal sculptures of the nymph Daphne and large-scale lilies created from old Cadillacs. Kirk's Daphne sculptures intended to represent strong women who have found freedom through faith, surrender and acceptance, themes "at the root of her work."

An accomplished skateboarder, Kirk took pride in her prowess on the street and in the waves. But her calling was to make sculpture. Her devotion to sculpture paid off when she landed a scholarship at The School of the Art Institute of Chicago, and was later commissioned to create an outdoor sculpture for the city of Columbus, Indiana. Kirk's sculptures found homes in major cities across America.

Surfing DNA

Like a majority of the surf industry women, shaper Valerie Dupont supplemented her craftwork with other means of support. In her case, it is the impressive occupation as a biotech scientist who sequences DNA. She got her start shaping when she found an old Bob McTavish board on the beach and set about repairing it. A native of France, she moved to San Diego's surf mecca in Encinitas where it was an easier transition from synthesizing DNA polymerase to sculpting foam polymers. Initially shaping for family and friends, natural talent and word of mouth brought her business to a steady growth mode.

"Being both a shaper and one of the few females in the industry opened doors in the most prestigious shaping rooms of master board builders in France, California, Oahu and Maui," noted Regina Nicolardi, a journalist for *Outside* magazine.

If female *shapers* are a rare breed, women working in the rest of surfboard manufacturing is an *even rarer* sight. But Dewi Malopsy moved from Indonesia to one of the surfboard manufacturing epicenters—the North Shore of Oahu—to learn how to glass surfboards. First apprenticing under shaper Jeff Alexander (who ironically, moved *to* Indonesia later) Dewi Malopsy learned the trade, moved on to California, and quite quickly opened her own factory, Tiger G. Glassing.

Carving in Multiple Mediums

Southern Californian Christine Brailsford Caro made her mark in the industry as a designer, shaper, wood carver and surfer. The Leucadia resident earned a reputation for her Furrow Surfcraft out of the Moonlight-Christenson Glassing Factory in San Marcos. "If shapers were a deck of cards—among the aces and jokers—Caro was an articulate queen high," commented Jeannette Prince. "Everything Caro has done relates back to her world view." She borrowed the name "Furrow" from the farming world (furrows are lines dug for seeds to grow).

Known for shapes inspired by the shortboard revolution, Caro incorporated her own interpretation of modern design.

"Foam volume and placement of foam are key," noted Caro. "For many of my boards, I like to hide volume under the rider's chest to help get into waves earlier. That thickness is foiled to thin rails, depending on the model, rider, or wave, and tail."

As a woman shaper Caro built boards primarily for women, sought after for her custom concepts.

A Citizen of the Surf

Born in South Africa, growing up in Australia, making a life and career in Hawaii while carrying numerous passports and multiple citizenships, Jodi Wilmott might have been the model for a citizen of the surfing world. Immersed in the surf life from birth by a father who shaped surfboards and a mother involved in surfing events, her family traveled from region to region.

Wilmott's first wave was at Queens, Waikiki on her dad's board, when her family moved to Hawaii, later living in Pauoa Valley with the Aikau family. "It was truly a blessing to grow up with the Aikaus and they remain a big part of my family's life," she said.

She first met Eddie Aikau in the early 70s when he was in South Africa for an international event in Durban, where Wilmott's family was then living. After South African legend Shaun Tomson's family (who had originally offered to host him) lost their house in a fire and were themselves living in a hotel, Wilmott's family took Aikau in.

"Eddie and his brother (Clyde Aikau) were tremendous representatives for the Hawaiian culture," Wilmott recalled. "They would come to my school and play music and teach the kids about Hawaii. They even learned a couple of Australian folk songs to play for the kids. Eddie used to love trying to mimic the accent."

That began Wilmott's lifelong affair with pro surfers and the World Tour which was barely in its infancy then. "My life has run parallel with professional surfing from my first day," Wilmott said. "Growing up, my family hosted a lot of the surfers from Hawaii, South Africa and Brazil in Australia when the Pro Tour had just begun. Being surrounded by the world's best surfers really made professional surfing a comfortable place for me to make a living—and a life."

Aspiring and self-assured, Wilmott earned an Associate's degree in Public Relations and Business Communications. That education—in addition to her knowledge and love for surfing—helped her launch Ocean Promotions, a Hawaii-based PR company. She was soon the communications director for both the Triple Crown of Surfing and Quiksilver in Memory of Eddie Aikau events, and in 2017 landed a position as the first ASP tour media director.

"Perhaps no one person in the history of our sport has had such a consistent hand in reflecting the big news and spirit of our culture," observed *Freesurf* magazine publisher Mike Latronic.

Inconspicuous Management

The role of women in top management was often overlooked in the surf industry. Margaret Yao Calvani and her husband Matt took Bing (the iconic 60s label started by Bing Copeland) and revitalized the entire brand, opening a new retail shop and a line of classic Bing shapes. Vicki Patterson took the responsibility of managing a board manufacturing and retail operation when she and her husband Timmy Patterson started their Orange County surf company after years of apprenticing at other surfboard brands. He had good roots: "Timmy's father and uncles are from Hawaii's most legendary transplant families to the mainland," Vicki Patterson explained.

Timmy earned a "premier shaper status" starting with 80s legendary free-stylist Matt Archibald. "It was a 'bromance,'" says Patterson, "but it put us on the map." With clients like three-time World Champ Andy Irons and 2019 World Champ Italo Ferreira, the Patterson's built a strong following.

"Timmy was the shaping guru, but Vicki ran the business," observed Courtney Conlogue, a longtime client and odds-on favorite to win a World Title in her lifetime. "Vicki did everything from scheduling, inventory, merchandising, accounts payable and receivable, to retail management, staffing, media and team relations," added two-time U.S. Champion Brett Simpson, who also rode Patterson's boards. "She was the Queen behind the throne." In an industry where there are few females involved, Vicki found the hardest challenge was standing up to guys who were not used to taking orders from a woman. "The surf industry operates on the 'bro principle'—everyone wants their equipment for free," Patterson said. "Craftsmen didn't like being held to tight deadlines, friends didn't like to pay, Timmy didn't like operating on a strict production schedule."

Patterson, like other industry women, took on managerial duties. They also tempered the masculine edge.

"If they were *too* obnoxious I had to take down the 'girlie posters' in the factory," Patterson laughed. "My daughters were not going to be brought up in the 'old style' boys environment—even in the factory."

Debbee Pezman knew this story well. She and her husband Steve left *Surfer* publications after nearly thirty years where he had been the helmsman. She had run various departments of the magazine group as well. They started the *Surfer's Journal* in 1992 with Steve as the editorial visionary and Debbee as—most of the rest of it. Her management experience in distribution, production, subscriber services and ad sales were crucial to the *Surfer's Journal* becoming the preeminent surf publication of its era.

Ardent and optimistic, Pezman's less-recognized role was to another kind of board—the kind that comprise the organizational structure of the surf culture. An Advisory Board member of the influential Surfrider Foundation, and a support system at her mother's soup kitchen, Pezman was a philanthropic spirit.

Her most lasting contribution might have been her visionary championing of the Surf Industry Manufacturer's Association which was eventually founded in 1989. As with *Surfer* and *Surfer's Journal*, Pezman worked discreetly to push forward the complicated framework of the organization while the surf brands often quibbled among themselves.

"Most people are aware of the beautiful images and words that they get from the finished product," Debbee remarked. "They don't see the behind the scenes work, the attention to detail, the organization, the paperwork, the finances." And that is often where the women are—where they make a huge, but typically inconspicuous difference.

Boss of the Boards

Not everyone could choose to be inconspicuous. Some women were forced to stand in the spotlight and stare down the glare—if they wanted to call the shots. Although female chief executives are rare in the surf industry, Caroline Weber (the wife of 60s icon Dewey Weber) is an example of what surfing's first surfboard factory CEO had to do to prove she could be the chairman of the boards. When Dewey Weber died in 1993, news of his passing spread around the world. Newspaper and broadcast eulogies appeared virtually everywhere from San Diego to Sydney. The California State Senate adjourned in his honor.

After a respectful mourning period, Caroline Weber dried her eyes, took a breath and convened with their two sons, Corey and Shea. It was the family's collective desire to keep Dewey Weber Surfboards alive. To succeed, Caroline had taken a hard look at the business and determined that some drastic measures were required to bring Dewey Weber Surfboards back to the stature it once commanded.

The negative rumors running throughout the surf community following Dewey's death created an even more challenging environment for Caroline. The first woman CEO in the decidedly "man's world" of surfboard manufacturing took on an uphill struggle.

No pushover, Caroline expected respect. Initially it was not granted. Caroline saw the future of the brand as needing a significant improvement both in the product and the image the brand presented. She insisted on quality surfboard construction. At first she was ignored. The male craftsmen working for the company considered her ignorant. Glassing rooms were, after all, an exclusively male domain. She was not deterred. Caroline knew what she wanted and demanded it. She bought the first ad in the new Longboard Magazine in 1993. It featured a great photo—a shot of Dewey by Leroy Grannis—and went on from there.

"It was tough," recalled Gail Motil, of *Longboard* magazine. "But the end result was a well-orchestrated recovery." Caroline persevered. Within eighteen months she had Weber Surfboards producing some of the finest equipment on the market again. "We took the company from virtual insolvency to thriving enterprise," says Caroline. "No one thought I could do it. But we did."

A Subtle Funster

It would have been hard for Danielle Beck to be inconspicuous. Blond, blue-eyed, a super-model Heidi Klum look-alike with intelligence, athleticism and ambition, Beck seemed destined to become a star in the industry while she was still the Roxy Core Marketing Manager.

Her first break came when she created MTV "Surf Girls" an early reality show set in the Roxy team surf house on the North Shore which she also co-produced and hosted.

Beck had a rare talent: she could negotiate, direct and strategize with serious aplomb while never seeming to overshadow the men she worked with—and for.

Coolly self-confident, she remained aloof without appearing haughty and commanded a respect among her peers—both men and women alike. She was one of the first women to climb to the top ladder of one of the biggest brands in the business; a billion dollar corporation of which she was a big part. In 2010 after almost a decade with the Quiksilver group she became the Vice-President of Marketing for Roxy, a top tier of the executives in the surf industry and one of the most influential positions in the women's market.

In 2015 she struck out on her own, cofounding Funsters, Inc., a full-service creative agency.

Surf Express

Originally from Emerald Isle, North Carolina, Carol Holland started tabulating for ESA contests, packing up kids for surf trips, organizing houses, food, money and transport, as soon as she had children in competition. For years Holland directed the OP Pro/Am Series in Florida, the Tropics Gran Prix and WSL contests in Panama and Puerto Rico. As the parent of budding surf star Todd Holland, she traveled extensively with surfers and surfboards. Observing how the entire surf market was being underserved and realizing how much experience she had in the field, Holland decided to go to travel school.

"Travel agents had no grasp on locations surfers wanted to go to," she remarked. "I knew nearly all of them." Shortly thereafter she opened Surf Express, an all-inclusive surf travel company, eventually offering trips to Central and South America, Mexico, the Caribbean and beyond. The first of its kind, the business was an immediate success. Predating the boom in group surf travel, it became one of the most successful niche market companies in the business, eventually serving a booming girls market.

Rhode Island's Chick on Sticks

In Rhode Island, Kira Stillwell was a surf entrepreneur of a different kind. From a passion for surfing Stillwell, her sister Hollie Stillwell, and Jennifer Sadoski formed Chicks on Sticks, a woman's surf club, in 1996. They had talked among themselves about creating a place "for a diverse, wonderful group of women surfers." But the concept blossomed, with members in Maine, Vermont, Connecticut, Massachusetts, Pennsylvania and New York.

Kira Stillwell and her sisters grew up sailing and snorkeling in the forty-degree Atlantic water of the small town of Narragansett. They started surfing late but caught on quickly. The club formed the backbone of beach cleanups, the instructional surf program and eventually the re-establishment of a robust Surfrider Foundation chapter.

"We originally thought that a club would simply act as an avenue for us to spend lots of time in the water together," Stillwell said. "But it took on a life of its own."

Millennium Stars

New Century, New Choices, New Benchmarks

2000–2007

Wahine Na koa

*"It took me quite a long time to develop a voice, and
now that I have it, I am not going to be silent."*
—Madeleine Albright, first female U.S. Secretary of State

A Woman's Worth

Anyone surfing the web in 1999 remembered the unsettling "Y2K" conspiracy theory: the new millennium's date-realignment would short-circuit the Internet infrastructure and personal data-systems. While paranoia reigned briefly, the computer cataclysm didn't happen; the emergency food packages stashed by doomsters in bomb-proof shelters were chucked into crock pots and surfers (in particular) continued to party like it was 1999.

As the information highway's rapid change ushered in the first decade of the 21st Century, women found themselves on a fast track that often bounced off the guardrails. Cori Schumacher—the first openly gay woman surfer—became the 2000 Women's World Longboard Champion with 1999 Champ Daize Shayne finishing second. Christina Aguilera's "What a Girl Wants" topped the charts and remained on Billboard's Hot 100 for 26 weeks. *Blue Crush*, a 2002 Hollywood film about surfing women, was released by Universal, making it the first general audience surf film in over twenty years.

Films with women protagonists in startling new roles were beginning to appear everywhere. *Bend it Like Beckham*, Kiera Knightley's breakout film role, displayed independent young soccer players finding their muse. *Erin Brockovich*, Julia Robert's Oscar-winning performance showed a working class woman become a successful legal advocate. And *Dreamgirls* made Jennifer Hudson a major star.

Her debut as a curvaceous, sexually assertive, self-confident black woman—not played for laughs or impersonated by a male comedian in drag—stole the show. Another singing star, folk rock phenom Sarah McLachlan took surf lessons from world longboard champ Izzy Paskowitz at the venerable Paskowitz Surf School and became a devotee. "I fell in love with it the first time I did it," she said to *Surfing GIRL* magazine in 2001.

Hawaiian surf prodigy Bethany Hamilton saw no limits at all after losing her left arm in a 2003 shark attack, making global headlines and shocking the surf community. As she courageously rehabilitated—returning to top competitive surfing and riding forty-foot Jaws—she set off a social media frenzy and inspired young women everywhere. That same year Layne Beachley of Australia made global headlines herself, winning a sixth consecutive WSL Women's World Shortboard title.

In American politics Condoleeza Rice became the first African American Secretary of State in 2005 and two years later Nancy Pelosi became the first female speaker of the House of Representatives. Things seemed to be moving forward—and in surfing progress seemed on the upward swing too: a South American woman, Sofia Mulanovich won a World Title for the first time since fellow Peruvian Felipe Pomar in 1964, broadening the female field of opportunity on a global scale.

And after twenty-nine years of operation, the California Surf Museum opened new city-donated facilities designed by architect and board rider Louise Balma, in Oceanside, California. As rock star Alicia Keys noted: "A real man just can't deny a woman's worth."

That worth was definitely increasing. By 2010 nearly 75 percent of women worked outside the home and there was broad agreement that a working mother could provide just as good a home-life for her children as a stay-at-home mom. Lisa Andersen had already proved that by winning a World Championship less than a year after she had borne a child. After seeing Andersen's effect on surfing, women on waves took their new options seriously. To be a world surfing champion in the new millennium, the level of ability—and significance—had risen to never-before-seen heights.

A Fierce and Gracious Competitor

The most unlikely of all women's world surf champions, Sofia Mulanovich was a fierce and gracious competitor. Born in Peru, a place long known for a wealth of waves and talent, but a dearth of infrastructure needed to produce surfing champions, Mulanovich began on a Morey Boogie at five. She moved to a surfboard at nine and began competing at thirteen—making it to the quarterfinal of the Op Pro in 1996.

Sofia just missed the cut to the WCT in her first year as a pro, but in 2004 Sofia won three consecutive events to become the first professional world surfing champion from South America. Warm and friendly, she won the coveted Surfer Poll Awards in 2007.

A national hero in her native country, where stadiums and children are named after her, Mulanovich can be considered the first great Latinx competitor.

When she won the WCT Women's World Championship at the Billabong Pro at Honolua Bay Maui, I was the brand's media director—responsible for getting the news out to the world. As I sent media releases out, the incoming live-streaming videos showed hundreds of thousands of Peruvian fans cheering in their sports bars. Before the trophy ceremonies were completed I received a telegram of congratulations to her—sent from the *President of Peru*. In her country Mulanovich was a celebrity on the scale of Beyoncé in America.

Following in the Footsteps of Her Mentor to a World Title

As a youngster charging around in the shorebreak of Sydney's northern beaches, Chelsea Georgeson caught the eye of Lisa Andersen.

Taking Chelsea under her wing, the multi-World Champion connected Georgeson with sponsors, media and coaches, springing the nineteen-year-old onto the World Championship Tour in 2002.

"This set of women—the momentum generation—were so much more savvy, intelligent, aware," observed *Wahine* publisher Marilyn Edwards.

By the 2005 season, Georgeson was a title contender, winning four WSL events. A dramatic showdown with reigning champion Sofia Mulanovich in the quarterfinals at the Roxy Pro at Honolua Bay captured the world's attention. Georgeson won the contest, the Triple Crown and the 2005 Women's World Title.

In the ensuing media crush, and at the height of her career, Georgeson married and postponed her tour schedule to have a baby. As a protégé of Andersen she carried the same independence and self-confidence. She didn't name the baby Lisa. But some thought perhaps she should have.

Crush, crush, crush

Small in stature, observers and colleagues alike considered Rochelle Ballard a giant of her era when riding big waves and deep tubes.

Ballard was credited with helping change the face of women's surfing, first as the star of a surf film that later became a Hollywood smash, then as a big wave charger and finally, as perhaps the best tube rider of her generation. While Layne Beachley dominated the early millennium tour contests, "Rochelle captured the imagination of women surfers with her tube riding," claimed Kate Bosworth, the actress who played Ballard in the big screen version of *Blue Crush*. "Her bravado behind the curtain and natural likeability made her a highly-esteemed star," added Ballard's heir apparent Keala Kennelly.

Ballard migrated to Kauai with her parents when she was six. Fellow California transplant Margo Oberg inspired her to surf at twelve and she began competing as a teenager. By 1991 she was surfing professionally, and soon after married Bill Ballard, a surf movie-maker. Their subsequent film based on their travels with other top women surfers resulted in the documentary *Blue Crush*, which became the basis for the hugely popular Hollywood film of the same name.

She competed on the Women's Pro Circuit for ten years, and from 1994 to her retirement in 2004, Rochelle made the top ten rankings of the Women's Pro Tour every year.

It was not without hardship: "Nothing develops your winning edge like being down to your return tickets," Ballard remembered. At the last tour event in South Africa one year, she found herself broke; the credit cards maxed out.

"I knew I had to win this one or we were going home—maybe for good," she recalled. She needed some magic. A chance encounter provided it.

"We met Cheyne Horan in the hotel elevator. 'Why don't you let me coach you?' he offered. 'I said yes. He did. And I won.'"

In 1997 Ballard mustered more magic: a women's world record for scoring two perfect ten's in a single heat, a world record that is not likely to be broken. She also served four years on the ASP Board as a surfer representative. But it was her fearlessness in big surf—from Teahupoo to Sunset Beach to Jeffreys Bay—that inspired the generation of women surfers who came after her.

"Rochelle was so grounded, and so good in big waves," Layne Beachley told me. "She was a great barometer too—she wouldn't let you get away with stuff—she would hold you accountable."

After leaving the pro scene, Ballard moved to Kauai, ran an annual surf contest, became a yoga devotee and created a surf/yoga/wellness retreat business that became her successful follow-up career.

Although she won the Wahine Women's Bud Light Tour in 1996 and captured the 2012 ISA World Masters fifteen years later, the women's World Title eluded her during her Pro Touring days.

In the end it did not matter. During her seventeen years as a professional surfer—and in the years before and since—Ballard remained what many consider "one of the most influential women surfers of all time."

The Danger Zone

With a nickname like "Danger Woman," it's of little surprise that Kim Hamrock's reputation for fearlessness preceded her. When a male surfer collided with her on a wave at Lower Trestles, an incendiary vocal exchange followed. Then he punched Hamrock in the face. He was hardly prepared for what happened next.

"I took both my fingers, jabbed them in his eyes and held him underwater," Hamrock demonstrated. "I wanted to make sure by the time he got up, he'd be too exhausted to want to get me."

To the credit of the locals, the ugly aggressor was sent packing, banished from the surf spot indefinitely.

The salient point? Hamrock could give as good as she got. But many women were either intimidated by the bullying behavior or simply too disgusted with it to put themselves in a position to be demeaned.

Born in 1960 in Whittier, California, Hamrock didn't start surfing regularly until the age of sixteen. Eventually a driver's license and a used car would take her the twenty miles down Beach Boulevard from inland La Habra to the beaches of Huntington and Trestles. But in the mid-70s, an era when female surfers were somewhat rare and often discouraged by Southern California's notoriously misogynistic lineups, it was not easy for an aggressive, fearless female.

Intent on taking as many waves as she could find, Hamrock was dropped in on constantly, had her lease yanked frequently. She was threatened and yelled at by surfers not half as good as she was in the lineup.

Despite the harassment factor and the constant hassle required to get waves, by the mid-90s, Hamrock had garnered six U.S. titles (four shortboards, 1993-96; two longboard, 1995–96.) After turning pro as a longboarder in 1998, just four short years later—*at age forty-two*—she was crowned Women's Longboard World Champion in 2002.

But it was her big wave prowess that earned her the name Danger Woman, a moniker she wears with pride. For years, she was the only woman invited to surf in a longboard tube riding contest held at the big-wave spot Puerto Escondido, Mexico.

At forty-five, Hamrock claimed a Banzai Pipeline Surfing Championships title, despite being the oldest competitor in the event, and was the only woman to be invited to the Red Bull Big Wave Contest at Dungeons in South Africa, where she both paddled and towed into some 30'-plus waves.

Continuing to focus on larger surf, Hamrock earned a runner-up title at the 2005 XXL Big Wave Awards. That same year she was inducted into the Surfer's Walk of Fame in Huntington Beach. Wanting to share her experiences and stories about surfing, Hamrock wrote a book in 2015, entitled *My Grandma Surfs*

Better Than You. And as a mother of three, that book title may be the maxim that defined her legacy.

Beck On Call

The multiple disciplines and varied avenues of success seemed to accelerate at the turn of the 21st Century. Holly Beck was perhaps the prototypical example of the change—well-marketed, multi-talented, highly motivated and always on call.

Beck began surfing at age fourteen after being told by her mother that surfing was only for boys. Rebelliously resistant, she fell so in love with the ocean it took over her life. Consumed with riding waves, six years of amateur contests fed her competitive spirit.

"By the 1999 season," Janice Aragon, executive director of the National Scholastic Surfing Association, stated, "she *dominated* women's surfing in the amateur ranks."

Graduating from UCSD with a degree in Psychology and an ISA amateur national surfing title that same year, Beck officially turned pro at twenty-one. The next decade was spent as a professional surfer and model, traveling for photo and video shoots, gracing the covers of surf and mainstream fitness magazines. At one point her passport had sixty-four pages filled.

Initially it was a dream. "But then it got to the point where I wasn't winning. I was placing in the middle—and I sort of lost motivation. . . . I decided I wanted more."

Equally adept in a boardroom or bikini—a beauty with an MBA in marketing under her belt—she convinced her sponsors her value would increase "by allowing me to function as a roaming billboard."

Determined and well-educated, Beck succeeded, maintaining her allure among sponsors while helping to break down surfer stereotypes. Camera-savvy and disciplined, Beck was an interviewer's dream, providing articulate responses and displaying true passion for a seemingly adoring media.

Beck became one of the surfing world's most visible stars, appearing on countless TV shows including *The Best Damn Sports Show*, *MTV*, and most notably as star of the WB's *Boarding House* in 2003. Despite immense media attention, Beck remained unassuming, claiming to "still be the dork she was in high school." Eventually tiring of the constant travel, Beck bought property in Nicaragua in 2007, a result of her affection for Central America and a desire to settle down.

In 2010 she retired from pro surfing and moved to Nicaragua full time.

"My favorite thing about traveling as a pro was having adventures with other women, so I founded a women's surf and yoga retreat called Surf With Amigas,"

Beck disclosed in a 2020 interview. "I wanted to continue my travel adventures, support my lifestyle—and inspire other women to do the same." Married in 2012 to friend Kim Obermyer, Beck began living full time in Central America splitting between North Nicaragua and Southern Costa Rica. The couple had two children and founded Hip-E Habitat, a residential home design-build, construction management company.

By Jupiter

Beck set a high bar, but she was not alone in using education, passion and talent to further a career in surfing. Jenni Flanigan launched from Jupiter Beach, Florida with a powerful surf style and a degree in English & Comparative Literature, graduating Cum Laude from the University Honors Program at Florida Atlantic University. On a surf safari with Holly Beck to Panama, her surf videos of the trip went viral, putting her in the spotlight. She quickly used her visibility to promote her passions: surfing, traveling and spreading awareness for sustainable, organic agricultural practices and water conservation in developed and developing countries alike.

"Knowledge is power, the world is in crisis," Flanigan said in 2010 "and there's so much work to be done to save our planet from the human race."

Adept at playing any number of stringed instruments, Flanigan adored the song "Stella Was A Diver And She Was Always Down" by Interpol, which might have described *her own* persona.

"First, it has a nautical theme which would go well seeing as I was stuck on a deserted island and all; and second, there are so many intricate and intriguing metaphorical messages." Flanigan continued: "It might take thirty days of food- and water-deprived speculation to figure them all out: 'She once fell through the street/Down the manhole in that bad way/The underground drip/It's just like her scuba days.'"

Witty and erudite, Flanigan saw life through the ocean, and the environmental sea vessel *Calypso* as a metaphoric symbol of purpose. It earned her respect. As she often said, "How very Jacques Cousteau."

Kiss and Make Up

As a professional makeup artist, respect was something Roxanne Saffaie received often in her career. Saffaie worked with leading photographers and stylists on shows, ad campaigns, N.Y. & L.A. fashion week and editorial work in magazines. Serving as the beauty editor of *Woman's Surf & Style* magazine, her work also graced the pages of *Vogue, People, Maxim, WWD* and *Nylon* among others. But she knew that that no matter her reputation in the fashion world, none of the males out in the Waikiki lineup were going to hand her any waves.

"When I go out at Kaisers where you have to really compete for waves, I have earned the respect for being out there all the time," Saffaie acknowledged. "I don't drop in on anybody, and guys give me respect for that."

Saffaie's multidimensional talent landed her on "The List" in *L.A Confidential* magazine with the likes of George Clooney and Dolly Parton. Roxy's client list included Tommy Hilfiger, Michelle Rodriguez, Michael Kors, Paula Patton and Russell Simmons. But her wave-riding ability set her apart from her peers.

Saffaie was one of a large cadre of college-educated professional women who at the turn of the millennium combined their careers with a surfing passion—despite the risks. Diane Tachera, a corporate businesswoman, hung up her Ralph Lauren outfits and opted for the casual look of khaki pants and T-shirts—and a job she loved. An avid longboard surfer, Tachera's previous careers included public relations and stock trading. She left that corporate world behind to cofound the Hawaiian Longboard Federation full time. Tachera became a one-person surf event operation, run out of her house.

"I'm a risk taker, and I value my lifestyle over financial rewards," she said.

Cécilia Thibier took a risk when she moved to the Basque region of France to pursue photography. "In Biarritz, I found my personal paradise, my happy place where I could finally live my dream of being a photographer and a surfer."

Although it meant leaving an exhilarating city like Paris and a promising career behind her, it was a risk worth taking. "Despite the struggles and the unknowns," she declared, "I was finally able to free my spirit and follow my path."

Half Moon Bay chiropractor Jo Stroud practiced her surfing in Pacifica, north of San Francisco. She met wetsuit mogul Jack O'Neill in Santa Cruz in 1980, at an art opening. O'Neill took her on her first surf session at Pleasure Point in Santa Cruz, starting her long voyage of "endless summers."

In 1990, Stroud was often the only woman in the lineup. By 2006 females sometimes outnumbered males. As a member of the Surfer's Medical Association (SMA) she attended an annual conference on Tavarua Island, and after falling in love with surf travel, chased waves around the world both with the organization and on her own.

It was a risk to step out of the comfort of her traditional physician role. But as Stroud treated numerous patients with back pain, she realized *her own* well-being was *surf* related. "It's like meditation with me," she said. "I love the contact with the ocean; it's necessary for my health."

Causing Effect

Surfers became active in a number of causes and issues as the Millennium gave sway to a thousand fresh perspectives on lifestyle and beach culture.

Born without hearing, Crystal "CJ" da Silva not only proved disadvantage could be overcome with talent, perseverance and pluck, she became an exemplar of triumph over a struggle. "I've surfed in many contests. I can't hear the horn, so I have to look for the flags." WSL contests were also difficult. "I couldn't hear the scores during the heat or what score I needed to advance." Disadvantages were balanced by friends and fellow surfers.

"When I surf local spots, I see mostly familiar faces and they wave or write in the sand."

After marriage and a child, da Silva developed CJ Waterwear into a bikini business, and remained an advocate for the deaf in surfing and other sports.

Big-wave rider and twelve-year veteran pro competitor Kyla Langen was one of the first gay rights activists to actually have an impact in the surf community. Ranked number eleven on the World Qualifying tour in 2006, by 2016 she had successfully run Queer Surf, a surf school primarily for lesbians, intending to bring diversity to the beach. "It's just such a privilege to be able to go to the ocean and be at the ocean and it's a shame that it's a privilege that's often reserved for straight white folks," Langen said.

Optimistic and approachable, Kimberly Ann Mayer was arguably the best female surfer to come out of Santa Cruz, California in the first decade of the millennium. With a passion for surfing and a degree at UCSC in Environmental Studies, Meyer took her second passion—ecological balance with the focus on sustainable agriculture—and fitted it into work with Orchard Keepers, a local company whose mission is to promote, encourage and create backyard food systems through holistic and sustainable land use practices.

But with surf being her first passion, Mayer eventually moved into the bur-geoning area of women's surf retreats, joining forces with her friend Holly Beck in Nicaragua. Mayer and Beck had spent years traveling the world together for competitions and photo shoots. Beck saw Mayer's addition to the Central American "Amigas" retreats as a gold standard for the enterprise. "Kim Mayer is probably one of the coolest people on the planet. She's always stoked, always positive, jams on the guitar, kills it with a soccer ball, is up for any adventure, is the one most likely to make friends with every random person she comes across, plus she totally rips at surfing!"

Enthusiasm was seemingly rampant in the Bay Area of California at the time. There were observers within the regions surfers who contended that if ever there were an ideal "Miss California," it would be Alayna Natty Scheibel. And *not* "to be mistaken with the Miss California pageant type," declared Clarkie Clark who edited Realskate.com in 2003. "Our local army of Santa Cruz feminists drove that pageant out of town a few years ago," Clark asserted. "I'm talking about a *real* California woman; Covergirl for Surfer Girl; the picture of health, natural beauty, brains, strong athletic ability and an edge for business success." One of the owners of Paradise shop in Santa Cruz, Scheibel competed in the inaugural World Longboard Championship in 1999, dated respected shaper Jed Noll and toured the USA with a woman's team sponsored by Margaritaville Tequila that was among the first to travel to wave pools like Six Flags and Big Surf.

Everywhere

Whether business, environmental efforts, events, surf camps or numbers in the lineup, the growth was apparent *everywhere*. Half Moon Bay High classmates Celina Pritchard, Molly Davenport, and Alisa Stegmaier were among many who roamed the San Francisco Peninsula; teenage girl-packs on a perpetual quest for good surf. "It's crazy, the amount of girls in the younger grades that are getting into it," Stegmaier remarked back in 2000.

Music, surf and awareness dominated the millennial psyche. Songstress Michelle Branch was the reason why half of the teenagers in America bought guitars in 2002 and tried to launch songwriting careers. Her single "Everywhere" won the Viewer's Choice Award at the 2002 MTV Video Music Awards.

And surfing was the reason half the girls seemed headed for the beach.

Not only were the surf numbers increasing, the quality of performances were too. And not just in California. *Everywhere.*

French surfer Caroline Sarran and longboarder Alexis Gazzo led a swelling crowd of participants from as far afield as Joan Duru competing in Tahiti to Pauline Ado winning the first of seven French National Titles.

"There are a lot more girls that *charge*," world tour pro surfer Rochelle Ballard contended in 2006. "They are getting more assertive, but not even close to the guys in aggression. The girls can still be polite."

Perhaps the greatest measure of just how many women were flocking to the waves was their participation in surf contests. A few years previous on Kauai, Ballard and fellow star Keala Kennelly had to compete against the boys because they couldn't round up enough girls to fill one heat.

"Now, talking to my friend Coral McCarthy," (an outstanding longboarder on Kauai) Kennelly marveled, "the Roxy event had a hundred girls."

More than 250 females entered China Uemura's 2006 longboard contest in Waikiki. At Makaha, Buffalo Keaulana's Big Board contest enjoyed similar growth in wahine participation, while that same year the Triple Crown of Surfing added another event to its stable of North Shore winter contests.

"I entered China's contest, and it was very aggressive," Diane Tachera contended in 2006. "But it was packed."

Along with the amateur events, a surge of competitors moved into the pro ranks at that same time. Holly Monkman's powerful low-center-of gravity style caught the attention of the media, eventually providing a surf academy and marketing career. Jodie Smith was among the band of sports women who took on a strenuous training regimen including everything from bike riding to circuit training to running. Even professionals from other disciplines got into the act. Kelly Clark, an Olympic snowboarder with a gold and two Olympic bronze medals under her belt, took up the surfing life. Despite being one of the most decorated women in snow sports, she could not resist the lure, becoming a respected waverider as time passed. Her first trip after retiring from pro snowboarding in 2019 was a warm-water surf safari with friends.

A Good Goodbye

Some competitors are lucky enough to leave the contest scene with a sweet goodbye kiss to their whole career. In 2005, after thirteen years on the World Championship Tour, Trudy Todd announced her retirement from pro surfing just before the opening heats of the second annual Malibu Pro, and two years after threatening to "go full Pamala Anderson." Winner of the 1999 Triple Crown, Todd's record included six state amateur titles and a third in the World Tour ratings. She finished first on the Australian Championship Circuit Pro Tour in 1993, 1994 and 1996. But as journalist Kim Stravers noted on *Surfline*, multiple injuries, two bouts with cancer and a burgeoning surf-fashion line prompted her decision to shift her priorities toward business and her life's second act. The sassy Australian, who was once fined $1200 for brawling with a fellow competitor and found celebrity fame on the reality TV show *The Hothouse* was never known to make a quiet exit. Famous on tour for her party girl reputation, Todd went out with well-deserved fanfare, in a memorable battle with her friend and Tour partner Samantha Cornish.

By the semifinals of Todd's last event, *Surfing* magazine noted that the entire beach looked like a high school fashion show, LA style. Pregnant model Helena Christiansen was blocking spectator views from the competitor's tent with her sundry entourage of waif-like Starbucks-toting girlfriends. The entire scaffolding area became a mob scene as well-known celebrities Ricky Schroeder (a previous 80s TV star on *Silver Spoons*) and Red Hot Chili Peppers bassist Flea Balzary prepared to paddle out for their 15-person celebrity heat.

In the finals Todd came through in what was later described as a "swaggering blaze of glory" to win her last contest. Her victory—among a party celebrity crowd on America's most celebrity-laden surf beach—was a fitting farewell to one of the era's most colorful Queensland characters.

United Kingdom: Surf Champion Champions the Surf

Five-time British National Champion Robyn Davies learned to surf at fourteen; her home break of Porthleven was a rarity in Britain: a hollow reef break with a consistent lineup and real island-style power. "Since the day I first dipped my toe in the ocean I knew that it had a hold on me." By the turn of the millennium she had risen to the UK's top woman in the sport.

Enthused and optimistic, Davies was expected to win a sixth national title when in 2005 she injured her back in an automobile accident. Unable to surf for nearly ten months, she looked for another involvement in the sport. She started to do volunteer work for the National Trust, and at the same time became an ambassador for Surfers Against Sewage.

In March 2006, Davies was appointed to a position as Surf Project Officer for the National Trust in Devon and Cornwall. The trust, which owns some seven hundred miles of top surfing spots, is dedicated to preservation. Unequivocal about her new role, Davies helped launch a campaign to make the Trust relevant to a new, much wider and younger audience.

"I am so passionate about the wonderful natural resource that is our unspoiled coastline."

By 2013 Davies's role had focused on organizing events and managing eco-surf lessons—arranging for students to meet local wardens who explain to them how the coastline is managed and point out the different wildlife habitats and coastal protection. "My middle name of Sunshine has become prophetic. I love passing along the knowledge—and the environment is a really important part of surfing that is overlooked."

There was a bit of a Renaissance in the Channel Islands as well, from where many early English surfers had hailed. Emma Skinner, a professional surfer and model, along with her brother Ben "Skindog" Skinner, a prominent surfer and shaper from Cornwall, England, generated media interest. Skinner originally grew up on the island of Jersey, a self-governing bailiwick located between England and France, and came from the family business Skinners Brewery but eventually worked with a group of top surfers at Nineplus Surfboards headquartered in St. Agnes Cornwall. "Surfing became a huge part of my life," she said in 2006. She moved to Dubai to pursue creating art of the natural ocean world.

Barefoot and Pregnant

One unique vulnerability men do *not have* to contend with: the possibility of pregnancy. "Barefoot and pregnant" was a long-standing derogatory term describing how to keep women controlled and helpless.

But professional surfers—who *already* went barefoot to work—were not on that career path. One woman was able to turn the phrase from an offensive remark to a triumph: Four-time World Champ Lisa Andersen, who didn't win her first title until after giving birth to her daughter Erica. Some, like World Champ Chelsea Georgeson and fearless Kim Hamrock, chose retiring from professional surfing to marry and start a family.

One retirement was particularly touching. Pregnant with her first child, Melanie Redman Carr, a veteran known for her formidable skills and phosphorescent blue eyes, quit the Tour in 2007 after reaching number two in the world rankings the year before. The no-nonsense Western Australian pro admitted the effects of pregnancy were interfering in her performance: "I feel a little slow and heavy and it's difficult with the weight distribution."

Redman Carr had joined the World Tour sixteen years earlier at the age of sixteen and had remained in that top echelon her entire pro career. She had been runner-up to the World Title twice—once in 2001 and again in 2006. But motherhood took precedence. Touted in a *Surfing Girl* article as "the most likely surfer to become a U.N. Ambassador" Redman Carr's solid contest record cemented her legacy.

In a bittersweet press conference held on the day of her retirement she said of her storied career: "It is quite a nice thing to be able to tell my child one day."

Pregnancy has certainly not been a finish to every career. Some women even returned to greater glory after taking time off to have children. Quiet-spoken Australian Yvonne Byron of Wollongong made a stunning comeback after five years away from competition. A savvy, unassuming mother of two, she created a major upset in her 2005 return by defeating six-times world champion Layne Beachley to win the women's Bico Classic at Margaret River, Australia. A former WCT surfer, Byron (née Rogencamp) had been absent from the contest scene since 1999 when she gave birth to the first of two children. During her string of comeback victories, this three-time Australian Open champion won two consecutive Australian Surf Masters titles in the over-30 division but was still unable to return to the Pro Tour due to family commitments and lack of sponsorship. Thwarted by obligations and financial hardship, the indefatigable veteran still saw winning an age-category State Title—under any circumstance—as "a major thrill."

Baby on Board

Maddie Peterson, an aspiring pro and fashion model, dealt with the dilemma of career and motherhood in a different way. While perhaps not a household name, Peterson is a rare beauty with respected talent as a competitor: she earned a fourth place copper medal at the 2015 ISA Games in Ecuador.

"In today's generation, especially for women, body image is such an important topic and something I feel very passionate about," she explained. "You know, the plan you have in mind isn't always what happens in life, so you need to be able to adapt and go with the flow."

One noticeable disparity across all professional sports, but surfing in particular, is the different way male and female athletes deal with having a baby in the family. Many of the Men's Contest Tour surfers have children. And although mothers and the little ones occasionally join them for events, for the most part the men go to the contests alone, leaving their family behind while they compete. Yet on the Women's CT, rarely does a child appear, nor seldom does a woman surf competitively full-time on the CT after having a baby.

Friends and fellow travelers, Peterson and her friend Alana Blanchard experienced pregnancies at the same time but with differing responses. While on a joint surf jaunt to Cabo San Lucas Mexico, Blanchard confided to Peterson that she was pregnant. Then a couple weeks later, Peterson found out *she* was pregnant as well. "So throughout our pregnancies we talked a lot, she told me what she was going through, I shared what I was going through." It was interesting, she noted, "to see Banks [Alana and Jack's son] and Brooks (Maddie and Blake's son) grow up—and compare them to one another. Alana was really helpful to me throughout the whole experience."

Together with the support of her sponsors Peterson was able to "use my platform as a younger mom to show the transition that occurs in that period, both to your body and your mindset as someone bringing life into the world."

Alana Blanchard did not end up feeling so lucky. After garnering massive media attention during her career, Blanchard was disappointed by her sponsor's support after her pregnancy became widely known. Blanchard, whose natural beauty and sexually attractive persona was often considered a significant value to her sponsors, felt she lost the appeal they were looking for after she became a married woman with a child.

"They no longer really wanted to use me," Blanchard divulged in March of 2020, "I want to be with a company that really supports me, who I am today and that just wasn't Rip Curl at the time." Her sponsor strenuously denied her version of the breakup, but Blanchard's perception was shared by many women in that situation.

There were women who declined to give up their hard earned professional career—and remained successful nonetheless: Melanie Bartels was predicted to lose her drive and focus when she decided to raise her child as a single mother. But she was back in the water just weeks after birthing and went on to become a top ten star on the World Circuit.

Lisa Andersen's first World Title win while she was pregnant may be the most impressive competitive achievement—matched only three other times in the entirety of modern sports.

Keala Kennelly, perhaps big-wave surfing's most distinguished woman, had a child in 2012 but she has continued her career (even increasing her multiple achievements) since then. Having a child *did* affect the overall equation for Kennelly. "When it comes to my son, I definitely think about him, and it just makes me calculate my risks a bit more," she told journalist Laia Garcia. "But at the same time, I want to make my son proud of me, and that makes me want to go bigger and charge harder." A string of championship titles made her case, even when the price was extracted in heartache.

Another woman had a story about motherhood as exceptional and fascinating as any in women's sporting history. Her record *seven* World Championships are only part of the emotional rollercoaster of her personal life: a search for fulfillment—and a quest to find her origins. She begins the next chapter.

Seven Wonders
2000–2007

"A woman's heart is a deep ocean of secrets."
—Rose Dawson,
protagonist of the film *Titanic*

The Sins of My Unknown Father:
Layne Beachley's quest for the truth, peace
and seven World Titles

Layne Beachley looked up at the man who had walked to the front of the line where she was signing autographs. She was surprised—he was not asking her for an autograph, he was giving her a photograph—of himself and another man in a boxing ring. There was a note with it. The folded scrap of paper had a phone number and a question: "Am I thirty-two years too late?"

It was Australia Day, January 26th and the holiday throngs attending the annual Surfboard Challenge at Blue Point were thick and in a celebratory mood.

When she looked up the gray-haired man had disappeared into the holiday crowd. Layne stuffed the photo and note in her handbag and quickly returned to signing autographs for a long line of fans. She took a break from the signings an hour or so later, walking over to watch the contestants jockeying for position in the modest swell off the point. *Was that my dad?* The sudden thought made her head swim. She lingered, lost in thought, gazing at the Harbor Bridge, the Opera House and the Sydney skyline in the distance. The more she considered the chance encounter the more it seemed there was only one plausible answer. *Am I thirty-two years too late?* the message said. She had turned thirty-two that May.

Heading back to the autograph area, she found herself walking quickly, anxious to look at the photo and copy the number into her phone. But her bag was not under the table where she had left it. A scrupulous search turned up nothing.

The bag was gone, with no trace. And with it the only fragment of hope that she would ever find the father she had never known.

It felt like the lyrics of "Seven Wonders," the Christine McVie-penned tune by Fleetwood Mac: "So long ago, certain place, certain time—but if our paths never cross, well you know I'm sorry."

The search for the truth would be long—and take more twists and turns than the Gold Coast Street Circuit motor race.

Layne Collette Beachley grew up surfing at Manly Beach, Australia. Since her first World Title win seven-time women's world surfing champion Layne Beachley's life has played out in public.

Her two-decade-long career on the professional circuit was a professional triumph. But it was also a struggle to overcome chronic fatigue, bitter loss and debilitating anxiety. Layne was adopted at birth but didn't know. When she was only six, her adoptive mother died. It wasn't until the age of eight she was told by her adoptive father that she had been adopted.

She suffered through the break-up of her relationship with Ken Bradshaw, her Hawaiian big-wave riding mentor. She married INXS band member Kirk Pengilly in a fairy tale wedding—and then had to help him through a serious struggle with cancer.

But through it all, the Australian women's champion kept one dark secret: *her birth was the result of her mother being date raped.*

It would be a haunting riddle she would struggle with—and discover the explanation to much later in her remarkable life story.

Athletic and naturally outgoing, Layne Collette Beachley battled the male-dominated line-up at Sydney's Manly Beach and began competing with the pros at age sixteen.

By twenty she was sixth in the world, and two years later she left home to compete on the World Pro Tour. Enamored with big waves almost immediately, Beachley found surfing contests in smaller conditions more problematic—finished as runner-up twice during Lisa Andersen's world championship reign. Andersen was the immovable object meeting Beachley's unstoppable force: "For quite a long time I saw Lisa as the *one thing* between me and *everything* I wanted." Their rivalry was legendary and their personalities starkly contrasting: Andersen tended to be more reserved publicly, guarded, with a wry, sometimes sarcastic humor. Beachley was gregarious and open, with a more brash humor, but whose need for affection and acceptance made her just as easily wounded.

Beachley met big-wave surfer Bradshaw on a winners podium in 1997, and a trusting friendship slowly turned to romance. "I craved affection and loving support," she admitted, "Ken gave me that."

The next year she moved into his Sunset Beach house. "He became my mentor, shaper, lover, sounding board, and coach," she laughed. "I learned a lot."

Bradshaw's tough training regime and competitive strategy welded Beachley's feet to the top rung of the competitive ladder. And as tow-in surfing came into play—surfers strapped into short boards and towed into waves via personal watercraft—Bradshaw and Beachley embarked on a number of missions to the North Shore's distant outer reefs. At one session Ken towed her into a legitimate twenty-five-foot wave at the Outside Log Cabins wave break, setting a standard for the time. While Beachley and Bradshaw eventually broke up in 2000 after her third World Title, they remained friends.

Bradshaw's confidence helped prepare Beachley for her duels, but it also fueled her enmity with Lisa Andersen. Their rivalry became so intense Beachley acknowledged, "we began 'trash talking' each other." But in 1998 with ten seconds left in the final heat of a ferocious contest at Snapper Rocks, Beachley finally defeated Andersen, igniting her six-string firestorm of titles.

Her six World Championships (1998–2004) set the women's record for consecutive titles. Her seventh World Title in 2006, earned her the most wins of any female in surf history—until Steph Gilmore tied her record in 2017. But her six *successive* championships is a record that may *never* be broken.

A serious neck injury hobbled Beachley to a fifth place finish in 2007 and fourth in 2008. As challengers and successors like Stephanie Gilmore moved in, Beachley retired from the WTC circuit in 2009, capping a record-breaking twenty-year professional career with the highest earnings ever in women's surfing.

"Retirement" hardly slowed her down: After starting her own clothing company, Beachley Athletic, in 2009, she decided to produce her own world tour event at her home break of Dee Why, Australia, creating the $100,000 Commonwealth Beachley Classic—the largest prize purse on the women's pro circuit.

While serving as the 2009 World of Difference program chairperson (which gives four Australians the chance to spend a year working for charity while still being paid) she started her own Aim for the Stars Foundation as well.

There is no question about Beachley's achievements—she is ensconced in the pantheon of all-time all-stars. And although her personal life had been rocky, she has been careful in her relationships—and the slow engagements have rewarded her: Not long after her break-up with Ken Bradshaw she acquiesced to a blind date with Kirk Pengilly the INXS rock star and—after seven years of courtship—married in 2010.

But Beachley still carried demons from the past. She was six weeks old when she was adopted by a loving a North Balgowlah couple Val and Neil Beachley. Her father taught her to surf at age four. She remembered her childhood with fondness.

"My dad would run on Manly Beach boardwalk towing me on my skateboard, holding on to his towel."

But her adopted mother died of a brain hemorrhage when Beachley was just six. Her father Neil remarried, only for her stepmom to die of cancer seven years later. Surfing was a refuge. "It's where I go to process my emotions, a place of solace where I run to escape life's troubles," she said. "When I'm in the water I feel safe from turmoil."

Beachley's search for her birth mother led to the discovery of Maggie Gardner, who as a young unmarried seventeen-year-old from Glasgow, had given birth less than a year after arriving from Scotland. Now she would need to confirm that Gardner was the women who had given her up for adoption three decades ago. She forged on with the search.

"My adopted family was wonderful, but I felt unworthy of love," she would confess later. "I wondered why my birth mother rejected me." But Beachley decided successful people use challenges, setbacks and obstacles as platforms for opportunity.

"I distinctly remember making the choice between being a victim of circumstance or a master of my own destiny," she remembered. "I decided to prove my worth and become a world champion. I didn't even know champion of *what*, but I knew it would happen."

The confirming adoption information came while she was in Indonesia, just six weeks away of winning her second World Championship. She now knew who her birth mother was and knew both of them had contact information. Beachley decided to postpone contacting her birth mother to focus on the competition.

But her birth mother Maggie was far more anxious to connect than Layne. She searched Beachley on the internet and called her in Indonesia, initially only hoping to hear her voice on her answering machine. But Beachley answered the phone and it caught Maggie off guard. A volley of information shot out including the story of being an aspiring model who had been raped by the owner of a Kings Cross modeling agency.

"I didn't know what to do with the information that she had been raped. It was bewildering at best."

"Maggie wanted me to have a mother and father," Beachley realized. "She was heartbroken, and guilt ridden." She needn't have been—Layne's life was *not* unhappy, as Maggie assumed—in fact quite the contrary.

"I was traveling the world, getting paid to go surfing for a living. I was a world champion, and I had a wonderful relationship with the family I was adopted into," Beachley continued. "She had nothing to feel guilty for."

Despite the jolting details, Beachley finally decided to meet her mother in 1999. "I felt I was looking in a mirror seventeen years on," she remembered, after flying to Maggie's residence in San Francisco. There was no question Maggie was her mother. "We sat down, and it was like two girls catching up over coffee." Expanding on what she had told Beachley when they had first spoken on the phone call to Indonesia, her birth mother explained the circumstances of her birth: Just seventeen, and newly arrived in Sydney from Scotland, Maggie had accepted a dinner invitation from the manager of a Kings Cross modeling agency. That evening he attacked her. Fatefully, it resulted in a pregnancy.

Maggie Gardner chose to have the baby and gave birth at Crown Street Women's Hospital in May 1972. She put Beachley up for adoption and left Australia, first for New Zealand and then the USA.

"One of the things I first asked was, 'Who was my birthdad?'" Beachley confessed. "Mum said, 'Well, I was raped, and I really don't know who he is.'"

That first meeting had answered a lot of questions. But not one crucial one.

Beachley had remained curious about her father—and Maggie resented her attempts to trace the man she claims had raped her. "I wanted to know who he was. Maggie only made one half of me."

"I wondered about so many things, like where I get my dark olive skin from. But I think finding him would raise more questions than answers."

Beachley also believes that the deaths of her mother and stepmother had caused her to "equate motherhood with loss." So, when Maggie told her she had a low immune system and had been ill, Beachley was too afraid to get close, fearing she would face grief all over again. A long period of estrangement elapsed. But after her wedding in 2010 she found the contentment marriage had given her brought out the desire to build a closer bond with Maggie.

"I have had a protective mechanism around my heart," she admitted. "I am aware of it and now I am willing to unlock that. Initially, I didn't want the distraction," she conceded. "When Maggie was in hospice, she called me from Canada. And I came, immediately.

"*She* had been the one who made all the effort, sending me gifts, emails and reaching out. So we both were so happy to be able to say goodbye."

But the yearning for the father she never knew remained. "When I first saw my birth mother, I remember her eyes and seeing myself," Beachley marveled. "But when I got to thinking about this bloke . . . I'd just like to know."

Layne Beachley finally *did* meet the man who had given her the note and who claimed to be her father. But the DNA tests showed they were not related. Over the years two other men have claimed to be her missing father but were not connected by blood either.

Beachley may never find the birth-father she so longed to know. Some things remain shrouded in mystery an entire lifetime. She reconciled with her birth-mom, and accepted Maggie's adoption choice. Finally she felt a lasting peace in her heart. "Surfing has been my life," she said, "but it's also saved my life. It brings me joy and energy."

In September 2018 she won the WSL Masters, her eighth World Title. "Winning the Masters enabled me to maintain a slender step ahead of Stephanie," Beachley mused after receiving the award. "But based on Steph's current focus, performance and competitive spirit it's only a matter of time before she matches me then smashes me."

Beachley seemed more content in 2020 than in any time in her career. She had health, a happy marriage and a sense of closure about her years in turmoil.

"I am one hundred percent grateful. I was adopted into a beach-loving family with the surname Beachley and became a pro surfer. And my dad was the best father ever." She paused with her trademark smile, and then concluded: "He taught me to surf. And loved me. What more could I have asked for?"

Blue Crush
An All-Girls Hollywood Film
Sparks a Wave of Female Water-women

In 1998, an *Outside* article about Maui surfer girls by Susan Orlean, titled "Life's Swell," landed in a Universal Pictures screenwriter's hands. The article and the popularity of women's surfing sparked the Hollywood adaptation of *Blue Crush*, which was released in 2002. Directed by John Stockwell, it told the story of three friends who have one passion: living the ultimate dream of surfing on Hawaii's famed North Shore. One of the biggest box office draws of any Hollywood mainstream film revolving around surfing, *Blue Crush* was hailed for its spectacular camera work and real-life danger for the surfer-girl stunt doubles. The first major film about surfing to star an all-women lead cast, it became the most influential surf film of the decade. Attracting interest from young women, the surfing audience, and mainstream movie-goers, it caught the attention of the world much the way *Gidget* had done a generation prior.

The original *Blue Crush* was an all-female surf video released in 1996, which hit the shelves thanks to Bill Ballard and his influential wife, Rochelle, one of the era's major surf stars. Featuring the best female short-boarders, the surf travel-action video showcased the women's undeniable talent and became one of the biggest selling surf titles of its time. Every surfer girl was inspired to go surf after watching it.

The professional female surfers featured in the original *Blue Crush* video were cast as stunt doubles and bit characters in the sensationalized coming-of-age Hollywood version. Rochelle Ballard, Megan Abubo, Layne Beachley, Kate

Skarratt and Keala Kennelly joined surfer-turned-actress Sanoe Lake, actress Kate Bosworth and actress Michelle Rodrigez in the movie, which spread the allure of women's surfing to the masses. The film is credited with helping push beach fashion into high gear as well.

"The whole surf culture started to embrace women a lot more," Michelle Rodriguez observed. "For good."

She Works Hard For the Money

Kate Skarratt felt the wave pushing her further under water, down to the reef, wedging her body into a cave. She felt stuck. She thought she might be close to drowning.

Professional surfer/body-double/stuntwoman Kate Skarratt was surfing on Oahu's North Shore—doing a stunt for a film being shot at Pipeline, one of the most feared surf breaks in the world. During filming of *Blue Crush*, this intrepid adventurer from Wollongong was hurt many times at this lethal location. But this incident—being shoved under the reef formations—was the worst. Yet without a hint of bravado, Skarratt told the Sydney Herald, "It wasn't the longest hold-down I've had, it wasn't that scary, it was just for that instant."

"I'd never been caught, I'd never been wedged before," she admitted. "It's a lava bottom and there's lots of little caves; my leg just got wedged into one, and that's the scariest thing, being held in there. Luckily a bit of turbulence got me and pushed me out."

She limped away from the accident with just a torn hamstring. It was certainly not the only one: there was the day for instance when she "hit her head on the reef" and "couldn't feel her elbow for a while" while filming a wipe-out. Although she ranked as high as number ten on the WSL World Tour and had appeared in Sheryl Crowe's number one hit music video for "Soak Up the Sun," her stunt work in *Blue Crush* pushed her into a completely different level of success. After the high-profile exposure from *Crush*'s huge box office, Skarratt worked on *Modus Mix* (2003) and *Beyond the Break* (2006).

But the fickle and fleeting big screen movie business was hard to depend on—and earnings from contest winnings were inconsistent as well. A knee injury in 2003, sustained while on tour in Hawaii, was a serious setback: "I landed on my head and I compressed my knee at Sunset Beach."

For a stunt woman/pro competitor an injury is a choke hold on the fiscal faucet. "It's quite disappointing," she acknowledged, lying on a bed and needing crutches to get around. "I can't finish the year with this injury." It was the last year she would compete on the world tour.

The Edge of Glory

2007–2011

"We need to reshape our own perception of how we view ourselves. We have to step up as women and take the lead."

—Beyoncé

Much More Gilmore

In the dying minutes of the Maui Pro's final heat—the last stop on the ASP Women's World Tour—Stephanie Gilmore held her breath awaiting the outcome. In a three-way race for the 2014 World Title the two other contenders—Carissa Moore and Tyler Wright—were battling wave for wave. The result could determine Gilmore's own fate. If Moore prevailed, Gilmore would take the title.

"It was," she recalled later, "the most emotional I've ever been watching someone else surf."

At the bell, Carissa Moore's formidable performance eliminated Tyler Wright from the World Title contention, cementing Gilmore in the annals of surf history with a sixth world championship. Tears streaming down her face, Gilmore accepted the title with appreciation. She had survived being beaten by a metal bar, suffered the agony of a fractured a knee while free surfing in Western Australia and withstood the controversial fallout from posing nude. But this was a moment when her tears were an expression of her "Happy Gilmore" moniker.

Most surfing careers are rockets breaking the chains of gravity. Stephanie Gilmore's was a moonshot. At seventeen she entered the WSL World Tour, winning it her first year; not only a landmark in her own career, but in the record books. Gilmore was the first surfer—man or woman—to ever win the title during his or her rookie year. A string of three more World Titles followed—four back-to-back championships from 2007 to 2010. At only twenty-two she became the youngest surfer—man or woman—to win four consecutive titles. In 2010 she was included in the Surf Hall of Fame, the youngest inductee ever. That same year she was awarded the Laureus World Sports Award, one of the most prestigious recognitions in the world of action sports.

"I'm in awe of her natural grace, style and bearing," her friend and admirer Layne Beachley noted in an interview. "She's beautiful but completely nonchalant about it."

In 2011 she was awarded the ESPN ESPY prizes for best female athlete in action sports which she repeated in 2013.

And with only a single year break she captured her fifth again in 2012. Another single year break and she took her sixth in 2014—six in eight years. And then, in 2018—a full eleven years after her initial win—she became only the second woman and third surfer ever to win seven WSL World Titles. Along with her predecessor Layne Beachley, this seemingly unpretentious hometown girl had achieved the most successful woman's competitive record in surf history.

"No one has changed the women's perception more than Steph," observed Laura Enever. "She is so cool but incredibly passionate. She is so relaxed, but the most competitive person imaginable."

Gilmore earned local hero status in numerous surfing communities, thanks in part, to this infectious optimism. Her hometown nickname "Happy Gilmore" became a reflection of both her personality and her life story. Growing up in the small town of Tweeds Heads in New South Wales, Australia, Gilmore started surfing at age eleven and won her first competition at seventeen. She still considered Australia home, but kept semi-permanent outposts in Hawaii and California as well.

In little more than a decade, Gilmore joined the rarified ranks of surfing's greatest competitors. Like Joyce Hoffman, she was a role model, a driven athlete and a spokesperson for half the surf world. Like Margo Oberg, she was a prodigy, breaking every record anyone had set. Like Lisa Andersen's epic duels with Layne Beachley, Gilmore found a remarkable rival in Carissa Moore. From 2010 to 2019 they traded World Titles eight times. And Gilmore tied with Layne Beachley in attaining more World Titles than anyone else in history.

"I call her the 'smiling assassin,'" Beachley said. "She's so friendly and inclusive—but deep down she has a demon desire to smash you in competition."

Nonetheless her humility and positive presence belies her killer instinct—and seven world championships. It is an admired and astonishing combination to her peers.

"Steph is the gold standard we all aspire to," confirmed Caroline Marks, her toughest new rival for a title.

Gilmore quickly became more than just a good-looking female World Title holder. "She's special—for those who know her closely, but also, for the average, anonymous surfing spectator," declared Zach Weisberg, editor and founder of The Inertia, one of the surf media's largest sites. "Stephanie is a genuine human being with a powerful competitive drive. She has the grace of a ballet dancer and the free spirit of a life explorer."

As her father puts it, "she looks majestic on a wave."

Her surf style has been compared to that of ultra-stylist Joel Parkinson, a fellow Australian and World Champ himself. Single Fin website editor described her surfing as "aggressive but precise, with both technique and grace—which inspired a lot of women."

Every Ride Has Bumps

Her meteoric rise was not all smooth. Several near crashes created enough turbulence to threaten her entire trajectory. In 2010, a deranged homeless man attacked Gilmore with a metal pipe, breaking her wrist and opening a massive head wound. The unsuspected assault came just before the start of the 2011 ASP World Tour. Just weeks after the incident, Gilmore returned to the surf, winning the Roxy Pro France later that year. Showing her physical and mental strength, Gilmore stormed the World Tour in 2012, earning her fifth World Title at just twenty-six.

She learned to handle controversy and in fact seemed to become the model of independence. Just as she was cementing her fifth title the backlash over blatant chauvinism in surfing began to erupt, coming from various angles all at once it seemed.

In 2013 pro surfer and model Anastasia Ashley rode one of her biggest waves, dropping into a twenty-five-foot face at Jaws. The feat was met with the headline: "Hot Surfer Chick Catches Huge Wave, Famous Butt Unscathed."

"It's insulting but it's a reality we live with," was the explanation Shannon Aikman gave. "Once when I was sixteen surfing 35th Street in Newport Beach a guy yelled at me 'You don't belong on the beach! Go back to the kitchen!' You ignore it but it stays with you." Other provocative issues came up as well culminating in a photograph session for the Sports ESPN Body Issue, and a racy video she modeled for her sponsor. The ad caused a public furor with a media ginning up the hullabaloo.

Gilmore took a raft of criticism in light of the debates already swirling in the women's movement. But despite thousands of petitioners demanding her sponsors remove the offending ad, Gilmore was unfazed. She saw it as nothing more than a freedom of expression issue. And her reply politely defied the denunciations: "I'm twenty-five now; I'm no longer a girl. I'm a young woman, and I want to embrace that and enjoy it. I've realized that you can be glamorous, and you can be fabulous and sexy. You're a woman; you can do whatever you want." And she did.

Out of the water, Gilmore revealed some surprising diversions. A passionate and serious electric guitar enthusiast, Gilmore was often accompanied by one of her two favorite guitars—a vintage Epiphone Crestwood or a Fender Jazzmaster—while traveling the globe. And she played them with some impressive colleagues.

Sharing the stage with Jimmy Buffett singing "Volcano" and "Margaritaville," was her first show in front of a live audience—and Gilmore's performance mirrored her surfing: strong, effortless and impressive. Gilmore also joined Foo Fighters's drummer Taylor Hawkins onstage for a version of the Rolling Stones song "Bitch" while on tour with his side project, Chevy Metal.

Unmarried and with no children, Gilmore's personal life remains private. But Gilmore has a very public persona, one she hopes can empower others, with not only her words, but also her actions—she spreads the good word of health and happiness wherever she goes.

"Never underestimate yourself. Work hard. We only have one body, so make sure you look after it and treat it well. No dream is too big; find a way to succeed." Gilmore, unlike many stars of her caliber, proved that kindness, class, and confidence were cornerstones in a happy life.

In 2017 she moved to Los Angeles, a more central global energy zone. As an environmental activist and humanitarian advocate, she is on the advisory board of Sea Shepherd. A natural-born traveler who loves to explore uncharted territories, waves and cultures, her fondness for the African continent prompted Gilmore to collaborate with the Coeur de Forêt foundation to create water wells in Senegal and worked with World Vision in Kenya in support of children.

Chosen to represent her nation in the first ever surfing competitions of the 2021 Olympic Games, Gilmore joined a long linage of Australian champions as one of the most influential in surfing history.

A Changing of the Guard

Gilmore was no solo artist, she was part of a movement. The growth of professional surfing cut a wide swath across the globe, producing a startling set of breakthroughs. By 2007 it appeared that an emerging generation of surfers might again revolutionize the quality and performance level of women's surfing. Despite a serious injury and against doctors' orders, Hawaiian Megan Abubo won the Triple Crown of Surfing posting a perfect ten-point score at the Hawaiian Pro event at her hometown Haleiwa. French native Caroline Sarran became the only European female on the Woman's World Tour, qualifying after winning several French National titles and a European Championship in 2005. She stunned the world with a performance at Cloudbreak, Fiji, when she turned a Wild Card invite into a win in the trials and a fifth place in the main event, taking out seven-time World Champ Layne Beachley in the process. Sixteen-year-old French surfer Pauline Ado—the European junior leader—was another sign of the times on the women's tour, with top athletes getting younger and younger by the year. A year later seventeen-year-old Paige Hareb became the first New Zealand woman to qualify for the WTC in 2008. Newcomer Silvana Lima shattered the Brazilian glass ceiling vaulting into the top pro ranks as well.

Australia had fielded a batch of outstanding talent built on the extraordinary seven-time World Title holder Layne Beachley. Jessi Miley-Dyer, seventeen, the 2006 women's world tour Rookie of the Year, came in second on the women's world tour. Rebecca Woods, already a World Junior amateur champ took first in the pro rankings of the World Qualifying Series.

"The days of Layne Beachley and that generation are over and a new generation of girls are starting to come through—capable of a level of performance which will drive the prize money up on the women's tour," said Rip Curl media manager Dane Sharp. "There are a group of young women who can radically change this sport and create so much outside-the-industry interest that drives new sponsorship."

Jessi Miley-Dyer was one who seemed to have destiny in mind from a very early stage. Chosen by Surf Lifesaving Australia as a 2000 Olympic Torch bearer—one of the youngest ever—she carried the flame on a surf boat onto Bondi beach. She had won a National Scholastic snowboarding title in 1999. But not before winning Lifesaver of the Year at age fourteen.

Quickly moving through the surf rankings, the New South Wales native won numerous national junior titles before becoming World ISA Under-18 champion in 2003. Declining a scholarship to study law at the University of New South Wales, Miley-Dyer turned professional in 2006 and won the Billabong Pro Maui in her debut season, beating seven-time world champion Layne Beachley in the process, on her way to an impressive fourth place overall in the ASP Women's World Tour rankings and the Rookie of the Year award.

A successful competitive career followed. But after six years on the circuit, Miley-Dyer transitioned from performer to management in the World Surfing league, becoming Women's World Tour Manager in 2012.

"Jessi always had a scholastic background," explained Rochelle Ballard, who was a colleague during Dyer's competitive career. "She was a lot more prepared for life after the circuit than most girls."

Completing a Master of Business degree in 2016, Miley-Dyer moved up to the job of Deputy Commissioner & Director of Athlete Development in the WSL organization. "Jessi knew she would need a career and she set herself up to do it," Ballard observed. "She always had the leadership personality."

In 2018 Miley-Dyer became the first surfer to be inducted into Australia's UNSW Sports Hall of Fame, another honor on her record. But perhaps Jessi's most lasting contribution to the sport was her lead role in bringing pay equity to the WSL in 2019—a first in sports history. That same year she was promoted to Vice President, Tours and Competition. "It was a big achievement," she said when she announced the negotiation to the media. "And I'm proud to have been part of it."

Perfect Illusion

Lady Gaga's smash hit "Edge of Glory" was the musical equivalent to the storm of cutting-edge performances from young professionals across the globe. Propelled by stabbing synthesizers exploding into a chorus of soaring vocals, pounding beats and a scorching solo from Bruce Springsteen's saxophone side-kick Clarence Clemmons, it was the perfect anthem to pump up their high-octane surf sessions.

But perfection had a cost. And in surfing it is sometimes accompanied by an illusion of progress when the core problem is "simply" disguised to appear more palatable.

"The portrayal of women as physically strong and healthy inspired many women to jump into surfing and offered them a chance to create an identity that was centered around ability rather than image alone," wrote Cori Schumacher in a *Huck* magazine piece. "These activities, while offering a more active, healthy lifestyle, can be truly empowering in practice.

"However, if image is emphasized and valued above ability and performance in the competitive realm, it is possible that a competitive form of shape-shifting will arise (distorting the spirit of achievement found in this realm). This is the exact tension within women's surfing currently." Lady Gaga's pop rock dance anthem delved into the "highest of highs and lowest of lows" as a commentary on modern society: "Trying to get control / Pressure's taking its toll / Stuck in the middle zone. Somewhere in all the confusion / It was a perfect illusion."

Hitting the airwaves in 2016, the hit song paralleled a controversial interview with top Brazilian star Silvana Lima, confronting the same dilemma Lady Gaga addresses—and with the same painful candor. A quick review if Lima's success illuminates the issue in surfing's realm.

Fleeting Flawlessness

If someone were to imagine a perfect 'first' in these women's groundbreaking performances they would do well to consider the longest running Brazilian competitor on the World Contest Tour: Silvana Lima. On December 8, 2009 at her *very first* WSL contest, in her *very first* professional heat, on her *very first* wave, the stalwart rookie dropped into a perfect hollow Honolua Bay wave—and received the highest score possible, a perfect ten.

It was no chance fluke—her performances would earn her eight Brazilian national titles, two World Title runner-ups and the unofficial title of Brazil's greatest-ever female surfer.

Life had not always been so fantasy-like. As a child growing up in a beachside shack, Silvana Lima could only dream of one day living in a real house. It was much the same in the water, where she first started surfing on a wooden plank, dreaming of one day riding a real board.

Even after injuries hobbled her for several seasons she remained a top contender who was never out of the running for a title. In the years she was fully healthy, Lima's position in the top rankings was a source of national pride and an inspiration to many upcoming female Brazilians.

Although initially well-supported by a large surf brand, Lima struggled with sponsorship as time went on, an issue Lima contended was in large part due to her physical appearance.

"I don't look like a model," Lima told the BBC in a 2016 television series. "I'm not a babe. I'm a surfer, a professional one."

"The surfwear brands, when it comes to women, they want both models and surfers," Silvana continued. "So if you don't look like a model, you end up without a sponsor, which is what happened to me." It's an issue she sees as exclusive to women: "You're excluded, you're disposable. Men don't have this problem."

Although roundly disputed by the surf industry, this issue is unquestionably resistant to an agreeable resolution and remains a thorn for women athletes in surfing and beyond. Financial assistance *did* come her way in 2018 from a most unusual source. Kore, a cryptocurrency company that had aligned with surf culture, negotiated a contract—making Lima the first woman ever sponsored by a brand in the crypto space.

Outside industry sponsors can be as brief and fickle as the seasons swells, but in scoring that sponsorship deal, Lima became one of the first athletes in the world to bridge the emerging cryptocurrency industry with sports.

And despite the struggle for surf brand sponsorship there is a bright spot in this saga: the contest earnings she accrued in competition helped her buy the dream home she envisioned as a child for herself and her family.

Another standout Brazilian from that era was Bruna Schmitz. In 2003, with over thirty surfing titles to her name, Schmitz became the youngest surfer to win a Brazilian pro event and soon after signed with Roxy at the age of fourteen, becoming the youngest Brazilian to turn pro. She then went on to qualify and compete alongside surfing's elite on the WSL World tour from 2008–2010 before choosing to shift her focus away from competition. With movie-star looks she seemed to make Lima's point about sponsor support and physical beauty by subsequently traveling globally as a Roxy athlete and international model, shooting with *Sports Illustrated* and Estee Lauder and dating French surf star Jeremy Flores. In 2013, she moved to Southern California where she made a foray into stunt work for films, including *Tribes of Palos Verdes* starring Jennifer Garner. She did campaign work with Verizon Wireless, Beats by Dre, Jose Cuervo, served as an ambassador for Sambazon, YogaWorks and major causes like Heal the Bay. Schmitz married former pro surfer and Hurley Global Marketing Manager Dane Zaun in Redondo Beach, California.

Hawaiian Grace

Hawaii had always produced a well of talent, but not since Margo Oberg in 1981 had a Hawaiian female come close to winning the title. Twenty years after Oberg's back-to-back wins, Hawaiian Megan Abubo made her international debut when she came within a hair's breadth of taking the World Title back to the Islands.

A formidable competitor, Abubo won seven national titles as an amateur, six WSL Tour victories and took Rookie of the Year honors as a pro in 1996. She was the 2001 World Champion runner-up and finished number four in 2005.

Born in Connecticut and raised in Hawaii, Abubo revealed a style honed on powerful reef-breaks in *A Girl's Surfing Addiction*, a 2004 surf film showcasing the new crop of talented women from a fresh perspective, focusing on travel and female camaraderie.

Her most dramatic moment came when, despite a rib injury, she won the 2007 Triple Crown of Surfing title, a status only exceeded by the World Championship itself.

Relaxed in public but intensely determined, Abubo created options for herself in various aspects of the culture: a stunt double in the widely acclaimed *Blue Crush*, yoga teacher with Rochelle Ballard on Kauai, and spokesperson on behalf of Roxy for Keep A Breast—an art initiative that raises money for breast cancer research by auctioning art-decorated breast casts of famous female athletes and artists. Abubo has developed a passion for breast cancer awareness since her sister, a two-time breast cancer survivor, was first diagnosed at age twenty-seven. After her sister's death Abubo headed up numerous Keep A Breast events and became a starring advocate for the cause in Hawaii.

Kiwi Conqueror

Paige Hareb entered the World circuit as a teenager, the first Kiwi to qualify for the pro circuit, and one of the first female competitors to take training seriously.

Humble and soft-spoken, Hareb was an all-round athlete in her youth, excelling in basketball, tennis, soccer and skiing. Joining her hometown Oukura Board Riders Club, Paige soon began winning dozens of national surfing competition events across both sides of the Tasman Sea. She placed in the top ten three times from 2009 to 2012 but missed the cut in 2014 forcing her to dig deep into her emotional core to requalify in 2018, a decade after her first entry into the top level of competition.

In the 2018 World Surfing games in Japan (a warm up for the Olympics) she nearly won a World Amateur title but had to settle for a Silver medal, unable to overcome a near-perfect run from Australian Sally Fitzgibbons in the final, denying Hareb a first world championship. Nonetheless, Hareb's inspired performance catapulted New Zealand to ninth on the final team standings, securing an easier draw for the 2021 Olympic qualifying event.

South African Cyclones

Sixty-nine million square miles across the Indian Ocean, a deep bench of South African standouts had formed. Blessed with a long coastline, the isolated nation almost dictated frequent travel for an aspiring talent to be recognized beyond their native country. From the earliest days of the 60s to the 80s generation of Wendy Botha, South African women have traveled the world to find their dream. But not until the 2000s did such a large talent pool emerge from the nation of Springboks and Nelson Mandela. Suddenly surfers like Bianca Buitendag (who ranked fourth in the World Surf League in 2015), Chanelle Botha (winner of the 2013 South African Junior Series) and Tanika Hoffman (a multiple World Games medalist) were finding wave fields and making headlines.

Growing up on the shores of Cape Town, Tanika Hoffman credits much of her success to the great waves of her local break—and her shaping guru, legendary South African Spider Murphy. A three-time South African National Champion, Hoffman and her South Africa teammates took home the Gold Medal at the 2013 World Surfing Games in Panama. Considered Cape Town's top female surfer,

Hoffman was featured in the big screen film *Blue Crush 2*, shot on location in South Africa, with a script that followed two young women pros back to their native homeland. In 2018 she helped raise funds for her nation's team to compete again in the World Surfing Games, took a surf trip to Barbados and starred in a Go Pro video.

The South African talent continued to build throughout the second decade of the century. A cadre of South Africa's top competitors was predicted as the "South African cyclone" by journalists and commentators in the global media.

Their predictions were confirmed when Zoe Steyn, as a sixteen-year-old, became the youngest female surfer to win the prestigious South African National title, beating her hero South African legend Heather Clarke and then in 2019 repeating her achievement.

Her most frequent rival for the top rankings was Capetown's Ceara Knight. And Sarah Baum, who moved to Australia's Gold Coast to train in warmer waters, won the World Surf League women's qualifying series top 50 after claiming victory in her native South Africa as well.

Ranked among the world's top seventeen female surfers on the ASP Women's WCT in 2013, Baum competed alongside fellow South African standouts Bianca Buitendag and Roxy Louw.

Staying Louw

Including surf, hockey, modeling, film and entrepreneurship, perhaps no one had more overall success than Roxy Louw. The daughter of Springbok rugby legend Rob Louw, this South African surfer learned early what competition meant and the importance of letting your internal voice guide you. "For a long time the dream was to play hockey for my country but as I fell more in love with surfing that dream began to change." Louw was playing for Western Province organization when she decided to quit hockey and pursue surfing full time.

At the age of seventeen Louw's surfing talents were recognized by Oakley where she became a team rider. A chance photo taken by the team photographer led Louw to become the face of Oakley's international campaigns and catapult her into the modelling world. "At the time I was so focused on surfing I never really considered doing anything else but when the opportunity came, I wanted to make sure I made the most of it."

She did. Louw found herself in the pages of *Sports Illustrated* and was voted sexiest woman in the world by *For Him* magazine in 2010. Her success in the modeling world opened doors for various other endeavors. She became the spokesperson for Kauai. French automotive maker Renault even named a car model after her.

By 2010, her modeling commitments and brand ambassador duties growing exponentially, she landed a role in Universal Pictures's *Blue Crush 2*. "I was cast as Acapulco Goldie. It was such a fun role. She was such a free spirit which I totally related to." The role lead her to being cast in *The Perfect Wave* alongside Scott Eastwood and Cheryl Ladd.

In 2017 Louw founded Green Leaf Vitality, a business dedicated to a healthy mind, body and soul. Specializing in yoga as well as general health and well-being, Louw focused her attention on making health and well-being accessible to everyone, hosting kids and adults yoga classes, workshops and surf/yoga retreats.

Long Story Short

A new cadre of longboarders emerged as well, following the path blazed by Kassia Meador, who by the mid-2000s had gained legend status. Brazil's Chloe Calmon was one of the younger generation who considered Meador an inspiration. On the World Longboard Tour just before the Coronavirus pandemic shut down sporting activities worldwide, she ended the season in third place. For nine years pre-Covid-19, Calmon ranked in the Longboard Tour top ten, slowly moving closer to her goal of a World Title.

Elegant and expressive, Calmon followed Meador's lead—keeping all her cards in play as she watched the future unfolding.

Placed on a board by her father as an infant, Calmon grew beyond basic proficiency at Macumba Beach, one of Rio's iconic surf spots, building a reputation as "a stylist who happens to compete," never sacrificing beautiful moves for a judging criteria.

Surfing from a young age "you learn how to connect with a wave but mostly you learn how to listen to your inner voice." And perhaps the subconscious voice of Meador.

Big Wave Matadoras
Women Take on the Challenge of Massive Surf

1950–2000

"Becoming courageous is the willingness to realize your true capacities by going through discomfort, fear, anxiety or suffering and taking wholehearted responsible action."

—Ruth Schimel, PhD,
author and motivational speaker

The Bigger the Better

Women have been challenging big waves as far back as the late 50s when a fifteen-year-old Linda Benson rode an 18-foot wave at Waimea on a borrowed board. Marge Calhoun, another early pioneer of women's big-wave riding, took on big Makaha on Oahu's West side. Joyce Hoffman rode what was then considered big, dangerous Pipeline. By the mid-70s Margo Oberg became the female master of Sunset, taking on its biggest swells and surfing on par with many of the men. There were; of course, many others.

Over the decades, female surfers—and bodyboarders like Phyllis Dameron—distinguished themselves at places like Makaha, Sunset Beach and Waimea Bay.

Petite, spirited, super-fit, Dameron has been described as an "utterly fearless bodyboarder," by big-wave legend Ken Bradshaw. In the late 70s she was the first female any of us had ever seen ride Waimea on a boogieboard, taking off on huge days and huge drops, literally skipping down the face where a standup surfer would have been pitched face first. She was impressive enough for me to write a coveted profile in one issue and my photo editor at *Surfer* to shoot a center spread shot at twenty-foot Waimea in another. Dameron never acquired a sponsor, never sought one. She did it for the pure thrill. And in a time when it was one of the only welcoming arenas openly available for women, Dameron took on Waimea, the biggest known wave in the world.

In the early 90s big wave spots were being discovered with increasing rapidity. Hawaii's Waimea Bay and Makaha had been the benchmarks for big wave surfing. But with the discovery of Northern California's Mavericks, Cortez Banks, Maui's Jaws and Portugal's Nazaré, the possibilities expanded dramatically. These expanded global wavefields generated significantly larger surf than had previously been experienced. A new definition evolved, classifying *truly* big waves as forty feet and above. Suddenly colossal new locales were readily available to test. And within a just a few years women began to enter their arena.

A History of Big-Wave History-Making

Big waves have always been the Disneyland of surfing and perhaps nowhere in surfdom was the perception of women's inferiority more embedded than in the mythology of big waves. "They are the stuff of fairy tales, the size of castle walls, dissolving into the clouds, but capable of turning into very real monsters," Andy Martin wrote in 2008. "Once upon a time, women were the Cinderellas of surfing, the downtrodden downstairs parlor maids, while the baggy-shorted princes were out there strutting their stuff."

But that fantasy underwent a metamorphosis at the turn of the century and by the second decade a new script was emerging—one in which dozens of Snow Whites were arriving as belles of the big-wave ball.

Surprisingly, big wave barriers were in some ways easier to break than those in crowded smaller surf, although men often saw women as neither brave nor competent enough to handle extreme conditions in earlier eras.

As big wave legend Buzzy Trent wrote in a 1963 *Surfer* magazine piece: "Girls are intended to be feminine, and big-wave riding is definitely masculine. . . . Girls are better off and look more feminine riding average-sized waves."

Trent's perspective was upended at the turn of the millennium, and there has been no turning back in the decades since. In 1994 when the Cranberries went unexpectedly multiplatinum with *Everybody Else Is Doing It, So Why Can't We?*, women surfers seemed to ask the same question. The Irish Alt band's lead singer Dolores O'Riordan's ethereal swoop rang deeper and harsher—with the hit song "No Need to Argue." And when the "girls" finally did paddle out into the big-waves, surfers didn't seemed to argue either.

Andrea Moller was the first to prove that Trent's claim had expired. In 1996 Moller's Brazilian tow partner Maria Souza towed her into a forty-footer at Peahi, and she became the first woman to ride the outside reef nicknamed "Jaws" off high cliffs on Maui's North Shore. A Brazilian transplant who had come to Hawaii and trained as a lifeguard, Moller prepared for a decade before this moment arrived.

At nearly the same time, Sarah Gerhardt began exploring a similar-sized wave spot in California. In 1999, while pregnant with her first child, Sarah rode a wave of significant size at Mavericks, becoming the first woman to do so.

Gerhardt was not a typical big-wave rider, nor a typical female one. Having earned a Doctorate degree in Physical Chemistry from University of California, Sara Gerhardt proved not to be your typical person—in any aspect of her life.

An amateur astronomer, Gerhardt's father moved his family to Hawaii Island in the late 70s. To be nearer to the observatories atop Mauna Kea was his motivation, but the family ended up homeless, camping in beach parks. "I spent my early years unsupervised, playing in the ocean," remembered Gerhardt in 2020. "That started *everything*."

By the time she was seven, her mother was dealing with increasingly degenerative muscular dystrophy. As Gerhardt told Rosemary Camozzi, she took her two daughters to California, so she could attend graduate school, while Sarah's father was working at sea. By then quadriplegic, her mother took seven years to complete a master's degree in counseling in San Luis Obispo. Meanwhile, Gerhardt cared for her, sleeping by her side, helping her get dressed every morning and accompanying her to college at night.

Gerhardt herself suffered from severe asthma and allergies, which frequently sent her to the hospital. She didn't make it back to the beach until the seventh grade. When playing in the frigid water and watching surfers ride the waves, she realized her allergies seemed to vanish. "I felt so alive. All my troubles disappeared," she recalled. "That was profound—because I had a lot of troubles."

The family often struggled financially, and she was bullied in school. But in 1987 Gerhardt's dad gave her a surfboard and wetsuit for her thirteenth birthday. She was immediately enthralled. A half-decade later, on a trip to Hawaii in college, she fell in with a crew of surfers that included big-wave icon Ken Bradshaw, and quickly found herself tackling bigger and bigger waves.

Pursuing her scientific studies at a college near her residence in Santa Cruz, Gerhardt also worked on the physical chemistry required for mastering the giant waves of Mavericks, a massive wavefield with jagged rocks in front of a high cliff. She married a big-wave surfer and in 1998 began to cautiously explore the terrain.

"I saw her sitting in the channel and I paddled up and asked her what was going on, and she said she was 'just watching her husband, Mike,'" remembered Frosty Hesson, a legendary big-wave surfer and mentor whose life was portrayed in the 2012 movie *Chasing Mavericks*.

"I told her, 'well, that's not what I'm seeing,'" Hesson recalled. What he saw instead, was "analysis and inquiry and questioning and resolve. She was studying the waves, cataloging them." Later that day, Hesson said, he told board shaper Bob Pearson he'd just met the woman who would be the first female to ride Mavericks.

In February 1999, Gerhardt did just that.

Featured in Stacy Peralta's Sundance-nominated big-wave film *Riding Giants*, Dr. Gerhardt talked about how she was both repelled by the danger but thrilled by the challenge. "I didn't know if I could deal with it," she conceded. "There is no easy entry, and it isn't forgiving if you have a wipe-out." But she found a scientific strategy for dealing with the fear: "I talk to myself. Every fearful thought that enters my mind, I rationalize it and then disqualify it."

After her second child Gerhardt took a full-time chemistry professorship at Monterey Peninsula College, while she and husband Mike (her favorite Mavericks surfer) remained deeply connected to the Santa Cruz surf scene.

Then in 2004, Andrea Moller once again broke the size barrier. Paddling in at thunderous Peahi, Moller became the first woman to drop in unassisted by jet skis, demonstrating that no fairy godmother was required for these women to dance at the ball. The viral video of her exploits threw open the floodgates. By 2010 the slow trickle of big-wave women had become a torrent of unexpected barrier-breaking riders bent on making a mark. Santa Cruz local Jamilah Starr—named one of the "Twelve Most Adventurous People in the World" by *National Geographic Adventure*—rode a giant left at Puerto Escondido in Mexico, making her a contender for the 2006 XXL awards a second time after winning the 2005 inaugural women's award the previous year. Athletically seductive, Starr was the only big wave finalist nominated twelve years in a row, and the only woman to win the Central American Longboard circuit competing against an all-male field of competitors. Her friend and Mavericks compatriot Jenny Useldinger followed her out into the lineup.

Useldinger had the kind of upbringing that gave her an edge in this arena. Her mother was a pro surfer and the young Jennifer followed her around the Grand Prix circuit from Bora Bora to New Zealand and Japan. Home schooling consisted of her mother winning the women's section while Jenny won the girls (or sometimes the boys). Jamilah Star met her at a contest and took her to Mavericks.

Hawaii and California were hardly the only performance locales. Down in Australia seven-time World Champ Layne Beachley made international headlines in 2010 riding an eyebrow-raising tube at Ours, a massive hollow wave in Sydney.

The next matadora was Brazilian Maya Gabeira, who in some ways was the first women's big wave superstar. Her stunning looks and total dedication made her an immediate media darling. But her performances legitimized the attention she received. Charging into every accessible big wave location, she captured the

XXL title from 2007 through 2010, in four consecutive year-long, record-breaking global campaigns.

Maya's assault was so dominant that it would take Keala Kennelly's "literally insane" performances (as World Champ Layne Beachley would describe them) in 2011 to break Maya's winning streak.

Maya Gabeira—the daughter of a well-known Brazilian fashion designer—grew up privileged but, after a period of adolescent rebellion, she discovered surfing. Her father, Fernando Gabeira, was also a political revolutionary—a member of MR8, the group behind the kidnapping of Charles Elbrick, American ambassador to Brazil in the 60s. Fernando was barred from the U.S., but Maya made it her base, dedicating the next two decades to chasing giant waves from South Africa to Tahiti, breaking taboos and records in the process. Fearless, gorgeous and committed, Gabeira's head-turning performances became definitive examples of a beautiful female capable of the most dangerous and challenging achievements.

Anyone requiring further evidence that women were riding bigger waves than ever need only look as far as the video entries for the Billabong XXL Big Wave Awards to get a defining answer. The year-long chase—which awards surfers for big wave surfing—had added more female nominees with more outstanding performances each succeeding year.

But on January 22, 2015, when Paige Alms paddled into one of the biggest barrels ridden at Jaws, the world really became aware of what had been building in the women's performances for a decade. It was not only a career highlight, but a historical achievement covered by media around the world and earning her an XXL Big Wave Awards "Ride of the Year" nomination. In 2016, she became history's first Women's Big-Wave Tour Champion following her performance at the Pea'hi Challenge. That year surf media giant Surfline called her "the world's best female big-wave surfer." Cinderella's glass slipper had found a perfect fit, turned into a fiberglass arrow.

The media adulation and peer group deference to heroic athletes like Alms, Kennelly and Gabeira belies the potentially lethal damage that collision with multiple stories of collapsing water can met out on the human body. In many cases there are injuries, health issues or physical challenges that these women have had to overcome. And some are not even due to accidents.

Brittany Gomulka—originally from Ocean County, New Jersey—moved to the North Shore of Oahu in 2005. In 2012 she started training to surf big waves. Unknown to most she had a special handicap: she battled Lyme Disease for nearly a decade, all throughout her big-wave sorties. With the help of dedicated doctors, a clean lifestyle and healthy diet she eventually made a full recovery and continued to surf.

Size Matters

Surfing's biggest threat has always been the danger of injury—nearly seventy times more common than fatalities. In the rarified world of truly big waves, the bigger the wave the more danger involved. When it comes to surfing, size really does matter. Since fellow surfers increase the risk factor, respect and caution usually keeps any blatantly risky behavior out of the picture when surfing the biggest (and most dangerous) waves. But not always.

For Jenny Useldinger there seemed little doubt that some fairly classic alpha-male behavior contributed to her worst wipeout at Mavericks one big day in the winter of 2006.

"They were hassling me," she explained, about a few aggressive guys, "and put me in a sketchier position than I would have liked." A rogue wave came steaming right at her. She paddled up the face, but it started to pitch out and over before she got to the top. She punched her way through the back and actually caught a glimpse of sunlight, other surfers, and the world beyond before the wave flicked out a tongue and sucked her back in. She was dragged backward over the falls and given the laundering of her life. She made it back to shore but was out of the water for the next seven months with an injured knee—and her favorite nine-foot four-fin big-wave gun was smashed to pieces. Perhaps it is no surprise that her sponsors expanded from Roxy and Ocean & Earth to CTI Knee Braces and Try-Star Medical.

In 2013, Maya Gabeira nearly drowned at Nazaré in Portugal in one of the most devastating wipeouts ever witnessed. Attempting to claim the record for biggest wave surfed by a woman, she was eaten up at the bottom of an estimated eighty-foot (twenty-four-meter) beast, breaking her ankle on impact on the third massive bump while still on her board. Trapped under a set of waves, she lost consciousness.

"I lost her," her Brazilian tow partner, big-wave rider Carlos Burlé said in an interview with *Stab* magazine. "She was gone for about five minutes. I finally saw her floating face-down in the shorebreak. I jumped off the Jet ski, grabbed her in an armlock, and we got to the beach that way. I don't know how. They administered CPR immediately, and she started breathing." CPR saved her life, but she had snapped her right fibula and herniated a disk in her lower back.

Keala Kennelly would experience a similar skin-of-your-teeth catastrophe in Tahiti. Three days after riding the biggest, most treacherous barrels of the decade at Teahupoo, she surfed a memorial heat in honor of her good friend World Champ Andy Irons. Exiting from a critically dangerous tube she face-slammed on Teahupoo's notoriously shallow reef. The gash in her face was "my red badge of courage," she joked later. "I didn't get awarded the medal for a purple heart," she laughed, "but the one I do have almost stopped!" She none-theless required reconstructive surgery and was inches from a smashed skull and snapped spinal cord.

Yet both these intrepid spirits were barely recovered when they returned to the field of carnage.

Maya's recovery is an inspiring story of resilience. Two years later, she returned to Nazaré to face the same monsters that almost killed her—continuing to push the limits of female big-wave surfing in quest of the ultimate prize.

On January 18, 2018, Gabeira successfully surfed a sixty-eight-foot (nearly twenty-one meters) wave at Nazaré becoming the first female big-wave surfer recognized with a Guinness World Record.

Kennelly appeared to treat *her* accident's brutal damage almost disdainfully.

"When KK was still in the IC unit the first thing she said was 'When can I get back out there?'" Bianca Valenti told me in April 2020. "It was like she wanted to slap that wave right back!"

"Keala and Maya are so dedicated, so committed," Bianca Valenti continued. "Both of them could have died from their accidents. Or just quit. Instead they rose up and totally conquered their fears. And triumphed."

To say Keala Kennelly rides big waves is like saying Beyoncé sings pop. Keala Kennelly doesn't ride big waves—she attacks them. She doesn't walk—she struts. She doesn't smile—she lights up the hall. "Keala may be the most courageous person in surfing, breaking the rules and rewriting them at the same time," claimed Kelia Moniz. Kennelly won the Billabong XXL Big Wave women's title three times, and in 2018 finished the WSL Big-Wave Tour ranked number one. But her journey did not come without struggle—or without emotional scars.

Becoming KK

"When I was six years old I actually had thoughts about ending my life—because I was a girl, and I knew I wanted to do what the boys did," she told Alex Haro in a 2019 interview with *The Inertia*. But her strength (like so many she has inspired) comes from an inner core belief: "We have this one life. I decided very early on that I would live mine the way I wanted to with no limitations put on me by other people. I was just going to see for myself what *could* and *couldn't* be done."

That youthful commitment became prophetic. And the awards became myriad: a Gold Medal in the 2000 Summer X-Games. An ESPN 2002 Female Surfer of the Year. A coveted Triple Crown of Surfing win in 2003. A star on the Surfing Walk of Fame in 2013. XXL Barrell of the Year and an ESPY nomination for athletics from ABC TV in 2016. That same year she was the first woman to be invited to participate in the Eddie Aikau event at Waimea Bay; a statement in itself.

Kennelly has her own statement: "I'd like to actually *compete* in The Eddie and beat some *hombres*. I don't want to be the token chick that finished last or second to last," she emphasized. "I want to take some guys *down*."

Her boldness, her determination to level the playing field and her sexuality have cost her financially as well as emotionally. When she left the tour and came out as gay, she lost three out of four of her main sponsors. The issues faced by her surfing foremothers regarding their sexuality clearly had not yet been vanquished.

"They weren't going to come right out and say that they were cutting me because I was gay," she has said. "No one's going to say that. But financially I've struggled ever since."

Money did not appear to stop Kennelly before or after her coming out *or* her sponsor debacle. For most big-wave surfers—man or woman—there is a deeper, more personal motivation.

"Not getting paid to do what I love has really made me realize just how passionate I am about it. I'm working other jobs to keep doing the thing that I used to get paid to do. It's helped me realize what I really love to do, and I'm really passionate about surfing big waves."

That realization also led to a wider set of sponsorship options. In 2019 Kennelly acquired support from a non-endemic feminine brand *Flex Fit*. The company wanted to reach out to the women in my market," Kennelly explained. "And I guess they felt like I was an influencer there." It was a first, and a nod to product makers growing awareness of niche markets for women.

Kennelly was the first woman ever to be towed in at Teahupoo, back in 2005. Five years later she charged the biggest swell to ever hit Tahiti, the infamous "Code Red" week and rode the deepest monster barrels a female had ever caught—except for the record-setter she garnered in Mexico the same year.

But Keala Kennelly was not just fearless in big waves. She was brave enough to come back from serious injury, charismatic enough to venture into film acting, playing herself in the big-screen hit *Blue Crush*; intrepid enough to win a role in the HBO show *John From Cincinnati*. As a successful DJ she was not afraid to play the music she liked or carry her own sexuality with confidence. A champion of LBGT rights, she had the courage to be the first woman to win the Open Gender category at the XXL Awards.

As Longboard World Champ Kelia Moniz concluded: "KK has chosen her own path. She's not sweet. She's *cool*. *The coolest*. Everyone respects her for being herself and being a barrier breaker in so many ways."

Keala Kennelly has lived her life fearlessly. And the world has loved her for it.

Making the Big Time

2007–2020

"If you don't risk anything, you risk even more."
—Erica Jong, *How to Save Your Own Life*

Lost in Translation

On February 11, 2020, at the inaugural WSL Nazaré Tow Surfing Challenge event in Praia do Norte, Portugal—*Maya Gabeira rode a seventy-three-foot (twenty-two-meter) wave into the history books.*

Gabeira didn't just ride the biggest wave ever ridden by a woman. It was the biggest wave surfed by anyone in the 2019–20 winter season, woman *or* man—a first for women in professional surfing.

"I think it's really important for the next generation of girls growing up to see women accomplishing these things," said Paige Alms, one of the world's best big-wave surfers. "You can only really dream as big as what you can see." It was a salve to any woman who had heard the phrase "that was a big wave . . . for a girl."

For female surfers who have heard that caveat attached to their accomplishments for so long, Gabeira's record breaker signaled that the time had finally arrived when their rides were no longer a loss on *anyone.*

Bigger Than Life

On that momentous Thursday in 2015 when the wave at Jaws pitched over Paige Alms's head, the "hollow space was big enough to drive a Winnebago through," said Buzzy Kerbox, one of the pioneers of the now legendary outer island reef.

"I just pulled up high into the barrel so I could get enough speed to get out," Alms confessed.

The ride—and the attending media frenzy as it went viral almost instantly—gave a young seventeen-year-old a spotlight that never left. It also gave Alms the 2015

XXL Women's Overall Performance Award as the first female to be barreled at Jaws—and the commitment to rise to the top level of big-wave riders in the world.

The daughter of a single mom, her peers see her as having earned every ounce of her attention.

"She is wise beyond her years," said Layne Beachley, "Down to earth; a truly solid psyche."

"Calm, cool, kind," was Keala Kennelly's description of Alms. "So helpful, she'd always pick me up from the airport, made sure I was set up."

"She elevates us," was how photographer Sachi Cunningham defined Alms's influence. "So patient, so steady. Such a strong, impressive athlete."

"Paige thrives on challenge, even danger," Rosy Hodge, the surf pro turned commentator noted. "She's suffered scary injuries too."

Alms's response was typical of her candor and dry wit: "Yeah, big-wave surfing is dangerous and scary, but I don't see why that makes it more masculine," Alms opined. "Women birth people—that's pretty much the gnarliest thing you can go through and no one's calling *that* masculine."

Alms's unusual childhood appears to have been a catalyst for her big-wave fascination. When she was seven, her mom sold their house in Victoria, British Columbia, where she was born, and flew to Australia, where they traveled the length of the country camping in their Volkswagen van for ten months. On their return ticket they stopped on Maui to visit her aunt and uncle. They never left. Instead they found a home on the quintessential village of Haiku in upcountry Maui on the slopes of Mount Haleakala. By chance it happened to be a five minute drive to the beach—at Peahi, the Mt. Everest of Hawaiian surf breaks. At ten she was cutting her big-wave teeth at Ho'okipa, the windy outside break famous for sailboarding on the island's north shore and had her first big-wave session at fifteen. "I was with Chris Vandervoort, who took me out on his borrowed 9-0 and I remember that day like it was yesterday. I was hooked from that day forward." Alms recounted. Although she has been nominated five years in a row at the XXL Awards, Alms finally won the "Women's Best Overall Performance" for the 2014–2015 season.

Although the Maui Film Festivals showing of *The Wave I Ride*—a documentary on her exploits—brought even further acclaim, the costs of her life work was hardly the life of a film star. She does not receive a million dollars a picture, or a percentage of the gross.

"Paige is not afraid to work for every surf trip," Rosy Hodge contended, "You can find her fixing dings in her garage to earn money." Far from poor, Alms's need to acquire sponsors was to finance a lifestyle that demands constant travel and a nearly unlimited open schedule—and she is not averse to finding creative ways to maintain it. Odd jobs—house painting, construction work, surf lessons and catering—supplied Alms with the funds to travel, compete and surf. Intensive physical training at her local gym kept her in shape in the off-season and making art, organic gardening or playing ping-pong offered the diversion from her big-wave obsession.

That obsession has earned her the 2016 Pe'ahi Challenge, 2017 XXL Female Performer of the Year and the first ever WSL Big-Wave World Title for the 2016–2017 season. In the process she became a leader among an elite group of surfers who dedicate their lives to riding giants. She not only collected the 2018 XXL Women's Overall Performance Award, and a second WSL Big Wave World Championship in 2017/2018, but went on to win the Jaws big wave event four years in a row.

"Paige is the champ," Sachi Cunningham stated. "She's the quarterback of this big-wave team."

As cofounder of the Committee for Equity in Women's Surfing in 2016, Alms was not afraid to speak up when the time came: "Men will look at women and be like, 'Who does she think she is?' A lot of the time they don't say anything, but you can feel it. The male bravado, the ego."

She continued to push herself to ride the biggest waves possible alongside her peers. Part of her motivation seemed to be a hope to inspire other women to push their limits and live their dreams too.

"We're at a time and place in our country, and in our world, and in this sport," Alms declared, "where we [women] are in a place of power, where we need to speak up."

Among her peers the consensus is that Paige Alms will be one for the history books. "She's the Gabby Reese of surfing," concluded Sachi Cunningham—"an Olympian in every way."

France's Surfing Pentathlete

The pace at which women's big wave records were broken in the late 20-teens seemed exponential—and the effect it had on women's surfing created a revolution in the sport. So to call Justine Dupont—the 2019 big-wave women's record holder—a "French Revolutionary" did not invite hyperbole. With top results in five separate disciplines she became known as a "Surfing Pentathlete." Not only National *and* European Shortboard *and* Longboard Champion—she clinched the title of four *additional* Championships—in the Stand-up Paddle and Paddleboard racing divisions as well. That was on top of a world record for women's big waves.

"Justine is dominant in *all* disciplines," said Sachi Cunningham, an Associate Professor in Journalism at SFSU. *"Dominant."*

Her natural ease on both small and massive waves often made it difficult to imagine how Dupont would have fulfilled any other destiny. Frequently touted as the First Lady of French surfing, her career evidenced achievements to more than justify that label.

Quiet and demure, Dupont's approach was once described as "Speak softly but carry a big sling blade."

Born in Bordeaux and brought up in Lacanau, on the forested west coast of France, Dupont was riding her first waves at eleven. Just four years later, in 2007, she finished second at the world longboard championships—a remarkable achievement for a fifteen-year-old.

National and European titles followed—and then a WQS victory in Portugal—making her the first European female to win that event. Along the way Dupont developed a passion for big-wave surfing which took her to a whole other realm. In 2013, she managed to surf a forty-foot monster swell at Belharra, just outside the St. Jean de Luz harbor—*twice*. It was a feat that earned her a prestigious record—no female surfer had succeeded in taming a wave this big before. At the beginning of 2016, she went back and did it all again.

"Big wave surfing is my thing," she would say with a calm, whispery voice that belied her starkly singular accomplishments in competition as well as leadership.

In 2018, Dupont was elected Chair of the Athletes Commission of the International Surfing Association. And in 2019, she was designated "Best Female Big-Wave Surfer of the Year" riding a seventy-foot wave at Nazaré, Portugal inching above Maya Gabeira's previous the record for the largest wave ridden by a female—and breaking several previous world big-wave records set by men.

In 2020 she received the "Ride of the Year" and "Performance of the Year" WSL Big Wave awards. But once again Maya Gabeira broke the world record for a woman riding a seventy-three-foot wave to regain the title of biggest wave surfed by a woman.

Savannah Shaughnessy had a similar story to Sara Gerhardt, but her entry was a decade later. Graduating from UC Santa Cruz with a degree in Biology, she followed up in 2016 with a nursing degree as a full-fledged RN. Like Sara, she paddled out to Mavericks for a full year before she took a wave, watching, waiting and wishing. There *was* a slight difference—Savannah was *sixteen* at the time. She was one of only three women invited to participate in the first ever women's exhibition in the men's Big-Wave World Tour at Nelscott Reef in 2010 and then to be invited to participate in the Coco Nogales Mexican Pipeline Tube Ride Invitational in 2011. And the first-ever woman to make it into the final cut for a Mavericks big-wave contest.

In 2011 she had a bad day there, taking not one wipeout but two. The second one left her starry-eyed and dizzy. When she threw up later that night, she decided she probably had a mild concussion. The next day she surfed Maverick's again. "It's how good big-wave riders calm their fears," was how Bianca Valenti explained it.

Writer Taylor Paul told the story of a big day when a wipeout of his own relegated him to observing from a boat in the channel: "It's 25 foot. [Shane] Dorian pulls into a bomb (again) and gets pinched. [Mark] Healey lays everything he's got onto a heel-side bottom turn. Then future World Champ John Florence takes one.

"John-John!" the guys on the boat cheer. But wait, "Who's that chick?" *That chick* drops in behind J.J., steeper, deeper and full of knee-knocking grace. Greg Long turns to me laughing, "Was that that chick Savannah?" I tell him it was. "Damn," Greg says. "She surfs *really good.*"

Shaughnessy herself noted that "2010 to 2016 were my peak years at Mavericks."

Shaughnessy had a serious injury in 2016, a reminder to all big-wave surfers about the risk inherent in their pursuit. She bore a child shortly after. Family and economics became priority, and so in 2018, she decided not to return to the big-wave lineup.

I'm No Angel

For her first taste of big waves Bianca Valenti paddled out at Ocean Beach, the stretch of San Francisco's shoreline that attracts open ocean swells.

"It was a beating like no other," she recalled. "My board was instantly ripped out of my hands. I was spinning in every direction imaginable, had no idea which way was up, and when I opened my eyes, I saw only blackness. I thought, if there's another wave after this one, I'm dead."

She got back to shore and stood there, "watching these amazing, giant, perfect waves, thinking to myself, 'I want to ride those waves. I can do this. I have to start preparing.'"

Within weeks she had moved to San Francisco, finding a pastel, salmon-colored flat in the Outer Sunset neighborhood about five blocks from the Great Highway, where frequent banks of Bay Area fog muffle the faint jangle of distant street cars.

"All I wanted to do I've been dreaming since I was seven years old—I have it written down in a third-grade essay—that I wanted to be a Pipeline Master [the winner of the renowned Hawaiian surfing contest]," she confessed. "And all my life I've never had the opportunity because they've never had women."

"Bianca is a one-of-a-kinder," Keala Kennelly told me. "She's funny, smart, bold—and so damned positive *all the time.* At first you almost can't believe she's for real," Kennelly laughed. "But after you know her, that's just the way she is. *All the time.*"

Valenti started surfing on a longboard but soon came to realize big waves were her true passion. In 2014, she became the first-ever champion of a women's big-wave competition, after competing in the Big Wave World Tour at Nelscott Reef, Oregon.

"Bianca is the rare person whose soaring ambition was matched by her formidable talents," concluded Sachi Cunningham, who spent many hours in dangerous situations with Bianca. Her peers agreed.

"Bianca spearheaded the effort to get equal access and equal prize money," Layne Beachley pointed out. "The great thing is she is so positive about her approach."

Armed with a quiver of eight-foot-plus guns Valenti built a solid level of performance skills while working as a sommelier at her dad's Italian restaurant, Valenti & Co., in Mill Valley.

"Bianca is a super-skilled big-wave barrel rider," stated Beachley without reservation. "She was definitely the best woman at [Mexican big-wave beach break] Puerto Escondido."

"It takes a tremendous amount of hard work to be out there—for anyone. But if you're a woman, you have exponentially more work, mentally and physically," Valenti explained. "To catch waves, you have to be able to match the speed of the wave and most men have an easier time with this, with more muscle mass up top and a longer wingspan. For every man's paddle-stroke, I have to do three."

In 2016, Valenti cofounded the Committee for Equity in Women's Surfing to create opportunities for women to surf in big-wave contests.

In November 2016, the Coastal Commission of California required the organizers of the Mavericks Challenge—a high-profile U.S. surfing contest—to open the event up to women in order to approve their permit. "I think what it boils down to is the question of how public resources are used," Valenti explained, "and it's important for everybody to have accessibility to public resources." For Valenti, competition access *was* the primary barrier to women in the sport. After deliberations on Valenti's case six women were invited to compete in the competition for the first time.

Valenti was a rare combination of sass, strength and social savvy.

"As a woman, you have to constantly prove yourself, whereas a guy—even of lesser experience—will paddle out and no one will say anything. Now I get cheered on [by the guys], but it took me a while. Psychologically, it was the hardest thing to deal with that hungry pack of wolves while I earned my place."

Self-confidence and determination were tempered with political intelligence and a sensitivity to the disparate parties involved to negotiate well without accruing acrimony in the process.

"I'm a female and I'm a surfer, therefore surfing is feminine," said Valenti. "Men feel like we're trying to take something away from them, but we're not. We're all in this together. Let's celebrate men and women."

Mavericks maestro Grant Washburn found Valenti a kindred spirit. He too moved to San Francisco in 1990 for the same reason Valenti had: to surf big Ocean Beach.

"You know she's in it for the love, because nobody really sees what you're doing out there," he said. "I remember one day she told me she was ready to try Mavericks—and she's done that over the years. I've seen her out at solid, serious Mavericks without any cameras around and just a few people out, having the best time. For the love."

The Girls From Brazil

As the big wave category ballooned from a few intrepid females to dozens of truly capable women several developments began to emerge. To some extent they paralleled the era's overall trends: local talent began to put on outstanding performances from emerging coastal nations. Second generation daughters are following their parent's (particularly their fathers) salty footsteps.

One of the most visibly striking changes in the century's second decade was the number of Brazilians who burst into the forefront of pro competition. Although the men received the most attention, a troop of Brazilian women have entered the big-wave area with the same enthusiasm and bravado of their male counterparts.

Some, like big-wave superstar Andrea Moller just seemed to rely on intense focus. Bianca Valenti described Moller as "amazingly calm, strong, intense, but with a soft energy at her core."

"Andrea is the elder statesman—not because she's so old but because she's so regal," said Sachi Cunningham, a video photographer respected by the big-wave women she works with. "She started so many of the achievements that are on the record for all time."

Considered Brazil's most accomplished water-woman, Moller can claim more than a few important firsts: she—with her team-mate Maria Souza—was the first women towed into legendary Jaws (a forty-foot swell) and was the first to paddle in too. When Moller took a group of Japanese tourists on an underwater outing there was a sudden earthquake. Calming some of her panicked clients who were walking on the bottom of the seafloor, Moller got them all back quickly—but safely. "Andrea is a total water-woman in every way," said Sachi Cunningham. "She's the one you want to be with when the shit hits the fan."

Born and raised on a small island of Ilhabela, Brazil, she "literally grew up in the water." She moved to Maui where she became a professional water-woman while working as a paramedic. "She is the most grounded of any of us," Bianca Valenti told me. "And she's super smart."

Stand-up paddle and outrigger canoe paddling were also passions; she has entered and won competitions in every category from one-man canoe to six-man teams, from long-distance races to channel crossings. Her SUP career started in 2005, when she crossed the Ka'iwi Channel competing among the men. She was part of the first female Stand Up team, together with Maria Souza, to cross the grueling thirty-two-mile Molokai to Oahu, Ka'iwi Channel. Moller held the world record and achieved numerous titles at the Battle of the Paddle and Olukai Ho'olaule'a long distance competitions in Hawaii.

But surfing was the primary focus. Winner of the 2016 WSL Best Performance Award, Moller claimed a world record for the biggest paddle-in wave surfed at the 2019 Big Wave Awards. Keala Kennelly has observed Moller as much as anyone: "Andrea's goal was to push the limits. She wanted to take Women's big wave surfing to a higher level."

Some seem to have a family DNA component that sets them on another level from the beginning. Silvia Nabuco was born into a family of Olympic athletes and there doesn't seem to be any sport that she doesn't compete, if not excel, in. A two-time XXL Big Wave Awards finalist, she holds the Brazilian Bike record and was runner-up for a spot on the Brazilian windsurfing team.

Raquel Hackett often positioned herself on waves as if in combat. Growing up in Niteroi, Rio de Janeiro, Hackett struggled every step of the way, bringing her young daughter with her on her journey. "My story, my sweat, my difficulties that I faced to be here made me not just a big-wave surfer but a warrior," she was quoted as saying to journalist Maria Fernanda.

"She has such a positive attitude about everything," noted Valenti, who was in many ways a hardscrabble comrade in arms. "I have a saying—'Tenacity trumps talent.' She's got both."

Another Rio native and late bloomer Michaela Fregonese didn't start surfing big waves until 2017 when she was already thirty-six years old. And like Hackett, she brought a son and daughter with her. A dual citizen of Brazil and Italy, Fregonese trained on jet skis in Peru, spent summers in Indonesia and scored a house on front of Pipeline where she attacked big waves with an intensity that brought "the *fierce* to the *feminine*."

Within three short years she had captured Brazil's Big Wave Champion award and had multiple entries at the 2019 WSL Big Wave event.

"She loves her sports and her kids," Valenti complimented. "She even plays football with them."

A recurring characteristic among the Brazilian big-wave riders seemed to be their proficiency in multiple water sports, often learned from their parents.

Nicole Pacelli was no exception. A world champion stand-up paddler, she moved to Sao Paulo from the beach town of Maresias. She is a regular at Jaws, and other big-wave spots. With a former body-boarder mother and an ex-pro surfer father, it was not a surprise when she captured the first ever Women's Stand Up World Tour championship and a second one at Turtle Bay, Oahu the following year. "She knows how to handle size," noted world big wave record breaker Paige Alms. "She was the only female to compete in the Sunset Beach SUP World Championships right along with the men."

Great Big World

Although not Brazilian, Hawaiian Makani Adric shared a multitude of familiar activities. She studied Brazilian Jiujitsu at Sunset Beach Jiujitsu; trained as seriously as the girls from Brazil: mountain biking, pull ups, sprints and breathing techniques to help prepare for surfing bigger waves.

Born and raised on the North Shore, at fifteen she realized she loved surfing big waves. Not long after she took her very first big wave—at Waimea Bay. No safety vest, just a bikini, her board and the feeling of excitement.

A Portuguese speaker but not Brazilian, Joana Andrade sealed her status as her nation's preeminent big-wave rider, winning her fourth straight title Portugal's XXL Big Wave Awards as Best Local Female Big-Wave Surfer. Tiny and humble, the Nazaré, Portugal local operated a surf school in her home town while training for the winter swells. Gaining international acclaim for her 2015 XXL Ride of the Year nomination, Andrade was invited to the Women's Waimea Bay Championship in Hawaii in 2017 and every subsequent year it was held. She was the subject of the 2020 film *Big vs Small,* a 45 minute documentary by Finnish-based Raggari Films.

Women from Central America were rarely seen riding big surf. But Polly Ralda is an unquestionable exception. The Guatemalan charger started surfing when she was fifteen-years-old, but it wasn't until she moved to Hawaii almost five years later that her passion for big waves started. Surfing in her backyard as often as she wanted seasoned her for the challenge. Her favorite wave became Waimea Bay where for years she was either training on the beach, rock running, swimming, free diving or surfing on bigger days.

The Queen of the Bay contest—first begun in 2018 with director Betty Depolito—provided the women a venue for surfing on Oahu at the queen of the big-wave spots—Waimea Bay. The contest was by invitation only and the list was understandably tough to determine. But it did highlight many women who otherwise would have had minimal visibility.

Not surprisingly, many of the invitees were long-time North Shore residents. Living in Hauula, Remi Nealon spent her entire life in the ocean watching her father surf Oahu's North Shore before taking on Waimea herself. A competitive swimmer in her youth, Nealon passed down her skills and her love for the ocean to her three boys.

Similarly, as a mom with two kids Momo Sakuma worked at Roy's Beach House at Turtle Bay Resort while honing her craft in the waves at Sunset Beach for fifteen years.

Blake Lefkoe, a freelance writer, editor, mother and big-wave surfer, graduated from the University of Hawaii, living on Oahu with her family. She began surfing in her twenties and then moved on to big waves in her early thirties.

Transplants from both coasts of the U.S. followed their big dreams to Hawaii. With two diverse obsessions—tomatoes and Pipeline—Emilia Perry learned to love the taste of both. A pro surfer and part-time nail tech at Salon Atlantis in Haleiwa, Hawaii, Perry knew her priorities: "Nails are fine, but surfing comes first."

A devoted Christian, Perry said surfing has kept her young: "To surf is to plug into the Fountain of Youth."

Australian born, Perry started surfing as a teen. "When I was seventeen, I was riding for Billabong and they sent me over to Hawaii. Two days into my trip I met [pro surfer] Tamayo Perry and we married three years later," she said. Her husband remains her inspiration. "We traveled the world," she said, "from Easter Island's reefs to riding a wave down a river in England."

A California native, Sheila Lee moved to from San Diego to Sunset Point to pursue her big-wave goals. An elementary school teacher, surf program coordinator, and yoga instructor by trade, she chose to be a music lover, nature explorer, and mermaid by heart.

Settling down on a farm outside of Haleiwa Hawaii was a long journey from the Jersey Shore where she was born. But a decade later Wrenna Delgado found herself still driven to chase her passion for big waves.

Others moved to the North Shore from far-flung regions but found a match with their passions and careers.

As former residents of Washington D.C. and Hong Kong, Siri Masterson's mother name her *Siri*—and without any connection, her uncle named Siri's cousin *Alexa*. Siri and Alexa were both born before years Apple and Amazon chose those names to represent the ultimate Internet concierge personalities. Masterson's moniker is a Scandinavian derivation of Sirius, the brightest star in the sky. Along with surfing, Masterson played polo and trained polo horses at the Hawaii Polo Club and Dillingham Ranch in Mokuleia, her home surf break. To help support her habits, she managed the Dillingham Lodge wedding venue as well.

Originally from Osaka, Japan, Kiyomi Sheppard always loved to surf but made a quantum leap when she married a young local surfer who showed her that the way to become a better surfer is by becoming a stronger paddler. A Sunset Beach,

Oahu resident, she took up prone paddle-boarding and SUP paddle-boarding. The training took her to the next level, able to be invited to most major events.

A keen interest in craft beer and a full-time job as a firefighter in her native Northern NSW Australia provided both passions and career beyond surfing for Shakira Westdrop. Surfing both shortboards and stand-up paddleboards she competed in the ISA SUP World Championship five times, and won gold in 2018.

A strong showing from the Kauai contingent surprised no one either. Born and raised on Kauai, Kelta O'Rourke began surfing at six years old and had her first big-wave session at twelve. Instantly enthralled, O'Rourke was driven to keep getting bigger and bigger waves. She moved to Oahu's North Shore to attend the University of Hawaii at Manoa and indulge her obsession with big Pipeline.

As a student at Kauai Community College, surfing big waves spoke to Kaya Waldman's soul. Spending every day in the ocean, surfing at her home break Kealia, the Kapa'a, Kauai native set a goal to surf the biggest waves around the world.

The one lone young charger from Maui, Skylar Lickle, was among the youngest of the women invited to the Queen of the Bay event. She grew up in Haiku, Maui where she and her elder sister McKenna attended Seabury Hall, a small private prep school on the slopes of Haleakala crater. Bubbly and energetic, her introduction to big waves began when her father (one of the first to windsurf Jaws) handed her the tow rope on an outside day. Her performances at Jaws were qualifying evidence of her talent. Not many get that chance.

The Big Picture

In the quarter century since women's big-wave performances began to be taken seriously, many spots previously surfed at smaller sizes—Mexico's *Puerto Escondido* and Todos Santos, Pico Alto in Peru, Punta de Lobos in Chile, and South Africa's Dungeons—added extra locations for contest events. As big-wave locations expanded globally so did the women who were challenging them.

This trend was even more pronounced in Hawaii, where families of great surfers and waves of serious consequence both abound. Once considered surfing's ultimate challenge, it has been the place of big-wave legend for more than seven decades. But for all its storied history it never had a contest for women until 2018. That winter a small group of big-wave women surfers competed in the "Queen of the Bay" the first ever Waimea Bay women's competition. The aim was not just another contest but a celebration of women and their progress in surfing.

The idea had first been hatched around 2014 when Betty Depolito, the contest's executive director and founder, saw how underrepresented the new wave of female big-wave riders were. While there were a handful of women's divisions in big-wave events around the globe, there was no tour and no women's only big-wave event. It elevated the Queen of the Bay contest into a moment in history.

The Naked Truth

In 2020 Felicity Palmateer brought her *own* moment in history: *Skin Deep*, a four minute film showcasing Palmateer surfing nude—in Fiji, Hawaii, Australia and Wales.

Earlier in her career she had earned the multi-moniker "big-wave activist artist." In *Skin Deep* Palmateer seemed to be exploring her own definition of herself and her interpretation of artistic freedom. Four years in the making, the film was "a journey toward uninhibited self-expression" linking her two passions—art and surfing.

Driven and dedicated, Palmateer seemed to lay claim to the idea that if a picture is worth a thousand words, then she had a lot more to say than just winning heats. With the ocean as her central inspiration, her father (an art and ceramics teacher as well as a passionate surfer) introduced her to both mediums. Raised on Western Australia's wild coast Palmateer became both a prolific painter and big-wave surfing prodigy. Even as a long-time top-ranked competitor she appeared to integrate every piece of her experience into a holistic lifestyle: surfing, healthy eating, travel, producing an eclectic body of art.

Then she won her record breaking "biggest wave by an Aussie female," and suddenly the big-wave passion overtook her art.

Unphased by others' judgements, she surfed nude in *Skin Deep* and charged big Pipeline with the same intense focus. But her purposeful actions often called attention to the serious causes she championed: her love for animals, body positivity, support of women's issues and defense of fragile ecosystems.

Living the Legacy

When a 2014 invitation-only big-wave event held at Mavericks failed to include Emily Erickson she flew from Hawaii to the contest anyway. A total unknown at the time, she talked the event's organizers into allowing her to compete nonetheless.

"I'd spent the last ten years surfing big waves and earning my way into surfing Waimea Bay," said Erickson.

Maverick's big-wave pioneer Jeff Clark saw her catch one of the break's heavy waves. "She definitely made a statement when she was out there," Clark remarked. "Big-wave riding is in her genes."

As a child Erickson had played on the beach at Waimea Bay, while watching her father, Roger, a big-wave Waimea Bay legend and former North Shore lifeguard, ride giant swells. A Vietnam veteran, Roger garnered the nickname "Tarzan" in his younger years for being something of a wild man as well as for his surfing prowess and physical intensity.

Though born in Hawaii, Emily Erickson's first stay was short—relocating to Virginia at six. A naturally gifted athlete, Erickson became a talented cross-country runner in high school. But the call of her birthplace was strong. Accepted to the University of Hawaii, she returned in 2006, this time with a wave-riding component to relieve the pressure of her studies.

At seventeen, her introduction to surfing began late, but once involved, she fell to the siren's call of big waves.

Erickson's best friend Wrenna Delgado, a fellow big-wave surfer involved in the formation of Queen of the Bay observed her closely for years: "It's in her blood. Her desire to surf big waves was probably always hiding inside her, but when she came back to the North Shore, she wanted to be in that energy. That's something you can't ignore."

A year later, seeing her passion, her father gave her his 10'6" big-wave gun. "Nothing hit me as hard as surfing did," she confessed.

Innate intelligence and almost aristocratic grace seemed to inhabit Erickson's being, an attractiveness as natural as her Hemmingway-like simplicity of speech. Described as a restless spirit, Erickson soon began traveling to surf around the world. The almost immediate attention—an *Outside* magazine article, the cover of *The Surfer's Journal*, nominations for two Billabong XXL Awards in Women's Overall—were positive confirmations, even if unexpected. But sponsors were hard to find and Erickson looked for other means of support.

For more than fifteen years, she worked at a sushi restaurant and a natural foods store, took modeling jobs and stunt work in films. In *Jurassic World*, she could be seen sitting on her surfboard until a dinosaur takes over the screen. In between stints of work, Erickson pinballed around the globe, chasing big swells.

"Emily works to surf," commented her colleague Laura Enever. "The way she juggles everything is amazing—her work, her training, her friendships, her equipment—even her single fins."

"Big-wave surfing takes so much time and requires so much experience that it doesn't do it justice to put it into just an hour heat," said Erickson. "I want to show the world this powerful image of women dropping into these massive waves. I hope to share that image with others and show the world what women can do."

That dedication and sense of purpose seemed to personify both the motivation and the legacy of Erickson's life. It was a simple perspective she said: "Riding big waves is where I am supposed to be."

Insult To Injury

"You could try and take us—But we're the gladiators—Everyone a rager— But secretly they're saviors Glory and gore go hand in hand—That's why we're making headlines."

—Lorde, "Glory, and Gore," March, 2014

American Carnage

When Mercedes Maidana arrived to take part in the Nelscott Reef Big-Wave Classic on March 12, 2014, she had no idea it would completely change her life. It seemed an unimportant and relatively new competition on Oregon's northwest coast of the U.S. But paddling out in her first heat of this invitational event it became an unexpected nightmare.

"I got caught by a thirty-foot wave and just froze," she told the BBC Sports network. "It took me all the way down under water and my surfboard crashed into my forehead." Although quickly rescued, Maidana was bleeding profusely. Once back on shore, she was taken to a hospital. The doctor glued the cut above her eye. He said she had a "mild concussion, nothing to worry about" and discharged her. But *something was wrong*. And Maidana knew it.

She started vomiting that night. Rushed back to the hospital where another scan was done, nothing tangible was detected. She was diagnosed with a mild concussion and told to rest. Yet a few days later her mind and her body began to fail.

At the time Maidana was one of the best big-wave surfers in the world. Since taking up the sport in her early twenties she had worked tirelessly, obsessively developing her skills on Maui's famous North Shore and building up her fitness. Within weeks of her board smashing into her forehead she struggled to get off the couch or hold a conversation, she told *Guardian* reporter Tom Dart. Her tongue was leaden. She was too weary to walk her dog. She couldn't carry on a simple conversation. Even sending a text message was exhausting. Each time she went to see a doctor, they told her to rest and gave her antidepressants. Constantly dizzy, confused, anxious, depressed and paranoid, her world crumbled.

"I lost my husband, my house, my sponsorship, I had a coaching business, I couldn't do it anymore. I lost everything," she acknowledged. "The cut, the cut in your eyebrow! We were all concerned about the blood, instead of what's happening underneath."

"While concussions in major contact sports, notably American football, attract most of the research and media attention, traumatic head injuries in surfing are the shadow amid the sunshine," Tom Dart wrote in his groundbreaking article for the *Guardian* newspaper, "rarely discussed and poorly understood despite their potentially devastating effects. Studies suggest a significant minority of surfers suffer head injuries that carry a risk of cognitive decline in addition to the immediate danger of drowning."

"Nobody talks about concussions in surfing," Maidana has asserted, "and nobody ever wants to talk about mental illness."

In hindsight, Maidana is sure that her injury in Oregon had its origins in hidden trauma from an accident in Maui the week before. "I got two fifty-foot waves right on the head in the impact zone [where the wave is most powerful]," she explained painfully.

"It was like a horror movie, so much time underwater, it was just so violent, the beating in my body and the lack of oxygen. I truly was one inch from dying. I really felt: OK, the next moment I'm going to be on the other side. In a way I wanted it to end because I was feeling really bad, I just wanted the peacefulness."

Still, she did not seek treatment. She thought she would be OK. But when Maidana arrived at the contest at Nelscott Reef the waves were much bigger than expected.

"That's when the terror started to creep in, I was very nervous, very uncomfortable in the water. A thirty-five foot wave, nowhere to go, that's the moment where you have to ditch your board and dive and get under the wave," Maidana said recalling the traumatic event. "I freaked out, that's when I think the PTSD came. I froze—I saw the wave and I just didn't do anything—and it just took me," she said. "It hit me underwater with the lip of the wave—imagine a thirty-five-foot wave bringing a ten-foot board that's like a table, into my forehead. I got hit, I felt a quick in-and-out, black stars, pulled my inflatable vest. When I went black, I was like, 'come back—because if you don't come back right now, you go.'"

For many years Maidana struggled to cope, enduring the pain of a long slow recovery. Eventually she channeled her experience into raising awareness of the big-wave danger. She decided to pledge her brain to the Concussion Legacy Foundation for research. "I wanted my legacy to be that I paid it forward, used my experience to help others navigate the seemingly impossible process of dealing with a traumatic brain injury. There wasn't a lot of research on brain trauma among surfers, and I wanted to be a leader in my sport, my community."

No Pain No Gain

To prove their gutsiness women often have taken chances that many men might not even contemplate. Emily Erickson did so in the Jaws event in 2019: "We went straight into the deep end," she said. "It's a pretty risky thing to have the first of these events at the most dangerous spot in the world. As for me, I took a chance. I went for the biggest, baddest wave I could find. That's kind of the point. It's what I choose to do. I've spent a decade pursuing this crazy, blind passion. I went out there because I want to support the whole women's movement."

By the end of the first forty-five-minute heat, Keala Kennelly and Emily Erickson were both headed to the hospital: Kennelly with torn ligaments—mowed down in exploding whitewater—and Erickson with a fractured leg bone from an elevator drop after a vertical wind shear took her board airborne.

While that episode at Jaws was more extreme than most, injuries of consequence are not uncommon. History is filled with incidents that threatened a surfer's career: Seven-time champ Layne Beachley tore knee ligaments and couldn't advance to the finals of the Jeffreys Bay contest in South Africa. She won four more titles. Courtney Conlogue, considered a top contender to win the 2019 World Title, took a freak face-smack on an inconsequential wave in Portugal's WTC event and missed the rest of the season. At the 1999 WCT event in Tahiti, Serena Brooke suffered a serious concussion. Stunned for a few minutes she paddled right back out, pushing through to the semifinals of the event. Sally Fitzgibbons perforated her eardrum in a wipeout at Cloudbreak, a serious shallow wave in Fiji. Defying the doctor's orders she refused to leave the heat, continued to surf—and won.

When Maya Gabeira took off on a fifty-foot peak in Portugal wiping out and nearly drowning, big wave iconoclast Laird Hamilton criticized her for "not having the skill to be in the water" that day. But the number of serious wipeouts suffered by unqualified males floundering in the lineup, begged the question of Hamilton's perspective.

Former World Surf League Hawaii General Manager Jodie Wilmot put it succinctly: "If a *guy* had been on that wave nobody would have said a *word*."

When asked about worst injuries, Daize Shayne joked that the insults were often worse: "Enduring Christian Fletchers encouraging jabs every winter; Joel Tudor getting me kicked off my wet-suit sponsor (serious injury, ha!) And there were physical ailments too: when I contracted chicken pox in Australia—and landing head-first into a peanut shark. All these things are way worse than getting eight stitches in my head from a small day at Pipe."

Close Encounters

Although surfing is an inherently dangerous sport in most studies it rates very low both in terms of serious or fatal injuries and for number of injuries per participant. More than two thirds of all injuries are from contact with a surfboard, more than half are from the injured person's own board.

According to several decades of research by a number of statistical studies, traditional surfing has never rated in the top thirty of dangerous sporting activities. But big-wave riding, on the contrary, has been rated as highly dangerous, often in the top ten category for acute injury and death.

Is it fair for men to say the sport is too dangerous for women?

"The ocean doesn't discriminate," noted Emily Erickson. "Why should we?"

"Big-wave surfing isn't about how strong you are on the outside," Keala Kennelly told me years ago. "It's what you are made of on the inside."

"Part of it is studying and learning and putting in the time. Another part is going with your instincts." Training, preparation, dedication—and what for centuries has been called "women's intuition"—appear to be as important as the courage.

For Keala Kennelly, "If women are going to be taken seriously and respected alongside the male big-wave surfing greats, then we should be held to similar performance standards."

Yet the spectacular rides on huge waves by Paige Alms at Jaws and Keala Kennerly in Tahiti or Maya Gabeira at Nazaré were a match for anyone. Those kinds of performances got men major bargaining power in compensation negotiations. They are frequently financially ignored when women achieve them. Keala Kennelly was the most obvious: "Even though I got more exposure since I left the WCT tour and just started focusing on big-wave surfing—like double-page spreads in the Big Issue of *SURFER* magazine, stuff that other women weren't getting—my salary kept getting cut every year," she explained. "The year they dropped me was the year that I won the *men's* award, was nominated for an ESPY and was the first woman ever to be an alternate in The Eddie. Nothing made sense," she said.

"I thought, 'If I was a *dude* getting all these accomplishments, I wouldn't be having money problems right now.'" Karelle Poppke from Tahiti agreed with the difficulty: "I have had a lot of trouble securing sponsors," she said.

Hailed in her own country as a "champion in the making," she still had trouble finding the financial support.

She thought she knew the reason: "I don't have the top model profile of the California surfer who attracts the sponsors." After placing seventh in the 2017 ISA World Games, Poppke thought she was on her way to breaking into the top pro ranks. She trained hard and had huge support from the Tahitian media. But without sponsorship, as so many find out, sometimes the points don't add up. "We're not all beauties paid to wear swimsuits," she stated, disappointment obvious for someone who had been called "Tahiti's best." "I have to make a living like everyone else." In 2018 she retired from pro surfing to join the French Polynesia Air Force. Ironically she took second in her last Qualifying Series competition in Japan.

At the 2005 Teahupoo event Laurina McGrath suffered a puncture wound to the thigh after brushing against the reef on her first wave. Undaunted, McGrath caught three steep pitching waves before her two adversaries in the heat were able to get even one ride on the scoreboard. She won the heat and made it two more rounds but lost in the semifinals. But in 2009 she did not return to the circuit. Plucky and unruffled, her injury was not the cause of her retreat—sponsorship was her obstacle.

Paige Hareb was forced to withdraw from competition after crashing into rocks in 2018 during a free surf in Mexico. "The wave slammed me straight into the side of a rock," Hareb recounted later. "I heard my ribs crack underwater. Broke ribs nine and ten." After being helped from the water, she was diagnosed with an abrasion on her lung and some liquid inside, but returned to competition after missing only two events.

"Every pro surfer gets injured," big-wave filmmaker Sachi Cunningham told me. "The key factors are: when in their career do they get hurt? What's the damage and how does it affect them?"

After finishing seventh at the ISA Junior World Championships in New Zealand in 2010, Cannelle Bulard, a French surfer from Réunion Island off East Africa who grew up on a sailboat in the Indian Ocean, came back in 2011 to take the ISA Amateur World Title. She turned pro and thought she was on the way to a successful rookie season. But then Bulard suffered a knee injury at the beginning of 2012 and was out of commission for most of the winter/spring competitions. She was required to take a two-month break from competition and training. Her rehabilitation included riding a bicycle, training as well as surfing for a solid month.

Early in her career, youth was on Bulard's side. By 2020 she had made a remarkable comeback, topping the rankings of the World Qualifying Series to qualify for a spot on the World Tour just before COVID-19 forced the global lockdown.

Injury has always been an accepted risk of competition, and as the physical limitations grow, athletes look for alternative methods of making a living. Some surfers even with debilitating injury have found post-competition avenues within the surfing community as satisfying as their active pro careers. A pioneer and visionary of her sport, Prue Jefferies spent twenty years as a fierce competitor on the Association of Surfing Professionals World Tour. But following a string of injuries that included torn ligaments and a broken neck, Jeffries put on her contest jersey for the last time in 2006. Intelligent and sometimes deceptively restrained, she became an internationally published writer, editorial consultant, ambassador, brand cocreator and filmmaker after retiring from the World Tour. Later Jefferies earned a certified message therapist degree and became a practitioner and creative director at the Biodynamic Therapy Association of North America, and continues to devote time promoting women's issues and championing sports opportunities.

Glory and Gore

Length of recovery time is often less important than its relationship to upcoming performances. While visiting with her friend Kassia Meador during a long break between contests, Perth local Claire Bevilacqua injured her ankle. "I was out for *four weeks*," she recalled. "But it seemed like forever."

But after her four weeks of recovery she was only back in the water *four hours* when she suffered another, more challenging injury: Just before the Pipeline Pro started she made a slight miscalculation and her board smashed into her body. "I think I was being a little too cocky, catching a wave in before the contest and trying to show everyone that I wasn't afraid," she admitted. "Then my board hit me. I thought I broke my leg."

Bevilacqua limped down to the water's edge for her first heat. Once out in the water she erased the pain. "The injury affected me because almost every wave I felt a little wobbly, but I was so psyched up I just tried to block it out," Bevilacqua remembered.

She didn't just compete—she got multiple barrels at the shallow hollows of Pipeline's Backdoor section during the final. The *Honolulu Star Bulletin* claimed she was "dominating her competition."

It should have been no surprise—Claire Bevilacqua was *no rookie*. In the years prior to this climatic peak Bevilacqua had a quick rise in the ranks. Compact and confident, after only four years of competing, she won the 2003 State *and* the Australian Pro Junior Women's Championships. With strong sponsor backing, she had set her sights on Pipeline and no near-broken leg was going to faze her. Now with another half dozen years under her belt she ignored the immediate problem, relying on her months of preparation to see her though. "I just eat, sleep and surf Pipe every day when I'm here in the winter," she was quoted at the time. The preparation paid off: despite a leg in agony Bevilacqua took the prestigious 2009 Pipeline Pro title with apparent ease.

In 2017 she won a major competition—the first-ever Barbados Surf Pro—fifteen years after winning her first event.

"The most important thing is how you *recover*," Bianca Valenti has explained to me more than once. But age, timing and extent of the damage are important factors:

Surfing her home break in 2012 when Honolua Bloomfield was only thirteen years old, her shortboard flipped and hit her nose-first on the forehead, leaving a gash that took thirty stitches to mend. She was back in the water three weeks later.

Samantha Cornish entered her first competition at the age of eleven. With a father, Peter Cornish, who was also a professional surfer, Samantha started young, entering her first competition at eleven. By fifteen she had won the 1996 World Junior Championships. Affable and even-tempered, she joined the World Championship Tour (WCT) in 2002. But then three years later she seemed to falter due to an injury that might have finished her career—without her determination. Cornish was awarded the ASP injury wildcard at the end of 2006 after nearly falling off the tour. But she returned the next year making a fiery title run that just missed, finishing fourth in the rankings in 2007.

Heather Clarke did her one better: At the end of 2003, the South African surfer was ranked third among female surfers in the world. But in 2009, she was seriously injured when the car in which she was traveling was struck by a drunk driver. After surgery and traction, Clarke finally was able to return to competition after recovering for almost a year. The affectionate outpouring of support was startling even to Clark but appeared helpful. Competing at the International Surfing Association World Masters Surfing Championship, in 2010 she won her second consecutive gold medal, and in 2011 she won the silver medal, turning tragedy into triumph.

Silver linings have not attended every dark cloud. The heir to Lisa Andersen's media frenzy, Serena Brooke was one of the surf world's brightest and best-liked stars in the late 90s and early 2000s. Super-fit, fresh-faced, the Queensland teen claimed ASP Rookie of the Year honors in 1995, won her first tour event the next year, and twice finished second in the world (1998 and 1999) a ranking surfers call the "bridesmaid's curse."

A romance with dashing surf photographer Tom Servais got her career off to a fast start with surf shots in *Surfer* that brought her international attention. But it would hardly have mattered if he hadn't. From early on, Brooke knew what she wanted to do and did it: skipped school, burst through the world amateur titles, went straight on to the Pro Tour and was soon knocking at the door of the number one spot.

Loved by her compatriots she was nonetheless formidable in competition.

"Serena could put on a savage game face and take it off just as quickly after the heat was over," said fellow competitor Rochelle Ballard. Full of "irresistible energy," she could elicit powerful performances. Brooke was also one of the most *marketable* athletes in woman's surfing, picking up sponsorships and television appearances along with prize money. Fit and freckled, with no doubts or regrets, a bright career seemed Brooke's likely future. But a string of injuries, excessive even for a competitive athlete, cut short her bright career. In 2002, she received a chin injury requiring twenty-six stitches. One day later she was back in competition. In 2003 while leading the rankings in the Foster's Pro Surfing Tour she had to withdraw for the tour after seriously hurting her hand and requiring lengthy therapy.

Then in 2004, in a freak accident during practice for an event, Brooke came very close to losing an eye; her board shot up from under her and the fin slashed her face. Her upper and lower eyelids were sliced through and another cut ripped through a tear duct. It took months for full recovery.

By March 2005 Brooke has been relegated to the bench for three seasons. The horror run of injuries didn't stop her, but the resulting damage had taken its toll.

After fourteen years of Tour life, Brooke bowed out of full-time competition after the 2008 season. In the years after, Brooke went on to open a foundation doing charity work, appeared in surf fitness videos and started her own clothes company. She and her partner Emma Sheldrake moved to Noosa Heads, Australia and in 2013, began what she called "the most important chapter of her life:" giving birth to twin girls. They made headlines in Australia in 2013 after coming out in support of gay marriage and requesting their union be legalized.

Between PT and PTS

Physical Therapy and Post Traumatic Stress can both accompany a serious injury.

Happy endings notwithstanding, what happens when an athlete suffers a setback at the top of their game?

Officially qualifying for the 2012 Women's Pro Tour, Sage Erickson wasted no time putting her many years of hard work to good use. Competing in the WSL 6-Star events that make up the qualifying rounds, she garnered enough points to finish fourth place and make the Pro Tour cut.

With plans to compete in the ISA amateur World Titles being held in China, she decided to head to warmer waters. Leaving her Ojai, California abode, she flew to Copacabana Beach in New South Wales Australia. It was not a fortuitous decision.

"I was doing a bit of cross training, 'bush running' as the Australians would probably call it and I sprained it over a decent sized rock. Straight to the ground I dropped, unable to really walk." Within minutes the ankle was double its original size and bruising rapidly. "I knew I was in for trouble."

The local doctors were on Christmas Holiday. The China event was just days away. With the Roxy Pro Gold Coast less than a month off, Erickson knew her priority was the WSL Pro Tour. She had worked so hard to qualify for it, there seemed only one choice. She returned home to heal and build strength in her ankle.

Erickson would spend the next five years battling to win her first Pro Tour event. She broke into the top ten rankings twice, but then she narrowly missed qualifying for the top thirty-two in 2018. Obsession with contests was not her mindset; she looked at other avenues to augment her pro status. Her sharp mind and petite but beautiful appearance gave her a multitude of options: as a model, spokesperson or free-surfer. But Erickson was not ready to simply walk away from the competition where she had fought so tenaciously. She won the U.S. Open of Surfing in 2017 and again in 2019, denying her longtime rival and friend Courtney Conlogue a repeat, while simultaneously helping her requalify for the 2020 World Tour. But one wonders what might have been different if the first year injury had not occurred.

So much of a top surfer's identity is wound into their professional career, injury can be as damaging to the mind as to the body. Do these circumstances affect the surfer's psychic perspective?

In 2016, a wave hit veteran Andrea Moller so hard that it ripped her hamstring muscle off the bone. Unable to walk for months, the veteran who had pioneered Jaws two decades earlier had to depend on her twelve-year-old daughter for help bathing. Still, Moller recovered and didn't stop surfing big waves. "I think it defines me, who I am," she offered. "Like, when I got hurt, I wondered:

"'Could I just settle down and make a garden, focus on projects at home?' Unfortunately, when I do that in my life, I feel incomplete."

31

The Long Way Around
2000–2021

The Longboard Artform Comes of Age

The dawning of the new millennium began an acceleration for surfing. For the first time ever a women's longboard world contest was on the table, four decades after the men's contest. Young girls had taken to longboards in mass. Demand was shattering records. Would it last?

Blood on the Tracks

Cori Schumacher never had a warning. As the Firestone tires on her Blue gray Explorer exploded she could not have anticipated the crash she was about to experience. Her SUV swerved, lost control and rolled over, crossing several lanes of traffic, smashed a pole and returned to an upright position on the side of the freeway. Her friend and passenger was bleeding from her ears. Cori's arm had no feeling in it. She remembered them sitting there in shock. "The same song was still playing on the radio," she told her mom later.

Rushed to the hospital, her mangled car nearly unrecognizable, she kept thinking about tomorrow. She was scheduled to fly to Costa Rica for the 2000 World Longboard contest.

Treated for a mild concussion, multiple leg gashes and gaping scabs where her arm had met the asphalt, she was released from the hospital the next day. The doctor ordered her to rest in bed for the next week. Instead Schumacher rescheduled her flight for the following day and flew to the Central American contest site.

Schumacher had lost the initial 1999 World Surf Contest the previous year when, through a fluke of scoring changes in the finals, she ended up placing second to a surprised Daize Shayne, who had surfed brilliantly but with her famously lackadaisical style.

"That was a fiasco," confessed Sherri Crummer one of the judges. "Everyone thought Cori had won." Including Shayne, who apparently was chagrined at the outcome.

Now wounded and exhausted, it appeared she might again be thwarted by this random turn of events.

Arriving at the site in Costa Rica, Schumacher initially thought she would compete as long as she could and then just watch. But she won her first heat. She thought she might be too dizzy to continue. Then she won her next heat. And another.

Somewhere in these early rounds, Schumacher made a decision: she did not intend to lose the World Title again, concussion, cuts or contusions notwithstanding. Heat after heat she gritted through the pain, somehow reaching the semi-finals. Her bruises turned black. Her stitches became soft. But not her focus. By the time she had reached the finals, again facing the inimitable Daize Shayne, the entire crowd of spectators had lined the shoreline. And when she came out of the water victorious, a cadre of emotional competitors carried her on their shoulders cheering as if the pain of her triumph was their own.

In an extraordinary feat Cori Schumacher had won the 2000 World Longboard Championship. As if to remove any doubt she returned the next year to repeat her title winning performance—sans the automobile accident.

Sisters of Avalon

Intertwined in the first three World Longboard Championships, Cori Schumacher, Daize Shayne Goodwin, and Sheri Crummer would become highly influential figures in Southern California surfing's future.

"Awakening in dark swells and mystery," like Cyndi Lauper's epic "Sisters of Avalon," these "daughters of Eve," were the first leading women of longboarding's 21st Century that began with the first World Longboard Contests.

Shayne-Goodwin had won the initial event, Schumacher took the next two and Crummer had judged them all. Their careers would continue to be linked through friendship and achievements, with many similarities and just as many completely contrasting characteristics. All three rode shortboards as well as longboards and grew up surfing and living at the beach from the time they were born. Each was mentored by longboard icon Joel Tudor in some fashion. Lissome and alluring, with an aura of carefree disinterest, Goodwin entered the inner circle of surf stardom as Tudor's girlfriend. But women with as many star-like qualities as Goodwin had every motivation to display them all, including her strong but effortless surf style. Schumacher's family had been best friends with the Tudor's when she was growing up. Born into a dedicated clan revered as community pillars as well as talented waveriders, Schumacher was competing alongside Tudor before she was in elementary school. And Crummer, born and raised in San Clemente—a quintessential California surf town—had a multitude of hometown surf spots and mentors like Tudor who helped her advance rapidly.

As often is the case for leaders in the culture, each of these women took sabbaticals at various key moments, an introspective phase to assess life's larger meaning.

Crummer took off for New Mexico, living in a small cabin among the cedars and pinons with a wood burning stove but no running water or electricity, a Thoreau-like examination of what was truly important.

Schumacher became so disenchanted with the demands from those who would bankroll (and control) her career she walked away from the cutthroat competitive surf ethos altogether, moving to San Francisco. "My whole self-worth as a human being became attached to how well I performed in the contests," she said in a film she posted online.

Crummer moved to Los Angeles to pursue music—a second calling that put drumsticks in her hands instead of fiberglass under her feet.

Goodwin didn't feel the need to remove the surfing component in order to engage *her* musical passion. She recorded an album *Living Your Dreams* in 2005. Her first hiatus from the mad mix of modeling, music and surf didn't come until her first baby in 2013.

As their stars rose, their widely differing ages did not separate their friendships or their influence—Goodwin still in her teens, Schumacher in her early thirties and Crummer already into middle age.

As their careers progressed each faced seemingly insurmountable crisis in their lives testing their spirit and beliefs across a broad spectrum of issues. And it struck each of them far more seriously than the average attractive white women living in the coastal environs of Southern California. For Goodwin—the most extroverted of the trio—experimenting with drugs entered her life early. Cigarettes, drinking and smoking pot at a really early age set the stage for additional challenges. "Daize was wild," noted Julie Cox who roomed with her on a surf trip to the Cook Islands.

"Surfing actually saved me from getting into the hard drugs," Goodwin has admitted, "but I was still doing drugs like acid and pot." Over time, the problem became so acute at one point she felt she might have lost her way altogether.

Crummer encountered a more instantaneous calamity. In October 1999, on her way to the U.S. Championships to qualify for the World Title, she was in a devastating automobile accident. The doctor's analysis indicated she would never compete again—and most likely never surf again.

And Cory, confronting the challenge of family breakup, religious doubt, sexual turmoil and a loss of faith in the very culture she had grown up in, faced a storm of angst-ridden life choices.

Yet each of these women managed to carve a path past the exposed reefs of their lives and find both redemption and achievement.

Sherri Crummer recovered from her massive injuries, fought back to peak physicality and went on to win three consecutive U.S. National Longboard Championships in the women's eighteen-and-over division from 2002–04 at ages fifty-two, fifty-three and fifty-four. "After my first U.S. win I signed a poster and dropped it off at the doctor's office who said I would never compete again," Crummer recalled. "Never did hear from her."

Daize Shayne Goodwin, after winning two World Championships in 1999 and 2004, turned her intense energy into a more focused game plan, embracing the family life with enthusiasm. Then came a hit single, music tours, modeling and eventually a marriage and children.

Cori Schumacher's world championship titles in 2000 and 2001 were followed by a dramatic comeback in 2010 after nearly seven years in self-imposed exile. Her surfing, though, was not what defined her in the surf culture. In 2011, in a highly publicized battle against the WSL, Schumacher boycotted the Hainan China contest, citing China's "human rights violations" as the reason. "I have deep political and personal reservations with being a part of any sort of benefit to a country that actively engages in human-rights violations," Schumacher wrote to the ASP, "specifically those in violation of women." A few years later, when Roxy released their now-infamous Stephanie Gilmore advertisement, Schumacher again took to the battlefield, collecting over 20,000 signatures for a protest against the surfwear giant's questionable portrayal of women.

A short poignant biopic *Waves of Disruption: The Cori Schumacher Story* chronicled her life and what has driven her. And, by most observers' opinion, the surfing world became a better place with her in it—not only for her talent on a surfboard but her willingness to call out falsehood and inequities where she saw them, no matter what the personal cost. These women's stories would continue to impact surfing culture—but not before a raft of developments and characters would enter the scene they had ignited.

A New "World"

In 2004, surf event impresario Hank Raymond passed along the Women's World Longboard Championship event he'd created to Linda Benson. Benson—respected world champ and long-time legend—held the 2005 event at Ocean Beach,

California, where Floridian Kristy Murphy won the thrilling final in 8–10' surf. Murphy would parlay her title legitimacy into Siren Surf Adventures, an international surf, Stand Up Paddle (SUP) and yoga tour and retreat she would—along with Cat Slatinsky—found a few years later. Slatinsky, an Imperial Beach local who moved to Hawaii to cut her teeth in the South Shore waters, became an accomplished surf photographer and helped Murphy expand their retreat business worldwide—to San Diego, Costa Rica, Hawaii and the Caribbean.

With a track record of successful results and Benson at the helm, the Association of Surfing Professionals (ASP) and Roxy clothing took notice of the World Longboard event's potential and in 2006 borrowed the contest's title from Benson. For the first time ever, the ASP sanctioned the Women's World Longboard Championship. Held in Biarritz, France, it was won by San Diegan Schuyler McFerran against fellow San Diegan Jennifer Smith.

Quiet and grounded, McFerran traveled the globe to compete, an effort that paid off handsomely with a World Title.

"Schuyler had a good her head on her shoulders," Mary Bagalso observed of her. "Schuyler was always ahead of most the competitors at that time," noted Smith.

"She was home-schooled, supported by her family, and had sponsorship. She had the absolute best single-fin style; smooth, feminine, and she was beautiful," Smith continued. "I never felt like I fit in like that."

Smith, like many of the girls striving to build solid pro careers, struggled with "the beauty complex" even though she had extraordinary talent.

Femininity and the continued emphasis on conventional physical attractiveness was not the only issue that began to percolate among these women in the new millennium. Ethnic diversity became a focal point as well.

Josie Prendergast, the daughter of a Spanish-Filipino mother and Scottish-Australian father, was a perfect representative of the multicultural connection surfing brought to light. Soulful and altruistic, Prendergast quickly refined her smooth style, emulating her shaper, legendary master-boardmaker Bob McTavish. Along with friend and fellow pro Alessa Quizon who was of Filipino decent, she was the subject of the surf documentary *Highsnobiety*. Eschewing the more commonly driven competitive side of the lifestyle, Prendergast dreamed of a higher calling: creating an orphanage home for children in the third world countries, then providing them with school materials for a better life.

She was not a singular case. Kassia Meador, who came from a tightly-woven, hardscrabble middleclass family, yearned to break the traditional mold. Total emersion in surf culture obscured her Latinx roots, but not her drive to succeed. In a sport traditionally dominated by blonde Nordics and Hawaiian/Asian ethnics, Summer Romero—like Kassia Meador—was one of the first Latinx women to enter the top ranks of competition. Romero won the 2004 Women's World

Longboard Championship and then in 2005 took the U.S. National title. The beach lifestyle pioneered in the Hawaiian and Californian cradle of surf civilization was not foremost in Hispanic heritage. Although Peru and later Brazil developed strong surf traditions, Latinx involvement in surf culture was rare in the U.S.

Meador could not have paddled out at a better moment to step into this new crucible and forge a fresh path in longboarding. Blending the glamour of the decade's cross-stepping stylistics with the street-smart energy of her own freestyle abandon, she would become an authentic force as powerful as any in the early-to-mid 2000s.

Many of Meador's performances were captured in some of the most respected surf films of the era, including Dana Brown's 2003 *Step Into Liquid* (in a segment titled "Surf Like a Girl") and Thomas Campbell's 2004 film *Sprout* (in a segment titled "Lady Slide").

The one soft spot on her resume is contest titles. For whatever reason Meador has not collected the championship trophies that many of her colleagues have.

"It's almost unexplainable," Jen Smith, her friend and fellow competitor mused. "The fact that she doesn't have multiple titles is crazy. Because in reality, she was *the best.*"

Meador has never seemed to worry about the accolades or the competitive results.

"I want to make surfing a holistic lifestyle for me," she told me in a 2003 radio interview. "It doesn't matter if its sponsorship, business, coaching, whatever." That singular passion has driven her life. "I knew the moment I rode a wave exactly what I wanted to be."

Like Meador, the day Jen Smith won her first contest at the age of ten she knew what she wanted to be: a competitor. That elevated sense of achievement sent her into the contest circuit. For Smith it was her means of ascent. "I wanted to be up on the podium," she confessed. "I wanted to take the big trophy home." Her dad, a highly regarded surfer himself, owned a skateboard shop near their home in Pacific Beach; she grew up surfing with him almost daily. "I was the youngest of three kids," Smith said, "so I grew up scrappy." The combination of supportive surf dad, beach town residence and focused motivation paid off.

At just twenty-one, Smith won the Roxy Jam Women's World Longboard Title in Biarritz, France in July 2007—and two years later she won again—her second WSL World Title in three years. Smith continued to compete, winning Australian titles in 2014 and placing highly in the tour events. An unabashed gardener, she also plays ukulele, cooks and "drinks a lot of tea." Smith started shaping in 2010 and "got really addicted to it." But she credits her friends—particularly the older ones—for mentoring her. Mary Bagalso, a respected surfer on premier shaper Donald Takayama's surf team, "would drive me up to Malibu or down to Baja,"

Smith remembered. "That Oceanside crew was one of the hottest in the 90s when everything was exploding in the surf scene," Smith continued. "Malia Fuertes, and Summer Romeo spent a lot of time being big sisters and friends."

Nicknamed "Squib," Fuentes had already been to Hawaii, "was living at my house," and as Bagalso recalled, was "quite a firecracker." Carefree and spontaneous, Fuertes "translated that spirit into her surfing," Bagalso laughed.

Bagalso, a San Diego State University graduate, was something of a firecracker herself. An ICU and CRNA (Nurse Anesthetist) with a black belt in tae kwon do, she managed to take a team of surf girls on a Margaritaville-sponsored tour around the U.S. giving demonstrations at wave pools.

Jen Smith's younger friends were no less impressive: Samantha Roper and Jenna Klein both came with deep roots in the culture—Samantha's father was renown La Jolla tube rider and board restoration guru Joe Roper. Jenna Klein's mother Julie had built a business making the best custom board bags in the industry. Klein's attorney father Craig—a high-caliber surf talent himself—had defended many a needy surfer in his career. Klein and Roper represent the deep underground faction of female surfers whose ability far outweighs their media visibility. They also epitomize the encouraging ties that bind these women in ways male surfers never need to contemplate when they aspire to a competitive career. Like all competitors, Smith needed loyal friends as auxiliary support. "It's true I had to fight for my place," Smith concedes. "But it was my path to success. Winning contests was the way I could do it."

Longboarder Mary Osborne blazed a different trail to success, focusing on the environmental side of the lengthy equation to bring awareness to a growing group of concerned women. She started the Women's International Longboard Organization, the first women's association in the surf subset of longboarding. After winning the Malibu Surfing Association (MSA) Surf Contest in 2009 and 2010 she spent thirty-three days crossing the Atlantic ocean to study the giant garbage patch floating in the circular currents of the Atlantic Gyre and other plastic pollution, and in 2010 became the Ambassador for 5 Gyres Institute and United Nations Safe Planet Campaign. Traveling to China in 2010 and 11, she became the first women to surf Silver Dragon tidal Bore in Hangzhou, resulting in a nomination for Action Girl of the Year and Teen Choice Award, along with winning the MTV Surf Girls competition.

"Mary was great with the media," and, as Mary Bagalso described Osborne, "an amazing combo—a surf-stylish, heavy-metal, motorcycle-riding, well-networked entrepreneur."

After appearing on the covers of *Surfer's Path*, *Surf Life for Women*, *Making Waves*, *Brass* and *Surfing Girl* magazine Osborne used her spotlight to found surf camps for kids and women's surf and yoga retreats. "Mary paved her path and then brought others along," Longboard maestro Julie Cox observed. "She could work on a farm delivering food to needy folks and make everyone want to do that too." By 2017 she had become a television host for various sports and travel shows as well as a writer for various surf and travel publications including *Self*, *Sunset*, *Women's Surf Style* and *Shape* magazines.

In contrast, third generation Emily Lombard remained close to her roots and family ties. With grandfather a San Onofre Surfing Club founding member, and father Bobby a top surfer of the 70s, Lombard had grown up literally under the famous shack on the beach at San Onofre. Moving through the Club's multiple age divisions she captured numerous titles and later served as the contest's director. "Emily studied to be a nurse, ran the San Onofre Surfing Club annual contest and continued to be ranked in the longboard hierarchy," said Sheri Crummer, one of her local mentors.

Immortalized in the San Onofre 50th Year Anniversary book (as a wave-riding three-year-old) she would surf both longboard and short while becoming a nurse to finance her commitment and passion for waves.

The Emancipation Proliferation

The path to independence was longer for some surfers, regardless of their obvious and varied talents. Meador remained with Roxy for fourteen years, competing in contests, appearing in surf films and shooting ad campaigns all over the world. She dabbled in wetsuit design, pushing the brand to experiment with more gender-specific cuts, and asking for color options. In 2009, Meador was able to persuade Roxy Japan to produce a capsule collection of wildly chromatic wetsuits. It sold out almost immediately.

Shortly thereafter, Meador stepped away from contests and her other professional surfing obligations. She wanted to create wetsuits on her own terms.

"When Kassia left Roxy to make her own brand," said Leah Dawson, a former pro and fellow longboarder, "That was *definitely* a powerful shift."

Dawson would know. She created her surf career as an influential voice in raising awareness of the women's surf culture, identity and community. If more strategically focused, Dawson at the same time approached her life in a holistic and Zen-like manner. The two-time winner of the Women's Pipeline Longboard Event, Dawson competed for over twenty years in both long and shortboarding around the world, yet her passion was "connecting with the wider surf culture around the world."

Exploring retro-to-modern single fins, twin fins, finless boards and shaping, Dawson developed into a true rarity among female surfers: one who rode all types of boards, and all types of waves.

Completing a BA degree in Creative Media from University of Hawaii drew her to work as a live-broadcast camera operator for eight years, filming the Triple Crown of Surfing and the Eddie Aikau Waimea Invitational, among others. Dedicated to living an eco-friendly life, with a passion for storytelling through filmmaking, she's a unique voice for the Changing Tides Foundation—and for surfing itself.

Dawson was accurate about Meador's theory that the new recreational surf activists in the thirties and forties age-group would value upscale products. Timing was on her side too. The strategy coincided with a seismic social trend: the feminine reckoning rippling through the surfing world.

In 2011, Cori Schumacher, then the reigning longboard champion, boycotted the WSL World Longboard Tour for planning an event on Hainan Island, China. In a letter to the organization, Schumacher cited China's human-rights violations, "specifically those in violation of women." In the press, Schumacher decried surfing's treatment of women, calling the sport "massively homophobic." To succeed as a woman surf pro "You have to look this particular way," she told the *New York Times*, "you have to have no views, have to be somebody who is basically like a blank billboard upon which a brand can assert their image."

Most Likely to Succeed

The first dozen years of the century would see women athletes with such a multitude of talents and achievements they were impossible to ignore. In a search for the world's most complete water-woman some observers saw Candice Appleby's performance record as proof of her entry into that rare sphere. Appleby not only won the 2006 National Longboard Championships, but became the captain of the championship shortboard division as well. She moved to Hawaii, earning a Bachelor of Science degree in Tropical Plants and Soil Science from the University of Hawaii in 2008. Over the next decade she would become one of the world's most formidable Stand Up Paddle competitors while also excelling in ocean triathlons, pro Longboard events, body surfing, canoe surfing, prone paddle racing, lifeguard competitions and WSL sanctioned events. Upbeat and gregarious, she earned the respect of competitors in almost every board sport category. Had Appleby remained focused exclusively on traditional surfing it is not hard to imagine what records she might have broken.

Lindsay Steinriede would never be described as an underachiever. Powerful and elegant, her 2011 World Title win came on her twenty-sixth birthday—at the Roxy Pro in Biarritz, France—where she edge out two-time previous winner Jen Smith. An all-around athlete who claimed she preferred team sports, it is surprising that Steinriede found the time to become a world champion long-boarder. In high school, she competed at the varsity level in volleyball, and track and field, where she held the Dana Hills High School pole vaulting record for over a decade and was the soccer team Offensive Player of the Year. But Steinriede loved surfing with a passion.

"At the end of the school year I used to give out the Doheny Jetty payphone number in my friends' yearbooks," she laughed, "because that's where you could reach me sun up to sun down in the summers." Those days at Doheny earned her the league's MVP in surfing three times.

As World Champ and contest rival Jen Smith attested, "Lindsay was one of those people who was good at *everything*."

After being crowned the Homecoming Queen her senior year, she went on to start on both the UCSB soccer and surfing team—on a scholarship.

An outstanding student throughout high school and college Steinriede earned a Master's Degree in Physical Education, becoming a full-time kinesiology instructor at Saddleback College, teaching kickboxing, pilates, yoga—and surfing. Gold and dancing are two additional activities she worked at mastering after her marriage in 2009. Her father, who taught her to surf and died in 2010, was the inspiration to take her surfing to the highest level. "He was my teacher, mentor, coach and friend."

In 2013 Steinriede starred in an all-girl surf film with three other outstanding surfers titled *Say No More*. Considering Steinriede's multitude of achievements it could be a fitting description for her own life.

Kelia Moniz stepped in to don the longboard crown next, taking back to back Longboard World Titles in 2012 and 2013. Chelsea Williams, Rachel Tilly, Tory Gilkerson, Honolua Bloomfield and Soleil Errico would be part of a new generation that would begin with Moniz.

For most athletes two consecutive championships would have been the crowning peak of their career. For Moniz it was just the first starring dance in a lifelong ballet.

As the ground grew more fertile for professional longboarders, opportunities for later career phases began to emerge. It would be a future chapter, but it would implement the template built by these revivalists of the new millennium.

One earlier revivalist this young crew saw as a model for success was Julie Cox. Cox epitomized the new wave of long board Renaissance women: a Jill of all trades and master of many. The Agoura Hills native got a Gidget-like upbringing at Leo Carrillo State Beach (substituting for Malibu, just as the original *Gidget* film did.) Graduating to Junior Lifeguards, she eventually learned retail skills working at the Beach Camp's store. Moving north for college, she began experiencing bigger waves while attending University of California Santa Cruz. While enrolled in

Environmental Studies at UCSC she found a great fit at Paradise Surf Shop, one of the first all-women surf businesses. But after finishing college Cox moved once again, this time to Central America to work at Las Olas, the legendary Costa Rican surf school. She continued to compete professionally, winning a berth on the Roxy surf team.

Becoming adept at surf instruction and coaching at Las Olas, she would expand even further, creating her own surfboard line, Jule Collection, under the umbrella of Jed Noll, a fine shaper (and big wave legend Greg Noll's son).

Understated but high-profile, Cox displayed an eclectic, distinctive style of dress and demeanor both in and out of the water. Combining many of her diverse skills, Cox served as the operations manager at the California Surf Museum for several years before embarking on her most impressive achievement in 2016: opening the Traveler Surf Club just outside San Francisco, in Pacifica, California.

In partnership with her wife Rel Lavizzo-Mourey, Traveler quickly evolved into a popular coastal outpost offering sporting-club-style facilities, serving as a cultural hub for surfers from all walks of life. Warm showers, board lockers; hot coffee, a sauna, heated garden seating and more amenities were all included in the monthly membership. Additionally, the space offered both new and seasoned surfers a place to stash their gear—especially those living in the crowded city—as well as a post-session respite from cooler northern waters. Several years later, and a few hundred miles south, Cox and Lavizzo-Mourey saw the opportunity for something similar, this time right across the road from Malibu's famed Surfrider Beach. The new clubhouse, located just steps from the world-class break, has offerings for surfers of all levels. Amenities mirror the Bay-area location, with a well-stocked shop up front and surf club facilities out back.

As Malibu became a surfing hotbed once again, Kassie Meador launched "Kassia + Surf" in 2015, introducing a wide range of products aimed at a burgeoning new segment of recreational consumers who would appreciate functional style and quality.

She collaborated with Dead Kooks shaper Eden Saul to make longboards for female proportions, and she made stylish surfboard wax spiked with the sweet scent of pine, mint and lemon from the palo santo plant. Leah Dawson credits Meador with setting a more supportive tone for women's surfing overall while raising the profiles of other women-owned independent surf lines.

Again, Dawson should know. *Outside* magazine called Dawson "Surfing's Champion, evoking her advocacy for women's increased involvement in the sport she loves."

Other boutique brands began to emerge: Seea, founded by Amanda Chinchelli, and SEPTEMBER the Line, launched by Erika Seiko Togashi and Ashley Lloyd Thompson, a board shaper (and former pro) out of Santa Cruz. Strong and fresh, these brands took a studied cerebral approach to their work just as their owner did in each of their endeavors.

Meador's style was more visceral: "Kassie really mothered that approach for our generation," Dawson said. "It had nothing to do with winning. It just had to do with enjoying the moment and doing whatever we can to help make the world around us a little bit better."

Brazil's Chloe Calmon is one of the younger generation who considers Meador an inspiration. On the 2019 World Longboard Tour she ended the season in third place, just before the Coronavirus pandemic shut down sporting activities worldwide. For nine years pre-Coved-19, Calmon ranked in the Longboard Tour top ten, slowly moving closer to her goal of a World Title. Elegant and expressive, Calmon followed Meador's lead—keeping all her cards in play as she watched the future unfolding. Placed on a board by her father as an infant, Calmon grew beyond basic proficiency at Macumba Beach, one of Rio's iconic surf spots, building a reputation as "a stylist who happens to compete," never sacrificing beautiful moves for a judging criteria.

Surfing from a young age "you learn how to connect with a wave but mostly you learn how to listen to your inner voice." And perhaps the subconscious voice of Kassia Meador.

No Cinderella Story

In the first post-millennial decade, longboard surfing amassed a level of enthusiastic participation rivaling the professional short board revolution. The spark ignited by women like Cori Schumacher, Daize Shayne Goodwin and Sherri Crummer at the turn of the century was now a bonfire of humble vanities: young women with pride, passion—even a bit of swagger. And these three women continued to advance—sometimes personally, sometimes for the entire culture.

"Despite many ongoing structural and ideological inequalities in action sports cultures there are signs of hope that feminist theorizing and politics are evolving and responding to the challenges of the times," Holly Thorpe and Rebecca Olive declared. "Indeed," the noted surf scholars continued, "there are some exciting developments in action-sports scholars and practitioners working together."

The trio's own groundbreaking record continued to prove the point: in 2011 Schumacher married her wife Maria after a long relationship. In 2012 Schumacher and Crummer cofounded The Inspire Initiative and History of Women's Surfing Project; Schumacher heading the Initiative and Crummer the History project. Goodwin—residing in Ha'ena Hawaii, with her husband of sixteen years, Aamion, and her three children—opened their own small business, Slow

Yourself Down, while simultaneously operating a successful health supplement business LifeVantage. Crummer was inducted into the San Clemente Sports Wall of Fame in 2019. Schumacher ran for Carlsbad City Council as the first openly gay candidate and won handily. Longboarding's legacy had taken a twenty-year-long growth curve, helping to invigorate the entirety of women's surfing.

Longboarding's renaissance had reinstated *elegance*—an old mode of feminine expressiveness—and established a new sense of *inclusion*. Schumacher and her generation had advanced forward by end-running conventional social customs. Their women's rights struggle, an entire generation after the civil rights movement, had real impact on the surf culture.

Like swells refracting around headlands, seeking a more perfect union with rocky points, the waves of change had pushed across a long turbulent watery universe. But ever so surely their refraction seemed to bend toward justice.

32

Shining Lights

"Courage doesn't mean you don't get afraid. Courage means you don't let fear stop you. Courage, sacrifice, determination, commitment, toughness, heart, talent, guts. That's what little girls are made of; the heck with sugar and spice."

—Bethany Hamilton

The altruistic urge runs deep in surfing's history. Newspaper accounts of both Duke Kahanamoku and early pioneer George Freeth using their surfboards to save dozens of lives on capsized boats during storms in California were well documented. Eddie Aikau's legendary lifesaving feats at Waimea in thirty-foot surf burnished his legend. Although the acts of generosity and courage by surfers worldwide would be too numerous to mention, women have played an outsized role in bolstering surfing's positive image.

Whether it was Rell Sunn putting on her annual Easter Egg festival for under-privileged kids, Surf Aid Executive Director Erin Miserlis managing the efforts to fight malaria in the coastal third world, or Surfrider Foundation COO Michelle Kremer helping protect the wave zones, altruistic behaviors are part of the glue that has bound the surf culture together.

For the women of surfing these selfless acts can be as simple as retrieving another competitor's board right in the middle of the heat, or as long-standing as spending a lifetime helping kids to surf. For some, the self-service comes by preserving the culture or protecting the natural world. Sometimes it is simply providing a good healthy meal to surfers for thirty years. But in all cases it is setting an example of courage, inspiration and generosity of spirit.

Love, Shine Glow
Sophia Bartlow's Motto was "Be a Local Wherever You Are"

The bands of heavy rain that had saturated the hillsides at dawn ended before the memorial for Sophia Bartlow began. Along the drive to the ceremony rainbows appeared, a signal to those heading to the amphitheater at the foot of the Huntington Beach Pier. "Sea Sister" Sophia Bartlow, the irrepressible California longboard champion, beloved Hawaii State shortboard champion, and the intensely driven national champion of the 2014 U.S. Stand Up Paddle Tour, had succumbed to injuries sustained in a car crash two weeks earlier near Waialua, on Oahu, Hawaii.

The tragedy had shaken the surfing community; stunned to lose such a gifted and gorgeous woman so full of achievement and unfulfilled promise. "Love, Shine, Glow." Those words were Sophia's mantra and she lived them like surfing's queen of hearts.

There is no activity that symbolizes surfing's tribal culture like the paddle out—and this one for the daughter of a regal surf family brought the full spectrum of waveriders: old and young, local and distant. But most notable lots of women. *Crowds and crowds* of women. Her joyous persona reached far and wide: Surf icon David Nuuhiwa recalled how during contests Sophia would paddle in and retrieve another competitor's board right in the middle of the heat. "I knew right then she was a different kind of girl."

Malibu's senior star Allen Sarlo reminisced about surfing South Africa with Sophia's mother, surf icon Jericho Poppler, and then, years later when they had kids, finding out that she had, "a daughter named Sophia Bartlow and I had a daughter named Sophia Sarlo—and the girls competed and became friends."

Jericho's deft touch ensured the memorial was orchestrated to perfection. From the haunting Hawaiian opening prayers, to the tearful friends' and family's remembrances, to the massive paddle out that followed the beachside observance—over a thousand people attended the service and many of those made their way through the pier to form three circles of celebration.

"Love, Shine, Glow," they chanted from the water and on the pier, as a lifeguard boat fired a cannon shot in honor.

Later that night, sitting with family and friends at the River's End Cafe in Seal Beach where Sophia had ridden her first waves, surfers reflected on her mother Jericho's words from earlier that day.

"I've never in my whole life been around so much love, it's incredible. It's because of what surfers do and what we love to do, which is to ride waves. Sophia is now riding waves for us up there," Jericho added, pointing toward the sky. "And she's ripping!"

Saints and Heroes, East and West

In the East Coast pantheon of saints and heroes Betty Marsh would get a nomination for being both. Although not a surfer herself, Marsh along with five other

East Coast visionaries founded the East Coast Surfing Association (ESA) in 1967, a milestone that sparked the formation of large-series competitive programs from New York to Florida. Comprised of six districts this venerable organization grew to become perhaps the finest (certainly the largest) competition-oriented surf organization in the world. One of the original trustees, Marsh was instrumental in the ESA's development serving as director of the Carolina district for 22 years, lobbying for coastal access for surfers and coaching the East Coast team in the U.S. Championships. Diligent, dedicated and well-liked, she opened her own Marsh's surf shop in 1972, but continued to work for and support the ESA until her death from complications of an auto accident in 1992. Almost from its inception she was dubbed the "Matriarch of East Coast surfing" a title seen by many as prestigious as a national championship.

If dedicating her career to the amateur surfing competition is a contribution, Janice Aragon may have no equal. After serving as the director of the National Scholastic Surfing Association for over four decades, Aragon has been widely credited as the driving force behind youth competitive surfing in America.

"She didn't just fall into being the head of NSSA," observed top professional Courtney Conlogue, a former national champion who rose through the ranks under Aragon's tutelage. "She has a national title herself—a champion who has mentored hundreds of champions,"

Aragon began surfing at age sixteen but didn't compete until she was twenty-nine, winning her first contest as a complete unknown. A year later, in 1984, Aragon was crowned the ISA Women's World Champion. She won the title in her hometown of Huntington Beach, helping lead the U.S. team to victory.

After having her second child in 1985, Aragon won the prestigious National Scholastic Surfing Association (NSSA) Nationals. The next year, she transitioned to NSSA judge and by 1986 became the first female to judge a Pro Tour event—the OP Pro in Huntington Beach.

In 1989, Aragon became Executive Director of the NSSA.

"Janice Aragon impacted our sport and generations of surfers in a huge, positive way," Surfers' Hall of Fame founder Aaron Pai said at Aragon's induction in 2019.

No professional escapes struggle, disappointment and sometimes outright criticism. Aragon had conflicts, fought battles and took some defeats over her long career. But the overarching mission remained.

"To help kids achieve their dreams and goals whether it be professional surfing or heading off to college and pursuing a career is very rewarding," Aragon said. "Hopefully it leaves a lasting impact on them. My goal each year is to continue to bring new and exciting things to the NSSA and focus on the progression of our contests and to bring the best quality events to our members. I am going to push on to help grow the sport."

When Tom Gibbons and his colleagues started the National Scholastic Surfing Association in 1976 they envisioned building a long legacy of surfers who could be successful as both students and champion waveriders.

Stacy Wood, a physical education teacher at Dwyer Middle School, the long-time volunteer surf club coach, honored that legacy on both counts. Instrumental in all aspects of the school's surf athletics—from teaching beginners water safety and surf etiquette to developing competitive strategies and training for the pros, she put her mark on the program. Wood's record as Dwyer's surf team coach is one of the best in history, winning multiple NSSA National Interscholastic titles.

But Wood is also credited for making sure her student-athletes remained on track in the classroom too, requiring team members to carry a 2.0 grade point average in order to participate.

A lifelong surfer from Huntington Beach, Wood was awarded Duke's Outstanding Educator Recognition Award at the 2012 Surfing Walk of Fame.

Like Wood, Carolyn Krammer was an unwavering organizational stalwart who burnished the legacy of amateur surfing. Involved with the sport since 1963, she competed through the 80s, then served on the board of directors of the Women's International Surfing Association. (WISA) She later became a member of the Western Surfing Association's board of directors as well as the Competition Director of the Scholastic Surfing Association, working tirelessly for the organizations she served.

A Surfing Passage to India

Ishita Malaviya became India's first and only professional surfer in the mid-teens of the 21st Century. Her nation could not have asked for a more gracious and respectful ambassador to introduce surfing to a nation with one of every seven souls living on earth.

Malaviya's love affair with the water started in 2007 when she met a German exchange student traveling in India.

"It was through him that we discovered an ashram, where the devotees were actually surfers from California. They were surfing at a spot that was only an hour away from us. A small chat and we found ourselves amid the waves," the Mumbai native told Financialexpress.com.

Immediately drawn to the waves she was nonetheless apprehensive at first.

"The ocean has always been a place for me, but women were to stay at home," she said. "It's never been a place for them. People were quite fearful about women getting in the water. It's about them getting dark because dark skin is looked down on in India."

When Malaviya was featured in the surf adventure documentary *Beyond the Surface* she not only became an immediate star, she popularized surfing to 1.2 billion fellow citizens while putting India firmly on the global surfing map.

Her heartfelt ability to communicate the value of wave-riding made her an almost overnight personality in the surfing world. Strong and spiritual, she and her husband witnessed the power of surfing to overcome class, religious and gender barriers in their community. Surfing environmentalist Lauren Hill, a friend and supporter, called Ishita Malaviya the "new story for women in India," a modern surfing pioneer "demonstrating how to gracefully navigate surfing swells, be they cultural or environmental."

Gentle but passionate, Malaviya exemplified how to create change without backlash. She took on the role of busy surfing ambassador, operating the Shaka Surf Club and Camp Namaloha in coastal Karnataka, which partnered with the Australian Life Saving Society and Rashtriya Life Saving Society as well as with local government schools to create "The Nippers Programme" training children to become junior life guards. Sponsored by Quiksilver, she was part of the first Summer Swell Challenge in Pondicherry.

Utterly unpretentious, Malaviya's carefree spirit represented surfing in the pure simple form.

"Surfing brought back that element of play in my life and gave me a sense of freedom and liberation I didn't know I was seeking but desperately needed," she said in 2019. "I encourage people to surf for the immense potential to bring joy and healing by developing a deep connection with the ocean."

Cause and *Affect*

In 2016 Lauren Lindsey Hill focused on raising awareness about the Maui dolphin, of which there are only fifty-five remaining in the world. That would be one of many causes she would affect with her energy and effort.

Born in the Sunshine State but spending equal time on the Sunshine Coast, residency claimed a tale of two cities— her hometown of St. Augustine, Florida and Byron Bay, Australia. Her beau, Dave Rastovich, a world class pro surfer—also known as a committed environmental activist—meant they were often pegged as the perfect eco-surf couple. But as is often the case with millennials, Hill is eclectic—no *single* obsession defines her many interests. She's volunteered at VDAY, an organization that benefits victims of domestic abuse. As the 2002 Woman's U.S. Longboard champ she earned enough respect in the line up to speak up for women's equal pay, and created *The Sea Kin*, a thought-provoking, articulate website astutely confronting surfing's male-dominated culture. Clean water, coral reefs and containing malaria would all be additional passions she pushed. When she swam with the whales in Tonga it was to help them not exploit them.

After having a baby in 2017 and rediscovering the surf, she starred in the well-received surf film *Church of the Open Sky* as well as her own film *Pear Shaped* about the birth experience.

"No one has carried the flag for more good causes than Lauren," declared Layne Beachley, who has earned a solid reputation for philanthropy herself. "She doesn't raise money. She does the *work*."

Hill released *She Surf* in 2020, a look at the rise of female surfing reflecting on what it means to be a water-woman. The book featured essays exploring the complex relationship between surfing, professionalism, sexualization and surf apparel.

It could be argued that it's easy to admire a woman with beauty, brains and nimble wave grace. What separated Hill was an intelligent humility, a depth of many fields and a commendable sense of real commitment.

Courageous Inspiration

It was a typical autumn day on the "garden isle" of Kauai. Alana Blanchard, Bethany Hamilton and Alana's father Holt had gone together for a surf session.

Hamilton began the story: "We paddled out to Tunnels (one of Kauai's premiere surf spots) and it was small, one to two feet. And I was laying on my board facing sideways toward where the waves were coming," she recalled. "The shark just came up from nowhere—I hadn't seen it—and it just came up and grabbed my arm and yanked back and forth. And then it let go of me and I started paddling with one arm."

The attack happened so quickly that none of the surfers around her ever saw the predator—a 14-foot-long tiger shark—or her struggle with it.

"We're just sitting there and all of a sudden Bethany goes, 'I got attacked by a shark!'" Holt recalled. At first, he said, he thought she was kidding because he never saw any splashing or struggle or heard her scream.

"All of a sudden she was paddling in toward Alana and myself," he said. "And I saw blood in the water. I paddled up to her and at that point I noticed *her arm was gone*."

Blanchard knew how critical the situation was. Still 200 yards from shore, he had to get her help before she bled to death.

Using his surfboard leash, Blanchard fashioned a makeshift tourniquet for Bethany and paddled her to shore.

Throughout the extreme ordeal, Bethany remained calm. "I think I figured out that, if I panicked, then things wouldn't go as good as if I was calm," she said.

"I was praying to God to rescue me and help me," Bethany said. "And then, I had this one pretty funny thought: *'I wonder if I'm going to lose my sponsor?'*"

In an extraordinary coincidence, Bethany was rushed to Wilcox Memorial Hospital, where her father, Tom Hamilton, was about to have routine knee surgery. When doctors told him his surgery would have to be delayed because there was a badly injured surfer en route, Hamilton feared the worst, knowing his daughter was out surfing.

Dr. David Rovinsky recalls telling Tom Hamilton the news. "I was crying because I knew it was Bethany. I knew how it would affect Tom, and it's the hardest news you can share with another parent."

"I just prayed to God that she'd survive," her father said. "They had to roll me out of surgery, and she replaced me in the same operating room."

In God's Hands

Bethany Meilani Hamilton was born on Kauai in 1990, to surfing parents who moved there from the mainland. She learned to surf young, helped by her brothers Noah and Timmy, and won a Quiksilver "push and ride" contest at eight years old. Bethany won her age group in longboarding and shortboarding at the Rell Sunn Menehune contest in 1998, the 1999 Haleiwa Menehune Championships and in February 2000, she placed first in the "eleven-under girls," first in the "fifteen-under girls," and second in the "twelve-under girls" division at the Volcom Puffer Fish contest. She was just ten.

Her mother Cheri Hamilton had been a standout surfer back in California. Bethany had innate aptitude, coupled with love and faith in her family's strong Christian upbringing. She was a rising star in Hawaii's constellation. Her plans for becoming the next Margo Oberg or Lisa Andersen were abruptly curtailed on October 13, 2003.

Less than a month after her ordeal she returned to the surf. Learning to adapt to surfing with only one arm, Hamilton showed the strength of her talent and determination when she won the 2005 NSSA National Championships.

In 2008, Hamilton began competing on the Association of Surfing Professionals World Qualifying Series, with a goal of making the World Championship Tour, and shooting for the World Title. It was impossible to rule her out.

In the winter of 2010, A-List stars Helen Hunt and Dennis Quaid were cast as Hamilton's parents in the movie version of *Soul Surfer*, based on the book of the same name, which documented the saga of her tragedy and triumphant return. She had become an inspiration to a new generation of surfers. Hamilton ended up writing eight books of her own, many of them bestsellers. *Bethany Hamilton:*

Unstoppable, a feature length documentary produced about Hamilton's life, inspired even more young girls. True to the film's title, she continued to surf at the highest level of professional competition, winning events and placing high in the ratings.

During work with her faith-based motivational speaking events, Hamilton met and, in 2013, married youth minister Adam Dirks. They had three children in 2015, 2018 and 2021.

The couple competed as a team on the twenty-fifth season of *The Amazing Race*, finishing third. Perhaps most impressive, she surfed Peahi (Jaws) in the twenty-five to thirty foot range. For Hamilton the commitment to speaking to young women and inspiring them to do the work of Christ was a high personal priority. Like many courageous women surfers before her, Hamilton overcame adversity with grit, style and as her family would proudly say, amazing grace.

A Most Beautiful Sight

While Bethany Hamilton triumphed over tragedy as a teen, Carmen Lopez was challenged from birth. A blind Asturian surfer from Oviedo, Lopez set an exemplary model of succeeding in the waves—*and in life*. At twenty-one, the Asturian prodigy became the first blind Spaniard to participate in an adapted surfing world championship, competing in the AS-6 category for visually impaired people at the World Championship in La Jolla, California.

Lucas García, Lopez's instructor, has guided her through the training for competition.

"It is essential that she trusts me," Garcia explained in 2018. "I tell her to be prepared for the wave, but also to enjoy every time she enters."

A congenital glaucoma stole her vision when she was very young. Her commitment took more than most might have endured—sight or no sight. From Oviedo, her hometown in the interior, Lopez traveled more than an hour each way, taking two buses every day to Salinas to be able to surf. "To watch her make her way to the beach was," supporters declared, "*a most beautiful sight.*"

Surf Museums
Preserving the Stoke

There are a number of Surf Museums around the globe—more than a dozen in all. The U.S. (as you might suspect) has the most: Huntington, San Clemente and Oceanside California; Cocoa Beach and West Palm Beach, Florida; Tuckerton, New Jersey; and Corpus Christi, Texas.

Other surf nations have splendid museums too: Durban and Jeffreys Bay, South Africa; Torquay and Curumbin, Australia; Mount Maunganui, New Zealand; Braunton, Great Britain; and even a new one in the big wave capital Nazaré, Portugal.

But two of these museums have an unusual aspect in common: they were founded and nurtured by women. Natalie Kotsch and Ann Beasley opened the International Surfing Museum at 411 Olive Avenue in Huntington Beach three years after founding the museum in 1987. For most of its existence these two women worked to display their rich heritage in the cozy Art Deco building that houses its collection. It would be fair to say that this esteemed institution would not have survived and thrived without Kotsch and Beasley's nurturing nature. Honored by the Surfing Walk of Fame and the city itself, they will be remembered for their contribution to preserving surf culture

Similarly, Jane Schmass, a former California schoolteacher and restaurant owner, cofounded the California Surf Museum, became its historian and—over the next three decades—turned it into one of the world's top destinations for surfing history. After several locations the California Surf Museum finally found a permanent home on the appropriately named Pier View Way. When the city of Oceanside donated a run-down structure just a block from the beach, the renovation of both the interior and exterior of the building was designed by architect and surfer Louise Balma. Its distinguishing roofline in a shape of a wave and its white and blue ocean colors, as well as the design of its inner galleries, giftshop and offices, make it one of the distinctive architectural landmarks in the North County of San Diego.

Few women become an institution in the surf industry, fewer still who are not champion competitors. Huntington Beach legend Jan Gaffney took over a small sandwich business, catered to surfers and established one of the most iconic and long-standing food institutions in Orange County. A Long Beach, California native who stepped onto her first board in 1962 after falling for a surfer at the beach, Gaffney bought her first surfboard at a neighborhood supermarket, and quickly became a regular fixture at Huntington's surf breaks.

Even after earning a college degree in Anthropology, Gaffney couldn't resist the call of the surf—she landed a summer job at the Good Earth Health Bar located in George's Surf Shop on Main Street right in the heart of California's 70s surf culture. For a Southern Cal woman who loved people, surfing and healthy, fresh food, Gaffney knew she had found her place. Learning the business from the ground up, she purchased the enterprise from Steve Pezman three years later and re-named it Jan's Health Bar. Although a back injury halted her surf career, Gaffney has fond memories of helping found the Women's International Surfing Association and once defeating Joyce Hoffman in big Baja surf. But she will always be best remembered for the thirty years she served healthy, fresh menu items as a beloved, successful surf entrepreneur. Gaffney retired in 2010 to travel the world on bird-watching adventures.

Judith Sheridan had another kind of challenge—one brought on by disease rather than injury. Sheridan, a geophysicist and passionate surfer who's been out at Mavericks and made a number of big wave sojourns to Hawaii, contracted multiple sclerosis around 2012. It required unique and courageous adjustments to get through normal life let alone ride double overhead waves.

The symptoms of MS vacillate erratically and activate unpredictably. Symptoms like facial paralysis, vertigo, non-functioning arms or a sudden fall from weakened legs can occur without much warning. Bruce Jenkins, a career-long chronicler of surfing and a champion of women's sports, said "she had optic neuritis in both eyes, a complicated way of saying, 'I'm pretty blind out there.' Articulate by nature, she found she was having to search for words."

"They have disappeared from my vocabulary and I talk around them," she admitted in 2016. Her struggles slowed her down but did not keep her from doing what she loved. She pursued her work in geophysics and continued to surf as often as her career and health would allow. She gained a huge following in the local beach community who held her quiet courage and determination in an almost loving awe.

Shunning sympathy or overt assistance, friends and surf companions who witnessed her sessions in the water often thought she was completely healthy. Fit, lithe and enthusiastic, she projected a robust joie de vivre and remarkable sense of humor.

"She does get tired in the water," wrote Bruce Jenkins, "sometimes feeling a bit tentative because her body just isn't cooperating." But she wastes no time on bitterness or regret. "I don't feel it's a hardship, and it's not about me overcoming things with willpower," she declared. "I'm co-existing with my condition. I go out there because I love bodysurfing, because I'm curious about how I'll feel that day," she explained. "That's how I'd like to be known as a person." Would any surfer not feel inspiration from this singular woman of character?

The Father-Daughter Dance
The 20-Teens

"I hope I can find a man that will treat me as good as my dad."
—Lady Gaga

The Descendants

They say great fathers don't tell their daughters how to live. They live, and let their daughters watch them do it. There is barely a woman in the top ranks of surfing whose father was not a strong influence on them—not just as a surfer but as a surf coach, mentor and professor of surf science.

Fathers have played other vital roles for most of these women as well—as friends, supporters and guardians. Age, region, or achievement level, most women surfers have a story about their dad.

"Some people don't believe in heroes. But," 2018 Juniors Champ Kirra Pinkerton insisted, "they haven't met my *dad*."

"My dad is my role model. He's a great influence," Queen of the Bay invitee Skylar Lickle declared. "He gave up big-wave surfing because he wanted to be with our family more, so that's a pretty big sacrifice."

"The first wave I rode was about three inches high and the fins were dragging in the sand with my dad walking alongside holding my hand," remembered Laurina McGrath. "I'm sure it lasted about two seconds but it's still a really vivid memory."

Two-time Longboard World Champ Jen Smith remembered countless sessions in elementary school when her dad pushed her into waves—"babying me," she admitted, "but giving me the total support."

Seven-time World Champ Stephanie Gilmore made the most concise statement about the importance of fatherhood: "As a kid I had an excellent teacher and role model," she said. "*My dad.*"

Coco Ho has had the same. Coco's family is Ohana royalty: Her father Michael Ho was a World Champ, her late Uncle Derek was a two-time World Champ, and brother Mason one of the best to surf Pipe in the 20-teens. Coco herself is considered by many observers to be one of the greatest talents to come out of the Hawaiian Islands in a generation.

"My dad always put the emphasis on teaching us about the ocean," she has explained when asked about her father's influence. "I want to ask, 'Was that cutback hot or what?' But he wants to talk about where to sit, where the peak lines up, what the swell direction is. And now I'm beginning to see that those things are the key to winning. Because you can't be the best surfer if you don't know how to get the best, highest-scoring wave."

"Coco's dad was so invested in her, such a buttress for her strength," said Layne Beachley, of Coco Ho. "Of course," the eight-time world champ admitted, "my *own* dad taught me to surf at *four*."

Brazil's Chloé Calmon might be one of a very few to top that. Calmon's father had been riding waves for over forty years and when Chloé was born couldn't wait to get her out on the water. "I can't remember exactly how old I was when I got my first wave," Calmon laughed, "but I have pictures of myself as a baby on his longboard!"

The Descendants, Kaui Hart Hemmings masterful novel of fatherhood and grief, explored the tangled relationship of daughters and their dads. The adopted child of World Champ Fred Hemmings, Kaui's portrayal of strength, love and bloodlines was as true to life as any family saga. The engagement between father, daughter and surf does not just pertain to the winners of World Titles. It appears to be one of the central foundations not only for achieving, but for the deep commitment to the love of surfing itself.

Following in the Footsteps

What path does a descendant take in a family whose patriarch is almost Hawaiian surfing royalty? In the case of Maluhia and Mainei Kinimaka from Kauai's most esteemed surf ohana, the answer was: *follow in their dad's footsteps.*

The daughters of legendary waverider Titus Kinimaka, these sisters grew up surfing with three-time World Champ Andy Irons. As Titus' reputation for big waves and Polynesian pride grew, he took on the mantle of the Garden Island's foremost surfing chieftain.

Both sisters became proficient at longboards, shortboards, stand-up paddleboard and big-wave riding as Titus passed the torch to his two daughters teaching them the ways of the sea.

Maluhia, a 2010 top-ranked Junior Division competitor, took the academic route first, graduating from the prestigious Stanford University. After graduating from high school sister Mainei decided to travel the world to surf Barbados, Australia,

France, Mexico and California. Her favorite locale was San Francisco where her mom is from.

"It gives us a different viewpoint," she noted. Not too many Hawaiian girls have earned so many options. Maluhia and Mainei's love for the sea isn't just following their father. Like his forefathers before him who traveled thousands of miles to these unique islands, these sisters follow in the footsteps of their ancestors.

Sally Fitzgibbons's first significant result as a surfer began at the age of fourteen when she became the youngest surfer to win an ASP Pro Junior (under twenty-ones) event in 2004. She also finished second at the World Qualifying Series (WQS) Billabong Easter Girls Festival on the same day. She credits her parents for everything that's happened in her career.

"My mum and dad worked so hard," she recalls. "I watched how they operated and thought, 'That's how you do it. You don't back down from a challenge.'"

The seventeen-year-old started to be noticed when she won gold medals in the 800m and 1500m at the Australian Youth Olympic Festival in Sydney. A place in the Australian athletics team for the World Youth Track and Field Championships in the Czech Republic was in the cards after Fitzgibbons registered qualifying times.

But there was another passion calling. At her home in Gerroa, New South Wales, her back door was the surf—a place where her athleticism truly felt free.

Her father Martin sat Sally down at the kitchen table knowing what the decision would be. But he left it up to Sally to choose.

"I love surfing and it wasn't really that hard to decide," Fitzgibbons recalled.

Fitzgibbons was runner-up in the 2006 ISA World Junior Surfing Championships in Brazil.

By 2008 she dominated the World Junior Championship at North Narrabean, adding a second World Title to her file, this time at the under twenty level.

"Sally is such an athlete," said Laura Enever, who was a rival in their early years. "She is super-competitive in contests, but so much fun on land that we just became friends. And her dad—and mum—are very close to her."

Enever broke off a three-year relationship to Australian professional rugby league footballer Trent Merrin in 2017, due in large part to the stress from the high profile media coverage of their relationship. Enever was a seasoned veteran of the pro circuit by now—ranked sixth in the world in 2018, and fifth in 2019. She has remained close to her father.

She would regularly call home: "'Hey Dad, I'm trying this new move, come down to the beach.' Or we've got a few breaks he can see from the house, and if I nail something I race back asking 'Did you see that? I've been trying eight hundred of those and I just stuck one!' And he says, '*I saw it.*' And you have a little moment together."

Third Generation

The number of third generation surfers continued to grow as time passed further from the beginning of the modern surfing era. As a granddaughter to Larry Gordon, a storied family patriarch and iconic brand name, Mele Saili may be high on that list.

Her father, Masi Saili, was born on Tonga, raised on Maui, moved to San Diego where he apprenticed under the cadre of legendary shapers at G&S—until finally breaking out on his own. Her grandfather was perhaps one of the most seminal figures in early surfboard-making.

Her father played an influential role in her early surfing career—from shaping her first boards to pushing her and her sister into waves at Tourmaline. "It has really given me a foundation to be involved with surfing from an early age."

With her surfing mother Debbie Gordon (Larry's daughter) and uncle Eric still running the surf and skateboard empire, she was an heir apparent; her skills and confidence no mystery.

Kind and modest, Saili acknowledged the value of her royal surf lineage. "I have been fortunate enough to be born into a family that has created an identity through surfing."

The Double Descendent

Like many of surfing's outstanding women, Lee-Ann Curren has a family bloodline of waveriders. But in her case it comes from both sides of her family, making it as rich as any in surf history. Her father Tom Curren was the era-defining three-time World Champion of the 80s and perhaps the most-loved pro surfer of all time. Her grandfather Pat was one of the original Waimea pioneers and influential shaper of big wave "Elephant guns"; a legend in early surf lore. Her mother Marie Pascal was among the best French females of her generation, taking second in the European Championships at sixteen. Her aunt Marie Paul won the French National title in 1967 and her Aunt Marie Christine was a French National Champion *six times*. Her uncle Joe (Tom's brother) is a well-respected photographer and a highly accomplished surfer in his own right.

Historians frequently mention "being in the blood" when referring to second or third generations who follow their parents vocation or calling. "It's simply in the DNA," is a term often used to describe the similarities between parents and offspring such as athletes, musicians and politicians. Is genetic legacy an actual fact? Can style and talent be passed down through generations?

There is strong evidence in Curren's case. An uncanny physical resemblance, interests in both music and surfing (her father's two passions as well) and a laconic persona mirror Lee-Ann's enigmatic father Tom. A charming effervescence yet patrician reserve showed her mother's attributes.

"I feel as if I have a real mixed identity," Curren divulged. "Living here in the Basque Country, there's a strong culture that I'm influenced by—but of course my nationality is French and a whole side of my family is Californian."

Lee-Ann has been described as a polymath: equally at home in the sea scoring waves, in the studio making music or performing for live audiences. Twice crowned as the French National Champion, she was rated twelfth in the world in 2010, impressive in itself considering only a few dozen women in surfing history have reached that level. Yet she constantly wrote music and went on tour with a band, playing to audiences from intimate to festival size.

In 2019 she was the jury president of the London Surf Film Festival, where she was also involved in three of the event's film entries: *Musical Voyages*, a recorded road trip with Curren and cinematographer Patrick Trefz. The world premiere of *Translate*, an immersive, audiovisual surf experiment from award-winning filmmaking team Chris McClean and CJ Mirra. She scored the soundtrack on a third film called *Tan Madonna*.

Although sharing her father's passion for music, Lee-Ann's method remains distinctly her own. A multi-instrumentalist like her father, she nonetheless forms her melodic structures based on the tone or feel of each instrument.

It is in her surfing where the comparisons seem to unfold most visibly.

The unique body moves—Tom's head fake, the signature bottom turn with a hint of hand drag, the cutback holding the back arm raised in a karate chop, have remarkable similarities. The smooth adaptive quickness in her transitions are eerily reminiscent of her father's.

The same sensitivity emanates from her music: an acoustic lightness of touch enhanced by practiced techniques and immersive creativity.

She has wondered herself what the comparisons between their surfing and their music means. "I grew up surfing with my dad, and playing music together," she speculated. "I wonder whether it's a genetic thing or if I unconsciously copied what he does. It does feel kind of natural when I do that bottom turn like him. . . . It feels as if I'm inhabiting his style."

While the debate is perhaps irrelevant, the result is the opposite: Lee-Ann Curren is a third generation surfer whose own independent achievements have been stamped irrevocably onto her family's linage.

"I was always conscious about who I was, and that kicked in when I scored my first sponsorship deal at fifteen," she has said before. "But I feel I have defined myself differently and been able to gain respect outside of what my family has been."

A Daughter's Watery Real Estate

A father can play with his daughter in the surf like a kid, give advice like a friend, coach like a champion and protect like a secret service agent. In Sophie Sarlo's case, her dad—Malibu icon Allen Sarlo—did all four.

"There really wasn't any choice in my family," Sarlo laughed when asked about how she got started. "With my dad I was going to be a surfer, no questions asked." She started in Venice where the family lived, and when she was ten, graduated to Malibu. There she was given lessons by Carla Rowland, the reigning elder of California's premiere point wave. Having battled her way into an iconic perch herself, Rowland was an ideal coach for a young girl breaking into the merciless crowd at "the Bu."

"She opened a lot of doors for me," Sarlo confessed.

Sarlo played water polo for Malibu High School and competed on the surf team too. She met Jericho Poppler's daughter Sophie Bartlow, then a rising star from Long Beach. They became inseparable friends, often finishing in the finals together.

"When we would be on the podium the announcer would say 'The winner is Sophie' and then pause before saying one of our last names!"

But Sarlo found she was more of a team sport person, and surfing was something she wanted to do for the joy of it. "I just never really pushed myself into the one-on-one competition of surfing," she admitted. "Competing just didn't make me happy." Some were surprised at Sophie's reticence considering her father had been a highly esteemed pro. An original member of the infamous Z-Boys surf and skateboarding team known for their aggressive slashing style, Allen earned the nickname "Wave Killer" during the 70s.

But demurring from competition did *not* mean being noncompetitive. With World Champs Lisa Andersen and Layne Beachley as role models, she established herself as one of the most respected surfers at Malibu where she spent most of her surfing life. And even as an adult she still found herself sharing sessions with her father. "I love surfing with my dad," Sarlo said. "It's too much fun not to—and we look after one another."

A Super Girl Ingénue

At age nine Samantha Sibley's much-loved father was deployed to Iraq. A natural athlete, Samantha was involved in a number of sports, from soccer to gymnastics, trying to decide what sport she would concentrate on.

But her dad was an avid surfer. So when Sibley received a grant from Our Military Kids, a charity providing grants to children of deployed National Guard and Military Reserve to take part in extracurricular activities, it was an easy decision.

By twelve she dominated her competition, winning four titles. At fourteen Sibley earned a World Surf League wild-card entry into the Shoe City Pro in Huntington Beach. A member of the United States national development surf team, Sibley set her goal of being on the U.S. team for the 2020 Olympics, as well as the World Surf League Women's Championship Tour. She ranked second on the WSL North American Women's Junior Tour 2018. In 2019 she broke through to the top, winning the Super Girl Pro taking down some of the world's best. Centered and focused, Sibley continued to progress, giving credit to her father: "He has always been an inspiration."

Sometimes the best thing a father can do is be the coach. When Bronte Macaulay was only nine years old, her father Dave—a consummate competitor and shaper who himself finished third on the World Tour twice, in 1989 and 1993—taught Bronte, her brother and older twin sisters to surf in the Margaret River area of Western Australia. Road trips chasing waves around Australia's coastline in the family's caravan were one of Bronte's fondest early memories.

Absorbing her father's fundamentals—particularly his inverted backhand snaps and powerful forehand cutbacks—helped her as she explored the World Tour Qualifying Series for several years, finishing fourteenth in 2014. After falling one spot short the next year she battled through the next two years, finally securing one of the coveted berths on the tour in 2017.

The first female from Western Australia in more than a decade, Macaulay was the *only* one on the tour that first season of full competition among the world's top seventeen female surfers. Homesick and feeling isolated, the Gracetown native found herself struggling and uncertain of how to return to form. She asked her father for help. Her results improved in rapid succession and suddenly her rookie year was back on track.

Macaulay credits subtle changes for the breakthrough, but most of all she acknowledged her father's role in propelling a shift in her mental game. As her coach, trainer and surfboard shaper he joined her at every stop on tour, providing what she described as "a stabilizing presence." The result was undeniable. In 2020 she won the first event of the season in her home base of Western Australia, just before the tour was cancelled in the impending worldwide Covid-19 crisis.

In 2020 her older sister Laura Macaulay made history as the first woman to surf a break simply called "The Right," one of the most difficult and dangerous waves anywhere in the world. Located near her home in western Australia, the feat was covered by major networks around the globe. Like Bronte, she credits her father with physical coaching and mental confidence. Laura, who competed in the World Qualifying Series saw the big wave session as a "natural progression" in her training.

Free Ocean Girl

Like her father, Moana Jones is a water-woman fulfilling a family legacy: competing in Molokai 2 Oahu paddle race with younger sister Kai Jones and father, Dawson Jones. Dawson founded the thirty-two-mile race in 2015, and the father-daughter relay team competed in the three person race.

North Shore born and raised, Jones's years of riding challenging surf earned her a list of best friends that read like a roster of some of surfing's most recognizable names.

Part of the third generation of young Pipeline specialists, Jones earned respect from her entire crew as well as the more established Pipeline regulars for her pinpoint timing and instinctive humility. No less than 2004 Pipe Master champ Jamie O'Brien decreed her, "the best female at Pipeline . . . ever."

Energetic and joyful, her playful hair flips and wide smile added to her feminine mystique. An avid competitor through the age of sixteen, Jones changed direction when she entered the University of Hawaii Biology program and started a path toward a possible Nursing degree. Although she still harbored World Tour considerations, her preference moved heavily toward academics and free-surfing sessions.

Considered the unofficial female Pipe Master, she nevertheless dismissed expectations that restricted her freedom of choice. Jones' name Moana (the Polynesian word for Ocean) was given by her dad—and her legacy became cemented the day she entered in her first father-daughter race.

Montauk's Leading Light

When Quincy Davis launched Quincy x MTK in the heart of *her* hometown Montauk, she had already loved the location for years. A quaint storefront with cedar shingles and French doors that lead to an outside courtyard, it always reminded her of the surfboard shack her dad built for her. And that's why, "my store sign is a Q, just like my surf shack."

By the age of twelve, Quincy was the first New Yorker, male or female, to break into modern competitive surfing's top tier. When she won the 2009 Open Women's NSSA Championships at fourteen, her parents—and the Long Island surf scene—took notice. Her mother, Paulette, was one of the design forces behind the successful Surf Lodge, a surf culture touchstone in the area.

With a winter home in Puerto Rico and a summer residence there were no shortage of waves for a lithesome, Darryl Hanna-style waverider to build a reputation as one of the East Coast's top young talents.

"Quincy got so good so young," said her contemporary Cassidy McClain, a multi-champion herself.

An ardent ocean environmentalist, Davis became a Surfrider Foundation ambassador, building a trophy case of wins as she continued to chase the pro circuit around the globe. In 2013, Davis collaborated with her sponsor Volcom, inspiring and designing a clothing collection. Exploring her entrepreneurial side, the local celebrity pro-surfer added shopkeeper to her resume, opening Quincy, a beach boutique in 2018.

Sometimes the father makes the experience terrifying instead of terrific. Tricia Gill told a story about her dad—a big wave surf ski aficionado—dragging her out into waves completely beyond her comfort zone. She was crying and sobbing to go in. His reply was masculine: "Catch a wave, or I'll really give you something to cry about."

Gill readily admits that in retrospect she was never in any *real* danger and the experience *did* make her realize she could do far more than she assumed of herself. But the line between pushing confidence and pushing a daughter over the edge is still a fine one. . . .

Gill was by no means the only girl whose first experience was less than sublime. The first Pas de Deux with dad doesn't necessarily mean that a daughter will immediately become enthralled with the ballet either.

"My dad took me out here for the first time when I was ten," remembered Tatiana Weston-Webb. "It was actually pretty big and scary that day, but I'm really good at hiding my fear. He thought I was chill when I was actually terrified."

The Little Princess

As a child Alessa Quizon loved *The Little Mermaid,* Disney's 1989 animated musical fantasy film about a princess of the sea. Girls growing up on the wind-whipped west side of Oahu are not born in a royal underwater grotto with a silver trident in their father's hand and a gold tiara on their head. Instead, they're gently placed on well-worn shortboards and sent out into the water like Alessa and her older sister Kristen Quizon, who also had a brief professional surfing career before becoming a police officer. Their father first paddled Alessa into the family's surf heritage at age seven, igniting a spark for wave-riding. Three years later she entered the *Rell Sunn Memorial* contest at her home break Makaha, and in a heartbeat the flame became a competitive wildfire.

Talent and support from her traditional Hawaiian surf family, made the first step automatic: a successful NSSA career, winning the 2008 NSSA Hawaii Open and Explorer division. Quizon started off 2012 with a win at the Billabong

World Junior title in Australia. One main ingredient defined her success: *dedication*. It earned her a slot on the 2014 Women's World Tour at eighteen.

But it took more than a good bloodline to maintain an elite level slot on the World Tour. Slipping out of the top seventeen female pros in 2016 was tough for a competitor who logged more time in the water than a Princess cruise ship. Stepping back, regrouping and being selective with her choice of events, she took the 2019 Sydney Pro—the biggest win of her career—vaulting her back into qualifying contention. She still seems on track to be a Hawaiian sea princess with her own fairytale fast track.

Mother's Nature

Mothers can teach their children to dance too. Quintessential yet unique, Laola Lake has a story that spans her own life along with her daughter's. When her home burned down in early childhood, she moved with her family to the Royal Hawaiian cottages right on the beach at Queens. Growing up with the Beach Boys of Waikiki, with Asian, Polynesian and European ancestry so common among Hawaiian locals, Laola was immersed in the cradle of surfing's culture from the time she could remember. One of the first six women who went on the first World Tour in 1976, Lake was a strong surfer and connected to the Hawaiian culture. Her daughter Sanoe came along after her competitive surf career had taken a back seat.

"Sanoe was named after my sister," Laola said, pointing out that Sanoe means "the mist."

"We lived in the misty valley, and there was a famous song by Queen Liliuokalani," she explained.

Shortly after Sanoe was born her dad passed away from multiple melanoma. Like her mother, Sanoe had a natural connection to surf and a wide range of other interests. More than anything she seemed to have her mother's special touch for the magic of the ocean lifestyle.

Introspective and fiercely loyal, Sanoe started modeling in *17* magazine, and easily moved into the media community where film, television, advertising and fashion integrated into the California scene. With the timing that seemed to come naturally for the family, the *Blue Crush* movie was being cast and Sanoe became a candidate for a character they were developing.

"Sanoe had been in California longer than she had been in Hawaii at that time," her mother Laola would remark. The night before the *Blue Crush* producers made their cast choices, on the cusp of a breakout opportunity but down to her last dollar, Sanoe bought a sandwich and decided to share it with a homeless man. The next day the producers called. She had been chosen to be in the film.

Originally scripted for two female leads, the film company decided that night to expand it to three to include a part for Sanoe.

She had a retirement party after having a child, but her philosophical approach to life's journey remained. With her husband she started Tropicali, a fast casual restaurant in Big Bear, a gentrifying local ski resort an hour outside of Los Angeles, where they had bought a home to enjoy the mountains. Eating establishments, as those in that industry have attested, rely on an indefinable ambiance as much as the food, presentation or service. Sanoe's "vibe" seemed to be the once again in tune. Tropicali was listed at number fifteen in Yelp's 2019 Top 100 Places to Eat in the USA.

Dancing On My Own
Breaking the Barriers in a New Age
2011–2021

"There's nothing more beautiful than the way the ocean refuses to stop kissing the shoreline, no matter how many times it's sent away."
—Sarah Kay, American poet

Turn the Beat Around

Coco Ho was not taking no for an answer. She wanted to compete in the surf contest, and she was willing to surf against the boys if she had to.

It was a clear, sunny Saturday at Turtle Bay on Oahu's North Shore and Coco's older brother Mason was competing in a surf event, while her dad and uncle helped as coach and beach marshal. Any local surf competition in Hawaii is always a family affair and since the rest of the family was deeply involved Coco wanted in too.

The moment she saw the contest scene there Coco's enthusiasm became relentless: *let me in the competition.* That there was no girls division was of no consequence to her; Coco wanted to participate. The problem was there were only two divisions for boys thirteen and under: 1A and 2A. The 2A division was for the older kids that were better, like Mason. The 1A was a step below, but still had very capable little surfers.

"I'll surf in the boy's 1A division," she offered. Coco was resolute. Her dad and brother were skeptical.

"Coco, you'd have to surf against the boys," Mason Ho explained. "Some of them are my friends. And they're going to beat you."

"I don't even care!" Coco shouted back, undeterred. "I don't even want to win; it's not about winning, I just want to surf it with you guys. I want to do contests too!"

Dad and brother were impressed: little sister was unyielding.

"Coco was *so* excited," remembered Mason, "so stoked to do her first 1A contest. She didn't have a clue what to do, so I walked her down and showed her where to check in and where to get her jersey."

Her uncle Derek was the Beach Marshall. Seeing her name on the entry forms he approached her standing in line with the rest of the boys waiting to get their jerseys.

"Coco!" he said, "You're going to surf against the boys?"

"Yeah, yeah, I'm gonna surf!" Coco answered, beaming.

"Well okay," Derek grinned. "You better make sure you give these boys a beating."

Coco's eyes went wide as he said it, then turned to a steely grimace. Without warning she spun around to the kid behind her and fired a lightning left-foot kick straight into his groin. In the same swift combination she threw a right-hand punch to the next kid's chin. Blindsided, both hit the ground. Coco charged at the other three boys, but they were already bolting from the line, scattering in every direction.

The entire crowd, watching in startled disbelief, erupted in laughter. Momentarily stunned, her uncle Derek began shouting "Woah! Woah, Coco! I never meant like *that*!" Coco looked up nonchalant and responded: "Oh, okay."

The crowd was uproarious. No one was really hurt, not even bruised really, but Derek, embarrassed that his cavalier comment had been taken literally by his niece, took action.

"Coco, you going postal or what?" Derek demanded—chuckling. *"Apologize or something."*

He was still a little astonished at her taking on five boys. Coco turned toward the guys. With a look of complete innocence on her face, eyes belying her little warrior spirit, she nodded and said, "I'm *sorry* guys."

Coco Ho may have received some great tips from her dad and uncle, but there is no favoritism on the World Tour where every point is earned in sweat and tears. She climbed into the top ranks with a multitude of significant wins: the Hawaiian Champion 2005 and 2006, and Triple Crown Rookie of the Year in 2007 and the same title on the World Tour when she entered in 2009. Her popularity matched her aptitude; she garnered a consistent spot in *Surfer* magazine top five most popular surfers in the Surfer Poll for more than a decade.

Surely her family was a help too. A world champion uncle Derek, a legendary father Michael, one of pro surfing's greats, and brother Mason considered one of the best Pipeline riders of his generation was certainly no disadvantage. Event empresario Jodie Wilmott stated it succinctly: "Coco is so entrenched in this culture—if you looked up surfing royalty in the dictionary you could just put a photo of the Ho family."

Gregarious and humorous, media savvy was a particular strong point for Ho. Her 679,000 Instagram followers and other social media platforms often received replies with a good-natured earthiness, complete with cute slobbering dogs. She created a sensation with her naked surfing photoshoot at ESPN but her boyfriend, Canadian snowboarder Mark McMorris, took no notice.

Despite the competitive ups and downs, her youthful enthusiasm showed no sign of the jadedness that a prolonged Tour life can bring. Ho seemed more driven than ever to win a title when World Champions Stephanie Gilmore and John Florence began rooting for her, buttressing her belief she had what it takes to become a champion. Nonetheless, her Hawaiian roots still prevailed. Despite her drive, Ho could shed the game face, let her hair down and be the little girl who first wanted to be in a contest—just for the joy of it.

Womentum Generation

Coco Ho's rise was concurrent with a whole set of talented surfers who earned the title "Womentum Generation." A clever wordplay on the "Momentum Generation," the label given to the star-laden crew of men a decade earlier. A feature film of their friendships, rivalries and exploits was released in 2018 to high praise for its depiction of a highly influential, tight-knit group who defined an era in the sport.

Like their male counterparts, the Womentum girls had a similar effect on the women's side of surfing in the 20-teens. Many had been friends since childhood and had been competing from a very early age. While fierce rivalries existed, so did a natural camaraderie.

The consensus was that these women each had a uniqueness that set them apart, but an ethos that bound them together. Coco Ho's legendary father and uncle made her a royal princess while Melanie Bartels was sponsored by an actual princess with royal Hawaiian blood.

Lakey Peterson's childhood round-the-world adventure allowed her to see life through a different window. Tyler Wright and her World Title contender brother Owen were so close they both give credit for saving each other's lives.

Bethany Hamilton lost her arm to a shark. Alana Blanchard, her best friend, became the most highly paid women in surfing and the most photographed women surfer outside of it.

The group had several World Champs (Sofia Mulanovich, Tyler Wright, Carissa Moore). Many more were child prodigies (Malia Manuel—or Courtney Conlogue and Sally Fitzgibbons, both two-time runner-ups). As a group they would dominate the top ranks of the Pro Tour and claim the lion's share of the media attention for more than a decade.

Moore Aloha

An innate *goodness* emanates from Carissa Moore's being, as naturally as that of Sally Field, the best Gidget of the bunch. The genuine empathy and emotional vulnerability exuding from Moore's radiant smile and spontaneous laugh always dissolved any suspicion that her old-fashioned values in any way rang false. Moore's Aloha spirit is pure maple syrup; it fits her like stonewashed 501 Levi denims. Her biography could be titled Little House on the Peahi.

At a very early age, Carissa Moore established herself as a driving force in women's surfing, a competitor with the combination of abilities to become a world champion. But that was not what made her stardom unique.

"Of all the pros on the World Contest Tour, the one I respect the most is Carissa," said Keala Kennelly, "as a surfer and as a human being."

Moore started surfing with her dad off the beaches of Waikiki in her native Honolulu, a five-year-old forming an ardent affinity for wave-riding. "He loved the ocean," Carissa recalled, "and he wanted to share that passion with me."

By age eight Moore's natural talent was unmistakable. Nuanced and incisive, her style seemed already timeless. Watching her earliest videos, almost every move appeared already baked into the DNA of her style. Images of Moore from that time show a tiny youngster with almost identical body posturing, stance and maneuvers to that of her adult years; basic building blocks of her competitive success.

"By the time I was twelve, I was having serious conversations with my dad, trying to determine if this was something I really want to do," Moore explained. "I knew it would take everything I had, but I also knew it would be amazing fun."

"When we were young she was always the most focused," noted two-time World Longboard Champion Kelia Moniz, a peer and friend. "Carissa couldn't wait to get out in the water at dawn."

The achievements speak for themselves. Collecting wins at NSSA junior surf competitions and top spots at the ISA World Junior Surfing Championships, Moore amassed a record eleven NSSA amateur titles before high school graduation. At age sixteen, she became the youngest champion at a Triple Crown of Surfing event when she won the 2008 Reef Hawaiian Pro.

Just two years later Moore qualified for the World Surfing Tour. In that 2010 debut season, Moore finished third overall and was named Rookie of the Year. Barely old enough for a driver's license, the initial pressures of a decidedly adult world required adjustment, even if her peers saw her as the new rival talent. Homesick, adapting to new surf spots, the outsider in an naturally hierarchal system felt deluged with challenges.

"The first year was a steep learning curve," she admitted, "but by the end of the circuit I started to find a place for myself."

The following season, Moore lived up to expectations, claiming her first World crown, unseating four-time defending champ Stephanie Gilmore in the process. At eighteen, she became the youngest person—male or female—to win a surfing World Title.

"What is impressive about Carissa," Layne Beachley attested, "is that she understood at a very young age what being the best in the world truly meant." Tenacious, resilient, Moore had all three pillars required for greatness: raw natural ability, disciplined practice and opportunity. She had something else, too: a bone-deep altruism: "I think we're all in it together. We all have our individual journeys, we're all in it to win of course. But you know, at the same time, we all want to elevate the sport together. There's a mutual respect for each other," Moore continued. "That's what the women's tour is." Moore—always deeply aware of her roots and surfing's culture—contended: "It's also about our heritage, the women that have come before, all the effort they put in. And Hawaii, where wave-riding started. It's about every single surfer on tour and. We're stronger together."

Openly optimistic and unabashedly joyous, Moore was nonetheless willing to confront the thorny contradictions facing female athletes: exploitation, sexuality and the ethics of the digital age. After winning her second World Title in 2013, Moore realized her position as a representative not just of surfing but of the legions of young women who looked to her not just as a surfing idol but as a role model for an entire new era where almost everything was being debated—and no one path was black or white.

At the start of the 20-teens controversies arose concerning unequal pay, frustration over prize money, charges of exploitation and the sexualization of surf women. Cori Schumacher boycotted the Longboard World Championships in China in protest of women's treatment in that nation. Keala Kennelly had her salary cut after coming out as an LGBT figure. Anastasia Ashley rode a huge wave and was mocked for having sexy photos on the Internet. That same year an especially egregious video ad sparked public outcry. The spot features a faceless blond getting ready for the beach. The camera pans over her bare backside as she lies in bed and tousles her hair; her naked leg entering a shower; her bikini-clad breasts hovering over a surfboard as she waxes it.

The faceless woman turned out to be Stephanie Gilmore—an articulate, vivacious and intelligent professional as well as an attractive seven-time world champion. Viewers never saw her face, never heard her name, never watched her surf. More than twenty thousand people signed a petition to put an end to Roxy's "all sex, no surf" ads.

With a loyal sensitivity Moore was never critical of Gilmore—or Alana Blanchard, Anastasia Ashley, Felicity Palmateer or a host of other beautiful surfers who had taken advantage of lucrative offers to pose in sexy images. She simply took a personal position. "I am not going to wear the small bikinis," Moore wrote in the

2014 January issue of *Surfer* magazine. "I realize there is also the male audience. The women are sexy and fun to look at. Alana Blanchard has brought thousands of eyes to our sport by wearing her small bikini bottoms. I just want everyone to appreciate that she is an athlete as well and she takes what she does seriously. There is a fine line when it comes to sexualizing our sport. If it is overdone we lose respect, but there is a way that the girls can be marketed tastefully."

"She has so much integrity," said Kennelly, "She never used her sexuality to sell herself. And that is a true heroine to me."

Despite her almost suspicious level of virtue, Moore never received the smug labels of "boring" or "sanctimonious" frequently foisted on straight arrows in a cynical society. "Carissa gets a bad girl hall pass because she is so damn genuine," said one critic.

Declared another: "She had the appearance of Sally Fields, with her humility and her talent to boot."

Places in the Heart

Moore's comparison to Sally Fields was not just her physical looks—observers noted the similarities to Fields's television role as Gidget: the small, innocent, irrepressibly likable ingénue, bent on becoming a good surfer. It would, in fact, be hard to find a better role model: Gidget surfed at dawn, expected nothing from anyone and earned every wave of her admittance to elite status. Her character was honest, generous and enthusiastic—all traits Moore reflected decades later.

"Carissa doesn't just have the *skills*," said Stephanie Gilmore. "She's got the *heart*."

There were many places in the heart for Moore. She married her longtime boyfriend and companion Luke Untermann in 2017. "Getting married hasn't made day-to-day life that much different, but there's another level of commitment and contentment. It's been awesome."

Named Adventurer of the Year by *National Geographic*, Woman of the Year by *Glamour* magazine, Moore was voted as a Top Female Surfer in the *Surfer* magazine poll for a decade, winning four times. Inducted into the Surfers' Hall of Fame at just twenty-one years of age, the State of Hawaii declared January 4th as Carissa Moore Day. Being as joyous as Gidget and as talented as Fields had its rewards.

No one, of course, lives a life free of struggle. The field of contestants in the second decade of the 2000s may have been the most competitive in surfing history. A four-year gap after Moore's third World Surf League title had critics wondering if she had finally peaked. She had not: Impressively returning to form in 2019, Carissa surfed to victory at Jeffreys Bay and Hossagor on her way to a memorable fourth World Championship, securing a place on the 2021 USA Olympic surf team on the way.

Her fourth title seemed to give Moore a chance to look at other aspects of her life and put energy toward other important interests. True to form, Carissa founded a charity that offers girls opportunities to learn about surfing and much more.

"The goal is to give back and encourage them to be strong, beautiful, confident young women—and also to give back in turn," she explained. "I think that's how you can really make the world better, by sharing your stories."

"It's really pretty simple," concluded Kelia Moniz. "Carissa worked harder than anyone, truly wanted to be the best surfer in the world and made the commitment to reach her goal. I think she represents the epitome of the professional athlete."

In the depths of the Covid-19 pandemic of 2020 she released her first film *RISS: A Film About More Love* a streaming documentary that took in everything from her "dark time" between her third and fourth titles to her triumphant final when she learned she had won and would be going to the Olympics—and breaks down in tears. At one point, "Moore Aloha" appeared on a sign in the film. The words would work as a subtitle to her life.

The Aerial Altruist

As a twelve-year-old, Laura Louise "Lakey" Peterson made history when she landed the first-ever aerial in an NSSA women's competition, winning her first National Title in the process. Then, at just fourteen, she won the NSSA National Open Championships.

"That was the start of my career."

But Lakey had already experienced a life few children see. In the year 2000—when Peterson was just five years old—her parents, along with her older siblings set out on a year-long, around-the-world adventure. It was during this trip that Peterson learned to surf. For three months, the Petersons set up shop in Manly Beach, Australia, where their littlest member instantly earned the nickname "Lakey Legend" from the locals for effortlessly catching wave after wave on her boogie board.

"That led me to skateboarding, and I think my aerials in the water came from skating maneuvers."

Soon her maneuvers began to come in flurries, staccato combinations resembling a female MMA fighter, which when executed without a slip, yielded a technical knockout.

"If you looked up *progressive surfing* in the Webster's, there would be a photo of Lakey next to it," Keala Kennelly claimed, laughing.

A long run of amateur titles put Peterson in the spotlight. She did not disappoint; completing her 2011 season by winning every event in the North American Junior Pro series, securing her a place on the official Women's World Tour. She was recruited for the Nike surf team and was lucky to star in *Leave A Message*, the first all girls surf film. By sixteen she had qualified for the World Tour, beginning her rookie year in 2012.

Peterson has been ranked as high as number one by the World Surf League, the highest professional level of women's surfing, and number six on the ASP Women's World Ranking.

In 2019 she married Australian surfer Tom Allen and made a valiant run for the World Title and a berth in the Olympics. In one of the most dramatic showdowns of the sports year, Peterson missed being a member of the first Olympic surf team by a single heat. The glory, the excitement and all the endorsements that came with them was a disappointment to miss out on. But the bigger reason for wanting to be in the Tokyo Games of 2021 was more personal.

"My mom held a swimming record. She qualified for the Olympics but that was the year the U.S. boycotted the Games in protest of Russia invading Afghanistan. So she never got to go. When I was a little girl I always wanted to be in the Olympics."

An all-around athlete and committed philanthropist, "Lakey is dedicated to both hard work and good works," said Rosy Hodge.

Peterson put her faith to practice supporting several non-profits: she raised $50,000 in one season for Hands4Others and used her *own* hands implementing clean water systems in third world countries. An advisory board member for Ocean Lovers Collective and a spokesperson for the Student Conservation Association, she helped build the largest volunteer organization for students keeping National Parks and trails pristine.

"To me, Lakey is such a role model," said Caroline Marks, the competitor that won the Olympic berth Peterson hoped to attain.

Deeply passionate about children's cancer treatment, she raised funds for several children's hospitals in Southern California and held an annual hometown contest in Santa Barbara to give kids a chance to experience the ocean from a young age.

"The world puts it in our heads that only guys can do certain things," Peterson explained. "But I'm this feisty little girl who didn't see why I couldn't do those things too."

The Ecstasy and the Agony

At twenty-three years of age, with seven years on the World Tour and two back-to-back World Title trophies on her mantel, reigning champion Tyler Wright seemed to have the world at her feet. Tournament prize money earnings rivaled that of her male counterparts. Awash in major endorsements, praised by her peers and adored by a legion of fans, Wright's first World Championship honored a promise she made to her uncle, Mark Morrison, before his death in 2017, that she would win a World Title at the last event he would be able to watch. At an early point during her second title run, her brother Owen reached number four in the world at the same time she was leading the rankings. The pair became a sibling poster child duo, garnering worldwide acclaim. Wright collected a second world trophy despite taking time to care for her brother, who was recovering from a head wound he received at Pipeline. A top competitor who has come close to a title himself at least three times, Owen suffered a traumatic brain injury and a minor brain bleed after colliding with the reef in December 2015, the day before the Pipeline Masters event began. After helping him through his initial recovery, in her first heat she wore Owen's jersey number as a tribute and rode in a switchfoot stance (like her brother's) on her first wave after she had claimed the World Title in France.

"Tyler Wright is the best female surfer is the world right now and she is going to be back with a vengeance," declared former World Champ Debbie Beacham in 2017.

Popular and determined, it was hard to imagine anything but the best for this prospective contender to multiple world crowns.

At the top of her game, laser-focused on her objective and well-supported by her sponsors, fans and the media, there was talk that Wright might run the table for a third World Title, a runaway train with seemingly unstoppable momentum.

Then in the summer of 2018, during a South African World Tour event, something went terribly wrong.

The Fast Track

Two hours south of Sydney in the small beach town of Culburra, Wright's father introduced Tyler to wave-riding as a toddler, riding "foamies" with her four siblings. Living right on the beach, surfing quickly became the family obsession. Wright recalls she and her brothers daring each other to take off on bigger waves. Traveling with her family around Australia's amateur contest circuit in a six-bed passenger van was one of her fondest early childhood memories. Surf was the consuming activity, and competition came naturally.

Then in 2008, at just fourteen, Wright became the youngest surfer ever to win a World Tour event; The Beachley Classic, hosted by world champion Layne Beachley. The startling triumph created a sensation on the pro surfing circuit. Her dramatic rise continued. Wright won the 2010 Junior World Championships, joining the World Tour the following year. Easily earning Rookie of the Year honors, she finished fourth in the rankings for her debut season amid national fanfare.

Catapulted into sudden stardom, the frenzy of media, pressure to perform and adjustment to a relentless world travel schedule nearly overwhelmed the young teenager. Struggling to cope, after four years of intense touring she found herself feeling disenchanted and exhausted at only eighteen. Supported by her family, Wright took a rest, rekindled her competitive fire and returned to the World Tour with a newfound drive. Older and more mature, she took her ambition on the road, winning her first World Championship definitively.

Her second title in 2017 was a rollercoaster race, the lead changing constantly.

In Portugal, Wright tore her MCL three-quarters of the way through, in what seemed a season-ending injury. The damage, however, did just the opposite, jolting Wright out of complacency. "Tyler's super-tough," marveled former pro Rosy Hodge, who was on the tour then as an announcer. "She surfed through the pain and just never quit."

"Tyler had to step up her game that year," said Layne Beachley. "She put her whole repertoire together every event. She has an awesome style."

Sometimes described as wonton abandon, Wright's style—bursts of speed and timing—recalled the originality of singer Amy Winehouse scatting—percussive and freeform, turning her injuries' limitations into virtuoso innovation.

Wright's second Title removed much of the stress she had felt in her early years. "When I walked into the career at sixteen it always felt a bit too big for me. And now that I have done it, it feels so settled . . . so settled, calm and cruisey."

The contentment would not last long. On track to win a third World Title, Wright contracted a severe case of influenza at a World Surf League event in South Africa in July 2018. Her health rapidly deteriorated. Soon the pain was so crippling Wright was bedridden for fourteen months and the agony so overpowering she had no recollection of her twenty-fifth birthday. At her worst, Tyler was having up to six emotional breakdowns a day, admitting in a *60 Minutes* interview she was a fraction of her former self.

"That fraction was the parts that didn't work. No brain, body constantly in pain, night terrors, six emotional freak-outs a day."

It wasn't until Tyler's older brother Owen suggested she see neuro-orthopedic rehab specialist Brett Jarosz that her life turned around. He diagnosed her illness as "probably the worst post-viral syndrome case I'd ever seen." Together the pair worked to steady her nervous system and link up her biomechanics, and—with the help of her girlfriend, Alex Lynn—slowly nursed her back to health.

Her return to the World Tour was once again something of a sensation. In December of 2020 Wright made surfing history when she slid into the waters of Maui's Honolua Bay to become the first professional surfer to compete with a Pride flag on her jersey. On one wave during the competition, she scored a perfect ten. At the final—which had been moved to Oahu due to a shark attack—Wright made history again, becoming the first woman to win a Championship Tour event at the Banzai Pipeline, where WCT competitions had been men only in the past.

Her post-trauma actions affirmed personal growth as well as a professional revival. Wright took a knee before paddling out at the Tweed Coast Pro with a clear message written on her surfboard—*Black Lives Matter*. When Covid-19 was taking hundreds of thousands of lives, she went to the media and pleaded for responsible behavior to protect those most vulnerable. She's been open about dealing with her body issues and sexuality, posting proudly online about surfing in the Maui event as an LGBTQ+ woman. For these selfless acts and her recovery, Luís Pito, Founder of *SurferToday* named her "Athlete of the Year." Layne Beachley said one of her proudest moments was seeing Tyler come through the post viral experience ordeal "so centered, grounded; such a strong, beautiful woman. She just came out of her skin and embraced exactly who she is."

The Water Warrior

In the chilly darkness just before dawn, anytime between 2003 and 2017, any surfer frequenting the long winding path leading to the cobblestone point waves at Lower Trestles was likely to see Courtney Conlogue. The freckled, athletic, sea-water blond would more than likely already be on the beach—counting waves, timing sets, choosing her place in the line-up.

The ninety minute drive from her restored Queen Anne-style home in Santa Ana was a near daily journey since she was eleven. She exhibited warm maturity, quiet modesty, friendly charm. But her performances revealed something altogether different: A forceful, focused discipline. It garnered her two back-to-back Bells trophies and wins in Brazil, New Zealand, Portugal, as well as Australia. With a number two ranking in the World Surfing League for 2015 and 2016, no rising star seemed more likely to be a World Title holder—it was a crusade. A *Sports Illustrated* profile and tasteful shots of her muscled body in *ESPN*'s Nude Athletes issue and a win in the world's largest women's surf contest came with the territory. Sometimes labeled as the outsider in a world of tangled alliances and shifting relationships, she remained the most aloof competitor on the tour.

Fellow competitor Sage Erikson saw Conlogue from a more nuanced perspective: "I wouldn't be the surfer I am today if it weren't for Courtney. I had a real good childhood rivalry with her. A lot of people say she's ferocious and aggressive out in the water, but on land Courtney is one of the sweetest, most genuine people there is. I always surf my best when I'm with her because I know I have to show up and perform."

"Her win at Huntington Beach was historic," noted Rosy Hodge, when she blitzed the U.S. Open in 2018. "She will not be stopped."

A broken foot later in 2018 *did* stop her momentarily but did not break her momentum; she returned in 2019 as a serious contender. But that year a freak accident resulted in a serious head injury at the WSL Portugal event in November—her board smashing into her face at the end of her heat. It slowed her—but it also seemed to amplify her defiant, driven resolve.

She nonetheless became far more reticent to share inner reflections. Asked about a variety of subjects she often deflected with a simple reply: "I'm saving that for my *own* book." From the outset of her career the multi-time National Amateur Champ focused with "a steely, studied tenacity on only one goal: Becoming the first Woman World Champion from California since Lisa Andersen's four-time reign in the mid-90s," concluded Hodge. *"And she pursued it—respectfully—but relentlessly."*

A *Real* Princess Waves a Wand

Royalty rarely reaches into the lives of ordinary citizens. But at least in one fascinating case a member of the ancient Hawaiian monarchy bestowed the equivalent of knighthood on a professional warrior on a world crusade. Melanie Bartels's career was boosted by an actual princess—one that as the niece of Hawaii's last Queen, Liliuokalani—would have been next line in the Royal Family. She was just the fairy godmother Bartels (and most women tour pros) were dreaming about in 2008: that season, a third of the surfers on the ASP Women's World Tour lacked major sponsorships. Bartels, struggling financially since losing her biggest sponsor in 2007, had only been able to attend six of the eight ASP World Tour events. Traveling on the full global contest circuit was an unaffordable expense without sponsorship. But even missing a quarter of the events, she had earned a seventh-place finish in the final ranking. Sensing a chance to win a title, but short on funds, Bartels was hoping for a magic wand.

The princess had the next best thing: real money. Not only would Abigail Kawananakoa have been queen had Hawaii remained a sovereign nation, as an heir to Campbell Estate—the largest and wealthiest landowners in Hawaii—she was in a position to be the best benefactor a surfer could dream of finding.

Interviewed by the *Honolulu Advertiser* during a contest, Bartels was asked about her status—and explained what a struggle it was to make the events without a sponsor. "I said, 'Oprah if you are listening I need help,'" Bartels told

Nancy Emerson, who mentored many of the young upcomers in that era. "I want to bring the women's World Title back to Hawaii—a feat that hasn't been done since 1981 when Margo Oberg held the torch—and more importantly, become the first women's world champ with Hawaiian lineage. And the *Hawaiian* Oprah heard me."

Indeed, Princess Kawananakoa read the story and then promptly contacted Bartels's family.

Shortly thereafter Princess Kawananakoa—whose philanthropic mission was to help people with Hawaiian ancestry achieve their goals—designated Bartels as a Hawaiian surfing ambassador and wrote a check to cover Bartels's travel and expenses, granting funding for the entire season. Bartels started off with a second place win and finished sixth overall for the season—her best showing ever.

Spontaneous and sometimes unpredictable, she was known to charge into a surf session in capris and a tank top, and as Prue Jeffries remarked Bartels and her partner Seramur were "the hot coals in the progression of aerial specialists."

Though she stayed on tour for six season altogether—an admirable achievement in itself—she was never quite able to bring home the World Title trophy to Hawaii. Fun-loving but also occasionally aggressive, Jeffries described Bartels as "an individual" to which future world champ Sofia Mulanovich added "with a complete surfing style."

Eventually her career turned to lifeguarding, a talent that kept her close to the beach and the waves. But her world class ability was not really ever in doubt.

"Melanie had the talent to be a world champion," Nancy Emerson claimed when asked about Bartel's talent. "The right set just didn't quite come into focus."

If Looks Could Kill

At the age of twelve, Alana Blanchard witnessed the shark attack that cost Bethany Hamilton her arm. Though Blanchard felt it wasn't her story to tell, she would carry the trauma of this experience forever. The two girls, best friends, had grown up on Kauai together. They pushed each other to surf competitively and reveled in their shared passion for the sport. Blanchard was still navigating the emotional turmoil of the attack's aftermath when she signed with her first sponsor as a professional surfer.

As is protocol for girls and women in surfing, Blanchard was expected to model in her sponsor's swimwear marketing campaigns. (The boys, meanwhile, were photographed surfing.) "For a young girl, I was only fifteen at the time, I never saw my body like that," Blanchard shared. "I've always had an athletic body, and it really, really made me just pick myself apart. I didn't even know that was bad at the time, but I just remember thinking I was disgusting." As she looked for the first time through the lens of the surf industry's expectations for women, her self-esteem eroded.

A talented surfer, Blanchard quickly rose through the competitive ranks and earned a spot on the world tour by the age of eighteen. She won some impressive competitions including the Surf Women's Pipeline Championship in 2005 and the 2007 Women's Pipeline Pro, both at one of the most demanding and difficult breaks in the world. She competed all over the world and modeled in high-profile sponsor photoshoots (including the *2013 Sports Illustrated Swimsuit Edition*). "It was super high stress, and I really didn't know how to deal with stress that well," Blanchard reflected. When Rip Curl—a dream sponsor for a young athlete—came calling, Blanchard experienced trepidation along with the thrill. Comparing herself with the thin, non-athlete models, Blanchard felt compelled to lose weight in order to meet her sponsor's standard. As her self-esteem eroded, she began a vicious cycle of disordered eating.

She sought professional help and eventually reclaimed her mental and physical health. Most importantly, she resolved to carve a path forward for herself and others in her shoes that could resist the unrealistic and unhealthy demands of the sponsorship game.

Alana Blanchard's surfing talent was long overshadowed by the surf industry's fixation with her physical appearance. Advertising campaigns have featured her modeling rather than surfing; magazines have marveled relentlessly at her physical features. Her image was carefully tailored; she became best known for the parts of her that the surf industry chose to help sell their products.

And Blanchard certainly profited from her participation in hypersexualized editorials and campaigns. With over four million combined social media followers she was, at the height of her surfing career, one of the most well-known and well-compensated female surfers in the world—despite being outranked competitively by lesser-known world champions. Luís Pito, Founder of *SurferToday* called her "the most followed surfer in the world, an exciting athlete, with a powerful front-side carve, and impeccable tube riding skills."

But Blanchard's fame and paychecks came at a steep cost: a toll to her self-esteem and her mental and physical health, stemming from the conflation of her value with her physical appearance. Her male counterparts in the industry were valued for their performance in the surf; she, for her body.

"We're constantly looking at these [images], what everyone else thinks beauty is, and we have such a high standard. I think it's good to be open about it and to be real, because if I was growing up now . . . I couldn't imagine how hard it would be."

Alana Blanchard's appearance in no way deviated from the idealized image of the female surfer—thin, blonde, bronzed. But her public persona has evolved: no longer the doe-eyed darling of the male-dominated surf media, she has adopted a more natural look and become an advocate for a healthy plant-based lifestyle. After giving birth to her child, Banks, in 2017, she was more muscular than ever—focused on peak performance and having surmounted the immense, internalized pressure to be skinny. As a mother she was still a force to be reckoned with in the surf.

Blanchard and Rip Curl were synonymous for over a decade: the brand that dominated in a hyper-competitive industry, and the athlete-turned-model who made it rain for them. Their lucrative My Bikini campaigns splashed images of Blanchard's body on storefronts all over the world, far from the ocean's shores.

Money in the Banks

Then, Blanchard got pregnant. Fans took notice of Blanchard's disappearance from Rip Curl's Instagram, once indistinguishable from her own, and of the conspicuous removal of the Rip Curl sponsor sticker from her boards.

Blanchard's pregnancy coincided with a greater shift in the surf industry: mergers and acquisitions, bankruptcies, the end of storied sponsorships. But according to Alana, the end of her contract had more to do with her pregnancy than with industry hardship or market forces.

"Things ended okay," she later maintained. "They stopped using me pretty much after I had Banks, or found out that I was pregnant," Alana revealed. "They really didn't like that I had a kid. We kind of both decided that we needed to go our separate ways."

From Blanchard's perspective, there was no interest in support as a mother.

Whatever the true reason behind Blanchard's severed sponsorship, it marked the end of an era.

Her son Banks became a huge focus in her life, and her money went into all the things a mother does for her child. She married top pro surfer Jack Freestone, the father of her child and took up her life on Kauai much as she had before her long run of fame. And her interests and options expanded.

Learning to master a camera herself, Blanchard created her own platform to share with the world. Her image was no longer controlled. The purposeful reinvention of her career image mirrored a broader change in the surf industry: women starting their own brands, publishing their own magazines and writing their own narratives. Her transition became a touchstone for possibilities as the 21st Century continued to unfold.

Indie rock band The Best Coast, headed by Los Angeles singer/songwriter/ guitarist Bethany Cosentino, released *The Only Place*, the first surf music album in decades. Beyond reviving the California sound, Cosentino was equally—and eerily—good at predicting the future. She released a track with the lyric "What a year this day has been" in 2012, well before the 24/7 news hellscape became a social stranglehold. Speaking out about sexual misconduct in the music industry in 2016, a year before #MeToo took off, she even wrote a new song called "Everything Has Changed."

Perhaps not everything: *Progress of the World's Women 2015* found that despite some significant advances toward gender equality, persistent gaps between males and females remained—hindering efforts to achieve their full potential.

Brave New World

The Global View

2000-2020

*"Feminism isn't about making women strong. Women are already strong.
It's about changing the way the world perceives that strength."*

—G. D. Anderson

Maps

With the advent of the new millennium, women's struggles became an increasingly frequent topic in the global conversation. The development of the worldwide web was a part of the quantum leap. "By that time," observed Layne Beachley, *"everyone* was surfing the Internet."

On every continent the rising awareness of equality began to show renewed vitality, particularly in more traditional cultures. Music, film—and surfing too—contributed to the dialogue, sometimes even accelerating positive changes in attitude.

Whale Rider, the 2003 academy-award nominated foreign film from New Zealand, depicted a young Maori girl who challenges the ancient custom of male ascendancy to the chiefdom of the tribe when her twin brother dies at birth. At age twelve, she claims her birthright, breaking tradition and invoking a battle that ends with a triumphant climax; cinematically setting the stage for women's governing rights everywhere. It became a worldwide hit.

Aided by the growth of the Internet previously unknown artists reached an expansive viewership. The success of breakout indie-rock group Yeah, Yeah, Yeahs was a result of this vast surge of global "web surfers" to explore fresh music. The power of this new online audience to be worldwide tastemakers vaulted the band's 2003 single "Maps" to the top of the music charts. Some critics saw the popularity of "Maps" as an artistic roadmap for many of the smash indie-pop crossover hits in the early 2000s. Of being in an "all dude's world," lead singer Karen O said: "I had to scream and break things to make people listen to me. But they did."

Women discovered the eternal joy of wave-riding in places where surfing was unknown less than a few years previously. Catching the wave toward the future, they entered a brave new world.

Taiwan's Tiny Town Triumph

The rippling effect of 2002's *Blue Crush* washed onto shores previously untouched by the beach culture that surfing spawned. The film's worldwide release to mainstream theaters exposed surfing's allure to entirely new regions of the globe. Wenling Chou had grown up in Heng Chung, a small beach town in southern Taiwan and was already seventeen when she caught her first glimpse of the excitement *Blue Crush* initiated.

Like the vast majority of seafaring societies, the Taiwanese saw waves—and the elements that caused them—as a threat to harbors, bays and the oceangoing trade on which their entire economy depended. Vessels avoided the shallows of reefs and points and saw swells as a danger to their fragile cargo.

Dismissing her society's aversion to the sea, Wenling Chou surfed by herself gaining knowledge and skill through persistent effort. With no coach, no sponsors and little support from the community at large, the WSL World Longboard Tour was a bewildering puzzle when she first entered the professional surfing competition in 2010. Taiwanese friends, often unable to understand surfing, were confused as to why any girl would want to surf, let alone compete in dangerous sporting events. Chou rose through the ranks nonetheless, winning the Taiwanese National Championship, and by 2014 reaching number thirteen in the WSL Longboard standings.

Determined and cheerful, Chou shrugged off the burdens of social disapproval and competitive pressure with what appeared to be universal surfer humor.

"Good girls don't get tanned," Chou declared in 2012, speaking of paternalistic Taiwanese mores that discourage athleticism in women. "But," she added gleefully, "they also don't get to surf in Bali."

A creative individual in a massive communal society, media drew attention to her originality. A 2013 *Time* magazine article described her automobile as "a friend's scrappy Ninja Turtle green Volkswagen bus that looks straight out of Scooby Doo. In it lies her neon pink surfboard, which has the words 'Classic Malibu' stamped on it."

The international attention she received coupled with her innate diplomatic skills offered Chou a career after competition: a self-made ambassador of Taiwan, teaching foreigners about Taiwanese culture and tourism.

"When I first started surfing, I just wanted to have fun," explained Chou. "When surfing became natural for me, I started to challenge myself in what I call the second stage of my surfing passion. Now I am at my third stage where I feel I have this responsibility to tell the world how great surfing is in Taiwan."

On opening day at the 2017 Jaileshuei Surfing Festival, Chou was there working with the head judge and building as much visibility for the sport as possible. She had come a long way from her tiny town in old Formosa.

"Taiwan is still very conservative," she said. "Even bikinis are still something of a novelty. But things are changing."

A Uruguayan Champion

Celia Barboza is only one of many surprises found in the small South American nation of Uruguay. The Uruguayan competitive surf scene was well established long before most of the wave-riding world knew it existed. A robust surf culture developed, culminating in 2019 when a very competent surfer was *elected President* of Uruguay.

Although over eighty surf breaks dot the coastline, the surf population is relatively small compared to neighboring Brazil. And while there are many accomplished women surfers in the country, only a handful have risen to the top ranks of global competition. Of those at the top, Celia Barboza may be the nation's most significant surfer.

As a member of the Uruguayan National Surfing Team, Barboza's performance at the ISA Masters World Championship achieved the best result in history for a Uruguayan surfer—of *either* sex. Placing fifth, she was just one step away from the medals.

Respected and nationally acclaimed, Barboza was the winner of the USU's National Surfing Circuit for eight years, from 1995 to 2009, taking a bronze medal in a Mar del Plata Pan-American and a fifth place at the World Masters of Surfing that was held in Ecuador in 2013.

"My family had a house in La Paloma, and we used to go there every weekend," Barboza said in 2020. "I grew up watching surfers on the beach and admired them for what they did," she continued. "I couldn't take my eyes out of the sea and that's when I asked my parents to give me a board."

A physical education teacher and surfing instructor, she was 2015 Ladies Open champion of the Samsung Life Cup in Playa el Emir, and participated in the Uruguayan Circuit in 2016.

Philippine Wave Field

One of the world's most overlooked and underutilized wave fields, the Philippines received little attention in the global media—and deserved more. Despite domestic tribulations, this archipelago of over seventy-six hundred islands hosted a series of competitions throughout the second decade of the 21st Century. The tropical island nation produced several female surfers of international caliber who enjoy consistent swells from the westernmost corner of the Pacific. Nilvie Blancada and Daisy Valdez spanned the era of contemporary Philippine surfing—one as a young pioneer turned champion veteran and finally a successful entrepreneur, the other as a challenger who eventually earned her own championship status. Each had a startling story on the way to the top of the Asian ranks.

Pregnant with her second child, Nilvie Blancada entered the 2019 Cloud Nine Masters Competition—and made it to the semi-finals. It was a statement of both her talent and determination. And her dominance.

Friendly and focused, Blancada started surfing when she was eleven and was quick to progress—a partial result of having a massive wave field nearby, most of them rarely crowded. Her competitive skills were immediately apparent. In 2012, Blancada won the Roxy International Women's Surfing Cup, taking down past World Pro Tour, Australian Kim Wooldridge, in the final, showing her local knowledge and strategic chops.

At nineteen the Siargao local took the shortboard title, delivering her country's second gold medal at the Southeast Asian Games in San Juan, La Union after taking the longboard title earlier in the contest, with her sister—Nilde Blancada-Reitenbach (herself a top ranked Filipino surfer)—cheering her on. A string of other victories proved she was no fluke.

After years as the nation's top competitor, Blancada—resolute and entrepreneurial—stepped into her next career move developing a new resort at Cloud Nine, considered one of the finest waves in the Philippine archipelago. It was an interesting introduction to the larger surf culture.

"Being in the water you forget about everything," she said in 2017. "When you're not happy, just jump in the ocean," she insisted. "It's just happiness being there."

Filipina Daisy Valdez had an equally interesting introduction to surf culture. It was not until meeting a one-legged surfer named "Poks"—another surfing legend—that Daisy Valdez decided to take surfing seriously. Athletic as a child, she was a competitive gymnast, where, despite being the tiniest participant, she would enter the biggest events and win.

Growing up by the water, surfing came naturally to her. Petite and humble, Valdez had been surfing professionally since 1999, winning local competitions and accumulating over fifty titles.

In the late 20-teens Valdez seemed to dominate every surfing competition she entered. She was a gracious winner and never pushed the competitive aspect of wave-riding: "Everyone has just as much fun simply surfing," Valdez stressed. "You need not be a pro to feel the stoke, the natural high that comes with surfing."

But as a fierce competitor Valdez had her sights set on international competition. In 2019 Valdez was chosen by the Philippine Surfing Championship Tour (PCST) to be one of the surf athletes to represent the country at that year's Sea Games.

Younger, up-and-coming talent began to infiltrate the Philippine women's surfing scene in 2017. They included Jolina Longos from Pacifico, Siargao Island, Vea Estrellado (Sorsogon) and the lone surfer from Mindanao Debie Gumanoy (Lanuza).

It was in that period that Philippine surfing came of age.

Bringing it All Back Home

As a native-born female raised on Rapa Nui, it would have been easy to take the slow sweet road of Easter Island life. But Alicia "Makohe" Ika—the lone female surfer there for more than ten years—had other ideas. After moving to Hawaii in the early 2000s, Makohe saw how women were part of the culture of surfing in Polynesia. She also expanded her second passion—singing—and began to perform professionally.

Returning to Rapa Nui two years later, she brought the idea of teaching surf to her home island, opening a surf school in 2005. She also brought a new sound to traditional Rapa Nui music, incorporating Hawaiian influences and a falsetto singing style that quickly gained attention as Easter Island's first female recording artist.

None of this was without controversy. To prove her methods, she broke tradition—but as women began to advance, her efforts were rewarded, and female surfers became accepted in the island's surfing community.

Simultaneously she became the most prominent female solo artist at Easter Island and has released several CDs, the first ever to incorporate original songs with Rapa Nui musical tradition. Known as *Makohe* from her participation in the 2007 Patagonia-supported Hollywood-produced environmental documentary *180° South*, she brought the film ecological lessons about the dangers of irresponsible actions that even a remote region can experience.

In 2014, she appeared with family in House Hunters International on HGTV, once again taking technology from the outside world and connecting it with the unique style of her native region. Whether it be surfing, music, film or architecture, Alicia has taken the island's unique culture, fused it with other influences and other mediums—bringing it all back home.

The Triumph and Tragedy of Morocco's
First Female Coastguard Surfer

A sad irony cloaked Zineb Zhor's appointment as the first female in the Moroccan coastguard: She was hired to replace her closest sibling. "Her brother loved surfing and thought his job as coastguard was his life's goal," Zhor's mother Ourmaina confided on a beautiful video in 2015. You hear the fragile sadness in her mother's voice.

Zhor's brother was also a beloved son. He died of sunstroke in a tragic accident. After the loss of their star lifeguard, the city chose Zhor—his sister—as his replacement.

The siblings were close as any brother and sister—living everyday surfing and in harmony with the sea. A few years older, her brother taught her not only how to surf but how to be adept in every aspect of the ocean—confidence, strength, astute observation. To be chosen by the city was an honor not just to her, but a tribute to her brother's mentorship as well.

Zhor, like her mother and the whole family, honored her brother's memory. "He used to take me to the beach with him every day. I first played with a surfboard on his watch."

Surfing, she found, was like therapy—it washed away the pain of the tragedy and made her feel happy each time she went out for her daily surf session. Her dream was to go abroad and open a surf club. "Tom Cruise will come to my surf club!" she laughingly claimed in 2019. She didn't end up leaving home. But the dream continued as did her surfing. And like her brother she loved it as if it was her life's goal as well. Her mother observed the path Zineb had taken and saw the future: "There are more opportunities today than when I was a young woman," her mother reflected. "Now things have changed."

For Meryem Elgardoum, Morocco's four-time National Champion, the surf dream became a reality. She first stood up on a bodyboard in 2009 and was immediately hooked. In just a few short years she rose to the top of her country's ratings, winning four consecutive National Titles in as many years. By 2017 she had opened a surf coaching business in Imouran, Morocco, teaching other young Moroccan women how to surf. She soon became a key member of the Imuran Surf Association in Tamraght, providing boards and wetsuits for local village children learning to surf.

As a supporter of her community and Moroccan woman, she helped establish the Moroccan Females Surfing Foundation with close friends from all professions—doctors, psychologists, yoga teachers, fitness coaches—all sharing the common bond of connecting other women to water sports in their country.

Surfing the China Sea

China's Monica Guo—another Asian surfer whose achievement for her nation was a first—was introduced to surfing by big-screen hit *Blue Crush*. After watching the girl-centric surf film at age twenty-one, Guo decided she'd pick up and move from her hometown of Yangshuo, located in mainland China, and head to Hong Kong to be a surfer.

A bold move in a restrictive society, she relocated to the island of Hainan in 2009, much to her parents resistance (her father thought that no one would want to marry her if her skin turned darker from the sun; her mother worried about the dangers of the sea). Competing at the Duct Tape Invitational in China, Gao made her way into the semi-finals with her graceful approach and local wave knowledge. Ten years later, she was running an all-girls surf camp and competing for China on the International Surfing Association's contests as one of the country's top talents.

And by 2013 she had won China's National Surf Championships, earning a reputation as the best longboard surfer in China, dispelling her parents worries that she had no career in the surf world.

Guo didn't grow up at the beach—in fact, she wasn't raised anywhere near the coast. Guo grew up in Yangshuo, located in mainland China's southern province of Guangxi. Yet in 2018, less than ten years after she pulled up stakes in the provinces, she represented her country at the ISA World Longboard Championship. Coming in as an underdog, Monica put on a dazzling performance, achieving a huge milestone for Chinese surfing: becoming the first Chinese surfer to win a heat in any ISA World Championship. Guo continued her path as an influential figure in Chinese surf culture.

Hurricane Heroine

Hurricanes and disasters are something most travelers seek to avoid. For adventuress Karina Petroni, exploring foreign locales and risking danger in her local region only seemed to sharpen her thirst for excitement.

Petroni took on modeling in Paris with fashion giant Versace and conducted relief flights in the Caribbean; she competed on the World Surfing Tour, jumped out of a helicopter in the Wayward passage; boarded an abandoned vessel and sailed it bare-bones back to the Bahamas.

Born in the Panama Canal Zone, Karina Elizabeth Bergheim Petroni started surfing in Atlantic Beach, Florida, later moving to the Bahamas' Central Exumas, where her husband David Mitchell was operating a marine salvage company that his family started in 1983.

But ever since they first met in 2009, Mitchell and Petroni wanted to add a new activity to their enterprise: using their vessels and planes to assist in critical rescue efforts. When Hurricane Joaquín struck the southern Bahamas back in 2015, they worked as a team, conducting relief flights, unloading supplies and distributing them to neighborhoods and churches in some of the most heavily damaged areas. And after Hurricane Dorian's near obliteration, Mitchell's rescue plane had to make an emergency landing after its engine cracked a cylinder, stranding him on a small island for several days until she could get the needed parts to him.

Petroni has credited some of her boldness to her bloodlines: Her mother was Norwegian, and father was of Italian descent. "I am fifty percent Viking and fifty percent Mafia, a very spicy combo," she said. "I was born and raised in the Canal Zone of Panama, where my father was a pilot taking ships through the Panama Canal."

Petroni quickly became involved in the local surf competitions which snow-balled into a full-blown professional surfing career by age twelve. Surfing professionally for eleven years, in 2008, ranking fifteenth, Petroni became the highest ranked Caribbean competitor on the world tour and one of the last women from the east coast of the USA to qualify for the WTC for more than a decade.

Petroni appeared in the 2009 Academy Award winning documentary *The Cove*. She has also represented Oceana, an oceans advocacy non-profit focusing on beaches and marine sanctuaries. She continued to ride waves and initiate rescue missions, doing good work while living a good life. In short, she affirmed, "It takes more than a village," and every action can make a difference.

As women's opportunities expanded, their effect on the world grew. In this first decade of the new century a momentum built in every corner of the globe. While surfers in this era were not able to take down the hardest barriers they were the first generation to create a wave of energy and inspiration that was picked up by those that followed.

Pure Heroines

"The sea does not reward those who are too anxious, too greedy, or too impatient. One should lie empty, open, choiceless as a beach—waiting for a gift from the sea."

—Anne Morrow Lindbergh

The Russian Surf Women
at the Edge of the World

Russian surfer Yekaterina Dyba knew something was seriously amiss. For a week in August of 2020 surfers had been getting sick. Dead porpoises floated in the shorebreak. Yellow smears streaking along the rip tides. Were these strange symptoms related—even connected by a danger?

Dyba finally realized there was a crisis when she and other shocked surfers discovered scores of octopuses, crabs, starfish, sponges, sea urchins and other marine animals washed up on the shoreline of picturesque Khalaktyr beach, a popular surfing spot on Russian's pristine eastern coast. A geographer who runs the Snowave Kamchatka surfing school, Dyba first raised the alarm on social media about a week earlier when the first signs appeared.

"For several weeks now, all surfers have experienced problems with their eyes after returning from the water. White shroud, blurred vision, dryness. Sore throat. Many had nausea, weakness, high fever," Dyba wrote in a Facebook post. Local surfers also noted a change in the water's color. Surfer Natasha Danilina revealed she suffered a corneal chemical burn after she went surfing.

Then the carpet of dead animals appeared. It was "like a graveyard," a photographer observed as he filmed a thick layer of carcasses covering the sand.

Dyba's surf school, located on a windy beachfront in Kamchatka—a large peninsula, in Russia's Far East—juts out into the Pacific Ocean stretching 780 miles along the Sea of Okhotsk. Kamchatka's locals rightly call Khalaktyrsky Beach "the edge of the world." With water temperatures around 34 and 37 degrees Fahrenheit, crowds are rare.

Russian surfer and rock-climbing instructor Lyudmila Tanachyova admitted that before she went to the water for the first time it took her two days to psychologically prepare herself.

"If you have the right equipment—a warm wetsuit is paramount—there will be no problems at all," she said.

A contingent of local surfers have emerged—braving the cold, ignoring their authoritarian government—including a talented lens-woman Anna Gavrilova. "I have always taken photos of everything, but nothing has caught my attention as much as surfing," Gavrilova said.

Located not far from the Radygino military training ground, the beach occasionally closed down due to naval drills taking place in the area.

According to Greenpeace the situation was an *"environmental disaster."* Meanwhile, authorities determined that the concentration of petroleum products in the water was 3.6 times higher than normal, and the amount of phenol was 2.5 times greater. Over 90 percent of the sea life died. But as the 2020 ecological catastrophe became public through Dyba's social media, Russia's Pacific Fleet denied any ties with the debacle.

Yekaterina Dyba continued to operate her surf school, and to press for the cause of the toxic substance that had polluted her beach. Despite a task force organized to tackle the situation—and a criminal probe launched as well—officials never determined the exact cause of the pollution.

But once again a surfer let the world know the oceans were in trouble. Another had documented the damage. Still another had persisted in trying to find the truth. *And each of those surfers was a woman.*

20-20 Vision

The year 2020 had some highlights in women's achievements. Following the World Surfing League's groundbreaking lead, six nations committed to equal pay for women soccer players. A fifteen-year-old scientist and inventor, Gitanjali Rao, was selected as *Time* magazine's first-ever "Kid of the Year." Singer Dua Lipa had a hugely successful year with three Top 40 singles: "Don't Start Now," "Physical" and "Break My Heart." Although Covid-19 decimated film attendances, director Eliza Hittman's *Never Rarely Sometimes Always* told an intimate bare-bones, authentic story that is also a potent argument about self-determination.

In October, two women—Emmanuelle Charpentier and Jennifer Doudna—were awarded the Nobel Prize in Chemistry for their work on a way of editing DNA, known as Crispr-Cas9.

In November of that year, Kamala Harris became the first woman vice president–elect of the United States, shattering barriers that have kept men entrenched at the highest levels of politics since America's first election in 1792. In January 2021, she joined the ranks of other world leaders.

In surfing from 2015 to 2020 a number of firsts were added in the international contingency, some almost astonishing. One, about a set of tiny sisters surfing Pipeline, Waimea and Mavericks before they were out of elementary school, did something the world had never seen before.

Another Toe in the Ocean

The Resano sisters—three of surf history's most empowered female surfers, with ties to Argentina, Europe and Central America—were children from a small fishing village who surfed some of the world's biggest wave spots.

The oldest of the Resano sisters, Valentina Resano was born in Spain (her mother's native country) but grew up surfing in Nicaragua with her two younger sisters. Earning a five-stitches scar above her right eye while surfing double-overhead second reef Pipeline, she followed her father (a big-wave Argentinian) chasing swells wherever it was big. "My dad surfs every day," she confirmed, "so it was natural for me to get into it as well."

Both her sisters followed suit, all three taking on legitimate Mavericks and Waimea as well as Pipeline. Originally from Popoyo, Nicaragua, where the family had settled, Candelaria Resano moved to the border town of Hendaye between Spain and France. Eating croissants and making sand castles became favorite diversions when not taking on nearby Belharra, the Basque Country big-wave spot The youngest sister, Maxima Resano, told Ellen Zoe Golden in *Howler* magazine, her favorite surf location was Pan Dulce, in Matapalo, Costa Rica, a place their family visited regularly.

"No more waiting for a new day. You've got to swim sometimes," the Pixies sang in "Another Toe in the Ocean." That was almost exactly what the Resano sisters' father said when encouraging his daughters to push their limits. It appeared that these young pixies took the message to heart.

Tubes in Tel Aviv

Tel Aviv surfer Anat Lelior, who represented Israel at the 2020 Summer Olympics, served as a soldier in the Israeli Defense Forces. The 2018 World Surf League (WSL) Europe Pro Junior runner-up began surfing at the age of five, when her father would take her down to the Mediterranean beaches in Tel Aviv. In 2019, she won the Pro International Trials in Australia at Surfest. as well as the Deeply Pro Anglet, a WSL Qualifying Series event, near Biarritz, France. Lelior qualified for the Surfing at the 2020 Summer Olympics by finishing as the highest-ranked surfer from Europe (Israel is considered part of Europe, according to International Olympic Committee protocol) and one of the top thirty surfers in the overall open division at the 2019 ISA World Surfing Games in Miyazaki, Japan.

Younger sister Noa Lelior followed in her sister's footsteps, becoming a professional competitor.

Puerto Rico's 1st World Tour Competitor

When Brisa Hennessy arrived in Queensland, Australia in 2019, she became the first Costa Rican to compete on the World Surf League's (WSL) Championship Tour—something no Tico—male or female—had ever accomplished. Hennessey, whose parents operated a surf school, grew up immersed in the ocean lifestyle, catching her first wave as a three-year-old. Raised in the jungle of Costa Rica until she was eight, transplanted to Hawaii for her school years and serving a stint on the tiny island of Namotu in Fiji, Hennessy defined the term "citizen of the world." Her transient childhood gave her access to some of the world's best waves, where she fell in love with surfing and honed her style to be both powerful and smooth.

Perpetually positive, Hennessy worked her way up the Qualifying Series ranks, finally reaching her goal of making the World Tour. At the 2018 Pan American Games held in Punta Rocas, Peru, she won the Women's gold medal, garnering an Olympic berth, and she'll proudly represent her nation in the Women's Surfing event at the 2021 Olympics in Tokyo.

Surfing in High Heels

Maud Le Car may have been the first (and perhaps *only*) woman to ride a wave in high heels and a cocktail dress. After losing a bet in 2015, she ended up winning everyone's respect by donning her evening outfit and ripping the waves to pieces, while looking like the model—and role model—she became.

Born on the Caribbean island of St. Martin, Le Car moved to Cap Breton, a surf-Mecca beach town in France. By 2016 she was rated fifteenth in the world. When the northern islands of the Caribbean were destroyed by Hurricane Irma in 2017, Maud returned to St. Maarten later that year to see the damage and assist in the recovery.

Straight to Video

Celebrating her sweet sixteen birthday, Frankie Harrer was filmed riding a triple overhead barrel in Tahiti that has garnered over 500,000 web-views. Instantly gaining notice in the lineup, she seemed like she had been surfing since she was the size of Shirley Temple—but her sweet face was misleading. As a member of the U.S. National team at thirteen, this goofy-foot teen held the record for the most wins in a single season.

With a family seemingly single-minded in the support of Frankie's calling, she became one of the few women to attain enough clout in the surf industry to skip the competitive route, instead traveling the globe, building her surf video parts and training with Laird Hamilton in his pool. Moving to the Frogtown district in Los Angeles, she explored the world of tattoo artistry and the local music scene, finding her identity in aspects of life outside of her Malibu environs, while maintaining a high profile surf career.

After Morgan Maassen shot the video of Harrer towing into big Teahupoo that first brought her international acclaim, the expert videographer recalled "Frankie is like a little sister to me, so I'm constantly torn between helping her excel as an athlete and being worried for her safety. As she rolled into that bomb, I couldn't help but think 'She might die!' immediately followed by 'Her mom is going to kill me!' But she made the wave, so we were both spared our lives."

Sister Samurai

Mahina Maeda hadn't planned on riding gigantic, record-setting waves. It was early November 2014, and the sixteen-year-old from the North Shore of Oahu had been watching the waves climb from five to ten to fifteen feet and higher at Nazaré, the big-wave hub off the coast of Portugal.

Almost a year to the day before, Brazilian surfer Maya Gabeira had lost consciousness and nearly drowned on a wave there. Fresh off winning the junior World Title in nearby Ericeira, Maeda was looking for something to keep up the momentum—and something people would remember her for. Maeda's "Uncle Garrett"—big-wave surfing legend Garrett McNamara, a close family friend—strapped her into not one, but two life vests and took her out to ride her first wave estimated at 30 feet. At that moment she had become only the second woman on record to drop in at Nazaré, a feat that earned her a nomination for Ride of the Year in the 2015 Billabong XXL Big Wave Awards. The daughter of Japanese immigrants, she credited her mother, Hitomi, a former competitor in kendo martial arts, for her in-water fierceness.

At twenty-two Maeda had already won three World Titles, reaching the number fourteen position on the World Tour by 2020. A holder of duel passports in Japan and the USA and fluent in Japanese, she was a candidate to enter the Olympic surfing exhibition on the Japanese team. Dedicated but camera-shy, Maeda trained under former World Champ Barton Lynch, continuing to improve her game.

On March 11, 2011, at 2:46 P.M. one of the largest earthquakes ever recorded sent a god-awful explosion of colors radiating across NOAA's Pacific wave-modeling chart. Inside thick bands of red, pink and purple there were two colors that most surfers had never seen: gray and black. They corresponded to wave heights of more than 240 feet and they sat like a pall against the coast of Japan. When the resulting damage of the Fukushima nuclear plant leaked radiation into the ocean, Japanese big wave veteran Takayuki Wakita decided to bring his family to Oahu's North Shore full-time so his children could surf in radiation-free waters. The move proved a good bet: Sara Wakita, the youngest professional surfer to come out of Japan, made five finals in regional WSL Junior and Qualifying Series contests. Perhaps the only top surfer ever to be rescued from a record-shattering earthquake (her father grabbed her out of her second-grade class before the Tsunami hit) Sara surfed under the Japanese flag but surfed almost exclusively on Oahu's North Shore.

Japanese Gold Coast–based professional surfer Ren Hashimoto scored her first major win in Australia at the 2017 Tweed Coast Pro. A member of the Alley Boardriders based at Currumbin, she was the Club's open women's champion. Hashimoto represented her home country, Japan, at World ISA games, finishing ninth overall in 2016. Hashimoto's big win at Currumbin rocketed the diminutive yet powerful competitor into number five on the world women's qualifying series ranking. She was a standout at the 2018 and 2019 World Games as well.

In Japan itself surf tourism gained momentum on Japan's beaches with significant increases in the number of international female visitors. Domestically, the independent beach lovers between the ages of twenty-five and forty became the most sought after market in Japan. Miyazaki—considered Japan's surf capital—was its epicenter. The beach town's clientele was at one point nearly ninety percent young women. The feminization of surf activity played an important role in revitalizing the local economy and created a greater sense of belonging among women in the surf.

On August 31, 2019, almost no one knew the name Amuro Tsuzuki. She was a young World Qualifying Series battler from Japan, ranked fifty-sixth on the rankings leaderboard. Four days later, on September 4, 2019, Tsuzuki won the ABANCA Galicia Classic Surf Pro, and in doing so, became one of the most accomplished WSL competitive surfers in Japanese history. The win propelled her to eighth position on the QS rankings—well within reach of qualifying for the World Tour. In December of that same year Tsuzuki claimed the 2019 World Surf League Junior Championship at the Taiwan Open of Surfing.

Kana Nakashio won the NSA Girls Class championship for two consecutive years in 2017 and 2018. Observers pegged her as an ace for Japan's competitive future that proved her mettle by taking second place at the Japan Open against Japan's top powerhouses.

Keen observers to the international competitors saw Shino Matsuda's small stature and sweet smile as deceiving. Hidden in her compact frame they spotted an elite talent with sights set for stardom. At the 2019 ISA World Surfing Games in Miyazaki, Japan, she finished in fifteenth place, and as the highest ranking surfer from Asia, was awarded a continental qualification slot for Tokyo 2020. Locally Matsuda was ranked second and Rookie of the Year of the 2012 JPSA tour.

Fujisawa, Kanagawa native Nao Omura first encountered surfing at age ten when she joined a surfing class during a family trip to Hawaii. The experience captivated her. Omura competed at an international level since first taking part in the world junior championships at age thirteen. She finished fifth at the women's ISA World Surfing Games in 2013 and 2014, and seventh in 2017. Surfing in her native Tokushima, western Japan, Minori Kawai finished second in her first ever tournament at that young age, then she became the youngest professional surfer in history at the Japan Pro Surfing Federation at the age of thirteen. Other Japanese standouts included Osaka born Reika Noro, now a Tokushima beach local; Byron Bay Boardriders surfer Hinako Kurokawa, who reached the final of the Gotcha Ichinomiya Chiba Open in Japan; Ryoko Sezutsu, a Japanese longboarder featured in *She Surf*; and Minami Nonaka, who took a bronze medal at the ISA 2018 Games.

The English Patience

If patience is a virtue the English have it. Enduring unreasonably cold winter water, fickle swells that can melt away, extreme tides and Atlantic storm conditions requires stamina, perseverance—and Biblical-level patience.

"The reality for many female surfers is a lot different, especially for women in the UK," photographer and surfer Philly Lewis said. "We are far more likely to paddle out when the water is grey and there's hail falling from the sky."

It took both patience and perseverance for County Devon native Lucy Campbell to win six British National Titles while attending college, working in the surf lifesaving association and competing in running events and cross-training in the Cornwall High Performance Centre and mountain biking to stay in shape. A self-confessed food lover, she baked the occasional cake in her *spare time*.

Modest and naturally entertaining, Devon county local Emily Currie stormed both the shortboard and longboard categories in the European Championship, taking runner up ranking in the 2017 UK Pro Surf Tour and a top ten placing in the 2018 ISA World Longboard Surfing Championships, where she was the youngest member to join Team England.

Another top Devon surfer, Peony Knight took back-to-back wins in the English surfing championships in 2020 after winning titles as British National Junior and Women's champion and a UK Pro Surf Tour Women's and Junior champion. Competing on the WSL World Qualifying Series, Knight was Britain's top ranked surfer in the league in 2017 and finished ranked as the fourth best European.

After winning the 2014 European Junior Surfing Championships title in the Azores, Keshia Eyre moved to Ericeira, Portugal where an expat British surf scene sprang up over the first decades of the 21st Century. Frequent travel and selected contests narrowed her focus. And ex-pro brother Luis's boutique surf lodge Surfiberia in the uncrowded region of Sintra offered an occasional getaway refuge.

Cornish surfer Megan Chapman aka "McMcSpoken," a critically acclaimed spoken word, rap artist and poet, returned to competition surfing in 2019 after a ten-year break.

Looking Beyond

Below the surface a much deeper surf culture beyond contests developed over decades of dedication. "I surf every day. It keeps you alert, and I love the challenge," said Jessie Tuckman from Newquay. Emily and Lucie Airton were second generation surfers, introduced to the sport by their father. Surfing together helped bring them closer as a family but the experience itself was unique.

"I love the way surfing makes me feel, physically and mentally," explained Gemma Pasierb from Porthtowan, Cornwall. "It helps me to think clearly about the world."

Cornwall surf stalwart Tassy Swallow opened Surf House, an iconic building in St. Ives providing a learning space for everything to do with surf/sea.

Other surfers found productive ways to make surf ventures positive and profitable.

In 2020, surfer Kylie Griffiths was inspired to create London Girls Surf Club, an all-female collective that helped city-based women rebalance by getting onto a board.

"Surfing is really good training for my work," noted beach lifeguard Holly Bendall from Falmouth.

The world of serious professional modeling does not often intertwine with truly competitive athletes. But Devon County's Laura Crane was able to fuse the good pay of modeling work, surf lifestyle and a part on the television hit *Love Island*. Like many millennials these surfers did not have the struggles many surfers of earlier generations encountered. "There's definitely way more space for being a woman in the surfing community than there used to be," Crane noted. "Before you used to have to wear baggy board shorts to fit in, now girls are all wearing really cute bikinis and looking like girls when they surf."

Photographer and surfer Philly Lewis saw it differently. "I hate how we're fed this imagery of girls in bikinis on boards. None of it's very real. It doesn't really portray surfing as it is for girls."

Most UK surfers seemed to split the difference, sometimes with a bit of Brit wit. Well-liked and respected model and solid surfer Corinne Evans took the top spot in *Wavelength* magazine's spoof "The Surfers Sexy List." Her full-length wetsuit was hardly risqué.

Joking aside, the late 2000s deep bench of talent definitely showed strong promise. With dedication, training and calm English patience, top competitors Ayls Barton, Lauren Sandland, Belle Betteridge, Georgia Timson and Tegan Blackford raised the bar with impressive performances that drew attention to UK girls across the international scene.

A Mother-Daughter Dance

In the southern hemisphere, New Zealand found a surfing family line that drew international interest of its own. While women's professional surfing offers few opportunities to qualify for the top echelons of competition on the World Tour, for twenty-one-year-old Northland surfer Wini Paul that chance came at the Jim Beam Big Break in 2011. Paul, a former Kiwi national champion who had migrated to the Gold Coast of Australia, entered the contest to finance her dream of becoming a professional surfer.

The competition, judged online from each contestant's individually-submitted video clip, was produced by Jim Beam. The brand would sponsor one man and one woman surfer to the ASP World Qualifying Series. Paul gained over one thousand votes to win the second tier of the competition.

After attending the Raglan Surfing Academy during her school years she had a run of wins including the New Zealand national women's title in 2007, a victory that had special appeal.

"My best result would have to be winning the national title," she explained. "My mum won it six times. So to get my name on the same trophy as her was amazing." Wini Paul's mother is Pauline Pullman, a Northland and national surfing icon and one of the matriarchs of New Zealand women's surfing.

Pullman dominated almost every event she competed in during her long career and has helped her daughter into the world of competitive surfing. The success was a triumph on a personal level, and a satisfying bridge in New Zealand surf history. "My mum is everything to me. She never pushed me into surfing; she just let it happen in my own time."

The Reign in Spain

While Britannia ruled the waves of the millennium's Anglo territories, Spain built a wave-riding armada as well. The reign of eight-time Spanish National Champion European Title holder Leti Canales was among the longest in surfing history. She earned a gold medal with the Spanish team in the 2018 ISA Surfing Games Aloha Cup and reached the top ten rankings in the World Qualifying series in 2020. Her twin sister, Loiola Canales (younger by a few minutes) managed to build an impressive array of championships herself: regional titles in Euskadi, Bizkaia and Maider Arostegui, the 2010 Spanish Junior champion in 2010, fourth in the Junior European championships in 2012 and Atlantic Nautical Games champ the same year. A teacher specializing in new technologies and special education, she has lived in Madrid and Albacete, but always seems to return to her native coast and her first love—surfing.

Identical twins, Loiola and Leti Canales were the first duo to become such accomplished surfers since the 80s. "They are beautiful. They are remarkable. They are amazing surfers," declared Jeremías San Martín, an astute observer of the Basque surf scene. "They are so close. But each one followed their own path." Their life-long sibling rivalry was good-natured and intense. Similarities and differences can be seen in every category: Leti taught herself guitar, Loio learned sign language. One turns her restlessness into hiking and climbing, the other into passionate studies. Their surfing style takes different forms—Leta more variety of maneuvers, Loio with more spontaneity. Like many lesser-known pros, after eight titles Leti will still struggle to raise funds for the Olympics. Persistent and persevering, the pair of sisters support one another unconditionally. Leti reached the top ten on the World Qualifying in 2021 "They are the best," said former Basque champ Maritxu Darrigrand. "Long may they reign."

Supporting oneself as a professional surfer is harder in countries where surfing is not such a major sport. Garazi Sánchez, the 2017/18 Spanish National Champ, frequently pointed out that female surfers are also hamstrung by a lack of financial support. No matter her outstanding performances, "having sponsors that can finance your career has become something far from reality," Sánchez explained. "Traveling the world to score points at competitions is expensive, especially for those from countries where the same culture of sponsorship does not even exist." Ariane Ochoa Torres, like Sánchez, one of Spain's top-ranked surfers, was awarded a grant by the Spanish Olympic Committee to fund her training for Tokyo 2020, surfing's Olympics debut. Though she has various brand endorsements—including surf brand Oakley—she admitted that "the bursary is my biggest sponsor at the moment."

Lucía Martiño had begun to be well-known throughout her region of Asturias, Spain as the National Surfing Champion but became a tabloid sensation in 2014 when she dated European superstar singer/actor Dani Martín, who she met at a festival concert. Notoriety was no hardship; the Gijón native took the Spanish Junior title and two Spanish Championships, and at twenty reached the third place ranking in the European Pro Circuit. The green-eyed blond, who many mistook for a Californian, went on to chase the World Qualifying tour, picking up major brand support in the process. Despite the sponsor volatility, Martiño said, "more and more girls are living off surfing."

Nadia Erostarbe, the 2018 European Junior Champion, and Alazne Aurrekoetxea, one of Spain's best all-round water-women, also made names for themselves.

Laura Coveilla, a top model from Spain's Canary Islands, would have been known for her looks were it not for her documented world-class performances against the best surfers in Europe. Other Canary Island standouts included Cabreiroá Tenerife Pro champion Daniela Boldini, Melania Suárez, Sara González, Marcela and Lucía Machado.

The other nation on the Iberian Peninsula developed strong new talent as well. In 2020 Teresa Bonvalot was considered the best woman pro surfer to ever come out of Portugal. At an early age Bonvalot demonstrated a serene confidence in the water. Born in 2001, Bonvalot grew up in the Cascais, a coastal surf community in northern Portugal. Guincho, her hometown beach, hosted the annual European women's and men's world class Prime and CT events. Athletically gifted, Bonvalot was already playing football for her hometown club and representing her school at badminton and cross country running, demonstrating an instinctive tenacity to excel. Passionate and persistent, riding waves was a natural step for this 5'7", 114 pound goofy-foot who was swimming, sailing and boogie boarding by the age of seven—and surfing at the age of nine.

Not surprisingly, in 2017 a seventeen-year-old Bonvalot was crowned European Junior surfing champion for the second year in a row. She continued, just missing the World Tour cut by one slot.

Shark Fins; Whales Tails

"Out of the corner of my eye I saw the shark moving on my left."

In 2020 Lindsey Baldwin made international headlines when she captured a video of sharks surrounding her board while surfing her home break of New

Smyrna Beach, Florida. Baldwin, whose three-year-old daughter was just starting to get into surfing, wanted to make sure her old GoPro worked so that she could use it to capture videos of her daughter catching waves. Instead she ended up with one of the year's most-shared web clips. A member of the Eastern Surfing Association All-Star team back in the late 90s, Baldwin was among the top rated surfers in Florida. Along with her sister Marcie Baldwin, who was both an East Coast Surfing and United States Surfing Champion herself, Lindsay opened the successful surf school, Surfin' NSB.

The daughters of two-time Florida State Champion Charley Baldwin, Lindsey became a successful real estate agent with a Bachelors of Business Administration from the University of North Florida. Marcia went on to become a highly-respected ocean and animal artist with paintings in galleries around the globe. Featured in *National Geographic, Sports Illustrated for Women, Surfing* and the revered *Eastern Surf* magazine, as well as television appearances, both sisters describe their surf experiences with fondness.

Asked by television news crews at the time if she was scared during her shark encounter, Lindsey replied immediately: "Oh no, not at all. I actually went straight back again. I mean when the water's that clear, you really can avoid them."

Surely South African surfer Bianca Buitendag has laid two unique claims, one including the largest exotic animal encounter: she was the first female to surf Skeleton Bay, Namibia, the remote fabled south west African point break—and to have surfed with a whale. Sent on a mission by Roxy's and Swox' short film "Ku Khangela" she and good friend pro snowboarder Lena Stoffel took off to surf the southeast coast of South Africa. Between Jeffreys Bay and Durban lay the land of Xhosa, formally known as Transkei—homeland of Nelson Mandela and perfect right hand point breaks. Calm and graceful, Buitendag, a Victoria Bay native who spoke only Afrikaans as a child, spent most of her surf career traveling,

While surfing on the Namibia trip she encountered an extraordinary sight. "One day we saw a whale mom and her calf out in the water. They are so big. I've never seen a whale before. They jumped out and we saw them a couple of days in a row." For days the whales surveyed the break, breaching and playing just outside the lineup. It was a spiritual experience and one of many that gave her comfort after losing her father in 2015, an experience that brought her to the depths of despair. But she maintains that continuing to travel on the World Tour helped her recovery. It gave her a focus, she disclosed, to finished forth in the world at the end of that same year. "I am just grateful for having my father until the age of twenty-one," she said. After spending years in France, she returned to her hometown near Cape Town in 2019 and qualified for the 2020 Olympics.

"Scariest thing in the water for me is definitely sharks," confessed Australia's Nicola Atherton, who grew up on Bronte Road in the Sydney suburbs and became passionate about surfing at age twelve. Bullied as a kid for her weight and dyslexia, she turned to surfing, going on to spend a decade as a professional surfer, winning the World Junior Surfing Championship, becoming a member of the Lifesaving Association and the only female working on Bondi and Bronte beaches, earning awards for her lifeguard service. She later attained a new level of fame as a cast member on the Australian lifeguard reality series Bondi Rescue.

But beneath the surface there was a conflict, constantly circling like a tiger shark. Feeling forced to hide her sexuality on the surfing circuit, she developed depression after breaking up with the woman she'd been dating secretly for two years. Bubbly and talented, she was plagued from a young age with substance abuse and her life spiraled into addiction after splitting from her long-term girlfriend.

She has been open about her struggles with addiction, having been hospitalized in Bali after overdosing on alcohol and sleeping pills.

But being rushed to hospital was the catalyst for changing her life, and she became a firefighter and spokesperson for improvements in mental health awareness. Atherton remained devoted to surfing and improving every day. "Resilience is all about preparation," she said, and her dedication has been lauded by observers everywhere. As for the sharks, Atherton remained on the alert, feeling that caution was being overlooked. "I do believe Bondi's got a bit of a bubble around it, and I don't think about it so much down here—It's not completely on my mind. But, if I'm traveling up or down the coast surfing, it's something that's definitely on the radar!"

When a seven-foot shark swam into the lineup during the last heats of the day at the 2006 Women's Pipeline Pro, Sena Seramur was not surprised. But it was enough to scare the bodyboarding finalists right out of the water. Seramur had given a number of contestants a scare earlier in the day as she knocked off one after another of her opponents taking several hollow Backdoor Pipeline tubes and rode them fifty yards down the beach to Off the Wall. It was for her a remarkable return to the contest scene. As a young teen Sena was well on her way to surf stardom.

Well-sponsored and gifted on a board she won five National Scholastic Surf Association Championships in as many years. But on the higher pressure professional arena she found the stress too intense and returned to her home in Kauai.

"I wanted a normal high school experience," she told Darlene Connolly at Surfline. "I missed out on having that, so I took some time off." The self-examination was a positive experience. "I said, 'OK, who am I?' and got a normal nine-to-five job. I learned the worth of a dollar." Her return was an impressive one but somewhat short-lived. As is often the case not every talented person who loves surfing also loves to compete.

Two years later Amee Donohoe's shark encounter was a little closer and a lot more uncomfortable. At the 2008 Drug Aware Pro event at Margaret River in

Western Australia, she spotted a "massive" shark just inside the break line after catching a wave. Only two days earlier a fatal shark attack had occurred at the northern NSW town called Ballina, which claimed the life of a sixteen-year-old bodyboarder.

"I was paddling back out through the channel and saw this massive fin, it was really wide. I got a pretty good look at it, good enough to not want to stay in the water," Donohoe said.

"I've surfed all over the world with dolphins hundreds of times before and at places like Ballina on the east coast, so I knew when I saw the fin it didn't belong to a dolphin. The width and the girth of the shadow was massive."

While sharks can be dangerous, the number of attacks and fatalities are far lower than many other sports-related activities. More people are killed being struck by lightning every year than die from shark bites. And whales, which are among the most intelligent and docile marine animals, pose no threat for surfers, and have become a symbol for an endangered natural world.

At Jenny Boggis' surf resort in Byron Bay, migrating whales spout and dolphins surf in the lineup. A local Lennox Head surfer and Australian Open Women's Champion, sea life is part of the special program Boggs developed to immerse surfers in a total positive environment. After traveling the world as a professional surfer for eight years, she transitioned into coaching and training elite surfers. Within the year she was approached by Billabong to take on the role as team coach for their women's team, mentoring and coaching their top athletes.

"I love to see women light up because of surfing," she told *Coastal Watch* in 2017. "I love breaking things down with them, analyzing their skills and delivering the assistance to take it a step further."

That same immersive element informed Hawaiian surfer Koral McCarthy's goal at the Polynesian Voyaging Society. The *Malama Honua*, an authentic reproduction of the ancient sailing vessels that sailed the Pacific, helps teach the methods early navigators used to traverse the oceanic regions.

McCarthy, a Kauai native helped the Society to engage with schools, organizations and community members.

Community is a word found in most of these women's resumes. Competitive surfer Jodie Nelson set out to become the first woman to stand up paddleboard solo from Catalina Island to Dana Point on Sunday, March 29. She accomplished her goal. On the journey she made a new friend—a thirty-foot minke whale.

Like her French counterpart Maritxu Darrigrand, Nelson, a longtime waterwoman, became deeply involved in the nonprofits Keep A Breast Foundation and Boarding for Breast Cancer. Her objective was single-minded from the start: to fight breast cancer. Her mother and aunt were cancer survivors; she inherited the strength of spirit she observed in them. Nelson, a former pro surfer, has competed in world-class competitions and was one of the first women to be towed in at Teahupoo. But her courage in the face of deadly disease will likely be her more lasting legacy.

Encounters with a shark can be a hard trauma that affects confidence. An attack on Minori Kawai, Japan's top female surfer, was unsettling enough to challenge her self-confidence in the water.

Kawai, who began surfing at just seven in her native Tokushima, western Japan, admitted on more than one occasion she still has to battle her phobias in the water after fearing she might become shark bait.

"When I was surfing in Australia once, I saw a flash of a dorsal fin and thought: 'Uh-oh, I'm going to get eaten,'" said Kawai, whose style combines lightning speed and seemingly effortless grace.

"They told me it was only a dolphin that time, but then in Gold Coast I got stung by a nasty jellyfish and couldn't breathe so they rushed me to hospital."

Just when she thought it was safe to go back in the water, Kawai had another brush with disaster at a competition in Indonesia.

"In Bali, I saw this big shark fin when I was paddling and carried on surfing in a bit of a fluster. I was petrified.

"The sea can be scary," added Kawai, who signed autographs for adoring young fans after finishing practice.

"When you go out alone and the waves are massive, sometimes you think you could die out there.

"But you can't become a better surfer if you don't get in the water."

At the event she was able to put aside her fear and focus on her surfing, finally winning her first major WSL Qualifying event in 2017 at Tsurigasaki, her home break in the town of Ichinomiya, Chiba and the site of the Olympic competition in 2021.

"I never imagined I could win such a big competition," added Kawai, after becoming the first Japanese woman to win a World Surf League 3,000 qualifying series event despite spraining her ankle in a heat.

"It was like a dream and it took a while to sink in. But to win at Tsurigasaki, where I surf every day, was amazing. I got a taste for how the Olympics will feel and I'm sure it will give me an advantage."

Her victory was all the more remarkable given that she surfed with a serious ankle injury, taking painkillers before defeating fellow Japanese contestant Hinako Kurokawa in the final.

On January 27, 2015, Australian surfer Dianne Ellis was filming a pod of dolphins from atop her longboard when something smashed into her. The incident happened at Byron Bay where she says she had paddled out into the path of the dolphins.

In the video it's unclear what struck the board. But you can hear Ellis cooing to the dolphins and then saying: "Ahhh they're beautiful. Here comes some just now" right before the strike which occurs at the one-minute mark.

"(There was) an immediate explosion and suddenly I was floundering around in the water with two pieces of board," she told the Daily Examiner newspaper at the time.

"I thought a dolphin broke my board, but a small shark was sighted," Ellis added later on her YouTube channel, requesting viewers to offer their take on the board-breaking aquatic life form.

A stand up paddler then helped her to shore on the two remaining pieces of longboard. Ellis said it looks there are teeth marks on one of the fins.

Ellis, who has written extensively about her struggle with Lyme Disease and is a certified breathwork practitioner, author and host of a radio show, continued to surf despite the incident.

Ocean Eyes
Capturing the Surf Culture in Images

"When you've learned to both see and not see the resemblance, then you see the uniqueness."
—Barbara K. Rothman, author of
Genetic Maps and Human Imaginations

No Shooting Pains

As Shannon Glasson pushed the shutter button on her water camera, the flash illuminated the dark caverns of water, sucking dry off imposing reef, well below sea-level. It was the dark of night, the freezing water numbed her hands, the slabs of rock glistened in the blackness. Sydney Harbor had seen multiple shark sightings and several attacks that summer. The set of waves were double overhead, pitching top to bottom. But there was something unusual about the young surf photographer capturing images in one of the world's most dangerous surfspots—*she did not feel fear.*

Just seventeen when she started shooting, Glasson's first subjects were from her hometown Cronulla, one of Sydney's southern beach suburbs which hosts powerful waves, notably Shark Island and Cape Fear. What is more impressive than Glasson's collection of surf images is what she overcame to capture them. Born with Congenital Adrenal Hyperplasia (CAH)—a condition where her body does not produce adrenaline—she doesn't feel *any* fear in treacherous, even deadly ocean conditions. Additionally born with a severe case of Congenital Talipes Equinovarus (CTEV)—a severe foot condition that meant she would possibly never walk—she required heavy surgery between the ages of two and four years old. Each surgery restricted Shannon to a wheelchair, being unable to walk during the early years of her life. Up to the age of seven, she was in foot braces, undergoing thirteen surgeries to correct her feet. To clamber up the rocks remained a challenge, as her feet, that now face forward, do not articulate with full flexion and extension. Living with CAH meant adhering to a rigorous daily medication schedule. But, she told HuffPost Australia, she has learned to "roll with the punches" and take each day as it comes.

Driven and unapologetic, Glasson considered her condition an advantage: the lack of fear made intense, precarious experiences something far less intimidating than they would be for most cameramen shooting big waves. "So I guess there is always an upside," she laughed.

Taught to swim at only three months old—long before she could walk—the ocean was where Glasson excelled. Her chemical intolerance of fear allowed Glasson to develop a skill set to comfortably enter extreme ocean situations, photographing some of the most challenging surf captured on film. "I just like big waves," she said, remembering past aquatic sessions. "It's all about the chase."

A Depth of Field
Women Surf Photographers

One outcome of the women's movement in surfing was the rise in female photographers. Documenting—virtually for the first time—the act of wave-riding from a feminine point of view, it changed both the inner circle of surfers and the wider public's perspective on what surfing involves. The upsurge of women photographers followed the same flood of wave-riding participation occurring around 2010.

There had been women photographers in the earlier eras. Just not many.

Shirley Rogers connected to the surf culture as one of the only female photographers on the North Shore during the mid-70s through the 80s. She cut a striking figure, and North Shore male surfers gaped like school boys in an arena where working women were rarely visible.

Her presence—and her boyfriend Fast Eddie Rothman, a heavy character in North Shore lore—almost overshadowed her talent behind the lens. But in my tenure as the editor at *Surfer* her image submissions were selected on their own merits, and her work still stuns.

Surf photographers, like surfers themselves, tended to be both unusual and archetypical at the same time. Born in the West Indies island of Curacao, Simone Riddingius lived in Holland for three years, starting her deep relationship with wave-riding in 1964 when her family moved from the Netherlands to California. She met surfer Denny Auberg, a lifeguard at Malibu, during her teen years camping with her family. Auberg would later write the screenplay to *Big Wednesday*, the major Hollywood film depiction of his brother Kemp, Lance Carson and other early Malibu greats in the early 60s.

While Auberg gave her tips in the lineup, and taught her guitar, Riddingius soaked in the entire cultural milieu emanating from the beach life, incorporating it into her own creative personality.

"I was always mesmerized by the breaking waves," Reddingius remembered. "I'd watch the surfers carrying their boards, waxing them up, and then dancing on the waves. I wanted that lifestyle." After learning on a decrepit one-dollar longboard, she bought a shorter shape and, "before you knew it, my girlfriend and I were ditching school to go to the beach."

Shock-white blond and effortlessly engaging, Reddingius turned out to be a prototype of 70s surf style: after high school she moved to Santa Barbara, trading Malibu for Rincon, exploring music, shooting budding surf stars Kim Mearig and Tommy Curren, then vagabonding to Maui through the 90s making jewelry, shooting Jaws and sampling the counter-culture.

"She's an awesome photographer," World Champion Kim Mearig attested. "She had great timing when shooting surfing, I think because she was an accomplished surfer herself. She knew exactly what the surfers were setting up to do."

Reddingius was perhaps more of an influence than a star, her template was one countless young women used to shape their own lives. In 2000 she won the Masters' Division of the Margaritaville Malibu Women's Longboard Open. When *Wahine* magazine published a surfing photo of her from the event, "it was the highlight of my contest career," she laughed. Twenty-two years after moving to Maui she returned to Santa Barbara, freelancing as an engineer, opening a photo gallery and playing music once again with Denny Auberg—this time as the Wrinkled Teenagers.

Another early lenswoman, revered professional sports photographer Martha Jenkins began shooting up-and-coming amateur female surfers in the late 80s. Married to award-winning sports writer Bruce Jenkins, she became interested while the couple were supposedly on vacation in Hawaii. But her husband's work ethic meant their time was really spent covering the North Shore winter surf season. Eventually Jenkins abandoned all attempts to enjoy her Hawaiian holiday and joined her husband in the work frenzy. While Bruce interviewed top stars, Martha shot action and portrait photos for the same American and European magazines. After eleven years of shooting pro baseball, she enjoyed mixing their vacation time with her passion for capturing athletes.

In Florida, New Smyrna local Heather Holjes was shooting surfers in the 90s, when she was one of only a handful of active women water photographers anywhere in the world. Perhaps just as rare, although she has been bumped by sharks, it was a dolphin who took a small chunk of her leg. A solid competitive surfer as well, Holjes spent more than a decade competing and shooting photos through the 90s and 2000s. When asked about which passion took priority she replied, "It's a hard choice, but I can always surf when the light is bad."

Sharp Shooters

As more female surfers entered the lineup, women from a variety of regions and from varying backgrounds and disciplines entered the field of surf photography. Part of their significance was an explicit sense of purpose beyond simply capturing the peak action of a ride. They were seeing the act of surfing through a new lens. A group who mostly started in the 2010 period and after, they brought the female performance into sharp focus. Their opinions and methods vary, but their aim is true.

Elizabeth Pepin Silva, credited as the first female photographer to use an underwater housing, has been surfing in Baja since 1992. She produced the award winning film *La Maestra* about a teacher in Mexico who becomes a surfer.

"*La Maestra (The Teacher)* is a continuation of my efforts through my films and photography to change the way all women are portrayed in the media and create an alternative voice in surfing by pointing my video and photo lenses at women surfers of all ethnicities and backgrounds, ages, and sizes and shapes."

Filmmaker Marion Poizeau went to Persia, capturing the birth of Iranian surfing in her *Into The Sea* documentary and its women leading the charge. Following Easkey Britton, the Irish surfer and artist, Poizeau was able to explore the cultural fascination Iranians have for surfing and women's empowering role within it.

Serendipity has also played a role in the career of some photographers. A college softball scholarship in Hawaii brought Cat Slatinsky to the epicenter of contemporary surfing. In 1997, Slatinsky's good friend Ian Masterson asked her to join a little class he had been working hard to initiate at Windward College. It was the first Surf Science class ever held in the U.S. and it had a huge impact; giving her the courage to go out and buy her first video camera and begin her career as a surf videographer and photographer. Slatinsky ended up shooting *Heart*, an entire full length surf movie starring Kassia Meador, Prue Jeffries, Keliana Woolsey and Melissa Combo. She also worked for Bill Ballard and Fuel TV, filming a variety of other projects. Slatinsky contributed to *Dulce* and *The Women and the Waves 2* and her surf photos were published in magazines and museums around the world. Eventually Slatinsky evolved into a management position with Siren Surf Adventures but continued to use her film skills there too; all started by a simple twist of fortune.

Sol Sirens Soul

When the surf film *Sol Sirens* premiered September 15, 2005 at the La Paloma Theater in Encinitas, California, it was the culmination of a project that consumed five years of Ashley Carney-Davis's life. Paid for by waiting tables and a large assortment of credit cards, the film's debut was, as Carney-Davis put it in the movie, the point where "dream and reality collide." The storied La Paloma theater, famous for premiering surf films since the 60s, was sold out. The audience that night was both judge and jury, and Carney-Davis was nervous about the verdict.

A story about surf culture—and how an average female surfer fits into it—Carney-Davis had filmed *Sol Sirens* at ten locations with a half dozen surfers over more than two years.

"I wanted to make something to let average girls know that they could go to all these places," Carney-Davis said. She knew there was an audience for regular girls wave-riding at the amateur level and exploring foreign surf spots.

"I think that about one percent of the female population is good enough to surf at the professional level. I wanted to show that there is a place for the average woman in the surfing world."

Although the film speaks to a wide swath of adventurous females, it has an autobiographical base. The plot closely follows Carney-Davis' own life: a land-locked Texas teen intent on experiencing surfing and exotic travel.

Leaving her hometown of Nacogdoches, Texas, after graduating high school, Carney-Davis convinced her parents to send her on a foreign exchange program. In reality, she went looking for surf, exploring Central America by herself.

"I would call my parents from pay phones all over Costa Rica and tell them that I wasn't coming home," Carney-Davis said.

Buoyed by her initial trip she expanded her travel to a full endless summer hunt for waves. Filming the entire journey felt like she was realizing her dream. But while playing with a group of children in Indonesia's Mentawai Islands, Carney-Davis had a health crisis.

"The palm trees suddenly started spinning," Carney-Davis remembered. "My head was getting really hot, and I almost passed out." She knew then that something was seriously wrong. Extreme fatigue followed, as did random bouts of what Carney-Davis called "craziness." During those episodes, she was too exhausted to surf and on some occasions coughed up blood.

The illness was never diagnosed, and the symptoms stayed with her even after she returned to California. They eventually disappeared, something Carney-Davis credits to the work of a holistic healer.

Once back to health, she began the long film-editing process. Carney-Davis shaved one hundred hours of footage down to ninety minutes. It was a labor of love, but she felt compelled to finish the project that had consumed a half-dozen years.

"I made this film to tell my parents what had happened to me," she said. Carney-Davis saw the world in a new light after returning from Costa Rica; she was obsessed with surfing and travel. "I loved my parents, and I wanted to show them what I was doing with my life." Now, as the film opened on the theater screen that night, she felt her whole life was wrapped up in it. Nerve-wracking as it was, she watched the audience absorb the film, anxious for their verdict. It was one of the most stressful experiences she could remember. In the end Carney-Davis need not to have worried. She received a standing ovation as the lights came up.

A Deep Funk

Like surfers themselves, women find the physical demands are often perceived as inappropriate for females in a field previously dominated by males. Addressing that has often required serious athletic preparation.

"The physical work is done months before," said Christa Funk, considered one of the world's leading water photographers, best known for her picture-perfect images from Pipeline. "I mix a lot of cardio and strength training with swimming, surfing and bodysurfing," Funk stressed. "That's the easy part of my preparation, and I've been doing it for the last twenty years." A Coast Guard Academy graduate with a degree in Marine Biology and a military commission, she is one of the only swimmers—starting in 2005—willing to paddle out on days when the shifty second and third reef Pipeline is breaking. "It's nice to see women supporting each other and working together." Still, she admitted being glad she started when she did. "I haven't had to carve a path as a woman trying to fit into the surf industry from scratch," Funk said. "Because I'm already on the path paved by the women that have come before me."

Shannon Glasson had a more philosophic perspective: "Yeah, guys have said things like, 'Wow, I didn't expect a chick to be out here.' And I think that's because girls feel they don't belong out there. But they *do* belong," Glasson emphasized. "Hopefully over the next few years, the numbers will even out in terms of guys and girls out in the lineup," she added. "I've never seen myself as being different from the guys."

Understanding being "different from guys" was a prerequisite for many women, or at least *artistically* different.

"I wanted to create photos of my friends that male photographers weren't taking," explained Luki O'Keefe, whose work has shown at the Annual New

York Women's Surf Film Festival. Womanhood has definitely affected the way she has captured women's surfing: "Because I'm a girl, I know the angles that my friends like, and I know how to highlight the feminine aspects of their surfing."

For this initial group of women photographers the feminine viewpoint seemed unavoidable.

"I try to fool myself into thinking that gender doesn't matter, but you create from who you are," stated Jianca Lazarus, an artistic South African transplant by way of New York City. "And gender is an essential part of identity."

That gender identity—the partnership forged between artist and subject—was a big part of capturing exquisite images for New Jersey coastal resident Magdalena Kernan: "The girls I shoot with have been so supportive of me which has always made me feel so comfortable in the water," Kernan told *Surfer* magazine in 2018.

Kernan, who started shooting for Ocean City's celebrated 7th Street Surf Shop in the summer of 2014, had rapid success. She credits the assistance and support from her subjects: "I remember the first time I swam at Snapper Rocks in Australia. I went with Nikki van Dijk and she was taking the time to tell me where to go and where to sit."

A former shortboard competitor, San Diego local Ivana Cook picked up surfing in middle school when her family moved to Oceanside. Through her high school surf team, she began taking photos of friends. Once equipped with water housing, she fell in love with shooting from the water perspective, developed her own style of minimalist photography traveling in Tahiti. "The idea," she said describing her minimalist approach, "is to capture something so simple but so intriguing—something you wouldn't see in the real world."

Smile for the Camera

Many of the women have helped lift each other's boats. Alana Spencer, a woman from the North Shore of Oahu who has shot land and water photography saw that close partnerships—capturing her subjects' uniqueness—made her output valuable far beyond just beautiful images.

Her favorite subject was big-wave rider Sage Erickson. Both love the ocean and being active and have formed a symbiotic friendship that advanced both their careers. "With her being one of the top-ten best female surfers in the world, she gets to travel to some of the most beautiful coastlines on the planet," said Spencer. "Me, being a water photographer, it's a perfect fit to travel with her to some of these places—France, Fiji, Australia and Hawaii."

"Alana constantly inspires me creatively," Erickson responded. "I've never met someone so talented and so quiet and humble about it. Whether it's street style, surf style, island life, cooking, graphic design—or now, watching her photography blossom—it's been incredible to see." Erickson saw the value each received as well. "It works out awesome for me because we are so close. She can document my life in a beautiful way, which I get to share with people online."

"There's a beautiful sisterhood among female surfers, and rather than competing with each other we support each other in the water," agreed Vera Nording, a Swedish photographer who discovered her passion for surfing on a trip to California. "There is uniqueness in the diversity we all share."

That diversity in not only in where the women come from, but what aspects of surf they pursue. Originally from Mexico City, Maria Fernanda Bastidas was a swimming competitor who fell in love with the ocean and the camera. In 2017 she was featured in a *Surfer* magazine issue. Inspired, she continued to document the big wave scene. "I'm just a Mexican water photographer chasing my dreams and shooting big waves," she has said.

Maria Cerdahas spent a good deal of her professional career documenting diversity in women surfers. In 2015 she mounted an exhibition of women surfers from around the globe celebrating International Women's Day, along with Waves of Freedom with over one hundred others at Bird's Surf Shed, the iconic board shop and cultural epicenter in San Diego.

"There is a substantial, undeniable groundswell movement," Cerdahas declared, "rising from within women's surfing that is gaining momentum and visibility." Sarah Lee, from Cronulla, Australia, invested her time into people, places, and situations, never really thinking of about being a "woman in a man's profession," she said. "I think women just need to focus on entertaining their curiosities and cultivating what they love."

From Russia With Surf

Producer, director and author Inna Blokhina entertained those curiosities with a passion. Born in Dresden, Germany, she moved to Moscow to pursue filmmaking and to Hawaii to capture surfers. Her first film *On The Wave* was the first full-length documentary about surfing in Russia and received numerous international awards. *She Is The Ocean*, Blokhina's second and more ambitious project, was filmed around the world and took over six years to make. Starring Keala Kennelly, Andrea Moller and Jeanie Chesser with cameos from Cinta Hansel and Coco Ho, it debuted in 2020 to critical acclaim.

Poetry, Art and Science

"In my photography, I want to present a poetic and ethereal view of the surfing life. I center my work on female subjects as a reflection of my own vision, and as a way to communicate through them." French-born photographer and filmmaker Camille Robiou du Pont based herself in Asia in 2012, eventually settling on a small island in the Philippines. "I find inspiration in nature's poetry—femininity, the ocean and the sky," she said, "and my body of work is a nod to these influences."

Originally from Austria, Karo Krassel started to shoot sports in the snow, until she changed winters for summers, skis for a surfboard and spent time abroad. Moving to Portugal's wild West-Algarve, she refined her voice in water photography. "I love the calmness, fluidity and the beautiful rhythmic dance with the ocean when longboarding," she said. "It's like poetry in motion."

Initially drawn to photography through seemingly opposing passions of art and science, Christina Garneau's technique required capturing precise images and transmitting emotion simultaneously. After finishing her PhD in Biology, the Tofino, British Columbia native spent several years between the mountains and the ocean of the Canadian west coast, finding inspiration and a unique perspective. "It's never too late for a big change of path," she stressed. "I have a doctorate in cancer research but now reside in a quiet ocean town where I do surf, adventure and lifestyle photography full-time. If you continue being open to different things around you, you'll find your path."

Another Tofino-based surfer and lenswoman, Bryana Bradley sees her photography as art. She seeks to capture "the cold Canadian water, the sweet smell of kelp, the many hues of my favorite turquoise and greens, the variation of the silence that accompanies the ocean or the sound of water exploding as surfers paint the canvas."

Across the hemisphere into the northern cold zone, the blistery nor'easters and snowstorms don't draw crowds to New Jersey's beaches. But for Fiona Mullen the waves, light and composition are perfect. With a five millimeter wetsuit, booties and gloves, Mullen walks across the snow-covered sand dunes and swims out through the near freezing waves with her camera in hand. "I would force my mom to drive me down to the beach in time for sunrise whenever there was a big swell," she remembered. "I was obsessed. If I missed documenting even a single swell, it seemed like the end of the world."

At twenty-three Mullen had already accrued a number of international awards and recognition in the surf world for her technical skills. A native of the east coast, Mullen's love for both the winters of the Northeast and the warmth of the tropics had her splitting time between Maui, Amelia Island Florida and the greater New York City area.

Ladyslider

Fashion was a path many surf photographers first started down. Hawaiian photographer/stylist/creative director, Tara Michie's moniker is "Ladyslider," a nod to her smooth style, on land or water. Described as a mix of goofy and cool, her images of female surfers have been highly regarded. "I love working with other really creative people in the industry on creative shoots. It is so inspiring to see other perspectives like makeup artists, models, fellow photographers and stylists," she told friends in a recent interview. There was no pressure to produce anything in particular and personally, "I can take risks with my creative direction, styling, or photo angles. Especially with surfing."

Likewise, Ming Nomchong, an avid surfer, built an international reputation with her feminine and highly emotive fashion and lifestyle images. Raised on the east coast of Australia, Nomchong incorporated surf and fashion in a familiar environment. With her rare combination of edge, nostalgia and style, Nomchong was credited with bringing something fresh to fashion photography.

It Ain't Pretty

Sachi Cunningham's life story carries every twist of a bestselling fictional drama, except her narrative is real—and without a false moment. She is one in a long line of women whose documentation of dangerous settings are often entangled in *their own* heroics, sometimes overshadowing those who they cover.

A pioneer water-photographer at San Francisco's notoriously treacherous Ocean Beach, an award-winning filmmaker and photojournalist with degrees from Brown University and UC Berkeley, she is a valuable female voice in the field of surf storytellers. Her work has taken her from the deserts of Iraq to the shores of the Amazon, to Maui's Jaw's. Her award-winning stories have been screened at festivals worldwide, and on outlets including PBS *Frontline,* the *New York Times,* the *Los Angeles Times* and top surf magazines. A Professor of Multimedia Journalism, she mentors young filmmakers at San Francisco State University and has been included in both *Surfline*'s list of top filmmakers and *Surfer Magazine*'s list of top water photographers.

Surfer magazine executive editor Ashtyn Douglas Rosa contends that Cunningham *changed the narrative* in big wave surf photography. Previously, there was a sense that "women didn't belong in these waves or they weren't strong enough, they weren't capable of it or they weren't ready to compete in these waves," Douglas Rosa says. "But Cunningham was there documenting it."

Nominated for a News & Documentary Emmy Award for New Approaches: Arts, Lifestyle & Culture, she has seen war zones, photographed forty-foot waves, and survived the most intense cancer.

As for the cancer, Cunningham had a powerful source of inspiration for her battle: her Japanese American mother, who was born and raised for four years in a World War II incarceration camp.

"She did it all with such grace, and I think I learned from that," said Cunningham. "But she was never very public about her story, and she died of ovarian cancer. Now that I've gone through it, my goal is to encourage others to look at their medical histories and proactively take care of their physical and mental health."

Cunningham's bold tenacious nature reflects the burgeoning women's big-wave movement she's helped illuminate through her photojournalism. It's a spirit succinctly captured in the closing theme song of *It Ain't Pretty*.

Cunningham discovered she herself had fallopian cancer in July 2016. While undergoing a bilateral mastectomy and total hysterectomy—eight hours of surgery, including breast reconstruction—doctors also diagnosed her with fallopian tube cancer. That meant receiving months of chemotherapy too.

By the time her treatment was finished she'd lost all her hair and endured many days when "everything came crashing down," she said. "Unable to sleep, pain deep in the bones, completely out of it."

We Can't Stop

Cunningham would not be slowed, cancer or no cancer. "My mother instilled this stamina and my father provided patience," Cunningham divulged. "It's a helpful combination." Between treatments, Cunningham shot a huge swell at Mavericks from a boat, took ocean swims at a measured pace and continued work on *SheChange*, a documentary about female big-wave surfers that debuted in June 2016.

Her "partners in crime" as she described her film subjects, became known as the "Outer Bar Babes." They included some of the most respected big-wave riders in the world—Keala Kennelly, Sara Gerhardt, Paige Alms, Justine Dupont, Andrea Moller and Bianca Valenti.

"We call her the 'Honey Badger'," Valenti said, referring to a notoriously fearless wild creature. "She gets so psyched up about being out there in big waves. Nothing's going to stop her."

Success was never sweeter than the *SheChange* project, which seemed almost a culmination of Cunningham's long road toward artistic achievement. But perhaps her proudest achievement was to be named the first person (male or female) in *Surfer* magazine's history to feature water perspective photos that were shot at Ocean Beach.

And even though the obstacles are numerous and the prejudice still strong, Cunningham always took the glass half-full approach:. "I view lack of diversity as an opportunity for growth." Cunningham, who is also a mother of two, has viewed it as two choices: "You can let it frustrate you, or let it fuel your fire to create change. But we can't do it alone. Feminism needs good men in and out of the water. Ultimately, we're all in this together."

Cunningham continued to document the women's big wave movement. She seemed to understand seizing challenge and immediacy—the carpe diem of life—as if she were representing womanhood in all its global splendor. "Survival is part of what I do," she said. "To me this is like an awakening: that I only have one shot in life, and I'm going to go out there more determined than ever."

Early woodcut by romantic French artist E. Riou, which appeared in an 1873 travel anthology titled *Four Years in the Sandwich Isles*. Females of all ages, abilities and classes rode waves in traditional Hawaiian culture. Surfing women were seen as spiritually and physically powerful and commanded great respect in society.

ABOVE: The oldest known standup surfboard in history, circa 1600. This *papa he'e nalu* (Koa wood surfboard) is believed to have been the prize possession of Princess Kaneamuna, a 17th Century Polynesian royal. It had been carefully placed next to her tomb. *Courtesy of the Library of Congress.*
BELOW LEFT: Woodcut image of Hawaiian goddess or queen. Sex, power, pleasure and courtship were intricately intertwined with the act of surfing in the ancient Polynesian culture. And women claimed an equal if not the lion's share of Mother Ocean's sensual, sacred experience. *Courtesy of The California Surf Museum.* BELOW RIGHT: Princess Ka'iulani, heir to the Hawaiian throne. She was an ardent and outstanding surfer. She helped preserved surfing during the period of near extinction, continuing to ride waves against the wishes of the missionaries.

ABOVE: Duke Kahanamoku with surfing friends in Waikiki. All surfers in the early decades of the 20th Century knew Duke. As Hawaii's aloha ambassador, the five-time Olympic medalist was one of modern surfing's earliest first-person observers of women's surfing. LEFT: Esther Williams with her personal bodyboard. She produced a line of wooden bodyboards and rode waves in Santa Monica as a young woman. One of the most famous film stars and water-women of her time, William's swimsuits were popular for decades. *Courtesy of The California Surf Museum.*

Isabel Letham, Freshwater Beach, Sydney, circa 1914. Letham's famous ride with Duke Kahanamoku has become one of Australian lore. She was instrumental in popularizing the sport of surfing in Australia. *Courtesy of The California Surf Museum.*

Faye Baird with surf companion Charlie Wright circa 1926. Baird was San Diego, California's first female surfer, and gave surfing demonstrations in Pacific Beach, sometimes for a crowd of thousands. *Courtesy of The California Surf Museum.*

ABOVE: Agatha Christie with her surfboard in Cape Town, South Africa, 1922. The world's best-selling author was a zealous surfer and one of the first stand-up surfers in British history. BELOW: Agatha Christie, paddling for a wave in Waikiki, circa 1922. She wrote that surfing was "one of the most perfect physical pleasures I have ever known." *Both images courtesy of The California Surf Museum.*

ABOVE: Annette Kellerman portrait, 1907. Kellerman was likely the finest water-women of her era. But became an international sensation when she risked jail to win what was then called "the trial of the century" for women's opportunities and athlete's rights. BELOW: Gidget at Malibu, circa 1958. Kathy Kohner was nicknamed Gidget while surfing Malibu. The book and screenplay written by her father featured thinly disguised surf characters from the era.

ABOVE LEFT: Kathy Kohner surfing Malibu, 1958. Her two summers as an avid Malibu waverider earned her respect from the surfing community. The movie *Gidget* introduced the world to the joys of surfing and Kohner became an iconic figure in surfing culture. ABOVE RIGHT: Mary Ann Hawkins, the 20th Century's first female superstar. Setting the bar in performance for generations to follow, Hawkins won competitions against men and won over mainstream skeptics who challenged her pioneering work in child swimming development. *Courtesy of The California Surf Museum.* BELOW: Women have been challenging big-waves as far back as the late 50s when fifteen-year-old Linda Benson rode an 18-foot wave at Waimea on a borrowed board in 1958. One of the first big superstars of the early 60s, she was the queen of the small-wave performance, a brilliant competitor, a big-wave pioneer and a free-surfing free spirit. Benson was the first female to break the gender barrier when she appeared on the 1963 cover of *Surf Guide* magazine.

ABOVE: Joyce Hoffman, Capo Beach, California, 2014. In the mid-60s, Joyce Hoffman was the most prominent female surf star in the world. She became the first multiple world-title holder, first female state lifeguard, first cross-trainer and the first to ride Pipeline. *Photo by Tom Servais.* BELOW: Rell Sunn, the Queen of Makaha, surfing her home break, 1982. Personifying the aloha spirit of surfing, Native Hawaiian Rell Sunn changed the visibility of women in surfing during the early 70s. *Photo by Jeff Divine.*

Rell Sunn on a trip to Tahiti, 1981. She deeply connected to her culture's values of spirituality in surfing, caring for the ocean and engagement with the community. *Photo by Jeff Divine.*

ABOVE: Candice Woodward, Malibu WISA Pro 1976. Considered the best female surfer in California in her prime, Woodward pioneered the role of professional surfing beyond the competitive realm. *Photo by Jeff Divine.* BELOW: Rell Sunn and Jericho Poppler, 1980. This dynamic duo were the stars of the late 1970s pro circuit road show. *Photo by Jeff Divine.*

Golden Girls. *Left to right:* Debbie Beacham, Jericho Poppler, Candy Woodward, Betty Depolito and Lisa Tomb (kneeling), These women were among the first to develop the image of female surf stars as professional athletes.

Competitors Brenda Scott, Margo Oberg, Linda Davoli, Rell Sunn and Jericho Poppler at the Jose Cuervo surf contest on Hawaii's North Shore, 1980. *Photo by Jeff Divine.*

ABOVE: Frieda Zamba, Huntington Beach, CA, 1984. Hailing from Florida, Frieda Zamba won four World Titles. She set the stage for the string of strong, confident women and was a key link in the chain that connected the East Coast passion to its emerging competitive power. *Photo by Jeff Divine.* BELOW: Margo Oberg, Kauai, 2001. Oberg retired in 1970 having won every major amateur championship, securing a World Title, placing number one in the *Surfer* Poll, pioneering women's big-wave riding and completely dominating four years of global competition—before finishing high school. *Photo by Tom Servais.*

ABOVE: Lynne Boyer, Haleiwa Hawaii, 1981. A two-time World Champion with a fiery red mane and flashing smile, Boyer's style—particularly in big-waves—was groundbreaking. She would execute multiple maneuvers rather than big sweeping power turns. *Photo by Jeff Divine.* BELOW: Debbie Beacham, Haleiwa, Hawaii 1983. A character of unwavering determination she oversaw the Women's Professional Surfing organization moving it forward positively while simultaneously winning a World Title in 1983. *Photo by Jeff Divine.*

RIGHT: Pam Burridge, Sydney, Australia, 1988. Burridge won a World Title in 1990 becoming the first Australian female pro to do so. A protégé of surf icon Isabel Letham, Burridge named her first child Isabel in tribute to her mentor. *Photo by Tom Servais.*
BELOW: Layne Beachley, Lance's Left, Mentawai Islands, Indonesia. One of the most successful female surfers in history, she won an unprecedented seven World Titles and was an outspoken proponent of women in surfing. *Photo by Jeff Divine*

Wendy Botha, Off the Wall, North Shore, Hawaii, 1991. The first great South African surf star, Botha changed her nationality to Australian, and went on to win four World Titles. *Photo by Tom Servais.*

Daize Shayne Goodwin, Pupukea, North Shore, Hawaii, December 1997. A two-time longboard World Champion, Daize created a successful role that included competition, music and modeling, paving the way for many women in surf careers. *Photo by Tom Servais.*

ABOVE: Lisa Andersen, Backdoor Pipeline 1997. A dominant figure in women's surfing in the 90s, Andersen is credited with helping design and popularize women's boardshorts and for raising the bar for performance surfing. *Photo by Tom Servais*. LEFT: Lisa Andersen, Backdoor, North Shore Hawaii, 1999. She won the *Surfer* Poll award six times and was named one of the "25 Most Influential Surfers of all Time." *Sports Illustrated* also named her one of the "Top Female Athletes of the 20th Century." *Photo by Tom Servais*.

Lisa Andersen, *Surfer* magazine Photo Annual cover, Sabastian Inlet, Florida, 1996. From 1994 through 1997 she won four consecutive world crowns. In 1996, she was the first female in fifteen years to be featured on the cover of *Surfer* magazine. *Photo by Tom Dugan.*

Layne Beachley at the ASP banquet receiving one of her multitude of world trophies, 2001. *Photo by Tom Servais.*

ABOVE: Pauline Menczer, ASP Banquet, December 1999. *Photo by Tom Servais.* BELOW: Pauline Menczer, Jefferey's Bay, South Africa. Menczer won the World Title while suffering from acute arthritis. Her courage and pluck made her a beloved icon among her peers in the surf world. *Photo by Tom Servais.*

ABOVE: Stephanie Gilmore in the channel at Cloudbreak, at the Fiji Pro, 2016. A seven-time World Title holder, she is tied with Layne Beachley for the most championships in women's surf history. *Photo by Tom Servais*. BELOW: *Blue Crush* cast, including stunt work surfers, 2002. *Top Row:* Megan Abubo, Michelle Rodriguez, Layne Beachley, Rochelle Ballard, Kate Bosworth. *Kneeling:* Sanoe Lake, Kate Skarratt, Keala Kennelly. The film is credited with creating a huge boom in women's participation in surfing.

Sofia Mulanovich, Namotu Lefts, Fiji, May 2002. The first great female surf star from South America, the Peruvian-born World Champion is an iconic figure in her native country. *Photo by Tom Servais.*

ABOVE: Kelia Moniz, Pupukea, Hawaii, 2010. Learning to ride waves at surfing's birthplace at Queen's Waikiki, Moniz is the only daughter in a storied surf family. A two-time World Longboard Champion, she is considered the most likely woman to take the mantle of aloha into surfing's future. *Photo by Tom Servais.* BELOW: Carissa Moore, backside slash at Cloudbreak during the Fiji Pro, 2016. Moore's outstanding performances are only matched by her level of enthusiasm and kindness of spirit. *Photo by Tom Servais.*

ABOVE: Tyler Wright, Tavarua, Fiji, 2018. Openly gay and popular on the World Tour, Tyler Wright fought through serious injuries and tragedy to win two World Titles. *Photo by Tom Servais.* BELOW: Brazilian-born Maya Gabeira won the XXL Big Wave Awards five times and, in 2020, rode the largest wave by a man or woman.

The Medea of Media

Surf Journalism and its Feminine Quandary

"Led by a new generation of edgy sportswriters, we found new purpose in the great issues of the day—race, equal opportunity, drugs, and labor disputes. We became personality journalists, medical writers and business reporters."
—Jane Leavy, award-winning sportswriter
for the *Washington Post*

History is Written by the Victors— And the Victors Were Men

The myth of Medea demonstrates the masculine power of the pen—and how male media produces prejudice in written history.

The granddaughter of the Sun God Helios, Medea was a strong, quick-thinking enchantress in her original role in Greek mythology. Her divine descent gave her the gift of prophecy. Marrying Jason—leader of the adventuring Argonauts—she put her magic to work. As partner in his quest, Medea skillfully overcame each obstacle, piloting Jason through the shoals of the Aegean Sea and yoking the fire-breathing oxen. Her strategies defeated an army of warriors and slayed the sleepless guardian dragon, finally leading him to the fabled Golden Fleece. Wily, ruthless and faithful, she not only stood by her man, she outperformed him.

But as storytelling moved from ancient androgyny to a masculine hero complex, viewpoints changed. Medea's infamous "hell has no fury like a women scorned" image came not only much later in Greek culture but in an extended version beyond her original legend. Influential Athenian playwright Euripides wrote his version of Medea—shrinking the legendary female's story to a later era in a different region (Corinth)—and focusing on a shocking act of infanticide.

"Much of this play is about men's images of women," wrote Classic's professor Shirley Barlow in 1989.

The Greeks were nothing if not complex, and Medea's story is far more intricate and her multi-faceted character far more fascinating. And as it evolved from Greek to Roman to French literature, Medea began to be viewed by modern critics as similar to the mythic male heroes Odysseus, Achilles and Hercules—ruthless, prideful and without mercy. From that viewpoint Medea can be seen as a revolutionary, resisting tyranny. Betrayed, exiled, threatened, her vengeance could be considered defensive—refusing to allow her woman's identity to be destroyed by society's dictates and defying the male dominance of her culture.

The 21st Century thankfully forced no such tragic decision on women. But the writers, editors and publishers of women's surf media were perhaps every bit as proud and persistent in their effort to present surfing's story from a female perspective.

Finding Their Voice

The first women's *Surf* magazine was a coming of age saga.

Marilyn Edwards and Elizabeth Glazner met after the death of their best friend who had always told them they should meet one another. At her memorial they did. Becoming friends in mutual mourning, Edwards took Glazner surfing for the first time. Their healing process and the joy of surf bonded them both as friends and compatriots.

Early in their friendship both could see the conspicuous void in women's surf magazines. They were not the only observers of the latent demand. But they were the first to act on it.

In 1994, they cofounded *Wahine,* the first successful periodical for female surfers distributed on newsstands across the globe.

Neither had any real money, but the passion was insuperable.

"I sold my 1964 vintage 356 Porsche to put the ink on the first printing," recalled Edwards of *Wahine*'s 1995 debut issue.

"We started this with no market research, just on a hunch," said Glazner. "We weren't supposed to be in business. We were an independent quarterly."

Neither had experience with publishing—or the insider world of the surf industry. What they *did* have was a trove of talent and an indomitable spirit. Glazner had studied art at New York School of Visual Arts and had a journalism degree from Fullerton College in California. She had worked and was editing for a newspaper in Santa Clara California. "Elizabeth was an incredible artist," Edwards said. "But most importantly she had be a journalist for ten years." Edwards was a dedicated surfer, speech pathologist, marathon runner and entrepreneurial risk-taker uncowed by the daunting challenge. She had often been woken by her dad as a child, carried affectionately downstairs and dumped in the pool—pajamas and all. Edwards *loved* it.

Converting Edwards's small speech pathology offices in Naples, California, into the *Wahine* headquarters, Glazner frenziedly built the audience and content while Edwards developed database programs to operate booming subscriptions and advertiser account programs. With their graphic designer Sheri Fournier they worked often till two in the morning, introduced to making magazines in a trial by fiery commitment. "We learned the literary and the *literal* maelstrom of publishing," declared Edwards. "Our passion and drive was motivating all of it."

Debuted to huge fanfare *Wahine*'s launch celebration was held at the International Surf Museum in Huntington Beach at the conclusion of the 2004 U.S. Open of Surfing. The magazine was popular from the moment of its unveiling. Published quarterly, *Wahine* quickly cultivated a following, eventually building a circulation of 30,000–40,000. Filled with a pent-up trove of content, the magazine was considered a leader in female sports publications of the time.

But it was not without unanticipated struggle. "We thought we would be embraced by the industry," Edwards noted. But there was an almost unconscious prejudice toward us—definitely related to our feminine nature. Like Medea, after assisting in paving a path to the "golden fleece" of the women's market, they were surprisingly met in some quarters with scorn and hostility. Twice sued over the name *Wahine*, they were castigated for not kowtowing to the advertisers and disdained by the established surf publications. Humility and perseverance prevailed,

An invitation to be included for a Women in Athletics exhibition at the Smithsonian Institute in Washington, D.C., was an unexpected high point, clearly illuminating the legacy they were documenting, issue by struggling issue.

"It made us understand our place in history," said Edwards. "Not so much our financial success, but our impact on the culture."

"We should have been long gone," said Glazner. "But we not only survived—we've thrived. We were in the black."

While the profitability of any periodical is tenuous, the economic volatility of the action sports industry took its toll. Then came the crisis of 9/11.

"We just lost too many advertisers in one swoop," recalled Edwards. "You can survive ups and downs but not a crash." The drop-off in ad revenue finally pushed the Long Beach, California-based mag to close its doors after a glory-filled seven year run.

Wahine published twenty-three issues and one special edition in its eight years of circulation. A visionary and passionate editor, Glazner's content "led women's surfing out of the dark ages and created an authentic brand for girls' surf, skate, snow."

"We're grateful to have been able to provide such a unique marketing venue, particularly for the smaller women-owned companies," said publisher Edwards, whose spirituality mixed with her business structure.

Dedicated and unflappable, Glazner went on to serve as editorial director for Plastic Pollution Coalition, a global alliance working to end single-use disposable plastics, and she moved to Bishop, California where she continued as a freelance writer, and volunteer at the animal rescue center.

Edwards continued her speech pathology practice, helping hundreds of troubled patients learn to speak and communicate.

"We were the first and the longest-lasting publication for women's surfing," Edwards mused. "And the whole progression of the women's movement in surfing is chain-linked together. Every movement is a crusade to raise consciousness. I think that's what *Wahine* may have started." Rarely are trailblazers recognized in their own era. But their impact would be seen as a milestone for women surf media even decades later.

Sitting On Top of the World

On Sunday evening February 4, 2001—with a waxing moon four days from full—*Surfing GIRL* magazine celebrated the publication of its first independent newsstand issue at the Sky Room in Long Beach, California. Filled with female surf stars, new advertisers, media moguls and surfing publications staff, the chic affair was a salute to the new feminine demand, waxing as brightly as the earth's only natural satellite. The moon's pull had created a surging late winter high tide, as if to mark the rising energy pulling toward the feminine audience.

Riding the nonstop penthouse elevator fifteen floors above the lights of the Long Beach Harbor aside party goers to the swanky top floor Sky Room bar, ingenue journalist Alison Berkley could not ignore the striking analogy that women's surfing had also reached new heights.

The concept of including women in *Surfing* magazine started three years prior in the form of a small swimsuit preview insert, a la *Sports Illustrated*. The initial content seemed targeted toward males; a collection of attractive women mostly posing in bikinis. The decision in a 1998 issue to use real surfers as models, helped turn the appeal toward women.

"I remember that issue well, because I dissected it, cut out every photo I could salvage and used it to make a collage that I put under the piece of glass that covered my desktop," Alison Berkley recalled. "I studied those photos every day for more than a year and took them out only because I had to move offices."

Enter Kai Stearns, a "firecracker of an editor" teaming up with other *Surfing* staffers who wanted to see *Surfing GIRL* become more than a swimsuit parade. Instead of packaging the girl's mag with the regular issue of *Surfing* magazine only four times a year, *Surfing GIRL* became available on the newsstand and to subscribers as its own independent bimonthly publication.

"Kai was one of those rare creatures who can balance humility with confidence—aggressive without being too abrasive," Berkley observed. "She was charming and knew how to get her way without being manipulative. Mostly, she had patience of steel and a sense of humor to match."

Swell.com was just getting started and its California offices were across the street from *Surfing* in San Clemente. Berkley was hired as the women's editor. "I would trot over there to check out photos or seek advice on various obstacles I'd run into trying to represent women's surfing against the odds. She could have charged me a therapist's fee for all the reassurance she gave me when I first started as women's editor," Berkley admitted. Schooled in the personalities of various pros, photographers and challenges of the mentality of the surfing world, Stearns became an invaluable resource. "She would warn me about this or that," Berkley confessed, "and whether I chose to listen or not, Kai was *always right.*"

Stearns helped take *Surfing GIRL* from a thin, once-a-year insert to a 130-page independent magazine. "By helping to give women's surfing a place on the newsstand, she helped give women's surfing a place, period," declared Berkley. Or in Stearns's own words: "It's the ultimate statement to all the naysayers who've put down women's sports in general and surfing specifically. In its very being, it contains the spirit of every person who's had to say, 'Alright then. I'll do it on my own.' It reflects not only the growth of our industry, but a substantial shift in the nation's consciousness. Finally, girl power really means something."

Both *Wahine* and *Surfing GIRL* pioneered the women's media. Success may have been fleeting but their impact is indisputable.

"It's strange to think it was only two years ago that photos of female surfers were so rare that I felt the need to preserve them under glass," Berkley said at the time. "Now I'll have enough material to poster *all four walls* if I want."

Pens and Needlers

Womens' demand for surf content was becoming inescapable. In a reversal of the usual scenario, *SurferGirl* began as a website in December, 1996, then became a print magazine. When creators Jennifer Ramsay and Pat Villyard informed web surfers they intended to create a print magazine, subscription orders began to pour in, some from as far inland as Dubuque, Iowa—for a magazine that didn't even *exist.*

They quickly realized they had met a need when surfers began dropping in on their website more than a million times a month.

Ramsay, just twenty-three, was an archetypical surfer girl, raised on Long Island, with a brother and a boyfriend who surfed. She was a lifeguard who viewed wave-riding as a male domain. Her attitude changed when Ramsay moved to Santa Cruz, a bonified surfing epicenter.

Publishing began in a tiny three-room office, crammed with Macintosh computer equipment, page layouts taped to the walls and an ocean view. A crew of six scurried from room to room, pausing often to dispel deadline stress with jokes and laughter.

Worries that they might not have enough material to fill a magazine every other month were quickly wiped out by a tsunami of stories and photos.

At the turn of the century the youth sports market was growing exponentially, particularly for women. Globally, corporations were in a mergers and acquisitions frenzy, gobbling up brands like the *Pacman* video game. Magazines became a prime target and surf media was seen as a hot sexy new consumer audience. *Surfer* and *Surfing* magazines merged, and the publications were bought and sold several times in the space of a few years. In the process *Surfing GIRL* was retitled *SG* to encompass the growing women's market various boardsports, broadening both the readership and the advertising base.

For *SG*'s editor Robyn Lass, the goal was "to continue to grow the sports of surfing, snowboarding and skateboarding. "Robin was a classically-trained journalist and a good surfer and snowboarder to boot," recalled Norb Garrett, the head of the *Surfer* magazine group at the time. "Robin and the publisher Alex Ota—who was also a women with strong business chops—had a very successful title with a huge creative presentation." Dedicated to providing coverage of professional and amateur female athletes in all three disciplines, the *SG* title debuted in October of 2002. A later editor, Melinda Larson, carried the magazine forward for several more years.

In 2002, Anne Beasley introduced *Surf Life for Women*. Beasley had been at the forefront of women's surfing for five years as the President of the East Coast Wahine Championships, and as editor in chief, felt she knew the audience she was aiming to please.

Working alongside Beasley was photo editor, Debra Colvin, whose images were published in all major surf publications, and reporters Katy Clark and Lauren Makarow, both avid surfers and skilled wordsmiths. *Surf Life for Women*'s publisher, Sunshine Makarow, was a member of the United States Surf Team from 1999 to 2001. The magazine lasted three years as a quarterly publication with a subscription base that was a little over 3,000 and a total circulation of 30,000 which included a mixed bag of subscribers, newsstand circulation and promotional circulation.

The English passion for literature is only matched by their zeal for all things surf—a good combination for Louise Searle, the editor of *SurfGirl* magazine an international surf and beach lifestyle magazine and website based on the Cornish coast. Along with serving as production manager for *Carve* magazine Searle was the editor of *The Surf Cafe Cookbook*, *The Surf Girl Handbook*, *The Surf Girl Fitness Guide*, and *Surf Cafe Living*. *SurfGirl* was the first independent magazine for Women's surfing in the UK.

Another publication, *Women's Surf Style* magazine, based in Honolulu, Hawaii, offered issues free in Hawaii, but held a paid subscription fee for readers around the globe. Editor Sandra Olson founded the publication in 2003 and operated it for more than two decades.

Some ocean eyes were able see the world around them with a different lens. Founded in 2006, based in New Zealand, and obsessed with women's surfing, *Curl* magazine's editor Lynne Dickinson offered advice to up and coming surfers on every aspect of surfing from 'how-to's' to competitions. *Curl*'s 2020 February issue was voted Magazine Cover of the Year by the prestigious Maggie awards, an international media group similar to the Oscars for film.

Pictures to Burn

Cooler magazine made its way around Europe as a hybrid surf/snow/skate women's edition for girls back in 2005, edited by Samantha Haddad.

Nina Zietman—the editor in 2015—wanted to inspire and encourage women to get outside and explore the outdoors. Essentially British in flavor and run by London publishing house Factory Media, it remains a relevant magazine in the 2020s.

While women's magazine's struggled for advertising, their audiences were loyal and dedicated, supporting them with a passion bordering on fanaticism. Running since 2006, online magazine *JettyGirl* covered the California lifestyle. Editor Chris Grant, one of the few males to produce media exclusive to women, focused on website development and in 1998 his enthusiasm for web design and photography merged with the creation of *Boardfolio.com: The Surfer's Directory*.

Surfer publications tried their hand at the female market too, and like the other men's surf publications, with varying degrees of success. *Salted*—Surfer's vision of an all-girls magazine—hit the newsstands in August of 2012. *Salted*'s editor Janna Irons was perhaps destined to be a set of sharp ocean eyes observing surfing. With seven older brothers she came from a storied surf family: Her father Jim and Uncle Phil moved to Hawaii in the 60s, Phil taking a job at Clark foam and siring her cousins three-time World Champion Andy Irons and his Eddie big-wave winner brother Bruce. *Surfer* Publisher and industry stalwart Rick Irons was also a cousin.

Her mother designed the graphics of George Greenough's cult surf film *The Innermost Limits of Pure Fun*, one of the truly influential photographic breakthroughs of surf cinematography. Inevitably, Irons herself took a position as Assistant Editor at *Surfer* in 2007 and later as the editor of the short-lived but much-adored women's surf magazine.

What Youth, a web-based, infrequently published in print magazine followed *Surfer* into the women's market—*again* with mixed results, not for any lack of female creative talent. *Herewith* (their print and digital women's surf magazine) helped several surf media talents elevate their careers.

Serena Lutton moved from the Basque region of France to the Newport Beach area in Southern California and was immediately drafted as the creative director for the Herewith media group. "Being close to the water opens your mind and gives perspective," Lutton observed. "I bought my first camera at the age of twelve and started to organize photoshoots with my friends. I'd buy clothes on the day of the shoot and then take them back to the shop the next day. It was fun!"

Born and raised on Oahu's North Shore, Tahnei Roy, another *Herewith* staff member, bought her first video camera and a water housing at thirteen. With Hawaii's pristine environment as a backdrop she began taking photographs and making short films. In 2011, she moved to Southern California to play water polo and swim competitively. "A couple years later, I transferred to film school to pursue my passion toward cinematography and photography." After graduating with a Bachelors in Film and Video Production, "I worked full time for *Herewith* as their online editor and videographer. In mid–2017 she decided to branch off, creating her own digital freelance company.

Commentators, Critics, and Chroniclers

Some eyes are about seeing the field of battle and capturing stories from heroines who engage in their combat. Often the best observers are those who have been in the line of fire themselves. Reared in East London, Rosy Hodge learned to surf at Queensbury Bay, where giraffes, zebra and an occasional lion might trespass on the sweeping lawns surrounding her parent's home. A widely-viewed youtube clip captured two Great White sharks attacking a friend on the righthand point in front of her house as she watched from the deck.

Rosy was also present when Greg Emslie, the former South African professional, was charged, bumped and circled by a four-meter Great White.

"I ran home crying and hid in a corner cradling myself," she confessed. These experiences gave Hodge a constant unsettled feeling, even when she's many thousands of nautical miles from her home country (Hodge admitted she has the

Great White tracking app on her telephone). She declined surf sessions when the sardines run at her home beach no matter how good the waves might be.

Hodge broke into the World Championship Tour at fifteen winning the Roxy Pro in Fiji, and enjoyed what she described as "some success." Fast forward a few years and Rosy found herself in Hawaii at the end of 2010, knocked off the tour and reassessing. Serendipitously she received a call from Kate Bain (WSL Producer who was working for Roxy at the time.) Bain asked Hodge to commentate at the upcoming Roxy Pro on the Gold Coast. Hodge suddenly saw another career pathway. She only too readily agreed.

Hodge quickly found herself commentating at multiple events that year. It wasn't all easy, but the tall, engaging South African relished the work. When the new WSL took over the events, she was offered a full time role.

"It's so much fun!," Hodge divulged in 2020. "Getting to travel and surf and have the whole experience without the stress of competing is awesome." She didn't mind missing the surf—even when it was good—preferring the microphone to the contest jersey.

On camera her conversational style was distinctive; her signature dimpled-smile disarming. Endearing traits of humility and grace connected her to the athletes as well as thousands of fans around the world. But her ability to draw out the stories kept her in the forefront of her second career.

The task of being an honest critic was another set of characteristics—but required an equal amount of talent. The explosion of women's surf media, initially a great thing, since it was by women for women, now also fed into the competitiveness and spiraled down on the issue of conventional beauty in competitive surfing/sponsorships. The internet meanwhile, was metastasizing every issue that women had been dealing with since the 50s, whether it was body dysmorphia or misogyny.

Despite opportunities in the media due to the growing female audience, the tough issues regarding women in surfing often still went unanswered. When asked in 2012 about the current state of women's surfing Darlene Conolly—who at twenty-one, conceived and managed Surfline.com's women's section for several notable years—divulged that "the infighting, eating disorders, and competing to be 'the whole package' has created this horrible, insular environment in the competitive scene." Then the even more worrisome statement came: "It is much worse than it used to be."

Connelly studied for a Master's of Social Work degree, but her social skills appeared instinctive.

"I remember Darlene had strong writing skills and a fantastic grasp of surfing and surf culture," said Dave Gilovich, the Executive Vice President at *Surfline*. "Great surfer, too. She came with us on a trip to Tavarua with her dad and she ripped!"

Talented and committed, she was at *Surfline* from the time she was twenty-one years old; involved in the entire process—writing and editing, picking and editing photos, managing the budget, determining the site's content "and a whole slew of other technical, boring tasks." The position enabled her to travel all over the globe and work with the world's best surfers, male and female alike.

After leaving *Surfline*, Conolly was offered a "women in surfing" retrospective in *TransWorld Surf* magazine. The piece was considered a landmark. "I opened the story by writing, 'This is my suicide letter,'" she recalled. "And it basically was. I don't write about women's surfing anymore. There are too many harsh realities about the industry that you simply must suppress if you want to succeed. I'd had enough of it and wanted to do something completely different with my life, but *TransWorld* was an opportunity to tell a slightly more in-depth, but still censored, story of the world of women's surfing."

Despite the frustration of the gender conflicts, Conolly saw the editor experience positively. "I basically transitioned from childhood into adulthood under Surfline's watch," she fondly remembered, "and it was the opportunity of a lifetime."

You Are the Camera

Chroniclers of surfing are rare and an even rarer few see the future. When Andrea Gabbard wrote *Girl in the Curl* at the turn of the millennium, she could not have guessed it would be the definitive history book on women's surfing for more than two decades. Although other works were published over the period they were either more narrow in subject or less serious in the treatment of the topic. When critically-acclaimed singer/songwriter Julia Hatfield wrote the intimate lyrics to "You Are the Camera" for her 1998 album *Bed*, she would have been putting down those words at the very same time Gabbard was penning her women's surf opus, becoming not just the camera but the image creator of women's surfing over the next twenty years.

Gabbard grew up surfing the California coast and hiking the Sierra Nevada Mountains, becoming an expert student of the lifestyle. Authoring *Da Bull* in 1989, the biography of Greg Noll, surfing's most colorful big-wave rider, she also served as a contributing editor to *Outdoor Retailer* magazine. An avid mountain aficionado as well, Gabbard wrote *Mountaineering: A Woman's Guide* and the best-selling *Lou Whittaker: Memoirs of a Mountain Guide*.

Although Gabbard's tome was the most comprehensive, other women surf writers contributed to the library of surf literature in more specific spheres. Women's books covered memoir, wanderlust, wave history, coming-of-age, mid-life angst, and even social studies into the intricate cultural conflicts for female surfers.

In *The Wave: In Pursuit of the Rogues, Freaks, and Giants of the Ocean* Susan Casey explored ancient mythology, recent natural disasters, and scientific research, introducing readers to the cast of characters who have dedicated their lives to surfing the world's largest, wildest, and most dangerous waves.

Chasing Waves: A Surfer's Tale of Obsessive Wandering by Amy Waeschle was a memoir of her journeys around the world, written beautifully about the art, athleticism and her obsession with surfing.

Similarly, *That Oceanic Feeling*, Fiona Capp's part surf biography/part travel memoir/part autobiography of a woman approaching the middle of her life, presented the challenge of choosing to rediscover her greatest passions all over again.

Known first as a pro surfer Nicole Grodesky worked hard to receive recognition for her photography. After graduating from Cal State University Fullerton in 2009, she revisited competition, but her photos and writing took prime position. "Surfers are interesting global citizens," Grodesky observed. "In search of waves, surfers live in the 'in between spaces' of continents, choosing to be untouched by politics that land ownership and borders impose on us."

Published in all the major surf magazines, her photography was exhibited at The Surf Indian Gallery, Gallery 104, The Huntington Beach Surf Museum, The California Surf Museum and the Surfing Heritage Museum.

Although oceanic adventurer Audrey Sutherland wasn't a die-hard surfer, *Paddling My Own Canoe*—her kayak journey along the coasts of Hawaii's most untouched of islands—resonated with female wilderness adventurers everywhere. Her son Jock and grandson Gavin are surfers of the highest caliber, world class in every way.

Some books became hits. In 2005, Izzie and Coco Tihanyi released what was dubbed as the nation's best-selling surf book, *Surf Diva: A Girl's Guide to Getting Good Waves*. Well-received critically it was aimed at their target market of young women entering the sport.

One of the few novels to find their way into the surfing genre, *The Tribes of Palos Verdes* was Joy Nicholson's intimate look into one of surfing's most thorny social milieus—and a *Blue Velvet*-like underbelly view of the cultural complexities. Translated to the silver screen in 2017, it was loosely based on the infamous Lunada Bay Boys and Nicholson's own life after moving to the fabled peninsula of surf.

From Vans Warped Tour pit reporter to CNN fact checker, Shelby Stanger has had a wide range of job experiences. An award-winning writer, producer, and podcast host, she covered the action sports field in the first decades of the 21st Century for ESPN, *Outside* and major surf magazines as well as a stint with the iconic shoe brand, Vans. Her contributions to *Shop Eat Surf* the business journal of surfing, were the work of a tireless and genial journalist.

In 2016, Stanger created Wild Ideas Worth Living, an REI-sponsored podcast show featuring interviews with world-class adventurers, authors, scientists, athletes, health experts and explorers. A life-long surfer, she served as a valued board member and volunteer for Outdoor Outreach, a non-profit that helps empower at-risk kids.

For esteemed feminist Krista Comer, surfing wasn't just a physical sport—it was also political. In *Surfer Girls in the New World Order,* a landmark work on the subject, Comer explored what it means to be a girl in surfing: the stereotypes, the expectations, the portrayal of surfer girls in pop culture, the rise of women-run surfing businesses and the ever-increasing rise of girls dominating in a sport once practiced primarily by men. Her well-researched volume spotlighted a corner of the world where women came, saw and conquered.

Perhaps the most recognized—at least to the millennial generation, who watched her story repeatedly on the Disney channel—was Bethany Hamilton's *Soul Surfer: A True Story of Faith, Family, and Fighting to Get Back on the Board,* an inspiring tribute to faith and determination.

New Rules

The Global View

2010–2020

"I haven't been everywhere, but it's on my list."

—Susan Sontag

Surfless in Gaza

With warm sunshine, light offshore winds, plentiful waves, and white sand beaches that stretch for miles, this shoreline could be mistaken for Northern Baja, in Mexico.

But the Gaza Strip is no Baja California. The Palestinian coast of Israel is known as a powder keg of Middle East tensions. At the borders visitors pass through military checkpoints to enter Gaza. Overhead, Israeli drones often buzz above piles of rubble from decades of conflict.

Despite the virtual wartime environment Gaza's twenty-five-mile Mediterranean coast developed a vibrant local surf scene. It's most prominent surfer was a young woman who many considered the best talent in the region. Sabah Abu Ghanim, who started surfing at age five, was featured in a 2016 German documentary called *Gaza Surf Club*, about the surfers in Palestinian.

But shortly afterward she quit the sport at seventeen under pressure from her parents. After completing high school, and withdrawing from surfing, she spent most of her days at home, inside a simple cinderblock house, with eleven relatives, waiting as her parents arranged her marriage.

"We're religious Muslims," her mother Sabrine Abu Ghanim asserted. "Sabah's future is up to her future husband."

Although more opportunities are available for Palestinian women than in many other parts of the Middle East only a handful play competitive sports.

Gaza's conservative society—run by the Islamist party Hamas—imposes strict limitations on women's roles in many traditional families like the Ghanim's. A few years previous, an older sister stopped surfing soon after she too was married.

Sabah dreamed of teaching others to surf. But she moved inland to be with her husband.

"When girls are young, nobody objects. In fact, I taught them to surf," her father, Rajad Abu Ghanim said. A lifeguard and boat repairman, he was an avid surfer himself before an injuring his legs. He spent three months' saved wages to buy a secondhand surfboard from Israel for the family's use. "But as Sabah matures," he said "it's just no longer appropriate."

Privately, Sabah disagreed: "I wish I could go back to being a child," she confessed. "That's when I felt most free—surfing."

Can't Stop Fighting

As the 21st Century entered its second decade, women's issues became a global focus. The anarchic power-pop of Sheer Mag's pointedly political "Can't Stop Fighting" began with lead singer Christina Halladay's righteous voice; its lyrics referencing the hundreds of unsolved murders in Ciudad Juarez, where poor, working-class Mexican women had historically been targeted on their way to and from the maquiladoras, the manufacturing factories that are primarily staffed by those women. The killers were rarely identified, and almost never convicted.

But for the first time they did not go unchallenged. The interconnectivity of the global village aided progressive protest statements like these, infiltrating cultures everywhere.

Commended by many for its female empowerment themes, English pop star Dua Lipa's 2017 number one hit "New Rules," was the most streamed song of the decade by a female artist, with 169.9 million plays in the UK, and is the fourth biggest song overall, including its 245,000 downloads.

In this environment the possibilities for women surfers—particularly in the less-developed nations—started to break boundaries deemed impossible only two decades before. Surfing, like radio, rode an international wave of female enthusiasm.

In 2016 a squad of Vanuatu's best girl surfers travelled to Australia for the Surfest High Schools Challenge in Newcastle. In the most remote region of Oceana, this tiny archipelago in the Coral sea, a new organization had formed—Vanuatu Surfing Association, aimed to give their young surfers more contest experience, a springboard for continued success in the sport. For women's surfing on a global scale, this group's journey from a distant corner of the southern hemisphere was a historic moment. Association secretary Stephanie Mahuk saw what a great opportunity it was for the squad: "The objective was to bring as many female members as possible." It was an *undisputed success.*

In the aftermath, Solwota Sista was conceived from the Vanuatu Surfing Association's vision: encouraging and promoting the sport of surf among girls and women in Vanuatu communities who were previously absent from the lineup. Charley Donchos, Marine Cugola, Zaridah Toleo, and Serah John were among the first top performers.

For Serah John it fulfilled a proud legacy of her own. Her grandmother, the late Katleen John from Pango village was the legendary "Grandmother of surfing" in Vanuatu, hosting many traveling surfers and encouraging the nascent sport among the local children.

Solwota Sisters and the Vanuatu Surfing Association challenged the community to accept surfing as a sport suitable for girls and women. Gender disparities—particularly the cultural view of a women's role, and the access to opportunities based on these views—were clearly visible across the surfing scene. The goal was to create a safe and inclusive community of girls around Vanuatu who had a special connection to the ocean and would be committed to gender equality and safeguarding the environment. Samantha Suendermann, a professional surfer who in 2016 headed the women's development program for Solwota Sista in Sierra Leone summed up what he viewed as the future: "It is a slow progression," she said. "But *the irresistible joy of surfing is changing the world.*"

Diversity issues were not limited to those far from the surfing capitals of the globe. Other collaborations occurred, some more visceral, some more academic: In Spain, Valeria Kechichian—the director of Longboard Girl's Crew—created an international longboard community in Madrid in 2010. Argentinian-born, Kechichian proclaimed their purpose as "aiming to get more girls and women into the sport and changing the way we've been portrayed and perceived, by society and ourselves." By 2020 Kechichian's Crew was considered the world's largest action-sports community, with 240,000 Facebook followers and representatives in 70 countries.

Formation

Few pop culture moments integrated like the 2016 anthem "Formation" and the formation of the black women's community in surfing. Beyoncé's two great obsessions—love and power—combined on her personal-is-political masterpiece "Formation," a defiant celebration of black womanhood. Dense with references to Hurricane Katrina, racist policing and the resilience of black society, the song's debut was followed a day later by dancers in Black Panther berets flanking Beyoncé at the 2016 Super Bowl performance. Released early in a year when overt racism and misogyny bum-rushed American politics, "Formation" remains the radical apex of a sui generis career.

As if carried by the energy of that music, ethnic women entering the sport "carved out a space for themselves in the surf world, helping to belie the notion that "surfing is just a White sport."

Forming in the same time as Beyoncé's album, Black Girl Surf and Brown Girl Surf added some long-needed diversity to the surf lineup. Rhonda Harper, founder of Black Girl Surf was at the forefront of that movement. An avid surfer since the 80s, Harper set out on a quest: to train the next generation of professional Black surfers. The inspiration had come when the Africa Surf International contest in Sierra Leone fell short of African female participants. Harper realized the surf world was lacking Black women—and she wanted to change that. In a small decision with long-lasting effects, she chose to help those who wanted to compete on a professional level. Harper already had a solid success story. She coached Senegalese surfer Khadjou Sambe, for the opportunity to represent her country at the Summer Olympics in Tokyo. It was a template for expansion—and success.

"I'm excited every time I see a new face or a new organization that specializes in getting the next generation in the water," Harper told Zora Media in 2020.

Lack of diversity in the sport prompted Brown Girls Surf to form for the same reason. Founder Farhana Huq noticed women like herself rarely appeared in mainstream surf media. "In 2010, if you Googled 'women of color surfing,' very little came up," said Mira Manickam-Shirley, executive director and cofounder of Brown Girl Surf.

Manickam-Shirley and Huq linked up, creating a community surf club emphasizing women of color surfers. Another achievement was made by their efforts: breaking barriers and defying stereotypes and—perhaps most importantly—providing—for perhaps the first time—a place for them in the surf community.

One of the BGS volunteers, Jamila Hubbard, declared that "imagination was the most attractive thing" about surfing—and the most important thing for entering its world: "While there may be financial or logistical barriers, one of the most powerful is the 'imaginative barrier," contended Hubbard. "Can you imagine yourself doing this? For many in our community, surfing is not something they could imagine themselves doing until something shifted. And a lot of time that shift has to do with *representation*," she emphasized. "As our community grows, we don't have to rely on gatekeepers to let us in." Suddenly they were making a difference.

Mexico's *Maestra*

Making a difference was a reoccurring theme of the era. In 2014 artist, filmmaker and longtime Baja surf traveler Elizabeth Pepin Silva produced the award-winning film about a strong Latinx role model Mayra Agulair. A teacher in a tiny rural fishing village in Baja, Mexico, she became the first Mexican woman surfer in her area. Through surfing, her deep connection to the ocean turned Agulair into an ardent environmentalist, teaching her students the importance of land and sea stewardship through hands on learning.

In the film, Mayra talks about the amazing surfing waves in her town—a gift of nature that has brought thousands of gringo surfers to the area over the years, forever changing Agulair's hometown in both positive and negative ways. In this regard, the film is also a subtle commentary on the impact outsider surf tourists can have on small communities around the globe and the need for all of us to be mindful of taking care of the environment, no matter where we are. "*La Maestra* (*The Teacher*) is a continuation of my efforts through my films and photography to change the way all women are portrayed in the media," Silva declared in a 2014 interview. Over time Silva worked to "create an alternative voice in surfing by pointing my video and photo lenses at women surfers of all ethnicities and backgrounds, ages, and sizes and shapes."

Native American Waverider

On the North Shore in 1980, Dina Gilio-Whitaker was one of the few women surfing Pipeline. "Was I well-received? Hell no. It was intimidating," related Whitaker.

Surfer, scholar, author, activist and teacher Whitaker was born a Native American of the Colville Confederated Tribes but moved to Hawaii on her own to study and surf, meeting a lanky surfer living on the North Shore. Eventually, she left Hawaii for academic life on the mainland, far from the ocean's waves. By 2009, the surfer-scholar was in New Mexico, deep in her studies of Indigenous culture—and reconnecting to her own Native identity. Out of the blue, Tom Whitaker—her boyfriend from her surfing days on the North Shore reached out, and the two rekindled their long-ago romance.

"It was definitely destiny," she says. The couple ended up marrying and moving to San Clemente, not far from where she'd lived as a child. Dina's return to Southern California and the beaches where she had first tried body surfing led her to San Onofre State Park. It's where she goes stand-up paddle surfing, not far from sites that have been sacred to Native peoples along the coast for more than ten thousand years.

Love brought her here, and she continues her scholarly pursuits and teaching—often focused on the intersections of indigeneity and surf culture. That includes documenting the work of Native activists in the "Save Trestles" campaign to stop a toll road from endangering the San Onofre park and its world-famous surf spot and writing an essay for *The Critical Surf Studies Reader* published in 2017. A policy director and senior research associate at the Center for World Indigenous Studies, she teaches American Indian studies at California State University at San Marcos.

Myanmar's Best

Barely known in Myanmar in 2014, surfing was first introduced at the Ngwe Saung Yacht Club where the Myanmar Waverider Cup was hosted with over thirty athletes from ten countries attending.

Thwe "Nida" Soe, the only female member of the National Team, made an almost immediate commitment to wave-riding—as deep as those in long-established surf nations.

Surfing in the tropical country (formally known as Burma) took a huge step when the Surf Association of Myanmar was established in 2019, and its national team entered the Southeast Asia (SEA) Games for the first time ever. Gifted and well-traveled, Soe surfed five to seven hours a day to reach a level of competitiveness in the international competitions.

"I can't live without surfing," Nida Soe said, after a day surfing in the waves off the small coastal resort town of Ngwe Saung.

"I did not expect to be chosen for the national team, but I'm thrilled at the opportunity."

Soe encountered the sport while studying in southern California and has been hooked since, saying she "always feels happy" on the water.

Soe and a small team of local surfers competed against the region's giants at the December games in the Philippines.

Although the Southeast Asian country is flanked by surf-ready coasts to the west and south, decades of military rule, lack of equipment and poverty kept aspiring athletes from testing the waters.

But the sport slowly gained prominence thanks to the impassioned surfers, particularly in Ngwe Saung, a small beach town that became the center of the growing surf after hosting several competitions. By 2020 it had fielded a team, hired a coach and prepared for future events to build their experience. Soe's advice then was: "try hard, be competitive, stay positive, and never forget to surf with style."

Guam—Deep in the Northern Pacific

Some regions had a surfing community for many years but had never seen the female sector emerge beyond its reefs until a dozen years into the 21st Century.

Often remote areas like Oceana found women's participation sparse. On the coral ringed atoll of Guam, the count was one.

The major island in the Marianas island chain, Guam was often described as six thousand miles from anywhere. That, however, did not stop Angel 'Lea Aguilar from getting where she wanted to go. By the time she was eleven, Aguilar had competed in Hawaii twice, California and the Philippines.

As a seventh-grader at Johnson Middle school and Hui Nalu Surf Club member, Aguilar participated in the Philippine Surfing Championship Tour, ranking fourth in the longboard division and seventh in the shortboard division.

Disciplined and patient, she was just sixteen when she won both divisions of the Wahine Classic.

But by that time Minami Cramer had entered the scene and was making a name for herself as well.

Barrels in Bangladesh

Women who surf in the Muslim nation of Bangladesh face disapproval and rebuke—those caught in the water are called whores and worse. But in the country that has the fourth-highest rate of child marriage in the world, with sixty-five percent of girls married before the age of eighteen, a handful of female surfers took to the ocean to challenge how girls and women are seen by the prevailing patriarchy.

In 2015 a group known as Cox's Bazar Lifesaving and Surf Club began to help young Bangladeshi women outflank repressive cultural conventions by surfing the Bay of Bengal—an act often in defiance of their husbands' wishes and societal restrictions.

Among their better-known members is eighteen-year-old Nasima Akter— Bangladesh's first female surfer and star of the upcoming documentary *The Most Fearless*. The documentary's writer and producer, Jaimal Yogis, discovered Akter after traveling to Bangladesh to write an article about her and her surf club.

"I was shocked by how freely some of the men, even the supportive ones, would sometimes refer to the girls in derogatory terms or talk about beating them as if it were normal in reprimanding them," Yogis told *TakePart*.

Akter is no stranger to disapproval. At seven, she found herself homeless after her family kicked her out for reportedly refusing to go into prostitution to make money. But the courage and focus it took to push away the pain of her upbringing showed the strength of Akter's character. "Nasima loves the sense of being out in the ocean, free of all the judgments or thinking about whether or not she is hungry," noted Heather Kessinger, the film's director. "She leaves that all on the shore."

Akter's husband, whom she married when she was sixteen, has at times for-bidden her to surf. His disapproval of her beloved sport is bound to have a major influence in whether or not she will be as involved with the club in the future, according to Yogis.

Documentaries like *The Most Fearless* have provided an inside look at the struggles of these Bangladeshi surfers, petitioning for a change in the way women are viewed and treated in male-centric societies.

"Akter and the other girls in the surf club are role models for people everywhere because they're breaking down the barriers that contain them," said Yogis. "The documentary was inspired by her courage to challenge cultural norms that are unfair or holding them back."

Back to Black—Peru

Deep in the Southern Hemisphere, Peru's Anali Gomez was vying to make his-tory too—in this case as the first surfer to be crowned three-time champion of the WSL South America. Determined and outspoken "La Negra," as she was nicknamed for her black skin, needed at least a second-place result to achieve this unprecedented feat.

Three years earlier Gomez led her Peruvian team to victory and individually earned herself a gold medal in the International Surfing Association's (ISA) 2014 World Surfing Games. Hosted in her hometown of Punta Hermosa, the site of many contests, she had been the amateur anchor whose performance had brought the entire Peruvian populous to their feet.

Now with the WSL 2017 South American competition in the fifth and final stage she needed to defeat fellow Peruvian, Melanie Giunta in the semi-finals to win an unmatched three titles in a row, this time in San Bartolo, Peru.

As the waning minutes of the semi-finals ticked down, it was still not clear if she would make a "threepeat." But as the last heat of Reef & Paris Women's Pro came to a close it appeared Gomez had done just that. Despite losing her final heat, the semi-final duel had earned enough points to reclaim the title of WSL South American champion, for the third time.

Most surfing careers receive immediate payoff from achievements like this. Yet despite her world champion titles and skill in the water, Gomez has spoken openly about her ethnicity and how it has affected sponsorship. "La Negra," as her nickname indicated, her dark skin seemed to lack the right appeal for surfing apparel and sponsors.

"It was because the brands were sponsoring people who fit what they were looking for as a model," she contended when asked why she struggled to find sponsors. "They were looking for 'gringuitas' with light eyes" to represent them, stated Gomez. "If I'd had blonde hair, light skin and blue eyes, maybe I would've had that opportunity, even though I didn't have the talent."

Growing up in a poorer part of Punta Hermosa and remembering her financial difficulties battling to fulfill her dream of becoming a champion surfer, Gomez was prompted to launch "Surf Para Todos." The non-governmental organization gives classes, run by Gomez, to low-income young surfers who are unable to afford the costs of surf academies.

She was crowned "Best Latin American Surfer in the Open Women" on the Latin Tour by the Association of Latin American Surfers in 2019. More than two hundred athletes from fifteen countries participated in the event.

Surfing Song Lines

For the pride of her people Jasmine McCorquodale was determined to make history. Surfing since she was just nine years old, Jasmine McCorquodale had been a Kamilaroi surfer with big dreams—to be the first female Indigenous surfer on the World Tour. For eight years Victoria's iconic Bells Beach had hosted the Australian Indigenous Surfing Titles, with the 2020 competition fielding eight females in the Open class and eight females in the Juniors.

In December 2019 she was one of four females selected from across Australia, Fiji and Tahiti to train with three-time World Champ Carissa Moore, as part of a global exchange program run through Moore's foundation.

Her mother Kirsty Zorić, a former Indigenous surfer and Western Australian state champion, viewed her daughter's accomplishments as "remarkable."

During her own era of competition there were no more than a handful of females competing in the events, but the growth was rapid.

Surfer and altruist Mary Slabb, the cofounder of Juraki Surf, predicted it was "only a matter of time before we see the first female Indigenous surfer in the Women's World Surf League." As an organizer (with her husband Joel) of the first indigenous surf competitions in Australia, May Slabb's prediction was a prescient although not altogether risky calculation. McCorquodale went on to compete in the WSL, setting up a career in pro surfing and entering the history books.

Introducing Indonesia

In May of 2019, Kailani Johnson became Indonesia's first ever World Surfing Tour Competitor. In a historic moment for women's surfing, Johnson's entry not only marked her debut on the elite level but also the first time an Indonesian woman competed in a championship event.

The Corona Bali Protected contest saw eight regions represented by eighteen surfers showcasing the depth of talent around the globe. Johnson was the wildcard local favorite. Facing off against three-time World Champion Carissa Moore, Johnson held her own through most of the heat, while Moore struggled with an unfamiliar spot. An interference call disqualified Johnson, but the moment was a remarkable one, nonetheless.

For Johnson 2019 was the year of confidence. Fearless and lovely, Johnson's breakthrough session at big Krui in her home nation garnered respect from everyone there including world champion Gabriel Medina. "She's not scared," observed Medina in 2019. "If she can build her strength to match her courage, she will take this very far."

Born and raised in Bali by an expat Hawaiian father and a Balinese mother, she and her sister Pua often battled for acceptance as Indonesian citizens. But their surfing prowess removed any stigma of a mixed heritage and won respect from even the men.

Building strength and holding one's courage in the face of resistance—a two-fold challenge—was what many women surfers faced in Indonesia's 17,000 island archipelago. In the world's most populous Muslim country surfing is also frowned upon for women where it is culturally prohibitive to bare their bodies and allow their skin to tan. Women in rural areas are expected to stay at home.

Diah Rahayu Dewi, an articulate college graduate, and devout Muslim, is often sought after by the Indonesian government for her cheerful sound bites. A successful entrepreneur, she became a Bali beachside bar owner, but still the highest paid female pro surfer in Indonesia.

Zahwa Ardika Utami is one of a small but growing number of girls breaking with Indonesian tradition to take up wave-riding. The worldwide exposure to come from surfing's debut at the 2021 Tokyo Olympics helped young girls like Utami to turn the tide on sexism in Indonesia and emulate pioneering professional women surfers like Diah Dewi. At XX Surf, a surf school on Lombok where Utami is a student is a popular social enterprise. It also has a civic mission: seeking to empower girls through the sport while also tackling issues such as child marriage and teen pregnancy.

Founded in June of 2019, XX Surf—which takes its name from the female chromosomes—offers lessons to tourists at a fee but it is also training local girls for free to give them a taste of life outside marriage.

"We want to empower them, so they know more about the outside world," said XX Surf's cofounder Dedi Susandra, a twenty-seven-year-old former hotel manager-turned-coach.

Susandra, himself from Lombok, said local girls are often discouraged from surfing due to "religious taboos about figure-hugging attire like wetsuits, pressure to do housework and fears that it will lead to wayward behavior, like casual sex."

It was a false concern for the nation of talented surf girls.

Salini Rengganis Ledewa from Pacitan in Java, Asmara Basunki, born in Italy of Javanese descent, and Bali local Dhea Natasya all showed their commitment and potential in 2020.

Natasya walked a tightrope between her Islamic beliefs and her own brand of sun worship. Like a stage player changing costumes, she felt constantly in flux. A top competitor in both shortboard and longboard events, her courage was a rare gem in the predominately Hindu world of Bali, sometimes bearing the scorn of her fellow believers who preferred her to dye her hair black when it showed even a hint of sun bleaching, and for participating in a "naked sport." She often competes in XL men's t-shirts, long boardshorts and full-length "burkinis."

One of the stars in the international documentary *She Is the Ocean*, Cinta Hansel featured her traditional Balinese dancing skills as well as her surfing prowess. Her father, Bruce Hansel, was one of the legendary "Pipeline Underground" of the 70s before moving to Bali in 1999, bringing his Hawaiian shaping skills with him. Daughter Cinta, the first Indonesian Junior Women's Champion two years running, has grown into a cultural force in Indonesia.

Likewise Taina Izqueirdo, a Puerto Rican by birth, lit up the competitive lineups of Indo for years. "I don't pay attention to all the noise," she commented. "*I am my own island.*"

Cuba Libre

Blond, vivacious Yaya Guerrero felt she was part of a mission: as the thawing of the relations between Cuba and the USA accelerated, she and a handful of diehard waveriders sought to make surfing not only legal—but popular—on the one coastline which remained inaccessible to locals and traveling surfers alike.

Fervent and resolute, she began surfing to escape the time capsule of Cuba's authoritarian government and chase the dreams every surfer feels.

Most surfers have been unaware of the potential surf in Cuba since the 1958 Fidel Castro-led revolution and most Cubans are unaware of surfing at all—a result of the cold war hostility that has restricted information in and out of the island nation for more than sixty years. For these Cuban surfers, surfboards—a waverider's most prized possession—carried an almost sacred significance.

"It doesn't matter if it's old or new, the mark or the brand," Guerrero declared, "when we have a surfboard in our hands it is a treasure."

In 2021 Guerrero was the subject of *Havana Libre*, a film about these surfers and their struggle to overcome the obstacles that stand in the way of their passion for surfing.

The Surfing Heart of Senegal

As a young teen growing up on Senegal's west African coast, Khadjou Sambe wanted to surf from when she could remember. But for more than two years, her parents forbid her from riding waves, afraid of the negative reaction from the proud ethic group of Lebou people, who live in the hardscrabble district of Ngor in Senegal's capital city.

But she kept asking: "My determination was strong enough to make them change their minds."

Even though the ethnic Lebou traditionally live by the sea, Sambe had never seen a Black woman surfing in her native country. "I would always see people surfing and I'd say to myself: but where are the girls who surf?" Sambe said. "I thought: why don't I go surfing, represent my country, represent Africa, represent Senegal as a Black girl?"

That opportunity came when she connected with the "Black Girls Surf" project (BGS), which helps Black girls and women around the world break into professional surfing. The BGS opportunity was the door. Commitment was the key. Her nearly daily trek through town to surf the powerful Atlantic swells gained a begrudging acceptance from her tightknit community. When she began training for the Olympics as a potential Senegalese surf team member, her performances became a point of pride.

Sambe began coaching other local girls, encouraging them to develop the skills and stamina to ride waves and soften the restrictive social roles of her traditional society.

In early 2020, she began using a house overlooking the ocean as a base during a visit by mentor and BGS founder American Rhonda Harper.

As Senegal's first female professional surfer, Sambe inspires a whole generation to defy cultural norms and take to the waves.

Like surfers in every corner of the globe, Sambe found the secret sensation only a surfer can know: "When I am in the water I feel something extraordinary, something special in my heart."

The High Tide Club in San Diego

Closer to the epicenter, the San Diego Surf Ladies—an all women's surf club—was founded in 2004 to create a supportive surfing community for women surfers in the San Diego area. Providing social surfing activities for its members, the club's monthly Waikiki sessions, Christmas, and end-of-summer parties kept their membership growing. Members travel together to destinations like Mexico, Costa Rica, Australia, and Hawaii for sessions that include all skill levels and generate camaraderie. Kim Masiello, Nicole Gergans, Chelsea Grace, Sarah Jasper along with Jen Sprogis, Lisa Valdez, Leslie Chiteroff, Judy Jones, Terry Denning, Kayla Salvas, Lisa Acierno, Hamy Pham, Molly Goforth, Elieha Schumacher, and Summer Thompson all spearheaded a growing trend for female surfers.

Were You Watching?

In 2015 the inaugural Surfing for Social Good Summit was held in Bali, organized by big-wave surfer Easkey Britton. In 2018 it convened again at Raglan organized by Lisa Hunter, Belinda Wheaton, Rebecca Olive and Easkey Britton, all affiliated with the University of Waikato, New Zealand.

"Were You Watching?" Nora Jones asked in her poetic song in May 2020. As it turned out women surfers—from Vanuatu, Spain, New York, Sierra Leone, Mexico, Myanmar—were *definitely* taking note. So were the Philippines, Guam, India, Peru, Indonesia, Senegal and Bangladesh. In fact, as the modern surfing era entered its seventh decade, the *whole world* seemed to be watching.

Rolling in the Deep
2015–2020

"You have such little control over the next wave, then you'll just kind of stay in the moment, find your gravity and be open to what's coming. Just don't turn your back on the wave—it's coming no matter what; you can't hide from it. So face the waves, try to catch one and ride it."
— Amy Poehler, actress, writer,
cofounder of Smart Girls

"Rolling in the Deep," Adele's 2011 cry of love, was the definitive mood of the late 20-teens. It's remembrance of slights received—and pain endured—captured both agony and ecstasy, the forgotten surf adventures and good times unchronicled by the media of a world in change. Some of the women in this chapter of surf history went on to become legends. Others simply lived the legendary life, unsung but personally fulfilled, enjoying what surfers know as the ineffable sensation—riding the energy of the universe.

Bridging the Gulf

In the most overlooked region of American surfing, it was not surprising that the women of the Gulf Coast went unnoticed in double measure. Down in Corpus Christie Texas, Lee-Lee Greenwell held a 5.06 grade point average while acting in numerous productions in the local playhouse and serving as vice president of her high school class—all while placing first in the Girl's Shortboard division of the Texas State Surfing Championships.

Aarin Hartwell, originally from Brownsville, made a name in Corpus Christi as an events promoter, organizer, model, competitive surfer and local Surfrider chapter's dedicated environmentalist. It was not a hard leap: her mother, a biology teacher of thirty-five years "coordinated all the Earth Day and beach clean-ups for the first fifteen years of my life."

Texas has usually been viewed from the Galveston, Port Arkansas, Padre Island region of the coast, called the Coastal Bend. Hometown hero Corpus Christi native Karen Mackay was the U.S. Champion in 1977, and Mary Lynn Magee as partner with her husband helped make Pat Magee's Surf Shop a long-time, thriving business, well-known throughout Texas.

But when the Texas Surf Museum in Corpus Christi opened its 2008 exhibit "Texas Women, Texas Waves" it also included several outstanding surfers from Port Arkansas who were far less known. One, Mary Goldsmith spearheaded a move in 1997 that made it legal to surf next to Horace Caldwell Pier. Goldsmith, then a member of the Port Arkansas City Council was credited with opening up one of the best surf spots in the Coastal Bend. Less than a decade later Goldsmith found herself vice-president of the Texas Gulf Surfing Association. She also is the mother of Morgan Faulkner, twenty-two, one of the most skilled competitive surfers ever to come from Texas.

Paulette Just, a top female surfer in the Coastal Bend, was a member of the Copeland Surf Team of Corpus Christi in the 60s.

Along with Goldsmith and Just, other surfers of note from the region Port Aransas included Mary Lynn Magee, Kate Prejean, Meagan Callaway, Christine Kreutziger, Gretchen Baughman, Patty Garlough, and Dorothy Turnbull Hill.

Brittany Tupaj and Kalani Balcom, both exceptional Texas talents were in top form surfing Horace Caldwell Pier just months before the exhibit opened.

Another honoree, Nicole Dodson never actually lived in Port Aransas but attended Port Aransas High School from 2002 to 2005, winning four titles in the annual Texas State Surfing Championships. "Women," Dodson said, "have been there alongside the male surfers in Texas since the beginning."

Although swells are less consistent and wave size smaller on average, the fervor of the Gulf competitors might be unmatched. From 2015 into the 20s it was hard to find a Texas surf competition where Olive Smith didn't take home a trophy—or several. Along with Maddie Garlough (a future Olympic hopeful) Kelly Scroggs (who studied at Texas A&M) and Brittany Tupaj, Smith was part of the Texas Gulf Surfing Association (TGSA) All-Star Team. Drummed up from the state's best competitors, each member of the team was highly-rated in several categories of competition.

Across the Floridian Peninsula to the Atlantic side, Lindsay Perry heard a different drumbeat. Described as a star voyager, singer/surfer Perry was noted for her "mouth like a sailor and a mind like a razor." That was not the most impressive thing in this Satellite Beach girl's orbit. A Taylor guitar tailored to parrot her voice—one as complex as a single-malt filtered by peat moss—helped her second album of original music *Dark Revival*, shoot to iTunes number one in the Blues charts in fifteen days. Shuttling to California, she surfed her tiny 5'6" Mayhem surfboard, built a website from scratch, assembled an intriguing collection of elephant oddities, designed graphics for ads, shot a music video and modeled her surf sponsors clothing.

How did a young woman from a small southern beach town on the Space Coast launch so many sub-categories of artistic exploration? Inspired by a voyage starting on the red-neck Riviera with a borrowed guitar and an adopted family, Lindsay found herself (*at thirteen*) composing songs—chronicles of boys, whiskey, and family tragedy that—rather than shatter her—instead shaped the dark lyrics heard on her albums and T.V. shows from ABC to Marvel Comics. Early in life Perry embarked on a journey. Maybe not a star trek. Perhaps more like a hitch-hiker's guide to the galaxy. *Her own.*

The Wizards of Aus.

Australia emerged as a center of strong women surfers in the 2000s. Previous decades talent seemed thin compared to the deep bench of *male* competitors who dominated the professional ranks from the mid-70s to the early 2000s. But from the mid-2000s Australia brought a host of standouts who showed a natural talent for the emerging social media platforms as well as surf performance.

Self-described media maven Laura Enever—fashionista, beauty regimen doyenne and clothing designer—became a star in a variety of ways. Winning the 2008 ISA Junior World Champion and the WSL Triple Crown Rookie of the Year at sixteen and the Women's World Junior Championship *barely a year later*, she was soon blogging and tweeting her followers on all things surf or fashion-related and making the covers of magazines at the same time.

Ice blond and statuesque, it surprised no one when she made *Playboy*'s "21 Hottest Surfer Babes" list on Instagram, or *Esquire*'s "Women We Love." Global visibility, though, had a price: balancing her sexuality as an advantage to career advancement without losing sight of the athletic performance necessary to back it up.

"I was so young," Enever recalled. "It was just as social media was accelerating as well. It was great to receive all the attention," but she realized something far more unsettling: "So many girls seemed to feel the only way to make it was to be sexy."

After the initial accolades, Enever began to resist the sexualization, deciding on a different almost opposite path. "I wanted," she stressed, "to be known for so much more."

The result? She spent six years on the professional World Surfing Tour consistently finishing in the top ten—and on the covers of the fashion magazines at the same time. An injury in 2017 forced her off the Tour but drove her to the big swells at Jaws and Mavericks. After being invited to the first World Tour event at Peahi in 2016, she spent six weeks training. So began a focused dedication to big-wave achievement.

"I just decided that I was going to chase swells," she said. "And make my own mark."

"Laura is such a charger!" big wave legend Rochelle Ballard exclaimed, explaining the dichotomy between beauty and bravery in women's surfing. "You watch this Barbie doll—and then she pulls into these giant barrels!"

A devotion to the craft of wave-riding established the athlete's side, Enever evolved into what she felt "was a difference person." But she had to make tough adjustments to do so. "Leaving the tour was the hardest, scariest thing I've ever done," she admitted, "but I had lost myself."

Enever's ability to transfer needed skills from other endeavors to successful big-wave riding created myriad opportunities. She used them well. Her generosity and mentoring paid back too. Young women everywhere were taken by her talent—and her commitment to causes. "My goal is to help amplify the amazing people who are using their voice to make things better."

When Pacha Light was just nine years old, Laura Enever gifted her a surfboard. It became the catalyst for a life-long love affair with the ocean, cultivated in the legendary waves off the Gold Coast of Australia that fostered adventure on both land and sea.

The daughter of environmentalist and writer Anja Light, she was educated by her mother, who taught her the greatest gift: self-confidence. Following in her mom's footsteps, Light became an ambassador for the Surfrider Foundation in Australia, campaigning to have her local Gold Coast point breaks be designated a National Surfing Reserve.

When Light and her friend—top surfer India Robinson—noted that one of the biggest junior surfing platforms—a competition previously called The King of the Groms (renamed Young Guns in 2016) was open only to boys, the two girls challenged it and created an equal opportunity surf contest.

In a serendipitous twist Light and her mentor Laura Enever were reunited on the Billabong Surf Team.

Macy Callaghan, the 2017 Junior World Champion, came out of nowhere and made a name for herself in a very short time. The aspiring Tokyo Olympian from New South Wales's Central Coast was touted as one of surfing's rising stars after winning the world junior crown at just fifteen and earning a World Tour wildcard invite to the Trestles event, mainland America's only Tour stop in 2017.

Opportunity arose again, this time at the WSL Hurley Ranch event when title contender Tyler Wright withdrew from the competition and Macy took her spot, just missing a chance to qualify for the Women's World Tour.

Callaghan was easily identified as one of the sport's brightest prospects, and at only sixteen, she embarked on a campaign to secure a berth in the world's top twenty.

"It seems more of a matter of timing, rather than talent, when she finally cracks the Tour," declared World Champion Layne Beachley in 2018. The following year Callaghan did just that.

Polynesian Prospects

Luana Coelho Silva's ehu-colored hair marks her as a descendant of the red-maned volcano goddess Pele. Focused and motivated, Silva became the 2018 Hawaiian State and USA Surfing National Champ in the u14 and u18 divisions, following that up with an Open Girls NSSA National Championship at Huntington Beach.

Born at Kapiolani hospital in Honolulu, raised in Waialua, Luana (which means "happy" in Hawaiian) Silva has graced the North Shore lineups since the age of three, continuing to move through the ranks of competition.

With Oahu's Backyards as her backyard and surfing parents who were veterans of Big Sunset, Zoe McDougall, another North Shore standout, seemed certain to develop a taste for serious surf. Competing throughout her childhood, by eleven, McDougall moved effortlessly into I and NSSA events, climbing the competitive ranks, eventually earning a first place finish in the Roxy Waikiki Classic (fourteen & Under division).

Inspired by her long-time neighbor, Coco Ho, she feel Ho "taught me so much. Everything I needed to know I learned from Coco."

Relaxed and matter-of-fact, McDougall gained mental confidence and through Junior Lifeguards became physically comfortable in the in larger waves. "I think being a really strong swimmer gives you a lot of confidence in the water," she noted. The two-time Hawaii State Champion trained with top coach Kahea Hart, using friendly rivals and fellow competitors Kai and Moana Jones, Brisa Hennessy and Honolua Bloomfield like shadow boxers in a virtual surf contest. "I like power," she confessed.

Outer Banks, Inner tubes

The Outer Banks of North Carolina had performers too: Nicolle Diggs, who grew up minutes from the beach along North Carolina's long strand of powerful beachbreaks, looked very strong in the first decade of the new century.

But in the second decade, there was one unquestionable East Coast standout: Cassidy McClain. For anyone imagining that women are not capable of living in men's shoes, consider this: At eighteen, McClain won the National Scholastic Surfing Association Championships *and* ESA Junior Girls Championships, in the same year. *That* was not the impressive achievement. In the same contest (immediately after winning her Eastern's title) McClain entered the open shortboard division—and beat every male *and* female competitor in the event.

"What she did was just mind-blowing," said Lisa, co-director of the ESA's South Jersey District. "You're talking about the best surfers on the east coast—and she beat them all." That was 2013. Just to be sure that her performance was not an outlier, she repeated it in 2014. *Twice,* she beat all comers, men or women.

What could motivate a young surfer from a small beach town just south of Atlantic City to reach that level of performance? McClain offered the answer: *Coming in dead last in your first contest at nine years old.*

"I cried after my first competition," McClain remembered. "But I never came in last again." Two short years later she had earned two titles.

Her fervor for surfing was not without sacrifices—her journey not always the traditional path. Cassidy lived out of her car for a period, and "took six years to get my AA degree," she laughed.

A passionate proponent of surfing in the snow, Cassidy loved her New Jersey home-town Ventnor Pier, and judging contests as much as surfing in them. That last love began a whole new career. Moving into that new role in 2018, she began judging ESA events up and down the coast, honing the skill set. Then her big break came—an invitation to judge a 2019 World Surf League Qualifying event at Nags Head North Carolina. It put her on a lifelong path. Like so many Eastern women competitors, it allowed McClain to give as much back to her organization as she received.

Did she feel the intimidation from men? "I got some looks at first, it can be a little intimidating," she admitted. "But as I got better I earned respect."

Islands in the Dream

"Living the dream"—a common adage among dedicated surfers—is often associated with tropical locales and warm water. Although Hawaii and Indonesia immediately come to mind, islands with surf are found in almost every region of the world's seven oceans. A fascinating cross-pollination has emerged as women from far flung isles have migrated to central hubs of surf culture and others from more mainstream surfing centers have relocated to outer archipelagos.

Growing up on the island of Ilhabela, a tropical rainforest reserve four miles off the coast of Brazil with miles of pristine beaches, Amanda Chinchelli developed her lifelong love of surfing as a kid.

But at ten, her family returned to Italy, where she developed an interest in fashion and a passion for design. Under the tutelage of her Italian grandmother Amanda learned to sketch, crochet and sew, building the skills needed to enter the field of fashion design.

The next step was moving to California. After setting down roots on the beach in San Francisco, she began developing a line of original swimsuits, bringing her creations to the women's surfwear market. Merging her design experience with her wave-riding skills, Chinchelli founded Seea, a community for style-oriented surf girls with surfing as their platform.

Tia Blanco, from the island nation of Puerto Rico, eschewed meat her entire life. Led by her life-long vegetarian mother, her entire family turned strict vegan in 2018. Surfing in the 2019 Pan American Games, she represented her surf-rich nation where she was born in 1998.

But with a father serving in the Coast Guard, tours of duty often took her to a new base before getting the previous locale fully mastered. The constant movement was challenging, but it did not stop Tia from winning two International Surfing Association World titles. In 2018 she won both the Rip Curl Pro Tofino Championships and the Corona Extra Pro Surfing Circuit O'Neill Series in Puerto Rico, garnering monikers that included the "Veggie Might" and Victorious Vegan.

If one is the loneliest number, French surfer Tessa Thyssen might have enjoyed being lonely: In her first world competition she ended up at number one in the 2015 Junior Championship—and took the win by less than one point. A native of the French-Caribbean island of Guadeloupe, Thyssen had already won the European title the prior year, and the World Title vaulted her into the pro scene, where she spent the next five years hunting down points in the qualifying events around the world, making headlines in the 2020 Super Girl Pro in Oceanside.

A Réunion Trio

The island of Réunion off the coast of Madagascar is known for its waves and weather. As a French territory it has produced some top competitors and some interesting free surfing stars.

Born in France, Victoria Vergara started surfing at four on the small French island of Oleron off the coast of France. "When I was young my parents took my sister and I around the world to surf and discover new cultures. When I was fourteen we moved to Réunion."

Almost immediately Vergara was forced to deal with the conflicting dualities of surfing and sexuality. With ads for her sponsor Roxy as her first modeling work, an agent from xcelled agency Elite scouted her in a supermarket and wanted her to move to Paris to become a model. Surprising everyone, she said no. "My life was at the beach, with my family, my friends, my bikini and my longboard. But things have changed, I became more confident with who I am, and started enjoying xcelled. I'm really living my dream, it's just hard for me to say that I'm a model, it feels more natural to say that I'm a surfer."

Modest but attention-stealing, Vergara competed around the globe on the WSL Longboard Tour, while appearing as a model in *Vogue*, *Elle*, and *Shape* magazines.

"If the surfer girls use what they have aesthetically to forge a career, then why not? I think it's super cool that things has changed. Every surf brand has created feminine and sexy clothing; showing the world that their surfer girls can still rip in a sexy bikini. Surfing gives you a fit body, the beach as a playground, and a bikini as a uniform. It's more escapism than sexualizing to have amazing, gorgeous ripper girls!"

"I try to show them though my social media that positivity, hard work, and having fun are the keys in life."

For Cannelle Bulard the transplanting was just the opposite. Although born on Réunion Island, it was in St. Martin in the West Indies that Bulard learned to surf. It was on a family boat trip around the world that lasted—*eight years*. She began competing early but the year 2011 marked a real turning point in her career: she won in quick succession the ISA Open and junior World Titles, the French Open and junior championships, and won her first two successes in Pro Junior (San Sebastian and Sopelana).

At the gates of the CT, in 2013 Bulard decided to put her career on hold for her studies as a physiotherapist in Spain. In order to support her friends from Réunion, she successfully participated in the French championships which she won in 2014 and 2016.

With her diploma in hand, Bulard had one goal: to win her berth in the 2020 Olympic Games.

The third of this trio of Réunion surfers—Alice Lemoigne—took the 2019 World Longboard Champion and is a five-time European Longboard Champion. Passionate about sports and painting, committed to the environment and the preservation of her island nation, her biggest fear was encountering sharks. From 2011 to 2020 there were twenty-four shark attacks, eleven of them fatal. "We have been deprived of our passion and can no longer enjoy our island. I was interested in protecting myself and watched many videos about Shark Shield Technology, trying to understand how it works. I also read an interview with Tom Carroll." After studying the subject she was enthusiastic to try Carroll's protective electrical field system. "It is just amazing how safe I feel with the shield around me. It allows me to surf safely and not to think about this fear of sharks around me."

Early Adapters

When Dani Burt woke up from a forty-five-day medically induced coma following a motorcycle accident to learn her right leg had been amputated above the knee, she was destroyed; angry; defeated. At nineteen years old, she had just arrived in San Diego after leaving a toxic family situation behind in New Jersey, where she was born and raised; the thrill of being on her own, her new life opened up before her, quickly turned to despair after her accident.

But Burt's life was really only just beginning. A World Adaptive Surfing Champion, Doctor of Physical Therapy and fierce advocate for gender equality in adaptive surfing—Burt is the picture of resilience.

In San Diego she started surfing just for fun. But her passion grew. She entered her first competition in Hawaii in 2010 after someone "randomly ran up to her" on the beach and invited her to join an adaptive surfing competition—and placed third against all-male competitors.

When the International Surfing Association debuted the World Adaptive Surfing Championships in 2015, the organization reached out to Burt and explained they were organizing a competition that they one day hoped to get into the Paralympics. In 2016, she was named the U.S. Adaptive Surfing Champion competing in a mixed-gender division. In 2017, Burt competed in the first-ever adaptive surfing all women's division—and won.

Alana Nichols grew up in Farmington, New Mexico, enjoying a passion for skiing and snowboarding. But in 2000 during a ski trip in Colorado, she suffered a traumatic spinal cord injury while snowboarding, paralyzing her from the waist down. Thinking her athletic career was over, she experienced a wheelchair basketball game her freshman year at the University of New Mexico. The physical and competitive gameplay reignited her athletic endeavors. She later transferred to the University of Arizona to participate in the intercollegiate program for disabled sports. She received her master's degree in Kinesiology from the University of Alabama.

An astonishing athlete, Nichols competed in several Paralympic Games, becoming the first woman Paralympian to win gold medals at both Summer and Winter games—and did so in three different sports—basketball, alpine skiing and canoeing.

Retiring from her Paralympic career, Nichols discovered a new passion—surfing. Like most sports she pursued, she quickly excelled. She has competed in the ISA

Worlds Adaptive Surfing Championship in 2015, placing seventh in an all-male field in the upright division. Nichols became the president of the Woman's Sports Foundation and continued surfing, working to implement adaptive surfing into the 2024 Olympic Games.

As a native of Hawaii, Ann Yoshida had a natural love for water sports. Her roots and connection with the ocean run through generations of family. Paralyzed in an accident in 2000 Ann found her identity as a water-woman in adaptive *surfing* and paddling. In 2018 she was the first adaptive athlete to be inducted into the Hawaii Waterman Hall of Fame.

Kazune Uchida from Kamakura, Japan was born with Osteoarthritis of the hip, where the bones and joints of the hips deform, creating walking disabilities. Growing up in Enoshima, by the sea, she learned how to swim as a young child, and became interested in surfing.

Registering as JPSA (Pro Surfing Association) Certified Pro Long boarder in 2010 Uchida was approved as an Adaptive Surfer (surfers with physical challenges) from ISA. Seven years later she won the ISA World Adaptive Surfing Championship in 2017, then won for a second year in a row in 2018.

Following her wins, Uchida worked the "Adaptive Beach House Project" to make beaches a more friendly place for the disabled.

In 2017 Kazune Uchida along with Hawaiians Ann Yoshida and State Adaptive Surf Champion Ava Heller, Alana Nichols and Dani Burt, wrote their legacy in the sport, becoming the first women Gold Medalists in adapted surfing.

Amateur Hour

The amateur governing body of surfing for over fifty years, the International Surfing Association provided not only a competitive structure, but broadened horizons for the participants. Working with the Olympic Committee for more than two decades, ISA President Fernando Aguerre and his staff finally brought surfing to the Olympics—even while Covid-19 postponed the event until 2021. Aside from nearly every outstanding professional star the ISA has produced a coterie of remarkable surfers—all with their own unique story.

Hawaii State Champion in 2012, Summer Macedo won the ISA World Juniors in 2015 and then the National Scholastic Surfing Championships as well as the U.S. National title, both in 2017. She went on to medal twice in the ISA 2018 World Surfing Games in Japan, a precursor to the 2020 Olympics.

Dax Minnow McGill the 2012 ISA champion went straight from her North Shore home to WSL professional competitions, with an X Games visit along the way. Her middle name—Minnow—came from her pregnant mother. Out surfing her mother suddenly felt McGill "flopping and kicking like a minnow." Called one of the most important women in surf by the X Games in 2014, she continued to compete throughout the decade.

The Gold medalist for the ISA World Games in 2013, Philippa Anderson knew she wanted to be a professional surfer after finishing second in the World Pro Junior for two years in row. "After coming so close to a win, I knew this is what I wanted to do," Philippa told Surf Europe in 2016. Named "the best surfer in the world not on the World Tour," Anderson grew up on the South African coast at Port Elizabeth with her brother, who is also a pro surfer. After losing her sponsor, she took some time off, regrouped, and returned to competition with a goal. Rated number thirteen in the World Qualifying Series, she began training in 2020 to requalify for the World Tour.

It isn't often that a surfer wins a World Title after having two children but that was exactly what South African Simone Robb did at the ISA World longboarding event in Peru. With the demeanor and performance of a teenager, Robb was crowned the 2013 ISA Women's World Longboard Surfing Champion. Robb, a multiple South African surfing champion and mother of two from Kommetjie, went undefeated throughout the entire event and posted the highest scores in the Women's Division.

Like the National Scholastic Surfing Association, the ISA helped legitimize surfing as an extraordinary sport. The innocence of the amateur was refreshing. While everything else seemed to be out of sync and illegitimate, the simple elegance of a backlit silhouette tiptoeing to the tip of a single-fin nose rider had a cleanness that helped disinfect the madness on shore.

But with much of the half-decade's music and movies either blending into ubiquitous obscurity or dulled through media over-promotion, some artists quietly broke that trend: With refreshingly original music, the Haim sisters debut album *Days Are Gone*, appealed to a burgeoning pop crowd without sacrificing a laid-back, LA surfer-sourced sound. The irrepressible groove of Haim's 2020 ode "Summer Girl" summed up that year's sense that while the world seemed to be going strangely dark, women could still choose to dance on the bright side of the sea.

Making Points

"I've been having a competition with myself and trying to be the best I could be."

—Judith Jamison

A Wave of Consequence

As the set bent around the corner of the point at Honolua Bay, seventeen-year-old Caroline Marks realized this might be the most important heat of her career. In the winter glint of a December late afternoon—at this fabled Hawaiian wave considered one of the best three right-hand point breaks on the globe—she was fighting not just for the World Title, but for one of her country's berths on the very first ever Olympic surf team. Three U.S. women were in contention for a spot the following summer in Japan: Three-time World Champ Carissa Moore, veteran pro and aerial specialist Lakey Peterson—and the newcomer Marks. Only two would be chosen. Entering the season Marks was already the youngest surfer, male or female, to ever qualify for the WSL Championship Tour, and the previous year had officially become the youngest surfer to be named WSL's Rookie of the Year at the age of sixteen. Despite her age, she had recorded three podium finishes and a total of five top-five finishes against the best surfers in the world during the 2018 WSL Women's Championship Tour. The San Clemente, California native had been dominating amateur competitions since the age of eleven; the adjustment to the pro level had not intimidated her. Now as the 2019 season wrapped at the Maui Pro, Marks knew what was at stake—and considered the wave coming into her path.

Since the 60s Honolua Bay has served as a modern day Colosseum, where surfriders pit themselves against the jaws of pitching waves like gladiators engaged with hungry lions. The studded stone cliff line overlooking Maui's legendary right point often appears to resemble a luxury skybox, offering the sweeping view of long range Pacific swells threading their way through the narrow channel between Molokai and Lanai, forming an oceanic playing field as grand as an NFL stadium.

But soon after the turn of the millennium "the Bay" became something else: the final contest site of the Women's World Surfing Tour. Like Oahu's Pipeline Masters (the last stop on the men's tour) the Women's Pro at Honolua became a season finale that frequently determined the World Title. The 2019 event was proving to be a climatic duel that would not only crown a world champion but decide America's two women Olympians as well.

The three top point leaders going into the final event were all from the USA: Hawaii's Carissa Moore, Californian Lakey Peterson and Caroline Marks, a Florida transplant now living in San Clemente. The stakes could not have been higher.

Incoming Outlier

Nestled beside the Indian River Lagoon along Florida's Space Coast, the tiny town of Melbourne Beach was Marks's childhood home. Growing up with five brothers her family's big pine-needled backyard consisted of a moto track, half-pipe, basketball hoop, and a surf break right across the street. "Being a tomboy I realized I was never going to be in the gang if I didn't learn to surf. I'd been into horseback barrel racing at first," she said. "But once I tried surfing I was so into it, I thought I'd give my brothers a run for their money."

Entering her first event she eviscerated the competition.

"There were not a lot of girls competing," Marks recalled. "I entered the event in the Open division against the top guys. When they announced I had taken the win I almost felt bad." She laughed sheepishly: "The guys who lost to me never lived it down. We're good friends now but jokes still get made at their expense."

By the time she turned thirteen, Caroline entered the ranks of professional surfing by winning the first of two Vans U.S. Open of Surfing titles in the Pro Junior division. Those performances earned her a chance to surf in her first Championship Tour event at Lower Trestles in 2015, making her the youngest surfer ever to compete in one.

In 2014, her father, Darren Marks, moved the family to San Clemente, California after her older brother, Zach, launched a successful social network specifically designed for kids. The move not only propelled her brother's business, but it also gave Marks the opportunity to surf World class waves along the Southern California coast. Immersed in a bigger pool of talent, she progressed at a faster clip, notching national NSSA titles in the girls' and womens' divisions, two Vans U.S. Open Pro Junior titles and the ISA World Title before setting out on the Qualifying Series in 2017. That year she made history by being the youngest woman to qualify for the Championship Tour (CT) at age fifteen, and earned her first Regional Title along the way. She followed that up with the

2018 Women's North America Qualifying Series (QS) Regional Title for the second consecutive year.

Her secret doesn't lie in her wave selection or her low center-of-gravity or her cat-like balance. "I love surfing. I'll surf eight, ten hours a day, just because I love it." That's how Marks explained her rise to surfing's pinnacle. In *Outliers*, the best-selling book by Malcomb Gladwell, he asserts the premise that mastery requires at least 10,000 hours to achieve. Marks crossed that threshold of predictive greatness before she reached driving age. Marks's first pro victory came in April 2018, in Australia, at the Pro Gold Coast championship. "I'll never forget it," Marks declared. Not only did she upset seven-time world champ Stephanie Gilmore, but her win marked the first time in surfing history that men and women were paid the same share of prize money.

Marks may represent an outlier in age and talent, but she exhibits many of her generations character traits. Post-millennial's often value adaptivity and eclectic experience over conventional wisdom and ridged maxims.

"Caroline is smart, and she had a maturity from the very beginning," observed Layne Beachley.

Gregarious and good-natured, her competitive rivals, Bronte McCauley, Sage Erickson, as well as Lakey Peterson—all at the top of the ratings themselves—became great friends.

Her coach, ex-pro and world big-wave recordholder Mike Parsons, had a more definitive observation: "Caroline's super-confident. She's an achiever, and she does exactly what she sets out to do."

Bounding effortlessly up the rankings ladder, Marks's nonchalance remained. As the limelight thrust her into a role in women's empowerment, she simply posited questions: "Why can't a woman go on that big wave? Why can a guy do that and not a girl? You just have to go out there and do it."

Back in the lineup at Honolua Bay on that wave of consequence in December, 2019, Marks answered her question. She took the wave, won the heat and went on to become the first of two females to compete as surfers in the 2021 Olympics.

Previous Prodigy

Caroline Marks was by no means the first prodigy to emerge in the surf world. Frieda Zamba won a World Title at nineteen, Lisa Andersen was a Rookie of the Year at seventeen, and Margo Oberg had actually *won* a World Title at fifteen, a record that may never be broken.

But in 2008 a fourteen-year-old neophyte "shocked the surf world by becoming the youngest national champion, a winner of the U.S. Open, and youngest surfer ever to win an ASP event, completing an unlikely underdog story worthy of a Hollywood film."

Malia Manuel, like most adolescent champions had started surfing early. Her father Selso, a well-known big-wave surfer on Kauai, met her mother surfing, and when Malia was three-weeks-old, her parents would take turns surfing and babysitting her on the beach. When Malia was three, she would ride tandem with her dad on his longboard in Hanalei Bay before she eventually was able to ride on her own.

"I would stand on his shoulders when he rode," remembered Manuel, who had never even seen a U.S. Open before competing and winning it that year. "I think that's where I lost my fear, standing up so tall above the water at a young age. I loved being out there."

Manuel's fearlessness comes from her father as well as the strong world-class surfers from Kauai, led by three-time world champion Andy Irons. "I tried to be fluid and surf like the Kauai boys," Manuel told journalist Arash Markazi in *Sports Illustrated*. "I inherited a lot of my dad's style, so I want to continue to be progressive in the same way. I grew up surfing with all guys and tried a lot of their moves. It's exciting to watch, something different I think."

While Manuel learned to surf in Kauai, she would often come out to Southern California and Huntington Beach with her mom, who was raised in nearby Seal Beach.

Elegant and precise, Manual was the second female to be featured on the cover of *TransWorld Surf* magazine and the next year in 2012, she qualified for the World Tour and took Rookie of the Year honors. By 2014 she was ranked number five in the world.

But Manual grew up knowing the beach and the world-class competition that descended on her hometown every winter over the past fifty years. It made her realistic about her own career. She was wary of the effects of stardom. So were her parents. While other standout surfers are often homeschooled, Manuel continued to go to a public high school, taking the same math and English classes as other fifteen-year-olds and going to the same dances and Friday night football games.

When Manuel won the Rookie of the Year honor in 2012, finishing number six, many thought a future World Title was all but inevitable. But after her seven years on tour, despite a handful of Qualifying Series wins and making five Finals, Manual was still searching for her first Championship Tour victory.

The media (including the WSL itself) described Manuel as the most underrated surfer on the women's side; long overdue for a serious breakout. An injury sustained at the 2017 Margaret River event sidelined her for four contests. The absence appeared to light a fire. That year she came back and ended the season with a runner-up finish at Honolua Bay on Maui, which she went on to repeat in 2018.

Her major sponsor Lululemon launched a swimwear collection with Manual in 2018 incorporating technical qualities like bonded seams that lie flat against your skin and firmly attached cups that won't shift or slide, allowing women to focus solely on their surfing.

"It's important to keep that femininity with this next generation," Manuel claimed. "Back in the day it wasn't like that. Barely any of the girls surfed. This new generation has really stepped up and made it a point to look good in the water and out."

South America's New Surf Status

The rise of the "Brazilian Storm" was an unexpected phenomenon in the surf world, finally fulfilling a long-spoken-about prophecy and emerged as the vanguard of all things surfing. From 2014 through 2019 a sudden assault of Latin storm troopers led by Brazilians Gabriel Medina, Adriano de Souza, and Italo Ferreira won four of the six WSL World Titles. The fanfare overlooked a cadre of South American females who had simultaneously vaulted into the top ranks of the women's division filling the positions previously held by Australia and the USA exclusively. The largest segment of this group were big-wave riders, followed by a strong contingent of bodyboarders who had already been invading the Hawaiian wave fields for several decades. But in the last half of the 20-teens, hailing from several Latin nations—Chile, Costa Rica, Argentina, as well as Brazil—made significant marks on international surfing.

Half & Half

On a Hawaiian winter morning in 1996, Tanira Guimaraes Weston-Webb— pregnant with her daughter Tatiana—sat on her bodyboard, waiting patiently for a solid set at Pipeline. Although she'd surfed the dangerous, challenging wave many times before, she was understandably anxious. Since relocating from Brazil to Hawaii, charging Pipe had become second nature to her, but pulling into heavy barrels while five months pregnant was uncharted territory.

As *Surfer* editor Ashtyn Douglas wrote: "A few years earlier, Tanira and her sister Andrea left their hometown of Porto Alegre to travel the world as professional bodyboarders. During a visit to Kauai, they met Doug and Kevin Weston-Webb, two handsome towheaded surfers who, as fate would have it, also happened to be brothers. Not long after, Tanira married Doug; Andrea and Kevin followed suit. The two couples bought a house together in Kauai on a tropical plot of land dotted with banana and avocado trees, which they'd use as a home base while chasing the occasional swell to the North Shore of Oahu."

As a set appeared back in the lineup at Pipe, Tanira positioned herself deeply dropping into a large womb-like hollow, her soon-to-be daughter secured within her own womb. Not many surfers experience a tube ride before being born. It is not surprising then, that Tatiana Weston-Webb would feel at home in the hollows of waves.

"It was so much fun surfing with my two kids when I was pregnant," recalled Tanira nineteen years later on a January morning on Kauai. "Because of that, I think they have water knowledge in their veins."

Although daughter Tatiana opted for the stand-up approach to riding waves, the passion for taking on heavy tubes seemed inherited; translating her skills into a competitive career seemed manifest. The only rookie on the WCT in 2015, the Brazilian-born, Hawaiian-raised prodigy was fiery and confident. An intimidating force on the women's tour, she won the U.S. Open in 2016, garnering her best WCT rank at number four. In 2019 she was rated number six, good enough to be an Olympian—just not for the USA.

Weston-Webb elected to represent Brazil in international competition—although she had several choices—she holds American and UK citizenship due to her parentage—her mother Brazilian, her father British.

The steely-eyed goofy-footer was invited to surf for Brazil by the Brazilian Sports Council and entered the Olympics under that nationality. But she was torn between her two backgrounds.

"I'd really love to surf for America, because I was raised here and it's what made me a surfer," answered Weston-Webb. "It's a really complicated question because I really feel half-and-half."

The South Rises Again

In 2016 Argentinian surfing superstar Ornella Pelizzari walked away from competition, taking a long hard look at what surfing really meant to her.

Competitively Pellizzari's professional career had been an indisputable success: as a two-time Latin American champion with nine Argentine national titles, she was in a rare league of international champions. But personal fulfillment frequently differs from the public history of competitive triumphs. "It is a very demanding industry, and the essence of surfing gets lost and wears out over the years.

"It was definitely a stage that I needed to go through, disconnect and finish some pending things in my life outside of surfing that allowed me to come back hungrier, more motivated," she said. It was a difficult decision to leave and even more so to return. "But I think it was the right thing to do." Proving her decision a fruitful one, Pelizzari returned in 2017 to win a Pan-American Championship and in 2019 collected her tenth Argentine National Title and become the first surfer (both female and male) to achieve that milestone.

Pellizzari's position on equality was a first for her nation as well: "There must be a social change at a global level beyond the awards or salaries of women compared to men. There must be respect above all else and acceptance of diversity."

Considered Argentina's greatest surfer, Pelizzari marked the pulse of female surfing for two decades and left a path that served to boost women's surfing there for future generations. "More love and less ambition, more union and less selfishness. The world is a beautiful place, and we are passing through to enjoy it," Pelizzari declared. "The challenge is in oneself, in clicking and changing what is within our reach."

Pelizzari was not a lone Latin in dealing with defeat and triumph. When Lorena Fica, Chile's only female on the World Tour, entered eleven contests in ten countries and lost every one in the first round, she had to dig very deep to find her inspiration to continue. She had lost the Chilean National Surf Championships for the first time after winning three straight titles from 2014–16. And her South American ranking had dropped from second to seventh.

"It was a year of pure defeats," Fica confided. The experience was a lesson the sport taught her, she realized, about humility and commitment. "Surfing is super individualistic, and when one is getting successes and triumphs it is very easy to fall into ego and arrogance."

Discipline, she recognized, was a mindset she could use to develop as a tool for life. "I realized that my achievements were all the result of perseverance and *perseverance*."

She set to work. By 2019 the native of Arica—Chile's surf capital—had positioned herself as one of the best national exponents of professional surfing in the Southern hemisphere. She re-took the National Chilean Title in 2018, and again in 2019, for an unprecedented fifth time, and was the odds on favorite to win the Latin circuit Women's Surf World Cup at Puta de Lobos, Pichilemu in her own country. Fica credited her impressive rebound to practicing visualization and the power of positive thinking.

Ranked number two in the WSL Latin American ranks Fica was slated to be the first Chilean in history to be a South American professional surfing champion. It was also the gateway to an Olympic spot. The worldwide coronavirus pandemic of 2020 postponed the entire year of WSL events, but Fica remained confident: "I think our country has shown itself much stronger internationally and women's power in Chile is almost on par with the men." Enterprising and influential, Fica was awarded the government's Golden Condor honors two years in a row; selected as a surfing pioneer, it is a recognition of her inspiration to women and young leaders.

Dark Horses

Like rockstar Katy Perry's number one hit single—2014's "Dark Horse"—
some surfers mixed a variety of elements in their repertoire that were often
underappreciated.

Considered a pioneer in women's Brazilian surfing, by 2018 Jacqueline Silva
garnered the best results for a Brazilian female in the nation's history. She began
at Florianopolis, the beautiful southern beach town when women's categories in
Brazilian surfing championships were non-existent. Among her notable accomplishments was winning the 1996 Brazilian Amateur Champion and winning the
World Qualifying Series in 2001.

"Jacqueline was a *dark horse* who didn't get enough credit," observed Rochelle
Ballard, retired top competitor and an astute observer of the pros. "But she could
take out the best competitors in any given heat."

Silva would see her toughest challenge when she met Julia Christian, an aspiring
young surfer from Carlsbad, California. Christian, a dark horse herself, had only one
professional waverider she looked up to: four-time world champion Lisa Andersen.
Andersen had been the only female from the mainland United States to qualify for
the elite World Championship Tour in the previous fifteen years.

"The majority of the women are from Australia, so Lisa was *it* for girls my
age," Christian said. "Usually you look up to people from your area, but when I
started surfing there was no one from California to look up to." Christian resolved
that she should fill that role. Her determination would bear fruit: in 2003 at the
age of twenty-one, Christian took Andersen's place in the hearts of young surfers
after becoming the first woman from the mainland U.S. since 1988 to qualify for
the WCT. It was an achievement that had seemed impossible just months before.

The top six women from the World Qualifying Series advance to the WCT
every year, and Christian wasn't in that class heading into the last WQS tournament of the season; an interference call in an earlier contest had knocked her
out. She called home, telling her parents she would probably be flying back to
California shortly. "I thought my chances of qualifying were over," Christian said.
"So I just surfed the final event because I was already in Hawaii."

What she didn't realize was that a first or second place finish at Turtle Bay
would give her the points necessary to qualify. She surfed each heat without pressure, quietly advancing to the finals.

And with just three waves in the final round—the fewest of the four
contestants—Christian racked up enough points to win the contest. She still
had no idea that she had qualified for the WCT. As the last event of the season
the awards ceremony included a presentation for the WCT qualifiers as well
as the trophy winners. As the last name of the qualifiers was announced she

suddenly realized it was *hers*. The momentousness of the prize brought her to tears.

Christian was not finished with taking prizes, however. In 2005 she won the U.S. Open of Surfing, considered a national title, alongside men's three-time world champ Andy Irons. Then in 2006 Christian claimed America's first gold medal in ten years after narrowly defeating her rival Jacqueline Silva by less than a tenth of a point.

Silva, ranked second in the world in 2002, had survived a head-on auto collision at Bells Beach Australia, and with fifteen years on the tour was the oldest surfer and only female competitor over thirty when she retired. A Brazilian National Champion and considered one of her nations best, she leapt to the top rank midway through the 2007 season only to see that ratings lead slip away in the last few events. Called a "fit, toned thoroughbred" by *Surfing for Girls*, she ran a good long race but often seemed to miss the finish line by a nose.

In 2002, the same year Silva had her highest ranking, an Australian aspirant, Rebecca Woods, won the Australian Junior Title at the age of sixteen, then went on to become the World Junior Surfing Champion two years later in 2004 at age eighteen. She debuted on the elite Women's ASP World Championship Tour in 2005 at age nineteen. She spent nine years on the competitive circuit, retiring with a bang with a party thrown by friend and fellow Tour competitor Rochelle Ballard.

Author Thomas Wolfe wrote the famous line "There are no second acts" for stars, but the consistent, intelligent Woods proved that old adage wrong. An accomplished photographer and writer, she was published in various surf magazines while studying for her degree at college. When she left the World Tour Woods enrolled at Southern Cross University, leading the team when they competed at the Australian University Surfing Championships Newcastle breaks not far from where she began surfing at Copacabana on the Central Coast. SCU became a powerhouse in Australian University surfing, winning three National Titles.

With a Bachelor of Clinical Science and a Masters of Osteopathic Medicine and almost a decade competing in the top of her sport, Woods's primary focus was to "help people heal with holistic and conservative approaches first. Osteopaths spend five years at University learning about the human body, health, injury and disease states," Woods explained.

Great Dane

Denmark-born, Australian-raised surfer Isabella Nichols planned to study archi-tecture at University when she was offered work on a major film as Blake Lively's body double for shark attack thriller *The Shallows*. At eighteen she won World Surfing League World Junior title, and the Los Cabo Open in 2015, following wins at the Under 18s Australian State titles, and the Aussie Pro Junior.

Nicknamed the great "Dane from Down Under"—Nichols garnered a *Teen Vogue* interview, global travel experience and World Tour pro invites all while moonlighting as a stunt double for Hollywood surf films. By 2020 she had risen to the eleventh place in the WSL ratings when the coronavirus pandemic shut the World Tour down for the season.

Tour de France

France made a significant leap in the World Tour ranks reflecting a nation with exquisite surf credentials and passionate support from participants and the national sports organizations as well. The number of French surfers on the tour literally quadrupled in the 20-teens and backing from the governmental bodies would make more powerful surf nations envious.

Basic hard work cannot be disregarded as a key element to success. Winning her first competition at ten years old, French competitor Johanne Defay quickly moved through the European amateur ranks to the WSL World Qualifying Series. Bubbly and enthusiastic, Defay nevertheless struggled to step up from the juniors to the World Qualifying Series. When the economy crashed in 2008 surf companies sharply reduced team-rider support. Defay, finding herself without sponsors and without decent results, almost gave up competing. Encouragement from her parents and personal commitment allowed her to qualify for the WCT two years later.

"Defay got over the edge by pure effort," claimed Lakey Peterson. "She's a winner by nature."

Winning three World Surf League events—the Vans U.S. Open of Surfing 2015, the Fiji Women's Pro 2016 and the Uluwatu CT 2018—Defay took her place, the top ten rankings for the next nine years, picking up a sponsorship from fellow French Pro Jeremy Flores.

"Johanne is so hardworking and dedicated," observed Rosy Hodge, a former pro surfer turned World Tour commentator. "She's respected for her training discipline." Defay developed her own skateboard model, a 32" concave deck used to simulate waves and train for specific maneuvers. Born in Auvergne, France, Defay began surfing off the beaches of Réunion Island, a French territory near Mauritius off the east coast of Africa, where she became a permanent resident in 2006. She qualified to represent her country in the 2021 Olympics in Tokyo.

Internationally in the amateur ranks France turned in strong performances in competitions from Panama to Ireland. Sarah Burel won the 2010 ISA World Title in Lacanau, France, while Marie Dejean scored well in Ireland in 2011. Véronique Hayon was impressive at the 2013 ISA Junior World in Nicaragua as was Joséphine Costes.

In the South American competitions, there were plenty of outstanding talents. Tessa Thyssen and Lisa Girardet both took a Bronze medal in their divisions in Ecuador's 2014 event. Anne-Cécile Lacoste took a bronze medal in the 2015 ISA World Games in Chile as did Kim Véteau in the junior division.

After winning the 2008 European Championship, Alizé Arnaud claimed the ASP Women's World Junior title at North Narrabeen in Australia the same year. One of the few French surfers in the 2000 aughts, she won the World Junior title for a second time in 2010.

Back in France Alice Lemoigne was the dominant presence in the longboard division. Winning her sixth European Longboard World Title in 2020, Lemoigne remained undefeated, her strongest rival Zoé Grospiron taking second place in both 2019 and 20.

French Polynesia

Tahiti may have an ancient lineage in women's surf history but its entry to the modern professional ranks is much more recent. The WSL event at the famed Teahupoo, on Papeete, brought global attention to the islands surf, but there was no women's division, As competitors, Marie Christine Sanford was impressive in the 90s, as was Patricia Rossi during the 2000s. Next in line to these pioneers were Lanikai Maro and Karelle Poppke in the 20–teens. Staking their countries' place on the international competition circuit brought them loyal Tahitian supporters, but their distance from the other surf capitals made it hard to maintain travel funds. And the nation's small population and lack of major brand sponsorship added to that difficulty. "Competition is tough, because women's elite level surfing is very well advanced," noted surfer Simoné Forges Davanzati, a top sports journalist and one of Tahitian surfing's most ardent patrons. "However, we must remember Karelle's excellent performance in Nicaragua, she reminded her fellow citizens in 2017, "when she finished second in the junior world championships."

Le Meilluer de France

Another French phenom, Pauline Ado, was not born into a surfing family—but she was born of the generation where anything seemed possible. Ironically, she disliked competition initially—until she started winning. Her first contest victory brought sponsorships and travel opportunities to explore exotic surf breaks with her surfing idols.

After a successful junior career where she claimed both the ISA world junior and the ASP world junior title, Ado's competitive focus, coupled with a flair for tactical surfing, elevated her into the top ten of the WCT in her rookie season.

In 2011 Ado set another benchmark by qualifying as the first ever European woman for a second year in the prestigious ASP World Tour. "I try to surf with people better than me as motivation, to push me to grow," she said. "I watch the top girls to work out their strategies, what maneuvers score them the highest points, and then I build that into my own performances."

Media shy with a strong work ethic, Ado finished ninth in the world rankings for the second time in her career in 2013.

Falling off the tour in 2015, after four consecutive years on the top seventeen, Ado requalified for the 2017 season. Winning the ISA World amateur title that year on her home turf, Ado returned to the pro circuit to claim her seventh WSL European title in nine years (2010–2019) cementing her legacy as one of the great French surfers in history.

Head Above Water

"The touch of the sea is sensuous, enfolding the body in its soft, close embrace."
—Kate Chopin

Ladies First

Ruth Bader Ginsburg, icon of the Supreme Court, was a tireless advocate for gender equality, But her words echo surfing's counterculture roots of individualism, creativity, and independence. Ginsburg would have no doubt admired the distinctive approaches adopted by the all-female cast of *Ladies First*, an episodic podcast by Bodega Boarder Crew and Log Rap. Set to Queen Latifah's late-80s feminist anthem of the same name, the clip features singular artists San Clemente standout Hallie Rohr, West Maui wunderkind Sierra Lerback, Hobie team rider Makala Smith from Dana Point, Haley Otto, the prodigious Hawaiian transplant from Chicago, and former Duct Tape winner Kelis Kaleopa'a, from Waikiki, each drawing their own unique lines as stylists. Dedicated to the late Ruth Bader Ginsberg, with effortlessly stylish surfing action interspersed with still-portraits of a dozen more feminist icons, *Ladies First* finds its cast heeding the late-justice's mother's advice: Be your own person. Be independent. Be a lady.

While perhaps more likely to be dedicated to their own grandmothers than a distant Supreme Court Justice, a part of this cadre of notable young surfers formed a bond in Waikiki. The self-dubbed "Waikiki Grom Squad"—at the median age of fifteen—were already considered some of the best and most stylish longboarders in the world. They grew up together on the beach, once playing hide-and-seek in beachfront surfboard racks, now spending countless hours sharpening their technical nose rides and smooth cutbacks along Waikiki's playful reefs. When they weren't surfing, they all did other activities together. And when not together they texted on a group chat.

Many of the girls were best friends and close neighbors.

As *Surfer* Managing Editor Ashtyn Douglas expounded in a groundbreaking piece in *Surfer*, "Most were homeschooled, most of them live in Waikiki, and they were born and groomed into some of the world's most beautiful, graceful humble surfers."

"They could literally surf a door if you give them a door," claimed Kelia Moniz, who watched many of them as children as she was an older teen. "They're just your typical local kids who love the beach and do everything that revolves around the ocean."

But what made this group unique wasn't just that they were a truly tight-knit group of surfers. Packs of passionate longboard enthusiasts were increasingly found all over the world from Malibu to Noosa, Bali to Cornwall. But this was by far the youngest of such groups to make such a serious mark on traditional longboarding.

Another aspect that distinguished these young surfers from other teens is the influence of Polynesian culture and the power behind Hawaiian longboard surfing. Longboarding in Hawaii, particularly in the 80s, was about surfing with power and grace in big waves. "These kids have drawn inspiration not only from the Hawaiian longboard style," contended Moniz, "they've embraced traditional single-fin style as well and blended the two together effortlessly."

Humble and talented, Kelis Kaleopa'a carried a huge legacy in Waikiki. At fourteen she won the highly-esteemed Duct Tape Invitational longboard event at the 2019 Vans U.S. Open of Surfing, becoming the youngest person to ever claim the title. Coming from a strong bloodline of beachboy heritage, she grew up following the footsteps of her parents and extended family. "My mom surfed with me in her belly, said Kaleopa'a "and I've been surfing Queen's ever since!" "She's the princess of Waikiki," declared Kelia Moniz, who has known her since she was born. "She carries herself with so much humility and grace."

Blond with a bold, buckle-knee style, Haley Otto moved to Honolulu with her family at the age of seven. "Kelis' grandma actually got me my first longboard," said Otto. "I caught my first wave at Baby Queens."

Her light-footed cross-steps and delicate nose rides earned her not just invitations to the world's most prestigious events—it made her a contender to win.

Originally a shortboarder, Samantha Rust started by watching longboarding videos because "it looked like so much fun." Then that Christmas, "I got my first longboard and immediately fell in love. I watched the other girls and copied what I saw." Queen's is (not surprisingly) Rust's favorite place to surf. Speaking for the entire group she declared "It's where my friends and family all are. Waikiki is my second home."

Another talent in the pack included petite goofy-footer Keani Canullo who developed what observers in Waikiki considered the most noticeably different approach out of all the girls. Billed as the "Princess of Queen's" she was sought after by photographers (as was the entire squad) for her surfing beauty.

Kind and thoughtful, but with a spunky style in the water, Canullo embodied what the aloha spirit is known for.

The youngest of the Grom Squad members, Sophia Culhane traveled to Australia in 20020 to compete in her first ever Women's Longboard Tour event and came in second. She showed how it was done with the most beautiful, flawless hang ten nose rides," noted Moniz. "She embodies what strong, gracious longboarding looks like."

Described as "graceful with a little sass in her style," Journey Regelbrugge claimed the top place in the fourteen & Under Girls 2019 Longboard National Championships. "She's got the sweetest voice," said Moniz, "and she's a joy to watch on a wave." Fellow Hawaii resident Mahina Akaka, claimed the eighteen-and-over titles in the girls longboard division in that same National Championships held in Oceanside, California. Akaka won prestigious contests in Australia, Mexico, Portugal as well as hometown Oahu. A hula enthusiast, yoga devotee and outrigger canoe paddler as well as an accomplished surfer, Akaka (true to her aloha spirit of this Hawaiian generation) told paddling legend Danny Kim "My only aspiration is to live my life in joy."

As the generations grow up, others move in to take their place. Crystal Dzigas Walsh grew up surfing Honolulu a few years ahead of the Waikiki Grom Squad. She is married to Australian pro surfer Anthony Walsh, raising her own son on the beach there, as generation's before her have done.

Royals in the Tudor Dynasty

While "Auntie Sister" Moniz was an inspiration to the Waikiki Grom Squad, Joel Tudor—the progenitor of traditional single-fin logging in the modern context and the creator of the Duct Tape Invitational events—had a different but dynamic influence on the trajectory of the current generation of Waikiki standouts.

A series of creatively-structured events (surfers can score points by spontaneously riding tandem or threading the pylons of the Huntington Beach pier, for example) the contest, which has become a favorite of both professional nose riders and their audiences, draws contestants from around the globe. But nowhere is it more popular than with the women of Waikiki, many of who have won the event over the years. Both Culhane and Kelis Kaleopa'a are Duct Tape winners, and all have "benefited from the opportunity to show their skills at the event," noted Moniz.

Tudor, a two-time longboard world champion himself, concurred: "Hawaiian style on a surfboard," he attested, "is a beautiful thing to witness."

Honolua Bloomfield, one of those in her generation influenced by traditional Hawaiian style, was the 2018 Duct Tape winner.

But the line of succession for women's longboarding goes back to the early days of World Championships when all boards were longboards.

Until 2015, the title of the youngest-ever World Champion was still held by one Carissa Moore, who at eighteen had already begun her climb to the pantheon of women's surfing. But in December, at just seventeen years old, Rachael Tilly became the youngest-ever World Title winner in the history of the sport, male or female. First came two WSL North American professional titles, 2013 and 2015. Then Tilly won the World Title for longboarding, WSL Women's, in China.

A 2016 graduate of San Clemente High School on Orange County, she was the female athlete of the year. In 2017 she finished fifth on the tour. Moving to Australia to pursue a business degree at Bond University on Queensland's Gold Coast she joined the Burleigh Longboard Club. She also became the surfers representative for the WSL longboard division. Coaching from her father she noted, was a large part of her success.

The very next year San Clemente native Tory Gilkerson rose to the top of World Longboarding and was crowned Team Gold Medalist at the 2018 ISA World Longboard Surfing Championship at Riyue Bay in Wanning, China.

American National team member Soleil Errico was the Junior Champ and Gilkerson's selection, "a reflection of the ISA's commitment to promote and develop more women judges in Surfing." The panel represents the highest levels of expertise and international experience in surfing.

Honolua Bloomfield—one of those in her generation influenced by traditional Hawaiian style—was the 2018 Duct Tape winner.

Athletically gifted, Bloomfield's surfing passion, confidence and support came from surfing parents—a flight attendant and a lifeguard. And not just any lifeguard—one whose respect was strong enough to have former pro Dino Andino name his son after Bloomfield's father—a high compliment considering Kolohe Andino was the winningest amateur ever, a top WSL pro and headed to the Olympics on the first USA surf team.

"Honolua is a whole generation younger than all the girls I grew up with," Jen Smith told me in 2020. "All those girls started where we left off."

Like so many others born around the turn of the century, Bloomfield doesn't focus solely on surfing like many of the earlier great women surfers.

"I like to do a lot of activities," she told managing editor Ashtyn Douglas at *Surfer* magazine. "Hiking, Running, Jujitsu, Free Diving, Stand Up Paddling, Music, Skateboarding, Cooking, I love doing them all." She had success with both short and long boarding but settled on the longboard when she started not just placing but winning multiple contests. In 2013 Honalua competed in a noseriding event at the MSA Classic Invitational in Malibu. She was the only female in the final—and took second place. Several weeks later Honolua competed in the ISA World Longboard Championships in Peru and won the gold medal. If winning the gold wasn't enough, she again was the only female in the Junior finals. She went on a spree winning the Turtle Bay Pro, Taiwan Open and the Duke's Pro twice. In the wake of that prior string of victories Bloomfield won the 2017 WSL longboard championships in Taiwan and the Duct Tape Invitational in Huntington Beach just months later. In 2109 she attempted a repeat of her World Title—once again in Taiwan.

"Bloomfield had all the odds stacked against her," noted Jen Smith, a two-time World Champ herself. "To win Longboard Tour she not only needed to win the event, she needed Chloe Calmon to be eliminated by the Semifinals." In an unexpected upset, Calmon—the odds on favorite—failed to advance and Bloomfield did win the event—collecting her second WSL World Title. Following her win Bloomfield's visibility shot up, giving her the critics view as a contemporary custodian of the classic Polynesian style.

"Hawaii will always grace the path forward," stated Joel Tudor. "Honolua is a living example of this island wave-riding dance."

San Clemente's Deep Bench Empire

The WSL Longboard Division had never seen a single city dominate the top ranks until the second decade of the 2000s. Lindsay Steinriede won in 2011, Rachael Tilly was the 2015 champion, as was Tory Gilkerson in 2016. All were San Clemente residents. Then native San Clementean Kirra Pinkerton secured the 2018's WSL World Junior title in Taiwan—four champs in eight years from one small town.

"Poised and composed beyond her years," the WSL characterized the sixteen-year-old Pinkerton's season as "stellar," after winning the WSL North America Junior Qualifying Series.

Then came the title battle: the 2018 World Surf League (WSL) Junior Championship at the Taiwan Open of Surfing on Thursday, December 6, at Jinzun Harbor. The daughter of 80s NSSA team member Jim Pinkerton, the young San Clemente native had to defeat yet another San Clemente local, Samantha Sibley in the semi-finals. In the final round it was touch-and-go in a deadlock duel with Keala Tomoda-Bannert of Hawaii in clean two- to four-foot waves. In the final, Pinkerton held a strong lead for the first half of the match up until Tomoda-Bannert found a perfect left which she smashed four massive turns on. The judges loved the young Hawaiian's commitment and awarded her an 8.20, requiring Pinkerton to reply yet again. With less than two minutes left on the clock, the young Californian found a left to snatch back the lead. Tomoda-Bannert had one more shot before the buzzer sounded but fell short, leaving the competitively aggressive but personally amiable Pinkerton to claim her maiden World Title.

With San Clemente's depth of talent even women without National or World Titles elicit world class performances. *Stab* magazine editor Derek Rielly described Karina Rozunko's style as "a unique grace complemented by the unpredictability of her maneuvers. It is neither formal nor boring. Just like her."

A San Clemente native, her father's stories of surfing's rich heritage helped Rosunko straddle the short and long version of modern equipment. But it was on the classic longboard models that Rozunko found her footing—and her heartbeat.

"In my opinion there is longevity in 'classic' longboarding. It has so much culture behind it, it's where current surfing evolved from," said Rosunko. "I think that the unique history is what has been keeping it alive and genuine." The effortlessness of her style made a name for Rozunko; her coveted aesthetic led to Vans asking her to design an apparel and shoe line. Her Jimmy Jazz and Ozzie Wright colab surf film, *Doll Riot* was nominated for best style at the 2019 Surfer Poll awards.

"Of all the women surfing in the classic style, Karina is the one," remarked Allan Seymour, a longtime observer of women's surfing from his day as an impresario of Roxy's early events. That was high praise.

California spawned more than one epicenter of contemporary surfing in this period. Cowell's Beach on West Cliff Drive is a famed beginner's spot in Santa Cruz. On any morning in the 20-teens as many women as men sat in the lineup. In the early 2000s, Kim Mayer was considered the area's top talent, a shortboarder sponsored by Trixie surfboards who won a string of professional events.

Micaela Eastman, an amateur longboarder known for her ability to hold maneuvers like "hang five" or "hang ten" for long periods of time, was another. Her graceful execution of classical moves punctuated by an aggressive, rapid-response style were more characteristic of male longboarders. Olsen thinks Eastman, who appeared in her first professional competition in 2003, was one of the best.

"We have a total sisterhood here of women surfers," said Liz Hess, business manager of Paradise Surf Shop.

Carolyn Swift, of the Capitola Museum, agreed. "The first feminists lived here in 1850—they didn't surf but they wore pants and built houses," she said. "Santa Cruz is known to be very unique in having very strong, independent women."

Island Continents, Island Nations, Island Epicenters

But it was not just in California. On the Australian continent, the first woman to grace the cover of *Surfer's Journal*, Belinda Baggs, a Newcastle, Australia, native who once placed third in the World Longboard Championships navigated her life as a mother and iconic-longboarder-ocean conservationist-turned-Patagonia-employee with similar aplomb. Committed and skillful, in 2020 she celebrated with other climate activists on their victory in protecting the Great Australian Bight from oil and gas exploration dangers, forming Surfer's for Climate shortly after.

Baggs (or Bindy, as she's often referred to) gained notoriety in the early 2000s starring in surf films like *Sprout, Dear and Yonder* or *Come Hell or High Water* for her delicate footwork and her ability to make just about anything she did on a longboard look inimitably elegant.

On the island nation of Japan, Natsumi Taoka earned the first-ever ISA Longboard World Contest Medal for Japan in 2018. In 2020 her home break of Taito, on the island of Chiba, offered her a chance to surf a once-in-a-few-decades typhoon swell. Warm and welcoming, with an infectious smile, Taoka was brought up in a family of ocean-lovers and surfers. Competing originally as a shortboarder, Natsumi gradually shifted toward competitive longboarding—something about the grace and finesse seemed to call upon her natural ability to maintain poise in even the most challenging of conditions.

On the outer island epicenter of Kauai, Gabriela Bryan claimed a Gold Medal in the Girls U18 division at the 2019 ISA World Junior Championships in Huntington Beach after steadily competing on the junior circuit for several years. With power and style well beyond her years, she was a rare junior surfer who transitioned smoothly into the pro ranks. Outer-island surfers frequently remain out of the spotlight, but Bryan consistently stacked up major results in making it clear that she was a force to be reckoned with.

Kauai-raised sisters Camille and Jackie Brady also have their roots in competitive surfing, but these days they spend most of their surfing time longboarding Malibu Point, just a few miles north of the Santa Monica storefront for their label, Cami and Jax.

The sisters were primed to create a business together after graduating college, Camille with a communications and marketing degree and Jackie with one in apparel design and merchandising. Cami and Jax crafts feminine styles like open-wrap tops and chevron-slit bottoms into fully performing surfwear.

Like so many other top surfers, especially in Hawaii, Rosie Jaffurs found herself teaching surfing almost without seeking it. A native of Pupukea, the rural high bluffs above the North Shore, Jaffurs credits legendary surfers for fostering her confidence and love of the ocean—a skill that's become her livelihood as a surf instructor on the North shore. Graceful and elegant, she was offered a job by Hawaiian icon Buttons Kaluhiokalani on the spot one year to teach at his surf school and never looked back. Of course the surf tips she received from her high school swim coach renowned big-wave pioneer Peter Cole couldn't have hurt her list of qualifications. Friendly and outgoing, her effortless style helped garner her a small role in *Blue Crush*. Two decades later she was featured in a series of 2018 surf film clips that included Hawaii State 2013 Longboard Champ Natalia Smith, Réunion-raised French pro Justine Mauvin, and 2018 Junior World Champ Soleil Errico, all outstanding talents. Shot by then fledgling videographer Roxy Facer, who—using her social media to drive, passion and messaging—aligned her projects with mini film reels that quickly became a sensation.

Crossing Boarders

There are many ways to cross borders—borders of countries, borders of experience or culture, and of course different types of *boards*, like those for surf, skate, and snow. In her career Chanelle Sladics crossed each of these.

Starting out as a competitive skateboarder, she quickly took those edge-sport skills to the mountains, competing in seven Winter X Games and earning a bronze medal in the 2007 slopestyle competition. Finishing in the top ten of the TTR World Snowboard Tour in 2009, the Newport Beach, California local won the Asian Open Championship and garnered a second a Bronze medal while serving on the Women's Sports Foundation Athlete Advisory Panel.

But growing up on the Orange County coast, in the heart of the surf industry meant putting her rail-to-rail performances to work in the water would be difficult to avoid. Crossing disciplines enabled Sladics to put her surfboard in different angles than the typical surfer—and to see the world from different points too. Her surfing took her to even more places than her snowboarding—both physically and in spirit.

"For me, and many people around me, I have noticed an abundance of gratitude," she observed. "So grateful we get to travel the world, open our eyes to new cultures and perspectives, give, and challenge ourselves in our respective sports."

Sometimes crossing borders has allowed for a life journey crossing the frontiers from fear to frustration to freedom. When Amy Kotch visited the Maldives in 2005 she said to a friend "Being a surf guide at a place like this would be a dream job." Three years later she found—quite by serendipity—that her wish had crossed the boundaries into reality.

She had traveled to the island kingdom of Sumba with friends. After a short stay she was offered a job working at Nihiwatu Resort on the fabled Indonesian island. That led to lead to a chance meeting with Tropic Surf owner Ross Phillips, who offered Amy her dream job of working as a surf guide in the Maldives. And that led to meeting her future husband in the lineup of its famous break.

After marrying and having a son, Curren, she traded being Surf manager at Phillips's Hudhuranfushi Surf Resort with her husband Richard a photographer and committed environmentalist, while she took on the pleasures and main responsibilities of raising their child. Together they turned surf guiding into a career many around the world look to emulate.

Sometimes crossing borders to other nations opened up new horizons at home. When Black journalist and adventurer Siraad Dirshe traveled to Ghana in 2019 she visited Kokrobite, a beach town just outside the capital city of Accra. Standing on the edge of the Atlantic Ocean, "I felt captivated, mystified even, watching kids surf."

It was an epiphany. Communities of the African diaspora, more specifically of Africa's Gold Coast, have been surfing for centuries—the earliest record dates back to 1640, nearly two centuries before it was practiced on American shores, according to Kevin Dawson in his book *Undercurrents of Power*. Yet Black people are almost always absent in historical and pop culture renderings of the aquatic pastime.

Just weeks after returning to New York, Dirshe "booked my first surf lesson despite the remnants of a frigid East Coast winter that hung in the air and clung to the water. It didn't matter that it took nearly two hours and a shuttle connection to journey from the cacophonous streets of Harlem to the murky forest-green waters of Rockaway Beach." The joy and peace she felt back in Ghana was now within her grasp.

"I believe it's the inextricable place of water in our history," Dirshe explained, "from the shores of Africa to our passage to America, that has led to women like myself and LA-based journalist Darian Symoné Harvin to embark upon a sport in which we rarely see ourselves represented."

Harvin agreed: "I've always loved the water and been a huge daredevil. Surfing felt like the sort of sport that would take some time to get good at. I was up for the challenge." Standing on a shoreline Harvin could forget her skin color and instead be reminded of the infinite possibilities available to her. Surfing became a reminder of her humanity in a society that doesn't give it willingly; inspiring her to take up space instead of feeling small. That soaring sensation is a universal border crossed by surfers everywhere no matter their color.

Model Citizens

French Tahitian model Hanalei Reponty Gudauskas began surfing for Rip Curl at age fifteen, enjoying a budding career as a competitive longboarder, which positioned her especially well for making a line of surfwear that touts as much function as it does fashion. Shy and gracious, her upbringing in Tahiti informed and inspired the surf label Abysse, that she founded with her mother.

Centering their brand around sustainability principles in harmony with the ocean environment, she made Abysse wetsuits from Yamamoto limestone neoprene (non-petroleum based) and swimsuits from ECONYL (derived from recycled fishing nets). Her husband Patrick Gudauskas was a well-known surfer on the WSL professional circuit.

Surfing magazine's swimsuit issue was just the beginning of Virginia Beach surfer Bree Kleintop's modeling career. Features in *Cosmopolitan* and *Shape* magazines, and ads for O'Neill wetsuits, Pac Sun retailers and Dragon sunglasses followed. With 462,000 (mostly women) Instagram followers in 2019 Kleintop was selected to star in the *Surf House* reality TV show filmed on Oahu's North Shore, a coveted media role that led to a gig modeling celebrity gowns on Runway. "I'm a model, yes, but surfing is what I do," Bree declared in the first episode of the 2013 season.

Opportunities opened up in a variety of places marking progress but the continuing controversy between sex and sports as well as sport vs lifestyle.

Laura Crane one of England's top surfers in the in the 20-teens, offers a look into some of the issues facing surfers who model. "At the age of twelve, I got sponsored which was literally a dream come true." By the age of fourteen, she became British National Champion, then went on to the European juniors and from there, the qualifying series—the next step to the World Tour.

"It was my passion," Crane insisted, "and it was something that I felt I was put on this planet to do."

But her modeling soon outstripped surfing's financial earnings magazine covers, TV appearances and social media mavenhood followed. Then came her stint on the worldwide TV series *Love Island*, and her visibility became almost blinding.

Balancing the opportunities offered by using social media and sexy images with a surf career wasn't easy, but it was an option previous generations never even had: "*Love Island* for me was a massive test. I went in to prove to myself that I've come a long way. Now that it's over, I wanted to tell my journey. That I had bulimia and an eating disorder since I was sixteen. That being a surfer and traveling the world and modeling put all these pressures on me as a girl growing up in that industry. Which, don't get me wrong, it is an amazing way to grow up, but it does weigh on you." Still her surf passion never wavered—in 2021 she was one of the British surf team qualifiers for the Tokyo Olympic Games.

Adept in 6' to 8' waves at Ala Moana, in Waikiki, Alisha Gonsalves, a South Shore surfer from Honolulu is still far more well-known for her season on *Surf House* than her impressive surfing. That her father was a pro surfer, and her boyfriend was world class WSL star Bruce Irons only complicated the debate about the road forward for women on waves.

Being a model has other meanings: Faith Lennox became a role model for triumphing over challenges. Suffering a "crush" injury to her left hand at birth, doctors eventually amputated her arm below the elbow.

Inspired by meeting Bethany Hamilton after watching her biopic *Soul Surfer*, Lennox saw her own body in a different light.

Lennox trained with Kelea Foundation founder Jennifer Gladwin, who had created the organization to make sports and the ocean more accessible to people of all abilities, especially young women. Quick to adapt, Lennox became one of the youngest surfers on the Hawaii Adaptive Surf team.

Lennox pushed herself to take a holistic health approach to her diet regimen but as a youngster still preferred fun food to fruits and vegetables.

While traveling for a 2018 competition, she enjoyed an acai bowl for nearly *every meal*. When her health coach pointed out "You know that's basically ice cream, right?" Faith responded. "A healthy ice cream!"

Triple Threat

Model, surfer and social media maven, Anastasia Ashley had a similar dual career course. A surf prodigy from age six, Ashley won her first major national title at sixteen, receiving the 2003 Triple Crown Rookie of the Year award. Two National Scholastic Surfing Association championships followed, along with a Professional Surfing Tour of America championship. And when Ashley won the 2010 Pipeline Women's Pro in Hawaii.

But when the California native appeared in the *2014 Sports Illustrated Swimsuit Edition* her public profile exploded, as did her opportunities. An appearance in season 14 of the TV series *Hell's Kitchen*, a feature in *Maxim* magazine and a jewelry line—all in 2014—made her singular rising star seem like an entire constellation. She took a class in social media and must have been the best student in the class as by 2019 she had nearly a million Instagram followers. The result has been more sponsorships, more earnings and more surf time. Ashley's surfing prowess while perhaps not at the World Title level, was none-the-less impressive—and should have eliminated any question of her legitimacy with regard to her surfing career. But her social media clips—often posing for photographers or caught in bikini-clad beach scenes—created controversy.

"I'm a little amazed even now after all this time that the response has been so incredible," she noted. "I'm proud of my accomplishments. I don't think there is any conflict in my approach. It's all built around being able to do what I want to do—surf, travel and have a great life."

Hot Coffey

A dark side inhabits the sexual atmosphere that can turn ugly in the surfing world—and because of the ubiquitous Internet—can travel far beyond the beach.

Ellie-Jean Coffey began a career as a pro surfer at ten and by fourteen she was a regular on the World Qualifying Tour, traveling the globe sponsored by a host of brands helping make her dream real. But as she got older misogyny became such a problem she felt afraid to continue.

Coffey said, "The abuse, both mentally and physically, I endured during my teenage years far away from home with adults in positions of power has haunted me my whole life. It was a pretty horrible time in my life. I think people in positions of power tend to abuse that power, and I was only a young girl, and it's taken me a long time to recover."

Coffey underwent "extensive, intensive therapy" as a young adult to recover from the trauma that "almost drove me to end my life."

Coffey, had spent her childhood living in a camper with her family on Australia's east coast, continued to surf but stopped taking part in competitions in 2017.

After coming out as bisexual, she developed her own X-rated business, starting a website with sexual "uncensored" content that shocked her fans but was wildly successful, generating over 900,000 followers on Instagram and thousands of subscribers who pay $10 per month to view her content. Her sister Holly Daze Coffey—a pro surfer who won the ASR Australian Junior Title in 2011—followed suit with equally high success. Dubbed the "Kardashian's of Surf," their two younger sisters, Ruby Lee and Bonnie Lou, have joined them in the X-rated web business. Backlash was intense, but the women have declared their independent empowerment and are both proud and unapologetic.

"They say you shouldn't be doing this, shouldn't be doing that, shouldn't be posting such provocative shots," she told the *Daily Telegraph*. "But I don't get that. I think people limit women's opportunities by thinking they have to be a certain way."

Class Acts

In her rookie season, Australian Nikki van Dijk finished thirteenth on the 2014 Women's Championship Tour. But a bad accident at Fiji's famous Cloudbreak that same year led her to re-examine her life—and adopt a vegan diet. "I hit the reef and it was really traumatizing. I had sixteen stitches on my eye and on my face. The whole thing was very scary. I came home, had plastic surgery." It was a couple of weeks before the next contest. She needed to get her body back in order and get healthy.

"After that I thought, 'Hang on, I do not need anything in my body that doesn't need to be there'. My sister had already gone vegan, she said, 'Give it a go'. Since that day I've never looked back. I have never felt better." The change appeared to pay off, 2015 was van Dijk's best year on the WSL tour, finishing the year with six quarter-finals in a row. She finished in nineth place for the season, won Los Cabos Open of Surfing at Zippers beach and qualifyed to compete on the WSL tour again in 2016.

A Victoria resident, she studied at New Haven college on Phillip Island where she was born and was always keenly aware of the American influence on surf culture. Lisa Andersen was her hero. "I used to watch videos of Lisa over and over again; she was my real inspiration," she said. "I know Lisa now. We talk about boards; she doesn't know how much of an idol she is to me."

Rethinking the options happens on campus as well. When Avalon Johnson found out her high school didn't have a surf team she did her research, asked her principal's permission, gathered interested students and submitted a proposal to her school. The proposal was accepted and in 2013 Classical Academy High School Surf Team began competing in the Scholastic Surf Series. In their very first season they tied for third place in the league. By holding bake sales, soliciting sponsors and cajoling a surf coach, Johnson helped the team finance their travel allowing them to finish strong in the events. Johnson went on to write a medical treatise as well. In 2013, she was invited to the Oncofertility Conference at Northwestern University to give a presentation on her paper "The correlation between decreased leptin levels and the onset of menarche."

Teen Surf Physicist

Zahli Kelly from New South Wales emerged as a wunderkind from Wooloowin, Queensland—and not just for athletics. Her long-term goal was to be a physicist, in early 2018 she won the opening event at the Hydrolyte Sports Series at Bells Beach. It was hardly a surprise—this Tweed Coast teen had dominated her local and regional comps for the previous five years. Besides her two-time State Champion and 2015 Australian Junior Champion U14 titles, Kelly placed third in the Open Titles—against women of *all* ages.

The science of biomechanics helped her understand how to advance her aerials—and she loved studying the subject at every chance. Homeschooled since grade three, she applied sport and movement studies to improve her surfing. training at the Surfing Australia High-Performance Centre. The facility—just down the road from her house—was home to some of the world's leading PDH students specializing in sport and athlete science and training.

Living in Casuarina, a small coastal town not far from the fabled Gold Coast points, she finished her first year surfing the WSL Qualifying Series with much fanfare—without missing a single exam.

From NSSA to UCLA

At eighteen, Taylor Pitz had already won the National Scholastic Surfing Association High School State Championship for a second time, surfing against girls who became top pros on the World Circuit where she likely would have qualified herself. Instead she chose to accept her admission to University of California Los Angeles campus to major in Political Science and minor in Environmental Systems and Society. She entered college with two close surfing friends, environmental law student Heather Jordan and Chandler Parr, both strong surfers and highly ranked competitors. The three grew closer as teammates on the club surfing team, aided, according to Jordan, by the fact that they knew one another before coming to Westwood. "We've competed together for five-plus years," Jordan said. "Girls that compete together are in that close-knit group, and it was interesting that we all went here at the same time."

Chris Zeitler, a member of the University of California Surf Team placed second in the National Championships while earning a degree in molecular Biochemistry. She was the coach of the year in 1989, eventually founding True Body Movement, a visual media company.

Irish Blood

With a doctorate in environment and society from the University of Ulster, Easkey Britton was expected to live the professorial lifestyle of tweeds and library hours. Instead this Irish surfer from County Donegal won the British ProTour twice and in 2010 won her fifth consecutive Irish National Surfing Championship title at her namesake wave in County Sligo

A lifelong surfer, Britton's parents taught her to surf when she was four years old along with her two sisters. Britton's younger sister Becky-Finn Britton took to longboarding. Older sister Tahlia Britton became the first female diver in the Irish Navy in August 2020.

Channeling her passion for surfing and the sea into social change. Easkey's work was deeply influenced by the ocean and the lessons learned while pioneering women's big-wave surfing in Ireland.

Britton became the first female surfer to ride the "big-wave," *Aill na Searrach*, off the Cliffs of Moher in 2007, riding the fifteen-foot wave featured in the Irish documentary film *Waveriders*. The first Irish woman to be nominated for the WSL Big-Wave Awards, Britton's tow-surfing performance at Ireland's premier big-wave spot, Mullaghmore, in February 2011, was a first for women as well.

A post-doctoral research fellow at the Whitaker Institute, National University of Ireland, Galway, Easkey helped lead the interdisciplinary NEARHealth work-package on nature-based solutions, exploring the use of blue and green space to restore health and wellbeing. In 2014, she starred in *Into the Sea*, a documentary film introducing the sport of surfing with women in Iran.

A Much Greater Salt Lake

When Joy Magelssen Monahan secured the 2008 Association of Surfing Professionals Women's World Longboard competition in La Côtes des Basques in Biarritz, France, she was the first Hawaiian to win the title. Taught to surf by her father at an early age, she has been competing since the age of thirteen.

Understated and joyous, with a beaming smile, Monahan combined her passion for surf with her commitment to her education—and to her faith. Attending Brigham Young University Monahan earned her bachelor's degree in accounting in 2011. She and her husband live in Hawaii, where she maintains close ties with her family. A member of the Latter Day Saints, her "I'm a Mormon" video has been viewed over one million times.

Double Dipping

There is always a balancing act between school and surfing, but in the case of Keenan Lineback there was an added balancing act: two sports—surfing and swimming. Introduced to swimming at four and surfing at eight in her small town of Conway, South Carolina, she loved the two with equal intensity—and talent.

Stradling her devotion to both sports created inherent conflicts. She frequently found herself putting one sport on hold as she pursued her goals in the other.

"My junior year of high school, it was my second year on the USA national surf team, competing in Ecuador," Lineback remembered. "I had to call the coach and tell him I couldn't do the team anymore because I was missing weeks at a time training for swimming. Junior year is when colleges scout evaluate high school athletes "They're seeing how you're doing at meets."

Torn between her passion and her responsibilities, Linebeck found the balance. After a discussion with her parents, she settled on pursuing swimming, accepting a scholarship offer from the University of San Diego. But there was another incentive to Lineback's decision: surfing the California coast when she wasn't swimming or studying. The choice was apparently a good one. As a top swim competitor she set college records in the 1650 Free, 1000 Free, and 800 Free Relay, and was awarded the USD Female Torero of the Year in 2014. And surfing took no backseat, whether surfing Trestles or Bali. Friends Kiana Fores, Colton Tisch, and Josè Manuel made good companions when she found her way to waves.

Lineback was not the only collegiate surfer at a top school to master two watersports. A dual sport athlete in surfing and water polo from Newport Beach, California, Kaleigh Gilchrist attended the University of Southern California majoring in communication and minoring in occupational science. Gilchrist co-captained the 2013 NCAA Championship team. She also won a national title for USC at the NSSA collegiate championships. Competing on the gold medal-winning U.S. Women's Olympic Team, Gilchrist scored six goals at the 2016 Summer Olympics.

At Newport Harbor High School she was part of the CIF winning water polo team during the 2008 season. Representing the U.S. Surf Team at *five* ISA World Championships, Gilchrist won back-to-back Surfing America titles in 2009 and 2010 crowning her the best eighteen and under female in America. She won another title as the NSSA high school champion. In 2010, she was the Orange County Register athlete of the year.

The Best Medicine

College doesn't eliminate surfing's fun factor. In fact the evidence shows it may enhance it. Haley Nemeroff, a San Diego State University graduate, might have been considered the poster-child for the old axiom "the best surfer is the one having the most fun," said Bill Schildge, a well-known bodysurfer and California Surf Museum Board member.

Joyous and energetic, Nemeroff lit up any beach with her energy and good-natured humor. From organizing a Dog Surfing Demonstration, to breaking a Guinness world record for the most bodysurfers on one wave, Nemeroff's indefatigable optimism and sense of fun garnered her a welcome spot in any line-up.

Colleagues often observed that one could always locate Haley by following the laughter coming from the crew she was with.

From organizing a Dog Surfing Demonstration, to breaking a Guinness world record for the most bodysurfers on one wave, Nemeroff's indefatigable optimism and sense of fun garnered her great affection. A strong competitor, Nemeroff became a fixture in the Southern California contest scene for two decades.

Along with her partner Meredith Rose—considered one of the best bodyboarder's in the world—Nemeroff enjoyed a classic beach house on the bluffs of Del Mar and used her education to develop a career in physical therapy.

No matter how healthy or how joyous, tragedy can strike even the most promising prodigies—without warning and in the strangest ways. Katherine Diaz Hernandez, a twenty-two-year old Olympic surfing hopeful from El Salvador died in 2021 after being struck by lightning at the popular El Tunco Beach.

Katherine was the daughter of the Federation's President Jose Diaz. The tragedy, which shook El Salvador's surf community, occurred while she was preparing for the ISA World Surf Games in El Salvador. The event served as a qualifier for the Tokyo Olympic Games. Hernandez was remembered fondly as "a great athlete who has represented our country."

Rachael Presti, a talented Sebastian Inlet surfer from Brevard County trained for the Olympics too. The ASF/NSSA East Coast champion and ISA medalist was shooting for a spot on the Tour next to her favorite surfer, Caroline Marks, who grew up nearby. "I'd love to see what the one-two east coast punch could do on the World Tour together," remarked *Eastern Surf* magazine founder, and astute talent observer, Dick Meseroll.

Deep in the Valley Isle

Monyca Eleogram remembers calling her home break in Hana the "mysterious beyond," because she never seemed to make it to the lineup. Many years and accomplishments later, Monyca has undoubtedly "made it." At fourteen, her athleticism culminated, and she solidified her place in the professional world of surfing. She represented Hawaii at the 2005 and 2006 Quiksilver World Junior Pro and qualified for the 2007 NSSA National Finals. Modeling and traveling with the Roxy surf team gave her a job that let her surf every day. Monyca's perception of surfing goes beyond the competitive elements, however. Her self-proclaimed greatest achievement is not her success as an athlete. Spending time with the people she loves is her mantra. She married her childhood sweetheart and best fried, Ola, on her family property in 2013, and she and Ola work together on their organic fruit farm in Hana, Maui.

The Future is Female
2000–2022

"There is no justification for present existence other than its expansion into an indefinitely open future."

—Simone de Beauvoir

Imua

As the third decade of the 21st Century began, a young Hawaiian surfer emerged as the first successor to the legendary Rell Sunn—perhaps the most celebrated—and certainly the most beloved—female surfer in history. To assume Rell Sunn's mantle was a large pair of slippers to fill. Two World Longboarding titles, a family considered Hawaiian royalty, and a reputation as "Honolulu's sweetheart" gave Kelia Moniz the start for a remarkable position as a global icon of the surfing culture.

An effortless ability to represent both Hawaii and surfing, the glamorous shimmer of her world-famous celebrity friends and her humility and natural grace under pressure added to her qualifications.

This resume comprised a rare collection of life experiences, imbedded in family and culture. There may be no more authentic or deeply rooted environment for a young woman to grow up in than surfing Waikiki daily with your family.

The legacy of Waikiki—Duke Kahanamoku and his brothers, Rabbit Kekai, Fred Hemmings, George Downing, the Aikau brothers, who all grew up surfing these beaches—are almost the definition of surfing's heritage. The Waikiki beachboys were a well-known symbol of Hawaiian culture for decades. Teaching the art of riding waves was a major part of that proud tradition. And the Moniz family became one of the most prominent families in that rich lineage.

Kelia's father Tony Moniz—a pro-level motocross rider, Golden Gloves boxer, as well as a highly respected big-wave rider may be remembered most for spearheading a generation of tuberiders at Pipeline who pioneered a new approach to backside surfing.

Kelia's mother Tammy, a gracious, shy young islander of Japanese descent worked at the Local Motion surf shop—one of the top brands of the 70s and 80s. The two met there and eventually married. Deeply committed to their Christian beliefs they opened the Faith surf brand in 1996 when their only daughter was just three. Shortly thereafter they opened the Faith Surf School and their children—four brothers and Kelia—grew up on the beach at Queens in the grand tradition that has been defining Hawaii since the turn of the 20th Century.

"My mom taught so many kids how to surf: not only local Waikiki girls who gain confidence in who they are, but girls from all around the world who take back the magic to their own global neighborhoods," Kelia declared. "It is a special gift."

Unlike many families where virtues of competitive success are forced on their children, often with less than positive results, her parents took a relatively laissez-faire approach to the children's own surf careers.

According to Kelia, her father's motto surrounding competition was really, "as long as you're having fun, you *are* the best."

But in the Moniz family, both talent and character is in the blood.

"Kelia has the perfect combo of strength, style and beauty," contended Laura Enever who met her in Tahiti. "We clicked and have been friends ever since."

As the only daughter in a houseful of males, the nickname "Sister" became synonymous with Kelia—for more than just her identity in the family.

"Kelia is the definition of sisterhood," observed Monyca Eleogram, one of Maui's premier talents. "That's why her name is so appropriate."

Kelia's generation was the first to truly integrate into the mainstream of popular culture—her husband was friends with Justin Bieber, and her friendship with Bieber's wife Haley garnered global media visibility. Kelia's relationship with Haley required balancing fame and family with the subtle ease with which Moniz learned to navigate her entire lifestyle. Kelia met Joe Termini, a New York–based photographer/artist who had developed major connections in the celebrity world. With trips to faraway destinations, nights spent roaming distant cities, and hanging with friends Justin and Haley Bieber, Joe and Kelia fell into a romance that grew into a happy marriage. It subsequently opened a new level of career opportunity.

The availability of a vast commercial sponsorship industry made a fundamental difference to a women with her achievements and stature. While Rell Sunn and previous generations struggled with finances constantly, Moniz had the good fortune to find support from a variety of roles: beauty product ambassador, clothing brand spokesperson, host to awards ceremonies, sponsored athlete, and bit acting parts. All these possibilities—which now earned real income—arrived or peaked during the new millennium. Such heady experiences have been the downfall of many young talents. But Kelia Moniz learned an old adage about fame early: *Walk with Kings but keep the common touch.*

And like the tradition of Hawaii and surfing both, she respected her heritage as the cornerstone of a strong life. "We don't know as much as we should about our history in surfing," she said describing her generation of women. "But we respect and appreciate what came before us. We know that the women who broke the molds helped us get where we are today."

As Kelia grew, it began to feel as though once again there was a female Hawaiian who could represent surfing's aloha spirit on the world stage.

In Hawaiian the word *Imua* means "to move forward with dignity." Rell Sunn personified that core value, a role Kelia Moniz was seemingly born to. And the Moniz family had always held a deep friendship with Duke Kahanamoku's successor, Rell Sunn. Filling Rell's slippers could be the biggest challenge of Kelia's life. But both friends and historian's considered her the heir to Rell's crown, with all the joy and struggle such a role brought.

"It's a price you have to pay for believing in yourself and choosing your own way," Moniz contended in 2021. "Making other people happy makes me *really* happy. I think that's what brings the most happiness, just making others smile." Moniz could have been quoting Sunn.

Kelia's conclusion? "Rell was the symbol of the surfing woman in Hawaii, the one my father always mentioned in every lesson he taught us."

Kelia has been in the spotlight most of her life. From a very young age, she seemed to instinctively understand her place in the surfing hierarchy; her responsibility to the Hawaiian way of life. "I feel the touch of the culture," she confided. "And if I can represent the aloha experience of wave-riding then I want to do that."

The Dog Days Are Over

Perhaps the generation of girls who are at the top of the charts in the early 2020s have experienced a different upbringing from the women who battled their way into the limelight during the 70s, 80s and 90s. While far from optimum, this new generation of women enjoyed a world where fighting for every scrap was no longer a requirement to survival. Yet surfing's intense focus on its roots and heritage meant that despite their opportunities, surfing women are indebted to the history that came before. Princess Ka'iulani lost her country but saved surfing. The legendary women of the 20s, 30s, 40s, and 50s blazed a trail that paralleled women's advancement across the world. Isabel Letham, Mary Ann Hawkins, Keanuinui Kekai, and Marge Calhoun were the giants of their eras.

Women from the 70s, like Jericho Poppler and Margo Oberg, paid homage to Joyce Hoffman and Linda Benson, the 60s first modern superstars. The first full generation of professionals like Debbie Beacham credit Poppler for "busting down the door like barbarians at the gates." Lisa Andersen and the boom time stars point to Beacham's era for "setting the cornerstones" of their edifice. And groundbreakers like Layne Beachley express gratitude to the 90s.

"Former world champions such as Wendy Botha, Pauline Menczer and Pam Burridge provided me with the platform to pursue my dream of becoming the best in the world, for a pittance of what the current champions earn today," asserted Beachley. "They competed for the love of it. They were the true pioneers, paving the way for future generations while inspiring a groundswell of "frothing towhead grommets," like me, to one day dare to dream that I could earn an honest living doing something I absolutely love."

Surfing's Equity and Equality

From 2010 to 2020—for the first time—women on waves achieved unprecedented accomplishments—not just in performance but in the culture of surfing itself. In 2010, Cori Schumacher, a fierce and beloved woman, was able to challenge surfing's governing body, fight for women's rights, win her third World Title, openly acknowledge her sexuality and be accepted as an equal *and* a champion.

In previous eras, differences in performance were used to make sense of the financial disparities in prize money. Women supposedly couldn't pull off the same tricks as men did—including airs, the breathtaking maneuver in which a surfer launches themselves completely out of the water and goes airborne. Nor were they assumed to surf big waves or endure intense wipeouts. But those assumptions have proven inaccurate. In 2011, Californian fourteen-year-old Lakey Peterson became the first woman to land an aerial in a competition. After her 2013 shark attack, Bethany Hamilton inspired the world by returning to ride thirty-foot waves. Paige Alms 2015 tube at Peahi became a milestone. Kassia Meador's longboard dances still rival all comers of either sex.

So what comes next for surfing's future? How do surfers move forward from the challenges their foremothers faced? Like almost all areas of modern society, surfing has a long and notorious history of sexism and inequality. Breaking through line ups dominated by men has always been difficult. Often the best competition conditions were reserved for men. As Layne Beachley famously proclaimed, "The story used to be 'The surf is two foot and junk, send out the girls!'"

Despite pulling in fewer sponsors and brands, women remain one of the primary consumers of the estimated $13.2 billion global surfing market. Surfing's inequity was most starkly evident, however, when it came to prize money. In March of 2018, the men's winner of the Gold Coast pro received $100,000, while the top woman was paid $65,000. A few months later, a photo of two junior surfers went viral, showing the two teens with their oversized checks. The female winnings were half those of her male counterpart.

But change was coming. And it was a powerful wave.

A Small Step for Women, a Giant Step for Womankind

In September 2018, surfing took a leap forward that startled the sports world: The World Surfing League announced that male and female winners would receive the same prize money.

"It's about not being afraid to stand up and use your voice for something and I've always been pretty quiet on that part," seven-time champ Stephanie Gilmore admitted. "I think for the WSL, it was just a matter of righting a wrong.

"When men and women are crowned champions and they stand on the podium together and they have an equal prize check, everybody can see that this should be normal," Gilmore declared. In addition to recognition by the Olympics, the progress tracks with the advancements made in more popular sports. For Gilmore, it's about legitimizing surfing with "more air time and more help to grow the sport," she said. "Young girls choosing the path of being a pro surfer, can now see it as a legitimate career.'"

With equal pay, Olympic inclusion and many hard-fought incremental battles along the way, surfing seemed as though it was finally, if slowly, becoming a good old girls' club too.

As surfing became the first sport in history to pay equal prize money for both sexes, the result was an explosion of interest in the women's surfing from both the media and the worldwide audience. It also spurred the commitment and determination of women to challenge the highest goals: After four years of success, the Queen of the Bay contest was finally firmly established, a big wave event for feminine warriors to carry their spears and enter the sacred waves of Waimea Bay. In 2020 Keala Kennelly was awarded the prestigious XXL Wipeout of the Year of the world's most dangerous wave—a category previously held only by men. In addition, 2020's XXL award for riding the largest wave on the planet was won for the first time in history by a woman—the formidable Maya Gabeira. In fact, *two* women rode record-breaking waves that year (Justine Dupont completed a wave just two feet smaller than Gabeira's) while Felicity Palmateer another barrier-breaker rode *au natural* in the liberating tradition of the ancient Polynesian queens.

And Kelia Moniz rose to take the baton representing the grand, regal wave-riding performances that the Hawaiian princesses—more than four centuries ago—held in such regal esteem.

Author Alvin Toffler, perhaps the world's most renown futurist, wrote a prophetic statement in 1971: "Surfing is a signpost pointing toward the future."

Not all barriers have been broken, and the arc of history still bends. But what Toffler foresaw has become reality. The great visionary imagined the future. And in surfing the future appears to be female.

How Professional Surfing is Scored

The World Surfing League formula for judging surf contest performances is relatively straightforward, intended to be simple enough for any viewer to understand easily. Man-on-Man contests were first conceived and implemented by former surf star, sex-change celebrity, and contest impresario Peter Drouyn in 1977. This format removed a long-standing tradition of four to six competitors being judged in each heat, replacing it with two contestants competing head to head. Surfers were now judged on their two highest-scoring waves out of ten to fifteen waves caught, and a priority system allowing each surfer to have an equal number of wave opportunities was instituted.

Before this change, when six competitors could all catch and ride waves, often simultaneously, it was often difficult for judges to agree on scores. And it was nearly impossible for the audience to know who was in the lead or even who had won until the results were announced—sometimes long after another heat was underway.

The simplicity of this two-person competition—essentially a duel as in boxing or tennis—created drama, suspense and most importantly, a clear immediate result. It also provided the two competitors and the spectators—on the beach and online—with real-time scoring updates.

The blow by blow presentation allows the contestants to know their status and what score they need to take or maintain the lead—and adds minute to minute drama for the audience.

Since the adoption of this format pro surfing contests have improved immeasurably.

This system has seemed to be perceived positively by women, who often eschew the confrontational aspects involved in intense professional competition.

"Women fight hard to win, but there's no blood lust," noted seven-time champ Layne Beachley. "Women almost never get physically aggressive during a contest. With the guys it happens all time."

"I'm not saying women don't get pretty intense during a heat," added Rosy Hodge, a former pro who became a staple commentator for the World Tour, "but there is a lot more camaraderie among the girls than the guys."

NAME INDEX